lonely planet

Iran

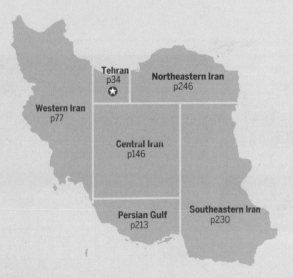

Tehran
p34
★

Northeastern Iran
p246

Western Iran
p77

Central Iran
p146

Persian Gulf
p213

Southeastern Iran
p230

THIS EDITION WRITTEN AND RESEARCHED BY
Simon Richmond, Jean-Bernard Carillet, Mark Elliott, Anthony Ham,
Jenny Walker, Steve Waters

PLAN YOUR TRIP

ON THE ROAD

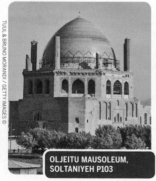

OLJEITU MAUSOLEUM,
SOLTANIYEH P103

TUUL & BRUNO MORANDI / GETTY IMAGES ©

PERSIAN RUG WEAVING
P316

JAMES STRACHAN / GETTY IMAGES ©

MASJED-E NASIR-AL-MOLK,
SHIRAZ P198

MOHAMMAD REZA DOMIRI GANJI / 500PX ©

Contents

Welcome to Iran

Welcome to what could be the friendliest country on earth. Iran is the jewel in Islam's crown, combining glorious architecture with a warm-hearted welcome.

In the Footsteps of Empire

Echoes of ancient civilisations resonate down through the ages in Iran. Some of history's biggest names - Cyrus and Darius, Alexander the Great, Genghis Khan – all left their mark here and the cities they conquered or over which they ruled are among the finest in a region rich with such storied ruins. Walking around the awesome and beautiful ancient capital at Persepolis, experiencing the remote power of Susa (Shush), and taking in the wonderfully immense Elamite ziggurat at Choqa Zanbil will carry you all the way back to the glory days of Ancient Persia.

The Beauty of Islam

Iran is a treasure house for some of the most beautiful Islamic architecture on the planet. The sublime, turquoise-tiled domes and minarets of Esfahan's Naqsh-e Jahan (Imam) Square gets so many appreciative gasps of wonder, and rightly so, but there are utterly magnificent rivals elsewhere, in Yazd and Shiraz among others. And it's not just the mosques – the palaces (especially in Tehran), gardens (everywhere, but Kashan really shines) and artfully conceived bridges and other public buildings all lend grace and beauty to cities across the country

Modern & Sophisticated

This is your chance to get to grips with Iran's modern history, too, particularly in Tehran. Enter part of the former US embassy, now called the US Den of Espionage; gaze up at Tehran's beautiful Azadi Tower, where hundreds of thousands of people gathered to mark the 1979 revolution and, in 2009, to protest against the regime the revolution delivered; and visit the haunting Iran Holy Defense Museum to learn all about the Iran Iraq war that so traumatised the country. Tehran is also where you can take Iran's contemporary pulse at creative contemporary art galleries and liberal cafe spaces.

Redefining Hospitality

Across Iran, a nation made up of numerous ethnic groups and influenced over thousands of years by Greek, Arab, Turkic and Mongol occupiers, you'll find the people are endlessly welcoming. Offers to sit down for tea will be an everyday occurrence, and if you spend any time at all with Iranians, you'll often find yourself invited to share a meal in someone's home. Say yes whenever you can, and through it experience firsthand, Iranian culture, ancient, sophisticated and warm. It's these experiences that will live longest in the memory.

Why I Love Iran

By Anthony Ham, Writer

What's not to love? The landscapes here are wonderful, from high mountains to deep deserts where the soulful presence of the Asiatic cheetah still roams. There's the architecture and the magic of the bazaars. There's the utterly civilised appeal of taking tea in a teahouse overlooking the river in Esfahan or with nomads out in the Zagros Mountains. Or wandering the mud-brick alleyways of Yazd then venturing to a Zoroastrian fire temple on the cusp of the desert. Yes, I love all of these things. But Iran's greatest gift is its people.

For more about our writers, see p384

Above: Masjed-e Shah mosque, Esfahan (p159)

Iran

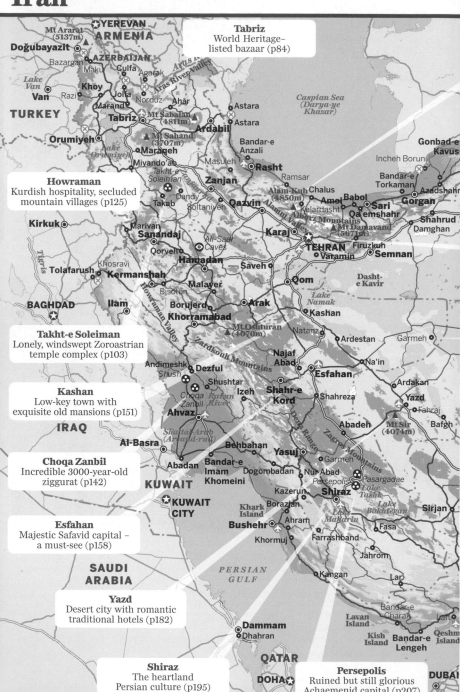

Tabriz
World Heritage–
listed bazaar (p84)

Howraman
Kurdish hospitality, secluded
mountain villages (p125)

Takht-e Soleiman
Lonely, windswept Zoroastrian
temple complex (p103)

Kashan
Low-key town with
exquisite old mansions (p151)

Choqa Zanbil
Incredible 3000-year-old
ziggurat (p142)

Esfahan
Majestic Safavid capital –
a must-see (p158)

Yazd
Desert city with romantic
traditional hotels (p182)

Shiraz
The heartland
Persian culture (p195)

Persepolis
Ruined but still glorious
Achaemenid capital (p207)

0
0
500 km
250 miles

Alamut Valley
Hike among the Castles
of the Assassins (p118)

UZBEKISTAN

Samarkand

TAJIKISTAN

Turkmenabat

DUSHANBE

Serdar

TURKMENISTAN

Chandir Valley

Ashgabat

Ashkhaneh Bojnurd
Tandoureh
National Park

Mary

Garmeh Shirvan Dargaz
Quchan

Esfarayen

Golestan National
Park & Protected
Wildlife Area

Tus

Sarakhs Saraghs

Sabzevar Neishabur

Mashhad

Mashhad
Shrine of Imam Reza,
Iran's holiest site (p257)

Torbat-e
Hedariyeh

Band-e
Fariman

Torbat-e
Jam

Tehran
Modern Iran – galleries,
cafes, restaurants (p34)

Taybad

Dasht-e Kavir

Khaf

Ferdows

Gonabad

Herat

Tabas

Qa'en

Garmeh
Desert oasis with
memorable homestay (p180)

Khur

Birjand

AFGHANISTAN

Lake
Sistan

Khash

Zarand

Kaluts

Zabol

Kaluts
Camp among 10-storey
sandcastles (p240)

Rafsanjan

Shahdad

Lake
Hamun

Kerman

Mahan

Mt Hezar
(4420m)

Rayen

Bam

Zahedan

Taftan

Fahraj

Mt Lalezar
(4374m)

Mt Taftan
(4042m)

Tahlab River

Qeshm Island
Sleepy Bandari villages,
amazing geology (p222)

Jiroft

Khash

Kahnuj

PAKISTAN

Iranshahr

Bandar
Abbas

Minab

ELEVATION

Larak
Island

Makran Mountains

3000m
2000m
1000m
500m
250m
0

Strait of
Hormoz

OMAN

Jask

Turbat

UNITED ARAB
EMIRATES

Gulf of
Oman

Chabahar

ARABIAN SEA

Iran's
Top 16

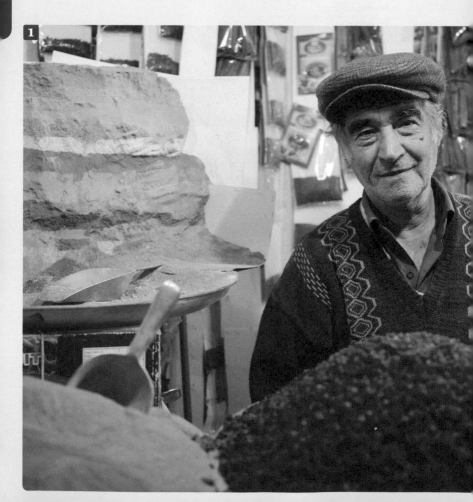

Meet the People

1 In any competition for the title of the world's friendliest people, Iranians would be definite finalists. It's the people that leave the most lasting impressions from any journey to Iran, their warmth and their hospitality, their willingness to set aside enmities between countries and welcome you with open arms and doors. Whoever you meet, you will regularly be asked what you think of Iran, told 'You are our guest' and brought tea and food. Meeting Iranians is, quite simply, the best experience in Iran. Below left: Spice merchant, Bazar-e Bozorg (p160), Esfahan

Esfahan, Half of the World

2 There are moments in travel that will long stay with you, and your first sight of Esfahan's majestic Naqsh-e Jahan (Imam) Square (p159) is one of them. This square is home to arguably the most majestic collection of buildings in the Islamic world: the perfectly proportioned blue-tiled dome of the Masjed-e Shah, the supremely elegant Masjed-e Sheikh Lotfollah and the indulgent and lavishly decorated Ali Qapu Palace. Far from being a static architectural attraction, the square and the nearby teahouses overlooking the river throng with life. Below right: Naqsh-e Jahan (Imam) Square

JAVARMAN / SHUTTERSTOCK ©

HL PHOTO / SHUTTERSTOCK ©

Yazd

3 Few places have adapted to their environment as well as the desert city of Yazd (p182). It's a gem of winding lanes, blue-tiled domes, soaring minarets, bazaars, and courtyard homes topped by badgirs (wind-towers) and watered by *qanats* (underground water channels). Several of these homes have been restored and converted into evocative traditional hotels. Many travellers declare Yazd to be their favourite city in Iran, and it's not difficult to see why, combining as it does a whiff of magic on the cusp of the desert.

Top: Amir Chakhmaq Mosque Complex (p183)

More than Kabab

4 Iranian food (p302) is one delicious surprise after another. Once you've tried several varieties of kabab, *khoresht* (stew), *ash* (soup) and flat bread, ask for *fesenjun* (chicken in walnut and pomegranate sauce) or anything with *bademjan* (eggplant), or try Gilan cuisine with its predominantly sour flavours. Then you can try the *shirini* (sweets)... As exquisite as so many Iranian flavours are, it's the buzz that surrounds eating, the primacy of food in so many social encounters that makes it truly one of life's great pleasures. Bottom: *Khoresht*

MARCIN SZYMCZAK / SHUTTERSTOCK ©

OPIS ZAGREB / SHUTTERSTOCK ©

Nomads of the Zagros

5 About two million Iranians from several different ethnic groups still live a nomadic existence, travelling with their goats in spring and autumn in search of pasture. Qashqa'i and Bakhtiyari nomads spend the summer months in the Zagros Mountains, before heading down to the coast for the winter. You can get a taste of nomad life on a day trip from Shiraz, or stay with the Khamseh (and eat their delicious hand-made yoghurt) in the hills above Bavanat (p211).

Ancient Persepolis

6 The artistic harmony of the monumental staircases, imposing gateways and exquisite reliefs leaves you in little doubt that in its prime, Persepolis (p207) was at the centre of the known world. These days it's Iran's premier ancient city. Built by kings Darius and Xerxes as the ceremonial capital of the Achaemenid empire, a visit to the World Heritage–listed ruins of the city also testifies to Alexander the Great's merciless destruction of that empire. Don't miss the monolithic tombs at nearby Naqsh-e Rostam.

7

CHRISTIAN ÅSLUND / GETTY IMAGES ©

8

VALERY SHANIN / SHUTTERSTOCK ©

9

OLEKSANDR RUPETA / ALAMY STOCK PHOTO ©

Skiing the Alborz Mountains

7 Think Iran and skiing is hardly the first thing that springs to mind. But Iran has more than 20 ski fields and most of the action is conveniently concentrated around Tehran. The Dizin (p72) and Shemshak resorts are the pick, with steep downhills and plenty of untracked powder to keep skiers of all levels interested. Chalets and ski passes are inexpensive compared with Western countries, and the slopes are relatively liberal, beloved as they are by Tehran's upper middle class.

Choqa Zanbil, Susa & Shushtar

8 Even if you don't normally seek out ancient ruins, these three World Heritage sites will make you reconsider. The great bulk and fascinating back story make the Choqa Zanbil Ziggurat (p142), which dates back a mere 34 centuries, one of the most impressive historical sites in a region full of them. Now excavated, some of the bricks look as if they came out of the kiln last week. Susa (Shush) is a fabulous ruin of a place with a castle, acropolis and palace remnants, while Shushtar impressively rounds things out. Top right: Choqa Zanbil Ziggurat

Tehran Art Scene

9 The capital's excellent museums and palaces provide great insights into Iran's past. However, to gain a handle on its present, don't miss the city's range of hip cafes and contemporary art galleries (p64). These provide an entree into a side of modern Iranian life – creative, challenging and liberal – that you seldom hear much about in the media. Even government sponsored institutions such as the Iran Holy Defence Museum and Qsar Garden Museum make inventive use of contemporary art.

Mashhad's Haram-e Razavi

10 Iran is an Islamic Republic and while most travellers find Islam is not nearly as all-pervasive as they had expected, the Shiite faith remains an important part of Iranian life. It is at its most obvious in the passionate devotion seen at monuments such as the huge Haram-e Razavi (p258) in Mashhad. The main draw here is the Holy Shrine of Imam Reza, the only Shiite imam buried in Iran. The passion and warmth you'll encounter here lends a powerful sense of Islam as a force for good in the world. Top: Holy Shine of Imam Reza

Desert Oases

11 The welcome is rarely warmer than in the vast, empty silence of Iran's two great deserts. Garmeh (p180) is the oasis village of your dreams, with a crumbling castle, swaying date palms and the sound of spring water. It's the sort of place you come for one night and stay four. Nearby Farahzad and tiny Toudeshk Cho, between Esfahan and Na'in, also offer memorable desert-style family homestays; think beds on the floor, basic bathrooms, fresh, delicious home-cooked food and endless horizons just outside your door. Bottom: Garmeh

Bazaar Shopping

12 In the age of the superstore, most Iranians rely on these mazes of covered lanes, madrasehs and caravanserais for much of their shopping. Tehran, Esfahan, Shiraz, Kerman and Kashan all have atmospheric bazaars where you can browse beneath domed ceilings, dodge motorcycles and stop in teahouses for a brew. But perhaps the greatest is the World Heritage–listed Tabriz Bazaar (p85), the world's largest covered bazaar and once among the most important trading centres on the Silk Road. Top: Tabriz Bazaar

Scenic Western Iran

13 With the slowdown in overland travel, few make it out west, but that's just the way we like it. Track down Unesco World Heritage–listed Armenian churches. Follow the route through Howraman on your way between Marivan and Paveh. Explore the Aras Valley. Or spend time getting to know the Kurds around Howraman, the Azeris in the northwest, the Gilan on the Caspian Coast, the Arabs of Khuzestan. Put them together and Western Iran (p77) is worth building your entire trip around. Bottom: Bridge on the Karun River

MATHESS / GETTY IMAGES ©

SHAHRAM KHORASANIZADEH / SHUTTERSTOCK ©

Hiking in the Alamut Valley

14 The fabled Alamut Valley (p118) offers a tempting invitation to hike, explore and reflect among the fabled Castles of the Assassins. Nestled on widely spread rocky knolls and pinnacles lie the shattered remnants of more than 50 fortresses that were once home to the medieval world's most feared religious cult. Choose a day hike from Qazvin or more extensive wanderings from Gazor Khan – a full trans-Alborz crossing to the Caspian hinterland. Either way, this is some of the most rewarding hiking to be found in the Middle East.

The Poets of Shiraz

15 Iranians like to say that even in the poorest home you'll find two books: a Quran and the poetry of Hafez. It's appropriate for a country whose most celebrated sons are poets, and where almost every person can quote their favourite millennium-old man of words. In Shiraz (p195), the city of nightingales and gardens, the tombs of Hafez and Sa'di draw pilgrims from around the country. Join them as they linger over tea, reciting the works of their heroes. Top right: Aramgah-e Hafez (Tomb of Hafez), Shiraz (p201)

Zoroastrian Fire Temples

16 Iran may be an Islamic Republic, but its Zoroastrian sites have an otherworldly charm. Chak Chak (p194), out in a deliciously remote location in the Yazd hinterland, has a superb fire temple with a stunning brass door, even more stunning views, and an air of ritual, ancient and deep. This was the Zoroastrian heartland and remains its most significant pilgrimage site. It's difficult to come here and not imagine yourself in the days before Islam arrived in Iran. There are other fire temples in Kerman and Yazd. Bottom right: Worshippers at Pir-e-Sabz Fire Temple, Chak Chak

Need to Know

For more information, see Survival Guide (p331)

Currency
Iranian rial (IR)

Language
Farsi (Persian) and ethnic languages, primarily Azari Turkish.

Money
Bring enough cash (in US dollars or euros) for the duration of your trip. You cannot use credit or debit cards, travellers cheques or ATMs.

Visas
A valid Iranian visa is required. Start the process at least two months before you plan to arrive. Some nationalities can get a visa on arrival if arriving by air.

Mobile Phones
You will need a local SIM card for cheap local and pricey international calls. Your home SIM will not work.

Time
GMT/UTC +3½ hours; daylight saving observed between No Ruz (around 21 March) and 22 September

When to Go

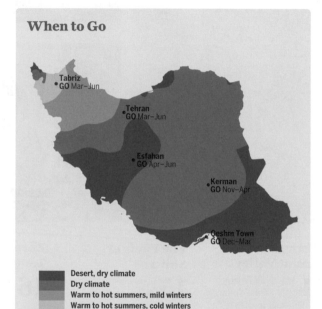

- Tabriz
  GO Mar–Jun
- Tehran
  GO Mar–Jun
- Esfahan
  GO Apr–Jun
- Kerman
  GO Nov–Apr
- Qeshm Town
  GO Dec–Mar

Desert, dry climate
Dry climate
Warm to hot summers, mild winters
Warm to hot summers, cold winters

High Season
(Mar–May)

➡ Ideal temperatures in most of Iran.

➡ Prices are highest and crowds biggest during No Ruz (21 March to 3 April), especially at Esfahan, Shiraz, Yazd and the Persian Gulf coast.

➡ Prices in hotels go up and availability goes down in April.

Shoulder
(Jun–Oct)

➡ Warmer weather in June means fewer travellers.

➡ September and especially October temperatures moderate; good for mountain trekking.

➡ Prices slightly lower than March to May.

Low Season
(Nov–Feb)

➡ Extreme cold, especially in the northeast and west, but good for skiing.

➡ Some mountain roads can be impassable.

➡ Hotel prices are discounted by 10% to 50% and there are fewer crowds.

Useful Websites

Lonely Planet (www.lonely planet.com/iran) Destination information, hotel bookings, traveller forum and more.

Iran Tourism & Touring Online (www.itto.org) As close as Iran comes to a tourism website with some informative links.

Iran Chamber Society (www. iranchamber.com) Good for high-level coverage of the arts.

Tehran Times (www.tehrantimes. com) Iran's English-language news site and newspaper.

See You In Iran (www.facebook. com/SeeYouinIran/) This FB group posts all kinds of useful stuff for Iran travellers.

Important Numbers

Drop the ⏻0 when dialling an area code from abroad.

Ambulance	⏻115
Fire	⏻125
Police	⏻110
Iran country code	⏻98
International access code	⏻00
Local directory	⏻118

Exchange Rates

Australia	A$1	IR29,700
Canada	C$1	IR30,200
Euro zone	€1	IR42,200
Japan	¥100	IR33,400
New Zealand	NZ$1	IR23,643
Turkey	1TKL	IR10,450
UK	UK£1	IR48,100
USA	US$1	IR38,180

For official exchange rates, see Central Bank of Iran (www.cbi.ir).

Daily Costs

Budget: less than US$50

➡ One-way bus Tehran–Esfahan: US$9

➡ Entrance fees to most sights: US$4

➡ Dorm bed or basic room with bathroom: US$10–40

➡ Meal in local restaurant: US$5–10

Midrange: US$50–200

➡ One-way flight Shiraz–Tehran: US$70

➡ Half-day trip from Shiraz to Persepolis by taxi/driver-cum-guide: US$40/50

➡ Double room with bathroom: US$40–149

➡ Meal in midrange restaurant: US$8–15

Top end: More than US$200

➡ Four-star hotel in Tehran or Esfahan: US$150 plus

➡ Main meal in top Tehran restaurant: US$25–50

➡ Guide and/or driver for day: US$70–100

Opening Hours

Opening and closing times can be erratic, but you can rely on most businesses closing Thursday afternoons and Friday (the Iranian weekend).

Banks & Government Offices 8am–2pm Sat-Wed, 8am–noon Thu.

Museums 9am–6pm summer, until 4pm or 5pm winter, some closed on Mon.

Restaurants noon–3pm, 6–10pm.

Shops 9am–8pm Sat-Thu, but likely to have a siesta between 1–3.30pm and possibly close Thursday afternoon.

Travel Agencies 9am-5pm Sat-Wednesday, 7.30am–noon Thu.

Arriving in Iran

Imam Khomeini International Airport (Tehran; p68) Fixed price taxi into town: IR750,000, depending on vehicle type; rip-offs are unusual if you use the official taxi queue. Bus to Metro station: IR75,000, plus IR7000 for Metro ticket to city centre

Shiraz International Airport (p206) Taxi into town: US$5

Turkish border at Bazargan (p81)Taxi to Maku: US$10. Onward bus to Tabriz: US$2

Getting Around

Services on most forms of public transport are frequent, fairly punctual and very cheap; airlines are often delayed. Book ahead if you're travelling on a weekend or, especially, any public holiday.

Air An extensive network of generally reliable domestic flights is a great way to avoid some *really* long drives.

Bus You can get almost anywhere by bus. Most buses are comfortable rather than luxurious; speed checks have dramatically improved safety.

Savari Shared taxis that are usually quicker than buses; far less comfortable.

Train Links most major cities but departures are much less frequent.

For much more on **getting around**, see p353

First Time Iran

For more information, see Survival Guide (p331)

Checklist

➡ Make sure your passport is valid for at least six months past your arrival date.

➡ Inform your debit-/credit-card company.

➡ Arrange for appropriate travel insurance.

➡ Check government travel warnings and make sure you're not travelling to any areas that will void your insurance.

➡ Check if you can use your mobile/cell phone.

What to Pack

➡ Farsi phrasebook

➡ Some pictures of your family to better communicate with your new Iranian friends

➡ Sturdy walking shoes

➡ Warm clothes in winter

➡ Hat, sunglasses and sunscreen

➡ Water bottle

➡ Electrical adapter (European, two round-pin type)

➡ Small gifts from home for new friends

Top Tips for Your Trip

➡ Plan your trip (including visa application process) well in advance.

➡ Don't be too ambitious – Iran is big and trying to see everything can lead to frustration.

➡ Learn some Farsi before you go – a sure way to make local friends.

➡ Take some small gifts from home to repay the many small acts of kindness and hospitality you're likely to receive while in Iran.

What to Wear

Few questions occupy the minds of first-time female visitors to Iran quite like the question of what to wear. Like all females aged nine and older, women travellers will need to wear hejab while in Iran. That means covering hair, arms and legs and wearing clothes that disguise your body shape when in public. Bring something long and loose from home and, if you want to look less like a tourist, shop for a *manteau* (an overcoat that covers your bottom, at least) once you arrive. Ditto for scarves, which will require constant attention lest you expose too much hair. As for men, the main dress restrictions are that you shouldn't wear shorts, or singlets that show your shoulders.

Sleeping

Choice is limited to fairly uninspiring hotels and basic local lodging houses away from the main tourist circuit and larger cities.

Hotels Runs the full gamut from budget cheapies to top-end behemoths; the upmarket end of things is limited but improving all the time.

Mosaferkhanehs Basic lodging houses or very basic hotels with dorm beds, shared bathrooms, and a predominantly local male clientele.

Camping With few official camping areas, camping is rarely appropriate.

Bargaining

In general prices in shops are fixed. But virtually all prices in the bazaar are negotiable, particularly for souvenirs and always for carpets. In heavily touristed areas, such as Imam Sq in Esfahan, bargaining is essential.

Bargaining tips include not showing too much interest at first when you find something you like. And don't buy the first one you see. Check out a few alternatives to get an idea of quality and price.

Remember that bargaining is not a life and death battle. A good bargain is when *both* parties are happy and doesn't require you to screw every last toman out of the vendor. As long as you're happy, it was a good deal.

Grilled *kubideh* (minced lamb kabab)

Tipping

Tipping is not a big deal in Iran. In upmarket restaurants (mainly in Tehran) a 10% gratuity might be expected – on top of the 10% service charge that's often built into the bill. But in most other places any money you leave will be a pleasant surprise. It's normal to offer a small tip to anyone who guides you or opens a building that is normally closed. If your offer is initially refused, persist. There is no culture of *baksheesh* (alms or tips) in Iran.

Etiquette

Iranians are generally quite forgiving of Westerners for any minor cultural transgressions – they don't expect you to know all of the rules. Some useful things to remember:

➡ When invited to dinner take a tin of the local sweets (eg *gaz* in Esfahan).

➡ Never use the thumbs up sign, which is the equivalent of the middle finger 'up yours'.

➡ Men should not offer to shake a woman's hand unless she offers first.

➡ Take off your shoes when entering a home or a mosque.

Eating

Iran is an excellent place to eat out (or in, if you're lucky enough to be invited to a meal in a local family home).

Teahouses Traditionally where Iranians would go to socialise and eat, with tea, *qalyan* (water pipe) and food.

Kebabis Simple kababis tend to be found around major *meydans* (squares) and serve, yes, kababs. Eat where the locals eat.

Take-away Fast food is popular and begins (and often ends) with bread-roll 'sandwiches'.

Restaurants Found across the country; most serve *ash-e jo* (pearly-barley soup) and salad as standard starters

If You Like...

Architecture

Church of St Stephanos, Jolfa One of three splendid Armenian churches that together form a Unesco World Heritage listing. (p96)

Oljeitu Mausoleum, Soltaniyeh A vast 14th-century mausoleum with the world's tallest brick dome is the most magnificent surviving Mongol structure in Iran. (p103)

Naranjestan, Shiraz Take the ultimate selfie in the exquisite winter *iwan* (vaulted hall), repeated ad infinitum in the mirror. (p197)

Mil-e Gonbad, Gonbad-e Kavus A soaring, almost unfeasibly bold 11th-century brick tower. (p256)

Museums

Treasury of National Jewels, Tehran Home to the Peacock Throne and a Shah's ransom of bling. (p40)

Isfahan Music Museum, Esfahan Stunning new museum that plays to the city's fine musical traditions. (p167)

Carpet Museum, Mashhad Admire exquisite carpets while on a pilgrimage to Mashhad's holy shrine. (p263)

Tehran Museum of Contemporary Art, Tehran Striking piece of modern architecture housing a fabulous but rarely seen collection. (p46)

Iranian Food

Ardabil Possibly the sweetest town in Iran, famous for its honeycomb, black halva ('pest') and myriad confectioners. (p99)

Hezardestan Traditional Teahouse, Mashhad Fabulous food, a memorable teahouse setting and live music make this the top choice for Mashhadis. (p265)

Haj Khalifeh Ali Rahbar, Yazd The mind- and taste-bud-blowing array of Iranian *shirini* (sweets) is the best in town. (p192)

Fereni Hafez, Esfahan Fereni is a classic Iranian dessert and this Esfahan institution is so popular people eat it for breakfast. (p172)

Ancient Civilisations

Persepolis The full glory of the Achaemenid period in one magnificent former summer capital. (p207)

Shushtar The Sassanian-era structures here include watermills, a 45-span bridge and a cliff-top castle. (p12)

Takht-e Soleiman History's foremost Zoroastrian fire-temple complex is set in a high, lonely bowl of mountains beside a crater lake. (p340)

Ardashir's Palace South of Shiraz, Ardashir's monumental palace was one of the earliest Sassanian architectural triumphs, and the most impressive of what's left. (p312)

Village Life

Ateshooni, one of Iran's original and best homestays in the classic mid-desert oasis village of Garmeh. (p180)

Tak-Taku Guesthouse Experience desert family life with Mohammad and his family in their atmospheric courtyard home in Toudeshk. (p178)

Bavanat Stay in a living museum of village life where profits return to the community. (p211)

Qeshm Island Experience the fast-disappearing Bandari Arab way of life in the coastal villages of Tabl or Shibderaz (p32)

Getting Active

Alborz trekking Iran's best hiking with trails possible from both the Karaj and Alamut sides. (p119)

Mt Damavand Trek to the summit of the Middle East's highest mountain. (p74)

Desert trekking Venture into the sands by camel or on foot from the desert villages of Farahzad or Mesr. (p181)

Rock climbing Tackle one of the region's classic climbing challenges at Farhad Tarash, in the shadow of the historic Bisotun rock inscriptions. (p339)

Bazaars

Bazar-e Bozorg, Esfahan Sprawling, historic and endlessly fascinating; feels like a Persian fairy tale. (p160)

Bazar-e Vakil, Shiraz One of Iran's best with brick-vaulted ceilings and a marvellously chaotic early evening vibe. (p196)

Grand Bazaar, Tehran Begin in the copper section, move on to carpets and inhale deeply in the nut-and-spice section. (p39)

Bazar-e Sartasari, Kerman Classic east Iranian bazaar with commercial lanes overlooked by mosques and museums. (p232)

Cultural Encounters

Kurdish hospitality, Howraman Valley Journey among the Kurds to experience singing and dancing in this ancient Kurdish bastion. (p125)

Zurkhaneh, Yazd Uniquely Iranian show of male strength with mystical undertones. (p183)

Religious pilgrimage, Mashhad Observe the passionate reverence for Shiite Islam that is nowhere more fully displayed than at the major holy shrines, particularly the huge shrine of Imam Reza in Mashhad. (p258)

Persian Food Tours, Tehran Learn how to cook Iranian-style and shop with locals to buy the ingredients. (p53)

Top: Carpet-seller's stall in Bazar-e Bozorg (p160), Esfahan
Bottom: Ruins of Persepolis (p207)

Month by Month

January

You'll see few travellers in mid-winter. Much of western Iran will be under snow and mountain roads can be cut off. Desert nights are very cold, but days are pleasant and sunny.

🏃 Skiing the Alborz Mountains

January and February are the ideal months for skiing. There are more than 20 ski fields in Iran but the best are Dizin (p72) and Shemshak (p73), near Tehran. The snow is great and skiing is cheap.

February

February is often the coldest month, which is good for skiing but otherwise not the most pleasant time to travel the country. The month also has a couple of stand-out events.

☆ International Fadjr Theatre Festival

The highlight of the Iranian theatre year centres around Teatre Shahr (City Theatre) and Iranshahr Theatre in Tehran.

🎊 Magnificent Victory of the Islamic Revolution of Iran

February 1 to 11 is known as Dahe-ye Fajr ('the 10 Days of Dawn'), a celebration of the days in 1979 between Ayatollah Khomeini returning to Iran and the fall of the Shah's government. Expect speeches and nationalist demonstrations across the country.

March

The whole country hits the road for No Ruz, the Iranian New Year, which is also the start of spring. For two weeks Iran virtually shuts down. Hotels are packed and travelling is tricky.

🎊 Chahar shanbe-soori

The Tuesday night before the last Wednesday of the Iranian year sees Iranians sing, dance and jump over fires to burn off bad luck as part of the controversial 'pagan' tradition of Chahar shanbe-soori.

🎊 No Ruz

The pre-Islamic celebration of No Ruz falls on the spring equinox on 21 March. It's a huge family celebration on a par with Christmas in the West and many people take two weeks off. Tehran is empty at this time.

April

It's spring, the temperatures rise, flowers bloom, Iranians return to work and weather-wise it's the best time to visit. April and May is peak season for foreign travellers; book ahead for rooms and flights.

🎊 Islamic Republic Day

The 1 April is a public holiday for the anniversary of the referendum that officially established the Islamic Republic of Iran in 1979. It's marked by rallies, speeches and military parades.

🎊 Sizdah be Dah

Sizdah be Dar ('13th day of the year'; 2 April) is a public holiday when the entire population heads to the countryside for a picnic. It's a pre-Islamic tradition that symbolises making a fresh start.

☆ Fajr International Film Festival

Iran's premier film festival features Iranian and international films and red-carpet events in more than 20 cinemas across Tehran. It has been held in February in previous years, so check the website for details.

May

With mild temperatures, May is a good month to travel in Iran but it's still high season. Wildflowers bloom from the west to the northeast, while anywhere close to the Persian Gulf coast temperatures are really starting to heat up.

📷 Ramazan (Ramadan)

During the month of Ramazan, Muslims are expected to perform a dawn-to-dusk fast that includes abstaining from all drinks (including water) and from smoking. Tempers can be shorter, but life goes on. In coming years it falls in May or April.

June

It's late spring and getting warmer and more humid, but as it's not crazy hot (except along the Persian Gulf littoral or the lowlands around Shush) and few are travelling, this is still a good time to visit.

📷 Kashan Rose Festival

Kashan is lovely at any time, but the rose festival in and around town in June, celebrates the picking of rose petals as a precursor to rose-water production.

📷 Eid al-Fitr

The Festival of the Breaking of the Fast marks the end of Ramazan and, after sunset, is celebrated with huge meals across the country. Depending on the year, it can also fall in May.

September

As summer segues into fall/autumn, the sun loses the worst of its sting (only the worst – much of Iran still bakes) and it's a good month to go hiking in the mountains.

📷 Ashura

Ashura marks the martyrdom of Imam Hossein and is the most intense, passionate date on the Shia Muslim calendar. It is celebrated with religious theatre and sombre parades in which men self-flagellate. In coming years it falls in September and August.

October

With moderate temperatures and no snow to block roads, October is a pleasant time to travel, and many Iranians take a break. Fierce summer temperatures are a thing of the past.

🏃 Nomadic migration

With summer over, nomads are on the move, heading downhill to warmer climes. The hills and back roads of the Zagros Mountains around Shiraz are a good place to find them.

November

Winter is coming and with it the cold and snow. Travel in the mountains of western Iran can be tough, but the desert, coast and cities of central Iran can be quite pleasant.

📷 Martyrdom of Imam Reza

The anniversary of Imam Reza's death is a huge deal in Mashhad, with Shiite pilgrims flocking from around the region to pay their respects at the vast Haram-e Razavi. It's in November or October in coming years.

December

A cold time to visit as the winter chill really kicks in (except on the Persian Gulf). Expect cold, clear skies, low golden light and snow-dusted hills – Western Iran in particular is at its most photogenic

📷 Yalda

Iran celebrates Yalda, the longest night of the year. It's a big deal as family and friends gather in homes to eat pomegranates, watermelon and recite Hafez and other poets.

Itineraries

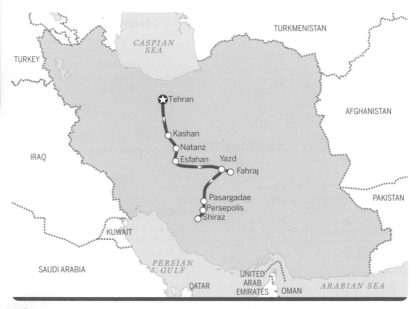

 Classic Iran

In two weeks it's possible to see the jewels of Iran's rich history, but you'll need to keep moving.

Start in **Tehran** and spend two days seeing the sights, including the Golestan Palace, the Treasury of National Jewels and Grand Bazaar. Take a bus to **Kashan**, where you can explore the bazaar, check out the Qajar-era traditional houses and chill out in the Fin Garden.

Make a pit stop at the mosque and tomb in **Natanz** en route to architecturally magnificent **Esfahan** and spend three days exploring the blue-tiled mosques of Naqsh-e Jahan (Imam) Square, the bustling Bazar-e Bozorg, the sublime bridges across the Zayandeh River and the Armenian community at Jolfa.

Head to the desert trading city of **Yazd** for three days wandering the maze of lanes, gaping at the Masjed-e Jameh (Jameh Mosque) and climbing to the Zoroastrian Towers of Silence. For a change of pace, stop in the desert village of **Fahraj** before spending a day visiting ancient **Pasargadae** and **Persepolis** on the way to Shiraz. Spend two days in **Shiraz**, where you can see the Zand-era gardens and bazaar, and wander the old city. Fly back to Tehran.

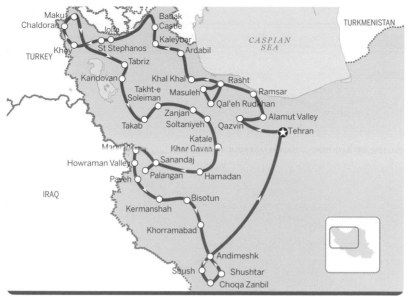

 **Go West**

This intriguing meander west is ideal for those who've seen the main desert city sights or are confident in navigating through areas often unaccustomed to foreigners. The route over mountains and valleys boasts nine World Heritage sites. The remotest sections will require charter taxis. Note that in winter, mountain roads can be cut off by snow.

Starting in **Tehran**, head west to **Qazvin** and spend the afternoon exploring the historic city, before driving into the **Alamut Valley** and hiking for two days among the ruined Castles of the Assassins. Continue across to the Caspian, recovering at a homestay near **Ramsar**, then onto vibrant **Rasht**, conquering the mountain fortress of **Qal'eh Rudkhan** before spending a pleasant afternoon strolling the teashops of photogenic **Masuleh**. Forsake the dull coast and jump a savari inland, up through nomad country to **Khal Khal**, then onto **Ardabil** to visit the magnificent Sheikh Safi-od-Din Mausoleum. Savari-hop the scenic back route to **Kaleybar** via Meshgin Shahr. Climb the breathtaking **Babak Castle**, then hire a driver for the sublime Aras River Valley run to **Jolfa** and the magnificent **Church of St Stephanos**.

Complete the Armenian church trifecta of **Qareh Kalisa** and **Dzor Dzor Chapel** on your way to **Maku**, via **Khoy** and **Chaldoran**. An easy half day to **Tabriz** and its bazaar leaves the afternoon for exploring troglodyte **Kandovan**. More savari-hopping across high landscapes due south to **Takab** and the starkly beautiful **Takht-e Soleiman**, once the world's greatest Zoroastrian fire-temple complex. Continue on across the incredible landscape to **Zanjan**. Hire a driver for the trip to **Hamadan** via the magnificent Mongol-era Oljeitu Mausoleum at **Soltaniyeh** and the remarkable **Katale Khor Caves**. Check out the BuAli Sina Mausoleum in Hamadan before taking a speedy savari to hospitable **Sanandaj**.

Spend an afternoon in **Palangan** before heading to **Marivan** and the scenic road thru **Howraman** to **Paveh**, via Kurdish mountain villages. At **Kermanshah**, sneak a peak at Taq-e Bustan's stone carvings and the scaffolding at **Bisotun** before you cross the mighty Zagros Mountains to **Khorramabad** and its fortress. Savari to **Shush** to wander ancient **Susa**, then hire a car to the 3000-year-old ziggurat of **Choqa Zanbil** and the Sassanian-cum-Roman engineering of the **Shushtar hydraulic system**. Take a savari to **Andimeshk** and your evening train back to Tehran.

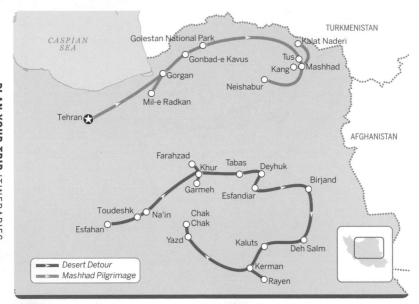

Legend:
- Desert Detour
- Mashhad Pilgrimage

10 DAYS Mashhad Pilgrimage

Take the train or bus from **Tehran** to **Gorgan**, nestled attractively in the Alborz Mountains. Gorgan makes a great base for visiting the Turkmen steppe and the remote Mil-e Radkan tower. If you're impressed by this tower, you'll want to visit the incredible 1000-year-old tomb-tower of Mil-e Gonbad, in **Gonbad-e Kavus**, before visiting the forested mountains of **Golestan National Park**, perhaps staying at the Turkmen Ecolodge.

Next up, travel to Iran's holiest city of **Mashhad**, where you can revel in the ecstasy of pilgrims in the stunning and massive Haram-e Razavi complex and visit the beautifully proportioned Boq'eh-ye Khajeh Rabi mausoleum. Mashhad is a great base for exploring the hinterlands by foot, bicycle or horseback. Nearby **Kang** is a photogenic stepped village of stacked mud-brick homes. The mausoleum of 11th-century poet, Ferdosi is found in **Tus**, while Omar Khayyam has his tomb in **Neishabur**. The impressive mountain cliffs of **Kalat Naderi** lie to the north.

Mashhad is a gateway to Central Asia; otherwise fly back to Tehran or continue south by bus or train into the desert.

12 DAYS Desert Detour

If you've ever dreamt of the oasis towns of *The Thousand and One Nights* or are drawn to hospitable homestays, this trip is for you. It's doable by taking infrequent buses, but the odd taxi *dar bast* can reduce waiting time. Avoid the summer heat by travelling between October and April.

Start in **Esfahan** and take a bus to **Toudeshk** for a night and a morning in the shifting sands of the Varzaneh Desert, before continuing to see the traditional houses of **Na'in**. From Na'in take the bus east to **Khur**, where you get a taxi to **Farahzad** and/or **Garmeh** for desert homestays that redefine hospitality; plan for three days all up.

From Garmeh, head west via **Tabas** and the remarkable 'forgotten' villages of **Old Deyhuk** and **Esfandiar**, continuing on to **Birjand** with its impressive fortress-restaurant. From there don't miss an oasis night at **Deh Salm** before crossing the Lut Desert with its extraordinaty **Kaluts** (giant 'sandcastles'). After bazaaring **Kerman** and daytripping to **Rayen fortress**, end your trip in a traditional hotel in **Yazd**, perhaps with a side trip to the fire temple at **Chak Chak**.

Plan Your Trip
Visas & Planning

Assuming you have a visa, most immigration and border officials are efficient and tourists rarely get too much hassle. Land borders can take longer if you're on a bus or train. Women need to be adequately covered from the moment they get off the plane or arrive at the border. Arriving without a visa is risky, as the visa-on-arrival process sees a lot of people turned away.

Who Needs A Visa?

Passport-holders of Turkey, Lebanon, Azerbaijan, Georgia, Bolivia, Egypt and Syria can travel to Iran and stay in the country without a visa from between 15 to 90 days.

Everyone else needs to arrange a visa in advance or seek a 30-day visa on arrival (VOA) at an airport. VOAs are not available to citizens of the USA, Somalia, the UK, Canada, Bangladesh, Jordan, Iraq, Afghanistan and Pakistan. If you hold a passport of one of these countries you will need to pre-arrange a tour or specially qualified private guide, or be sponsored by a friend or relative in Iran (who will take legal responsibility for you) to obtain a visa.

Israeli passport holders, and anyone with an Israeli stamp in their passport (or exit stamps at the Jordanian or Egyptian crossings into Israel), will not get a visa.

Which Visa? Pros & Cons

First, it's important to understand the process. Except with transit visas, all visa applicants must be 'approved' by the Ministry of Foreign Affairs (MFA) in Tehran. This includes those seeking a visa on arrival, who can be approved either in advance or, with a longer wait, on arrival.

If you're approved, the MFA sends an authorisation number to the consulate, which takes your application form, passport

Types of Visa

Tourist visa Issued for up to 30 days and extendable. Must be obtained before coming to Iran and valid to enter for 90 days from the issue date. This is the surest option.

Tourist visa on arrival (VOA) Issued for 30 days on arrival at any Iranian international airport. Convenient but relatively risky, as you may be denied entry. Not available to US, UK or Canadian nationals.

Transit visa Issued for five to seven days, this is the last resort. You must enter and exit via different countries, and have a visa or a ticket to an onward country. Transit visas are not available to US passport holders. To most other nationalities, the visas can be obtained in one or two days and no authorisation number is required.

How Do I Do It?

DIY Deal with an Iranian embassy or consulate directly.

Agency Pay an agency to obtain a visa authorisation number, which is sent to an embassy where you pay for and pick up the visa. Recommended.

VOA Works best if you get a visa authorisation number in advance and have at least your first night's accommodation confirmed.

photos and fee and issues the visa. Fees vary depending on your country of origin; see the Iran embassy website.

Transit visas are only fractionally cheaper than tourist visas and, while they don't require authorisation from Tehran, only give you up to seven days. The choice is whether to get a tourist visa in advance or on arrival.

Tourist Visa

There are two ways to get a tourist visa.

➡ **Do It Yourself** You can go through a consulate, which saves an agency fee but takes three weeks and often longer. In theory, you download and fill out the application form from the Iran consulate in your home country; you then take or send the forms and your passport, photos, money and proof of your travel insurance to the embassy and they will send your details to Tehran for approval. Several weeks later you might be contacted with the result. Otherwise you'll need to contact them, which is not always easy. If all goes to plan, you will eventually either pick up the visa in person (some embassies require women to cover their hair), or have your passport returned in a registered-mail envelope. Exceptions abound. In rare cases this method can take just a few days. However, we've also heard of cases where weeks after submission the consul has directed applicants to a visa agency to get the visa authorisation number. With so much uncertainty, if you choose this option, give yourself six weeks or longer to be sure.

➡ **Use an Agency** Visa agencies charge from €30 to UK£120 to get you an authorisation number. In most cases you fill out an electronic form with details of your itinerary and where you'd like to collect your visa, attach digital copies of photo and passport, and the agency sends this to Tehran. The MFA claims that for most nationalities it takes between five and 10 working days to assess the application. When it does take longer, the visa agency often won't know why, which might explain (if not excuse) the agency being slow to reply to your follow-up emails. There is no refund if your application fails, but few are rejected. Once the authorisation number is received, the agency will forward it to you and your nominated Iranian embassy/consulate. You then need to go through the application process as a formality, and in most consulates the visa is issued on the spot.

If you're British, Canadian or American, expect both methods to be slower, more costly and more arduous. When it's open, the Iranian Embassy in London will often request an interview and requires fingerprints from British applicants. For US citizens, allow three months to be safe.

Tourist Visa on Arrival

Iran usually issues 30-day tourist visas on arrival to people from about 65 countries, including most European, ASEAN, Gulf Arab and Central Asian countries, several South American countries, Australia, China, India, Japan, New Zealand and South Korea. Notable absentees are Britain, Canada and the USA.

Tourist visas are available at all international airports, but it is recommend to fly into Tehran's Imam Khomeini International Airport to avoid problems. At the time of writing, to obtain the visa on arrival the following were required:

➡ a printout of your travel insurance. If the printout doesn't specifically mention Iran, you may need to purchase insurance at the airport;

➡ insurance can be purchased (US$16) at the counter opposite the visa desk; it is strongly recommended that you purchase your insurance before starting the visa process;

➡ the name and telephone of a sponsor. In practice this can be a hotel; it is strongly recommend you have a night booked at the hotel you name and that you carry a printout of an email from the hotel confirming your reservation, although this is not an official requirement to get the visa;

➡ the requisite fee. For most Western nationalities, the fee is €75 (Australians pay €145) or the US dollar equivalent. Visa fees can be paid in euros or US dollars.

Entry Visa (Business Visa)

To get a 30-day (extendable) business visa you must obtain an invitation letter from the company or organisation you plan to visit. The process is otherwise the same as getting a tourist visa (DIY or using an agency). People coming for a conference or to play in a sporting event need an 'entry visa'.

Sponsors & Visa Agencies

Any Iranian can sponsor your application, which means they submit the paperwork for an authorisation code. But in most cases it's easier to use a travel agency or a specialist visa agency. Keep in mind, though, that even with an agency there are no guarantees, and the visa agent will take their fee regardless of whether a visa is issued or not. Seek up-to-date recommendations from other travellers before you choose one – Lonely Planet's Thorn Tree forum (www.lonelyplanet.com/thorntree) is a good place to start.

Two recommended visa agencies include:
→ **Persian Voyages** (p30)
→ **Iran Visa Authorization Code** (www.iranvisacode.com)

Before You Go

One of the main considerations when planning a trip to Iran is whether to travel independently, take a tour or do a bit of both.

To Tour or Not to Tour

Independent Travel

Travelling independently in Iran has more ups than downs. It's easier as a man or as part of a couple than as a woman, but is eminently doable regardless of your sex. Air, rail and bus transport is efficient and safe, sights are cheap and enough people speak English, or are willing to help, that it's hard to get into too much trouble. To top it all, as a visitor most Iranians consider you a 'gift from God' and you will be bowled over by the kindness of strangers.

Private Guides & Drivers

Freelance drivers and guides are a cheaper, more flexible alternative to group tours and plenty of readers have written to recommend this way of travelling – some for a month or more.

Check that your guide is a qualified one. It takes years of study to become a fully licensed guide. The experience, knowledge

VISA EXTENSIONS

First the good news: there is *usually* little difficulty in extending a 30-day tourist visa to 60 days. It's possible, but harder, to extend again, up to a maximum of 90 days. The following summary of how the process works is notoriously prone to change. Check the Thorn Tree (lonelyplanet.com/thorntree) or a specialist visa agency for the latest.

Choose Your City

If you want a long extension it's worth planning your itinerary to be somewhere friendly when the extension is needed. In general, cities familiar with tourists are best: Shiraz has for years been the city of choice, with Esfahan also getting positive reports. Second-string options include Kerman, Yazd and Tabriz, but these don't always issue the full 30-day extension. Tehran, Mashhad and other cities are less reliable. Check the Thorn Tree (www.lonelyplanet.com/thorntree) for recent reports.

The Process

Head for the Police Department of Aliens Affairs (*edareh gozannameh*). Note that the office might have changed name to the Passport & Immigration Police by the time you arrive. You'll need:

→ your passport and two or three mug shots;

→ two photocopies of the picture page of your passport, your current visa, entry stamp and any other extensions you've had (most offices have a photocopy service);

→ fee for the extension (check the current fee with the office in question, but IR500,000 at the time of research), plus small notes for forms.

Pay for two copies of the appropriate forms. You'll then be directed to a Bank Melli branch to deposit the cash – just say 'visa' and the bank staff will fill in the forms for you. Return with your bank receipt and the visa extension will be issued within an hour or two, though in some cases (hello Tehran) it can take several days.

Timing & Overstaying

In theory, you can only apply for an extension two or three days before your existing visa is due to expire, and your extension starts on the day it's issued, not the end of your original visa. Cross-check the Persian calendar dates so you know exactly when your visa expires.

If things go awry, a doctor's note on official stationery stating you were unwell might act as a quasi-extension at the border, or be used for a short extension in the nearest Aliens Bureau. But don't rely on this. If you do overstay, even by a few hours, expect to be detained.

GETTING THE PAPERWORK RIGHT

While we don't advocate lying on your application form, try to avoid unnecessary complications. Tricky questions:

Email If asked for one, opt for something generic and avoid .gov accounts.

Itinerary If you want a 30-day visa, write a 30-day itinerary. Keep controversial places such as Bushehr, Natanz and border regions off your agenda. Once in Iran you can go where you want.

Occupation Teachers, nurses and data-entry clerks are more welcome than unloved journalists, military personnel or, according to one reader, anything to do with fashion (very dangerous!). Be aware that the MFA might Google your name.

Purpose of your visit Tourism. One guy, applying for a visa on arrival, wrote 'to see Iranian girlfriend'. He was deported. What was he thinking?

Photographs Women will probably need to have their hair covered (any scarf will do) in their visa-application photo. Check embassy websites.

and language ability of these guides can transform a simple excursion into a memorable adventure. Bona fide guides must carry a license (with photo ID and hologram with the date of expiry clearly displayed).

Group

Most organised tours start and finish in Tehran, with a quick look around the capital before concentrating on the must-sees: Shiraz and Persepolis, Esfahan and Yazd, with some short diversions thrown in. There are plenty of other itineraries, and agencies will happily build a trip to suit your interests. Costs depend on length, mode of transport, type of accommodation and the exchange rate. Expect to pay in dollars or euros.

Iranian guides are generally very good so you can expect comprehensive explanations of sights and cultural happenings, and answers to all your questions. And best, they act as a translator when you meet locals. However, you are less likely to meet locals on a tour, which is a big downside in a country where interactions are so rewarding.

Iranian tour operators also act as local handlers for foreign-based agencies selling tours to Iran, so booking direct should give you the same tour (without the foreign tour leader) for less money.

Iranian Operators

Also see the Tours listings in the On the Road chapters for recommendations of individual guides and other local operators.

Abgin Cultural Tours of Persia (☑021-2235 9272; www.abgintours.com; Tehran) Fixed itinerary cultural, desert and trekking tours plus flexible, personalised trips. Respected.

Cyrus Sahra (☑021-8819 4619; www.caravan sahra.com; Tehran) Big local organisation with a wide range of tours.

Pars Tourist Agency (www.key2persia.com) Dozens of inexpensive tours specialising in areas around Shiraz.

Up Persia (www.uppersia.com; Kerman) Young company, good feedback.

Foreign Operators

Bestway Tours & Safaris (www.bestway.com; Canada) Upmarket trips, some combining nearby 'stans.

Clio (www.clio.fr; France) French operator of cultural tours.

Distant Horizons (www.distant-horizons.com; USA) Small groups accompanied by a scholar.

Geographic Expeditions (www.geoex.com; USA) Includes nomad and bespoke tours.

Iranian Tours (www.iraniantours.com; UK & Iran) Iranian operator with offices in UK.

Lupine Travel (www.lupinetravel.co.uk; UK) A professional and very well-priced outfit offering group tours of Iran's highlights as well as tailored itineraries. The guides are excellent.

Magic Carpet Travel (www.magic-carpet-travel. com; UK) Iranian-owned, has a good reputation.

Passport Travel (www.travelcentre.com.au; Australia) Australia-based operator; includes a carpet-themed tour.

Persian Voyages (www.persianvoyages.com; UK) Iran specialist with a range of tours, but can also help with arranging visas for independent travellers.

Regions at a Glance

Iran is a big country and while cheap, efficient transport means nowhere is beyond reach, few people make it to all corners in a single trip. Almost everyone spends time in Tehran, the bustling capital, en route to or from the historic cities of Esfahan, Shiraz and Yazd in central Iran. These cities, and the mountain and desert towns around them, rank among Iran's main attractions.

Western Iran is also popular, with mountains in the north ideal for trekking and a spread of ancient sites and ethnic groups keeping things interesting. More remote and less travelled are the Persian Gulf coast, with its Arabian feel, and the deserts and Silk Road trading cities of northeastern Iran. Much of southeastern Iran is currently off-limits – check before setting out.

Tehran

Culture
Museums
Activities

First Impressions

Trump preconceptions by sipping tea with students, seeing contemporary art, joining pilgrims at the shrine of Ayatollah Khomeini and walkers on a trail from Darband.

Windows on the Past

Highlights include the National Museum, the last shah's Niyavaran Palace, the Qajars' Golestan Palace and the National Jewels Museum, where diamonds (and rubies, emeralds etc) are indeed forever.

Active Pursuits

Depending on the time of year Tehran's proximity to the Alborz Mountains provides the option for skiing or hiking. At any time you can ride the cable car to near the summit of Mt Tochal or arrange a cultural cooking experience with Persian Food Tours.

p34

Western Iran

History
Culture
Mountains

Cradle of Civilisation

This region was the cradle of many civilisations. See the Elamites' Choqa Zanbil, the Achaemenid legacy at Shush and Hamadan, the Sassanian water mills at Shushtar and the massive Mongol mausoleum at Soltaniyeh.

Ethnic Culture

Azari Turks, Kurds, Lors, Assyrians and nomad groups share western Iran with the Persians. Feel Turkish nationalism at Babak Castle or visit Kurdish villages in the Howraman Valley.

Scenic Roads

Wind through the sublime Aras River Valley, hunt lost Armenian churches and Assassin castles, explore hoodoo'd badlands and cling precariously to Howraman mountainsides on the wildest roads in the country.

p77

Central Iran

History
Architecture
Deserts

Footsteps of Empire

Empires have bloomed and withered here. Top sights are the Achaemenid capitol of Persepolis, the Sassanian centre at Firuz Abad, Safavid glories in Esfahan and the preserved desert city of Yazd.

Beautiful Buildings

Architectural gems include: Esfahan's wondrous Naqshe Jahan (Imam) Square, the Jameh Mosque and bridges; Kashan boasts extravagant Qajar mansions; and in Yazd there are courtyard homes turned hotels.

Desert Hospitality

Experience desert hospitality: Garmeh is a classic oasis, Zein-o-din a restored caravanserai and Bavanat a somnolent town. Or stay with a family in Farahzad.

p146

Persian Gulf

Islands
Environment
Activities

Qeshm Island

Dolphin-shaped Qeshm is home to 60 Bandari villages, including photogenic Laft with its wind towers and minarets, and homestays in Tabl and Shibderaz.

Geology & Wildlife

Qeshm's geology is so exotic it's recognised as a Unesco Geopark, and in season you can spot hawksbill and green turtles at Shibderaz village and migrating birds in the Harra Sea Forest. Go to Hengham Island for dolphins and gazelles.

Island Adventures

Up the heart rate by diving the reefs around Larak, taking a boat tour through the Harra Sea Forest, cycling around Kish and taking a ferry to Hormoz.

p213

Southeastern Iran

History
Deserts
Adventure

Tracing Trade Routes

The ancient Silk Route city of Kerman is a big draw. Kerman's bazaar, with its teahouse and caravanserai, evokes millennia of trade and is bathed in the clear light of Iran's southeast.

Arid Landscapes

The whole southeast is desert or semi-desert. Highlights include the huge natural 'sandcastles' of the Kaluts, nearby desert campsites and Mahan's famous gardens at Bagh-e Shahzde.

Off-the-track Travel

This is frontier territory and it's easy to get off the beaten track. Stay in a centuries old cave village at Meymand or explore the careworn but rather beautiful mud-built villages of South Khorasan.

p230

Northeastern Iran

Architecture
Adventure
Culture

Architectural Wonders

The Haram-e Razavi shrine has a profusion of architectural styles and the 1000-year-old brick tower at Gonbad-e Kavus is a magnificent, significant landmark. Watch also for fine caravanserais dating back to the Silk Road's heyday.

Journeys

Take a 4WD over mountain roads to the 'secret valley' hiding Mil-e Radkan or hike over the Binalud mountains to the stepped village of Kang.

Poetic Pilgrimages

Tus is linked with epic poet Abulqasim Ferdosi, while Neishabur is the birthplace of poet and mathematician Omar Khayyam. At their tombs, expect Iranian pilgrims to recite poems of their heroes.

p246

On the Road

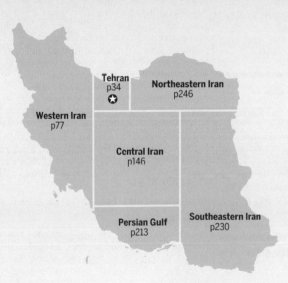

Tehran تهران

POP 8.43 MILLION / ☎021 / ELEV 1300M

Best Places to Eat

➡ Divan (p61)

➡ Dizi (p60)

➡ Gilaneh (p61)

➡ Khoone (p59)

➡ S.P.U Restaurant (p61)

➡ Azari Traditional Teahouse (p59)

Best Places to Sleep

➡ See You In Iran Hostel (p55)

➡ Howeyzeh Hotel (p56)

➡ Sepehr Apartment Hotel (p58)

➡ Firouzeh Hotel (p54)

➡ Ferdowsi International Grand Hotel (p55)

Why Go?

Hugging the lower slopes of the magnificent, snowcapped Alborz Mountains, Tehran is Iran's most secular and liberal city. Spend time here – as you should – and you'll soon realise that the city is so much more than a chaotic jumble of concrete and crazy traffic blanketed by a miasma of air pollution. This is the nation's dynamic beating heart and *the* place to get a handle on modern Iran and what its future will likely be.

Exploring this fascinating metropolis will transport you on a journey through more than 250 years of Iranian history – from the glittering Golestan Palace and the adjacent Grand Bazaar to the beautiful Azadi Tower and the notorious former US embassy. Then there are the city's many excellent museums and serene gardens. In such places, as well as in contemporary cafes, traditional teahouses and on the walking trails in the mountains, you can relax and enjoy all that's good about Tehran.

When to Go

The best time to visit Tehran is during the two-week No Ruz (Iranian New Year) holiday from 21 March. Given more than 60% of Tehranis come from somewhere else and head for home for the holiday, the usual traffic chaos is replaced by relative calm.

During April and May, and September to early November, the weather is relatively mild. Summer is hot and can be very humid, and while winter isn't as cold as some places, air pollution tends to be at its worst during December and January.

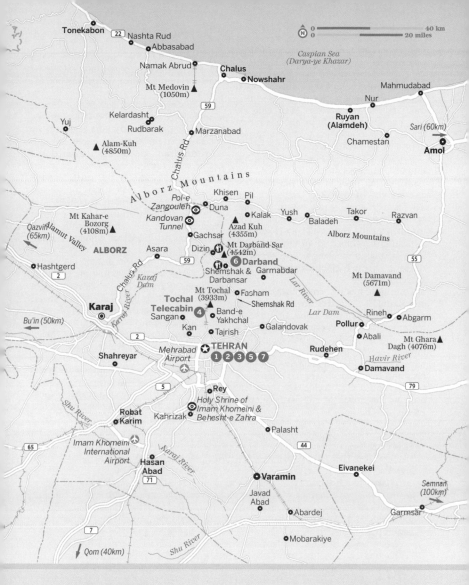

Tonekabon
22
Nashta Rud
Abbasabad
Namak Abrud
Chalus
Nowshahr

Caspian Sea
(Darya-ye Khazar)

Mahmudabad
Nur
Ruyan
(Alamdeh)
Chamestan

Sari (60km)
Amol

Mt Medovin
(1050m)
59
Kelardasht
Rudbarak
Marzanabad
Yuj
Alam-Kuh
(4850m)

Alborz Mountains

Khisen
Pil
Duna
Kalak
Yush
Baladeh
Takor
Razvan

Alborz Mountains

Pol-e
Zangouleh
Kandovan
Tunnel
Gachsar
Azad Kuh
(4355m)

Qazvin
(65km)
Alamut Valley
Mt Kahar-e
Bozorg
(4108m)
ALBORZ
Asara
Dizin
Mt Darband Sar
(4542m)
55

Hashtgerd
2
59
Shemshak &
Darbansar
6 Darband
Garmabdar
Mt Damavand
(5671m)

Karaj Dam
Tochal
Telecabin
Mt Tochal
(3933m)
Fasham
Shemshak Rd
Lar River
Lar Dam

Karaj
Bu'in (50km)
Karaj River
Chalus Rd
2
Sangan
4
Band-e
Yakhchal
Kan
Tajrish
Galandovak
Pollur
Rineh
Abgarm
Abali
Mt Ghara
Dagh (4076m)

Shahreyar
Mehrabad
Airport
TEHRAN
1 2 3 5 7
Rudehen
Havir River
Damavand

5
Rey
Holy Shrine of
Imam Khomeini &
Behesht-e Zahra
79

Robat
Karim
Kahrizak
Palasht
44
Eivanekei

65
Imam Khomeini
International
Airport
Hasan
Abad
71
Karaj River
Shu River
Varamin
Semnan
(100km)
Garmsar

7
Qom (40km)
Javad
Abad
Abardej
Mobarakiye
Shu River

0   40 km
0   20 miles

Tehran Highlights

① **Golestan Palace** (p37) Taking in the opulence of this monument to Qajar excess.

② **Grand Bazaar** (p39) Exploring the mother of all Iranian markets, which sells it all – from skimpy knickers to antique carpets.

③ **Treasury of National Jewels** (p40) Gazing at the Peacock Throne and a shah's ransom of bling.

④ **Tochal Telecabin** (p50) Riding the gondola to near the summit of Mt Tochal, where there's a small ski resort.

⑤ **Persian Food Tours** (p53) Getting a hands-on experience of making an Iranian meal with an expertly run cooking class.

⑥ **Darband** (p51) Enjoying a gentle hike up into the foothills of the Alborz Mountains at this north Tehran village packed with teahouses.

⑦ **Islamic Museum** (p40) Feasting your eyes on a gorgeous collection of arts and crafts from down the ages.

History

Back in ancient times, the village of Tehran was overshadowed by Rey, now a suburb of the city, but then one of the capitals of the Seljuk dynasty. In 1220 the Mongols sacked Rey as they swept across Persia, executing thousands in the process. Most who escaped wound up in Tehran, and the future capital's first population explosion turned the village into a prosperous trading centre.

In the mid-16th century Tehran's natural setting, numerous trees, clear rivers and good hunting brought it to the attention of the early Safavid king, Tahmasp I. Under his patronage, gardens were laid out, brick houses and caravanserais built and the town fortified by a wall with 114 towers. As Tehran continued to grow under later Safavid kings, European visitors wrote of the town's many enchanting vineyards and gardens.

Threatened by the encroaching Qajars, regent Karim Khan Zand moved his army from Shiraz to Tehran in 1758. At the same time, he refortified the city and began constructing a royal residence. Perhaps he had intended to move his capital here, but when Qajar chieftain Mohammad Hasan Khan was killed and his young son Agha Mohammad Khan taken hostage, Karim Khan decided the threat was over and abandoned the unfinished palace to return to Shiraz.

But things didn't work out quite as Karim Khan would have liked. By 1789 he was long dead and his one-time prisoner, Agha Mohammed Khan, was shah. The new shah declared this dusty town of 15,000 his capital.

As the centre of Qajar Persia, Tehran steadily expanded. By 1900 it had grown to 250,000 people, and in the 20th century it became one of the most populous cities on earth. Iran's capital has fomented and hosted two revolutions, two coups d'état and much intrigue. As the setting for the CIA's first coup in 1953, it had a profound impact on post–WWII world politics. And as pronouncements from Tehran have been the driving force behind the growth of radical Islam since 1979, that influence has not waned.

Mohammad Bagher Ghalibaf has served three terms as Tehran's first elected mayor since 2005. Under the stewardship of this conservative politician (who lost out to the more moderate Hassan Rouhani in the 2013 presidential election), Tehran has undergone many redevelopment and beautification projects. However, Ghalibaf's administration has also faced criticism for its woeful neglect of the environment: of the 15,000 plane trees that once lined Valiasr Ave only 7000 remain and many of them are suffering due to lack of water.

TEHRAN IN...

Two Days

Explore the **Grand Bazaar** (p39), Iran's biggest market. Stop in **Imam Khomeini Mosque** (p39) to watch Islam in action, then join the line for lunch at **Dizi** (p60). Spend the afternoon admiring ancient wonders at the **National Museum of Iran** (p40) and splendid **Islamic Museum** (p40). As the sun sets, join locals promenading on the **Tabiat Bridge** (p41) and grab dinner at the charming restaurant **Khoone** (p59).

On day two, check out the **Golestan Palace** (p37), take lunch at either **Khayyam** (p59) or the teahouse **Timcheh Akbarian** (p62), keeping the afternoon free for the bling-tastic **Treasury of National Jewels** (p40). Round the day out with drinks at **Sam Cafe** (p63) and dinner at **Divan** (p61) in northern Tehran.

Four Days

On day three, go hiking in the mountains at **Darband** (p51), followed by lunch at **Koohpayeh** (p61). Spend the afternoon exploring the leafy **Sa'd Abad Museum Complex** (p48), with its many palaces and galleries. Sample regional Iranian cuisine at **Gilaneh** (p61).

If the weather's fine, use your last day to ride the **Tochal Telecabin** (p50). If not, then spend a relaxed morning in the **Tehran Museum of Contemporary Art** (p46) and **Carpet Museum** (p47), perhaps take in a show at a commercial art gallery (p64) or wander around the **Qsar Garden Museum** (p42). Or go shopping at **Tajrish Bazaar** (p66).

⊙ Sights

Tehran is vast and many neighbourhoods are never visited by other Tehranis, let alone foreign travellers. Most streets have signs in English, but getting lost is still easy. It's worth remembering the Alborz Mountains are known locally as the North Star of Tehran because they are, yes, in the north. And as the whole city slopes down from these mountains, if you're walking uphill that usually means you're going north.

Valiasr Ave, running for 17km from the posh suburbs around Tajrish in the foothills of the Alborz Mountains to Tehran train station in the south, is Tehran's most famous street. Before the revolution it was known as Pahlavi Ave, a name which is now part of the city's history. However, another major north Tehran road – Afriqa Blvd – continues to be referred to by its pre-revolutionary name of Jordan. To complicate matters further Afriqa Blvd was renamed Nelson Mandela Blvd in 2015, even though you'll still mainly see many street signs calling it Afriqa Blvd!

⊙ Southern Tehran

This was the city centre until the mid-20th century, and the area south of Jomhuri-ye Eslami Ave is home to many of Tehran's best museums, as well as the Golestan Palace and the Grand Bazaar.

★ Golestan Palace PALACE
(کاخ گلستان); Map p38; ☑ 021-3311 3335; www.golestanpalace.ir; Arg Sq; general admission IR150,000, main halls IR150,000, other galleries & halls IR80,000; ⊙ 9am-5pm; Ⓜ Panzdah-e Khordad) The glories and excesses of the Qajar rulers are played out across this complex of grand buildings decorated with beautifully painted tiles and set around an elegant garden that's worth visiting in its own right. There are separate tickets for nine different sections, which you need to buy at the gate: the ones worth paying extra for are the Main Halls, which includes the spectacular Mirror Hall, and the Negar Khaneh (Iranian Painting Gallery).

Although there was a Safavid-era citadel on this site, it was Nasser al-Din Shah (r 1848–96), impressed by what he'd seen of European palaces, who created the 'Palace of Flowers' you see today. Originally it was much bigger, with inner and outer sections to encompass offices, ministries and private living quarters, but several surrounding buildings were pulled down under the Pahlavis.

➡ Takht-e Marmar
Heading in a clockwise direction around the courtyard from the ticket office, a long reflecting pool to leads to the Takht-e Marmar (Marble Throne Verandah), a mirrored, open-fronted audience hall dominated by a magnificent throne. Made in the early 1800s for Fath Ali Shah (r 1797–1834), the throne is constructed from alabaster mined in Yazd and supported by carved human figures. This hall was used on ceremonial occasions, including the Napoleon-style self-coronation of Reza Shah in 1925.

➡ Khalvate-e Karim Khani
On the corner of the same building is the gorgeous Khalvate-e Karim Khani (Karim Khan Nook), all that remains of a 1759 structure that served as the Terhan residence of Karim Khan Zand (r 1751–79). But it was Nasser al-Din Shah who enjoyed this elevated terrace most, smoking qalyan (water pipe) and perhaps contemplating his next asset sale as qanat (underground channel) water bubbled out of the marble fountain nearby. His marble tombstone now stands on the terrace.

➡ Negar Khaneh
Next is the Negar Khaneh (Iranian Painting Gallery), which displays a fine collection of Qajar-era art. Especially interesting are the portraits of the shahs wearing the jewels and crowns you can see in the National Jewels Museum, and pictures of everyday life in 19th-century Iran.

➡ Royal Museum
The next set of rooms comprises the Royal Museum (also called the Special Museum), a fascinating treasure trove of decorative art pieces and objects amassed by the shahs.

➡ Main Halls
The palace's highlight are the Main Halls, including the dazzling Talar-e Ayaheh (Mirror Hall). Built between 1874 and 1877 the Peacock Throne was housed here before it was moved to the National Jewels Museum. It was used for the coronation of Mohammad Reza Shah in 1967 (25 years after he came to power) and royal weddings. Today it and two adjoining halls house gifts, including a set of green malachite table decorations from Russia and fine porcelain from France, Germany and the UK.

➡ Howze Khaneh
Further east is the Howze Khaneh (Pool Room), named for the small pool and fountain in its centre. It houses a collection

TEHRAN SIGHTS

Southern Tehran

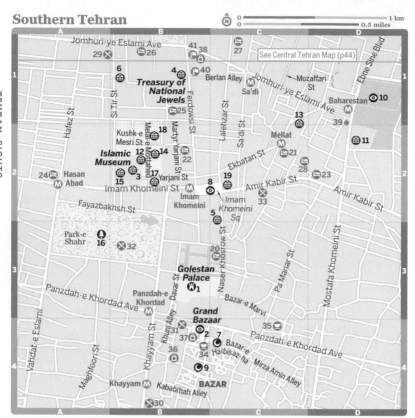

of paintings and sculptures of 19th-century European royalty given to their Qajar counterparts by the same European monarchs.

➡ Talar-e Berelian

Next door is the aptly named Talar-e Berelian (Brilliant Hall), where the use of mirrored glass on all surfaces and twinkling chandeliers reaches its apogee.

➡ Shams-Al Emarat

At the east end of the garden, the imposing Shams-Al Emarat (Edifice of the Sun) blends European and Persian architectural traditions. Born of Nasser al-Din Shah's desire to have a palace that afforded him a panoramic view of the city, it was designed by master architect Moayer al-Mamalek and built between 1865 and 1867. Only part of the building's ground floor is open for view, showcasing yet another sequence of mirrored and tiled rooms.

➡ Emarat-e Badgir

Next door stand four soaring *badgirs* (wind towers; used to catch breezes and funnel them down into a building to cool it), rising above the restored Emarat-e Badgir, first erected in the reign of Fath Ali Shah. The interior has typically ostentatious mirror work and is worth a quick look.

➡ Aks Khaneh

In the basement, the Aks Khaneh (Historic Photograph Gallery) exhibits a collection of historic photographs; one picture shows the inside of a Zoroastrian tower of silence, with bodies in varying states of decay.

➡ Talar-e Almas

Next up, the small Talar-e Almas (Diamond Hall) offers more blinged-to-the-max decoration. The more subdued teahouse and restaurant underneath might well be more appealing.

Southern Tehran

➡ **Abyaz Palace**

Finally, back near the entrance, the Abyaz Palace houses the Ethnographical Museum featuring a range of mannequins in traditional ethnic costumes.

⭐ **Grand Bazaar**   BAZAAR

(بازار بزرگ; Map p38; main entrance Panzdah-e Khordad Ave; ⊙7am-5pm Sat-Wed, to noon Thu; ⓜPanzdah-e Khordad) The maze of bustling alleys and the *bazaris* (shopkeepers) that fill them make this a fascinating, if somewhat daunting, place to explore. Despite being known as the Grand Bazaar, most of the architecture is less than 200 years old and pedestrian, although there are some gems to be found. Visit in the morning, when business is brisk but not yet frantic – later in the day the chance of being run over by a piece of fast-moving haulage equipment is high.

The bazaar's covered stores line more than 10km of lanes and there are several entrances, but you get a great view down a central artery by using the **main entrance** facing the square Sabzeh Medyan. The warren of people and goods is a city within a city and includes banks, a church, a fire station and several mosques, most notably the impressive **Imam Khomeini Mosque** (مسجد امام خمینی; Map p38; Panzdah-e Khordad St), and the ornately decorated **Imamzadeh Zeid** (امامزاده زید; Map p38; off Bazar-e Bozorg), a shrine to a descendant of the prophet.

Most lanes specialise in a particular commodity: copper, paper, gold, spices, and carpets, among others (note though you won't find fresh food here). The carpet, nut and spice bazaars might be the most photogenic, but the lane of stores selling fake designer labels (literally labels, not clothes) also catches the eye.

In our experience there are two ways to visit the bazaar. One is to simply wander the labyrinth of streets and alleys, taking whichever turn you fancy and going with the flow. If you get lost, remember to walk uphill to the main exits on Panzdah-e Khordad Ave.

Alternatively, allow yourself to be befriended by one of the carpet salesmen. Tell them what sections of the bazaar you'd like to see and they will lead you. When you're done, they will expect you to visit their carpet shop, drink some tea and view a few rugs – which in itself can be fun.

★ **Treasury of National Jewels**   MUSEUM
(موزه جواهرات ملّی; Map p38; ☑ 021-6446 3785;
www.cbi.ir; Ferdowsi St; IR200,000; ⊙ 2-4.30pm
Sat-Tue; M Sa'di) Owned by the Central Bank
and accessed through its front doors, the cavernous vault that houses what is commonly
known as the 'Jewels Museum' is not to be
missed. The Safavid, Qajar and Pahlavi monarchs adorned themselves and their belongings with an astounding range of priceless
gems and precious metals, making this collection of bling quite literally jaw-dropping.
Star pieces include the Globe of Jewels and
the Peacock Throne (p41).

Pick up a guidebook (IR40,000) at the
shop as you enter, or take one of the regular
professional tours in English, French, German or Arabic – it's included in the ticket
price and worth waiting for as there are few
descriptions in English.

Cameras, phones, bags and guidebooks
must be left at reception. Be careful not to
touch anything or you'll set off ear-piercing
alarms.

★ **Islamic Museum**   MUSEUM
(موزه دوره اسلامی; Map p38; ☑ 021-6670 2052;
www.nationalmuseum.ichto.ir; 30 Si Tir St; incl National Museum IR500,000; ⊙ 9am-7pm Apr-Sep,
to 6pm Oct-Mar; M Imam Khomeini) Next door
to the National Museum, and part of the
same complex, this museum offers a stunning collection of arts and antiquities from
throughout the Islamic period, including
calligraphy, carpets, ceramics, woodcarv-
ing, sculpture, miniatures, brickwork and
textiles. The collection includes silks and
stucco-work from Rey, portraits from the
Mongol period, a collection of Sassanian
coins, and gorgeous 14th-century wooden
doors and windows.

National Museum of Iran   MUSEUM
(موزه ایران باستان)موزه ملّی ایران; Iran Bastan Museum; Map p38; ☑ 021-6670 2052; www.national-
museum.ichto.ir; 30 Si Tir St; incl Islamic Museum
IR500,000; ⊙ 9am-7pm Apr-Sep, to 6pm Oct-Mar;
M Imam Khomeini) This modest museum is
no Louvre, but it is chock-full of Iran's rich
history. The collection includes ceramics,
pottery, stone figures and carvings, mostly
taken from excavations at Persepolis, Ismail-
abad (near Qazvin), Shush, Rey and Turang
Tappeh. Unfortunately, the presentation of
these treasures is less than inspired, and the
lack of useful explanations underwhelming
(ask for an English 'brochure' when buying
the ticket).

Malek National Library & Museum   MUSEUM
(کتابخانه و موزه ملک; Map p38; ☑ 021-6672 6613;
www.malekmuseum.org; Melal-e Mottahed (Bagh
Melli St); IR50,000; ⊙ 8.15am-4.15pm; M Imam
Khomeini) On display at this private museum
and library are pieces from the collection of
Hadji Hussein Agha Malek, in the 1930s one
of the richest men in Iran. The watercolour
paintings, delicate calligraphy and decorative
arts, including incredibly detailed lacquer-
ware boxes painted by 19th-century masters
of the art of the miniature, such as Mohammad Zaman and Abu Taleb Modaresi, are
exquisite.

Glass & Ceramics Museum   MUSEUM
(موزه آبگینه و سرامیک, Musee Abghineh; Map p38;
☑ 021-6670 8153; www.glasswaremuseum.ir; Si
Tir St; IR150,000; ⊙ 9am-6pm Apr-Sep, to 5pm
Oct-Mar; M Imam Khomeini) The Glass & Ceramics Museum is, like many of its exhibits,
small but perfectly formed. The galleries
walk you chronologically through the ages,
with detailed, lucid explanations in English
that chart the history of the country and
the region through the lovingly displayed
glass and ceramics that remain. The late
Qajar-era building's graceful wooden staircase and classical stucco mouldings are
particularly delightful, and there are many
delicate carvings and decorative flourishes.

Masoudieh Palace   HISTORIC BUILDING
(عمارت مسعودیه; Map p38; Ekbatan St; IR200,000;
⊙ 9am-4pm; M Mellat) Built in 1879 for Naser
al-Din Shah's son, who was also the governor
of Esfahan, as his residence in Tehran, this
lovely building and garden is in the process
of restoration. Recently there was a cafe operating in the dining hall, but it was closed
at the time of writing. It's still worth visiting
for the building's beautiful decoration and
peaceful grounds.

Madraseh va Masjed-e Sepahsalar   MUSEUM
(مدرسه و مسجد سپهسالار, Masjed-e Motahari; Map
p38; Mostafa Khomeini St; M Baharestan) Just
south of the Iranian *majlis* (parliament),
this Islamic college is arguably the most
noteworthy example of Persian architecture
of the Qajar period, as well as one of the
largest. Built between 1878 and 1890, it is
famed for its multiple minarets, high domes
and *iwans,* and poetry inscribed in several
ancient scripts on the beautiful tiling. It is
closed to the general public.

However, you may be lucky with the door
guards, and some local guides are able to
talk their way in (male guests only). A ban

on photography both outside and inside the complex is vigorously enforced.

Park-e Shahr
PARK

(پارک شهر; Map p38; http://parks.tehran.ir; cnr Fayazbakhsh & Vahdat-e Eslami Sts; ◔5am-midnight; Ⓜ Imam Khomeini) If you're staying in southern Tehran and need a break from the traffic, head straight for this pleasant, leafy park where you can take a boat trip on the pond (in summer), see various birds, including peacocks, silver pheasants and flamingos in enclosures, and enjoy tea or *qalyan* at the **Sofre Khane Sonnati Sangalaj** (Map p38; ☎021-5569 3505; mains IR180,000-400,000; ◔9am-11pm) teahouse. Or just sit and watch Tehranis relaxing.

◉ Central Tehran

★ Tabiat Bridge
BRIDGE

(پل طبیعت; Nature Bridge; Map p44; Ⓜ Shahid Haghani) It's easy to see why this multilevel, sculptural pedestrian bridge, designed by Iranian architect Leila Araghian, has won

awards and been a huge hit with locals. The 270m long walkway connecting Park-e Taleghani and Park-e Abo-Atash over the busy Modarres Expwy is a fun space to relax and, in good weather, it provides superb views of the north Tehran skyline against the Alborz Mountains.

There's a decent food court (p60) at one end and an OK restaurant at the other, as well as plenty of places to sit and socialise, making it a highly popular place to hang out in the evenings.

★ Iran Holy Defense Museum
MUSEUM

(Map p44; ☎021-8865 7026; www.iranhdm.ir; Sarv St; IR200,000; ◔9am-5pm Sat-Thu, 11am-5pm Fri; Ⓜ Shahid Haghani) This epic-scale museum, on a landscaped site of 21 hectares, is dedicated to the Iran–Iraq War, a bloody eight-year conflict that claimed a million lives. The main building consists of seven halls that commemorate the war's martyrs and run you through the history of the conflict in forensic detail. It may sound harrowing, but it is, in fact, a fascinating

---

THE PEACOCK THRONE & OTHER BAUBLES

Most of the collection in the **Treasury of National Jewels** (p40) dates back to Safavid times, when the shahs scoured Europe, India and the lands of the Ottoman Empire for booty with which to decorate their capital, Esfahan. But as the Safavid empire crumbled, the jewels became a high profile spoil of war.

When Mahmud Afghan invaded Iran in 1722, he plundered the treasury and sent its contents to India. On ascending the throne in 1736, Nader Shah Afshar dispatched courtiers to ask for the return of the jewels. When their powers of persuasion proved unequal to the task, he sent an army to prove that he was serious. To get the soldiers off his back, Mohammed Shah of India was forced to hand over several treasures including the **Darya-ye Nur (Sea of Light)**, a pink diamond weighing 182 carats and said to be the largest uncut diamond in the world. This bauble remains part of the Treasury's collection, but the Koh-i-Noor (Mountain of Light) diamond that was also part of Nader Shah's haul has long since been part of the British crown jewels.

During the expedition Nader Shah also bagged the Moghuls' famous Peacock Throne. But during the trip back to Persia, this piece of booty fell into the hands of rebellious soldiers, who hacked it up to spread the wealth among themselves. The **Peacock Throne** on display outside the vault door in the Treasury is the one ordered by Fath Ali Shah in 1798. Taking a daybed-style *takht* (table in a teahouse) they adorned it with 26,733 gems, including an extravagant carved sun, studded with precious stones. Before long it became known as the Sun Throne. Later Fath Ali married Tavous Tajodoleh, nicknamed Tavous Khanoum or Lady Peacock, and the throne became known as the Peacock Throne in her honour.

The Qajar and Pahlavi rulers enthusiastically added to the royal jewels collection, which grew to be so valuable that in the 1930s it was transferred to the National Bank of Iran (now the Central Bank of Iran) as a reserve for the national currency. Among the other standout pieces here are the tall **Kiani Crown** made for Fath Ali Shah in 1797; the crowns worn by the last shah and his wife, Farah; and the incredible 34kg **Globe of Jewels**, made in 1869 using 51,366 precious stones – the seas are made from emeralds and the land from rubies except Iran, Britain and France, which are set in diamonds.

and imaginative response to a deeply scarring episode in modern Iranian history.

At times the displays swerve into the surreal, such as the section that depicts the glittering vision of heavenly paradise the soldiers (many no more than teenagers) were sent to their deaths believing, and the one that places you at the heart of an aerial bombardment complete with sensory effects.

Outside, huge rockets and tanks flank the Garden Valley, at the centre of which is a 6000-sq-metre lake where, in the summer months, a fountain and laser-light show plays. The complex also includes a separate silver-sphere building where you can view a 15-minute film shown on a panoramic screen that depicts the besieged town of Khorramshahr before, during and after the conflict. Near the exit to the subway station is a replica of the Khorramshahr mosque covered in yellow and turquoise patterned tiles.

★ **Azadi Tower (Borj-e Azadi)** MONUMENT
(برج آزادي, Freedom Tower; Map p56; ☑ 021-6606 4121; www.azadi-tower.com; Azadi Sq; IR150,000; ⊙ 9am-5pm; Ⓜ Meydan-e Azadi) The inverted-Y-shaped Azadi Tower, built in 1971 to commemorate the 2500th anniversary of the first Persian empire, is one of Tehran's visual icons. Designed by Hossein Amanat, it ingeniously combines modern architecture with traditional Iranian influences, most notably the *iwan*-style of the arch, which is clad in 8000 pieces of white marble. It's worth going inside to see the complex structural engineering that forms the bones of the design and for the view from the gallery at the top.

You can reach the top by stairs or lift. At the base are galleries with changing exhibitions and a cafe.

To reach the tower, which sits in a large oval park, you'll need to tentatively negotiate the maelstrom of traffic that is an almost constant feature of the square.

Azadi Sq was the scene of much protest during the 1979 revolution and remains a focal point for demonstrations today, including some huge demonstrations during the post-election crisis in 2009.

★ **Qsar Garden Museum** MUSEUM
(موزه باغ قصر; Map p44; ☑ 021-8844 3311; www.qasr.ir; Motahari Ave; ⊙ 9am-8pm; Ⓜ Shahid Mofatteh, then taxi) ᶠᴿᴱᴱ This imaginative sculpture park and museum occupies two former prisons, one for criminals and one

for political prisoners, and the grounds surrounding them. The architects Experimental Branch of Architecture have done a cracking job on working with the historic site, placing quirky, contemporary artworks in cells and around the landscaped gardens, which include two pleasant cafes and a mosque.

Qsar means 'castle' and during all of the 19th century there was a royal palace here, but it eventually ran to ruin. In the early 20th century a prison, designed to meet international standards by the Russian architect Nikolai Markov, was constructed and it's this building that forms the first part of the museum. Lawrence of Arabia was held in Qasr for a very short time, which accounts for the cut outs of his image in one cell.

A second more modern complex was where political prisoners were housed during the time of the last shah. This was the first prison liberated during the Islamic Revolution.

Tehran's mayor Mohammad Bagher Ghalibaf is so impressed with the project that he now wants to turn the city's notorious Evin Prison in northwest Tehran into a similar family-friendly park.

US Den of Espionage MUSEUM
(لانه جاسوسی آمریکا; Map p44; Taleghani Ave; ⊙ 9am-noon & 1-4pm Sat-Wed; Ⓜ Taleghani) ᶠᴿᴱᴱ The former US embassy was the focal point of the 1979 revolution, when it was stormed by students who then held 52 diplomats hostage for 444 days. Today the compound is occupied by the Student Basij Organisation dedicated to defending the revolution. It's a fascinating place to visit: the front grounds (now called the 'Museum Garden of Anti Arrogance') are plastered with colourful anti-Western propaganda posters. Part of the chancery is a museum, highlighting the spying which went on there.

This is where the 1953 coup that brought down Mohammad Mossadegh was orchestrated, and from where the last shah was supported. Anti-US and Israel, and pro-Islam murals and displays decorate the corridors and former offices. Waxwork dummies are posed in the 'glassy room' where top-secret meetings were held. Step back in time as you view the antiquated telex machines, computers and shredders used by the embassy staff in vault-like rooms.

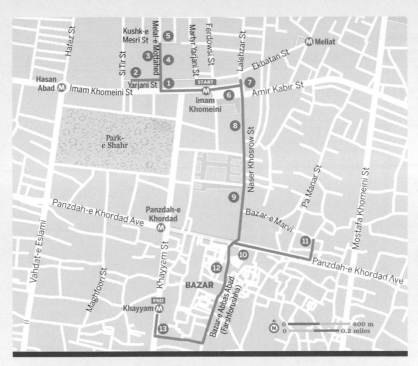

Walking Tour
Museums to the Grand Bazaar

START METRO STATION IMAM KHOMEINI
END METRO STATION KHAYYAM
LENGTH 2KM; THREE TO FOUR HOURS

From Imam Khomeini Metro station navigate along Imam Khomeini St west towards the **1 Portal of Bagh-e Meli**, an impressive gateway dating from 1906 and decorated with painted tiles. Pass through the gate to the old National Garden complex of museums and government buildings. If you have time, explore the **2 Islamic Museum** (p40) and the **3 Malek National Library & Museum** (p40). If not, admire the grand architecture flanking pedestrianised Melal-e Mottahed, including Building No 9 of Iran's **4 Ministry of Foreign Affairs**, and **5 Qazaq Khaneh**, the former Cossacks' Quarters.

Return to the maelstrom of motor vehicles encircling **6 Imam Khomeini Sq**. Little Qajar-era grandeur remains although there is still a fountain in front of the plinth that once held up a statue of Reza Shah. On the square's eastern side, the **7 Tejarat Bank**, a late 19th-century building that housed the first public bank in Iran, has an entrance that's decorated with traditional tiles.

Continue south along Naser Khosrow St. Once one of Tehran's grandest avenues it is lined with impressive buildings, such as **8 Dar ul-Funun**, established in 1851 as Iran's first modern university. Peek into the courtyard where there's a garden designed in the shape of the Union Jack. Further south, Naser Khosrow is pedestrianised and runs along the back of **9 Golestan Palace** (p37).

Naser Khosrow lead you to the entrance to the Grand Bazaar. Before exploring this centuries-old maze, take a moment to admire the beautifully restored interior decoration of the **10 Imam Khomeini Mosque** (p39). A short walk east along Panzdah-e Khordad Ave look for Eudlagan, a recently restored alley of the bazaar that leads towards the teahouse **11 Timcheh Akbarian** (p62), occupying a building that was a bank some 260 years ago.

Return to the **Grand Bazaar** (p39), where you could happily lose yourself for several hours of exploring and shopping. After all that you'll be glad of a rest at the gorgeous teahouse and restaurant **Khayyam** (p59), by Khayyam metro station.

Central Tehran

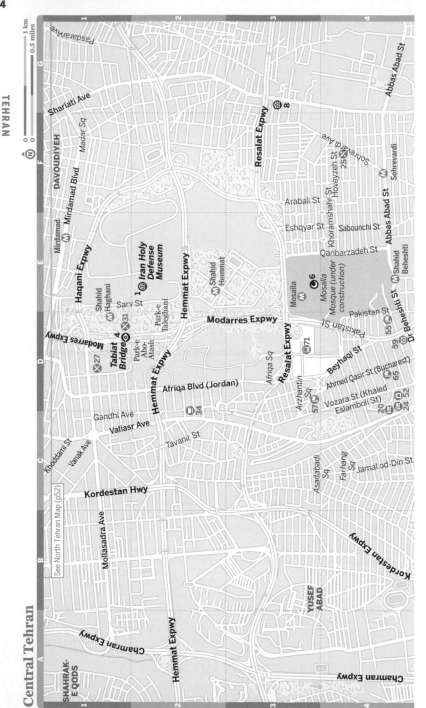

SHAHRAK-E QODS

DAVOUDIYEH

YUSEF ABAD

Pasdaran Ave

Shariati Ave

Madar Sq

Mirdamad Blvd

Mirdamad

Haqani Expwy

Shahid Haqhani

Sarv St

Parke Taleghani

1 Iran Holy Defense Museum

Modarres Expwy

Hemmat Expwy

Parke Abo-Atash

Tabiat Bridge 4

Hemmat Expwy

Afriqa Blvd (Jordan)

Gandhi Ave

Valiasr Ave

Tavanir St

Khoddami St

Vanak Ave

Kordestan Hwy

Mollasadra Ave

See North Tehran Map (p52)

Chamran Expwy

Hemmat Expwy

Chamran Expwy

Kordestan Expwy

Resalat Expwy

8

Sohrevardi Ave

Abbas Abad St

Arabali St

Eshqyar St

Khoramshahr St

Hoveyzeh St

25

Sabounchi St

Qanbarzadeh St

Pakistan St

Pakistan St

Mosalla

Mosalla Mosque (under construction)

6

Shahid Hemmat

Shahid Beheshti

Abbas Abad St

Sohrevardi

Dr Beheshti St

Shahid Beheshti St

55

59

65

24 52

20

Pakistan St

Beyhaqi St

Ahmed Qasir St (Bucharest)

Vozara St (Khaled Eslamboli St)

Azhartin

57 Sq

Resalat Expwy

Afriqa Sq

71

34

Asadabadi Sq

Farhang Sq

Jamal od-Din St

27

1 km
0.5 miles
0 0

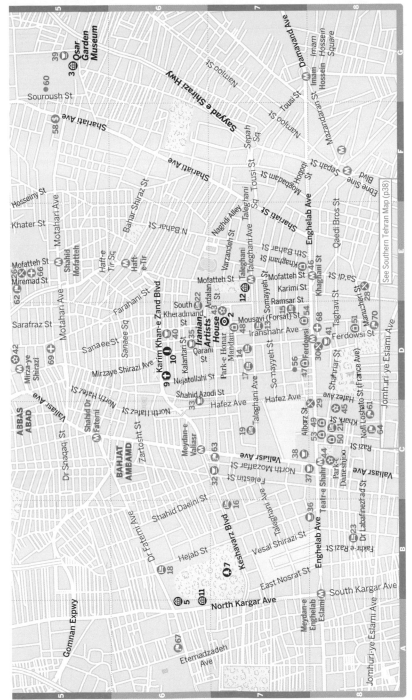

G

Qsar Garden Museum
39
3
60
Souroush St
58
Shariat Ave
Sayyad e Shirazi Hwy
Namjoo St

Namjoo St
Tousi St
Imam Hossein Square
Damavand Ave
Imam Hossein Square
Mazandaran St

Sepah Sq
Moghadam St
Tousi St
Hoghoqi St
Sepah St
M
Ebne Sine Blvd

Hosseiny St
Khater St
Motahari Ave
Bahar-Shiraz St.
N Bahar St.
Naghdi Alley
Varzandeh St
TalEghani Ave
Talaghani St
Sth Bahar St
Shariat St
Enghelab Ave
Qaedi Bros St

Mofatteh St
Miremad St
Shahid Mofatteh
Haft-e Tir Sq
Haft-e-Tir
Mofatteh St
Khaghani St
Sa'di St
Sepah St

62
66
Motahari Ave
Farahani St
South Kheradmand St
Ardalan St
12
Mofatteh St
Mofatteh St
Karimi St
Ramsar St
Khaghani St

Sarafraz St
Sanaee St
Sanaee Sq
Iranian Artists House
43
35
22
2
Mousavi (Forsat) St
Somayyeh St
Iranshahr Ave
54
68
Taghavi St
Manuchehri St
Ferdowsi St
28

42
Mirzaye Shirazi
Karim Khan-e Zand Blvd
40
10
Kalantari St
Qarani St
Park-e Honar
Mandari
14
48
17
Somayyeh St
Ferdowsi St
47
56
30
41
51
70

69
9
Nejatollahi St
Shahid Azodi St
33
North Hafez St
Hafez Ave
Hafez Ave
Hafez Ave
Shahriar St
Shafariar St (France Ave)
45
61
Jomhuri-ye Eslami Ave

ABBAS ABAD
Valiasr Ave
Shahid Dr Fatemi St
Zartosht St
19
Talaghani Ave
Alborz St
29
Nofl Loshato St (France Ave)
49
53
50
21
Khark St
64
Razi St

BAHJAT AMBAMD
Meydan-e Valiasr
63
32
North Mozaffar St
Felestin St
Valiasr Ave
38
37
M
Park-e Daneshju
44
23
Dr Labafinezhad St
Valiasr Ave

Dr Fatemi Ave
Shahid Daeini St
16
36
Vesal Shirazi St
Talaghani Ave
Teatr-e Shahr
Enghelab Ave
Fakhr-e Razi St

Hejab St
Keshavarz Blvd
18
7
East Nosrat St

Gomnan Expwy
5
11
North Kargar Ave
Meydan-e Engheleb
South Kargar Ave
M
Jomhuri-ye Eslami Ave

67
Etemadzadeh Ave
Jomhuri-ye Eslami Ave

See Southern Tehran Map (p38)

Central Tehran

◉ Top Sights
1 Iran Holy Defense Museum E2
2 Iranian Artists' House............................ D7
3 Qsar Garden Museum G5
4 Tabiat Bridge..D1

◉ Sights
5 Carpet Museum Of Iran A6
6 Mosalla Mosque E3
7 Park-e Laleh.. B7
8 Reza Abbasi Museum............................ G3
9 Sarkis Cathedral D6
10 Stars & Stripes Mural............................ D6
11 Tehran Museum of Contemporary
    Art (TMOCA) A6
12 US Den of Espionage..............................E7

◎ Sleeping
13 Amir Hotel..D7
14 Atlas Hotel D7
15 Eskan Hotel Forsat D7
16 Espinas Khalige Fars Hotel...................B7
17 Howeyzeh Hotel D7
18 Laleh International Hotel B6
19 Parsian Enghelab Hotel........................ C7
20 Raamtin Residence Hotel D4
21 Roudaki Hotel... C8
22 See You In Iran Hostel...........................D6
23 Seven Hostel B8
24 Simorgh Hotel D4

✖ Eating
25 Alborz F4
26 Cingari E5
   Coffee Shop & Veggie
    Restaurant of Iranian Artists'
    Forum.. (see 43)
   Dizi ....(see 35)
27 Khoone D1
28 Khoshbin E8
   Monsoon .... (see 34)
29 Pasta Charmy's C8
30 Sofre Khane Ayaran D8
31 Tabiat Food Court..................................D1

◎ Drinking & Nightlife
32 Agha Bozorg C7
33 Cafe 78 .... C6
34 Cafe de France D2

Cafe Gallery...............................(see 43)
Cafe Opera ....(see 21)
35 Cafe Upartmaan D6
36 Cake Studio Vorta B8
37 Godot Cafe C8
38 Lamiz...C7
39 Markov Cafe Gallery...............................G5
40 Nazdik Cafe D6
41 Romance Cafe D8

◎ Entertainment
42 Azadi Cinema Center D5
43 Iranshahr Theatre D7
44 Teatr-e Shahr...C8
45 Vahdat Hall..C8

◎ Shopping
46 Ab Anbar...E7
47 Alma Nuts...D7
48 Assar Art Gallery D7
49 Bottejeghe..C8
50 Gita Shenasi...C8
51 Moses Baba...D8
52 Seyhoun Art Gallery D4
53 Tanedorost..C8
54 Varzesh Kooh...D7

◎ Information
55 Afghan Embassy....................................D4
   Armenian Embassy......................(see 50)
56 Asia 2000 ....D7
57 Australian Embassy D3
58 Bank Melli F5
59 Central Post Office D4
60 Foreign Intelligence Office G5
61 French Embassy.....................................C8
62 Indian Embassy E5
63 Iraqi Embassy C7
64 Italian Embassy C8
65 Japanese Embassy D4
66 Mehrad Hospital E5
67 Pakistani Embassy.................................A6
68 Ramin Drug Store..................................D8
69 Tehran Clinic D5
70 UK Embassy..D8

◎ Transport
71 Terminal-e Arzhantin..............................D3

Tehran Museum of Contemporary Art (TMOCA)
GALLERY
(موزه هنرهای معاصر تهران; Map p44; ☎021-8898 9374; www.tmoca.com; North Kargar Ave; IR50,000; ⊘10am-7pm Mon-Thu, 3-7pm Fri; Ⓜ Meydan-e Enghelab Eslami) In a striking concrete modernist building on the western side of Park-e Laleh, this museum's impressive collection boasts works by Picasso, Matisse, Van Gogh, Miró, Dalí, Bacon, Pollock, Monet, Munch, Moore and Warhol, among many others. Unfortunately, they are not always on display, but do not be put off, as there are still some interesting exhibitions and events to see here, including films and performance art.

The architecture itself is impressive, as are the surrounding sculptures. A swirling walkway leads down to the darkly reflecting oil pool *Matter & Mind* by Noriyuki

Haraguchi and off to the nine major galleries. Art-loving Queen Farah Diba was the driving force behind the museum, which opened in 1977; her cousin Kamran Diba was the architect.

Carpet Museum Of Iran MUSEUM
(موزه فرش ایران; Map p44; cnr Dr Fatemi & North Kargar Aves; IR150,000; ⊙9am-5pm; Ⓜ Meydan-e Enghelab Eslami) Housing more than 100 pieces dating from the 17th century to the present day, this is a great place to see the full range of regional patterns and styles found in Iran. Look out for unique designs such as the Tree of Life with Kings and Notables. The permanent collection is downstairs, while upstairs is sometimes open for temporary exhibitions.

Reza Abbasi Museum MUSEUM
(موزه رضا عباسی; Map p44; www.rezaabbasi museum.ir; 892 Shariati Ave; IR150,000; ⊙8am-5pm; Ⓜ Shahid Sayyad-e Shirazi) Named after one of the great artists of the Safavid period, this museum showcases Iranian art from ancient times and the Safavid-era paintings of Abbasi himself. If you're interested in Iranian art, it's one of the best and most professionally run museums in the country. It's a bit of a walk from the nearest metro, so perhaps take a taxi.

The exhibits are organised chronologically starting with the top-floor Pre-Islamic Gallery, where you'll find Achaemenid gold bowls, drinking vessels, armlets and decorative pieces, often with exquisite carvings of bulls and rams. Here, too, you'll find fine examples of Luristan bronzes.

The Islamic Gallery exhibits ceramics, fabrics and brassware, while the Painting Gallery shows samples of fine calligraphy from ancient Qurans and illustrated manuscripts, particularly copies of Ferdowsi's *Shahnamah* and Sa'di's *Golestan*.

Milad Tower TOWER
(برج میلاد; Map p56; ☑021-8436 1000; www.teh-ranmiladtower.ir; South Sheikh Fadlallah exit, off Hemmat Expwy; cafe IR50,000, open observation deck IR120,000, all areas IR350,000; ⊙9am-8.30pm Mar-Sep, 10am-9.15pm Oct-Feb; Ⓜ Mosalla, then taxi) Dominating the skyline of Tehran's western suburbs, Milad Tower is 435m high, including 120m of antenna, making it, in 2017, the world's sixth-tallest free-standing tower. Bearing a striking resemblance to Menara Kuala Lumpur, its octagonal concrete shaft tapers up to a pod with 12 floors, including both enclosed and open observation

decks, a gallery, a cafe and a **revolving restaurant** (IR600,000/1,080,000/1,508,000 for breakfast/lunch/dinner).

Whether you should visit or not depends largely on the weather; on a rare clear day the views are worth it, but otherwise probably not. You need a taxi to get here.

At the base of the tower is the separate **Tehran Milad Tower International Convention Centre**, where concerts are occasionally held.

In 2012, Zaha Hadid won the design competition for the second phase of the site, a plan which would involve a couple more lower-rise towers. So far, though, construction is yet to commence.

Sarkis Cathedral CHURCH
(کلیسای سرکیس; Map p44; ☑021-8889 7980; cnr Nejatollahi St & Karim Khan-e Zand Blvd; ⊙8am-5.30pm Mon-Sat; Ⓜ Meydan e Valiasr) This white, twin-spired church, a centre for Christianity in the Islamic Republic, sits at the southern edge of the city's Armenian quarter. Built between 1964 and 1970 and paid for by benefactor Markar Sarkissian, the cathedral's interior is attractive, with giant glass chandeliers hanging over the pews.

Park-e Laleh PARK
(پارک لاله; Map p44; http://parks.tehran.ir; Keshavarz Blvd; Ⓜ Meydan-e Enghelab Eslami) Near the centre of Tehran, Park-e Laleh is a well-designed green space that because of its location amid so much traffic becomes an urban oasis. It's a great place for people-watching. As you wander through, perhaps on your way to the adjoining Carpet Museum or Tehran Museum of Contemporary Art, keep an eye out for young Tehranis refining their flirting techniques over soft-serve ice creams.

Northern Tehran

Almost everything in northern Tehran has been built in the last 50 years, so aside from the two palace complexes there are few historic 'sights'. Instead, this is modern Tehran, home to hip coffee shops, fancy restaurants and embassies.

Given the diabolical nature of traffic in northern Tehran, go as far as you can by metro or the Bus Rapid Transport (BRT), which runs in both directions the full length of Valiasr, and then either walk or take a taxi to your ultimate destination.

TEHRAN SIGHTS

`DON'T MISS`

TEHRAN'S STREET ART

Tehran's highway flyovers, high brick walls and jumble of concrete housing complexes and towers win no awards for visual appeal. However, those same structures do provide enormous canvases for striking, colourful and highly imaginative street art.

Such public daubings date back to the early years of the Iranian Revolution and the anti-West propaganda public art, such as the wall fronting the **US Den of Espionage** (p42) and the iconic **Stars & Stripes mural** (Map p44; Karim Khan-e Zand Blvd; M Meydan-e Valiasr) that towers over Karim Khan Zand Blvd in central Tehran. There are countless stories-tall portraits of Ayatollah Khomeini and of current Supreme Leader Ayatollah Khamenei. In the wake of the Iran–Iraq War, favourite subjects also include that conflict's many martyrs.

In recent years, Mayor Ghalibaf's administration has stepped up its program of beautifying Tehran by handing out gallons of paint to approved muralists such as Mehdi Ghadyanloo (www.mehdighadyanloo.com), who painted over 100 large-scale works across the city between 2004 and 2011. Ghadyanloo's surreal Magritte-like murals are typically whimsical, featuring figures walking across ceilings, twisting giant bolts or cycling or driving through the sky.

Of course, there's also an underground army of non-approved street artists turning out works that tackle social and political issues and which are often quickly blanked out by the authorities. Among them is Black Hand (www.facebook.com/black.hand.graffiti), who is often labelled as Iran's Banksy, and the Tabriz-born brothers and stencil artists Icy & Sot (www.icyandsot.com) now based in New York City.

★ **Sa'd Abad Museum Complex** MUSEUM (مجموعه موزه سعد آباد; Map p52; ☑ 021-2794 0491; www.sadmu.ir; Taheri St; IR150,000; ⊙9am-5pm, last entry 4pm; M Tajrish) Sprawling across the foothills of Darband, this estate was a summer home to royals since the Qajar dynasty, although it was the Pahlavis who expanded it to the site you see today. Covering 110 hectares and comprising 18 separate buildings, it will take you a good three hours to see everything. For a glimpse into the luxurious life of the shahs, don't miss the extravagant 54-room White Palace, built in the 1930s. The more classical-looking Green Palace (p49) dates from the end of the Qajar era

All tickets must be bought at either the front gate near Tajrish or at the northern entrance from Darband; entering from the north makes sense if you've previously spent the morning and had lunch in Darband. Ask at either ticket office for the useful English map.

There's a minibus (IR10,000) that shuttles regularly from the front gate, pausing at the White Palace on the way up to the Green Palace, then back again.

For refreshments, there are two pleasant but unexceptional cafes inside the grounds.

To get to the front gate, walk or take a taxi (IR80,000) 1.5km northwest from Tajrish Sq, beginning on Ja'fari St and turning left and

right (ask anyone for 'Musee Sa'd Abad'). Or go to Darband and enter from there.

The following are the key parts of the complex; the grounds are also a pleasant place for strolling.

White Palace MUSEUM (Map p52; www.sadmu.ir; Taheri St; IR150,000, incl Nations Art Museum IR230,000; ⊙9am-5pm, last entry 4pm; M Tajrish) Built in the 1930s, and one of the highlights of the Sa'd Abad Museum Complex, most of what you see in this 5000-sq-metre, 54-room palace dates from Mohammad Reza Shah's reign (1942–79). Little has changed since the revolution – the palace is filled with a hodge-podge of extravagant furnishings, paintings, a tiger pelt and immense made-to-measure carpets. In the upstairs Ceremony Hall is a 143-sq-metre carpet that is said to be one of the largest ever woven in Iran.

The nearby Dining Hall contains a similar carpet, and it is here that the shah, convinced the palace was bugged, dragged a table into the middle of the room and insisted both he and the American general he was entertaining climb on top before they spoke.

The two bronze boots outside are all that remain of a giant statue of Reza Shah – he got the chop after the revolution.

Don't miss the trippy stainless-steel staircases at the back of the White Palace's ground floor, which spiral down to the **Nations Art Museum** in the basement. This eclectic collection of works was gathered by Farah Diba, the last Shah's wife, and includes works from across the Islamic world.

Green Palace   MUSEUM

(Map p52; www.sadmu.ir; Taheri St; IR150,000; ⊙9am-5pm, last entry 4pm; M Tajrish) A hike up the northwest end of the Sa'd Abad Museum Complex, the classical-looking Green Palace was built at the end of the Qajar era when it was known as the Shahvand Palace. Extensively remodelled by the Pahlavis, the building's current name comes from the mossy green stone that covers the exterior. The design is over-the-top opulent, with wall-to-wall mirrors in the appropriately named Mirror Hall and the bedroom. Be sure to wander around the building to take in the view from the back.

Fine Art Museum   MUSEUM

(Map p52; www.sadmu.ir; Taheri St; IR80,000; ⊙9am-5pm, last entry 4pm; M Tajrish) Near the front gate of the Sa'd Abad Museum Complex, this museum exhibits many excellent paintings, including a dazzling full-sized portrait of Fathi-Ali Shah in full regalia by the early 19th-century artist Meh Ali Isfehani. There are also European works from the 18th to 20th centuries, including paintings by Salvador Dalí.

Royal Costume Museum   MUSEUM

(Map p52; www.sadmu.ir; Taheri St; IR80,000; ⊙9am-5pm, last entry 4pm; M Tajrish) Located at the northern end of the Sa'd Abad Museum Complex and occupying the 1939 vintage Shams Palace, once the Shah's sister's residences, this museum houses an exquisite range of clothing, including colourful tribal costumes and bejewelled evening gowns from the 1950s and '60s created by top European couturiers. Look out for the the Yves Saint Laurent–designed wedding dress of Farah Diba. The building itself combines Iranian and European architectural styles.

★Niyavaran Cultural-Historic Complex   MUSEUM

(موزه کاخ نیاوران; Map p52; ☑021-2228 7026; www.niavaranmu.ir; Niyavaran Ave, off Shahid Bahonar Sq; grounds IR15,000; ⊙9am-6pm Apr-Sep, 8am-4pm Oct-Mar; M Nobonyad, then taxi) In the Alborz foothills is the palace where Shah Mohammad Reza Pahlavi and his family

spent most of the last 10 years of royal rule. It's set in 5 hectares of landscaped gardens and has six separate museums, the best of which is the elegant 1960s Niyavaran Palace, with its clean lines, opulent interior and sublime carpets. Tickets must be bought before entering at the main gate. There's also a pleasant **cafe** with outdoor seating.

To get here, take a shuttle taxi or bus east of Tajrish Sq, and ask to be dropped at Shahid Bahonar Sq, near the museum entrance.

The following are the complex's main elements; note the Qajar-period **Sahebgharanieh Palace**, which was once Nasser-al Din Shah's harem before later being transformed into Mohammad Reza Shah's office, is closed for renovations until 2018.

Niyavaran Palace   MUSEUM

(Map p52; www.niavaranmu.ir; Niyavaran Ave, off Shahid Bahonar Sq; IR150,000; ⊙9am-6pm Apr-Sep, 8am-4pm Oct-Mar; M Nobonyad, then taxi) Built between 1958 and 1968 this remarkable palace contrasts clean-lined functionality on the outside with opulent, European-royal-style furniture and enormous, intricately woven carpets inside. Highlights include the magnificent Kerman carpet showing Iranian kings right back to the Achaemenids as well as some European sovereigns, including Napoleon Bonaparte; the shah's walk-in wardrobe full of dozens of uniforms; a selection of Farah Diba's very stylish gowns; and the retractable roof that opened the centre of the palace to the sky.

Imperial Library Museum   MUSEUM

(Map p52; www.niavaranmu.ir; Niyavaran Ave, off Shahid Bahonar Sq; IR80,000; ⊙9am-6pm Apr-Sep, 8am-4pm Oct-Mar; M Nobonyad, then taxi) East of the Niyavaran Palace this impressive two-floor library that was for the exclusive use of Farah Diba proves she had good design taste. Floor-to-ceiling windows throw light on a collection of 23,000 volumes, comfy Knoll sofas, sculptures by the likes of Picasso and a dazzling ceiling feature of 4356 glass rods designed by famed interior designer Charles Sevigny. Look out for the *Cinderella* picture book signed by Walt Disney.

Jahan-Nama Museum & Gallery   MUSEUM

(Queen's Private Museum; Map p52; www.niavaranmu.ir; Niyavaran Ave, off Shahid Bahonar Sq; IR150,000; ⊙9am-6pm Apr-Sep, 8am-4pm Oct-Mar; M Nobonyad, then taxi) Part of the sprawling Niyavaran Cultural-Historic Complex, two rooms here are filled with a small but well-displayed example of the eclectic collection of modern and ancient art gathered by Farah Diba, mainly during the 1970s. Works by Warhol, Picasso and Joan Miró share space with Iranian archaeological artefacts and finds from sites in Mexico and Egypt, and rotating exhibits of contemporary Iranian art.

Ahmad Shahi Pavilion   MUSEUM

(Map p52; www.niavaranmu.ir; Niyavaran Ave, off Shahid Bahonar Sq; IR80,000; ⊙9am-6pm Apr-Sep, 8am-4pm Oct-Mar; ⋔Nobonyad, then taxi) Immediately west of Niyavaran Palace in the cultural-historic complex, this attractive two-storey mansion dating from the early 20th century was last used as the residence of the crown prince Reza. The prince's white leather–themed living quarters are a time-warp to the 1970s. Reza's belongings range from childhood drawings to model planes (he was a pilot), a rock collection (with a moon rock gifted by Richard Nixon) to a polar-bear skin (a gift of the Canadian government).

Automobile Museum   MUSEUM

(Map p52; www.niavaranmu.ir; Niyavaran Ave, off Shahid Bahonar Sq; IR80,000; ⊙9am-6pm Apr-Sep, 8am-4pm Oct-Mar; ⋔Nobonyad, then taxi) Just before the exit of the Niyavaran Cultural-Historic Complex is this small collection of cars and toy motorbikes used by Shah's family. There are two stately Rolls Royces but, sadly, only a photo of the scale model Aston Martin (number plate JB007) that was a plaything of the royal kids.

Film Museum of Iran   MUSEUM

(موزه فیلم ایران; Map p52; ☑021-2271 9001; www. cinemamuseum.ir; Bagh-e Ferdows, off Valiasr Ave; IR200,000; ⊙9am-5pm Sat-Thu, 2-5pm Fri; ⋔Tajrish) Housed in a beautiful Qajar-era mansion surrounded by a pleasant garden, this interesting museum has well-displayed and explained (in English) exhibits of equipment, photos and posters from Iran's century-old movie industry. The highlight is a working cinema, Iran's first, with ornate moulded plaster ceilings.

New and classic Iranian films are screened here (usually without subtitles) at 1pm, 3pm, 5pm, 7pm and 9pm daily; get a Farsi-speaker to call to see what's on. A shop also sells hard-to-find Iranian films on DVD.

The museum is a 10-minute walk down Valiasr Ave from Tajrish Sq; look for the broad street with a garden down the middle leading to the museum.

Iranian Art Museum Garden   GARDENS

(Map p52; ☑021-2645 8061; Dr Hesabi St; IR10,000; ⊙10am-10pm; ⋔Tajrish) Scaled-down architectural models of famous Iranian buildings are dotted around this lovely, spacious walled garden surrounded by small boutiques, cafes and a restaurant. The models include such landmarks as the Si-o Seh bridge in Esfahan, the Gonbad Soltaniyeh and Tehran's Azadi Tower. It's a very pleasant spot to relax, do some shopping and mingle with locals.

Park-e Jamshidiyeh   PARK

(پارک جمشیدیه; Map p52; ☑021-2228 7793; http://parks.tehran.ir; Shahid Omidvar St; ⊙7am-midnight; ⋔Tajrish, then taxi) Also known as Stone Garden, Park-e Jamshidiyeh climbs steeply up the lower reaches of the Alborz Mountains and offers a clean, quiet atmosphere in which to enjoy the views and escape the smog. It's the sort of place you could happily while away an entire afternoon sipping tea, chatting with random Tehranis and watching the lights of this huge city slowly come to life.

Park-e Mellat   PARK

(پارک ملت; Map p52; http://parks.tehran.ir; Valiasr Ave; ▣BRT to Niayesh) Many Tehranis say Park-e Mellat is their favourite in-town getaway, and if you're here around dusk on any spring or summer afternoon you'll find plenty of people enjoying the shaded areas around a small lake. On weekend nights you'll find just as many young people cruising up and down Valiasr Ave, several to a car, eyeing each other off and swapping phone numbers through car windows.

Imamzadeh Saleh   ISLAMIC SHRINE

(امامزاده صالح; Map p52; ☑021-2274 8010; Tajrish Sq; ⋔Tajrish) One of Tehran's most attractive shrines, Imamzadeh Saleh provides a photogenic focus to Tajrish Sq with its twin minarets and dome covered in beautiful patterned turquoise tiles: it looks especially stunning towards sunset.

🏃 Activities

★Tochal Telecabin   CABLE CAR

(تله کابین توچال; Map p52; ☑021-2387 5000; www. tochal.org; Yaddeh-ye Telecabin, off Velenjak Ave; one-way/return Station 2 IR100,000/150,000,

Station 5 IR130,000/270,000, Station 7 IR380,000/650,000; ⊙ from Station 1 8.30am-2pm Sat, Tue & Wed, to 3pm Thu, 7am-3pm Fri; Ⓜ Tajrish, then taxi) Taking 45 minutes to run 7.5km up to within a short hike of the summit of Mt Tochal (3933m), the Tochal Telecabin provides a spectacular ride at any time of year. You don't have to go all the way (and you'll need to change gondolas at Station 5 anyway), but there's a ski resort up top where you'll find snow between six and eight months of the year. The mountain is also a highly popular hiking destination in the warmer months.

The telecabin is super busy on Thursday, Friday and public holidays when Tehranis flock here as much for the socialising as the skiing or hiking; on such days waits of an hour or more in line are not uncommon. On other days, however, it's virtually empty. Note the telecabin doesn't run in windy weather; it's worth calling ahead to check.

To get here, ask for a shuttle taxi to Tochal Telecabin from the north side of Tajrish Sq. From the entrance you can walk (10 minutes) or catch a bus (IR10,000) to the telecabin itself. On the way you'll pass several cafes, a single zip line operation and the **Alpine Coaster** (Map p52; IR200,000; ⊙ 9am-4.30pm Sat-Wed, 8am-8pm Thu & Fri), a bob-sleigh-style ride on metal tracks. Beside the telecabin there's also a **chairlift** (IR100,000 return) running to Cheshmeh, a popular hiking location not as far up the mountains.

The telecabin stops twice en route to the top Station 7 at 3740m – first at Station 2 (2400m), then Station 5 (2935m), where there's a cafe.

★ Darakeh   WALKING
(درکه; Map p56; Ⓜ Tajrish, then taxi) This village, at 1700m elevation and just north of the notorious Evin Prison, is one of Tehran's most pleasant urban escapes. From the cluster of riverside restaurants near the central car park, paths head up through the village and connect with hiking trails across and up the mountainside. It's possible to hike from here to Station 1 of Tochal Telecabin and beyond.

★ Darband   HIKING
(درب; Map p52; Ⓜ Tajrish, then taxi) Three kilometres uphill from Tajrish Sq, the road ends, becoming a path winding up a narrow rocky valley, with water cascading down the slope. The trail heads up into

---

ⓘ CLIMBING MT TOCHAL

The **telecabin** (p50) runs limited hours, but you can choose to torture your legs and climb 3933m Mt Tochal at any time, as locals like to do on Fridays. From Station 1 to Station 5 of the telecabin will take around six hours and is an easy route to follow. From Station 5 to the summit is more tricky and is best done in the company of experienced mountaineers – contact **Varzesh Kooh** (p66) for details of various routes and guides.

---

the hills past a picturesque succession of teahouses, restaurants and fruit-conserve stalls: it's one of the most relaxing places in Tehran to kick back with tea and a qalyan, with a mountain-village feel.

Near the entrance to Darband village is a **chair lift** (Map p52; IR70,000; ⊙ 7am-4.30pm Thu & Fri), which will cut out some of the slog uphill (although it was closed for renovation at the time of writing). Serious hikers can continue east across the mountain for around 5km to Park-e Jamshidiyeh (p50).

A visit to Darband can easily be combined with Sa'd Abad (p48): exit the palace complex via the top entrance and keep going up the hill.

Tochal Ski Resort   SKIING
(☑ 021-2387 5000; www.tochal.org; day pass incl Tochal Telecabin IR650,000; ⊙ 5am-midnight Dec-Apr; Ⓜ Tajrish, then taxi) Hugging the peak of Mt Tochal, and reached via the Tochal Telecabin (p50), this is the easiest ski resort to access from Tehran. The location at 3500m is spectacular, but the gentle slopes, accessed via a couple of chair and drag lifts, are not so long and mostly for beginners and intermediate skiers and snowboarders.

If there's sufficient snow it's possible to ski down from the top Station 7 of the telecabin to Station 5.

Ski passes are sold at Station 1, where it's best to rent any equipment you need, too (there is very limited equipment available at the resort). If you book to stay at the comfortable **Tochal Hotel** (☑ 021-2240 8000; www.tochal.org; Mt Tochal; s/d/ste IR2,120,000/ 3,150,000/3,540,000; 🖢; 🚡 Tochal Telecabin), your return telecabin journey and two days of skiing at the summit are covered. There's also a self-serve cafe at the hotel as well as another cafe at Station 5.

North Tehran

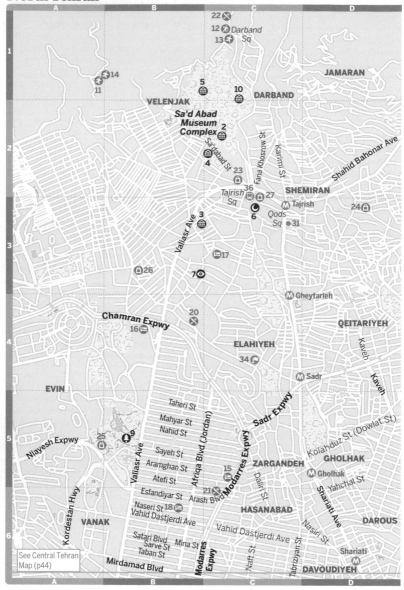

Tochal Ski Club SKIING
(Map p52; ☎021-240 3999; Yaddeh-ye Telecabin, off Velenjak Ave; ski equipment rental IR750,000 per day; ☺8am-5pm; Ⓜ Tajrish, then taxi) The club runs a busy equipment rental station at the base of Station 1 of the Tochal Telecabin; on Thursday, Friday and holidays make sure you get here as soon as it opens or you'll be in a long line for service. It can also arrange lessons at Tochal ski resort from IR350,000 per hour.

Styled after an onsen (natural hot-spring) resort, Hana has four soaking pools into which the salts and minerals have been added. There's also a salt sauna room, various massage therapies, a cafe and a Japanese restaurant on the well-designed premises.

☞ Tours

Ali Taheri
TOURS

(☑ 0912 303 0590; www.iran-tehrantourist.com; tours per day US$70) Personable guide Ali and his sons speak excellent English and know Tehran (and much of the rest of the country) well. They have a variety of cars and even a van in which to arrange tours.

Houman Najafi
TOURS

(☑ 0912 202 3017; houman.najafi@gmail.com) Tehran-based Houman conducts tours around Iran. He is well connected with local environmental groups and specialises in arranging a variety of outdoor adventure and nature tours.

Ali Reza Javaheri
TOURS

(☑ 0912 335 1830; www.viajariran.es; tours per day US$80) This Tehran-based guide speaks extremely good English and Spanish.

🎓 Courses

★ Persian Food Tours
COOKING

(www.persianfoodtours.com; per person 2-4 people €80, 5 or more people €65) Tehran-based Matin and Shirin run this superb cooking course that starts with a morning shopping expedition around Tajrish Bazaar then moves on to their beautiful purpose-built kitchen, where four local dishes and a special drink are prepared for a late lunch. It's hands-on, great fun and an ideal way to learn about Iranian cuisine.

Loghatnameh Dehkhoda Institute
LANGUAGE

(☑ 021-2271 7120; www.icps.ut.ac.ir; 4th floor, 3011 Valiasr Ave, Shemiran, Tehran) The International Center for Persian Studies here is affiliated with Tehran University and offers six-week (US$470 tuition only) intensive and longer, less intensive courses in northern Tehran.

🛏 Sleeping

Tehran's accommodation largely follows the city's social breakdown, so budget places are in the poorer south and the options get more expensive as you go north.

Hana
SPA

(☑ 021-2219 6951; www.spahana.ir; 24 Golbahar St, off Nobahar Ave; IR1,450,000; ⊘ 9am-4pm women, 5pm-midnight men) Tehran is constantly throwing up pleasant surprises and this Japanese-themed spa is one of them.

North Tehran

Because of continuing international sanctions, Tehran is an Airbnb-free zone; there are local alternatives, such as OrientStay (www.orientstay.com/en), but it has little in the way of budget or even midrange options for short stays.

Southern Tehran

Because it's near most of the major sights, southern Tehran is a good base, but it lacks much other than budget and less-than-sparkling midrange choices. Budget hotels cluster Amir Kabir St (east of Imam Khomeini Sq), where dozens of shops selling car paraphernalia and five lanes of cacophonous traffic create a terrible din. There are also few restaurants and little action after dark.

★**Firouzeh Hotel**　　　　　　HOTEL $
(Map p38; ☑ 021-3311 3508; www.firouzehhotel. com; Dowlat Abad Alley, off Amir Kabir St; s/tw without bathroom US$26/38; ❄ @ ⚘; Ⓜ Mellat) If ever there was a hotel the atmosphere of which revolved around one man, this is it. Mr Mousavi is the personification of Persian hospitality, and his enthusiasm, useful information and help with travel bookings make an otherwise unremarkable little hotel in an unlovely part of town into a backpacker centre. The small rooms come with cable TV, fridge, and bathrooms with shower and basin; toilets are shared.

Asia Hotel　　　　　　　　HOTEL $
(Map p38; ☑ 021-3311 8551; http://asiahotel.biz; Mellat St; s/d without bathroom from IR700,000/1,000,000; Ⓜ Mellat) Located opposite the metro station, this cheapie couldn't be more convenient. The street is on the noisy side, so ask for one of the plain but functional rooms facing away. Toilets are squat and you'll pay a bit extra if you want a private bathroom.

Hotel Naderi   HOTEL **$**
(Map p38; ☑021-6670 8610; hotelnaderi@
yahoo.com; 520 Jomhuri-ye Eslami Ave; s/d/tr
US$27/40/50; ❄; ⓂFerdowsi) The charm of
high-ceilinged rooms, 1950s-era Bakelite
telephones, a manual switchboard and
decades-old furnishings in this historic hotel is offset by dripping taps, grubby floors
and grumpy service. Still, when we visited, renovations were under way in some
rooms, the price was low and the location,
above adjoining Cafe Naderi, is good, if
plagued by traffic noise.

Built in 1929 and listed as a historical
monument, the Naderi was once the place
to party in Tehran (look for the bandstand
and dance floor in the overgrown back
yard). If you do stay, ask for a rear room
(room numbers 107 to 112 or 207 to 212),
because the front rooms are crazy noisy.

Amir Kabir Hotel   HOTEL **$$**
(Map p38; ☑021-3397 8970; hotel_amirkabir@
yahoo.com; 220 Naser Khosrow St; s/d/tr IR1,6
00,000/1,800,000/2,300,000; ❄⚲; ⓂImam
Khomeini) The standout feature of the Amir
Kabir is its traditional restaurant, but the
rooms are also worth consideration, too.
Decoration is hardly hip, with flocked wall-
paper and marble floors and a mixture of
squat and Western-style toilets in rooms.
There is, however, some Iranian identity
here, and you couldn't be better placed for
forays into the bazaar.

Khayyam Hotel   HOTEL **$$**
(Map p38; ☑021-3391 1497; www.hotelkhayyam.
com; 3 Navidi St; s/d/tr US$37/55/70; ⓅɃ❄@⚲;
ⓂMellat) In a brightly painted yellow building well set back from busy Amir Kabir St,
this well-kept budget hotel has clean, spacious and functional rooms and friendly
staff. Peyman, the Farsi-speaking pet parrot,
keeps watch over the lobby.

Gollestan Hotel   HOTEL **$$**
(Map p38; ☑021-6671 1417; www.gollestanhotel.
com; 14 Hasan Abad Sq, Hafez Ave; s/d US$50/70;
❄⚲; ⓂHasan Abad) Handily located in an
area around historic Hasan Abad Sq, the
Gollestan offers good value. Rooms are com-
pact and clean and, although far from the
most modern in design, they are perfectly
comfortable.

Hafez Hotel   HOTEL **$$**
(Map p38; ☑021-6674 3073; www.hafezhotel.
net; Bank Alley, off Ferdowsi St; s/d US$49/74;
❄@⚲; ⓂSa'di) In a lane beside the big

Bank Melli, the rooms here are quiet and
clean and have fridges, fans and pokey
bathrooms (some squats, some thrones).
Management speaks English and there's a
decent if unremarkable restaurant that's
open for lunch and dinner.

★**Ferdowsi International
Grand Hotel**   HOTEL **$$$**
(Map p38; ☑021-6672 7026; www.ferdowsihotel.
com; 20 Kushik Mesri St, off Ferdowsi St; s/d from
US$143/201; Ⓟ❄@⚲✂; ⓂImam Khomeini)
This is the only international-standard hotel
within an easy walk of the museums, Golestan
Palace and bazaar, and as such is popular with
tour groups. The quiet, mostly spacious rooms
are well-equipped and fair value (ask for a
renovated room). Service is professional and
facilities include a decent size men-only pool,
sauna and gym.

The 6th-floor rooms will appeal to those
with super-kitsch taste in style. There's also
a lively Iranian restaurant in the basement
with live music.

🛏 Central Tehran

Near the business district, between Enghelab
Ave and Keshavarz Blvd, but within striking
distance of the museums and bazaar, this
area has loads of midrange hotels, several
good new hostels, and plenty of transport
links via the metro and BRT.

★**See You In Iran Hostel**   HOSTEL **$**
(Map p44; ☑021-8883 2266; www.seeyouiniran.
org; 2 Vahdati-Manesh Dead End, off South Kherad-
mand St; dm/s/d without bathroom €15/45/80;
❄⚲; ⓂHaft-e Tir) What started as a Face-
book forum for helping travellers in Iran
has blossomed into Tehran's first fully-legit
hostel. Run by a clued-up, youthful and
open-minded team, this place was just open-
ing up when we were in town, but already
looks fantastic, with charmingly decorated
rooms and super-comfy beds.

There's a cafe, a gift shop (stocking col-
ourful craft products made by mehr-o-mah.
com, an NGO helping women and children
in poverty) and a spacious garden shaded
by trees. In the works are a movie screening
room in the former swimming pool and a
rooftop garden to grow some food. Check
the website for news of regular cultural and
social events.

Seven Hostel   HOSTEL **$**
(Map p44; ☑021-6696 0192; www.sevenhostels.
com; 5 Dideh Baan Alley, off Fakhr-e Razi St; dm

Greater Tehran

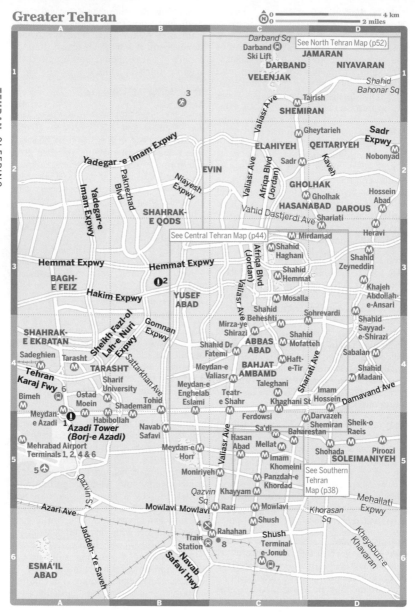

US$12; ❄❋; ⓂMeydan-e Enghelab Eslami) There are separate male and female bunk bed dorms at this popular hostel. Rooms are far from spacious (and the male dorm on the ground floor shares space with the common kitchen), which means things can get messy, but in its favour are price, location and super travel-savvy, friendly staff.

★**Howeyzeh Hotel** HOTEL $$
(Map p44; ☎021-8880 4344; www.korsarhotels. com; 115 Taleghani Ave; s/d US$120/160; P❋❄;

Greater Tehran

M Taleghani) It's worth paying a bit extra for the Howeyzeh's contemporary-styled grey-marble lobby and restaurant area with accents of teal and gold. Rooms don't disappoint either, being equally pleasant, and there's also a spa with jacuzzi and sauna.

Amir Hotel HOTEL **$$**
(Map p44; ☑ 021-8830 4066; www.amir-hotel. com; 278 Taleghani Ave; s/d from $120/152; ✹ ☎; M Taleghani) With a decent location and a pleasant 1960s design that has been well preserved in common areas (check out the water-grotto feature in the dining area) and most rooms, the Amir is a solid midrange choice. It's worth paying a bit more for the 'special rooms' on the 1st floor with their elegant contemporary design featuring calligraphy of Omar Khayyam poetry.

Atlas Hotel HOTEL **$$**
(Map p44; ☑ 021-8880-0407; www.atlas-hotel. com; 206 Taleghani Ave; s/d US$63/102; ✹ @ ☎; M Ferdowsi) The big, comfortable rooms here, some with balconies overlooking a courtyard garden, are good value, but you will hear some traffic noise whichever side of the building you're on. The combination of space, friendly service and facilities, though, do make it an oasis to come home to. The restaurant is also open for dinner.

Parsian Enghelab Hotel HOTEL **$$**
(Map p44; ☑ 021-8893 7251; www.enghelab.pih. ir; 341 Taleghani Ave; s/d IR2,800,000/4,800,000; ✹ @ ☎ ☒; M Meydan-e Valiasr) Set back from the busy main road, the Enghelab looks a bit dowdy in its lobby, but perks up considerably when you enter the revamped rooms, which are spacious, comfortable and stylishly decorated. A plus is the heated outdoor swimming pool (men only), which you have to pay a small fee to use.

Eskan Hotel Forsat HOTEL **$$**
(Map p44; ☑ 021-8834 7385; www.escanhotel. com; 29 Mousavi St; s/d US$116/162; ✹ @ ☎; M Ferdowsi) There are 42 sizeable, well-equipped, very clean and quiet rooms here that remind of modern three-star hotels elsewhere, but are unusually well-finished by Iranian standards. Rooms come with a safe, a good bathroom and comfy beds. Service is professional.

Roudaki Hotel HOTEL **$$**
(Map p44; ☑ 021-6670 9421; www.roudaki-hotel. com; 12 Shahriar St; s/d US$130/150; ✹ ☎; M Teatr-e Shahr) In a quiet part of central Tehran, the 49 renovated rooms here are a little on the pricey side, but offer plenty of space and come with a kitchenette (though without any form of cooker) and lounge area. There's a choice of double or twin beds.

Simorgh Hotel HOTEL **$$**
(Map p44; ☑ 021-8871 9911; www.simorghhotel. com; 1069 Valiasr Ave; r from US$167; ✹ @ ☎ ☒; M Mirza-ye Shirazi) This efficiently run medium-sized hotel is popular with business visitors. Downsides are that rooms are dimly lit with somewhat old-fashioned decor. On the plus side, they are spacious and quiet. Facilities include a gym, jacuzzi, pool and meeting rooms. A nice touch are free cakes for guests at reception.

Iran Markazi Hotel HOTEL **$$**
(Iran Central Hotel; Map p38; ☑ 021-3399 6577; www.markazihotel.ir; 419 Lalehzar St; s/tw US$50/70; ✹ ☎; M Sa'di) There's no lift at this small hotel with compact, functional rooms and old-fashioned furnishings. The price is reasonable for the centrally located area, though, and it's on an interesting street lined with spectacular chandelier and light-fitting shops. Bathrooms have Western-style toilets.

Laleh International Hotel HOTEL **$$$**
(Map p44; ☑ 021-8896 5021; www.lalehhotel.com; cnr Dr Fatemi & Hejab Sts; r from US$185; P ✹ @ ☎ ☒; M Meydan-e Valiasr) One of the best choices among the fading pre-revolution luxury hotels due to its fine location north of Park-e Laleh. The large rooms and suites offer fine park or mountain views, and

while the decor and service are both a bit tired, all up it's fair value.

The outdoor swimming pool is open late May to late September.

Espinas Khalige Fars Hotel HOTEL $$$

(Map p44; ☑ 021-8899 6658; www.espinashotels. com; 126 Keshavarz Blvd; r from US$282; P ✳ @ 🛜 ☒; M Meydan-e Valiasr) Polite service marks out the well-located Espinas, where the rooms and suites combine modern comforts with an understated dash of Iranian style in the decor. There's an underground gym, sauna and pool; women may be able to use these facilities before 3pm, otherwise it's men only.

Raamtin Residence Hotel HOTEL $$$

(Map p44; ☑ 021-8872 2786; www.raamtinhotel. com; 1081 Valiasr Ave; r from US$170; ✳ @ 🛜; M Mirza-ye Shirazi) White leather couches might not be your thing, but the Raamtin's 55 spacious rooms are otherwise reasonably well-equipped, and double-glazed windows cut most of the noise of Tehran's main commercial strip. Hotel service is efficient and the location ideal for business.

🛏 Northern Tehran

More upmarket hotels and apartment hotels are found in this part of town, where all accommodation falls into the midrange and top-end categories. It's too far to walk to the museums and bazaar, but you can take the Metro, BRT bus or brave the traffic. You will be closer to more fashionable restaurants and cafes.

AIRPORT ACCOMMODATION

Ibis Tehran (☑ 021-5567 7900; www. ibis.com; Imam Khomeini International Airport; s/d €108/150; P ✳ @ 🛜 ☒; M Imam Khomeini International Airport) Directly opposite the airport and sharing a building with the slightly more upmarket Novotel is this slick, contemporary-design business hotel that takes the sweat out of a late-night arrival or an early-morning departure. With the metro link up and running you could also use it as a base for a few days in Tehran minus the traffic!

A delicious buffet breakfast is served in the Novotel's restaurant. Stays of under six hours are €50.

★ Sepehr Apartment Hotel APARTMENT $$

(Map p52; ☑ 021-2224 5050; www.melal.com; 11 Salour St, off Dr Hesabi St; studio/1-/2-bedroom apt US$175/185/230; ✳ @ 🛜 ☒; M Tajrish) In a peaceful north Tehran neighbourhood that's a short walk from the metro or Valiasr Ave, the Sepehr is a stylish hotel made up of good-quality self-catering apartments. There are plenty of facilities, including a pool and jacuzzi, that can be exclusively reserved for private use by couples and families. A buffet breakfast is included in the price.

Parsian Esteghlal Hotel HOTEL $$

(Map p52; ☑ 021-2266 0011; www.esteghlalhotel. com; cnr Chamran Expwy & Valiasr Ave; d/tw from US$109/136; P ✳ @ 🛜 ☒; 🚍 BRT to Parkway) In the pre-revolutionary era this was the Hilton. The west tower rooms, which are cheaper, retain a faded 1960s glamour in the furnishings that will appeal to retro fans. Otherwise it's a functional and popular business hotel with good views from the rooms and plenty of facilities including a pool and gym.

Tooba Boutique Hotel APARTMENT $$$

(Map p52; ☑ 021-8820 7000; www.toobahotel. com; 17 Naseri St; studio/1-/2-bedroom apt from US$175/229/273; 🚍 BRT to Niayesh) As long as you're not expecting a boutique hotel in the Western sense, you won't be disappointed by the Tooba. It's a pleasant addition to north Tehran's range of apartment hotels, although only the one- and two-bedroom apartments have working kitchens. Good facilities include a roof-top restaurant, a sauna, a jacuzzi pool and a gym.

Media Hotel Apartment APARTMENT $$$

(Map p52; ☑ 021-2620 1610; www.hotelmediaap. com; 58 East Armaghan St, off Afriqa Blvd; s/d from $201/232; ✳ 🛜; 🚍 BRT to Niayesh) A good choice among the several upmarket modern apartment hotels in northern Tehran, the Media is tucked away in a dead-end street. Enormous one-bedroom apartments come fully furnished with desk and executive chair, comfortable bed and fully equipped kitchen. Service is good and there's a cafe and decent restaurant.

🍴 Eating

Tehran's range of foreign cuisines make a refreshing change from the Iranian staples. The wealthier central and northern suburbs offer more international flavours, served in highly designed spaces by sharply dressed, English-speaking waiters. Not surprisingly, such restaurants are relatively expensive by Iranian standards. Nearly all cafes serve food as well as drinks.

Southern Tehran

★**Azari Traditional Teahouse**   IRANIAN $
(Map p56; ☑ 021 5537 3665; 1 Valiasr Ave; mains IR110,000-150,000; ☺teahouse 6am-midnight, restaurant 11am-5pm & 7-11pm; ☎; Ⓜ Rahahan) Just north of the train station, this large and wonderfully atmospheric *chaykhaneh* (teahouse) is justly popular with locals. The *dizi* (lamb, potato and chickpea stew) and *kashk-e bademjan* (eggplant fried and mashed and served with thick whey and mint) are excellent, making it a great lunch venue. In the evening there's live music from 8pm.

If you prefer a quieter atmosphere the cosy restaurant next door offers a wider menu including kababs.

Amir Kabir Restaurant   IRANIAN $
(Map p38; ☑ 021-3397 8970; 220 Naser Khosrow St; mains IR150,000; ☺noon-9.30pm; Ⓜ Imam Khomeini) Carp swim in the rectangular pool at the centre of this atmospheric restaurant with wood-carved pillars holding up a gallery floor. It's a good choice for kababs, chicken and rice dishes. There's no English menu, but there are a few pictures on the Farsi menu you can point at, and the staff are friendly.

Moslem   IRANIAN $
(رستوران مسلم; Map p38; ☑ 021-5560 2275; Panzdah e Khordad St, Sabzeh Meydan; mains IR200,000; ☺11am-5.30pm; Ⓜ Panzdah-e Khordad) There's almost always a long line (which does move reasonably quickly) snaking out of this famous restaurant that's located on a couple of upper floors of a building overlooking the main entrance square to the Grand Bazaar. It's famous crispy rice dish, *tahchin*, comes in gut-busting portions along with chunky pieces of chicken or bean stew.

Don't want to line up? Takeaway is available at the street-level stall.

Gol-e Rezaieh   IRANIAN $
(Map p38; ☑ 021-6670 7290; 30 Si Tir St; mains IR80,000-100,000; ☺7.30am-4pm; ☎ ✐; Ⓜ Sa'di) Photos of Western rock and movie royalty (Freddie Mercury in particular) gaze down from the walls of this compact cafe, one of

Tehran's oldest. It's a favourite of intellectuals, journalists, writers and artists, and a great place to enjoy a breakfast or lunch of traditional dishes (such as the stew *khoresht*), including vegetarian options.

Tarighat Restaurant   IRANIAN $
(Map p38; ☑ 021-3311 3836; 482 Amir Kabir St; mains IR115,000-195,000; ☺noon-4pm Sat-Thu; Ⓜ Mellat) Handy to the budget accommodation, this lunchtime place serves reliably good interpretations of the standard kababs, *khoresht* and *zereshk polo ba morgh* (roast chicken served with rice and barberry). Look for the Chinese red lanterns hanging above the door and you've found the place.

Khayyam   IRANIAN $$
(Map p38; ☑ 021-5580 0760; Khayyam St; mains IR170,000-480,000; ☺noon-11pm; ☎; Ⓜ Khayyam) This beautifully restored 300-year-old building was originally part of the Imamzadeh Seyyed Nasreddin shrine opposite before being separated when Khayyam St intervened. The Iranian fare (mainly kabab, chicken and fish) is well prepared and plentiful, though service is hit and miss. Still, for tea, water pipes and sweets (IR50,000) before or after an outing in the bazaar, it's hard to beat.

Central Tehran

★**Khoone**   IRANIAN $
(خونه; Map p44; ☑ 0912 838 3437; www.facebook.com/restaurantkhoone; Kaman Dead End, Shahidi St; mains IR150,000-300,000; ☺noon-4pm & 7-11pm; ☎; Ⓜ Shahid Haghani) The next best thing to getting invited to a Tehrani's home for a meal is sampling the lovingly made dishes at this cute, cosy cafe. Khoone means 'home' in Farsi and the place is deliberately designed to put guests at ease. The short menu changes daily and features classic Iranian dishes such *tahdig* (crispy rice pies) and sweet drinks.

It's also perfectly located beside the landmark Tabiat Bridge.

Khoshbin   IRANIAN $
(Map p44; ☑ 021-3390 2194; 510 North Sa'di St; mains IR130,000-300,000; ☺noon-3.30pm; Ⓜ Sa'di) Tiny, no-frills Khoshbin is an institution among Tehranis, who cram onto the fast-turnover tables for an authentic Gilaki (food from the Gilan region) lunch. Try the *mirza ghasemi* (mashed eggplant, squash, garlic, tomato and egg), *kuli* (carp roe), *zeytoun parvardeh* (green olives marinated in

pomegranate molasses, walnuts and herbs) and particularly the fried whole fish.

Usually known as Hassan Rashti, after the restaurant's founder, it's next to the Mikhak shoe shop.

Sofre Khane Ayaran
IRANIAN $

(سفره خانه سنتی عیاران; Map p44; ☑ 021-6676 0376; 784 Enghelab Ave; mains IR150,000-300,000; ⊙ noon-midnight; Ⓜ Ferdowsi) This subterranean *chaykhaneh* (teahouse) is an appealing escape from the fumes of Ferdowsi Sq. Head to the ornate restaurant area rather than the smoky tea and water-pipe section. The menu has some hard-to-find dishes and some that you might not expect in your standard Tehran basement, such as 'submissive' (a delicious eggplant dip with fried onions).

Coffee Shop & Veggie Restaurant of Iranian Artists' Forum
VEGETARIAN $

(Map p44; ☑ 021-8831 0462; www.iaveg.com; Park-e Honar Mandan; mains IR190,000-300,000; ⊙ 11am-11pm; ✍; Ⓜ Taleghani) Wholesome vegetarian meals are served in this popular place where the produce is bought fresh each day and the kitchen is completely meat-free, so there'll be no surprises in the salads, pizzas or *khoresht* (stew). There's a convivial, romantic indoor-outdoor terrace plus the bright dining area.

There are several restaurants in the Iran Artists' Forum; the entrance is around the right-hand side as you approach from the front.

Pasta Charmy's
VEGETARIAN $

(Map p44; ☑ 021-6649 8510; www.charmyspasta. com; 2 Alborz St, off Hafez St; mains IR150,000; ⊙ noon-4pm & 8-10.30pm Sat-Thu; ☎✍; Ⓜ Ferdowsi) Cosy little Charmy's squeezes seats for about 20 around gingham-tableclothed tables into a room with an open kitchen. It dishes up simple but delicious creamy vegetarian pastas, salads, soups and drinks.

Tabiat Food Court
FOOD HALL $

(Map p44; Tabiat Bridge, Park-e Taleghani; fast food IR120,000-300,000; ⊙ 11am-midnight Sat-Wed, 10am-1am Thu & Fri; ☎; Ⓜ Shahid Haghani) On the lower level at the eastern end of Tehran's showstopper pedestrian bridge is this colourful and relaxed food court with outlets offering the usual range of fast foods, drinks and desserts. We liked the look of the baked potatoes with all kinds of toppings at the Istanbul Kumpir stall.

★ Dizi
IRANIAN $$

(دیزی; Map p44; ☑ 021-8881 0008; 52 Kalantari St; set meal IR450,000; ⊙ noon-4pm; ☎; Ⓜ Hafte-Tir) The name gives a clue to the menu: that's right, it's Iran's favourite lamb, potato and chickpea stew. Here they do it damn well, served with all the trimmings including fresh herb salad and a jug of the minty yoghurt drink *dugh*. The staff will show you how to eat it, if in doubt, and take photos of you.

It's been around for decades and the characterful interior is plastered with traditional paintings. Look for the bare brick facade and get here early or be prepared to queue.

Alborz
IRANIAN $$

(Map p44; ☑ 021-8853 4757; www.alborzrest.com; cnr Nikou Khadam St & Sohrevardi Ave; mains IR300,000-600,000; ⊙ 11am-11pm; Ⓜ Shahid Beheshti) Popular with well-heeled Iranians for business dinners and family celebrations, Alborz serves beautifully presented kabab platters with, especially, very toothsome lamb. The salad bar is brilliant – worth the trip in itself. There are lots of nice touches – they ask your nationality for a reason.

Cingari
INDIAN $$$

(Map p44; ☑ 021-8832 7075; 6 Zohreh St, off Mofatteh St; mains IR425,000-985,000; ⊙ noon-2.45pm & 7-10.45pm; ☎✍; Ⓜ Shahid Beheshti) Cingari is the pick of the Indian restaurants because it gets the Mughlai cuisine just right, with tasty tandoor dishes, flavourful curries and plenty of vegetarian options. The elegant, subdued lighting and efficient service would be at home in Sydney or London.

✗ Northern Tehran

Cinema Cafe
INTERNATIONAL $

(Map p52; Bagh-e Ferdows, off Valiasr Ave; mains IR200,000-300,000; ⊙ 8am-11pm; ▣ BRT to Bagh-e Ferdows) Of the two cafes that flank the Film Museum of Iran, this one has the more appealing food menu with a wide range of local and international dishes including omelettes, sandwiches, salads and pasta. It attracts a privileged, liberal crowd who like to hang out in the pleasant courtyard setting.

Markazi Jamshidiyeh Restaurant
IRANIAN $

(Map p52; Park-e Jamshidiyeh; mains IR180,000-380,000; ⊙ noon-midnight; Ⓜ Tajrish, then taxi) The first of several teahouses you'll see as you head uphill from the entrance of the park, is also the busiest, with tables offering great views from several levels. Prices are also relatively reasonable for the standard menu of kababs, chicken and rice as well as Western dishes such as pizza, burgers and sandwiches.

★ **Gilaneh**   IRANIAN $$
(Map p52; ☑ 021-2205 5335; www.gilaneh.co; Saba Blvd, off Afriqa Blvd; mains IR365,000-500,000; ⊙ noon-4pm & 8-11pm; 🐾; ☐ BRT to Niayesh) Rustic wooden beams, glazed tiles and a lively, friendly atmosphere all set the scene for the delicious Gilan-region food served at one of Tehran's most popular restaurants. Sample the mix of dips and the deep fried zander, a type of fish, or go for either the duck or chicken *fesenjan* (a dish with a rich nut and pomegranate sauce).

★ **S.P.U Restaurant**   IRANIAN $$
(Map p56; ☑ 021-2241 9494; www.spu-restaurant. com; Darakeh Sq, Darakeh; mains IR250,000-640,000; ⊙ noon-4pm & 7-11pm; 🐾; Ⓜ Tajrish, then taxi) One of the pleasures of a visit to leafy Darakeh, high in northern Tehran, is to enjoy a meal at its riverside restaurants. This is the best one, with both a main dining hall and private cabins where you can sit on the carpeted floors and recline on cushions while tucking into expertly made kababs and freshly baked bread.

★ **Koohpayeh**   IRANIAN $$
(Map p52; ☑ 021-2271 2518; Khoopayeh Sq, Sarband, Darband Ave; mains IR250,000 680,000, ⊙ 11am-11pm; 🐾; Ⓜ Tajrish, then taxi) There's fierce competition for diners at the many restaurants and teahouses that line the babbling river that flows through Darband, but most in-the-know locals favour this elegant place near the start of the village. Sit on the outdoor terrace and enjoy the view as skilled waitstaff in red waistcoats deliver all kinds of kababs and other local dishes.

Khaneh Azarbaijan   IRANIAN $$
(Map p52; ☑ 021-4614 0367; Park-e Jamshidiyeh; mains IR260,000-380,000; ⊙ 10am-midnight; Ⓜ Tajrish, then taxi) The most atmospheric of several teahouses in the popular hillside park at Tehran's northern edge is based in a cabin with stained-glass windows that's built into the rocks. Outdoor tables boast amazing views. The kababs, *ash-e reshte* (pasta and herb soup) and *dizi* (lamb, potato and chickpea stew) are fair value.

FAST FOOD & FOOD COURTS

For fast food, cheap *kababi*s (kabab shops) and other burger/pizza/sandwich joints can be found around the major squares and in the underground passages of some metro stations. There is a good food court at the **Tabiat Bridge** (p60), as well as at the **Palladium** (p66) and **ARG Centre** (p66) shopping malls.

Monsoon   ASIAN $$
(Map p44; ☑ 021-8879 1982; Gandhi Shopping Centre, Gandhi Ave; mains IR270,000-550,000; ⊙ noon-3pm & 7-11pm Sat-Thu, 1-3pm & 7-11pm Fri; 🐾; ☐ BRT to Pol-e Hammat) The Monsoon group has many restaurants across Tehran. This, one of their first, offers decent (but not authentic) Asian food including Thai-style curries, Chinese noodle dishes and sushi rolls – all of which makes a welcome change to kababs. It's smart, sophisticated and very 'new Tehran'.

Ananda Vegetarian Restaurant & Coffee Shop   VEGETARIAN $$
(Map p52; ☑ 021-2255 6767; 18 South Ekhtiyariyeh Ave, off Pasdaran Ave; mains IR300,000; ⊙ 8.45am-10.45pm; 🐾📶; Ⓜ Nobonyad, then taxi) Tofu vegan kababs, veggie pasta dishes and excellent salads are on offer at this gem of a restaurant. The pleasant garden courtyard setting and good service also make it appealing to meat-lovers.

★ **Divan**   IRANIAN $$$
(Map p52; ☑ 021-2265 3853; 8th fl, Sam Center, Fereshteh St; mains IR650,000; ⊙ noon-4, 7.30-11pm; 🐾; ☐ BRT to Mahmoodiyeh) Plush Divan is the pick of several restaurants operated by the Monsoon Group on the 8th floor of the swanky Sam Center. Chic furnishings, including striking portraits by Iranian artist Fataneh Dadkhah, set the luxe tone. A tempting menu of traditional Persian dishes with a modern twist delivers both on flavour and presentation.

There's a broad balcony with mountain views and a boutique by the entrance selling colourful, creative jewellery, accessories and interior design goods.

🍷 Drinking & Nightlife

Tehran has no shortage of cafes and traditional *chaykhaneh* (teahouses). The cafe scene is particularly vibrant, with numerous mod-chic places serving Tehranis looking for European, rather than Middle Eastern, influences. Cafes and teahouses also serve food, are often open till late, and are fun places to hang out and meet people. Bars, pubs and nightclubs? Dream on.

Southern Tehran

★ Haj Ali Darvish Teahouse TEAHOUSE
(Map p38; ☑ 021-5581 8672; www.facebook.com/kazemmab; Grand Bazaar; ⊘ 7am-5pm Sat-Wed, to noon Thu; Ⓜ Panzdah-e Khordad) There's been a teahouse here next to Abdollah Khan Madrassa since 1917, and Haj Kazem's father Ali took over the business in 1962. It's now a stand-up 2m-wide stall rather than a sit-down teahouse, but still worth searching out for its six types of tea (IR20,000), hot chocolate and coffee – all lovingly prepared by the genial Kazem.

With a very active Instagram account, he's no slouch when it comes to social media and marketing, making this little gem one of the most popular pit-stops in the bazaar.

Timcheh Akbarian TEAHOUSE
(Map p38; ☑ 021-2291 9600; 82 Eudlagan, off Panzdah-e Khordad Ave; Ⓜ Panzdah-e Khordad) This traditional teahouse occupies what was the first Iranian bank some 260 years ago during the Qajar era. Carpeted booths on two levels look on to a long thin pool with a fountain. The traditional lunch of *dizi* (lamb, potato and chickpea stew; IR150,000) is served 10am to 3pm, but the rest of the time its tea and water pipes only.

You'll find it opposite the Grand Bazaar, down a recently restored brick-vaulted passage that's worth a look in its own right.

Cafe Naderi CAFE
(Map p38; 520 Jomhuri-ye Eslami Ave; ⊘ 10am-7.30pm Sat-Thu; ☏; Ⓜ Sa'di) On the ground floor of the Hotel Naderi, this pastel-shaded cafe has long been a favourite, attracting a curious mix of students, artists and grannies in a setting that is circa 1950s Paris (unrenovated). The cafe fare is limited to Turkish and French coffee and a cake or two. Don't expect much service (or change) from the grumpy waiters.

The adjoining restaurant has a full menu (mains IR480,000 to IR660,000) and is known by generations of Tehranis for its chateaubriand and schnitzel.

Central Tehran

★ Cafe Upartmaan CAFE
(Map p44; ☑ 021-8886 0439; 48 Kalantari St; ⊘ 8am-midnight; ☏; Ⓜ Haft-e Tir) Although it's plagued by cigarette smoke, this large, multisectioned cafe is still well worth dropping by for its wide-ranging drinks and food menu, liberal vibe and the excellent crafts shop by the entrance selling artisan homewares from across Iran. Upstairs are separate galleries where you might also be able to catch an exhibition or some kind of show.

★ Lamiz CAFE
(Map p44; ☑ 021-6646 2204; www.lamizcoffee.com; 1435 Valiasr Ave; ⊘ 7am-11pm Sat-Thu, 8am-11pm Fri; ☏; Ⓜ Teatr-e Shahr) Lamiz has several outlets of its Seattle-style cafes around Tehran. This super-chic branch is the most central and boasts a wide range of drinks, including unusual ones such as matcha (powdered green tea). It also offers soy milk, a rarity in Tehran.

Baked goods and an excellent yoghurt, granola and fruit pot make it a decent breakfast option, too.

★ Cake Studio Vorta CAFE
(Map p44; ☑ 021-6647 5300; 979 Enghelab Ave; ⊘ 8.30am-10pm Sat-Thu, 3-10pm Fri; ☏; Ⓜ Teatr-e Shahr) Who doesn't love a cupcake? At this cute and buzzy cafe close by Tehran University, they're made well-slathered with butter-cream icing, plus there's several other sweet confections to go with the good coffee and excellent range of herbal and fruit teas – displayed in glass pots on the counter.

Agha Bozorg TEAHOUSE
(Map p44; ☑ 021-8890 0522; 40 Keshavarz Blvd; ⊘ noon-midnight; Ⓜ Meydan-e Valiasr) Tucked away down an ornately tiled staircase, this cosy underground teahouse is full of young Iranians flirting, drinking tea, smoking hookahs and eating (in that order) under attractive vaulted and tiled ceilings. The Iranian food is reliably good (mains IR130,000 to IR350,000), particularly the *dizi* (lamb, potato and chickpea stew).

Markov Cafe Gallery CAFE
(Map p44; ☑ 0919 387 2207; Qsar Prison Museum, Motahari Ave; ⊘ 10am-11pm; ☏; Ⓜ Shahid Mofatteh, then taxi) Occupying a small wing of the old red-brick prison at Qsar Garden Museum, this is one of two pleasant cafes

overlooking the surrounding sculpture park. Named after the prison's Russian architect, Markov has the slight edge due to its dual use as a gallery space and its rather good chocolate cake.

Nazdik Cafe
CAFE

(Map p44; ☑ 021-8849 0726; www.facebook.com/nazdikcafe; 1st fl, 134 Karim Khan-e Zand Blvd; ⊙ 8am-10.30pm Sat-Thu, 10am-10.30pm Fri; ☏; Ⓜ Haft-e Tir) One of central Tehran's most pleasantly designed cafes, Nazdik has both indoor and outdoor areas and a contemporary vibe. It's a popular spot for breakfast, and there's a good choice of herbal teas as well as the usual coffees and other soft drinks.

Find it above the also appealing **Kiosk Cafe** on the ground floor.

Godot Cafe
CAFE

(Map p44; ☑ 021-8888 3940; Enghelab Ave; ⊙ 10am-11pm; ☏; Ⓜ Teatr-e Shahr) Hanging baskets of plants create a fresh, garden feel to the arched entranceway to this cafe named after one of Samuel Beckett's most famous characters. Whether or not you end up waiting for eternity here for your friend to arrive, you'll be able to enjoy the usual range of drinks and some light snacks and meals.

Romance Cafe
CAFE

(Map p44; ☑ 021-6674 9574; www.cafe-romance.com; 4 Zarrabi Alley, off Ferdowsi St; ⊙ 9am-11pm; ☏; Ⓜ Ferdowsi) Upstairs in an alley, this charming multiroom cafe is an ideal place to escape the traffic mayhem around Ferdowsi Sq. The Middle European atmosphere, with patterned wallpaper, high ceilings and dark wood chairs and sofas, is indeed romantic. As well as Persian teas and Turkish coffee and the like it has a menu with several vegetarian dishes.

Cafe Gallery
CAFE

(Map p44; ☑ 021-8834 9366; Park-e Honar Mandan, Baroroushan St; ⊙ 10am-11pm; ☏; Ⓜ Taleghani) Located above Iranshahr Theatre in Artists' Park, Cafe Gallery is hard to beat in central Tehran as a place to sit and soak up the scene. You can soak up some art (it's a functioning gallery) and some sun, too, if you get a seat on the balcony. The food menu includes pastas, salads, burgers and soufflés (mains IR250,000) that satisfy without stunning.

Cafe 78
CAFE

(Cafe Haftad-o Hasht; Map p44; www.facebook.com/cafe78iran; 38 South Shahid Azodi St; mains IR140,000-180,000; ⊙ 11am-11pm Sat-Thu, 4-11pm Fri; ☏; Ⓜ Meydan-e Valiasr) A good place to get in touch with Tehran's hip young artistic community is this arty cafe plastered with posters for events and a wanderlust wall of tourist maps from across Iran. The coffee, wide range of teas, snacks and service are all good.

Cafe Opera
CAFE

(Map p44; ☑ 021-6673 3469; cnr Khark & Ostad Shahriar Sts; ⊙ 8am-10pm Sat-Thu, 4-10pm Fri; Ⓜ Teatr-e Shahr) Brick-walled and attractively decked out with old projectors, cameras and radios, this is a cosy little place to stop for coffee or hot chocolate, particularly if you've been to a concert or play at nearby Vahdat Hall.

Northern Tehran

★ Sam Cafe
CAFE

(Map p52; ☑ 021-2265 3842; www.samcafe.ir; 1st fl, Sam Center, Fereshteh St; ⊙ 9am-10pm; ☏; 🚍 BRT to Mahmoodiyeh) A coffee roaster dominates the entrance to the slickest of north Tehran's many fashionable cafes and chief hang-out of the city's privileged. Down your third-wave brew at the long shared table or lounging in a low-slung comfy chair while admiring the chic industrial interior of rough cement walls, distressed orange-painted iron beams and open kitchen.

Cafe de France
CAFE

(Map p44; ☑ 021-8879 2038; Gandhi Shopping Centre, Gandhi Ave; ⊙ 10am-11pm; ☏; 🚍 BRT to Pol-e Hemmat) On Ghandi's upper level, Cafe de France whisks you to the Left Bank with its dark wood, retro tables and chairs, messy display of books and cosy ambience. It serves all kinds of caffeinated drinks, cakes, sandwiches, pasta and ice cream.

If the cafe is too busy or not your scene then there several other cool little cafes peopled largely by young and fairly liberal Tehranis, making Ghandi a one-stop cafe-society shop.

Chai Bar
CAFE

(Map p52; ☑ 021-2221 0313; 145 North Salimi Ave, off Andarzgoo Blvd; mains IR200,000-300,000; ⊙ 10am-11.30pm; ☏; Ⓜ Tajrish) Occupying a pavilion in the grounds of a grand old mansion that now houses Art Centre Galleries (p64), Chai Bar blends traditional Iranian style with a superb garden location (outdoor seats are warmed by heaters in winter). It's ideal for lingering beneath the

DON'T MISS

CONTEMPORARY ART GALLERIES

Iran's vibrant contemporary art scene and the growing local and international profile of Iranian contemporary art has spawned dozens of commercial galleries across Tehran. The following is a small selection; look for the free bi-monthly booklet *Preview* at the galleries for information on others.

Iranian Artists' House (خانه هنرمندان; Map p44; ☎ 021-8831 0457; www.iranartists.org; Park-e Honar Mandan; ⊙1-8pm; Ⓜ Taleghani) FREE A hub for the contemporary and traditional arts in Tehran, this complex has several gallery spaces over two levels exhibiting works in all media on a monthly rotation. Within the building there's also a cracking arts and crafts shop, a cafe and two restaurants, including an Italian one on the roof and another that's vegetarian.

Seyhoun Art Gallery (Map p44; ☎ 021-8871 1305; www.seyhounartgallery.com; 11 4th St, off Khaled Eslamboli St; ⊙10am-6pm; 🚍 BRT to Pelle Avval) Founded by the painter Massoumeh Noushin Seyhoun in 1966, this is one of Tehran's longest running commercial art spaces showcasing contemporary Iranian artists. It hosts regular exhibitions of painting, photography, sculpture and graphic art in its original distinctive, black-fronted gallery.

Ab Anbar (Map p44; ☎ 021-8886 0703; www.ab-anbar.com; 2 Roshanmanesh Alley, off Khaghani St; ⊙noon-8pm Sun-Fri; Ⓜ Darvazeh Dowlat) Established in 2014 this is one of Tehran's more ambitious contemporary art galleries, with a focus on showcasing Iranian artists working outside of the country. Exhibitions change roughly every month and you can browse catalogues of past shows at their pleasant cafe on the top floor, which includes an outdoor terrace.

Assar Art Gallery (Map p44; ☎ 021-8832 6689; www.assarartgallery.com; 16 Barforoushan Alley, off Iranshahr Ave; ⊙Sun-Thu 11am-8pm, Fri 4-8pm; Ⓜ Taleghani) This gallery has a reputation for supporting contemporary artists and has a program of exhibitions that change every three weeks at its central Tehran space.

Art Centre Galleries (Map p52; ☎ 021-2665 5590; www.art-center.ir; 145 North Salimi St, off Andarzgoo Blvd; ⊙11.30am-8.30pm; Ⓜ Tajrish, then taxi) This gallery and crafts shop in a handsome century-old mansion in north Tehran represents several well-established, as well as up-and-coming, Iranian artists. Alongside canvases and sculptures, you can pick up glazed ceramic pomegranates and bronze ornaments.

Gallery Mellat (Map p52; www.cinema-mellat.com; Mellat Cinema Complex, off Niayesh Expy; ⊙10am-11pm; 🚍 BRT to Park Mellat) In the basement of the multiplex cinema that occupies a sinuous contemporary building in the western corner of Park-e Mellat, this gallery hosts regularly changing shows by local artists.

trees sipping the wide range of teas and Illy coffee; it also sells salads, soup and sandwiches (mains IR200,000 to IR300,000).

☆ Entertainment

Although there are restrictions on what can be performed in public, in Tehran you will have a chance to attend a wide variety of entertainments, including plays, movies, documentaries and concerts. The theatre scene is particularly dynamic, with many productions of local plays, as well as inventive translations of regime-approved foreign works, from Shakespeare to Arnold Wesker. Booking website Tik8 (www.tik8.com) lists events.

★**Iranshahr Theatre** THEATRE
(تماشاخانه ایران شهر; Map p44; ☎ 021-8881 4115/6; www.tamashakhaneh.ir; Park-e Honar Mandan, Baroroushan St; tickets IR200,000-400,000; Ⓜ Taleghani) One of Tehran's oldest theatres, this beautiful building in peaceful Park-e Honar Mandan typically has four different shows playing in its complex with two stages. While most of the shows here are performed in Farsi, some are more visual and internationally accessible than others. Use Google translate to see which plays are coming up.

Teatr-e Shahr THEATRE
(تئاتر شهر; Map p44; ☎ 021-6646 0595; cnr Valiasr & Enghelab Aves; tickets from IR160,000; Ⓜ Teatr-e

Shahr) Opened in 1968, this circular building covered in beautiful tiles is, visually, Tehran's most impressive playhouse. Come here to see Iranian stage actors performing in Farsi, of course. Some booking staff speak English, so call to find out what's coming up. Performances are normally at 6.30pm or 7.30pm.

☆ Cinema

Movie halls, old and new, are all over town, with a concentration along southern Lalehzar St and eastern Jomhuri-ye Eslami Ave, in southern Tehran. Films screen about every two hours between 10am and 8.30pm, for around IR80,000 a show. All films will be in Farsi or dubbed into Farsi, and don't expect anything remotely controversial.

The Film Museum of Iran (p50) has five films a day in Iran's oldest cinema. The best chance of catching international cinema is at events such as the Fajr International Film Festival (www.fajriff.com) in April, the Tehran International Short Film Festival (www. tisff.ir) in November, and the documentary festival Cinema Vérité (www.irandocfest.ir) in December.

Azadi Cinema Center   CINEMA
(Map p44; ☑021-84480; www.cinema-azadi. com; cnr Dr Beheshti & Vozara Sts; ☉10am-9pm; Ⓜ Mirza-ye Shirazi) There are seven large cinemas at this famous multiplex, all screening Iranian movies.

☆ Music

The tussle between moderate and conservative forces in Iran over organised public performances of modern music continues to plague Tehran's live-music scene. Getting approval for a rock concert, for example, is prohibitively hard, but performances of traditional and classical music are becoming more common with information on sites such as www.iranconcert.com.

The Tehran Symphony Orchestra (www. tehransymphony.com) has been revived under world-class conductor, Alexander Rahbari and is performing concerts at Vahdat Hall and the Tehran Milad Tower International Convention Centre.

Otherwise, musicians take to parks and streets for free concerts. You could also check with See You In Iran Hostel (p55) about regular jam sessions on Wednesday as well as other musical events.

Vahdat Hall   THEATRE
(Roudaki Hall; Map p44; ☑021-6673 1419; Shahriar St; Ⓜ Teatr-e Shahr) The centrally located Vahdat is a beautifully designed traditional horseshoe-shaped theatre venue dating from 1967. Look out for classical or pop music concerts here as well as drama.

☆ Sport

Iran's favourite sport is football (soccer), which is played at several smaller stadiums and at the 100,000-capacity **Azadi Sports Stadium** (☑021-4473 9022; www.azadisportcomplex.com; Azadi Stadium Blvd; Ⓜ Varzeshgah-e Azadi). Matches are normally played on Thursday and Friday, but to find out where, your best bet is to ask a man working in your hotel. If the big Tehran derby between Esteghlal and Persepolis is on, go – assuming you are not a woman, as only men are allowed in.

🔒 Shopping

Souvenir shopping in Tehran doesn't compare to working your way through the atmospheric bazaars of Esfahan and Shiraz. However, the range is bigger and the prices usually lower. As well as at the Grand Bazaar, plenty of souvenir shops can be found along Ferdowsi St and Taleghani Ave. Prices are 'fixed' but fall fast if you show any bargaining form.

🛍 Southern Tehran

★**Iran Termeh**   GIFTS & SOUVENIRS
(Map p38; www.irantermeh.com; Grand Bazaar; ☉7am-5pm Sat-Wed, to noon Thu; Ⓜ Panzdah-e Khordad) Head upstairs from the ground floor stall on the main artery of the bazaar to discover women creating gorgeous table runners and other decorative fabric pieces from *termeh,* local handwoven cloth in dazzling floral patterns. You can buy the cloth by the metre here, too, as well as souvenir products made from it.

Carpet Bazaar   HOMEWARES
(Map p38; Grand Bazaar, Panzdah-e Khordad St; ☉7am-5pm Sat-Wed, to noon Thu; Ⓜ Panzdah-e Khordad) There are carpet stores all over Tehran, but nowhere is the experience as memorable, and the price as negotiable, as in the bazaar. There are literally thousands of merchants to choose from selling carpets from luggage-friendly prayer mats

to gigantic antique pieces that you'll need to ship home.

Don't worry about finding the stalls – there's a high probability that at least one merchant will approach you soon after you arrive. Go with it, remembering you are under no obligation to buy.

Central Tehran

★ **Jomeh Bazaar**   MARKET
(جمعه بازار, Friday Market; Map p38; Jomhuri-ye Eslami Ave; ☉8.30am-2pm Fri; M Sa'di) All levels of this car park are transformed every Friday morning when traders from across Iran and Central Asia and members of the general public lay out their stalls to sell whatever they can. It's a lively, social scene, where you can find almost anything, from old gramophones, radios and books to tribal costumes, colourful carpets and trendy bags.

Come early to snap up the best bargains and unique souvenirs and crafts. Later in the day it can get really busy.

★ **Tanedorost**   FASHION & ACCESSORIES
(Map p44; ☑021-66718101; www.tanedorost.com; 1000 Enghelab Ave; ☉10am-10pm; M Teatr-e Shahr) Organic cotton and other fabrics are used for clothes at this rustically stylish Iranian fashion store serving both men and women. It does good shirts, trousers and jackets, as well as colourful head scarves and fabric bags.

★ **Bottejeghe**   FASHION & ACCESSORIES
(فروشگاه رخت ایرانی بته جقه; Map p44; www.bottejeghe; 972 Enghelab Ave; ☉10am-9pm Sat-Thu, 11am-9pm Fri; M Teatr-e Shahr) Nailing a trendy Iranian fashion look with attractive shirts, gilets and jackets in cotton, linen and soft wool, Bottejeghe also sells a rainbow selection of scarves and an attractive selection of cushion covers and other local crafts and knick-knacks – all great as gifts.

Alma Nuts   FOOD
(Map p44; www.almanuts.com; 21 Nejatollahi St; ☉9am-9pm; M Ferdowsi) Shops selling nuts, dried fruit and sweets are popular across the city. This centrally located one has an excellent, appealing selection of all these nibbles, which you can buy by the kilo or already packaged up.

Varzesh Kooh   SPORTS & OUTDOORS
(ورزش کوه; Map p44; ☑021-8882 6642; 1st fl, 595 Enghelab Ave; M Ferdowsi) Look for the green door next to the Tourism Bank and

go upstairs to the first floor to find this mountaineering and trekking gear shop selling the basics of what you need to tackle Iran's great outdoors. The English-speaking climbers who run the shop are super helpful and can put you in touch with guides and the local climbing community.

Moses Baba   ARTS & CRAFTS
(Map p44; ☑021-6671 3146; 213 Ferdowsi St; ☉10am-5pm; M Ferdowsi) Moses Baba, founder of this atmospheric old curiosity shop, is long gone, but his relatives (members of Tehran's small Jewish community) still run the shop. They'll do their best to ensure you don't leave without having purchased a dusty item, including lacquerwork, old coins, jewellery, enamels, pottery and paintings.

Northern Tehran

★ **Tajrish Bazaar**   MARKET
(بازار تجریش; Map p52; Tajrish Sq; ☉9am-10pm; M Tajrish) When it comes to classic Iranian shopping experiences, browsing the food stalls at this photogenic bazaar in upmarket Tajrish pretty much nails it. It's ideal for ingredients for Iranian cooking, including all kinds of nuts, dates, spices (such as saffron) and tea. You can also pick up a pretty teapot or some other souvenir while you're at it.

ARG Centre   MALL
(Map p52; ☑021-2239 6121; www.argetejari.com; 1 Sa'dabad St; ☎; M Tajrish) Easily accessible from Tajrish Sq and one of the more modern and well designed of Tehran's new breed of shopping malls, Arg offers plenty of trendy local and overseas fashions, jewellery, homewares etc.

There's an excellent **food court**, too, with a seating area that provides a panoramic view of the Alborz Mountains.

Palladium Shopping Centre   MALL
(Map p52; ☑021-2201 0600; www.palladiummall.com; Alef Sq, Moqadas Ardabili Ave; ☉9am-11pm; ☎; ⬛BRT to Mahmoodiyeh) Come mingle with well-off Tehranis at one of north Tehran's most popular malls. It's a slick consumer experience, packed with international fashion brands, such as Mango and Superdry, a supermarket, a sports centre, an amusement arcade, cafes, restaurants, and a pricey **food court** serving everything from freshly pressed juices to tacos and sushi rolls.

ⓘ Information

DANGERS & ANNOYANCES

Tehran is a very safe place for travellers, with low levels of street crime. It's generally OK to walk down most central and northern Tehran streets late at night, but be more careful in the southern areas of the city, where drug use is prevalent.

Traffic

Tehran's chaotic traffic is likely to come as quite a shock. It is normal to see motorcycles weaving between pedestrians on the footpath in an attempt to escape the gridlock; cars reversing at speed along an expressway to reach that missed exit; and all manner of automobiles hurtling towards each other in a Darwinian game of chicken.

The sheer volume of traffic can be overwhelming and makes crossing the street seem like Russian roulette. As a pedestrian, the best way to ensure a safe crossing is to do what the locals do. Safety in numbers is the usual tactic – wait for one or two other road-crossers to appear and, with them between you and the traffic, step boldly out into the flow. Although you will be sorely tempted to run, the best tactic is to proceed slowly so that drivers have time to react to you crossing their path. Be aware of contra-flow bus lanes, which turn relatively harmless one-way streets into a more dangerous street-crossing challenge.

Visitors are often surprised there are not more accidents. You might feel as if you've had three near-death experiences in the course of a single cab ride, but in reality drivers are adept at getting you near to death without actually killing you.

Pollution

Tehranis have to deal with some of the worst air pollution on earth. Around 80% of the smog that covers Tehran for about 200 days a year comes straight out of the exhaust pipes of the millions of vehicles that course through the city. It doesn't help that most of them run on poor-quality fuel.

When pollution levels reach crisis point (as they did in November 2016 when it was claimed that they had directly led to the deaths of 421 citizens over 23 days) schools are closed and there are radio warnings for the old and unwell to stay indoors. The worst time of year for such crises is winter, when the Alborz Mountains and a lack of wind prevent the air from clearing.

A 10-year plan to curb pollution has seen traffic restrictions introduced and billions pumped into the Metro network, so far with little impact on air quality. When the pollution really starts to hurt your throat, head for the hills and relative purity of northern Tehran villages such as Darband and Darakeh.

EMERGENCY

If your emergency is not life threatening, ask your hotel's front desk for the most appropriate hospital or police station and help with translation.

Ambulance	☏ 115
Fire	☏ 125
Police	☏ 110

INTERNET ACCESS

All hotels and many restaurants and cafes offer free wi-fi. For a map showing hot spots, see https://wifispc.com/iran.

LEFT LUGGAGE

Most hotels are happy to hold luggage at no cost.

MEDICAL SERVICES

Hospitals

The quality of care in Tehran's hospitals is reasonably high by international standards. Many doctors are Western trained, with English-, French- and German-speakers among them. Embassies and hotels can recommend a doctor or hospital. Alternatively, **Mehrad Hospital** (Map p44; ☏ 021-8874 7401; www.mehradgeneralhospital.ir; Miremad St, off Motahhari Ave; Ⓜ Shahid Mofatteh) and **Tehran Clinic** (Map p44; ☏ 021-8871 2931; www.tehranclinic.ir; Farahani St; Ⓜ Mirza-ye Shirazi) are accessible, clean and reputable.

Pharmacies

Tehran is well stocked with pharmacies, and medications (often generic brands) are cheap. For the nearest 24-hour pharmacy ask your hotel to phone the **pharmacy line** (☏ 191), or head for **Ramin Drug Store** (Map p44; ☏ 021-6673 8080; Ferdowsi Sq; ⊙ 24hr; Ⓜ Ferdowsi).

MONEY

Overseas cards cannot be used in local ATMs; instead, exchange money at the official money-exchange bureaux on Ferdowsi St south of Ferdowsi Sq.

Tehran is littered with bank branches – perhaps more than any other comparable city on earth. However the rates of exchange (the Central Bank rates) are usually poor – use money-exchange bureaux instead.

Avoid the black-market money changers who ask you to 'change' on the street before you reach an official shop.

POST

Central Post Office (Map p44; ☏ 021-8853 2387; www.post.ir; 267 Abbas Abad St; ⊙ 8am-2.30pm Sat-Wed; Ⓜ Mirza-ye Shirazi)

TELEPHONE

SIM cards are widely available, but best purchased on arrival at the international airport, where you can quickly sort out a package covering data for a smart phone and calls for around IR500,000.

Recharging is easy: a friendly local will be able to do it for you via their own phone, or by buying credit via a bank ATM – you can then repay them.

TRAVEL AGENCIES

Travel agencies abound, with several on Nejatollahi St in central Tehran. For domestic and international ticketing, reliable agencies with English-speaking staff include the following:

Asia 2000 (Map p44; ☑ 021-8889 6949; www. asia2000.ir; 36 Nejatollahi St; ☺ 8.30am-5.30pm Sat-Wed, to 1pm Thu; Ⓜ Ferdowsi)

Baharestan (Map p38; ☑ 021-3395 4243; parvazebaharestan@yahoo.com; 986 Baharestan Sq; 9am-7pm Sat-Wed, to 2pm Thu; Ⓜ Baharestan) Can handle bookings for flights, buses and trains; handy to budget accommodation.

Sarvineh Parvaz (Map p52; ☑ 021-2274 4017; www.welcometoiran.com; 1983 Qods Sq, off Shariati Ave; ☺ 8am-5pm Sat-Thu; Ⓜ Tajrish) In business since 1973, this full-service travel agency is a handy place to sort out travel plans in northern Tehran. It also organises ski tours and packages with full details under www.iranskitours.ir.

VISA EXTENSIONS

Try not to extend your visa in Tehran, unless you cannot avoid it – the process tends to get more difficult whenever there is an international-relations issue. If you must, head for the **Foreign Intelligence Office** (Map p44; Soroush St, near Shariati Ave; ☺ 8am-1.30pm Sat-Wed, to 11.45am Thu; Ⓜ Shahid Mofatteh, then taxi), go through the gate and get your forms from the building on the left, and make photocopies if necessary. Pay the fee at the **Bank Melli** (Map p44; Shariati Ave) five minutes away down Hamid Alley and across Shariati Ave. Return for security check and, *insh'Allah*, the extension.

❶ Getting There & Away

Tehran is Iran's transport hub and every town and city of any size is directly linked to the capital – always by bus, usually by air and sometimes by train. Tickets from Tehran can sell fast, so book ahead if you can.

AIR

Imam Khomeini International Airport

All international services use **Imam Khomeini International Airport** (IKIA, IKA; www.ikia. airport.ir; Ⓜ Imam Khomeini International Airport), 35km south of Tehran.

Customs and immigration procedures at IKIA are slow but generally hassle-free if your papers are in order. Bags are X-rayed as you leave the baggage hall, but tourists are seldom hassled.

You'll need cash to leave the airport and several banks in the arrivals hall can change money at poor rates. However, it will get you an official exchange receipt, which is worth having should you wish to exchange any unused rials back into foreign currency before you leave. Otherwise, you'll get a better rate from the money-changer booths at the departure level of the airport.

Mobile phone operator MTN has two booths selling Irancell SIM cards more cheaply than you'll get them in town, and with less hassle (staff can register the SIM while you wait). All these services are open 24 hours (in theory).

Unless your flight is very early or very late (as many are), give yourself well over an hour to get to IKIA from central Tehran, then an hour to get through customs and immigration. If you have changed money legally at a bank, and have a receipt, you can, in theory, convert unused rials into cash euros or US dollars. However, some travellers have reported being unable to do this.

International Departures

Mehrabad Airport (Map p56; ☑ 021-61021, flight information 199; http://mehrabad. airport.ir; Ⓜ Mehrabad Airport Terminal 1&2), south of Azadi Sq in the west of Tehran, is used for domestic flights. Every day there are flights between here and almost every provincial capital in Iran. **Iran Air** (p351) flies most routes and is complemented by a number of smaller airlines. Domestic flight prices are fixed by the government so with no price differential between airlines, it's best to buy tickets from travel agencies where you'll have more options.

BUS

Tehran has four bus terminals, each generally serving different parts of the country, so you'll need to work out which one you will either be arriving at or leaving from:

Terminal-e Arzhantin (Terminal-e Beyhaghi, Central Terminal; Map p44; ☑ 021-8874 2622; http://terminals.tehran.ir; Arzhantin Sq; Ⓜ Mosalla, then taxi) The most central bus terminal; easily accessible by either public transport or taxi. Many VIP services start and finish here.

Terminal-e Shargh (Eastern Terminal; ☑ 021-7770 0590; http://terminals.tehran.ir; Damavand Rd; ◰ BRT to Tehran Pars) Has buses to Khorasan province and the Caspian region. To get there, take the BRT east from Enghelab Ave, or take a taxi (IR325,000 from central Tehran).

Terminal-e Jonub (Southern Terminal; Map p56; ☎ 021-5518 5556; http://terminals.tehran.ir; Abassi St; Ⓜ Terminal-e Jonub) Has buses heading to all points south and southeast. To get here take Metro Line 1 to Terminal-e Jonub then walk about 300m through a tunnel, or grab a taxi heading south.

Terminal-e Gharb (Terminal-e Azadi, Western Terminal; Map p56; ☎ 021-4464 6269; http://terminals.tehran.ir; Ⓜ Meydan-e Azadi) Tehran's busiest terminal; caters for the Caspian region and western Iran, as well as international destinations including Ankara and İstanbul (Turkey) and Baku (Azerbaijan). To get here take Metro Line 4 to Meydan-e Azadi and walk the last 250m, or from central Tehran ask any westbound shuttle taxi for 'Meydan-e Azadi'.

Services typically run from around 7am to 11pm with the exception of Esfahan, which has hourly departures around the clock from Arzhantin.

Tickets are usually bought at the bus terminal. Services to major destinations leave so frequently you usually won't need to book ahead (peak holiday periods such as No Ruz being the exception).

TAXI

Most towns within a three- to four-hour drive of Tehran are linked by savari (shared taxi), including Amol, Sari, Kashan, Qom, Qazvin, Zanjan, Rasht, and anywhere along the way. Savaris leave from designated areas at the appropriate bus terminals. For example, for Kashan and Esfahan they leave from near the southern entrance to Terminal-e Jonub (southern bus terminal); savaris to Sari and Amol leave from outside the eastern terminal; and anything west to Qazvin or Zanjan from the western (Azadi) terminal. Just say your destination and 'savari' and you'll be pointed in the right direction.

TRAIN

Tehran is Iran's rail hub and many services start and finish at the impressive **train station** (Map p56; ☎ 021-5149, 139; www.raja.ir; Rah-Ahan Sq; Ⓜ Rahahan) at the south end of Valiasr Ave. Destinations and arrival and departure times are listed in English, and staff at the information counter are walking timetables. Departures are punctual.

It's advisable to book tickets (which you can do a month in advance) either via a local travel agency, online via at www.iranrail.net, or at the station itself.

Schedules

Prices and days of departure are liable to change; in particular, daily services in summer usually become less frequent in winter.

There are many services along the dual tracks between Tehran and Mashhad. They range from the Zendegi, with four-bed 1st-class berths and food (IR800,000), to the slow, all-seat bus train (IR400,000). Services often arrive at their destinations in the middle of the night – check before you book.

It is also be possible to buy tickets to intermediary stops, such as Yazd, on the Bandar Abbas or Kerman trains.

ⓘ Getting Around

TO/FROM THE AIRPORT

Imam Khomeini International Airport

Metro Line 1 (red) between IKIA and the city is the cheapest and fastest route (IR7000, 30 to 55 minutes) into or out of Tehran.

Otherwise take a taxi from IKIA for a set price of IR750,000. Going to IKIA you'll probably pay IR1,000,000 from northern Tehran, but from the south it should cost less.

Mehrabad Airport

Metro Line 4 (yellow) runs to Mehrabad: there are two stops serving different terminals so check which one you will need if you're heading here for a domestic flight.

Taxi fares are fixed: to southern or central Tehran costs about IR300,000, rising to about IR450,000 to northern and eastern Tehran. If it's peak hour, the price will be higher, which is fair considering the trip will probably take twice as long.

You can also opt for a shuttle taxi – tell a taxi driver *na dar baste* (no closed door) and he will look for other passengers going the same way – or public buses to Enghelab and Vanak Sqs.

BUS

Tehran has an extensive local bus network, but given buses are segregated by sex, crowded, slow compared with the Metro, and that there are relatively cheap taxis, few travellers bother. If you do, you'll find buses run from roughly 6am to 10pm or 11pm, finishing earlier on Friday and public holidays. Tickets cost slightly more than nothing and you buy them from ticket booths near bus stops or at bus terminals, and then give them to the driver when you board the bus. Buses never show their destinations in English; ask your hotel for route details or anyone at the bus stop.

Bus Rapid Transport (BRT)

More useful than local buses is the BRT system of rapid buses along 10 routes with dedicated lanes. On most routes buses depart every two or three minutes (although that still doesn't stop them becoming packed at peak times). Tickets cost IR7000. Two lines are particularly useful to travellers:

Rah-Ahan (train station) to Tajrish Good for hops along Valiasr up to **Tajrish bus station**

(Map p52), but the traffic lights and bus bank ups at major stops mean it's less than rapid.

Azadi to Tehran Pars Links the centre of town with Azadi Sq in the west and, most usefully, Terminal-e Shargh (Eastern Bus Terminal).

CAR & MOTORCYCLE

If you're crazy enough to want to drive yourself in Tehran, **Europcar** (☑ 021-8836 6615; www. europcar.ir; per day from US$115) has pick-up points at Imam Khomeini International Airport, Mehrabad Airport and in central Tehran.

For private car hire, the cost depends on vehicle type, how far you're going and whether you want an English-speaking driver who can double as a guide. Reckon on paying between US$70 and US$100 a day. One highly recommended English-speaking driver and guide is **Ali Taheri** (p53).

Just about any taxi (indeed, any car) in Tehran is available for hire (known locally as *taxi service*, *agence* or *dar baste*). For a driver who speaks no English expect to pay about US$50 for the day, depending on your bargaining skills and how far you plan to go.

METRO

The best way to get around is Tehran Metro (http://metro.tehran.ir), which has transformed the way the city moves by cutting journey times by up to an hour on some cross-town trips. At the time of writing five lines were complete and another two under construction.

There are two main ways you can pay for tickets. **Magnetic tickets** cost single/two-trips IR7000/11,0000 between any two stations on the system. Better value and more convenient are **stored value cards**, which cost an initial IR50,000 including IR35,000 of travel credit.

BUSES FROM TEHRAN

DESTINATION	STATION	FARE (IR)	DURATION (HR)	FREQUENCY
Ahvaz	Jonub	690,000	15	hourly 2-9pm
Ardabil	Gharb	400,000	9-10	hourly
Astara (Ardabil bus)	Gharb	370,000	8	hourly
Bandar Abbas	Jonub	*mahmooly*/VIP 530,000/890,000	15-20	3 daily
Chalus	Gharb	*mahmooly*/VIP 270,000/350,000	5-6	every 20min
Esfahan	Arzhantin, Jonub	330,000	5-6	hourly
Gonbad-e Kavus	Shargh	*mahmooly*/VIP 290,000/455,000	9	hourly
Gorgan	Shargh	260,000	7-8	3 daily
Hamadan	Gharb	330,000	5-6	every 30min
Kashan	Jonub	180,000	3½	every 20min
Kerman	Jonub	690,000	15	hourly 3-9pm
Kermanshah	Gharb	460,000	9	every 30min
Mashhad	Arzhantin, Shargh	680,000	13-14	hourly
Orumiyeh	Gharb	590,000	12	hourly
Qazvin	Gharb	*mahmooly*/VIP 200,000/700,000	2-2½	every 20min
Qom	Jonub	95,000	1½	every 30min
Rasht	Gharb	*mahmooly*/VIP 245,000/95,000	5-6	every 30min
Sanandaj	Gharb	460,000	8	hourly 3-11pm
Sari	Shargh	290,000	5	hourly
Shiraz	Arzhantin, Jonub	680,000	12-15	hourly 2-11pm
Tabriz	Arzhantin, Gharb	460,000	9-10	hourly
Yazd	Arzhantin, Jonub	490,000	9-10	hourly

Fares listed are for VIP services unless otherwise specified; *mahmooly* buses are less luxurious.

You can buy these and have them topped up at metro stations; using them, each trip fare is significantly cheaper.

Stored value cards can also be used on the buses, including BRT services. Be sure to tap in and tap out with these cards: at some stations, the place to tap out is on the wall not at the ticket barrier – watch what other passengers do.

Trains start at about 6am (7am on Fridays and holidays) and stop by 11pm. Services are most frequent and crowded during peak hours (7am to 9am and 3pm to 5pm). The first and last carriages of every service are for women only, though women are free to travel in any other carriage. Station announcements are in Farsi only, so keep an eye on the English maps inside the trains.

Line 1 (Red)

Line 1 is the most useful for travellers. It runs between Imam Khomeini International Airport and Tajrish in the far north. Tajrish is the jumping-off point for Darband, Tochal and the Sa'd Abad and Niyavaran palaces. Heading south, Line 1 stops at Terminal-e Jonub, Rey and Haram-e Motahar for both the Holy Shrine of Imam Khomeini and the Behesht-e Zahra martyrs cemetery.

Line 2 (Dark Blue)

Line 2 runs between Tehran (Sadeghieh) in the west – where it connects with Line 5 (Green) to Karaj – and Farhangsara in the city's east. It connects to Line 1 at Imam Khomeini, and is handy to the Amir Kabir St cheap hotels (Mellat station).

Line 3 (Light Blue)

Line 3 runs from Azadegan in the southwestern suburbs to the far northeastern suburb of Ghaem. Useful stops include Rah Ahan for Tehran Train Station; Teatr-e Shahr and Meydan-e

Valiasr for central Tehran; and Nobonyad for Niyavaran Cultural-Historic Complex in the northeast.

Line 4 (Yellow)

Line 4 runs between Mehrabad airport in the west and Shahid Kolahdooz in the southeastern suburbs. It's also useful as a link between central Tehran and Meydan-e Azadi, for Azadi Tower and Terminal-e Gharb.

Line 5 (Green)

Line 5 is largely above ground and is, in effect, an extension of Line 2. It runs from Tehran (Sadeghieh) to the west passing via Karaj to Golshahr.

TAXI

Taxi fares in Tehran are higher than elsewhere in Iran, and no taxis offer metered fares.

Motorcycle Taxi

Motorcycle taxis loiter on major corners all over town and make an adrenalin-inducing way to get across town in a hurry. They cost as much as taxis but take half the time. Don't expect a spare helmet to wear!

Private Taxi

If hailing a taxi, yellow and green cars are typically official private taxis. However, many locals use the app Snapp (https://snapp.ir) to arrange rides with any driver who's part of the service – it works similarly to Uber, but you will be given a fare estimate when you confirm the ride and can pay in cash.

Alternatively, get your hotel to call a **Wireless Taxi** (133), which cost a little more. You could also call the **Women's Taxi Company** (1814), whose green taxis are for female passengers only.

TRAINS FROM TEHRAN

DESTINATION	FARE (IR)	DURATION (HR)	FREQUENCY
Bandar Abbas	4/6 bed 800,000/600,000	20	2 daily (1.35pm & 2.45pm)
Esfahan	6 bed 350,000	7½	every 2 days (11pm)
Gorgan	4/6 bed 500,000/300,000	10	daily (10pm)
Kerman	4/6 bed 700,000/500,000	14	daily (11.55am)
Mashhad	4/6 bed & seat 800,000/500,000/400,000	10-12	16 daily
Qom	seat 40,000	2	3 daily (6am, 3.15pm & 5.45pm)
Sari	seat 180,000	6	daily (9.20am)
Tabriz	4 & 6 bed 500,000	12	2 daily (4pm & 5.45pm)
Yazd	6 bed 400,000	6-8	3 daily (6.15am, 4.35pm & 10pm)

Unless you're familiar with the going taxi rates, agree to a price before getting in the vehicle. Most drivers won't go anywhere for less than IR100,000. Negotiation is encouraged.

To get from southern Tehran to the north takes a minimum of half an hour, much longer in peak hour, when prices rise accordingly. Sample fares include Imam Khomeini Sq to Valiasr Sq (about IR100,000/150,000 in off-peak/peak hour), and Imam Khomeini Sq to Tajrish Sq (about IR250,000/500,000). Around town you can charter a taxi for about IR400,000 an hour.

Shuttle Taxi

Shuttle taxis ply main thoroughfares between major *meydans* (squares) and the best way to use them is to learn the names of the *meydans* and know which one you want to go to. *Meydans* such as Imam Khomeini, Vanak, Valiasr, Tajrish, Arzhantin, Azadi, Ferdowsi, Enghelab, Haft-e Tir, Rah-Ahan and Imam Hossein are major shuttle-taxi hubs. However, even these may have several ministations for shuttle taxis heading in different directions. For longer trips you will usually need to change shuttles.

AROUND TEHRAN

Alborz Ski Resorts

Between December and March, Tehran is blessed with five ski resorts within day-trip distance. The easiest to access is Tochal (p51), connected directly to northern Tehran via the Tochal Telecabin (p50). In good weather, even if you're not skiing, Tochal is a delight to visit, providing a spectacular, scenic escape from the city.

The next closest resorts are **Abali** (پیست اسکی آبعلی; chair lift per ride IR150,000, drag lifts per day IR250,000; ⊘8am-6pm Dec-Mar), around 50km northeast of Tehran on the way to Mt Damavand, then the neighbouring villages of Shemshak and Darbansar, 62km north of the city. The largest resort, and the pick of the bunch, is Dizin. It is, however, the furthest away – sitting 125km north of Tehran via the Chalus road – the only route usually possible during the ski season.

Dizin   دیزین

026🗗 / ELEVATION 2700M

Iran's largest ski field, **Dizin** (پیست اسکی دیزین; 🗗 0912 818 3454; www.dizinskiresort.com; lift pass IR1,060,000; ⊘8am-4pm Dec-May) is an international standard resort with three gondolas and numerous chair and drag lifts

(note the full system of lifts is usually only open on Thursday and Friday). With base camp at about 2700m and a vertical drop of about 900m, it will appeal to anyone feeling the need for speed, although overall the slopes are not so challenging.

Dizin's ski season can stretch from December to May, but it's usually safest to plan your visit between January and March. Pistes are sometimes groomed and there is plenty of scope for off-piste if you get a fresh snowfall. Apart from Thursday and Friday, waiting for the gondolas and ski lifts is not really an issue. Ski instructors can be hired for US$100 a day.

It's possible to rent all equipment, including snowboards and clothing, at ski hire shops both at the resort and in nearby Velayat Rud. A set of skis, boots and poles starts at IR450,000 per day.

🛏 Sleeping

★**Seven Hostel in Dizin**   HOSTEL $
(🗗 021-6696 0192; www.sevenhostels.com; Velayat Rud; dm/r US$20/45; 🛜) A brilliant deal for backpackers wishing to hit the slopes at Dizin, this cosy chalet-style hostel in the village of Velayat Rud, around 5km from the ski resort, is a winner. Managed by a friendly couple who can also cook you meals (extra cost), rates include a basic breakfast, drinks throughout the day and transfers to Dizin.

Dizin Hotel   HOTEL $$
(Hotel Jahangardi; 🗗 026-3521 2978; www.hoteldizin.ir; r/cabin/chalet from US$130/295/355; 🅿@) Right at the bottom of the ski field, the comfortable Dizin Hotel is split over two complexes. The rooms aren't bad and those in the main building (Dizin 1) have better views. Four- and five-bed cabins and chalets are also available. Prices are very negotiable in low season.

❶ Getting There & Away

The main way to reach Dizin is via the road to Chalus from Tehran. This route is around 125km and in winter you'll need chains or a 4WD for the last 10km or so. A taxi to/from Tehran is around IR1.5 million one way.

Alternatively you can take a bus bound for Chalus (VIP/*mahmooly* IR350,000/270,000) from Tehran's Terminal-e Gharb (Western Terminal); ask to be dropped at the 'Dizin slop' turn-off from where you'll have to hitch a ride for the remaining 15km.

Dizin can also be accessed from its upper parking lot (7am to 5pm) on the road from Shemshak and only 52km to Tehran. However you should check weather reports before using this access point at 3010m as you might be blocked by snow or snowed in. From June to October only there's also a treacherous zigzag road connecting this upper parking lot with the main lower one next to the Dizin Hotel.

Tehran travel agencies sell packages that include transport, accommodation and lift passes.

Shemshak & Darbansar شمشک دربندسر

☑ 021 / ELEVATION 2550M

The neighbouring ski resorts of Shemshak and Darbansar, in a steep-sided valley around 50km north of Tehran, both boast slopes that will get hardcore skiers and snowboarders most excited. Outside of the ski season (late December to March) the villages here are also a popular quick escape from the pollution, heat and stress of Tehran.

In winter, on the way to Shemshak, look out for the frozen waterfall at **Meygoon**, where it's possible to go ice-climbing.

🏃 Activities

Boots, skis and poles can be hired in both villages from IR450,000 a day.

The resorts' proximity to Tehran mean that the slopes can get very busy here on Thursday, Friday and public holidays.

Shemshak Ski Resort SKIING
(پیست اسکی شمشک); ☑ 021-2652 7445; www.skicomplex.ir; lift pass Sat-Wed/Thu & Fri IR600,000/660,000; ⊗ 8am-3pm late Dec-Apr) Government-operated Shemshak, Iran's second-largest ski field after Dizin, offers challenging terrain with mainly black-rated runs. Vertical descents are about 500m (some of it at an adrenalin-inducing 45-degree angle) and there are plenty of moguls. There are no gondolas, just two chair lifts and four drag lifts to get you up its two main slopes.

Darbansar Ski Resort SKIING
(پیست اسکی دربندسر); ☑ 021-2652 5175; www.darbandsarski.ir; lift pass all day/8am-3pm/4-9pm IR1,200,000/ 940,000/710,000; ⊗ 8am-9pm late Dec-Mar) At an elevation of 2650m, rising to 3150m, Darbansar is privately run and more modern than nearby Shemshak. The runs are moderately challenging and

there's plenty of scope for off-piste skiing, including across to Dizin on the other side of Mt Kashoolak. There's also a ski school and night skiing here.

🛌 Sleeping

The **Shemshak Tourist Inn** (Hotel Jahangardi; ☑ 021-2652 6912; www.ittic.com; s/tw IR1,800,000/2,600,000; ☜) is a small chalet-style hotel about 400m downhill from Shemshak's ski lifts. It's pleasant enough, but note that in ski season there is no direct car access to the hotel – you'll need to climb up 300 steps from the main road.

Ask around both villages about apartment rentals (summer/winter from US$50/70); Saturday to Wednesday will be cheaper and less busy at both resorts.

🍴 Eating & Drinking

Chillax Cafe & White Lounge Restaurant INTERNATIONAL $
(☑ 021-2652 7936; www.facebook.com/chillaxcafe.ir; 3rd fl, Sierra Bldg, Shemshak; mains IR180,000-320,000; ⊗ 8am-midnight; ☜) As chic as it gets when it comes to dining in Shemshak and Darbansar, this is the place to see and be seen by Tehran's liberal ski set. Waiters in fashionable black-and-grey outfits, *Vogue*-ish interiors and reasonably well-prepared local and international dishes and drinks hit the mark.

Siavash CAFE
(☑ 021-2652 4109; Darbansar; ⊗ 8am-11pm; ☜) This pleasant cafe, a short walk downhill from Darbansar Ski Resort, is where locals hang out, sipping coffee or tea, tucking into cakes and puffing on water pipes. It's also a good spot for enquiring about short-term rental accommodation in the area.

ℹ Getting There & Away

Shemshak and Darbansar are about 55km north of Tehran. A taxi here from Tajrish in northern Tehran will cost between IR400,000 and IR600,000 depending on your bargaining skills.

From Shemshak the road continues to the upper parking lot at Dizin and, from June to October only, down to the main Dizin resort area itself. Check with locals about whether this road is open, as part of it is unsealed and travelling safely along it depends on the weather and if you driving in a 4WD or a car with snow chains.

Mt Damavand کوه دماوند

♪ 011

The dormant volcano Mt Damavand (5671m), northeast of Tehran, is the highest mountain in the Middle East. Shaped a little like Mt Fuji, it is one of Iran's most recognisable icons, appearing on the IR10,000 note, on bottles of Damavand spring water and on numerous other commercial items.

In good weather, the dramatic mountainous vistas around Damavand are attraction enough, and there are pleasant hot springs for a soak in nearby Abgarm village, and skiing in season at Abali, on the way from Tehran. Most people who head out this way, however, will do so to climb the peak. Start by heading to the large, comfortable Polour Mountain Complex (2270m), built by the Iran Mountaineering Federation – the best place to acclimatise before attempting the south and west face routes. The climbing season is from June to September, or May to October for experienced climbers.

Climbing the Mountain

There are 16 routes up Damavand, but the vast majority of people take the classic southern route. For information on the northern route, talk to the English-speaking owners of Varzesh Kooh (p66), who are happy to share their knowledge and put you in touch with guides.

From a technical point of view, Damavand is basically a walk-up. Climbing so far so quickly is its most dangerous aspect, with altitude sickness (watch for dizziness, headaches, nausea and swollen fingers) claiming lives every year. The volcano last erupted about 7300 years ago, but it still belches out sulphuric fumes from near the summit, strong enough to kill unfortunate stray sheep and ward off mountaineers.

Most first-timers use a guide and you can expect to pay about US$550 for an all-inclusive (guide, transport, food, lodgings, donkey etc) three-day tour from Tehran. This includes the US$50 fee foreigners must pay to the government to climb the mountain. A guide alone for a two-day climb will cost about US$100 per day.

Damavand is best climbed in three days, starting at Polour Mountain Complex and going 11km by road to Camp 2, then trekking from there to Camp 3 or Base Camp, before making the ascent; www.damawand. de has maps and details of the various routes. There's no water en route and no way of booking the hut; on Thursday nights and holidays it is packed with students from Tehran. Bringing a tent, sleeping bag and perhaps a stove (and leaving it in camp during the final ascent) is recommended. Even in July, nights are freezing, and it can be -10°C at the summit. It's recommended to fill water bottles during the day, as the water will be frozen when you first get up.

In August you should be able to climb to the peak without special equipment. The summit doesn't require any technical gear, but it does require fitness, warm clothes and hiking boots for the loose rocks. Bear in mind that the weather can change suddenly and snowfalls are a possibility, even in summer. Most people return from the summit to Tehran in one day.

Hot Springs

After expending all that energy climbing Mt Damavand, you'll be pleased to know that in the upper part of Abgarm village, about 6km east of Rineh, several hotels have been built around hot springs. **Almase Shargh Spa Complex** (East Diamond Spa Complex; ♪ 0911 220 0025; www.larijanhotwater.ir; Abgarm-e bala, Larijan; IR150,000; ⊙ 8am-midnight) is a modern public complex open to men; women have to hire the place as a group. Alternatively, ask around about renting a room for the night in the village, for around US$25, which will including breakfast, tea and a dip in a private hot-spring bath.

🛏 Sleeping & Eating

Polour Mountain Complex HOSTEL $
(♪ 011-4334 2802; www.msfi.ir; Polour; dm/r from IR940,000/1,100,000) Run by the Iran Mountaineering Association, this large utilitarian hostel is base camp for many of those aiming to summit Mt Damavand. Bunk beds in the simply decorated rooms are comfortable. It's IR50,000 extra for a shower, but if you rent a room (which has six bunk beds in it) there's an attached shower. No cafe, but there's a kitchen for self-catering.

This is also where you will have to pay US$50 for the permit to climb Damavand. The association also has a smaller dormitory complex in the nearby village of Rineh.

★**Koohestan** IRANIAN $
(♪ 0912 318 9437; camp.polur@gmail.com; Manzarieh, Polour; meals IR350,000; 🛜) Run by clued-up, English-speaking mountaineer

TEHRAN REY

HOLY SHRINE OF IMAM KHOMEINI & BEHESHT-E ZAHRA

The **mausoleum of Ayatollah Ruhollah Khomeini** (مرقد مطهر امام خمینی; 021-5522 7578; www.harammotahar.ir; 24hr; Haram-e Motahar) is one of the grandest architectural endeavours of the Islamic Republic. Built on an enormous scale – which necessitated the moving of many existing graves at the giant **Behesht-e Zahra** (بهشت زهرا; www. beheshtezahra.tehran.ir; Haram-e Motahar) cemetery – the Holy Shrine also contains the tombs of Khomeini's wife, second son and several other important political figures; in 2017, former president Akbar Rafsanjani was buried here.

The shrine is flanked by four 91m-high towers symbolising Khomeini's age when he died. The huge gold central dome is adorned with 72 tulips, which symbolise the 72 martyrs who fought and died with Imam Hossein in Karbala.

Inside the vast main hall, covered with 12,000 carpets each 12 sq metres, Khomeini's tomb itself is enclosed in a stainless steel zarih, a cage-like casing through which pilgrims pay their respects and no small number of bank notes. Men and women approach respectfully from different sides.

Construction of the complex, covering 20 sq km, began in 1989 following Khomeini's chaotic funeral which devolved in a riot of some 10 million inconsolable mourners. It is yet to be completed, with the plan for the ceiling of the interior to be covered with tiny mirrors, as is the case with many other Shia shrines.

Avoid the shrine on or around 4 June, the anniversary of the Ayatollah's death, when hundreds of thousands of mourners visit the shrine. During the holy month of Muharram, the fountains surrounding the shrine run with red dyed water.

If you have time, wander over to Behesht-e Zahra. Tehran's biggest cemetery is interesting primarily because it's the main resting place for those who died in the Iran–Iraq War (1980–88). Like windows into another time, roughly 200,000 small glass boxes on stilts each contain a small memento – a watch, a knife, a letter – that once belonged to the lost father/son/husband staring out from a yellowed photograph.

Amir, this cosy log-cabin-style restaurant serves up excellent kababs, braised lamb shanks and vegetable dishes. It's on your left near the top of the hill as you enter the village, with an English sign and a grill outside. You can stay here, too, for free – as long as you pay for food and the shower (IR100,000).

Amir can also arrange a house in the village, sleeping up to five people and including dinner for IR2,000,000.

ⓘ Getting There & Away

The easiest way to get to Polour village and on to the Polour Mountain Complex is by taxi (IR2,000,000 *dar baste*, two hours, 80km). Alternatively, take a bus (IR200,000) from Tehran's Terminal-e Shargh and get off at Polour, then take a local taxi to the camp.

Rey   ری

☎ 021

In the 11th and 12th centuries Rey (also known as Shahr-e Rey) was one of the capitals of the Seljuk empire. It was devastated in the 13th century when the Mongols swept

through and, these days, has been swallowed up by the urban sprawl of Tehran.

Rey, however, retains enough history to give it a different sensibility, its key sight being the elaborately decorated shrine of a 9th-century Muslim saint. Beside the shrine complex is a lively bazaar, while further afield are a couple of minor historical attractions.

Rey can easily be combined with a visit to the Holy Shrine of Imam Khomeini and the neighbouring cemetery Behesht-e Zahra.

⊙ Sights

Rey's main attraction is the **Imamzadeh Shah-e Abdal-Azim** (شاه عبدالعظیم; http:// abdolazim.com; 24hrs; Shahr-e Rey) FREE. This mausoleum was originally built for a 9th-century descendant of Imam Hossein and has elaborate tilework; a golden dome; a pool in the courtyard; a 14th-century sarcophagus with intricate carvings, constructed from betel wood; and enough mirror tiles to make you dizzy. In the same complex is a shrine to Imam Hamzeh (brother of Imam Reza). Women need to wear a chador, available at the entrance.

Part of the complex is a small **museum** where you can see models of how the complex has evolved over the centuries and old photos of what the place looked like back in the 19th century.

The adjacent **Rey Bazaar** (بازار قدیم ری; Tabrizi St; ⊘ 8.30am-7pm; Ⓜ Shahr-e Rey) is lively, compact and architecturally attractive. If you have more time, hop in a taxi to see the natural mineral spring **Cheshmeh Ali** (تپه چشمه علی; Taqaviniya St; Ⓜ Shahr-e Rey, then taxi). In the past, locals used to clean their carpets in the pool here. On the rocks above is an elaborate **inscription** made during the reign of Fati Ali Shah (r 1797–1834), while higher up the hill are the ruins of Rey's ancient fortress wall, **Qal'-e Tabarak**. Not too far away is the 12th century **Toghoral Tower** (برج طغرل; 38 Nabi Pour St; IR100,000; ⊘ 9am-5pm Tue-Sun; Ⓜ Shahr-e Rey, then taxi). This brick structure rises up 20m and was originally topped by a conical dome that has long since collapsed. The tower, surrounded by a small walled garden, also marks the tomb of the Seljuk king Toghoral Beg.

✗ Eating

Bam-e Rey IRANIAN **$$**
(☎ 021-5596 7000; Fadaiyan St; mains IR160,000-560,000; ⊘ 10.30am-10.30pm; Ⓜ Shahr-e Rey) Rey's fanciest dining option combines both a restaurant and casual cafe. The waiters will bring the flag of your nation to the table along with your kababs, deep-fried fish, pasta and the like. There's also a roof-top dining area with a view towards the bazaar and the minarets of the mausoleum.

ℹ Getting There & Away

Shahr-e Rey (City of Rey) station is on Metro Line 1. Taxis can be hired in Rey for a negotiable IR300,000 per hour.

Western Iran ایران غربی

Best Places to Eat
➜ Paradisa Ahura Daniel (p141)

➜ Mostofi Restauant (p143)

➜ Negarossaltaneh (p117)

➜ Doorchin (p102)

➜ Shahriar (p91)

Best Places to Sleep
➜ Shushtar Traditional Hotel (p143)

➜ Gileboom Eco Lodge (p111)

➜ Hotel Anza (p97)

➜ Bam-e Sabz (p112)

➜ Navizar Hotel (p121)

Why Go?
A land of wild extremes and wilder history, Western Iran is the independent traveller's adventure playground. From the fecund Caspian coast to the stark, mountainous north-ern borders and the crumbling desert ruins of the southern plains, the region hosts everything from paddy fields to bliz-zards to the original Garden of Eden. Bordering Mesopota-mia, Ottoman Turkey and Czarist Russia, its fortunes have oscillated with the rise and fall of many great empires. This deeply historic, starkly beautiful and incredibly hospitable place is also home to almost half of Iran's Unesco sites.

The region is a linguistic and cultural patchwork: Kurds predominate in Kordestan and Kermanshah; Lors in Ilam and Lorestan; Arabs inhabit southern Khuzestan; Talesh and Gilaki are the traditional languages of Gilan; and Azeris, whose language is more Turkish than Persian, predominate in the northwest. In remote regions, and in Kurdish towns, traditional dress is still worn.

When to Go
The craggy peaks of the Zagros Mountains from Hamadan northwards see snow arrive early and leave late – falls are from about November to March, while the sweltering low-lands around Shush begin to boil in June.

To make the most of the region, try visiting for the spring flowers, which bloom in April or May, or the autumn harvest of juicy grapes and delicious mulberries in September or early October.

The crisp, clear air and low, golden light of winter make it the best time for photographing those epic landscapes.

Western Iran Highlights

1 Castles of the Assassins (p122)

Hiking between flower-filled valleys and snow-capped peaks amid ruined 12th-century castles.

2 Masuleh (p110)

Wandering through Gilan's verdant forests above an amazing stacked village.

3 Aras River Valley (p95)

Exploring ancient churches, mud-walled castles and grand canyons along a sublime river valley.

4 Qal'eh Babak (p97)

Launching an assault on majestic Babak Castle, the emotional heart of Azerbaijan.

5 Howraman (p125)

Venturing into a magical, rarely visited valley of

traditional Kurdish villages.

6 Choqa Zanbil (p142) Being awed by a massive brick ziggurat (stepped pyramidal temple) that managed to get 'lost' for 2500 years.

7 Qezel Owzan (p100) Getting right off the beaten track by following this river from nomadic Khal Khal to the Colourful Mountains.

8 Takht-e Soleiman (p103) Watching the sunset glow golden on snow-dusted peaks from these lonely temple ruins.

Bazargan بازرگان

🎵 044 / POPULATION 11,500 / ELEVATION 1417M

Car-repair yards, shops and a string of hotels line Bazargan's Imam St, a gun-barrel-straight strip fired towards the striking silhouette of Mt Ararat. About 2km short of the immigration posts, the village ends at the outer border gate.

Most visitors don't stay the night, but if you do, **Shahriyar Hotel** (🎵 044-3437 2618; Imam St; d/tr $60/70; P 🛜) is the pick of the basic hotels and has the best restaurant.

Maku, where you can get onward buses, is only 20 minutes away, so look for a savari and bargain hard – expect to pay at least US$3. The price drops the further you walk from the custom gates.

Maku & Around ماکو

🎵 044 / POPULATION 46,000 / ELEVATION 1218M

Scattered like rubble at the bottom of a towering ravine, Maku makes an atmospheric overnight stop and a good base for hunting Armenian churches in the austere, lonely countryside. Long a key fortress guarding the Ottoman–Persian frontier, Maku was one of many Azerbaijani khanates that gained semi-independence in the chaotic period following the death of Nader Shah in 1749. Although it rejoined Iran in 1829, the khanate was only finally abolished a century later. There's a handful of interesting sites.

Chahara Sq on Imam Khomeini St is the heart of town, and everything you'll need is close by. The bazaar is off Taleqani St one block north, while the bus terminal is 3km southeast. The wind blows a dust storm through town most afternoons.

👁 Sights

★ Qareh Kalisa   CHURCH

(Black Church, Church of St Thaddeus; IR200,000; P) Sitting photogenically aloof on a barren knoll, 8km off the lonely Shot–Chaldoran road in the middle of nowhere, behind the low-rise village of the same name, Qareh Kalisa is the best maintained of all Iran's medieval churches. Mostly rebuilt after an earthquake, the smaller black-and-white-striped chapel section dates from 1319–29, and the whole site is Unesco listed. Ring the bell if it's locked.

There's no public transport. Taxis from Maku via Shot ask US$25 return including waiting time.

Maku Fortress   FORTRESS

Above the town, under the huge overhanging cliff, lie the ruins of Maku's former citadel, where the Baha'i faith's Bab was imprisoned for nine months in 1848. Head north from the bazaar on Taleqani St and follow the footpaths and steps up past the Abu Fazl Mosque. The walk will take around 25 minutes, but the views are stunning.

Dzor Dzor Chapel   CHAPEL

(Chapel of the Virgin Mary) Amazingly photogenic, this Unesco-listed Armenian chapel was relocated to higher ground once the nearby dam filled up. It's a hilly, sometimes snow-covered 40km from Maku; an agency taxi from the Tourist Inn will cost around US$17 return. Take care which way you point your camera as the dam is considered sensitive.

Baghcheh Juq Palace Museum   MUSEUM

Built for the *sardar* (military governor) of Qajar Shah Muzaffar al-Din (r 1896–1907), this striking two-storey mansion sits amid 11 hectares of orchards and walled gardens in the village of Baghcheh Juq, 7km from Maku along the Bazargan road. With a nod to Versailles, the interior rooms, halls and atrium glisten and sparkle. Savaris from Maku's Chahara Sq charge US$2 one way.

🏃 Activities

Rock-Climbing Wall   CLIMBING

There's a load of routes (both sport and trad) on the big overhanging wall about 100m west of ruined Maku Fortress.

🛏 Sleeping

Hotel Alvand   HOSTEL $

(🎵 044-3422 3491; Imam Khomeini St; s/tw without bathroom IR400,000/600,000) Just west of Chahara Sq, the Alvand is probably the best of Maku's cheapies. The rooms are OK, but the shared facilities are not so flash.

Maku Tourist Inn   HOTEL $$

(Mehmansara Jahangardi; 🎵 044-3422 3212; Imam Khomeini St; s/d IR980,000/1,340,000; P ❄ 🛜) By far Maku's classiest option, the Tourist Inn has comfortable rooms, hot water, friendly English-speaking staff and a reasonable restaurant. Staff will also organise agency taxis to surrounding sites, including Qareh Kalisa church and Dzor Dzor Chapel.

ⓘ CROSSING THE TURKISH BORDER AT BAZARGAN

If you're travelling solo, crossing this 24-hour border usually takes under an hour. The hilltop **immigration posts** (⊙24hr) are 2km above Bazargan, IR50,000 (plus IR50,000 for bags) by shared taxi or minibus. The posts are just 600m from **Gürbulak** in Turkey (no facilities). The nearest Turkish-side accommodation is 40km east in Doğubayazıt, famous for its 1784 Işak Paşa palace and not a lot else.

Eastbound from Doğubayazıt to Gürbulak, take a *dolmuş* (minibus; 25 minutes, last service 5pm) from the junction of Ağrı and Sehiltik Sts, 100m east of the Kara-han Petrol Ofisi station (where Ağrı *dolmuşlar* wait). That's about five minutes' walk from Doğubayazıt's little bus terminal and cheap hotels. Westbound buses go from Doğubayazıt.

Arriving in Iran during office hours, you're likely to be welcomed by a charming Iranian tourist officer. The bank within the Iran-side customs building offers full rial rates for US dollars and euros. It won't change UK pounds or Turkish lira, for which you'll have to risk the scam-a-lot guys outside or, more safely, ask hoteliers in Ba-zargan village. Be aware that Turkish lira are effectively worthless anywhere else in Iran, except Orumiyeh.

Well-connected Tabriz guide-fixer Hossein Ravanyar (p87) is experienced at sorting out motorists' border-formality problems.

🍴 Eating & Drinking

Dr Nadim IRANIAN **$**
(☑044-3422 7771; Taleqani St; meals from IR150,000) The good doctor's traditional dishes are a cut above the local fast food. Set back from the street in a courtyard near the corner of Saadi St.

Cafe Ido CAFE
(Imam Khomeini St; ⊙noon-10pm) The most upmarket caffeine and nicotine den in town has huge windows as dark as its cof-fee. It's in front of Maku Tourist Inn (p80).

Khoy خوى

 044 / POPULATION 210,000 / ELEVATION 1149M
The ancient town of Khoy (Salt), named for the salt mines that once made it an important spur along the Silk Road, sits at the cross-roads of several alluring secondary routes and you may end up here needing a bed for the night. The most interesting road heads northeast up winding curves and across a high alpine plateau ringed by mountains to the lonely town of Chaldoran (Siah Chesh-meh) and nearby Qareh Kalisa (p80) church.

In the west of Khoy is the tomb of the dervish-philosopher **Shams Tabrizi** (Shams Tabrizi Blvd), one of Iran's inspirational Mus-lim thinkers whose brief relationship (1244 to 1246) with the poet Rumi was arguably as significant to Sufi history as Jesus' encoun-ter with John the Baptist was to Christianity.

Dependable places to stay and eat in Khoy include the comfortable **Zomorod Apartments** (☑044-3634 3733; Amir Beyk Sq; s/d/tr IR1,150,000/1,520,000/1,920,000; ᴘ ❄🛜) and the slightly worn **Tourist Inn** (Hotel Jahangardi; ☑044-3644 03552; www.ittic.com; Golestan Gardens, Engelab St; tw/tr IR1,450,000/2,550,000; ᴘ🛜).

ⓘ Getting There & Away

Iran Aseman (☑044-3622 2499) flies to Tehran (US$40)

All buses, minibuses and savaris leave from the main **terminal**, on the ring road south of the city, near Ghorubi Blvd. There's an 11am minibus direct to Van (p91) in Turkey; look for Turkish licence plates. Buses leave frequently for Tabriz (IR110,000, 2½ hours) and Orumiyeh (IR80,000, two hours), less frequently for Maku.

Savaris leave for Tabriz (IR150,000, two hours) and Salmas (IR50,000, 40 minutes); change at the latter for Orumiyeh. While some maps place Khoy on the road between Tabriz and Maku, it's actually 25km from the motor-way; the junction is a good place to pick up unofficial savaris heading to Tabriz and Maku, and even to catch through buses.

To visit Qareh Kalisa church via the haunt-ingly beautiful Chaldoran road (and, ideally, go on to Maku), you'll need to hire a private taxi (US$20 to US$30).

Orumiyeh

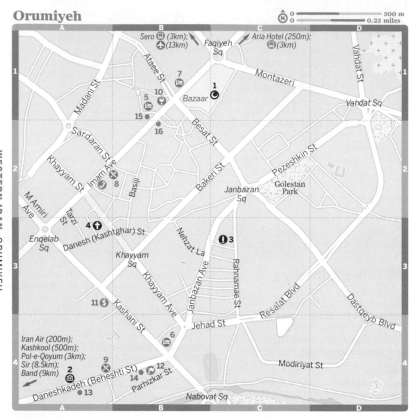

Orumiyeh

ارومیه

044 / POPULATION 669,000 / ELEVATION 1380M

Known as Rezayeh during the Pahlavi era, Orumiyeh (Urmia, Urumiyeh) is a logical stop en route to southeastern Turkey. It's a large, very historic city but offers no must-see sights. The main commercial streets, Imam Ave and Kashani St, form a 'T' at attractive Enqelab Sq. Beheshti St, unanimously known as Daneshkadeh St, continues west to Pol-e-Qoyum junction, around 3km beyond the **museum** (Map p82; 044-3344 6520; Daneshkadeh St; IR150,000; ⊙8am-5pm Tue-Sun).

If you have time to kill, you could check out the **Seh Gonbad** (Map p82), a two-storey tomb tower dating from 1115; the impressively large brick-domed **Masjed-e Jameh** (Masjed-e Rezayieh, Friday Mosque; Map p82) beside the bazaar; and **St Mary's** (Kalisa Neneh Mariyam; Map p82; off Kalisa Lane; ⊙8am-4pm or

by request), which some Assyrian Christians claim is the world's oldest still-standing church – even though it doesn't look that old. Around 6km from town in the hillside hamlet of Sir is the atmospheric **Marsarjis Church** (Sir; P).

🛏 Sleeping

Khorram Hotel
HOTEL $

(Map p82; 044-3322 5444; Sardar Camii Lane; s/tw IR600,000/900,000; 🛜) In the peaceful laneway behind Sardar Mosque, the Khorram has clean, simple rooms. It's just a short stroll from the delights of Imam Ave.

Orumiyeh Tourist Hotel
HOTEL $$

(Map p82; 044-3222 3085; www.ittic.com; Kashani St; d IR2,345,000; P❄🛜) At the fast-food end of Kashani St, this reliable place, with its friendly, English-speaking staff, large, very comfortable rooms, satellite TV and on-site restaurant, is a step up from

Orumiyeh

most other midrange options and is just the spot to erase memories of that epic 36-hour Turkish bus trip.

Aria Hotel BUSINESS HOTEL **$$**
(☎044-3332 2222; http://ariahotel.ir/; Taleqani St; d/tr IR2,360,000/2,980,000; ▣✳✳) A newer hotel on upper Taleqani St, the friendly Aria has very comfortable rooms with a slight '70s psychedelic vibe. Try to get an upper room with a view. Its restaurant is good, though expect surcharges.

Park International Hotel BUSINESS HOTEL **$$$**
(Map p82; ☎044-3224 5927; www.parkhotel.co/en; Imam Ave; d/tr/apt IR3,330,000/4,430,000 /5,390,000; ▣✳✳) In a fantastic central location opposite the bazaar, this opulent lair has heavy, almost baroque rooms with Jacuzzis. The staff is professional, and there's even a money-exchange service.

✖ Eating & Drinking

Kashkool IRANIAN **$**
(☎044-3345 6666; Bargh St; meals from IR150,000; ⊙8am-4pm) Traditional home-style Persian comfort food such as *dizi* (fatty lamb, potato, chickpea and tomato

dish that comes with its own pestle to grind into paste) and *abgusht* (hearty lamb stew) really hits the spot at this small, family-run restaurant with muted, stylish decor.

Reza Restaurant IRANIAN **$**
(Map p82; meals IR250,000; ⊙11am-late) This place dishes up cheap and cheerful *kababs* without a surcharge in sight. It's just off Daneshkadeh St.

Noghl Torabi SWEETS
(Map p82; Imam Ave; ⊙8am-10pm) Sells fabulous carrot-and-walnut halva (a sweet made of sesame flour and honey) and *noghl* (icing-sugar-coated nuts or fruit), the latter made in big, copper cement mixers.

Asal Coffee JUICE BAR
(Map p82; ☎044-3222 9988; cnr Imam Ave & Besat St; espresso IR50,000) Best espresso in town, and the juices aren't bad either.

ℹ Information

Exchange Reyhani (Map p82; ☎044-3544 7044; Kashani St; ⊙10am-10pm Sun-Thu)
Miras Ferhangi (Map p82; ☎044-3340 7040; Daneshkadeh St; ⊙8am-2pm Sat-Thu) West Azerbaijan's keen, English-speaking tourist-information office is beside the museum.
Turkish Consulate (Map p82; ☎044-3347 8770; http://urumiye.bk.mfa.gov.tr/; Daneshkadeh St; ⊙9am-noon Sun-Thu) Very security conscious.
Telephone Office (Map p82; Imam Ave; ⊙7am-7pm)

ℹ Getting There & Away

Espoota Travel (Map p82; ☎044-3345 5555; espoota@espootatravel.com; Daneshkadeh St; ⊙8am-8pm Sat-Thu, 9am-noon Fri) and **Donyaye Faraz Air Travel** (Map p82; Daneshkadeh St; ⊙8am-6pm Sun-Thu) sell air and train tickets.

AIR

Istanbul US$120, weekly with **Iran Aseman** (☎044-3343 4242).
Tehran IR1,925,000, daily with **Qeshm Air** (☎021-4764 0000; www.qeshm-air.com) and **Iran Air** (☎044-3344 0530; Daneshkadeh St), several times weekly with **ATA** (www.ataair.ir).
Mashhad IR2,225,000, weekly with Iran Air and ATA.

BUS, MINIBUS & SAVARI

All long-distance buses leave from the **terminal** (Haft-e Tir Blvd). **Seiro Safar** (Map p82;

☑ 044-3222 8399), **Hamsafar** (Map p82; ☑ 044-3224 4562) and **Iran Peyma** (Map p82; ☑ 044-3222 2954; www.iranpeyma.info) have central booking offices on Imam Ave. Hamsafar and **Vangölu** (☑ +90 850 650 6565; www.vangoluturizm.com.tr) both operate 9am services to Van (Turkey; IR120,000, eight hours) – expect long border waits.

Savaris and buses to Tabriz cross Lake Orumiyeh by bridge – there are great views.

From the **Sero terminal** (Mirza Shirazi St), 3km northwest of Faqiyeh Sq, minibuses run to villages of the Gonbadchay Valley, strung along the loop road that leads up to the dam reservoir and beyond, turning north 6km before the border. Taxis to Sero cost IR400,000 from outside the terminal.

❶ Getting Around

The airport is 13km up the Salmas Hwy (taxi IR200,000, 20 minutes). The most useful shuttle-taxi routes run from Faqiyeh Sq, either along Imam Ave then along Modarres Ave or up Taleqani St to the terminal.

Maraqeh
مراغه

☑ 041 / POPULATION 165,000 / ELEVATION 1470M

Just east of Lake Orumiyeh lies the historic city of Maraqeh (Maragheh, Maraga), which was briefly the capital of Ilkhanid Iran. It's famous for five distinctive 12th-century tomb towers, and for the ruins of the **Maraqeh Observatory** (Rasad Khaneh), the world's greatest medieval observatory, located on a windswept hill 3km northwest of town, and protected by a white golf ball–like geodesic dome.

You might struggle to find a cheap room, though you could try the student dormitories at either end of long Ohmid St. Otherwise recommended places to stay include the comfortable **Alliance Hotel** (☑ 041-3725 4477; Tarbiat Blvd; d/tr IR1,500,000/2,000,000;

P ✳ ☗) and **Darya Hotel** (☑ 041-3325 0304; Shekari Blvd; s/d/ste IR1,490,000/1,980,000/ 2,720,000) and the **Grand Hotel** (☑ 041-3745 7650; www.maraghehotel.net; Shekari Blvd; s/d/tr IR2,040,000/3,140,000/4,040,000; P ✳ ☗ ☒), Maraqeh's top digs.

Lilipar Traditional Restaurant (Pasdaran Sq; ☺ meals from IR150,000) is a hip spot where where Maraqeh's young gather to eye each other over some *qalyans* (water pipes).

❶ Getting There & Away

Savaris (IR100,000, 1¾ hours) and buses (IR60,000, 2½ hours) go to Tabriz. For the Takht-e Soleiman ruins, savari-hop via Bonab (IR15,000, 25 minutes) or Miyando'ab (IR30,000, 45 minutes) to Shahin Dezh (IR30,000, 45 minutes) and then to Takab (IR50,000, one hour).

Tabriz
تبریز

☑ 041 / POPULATION 1.6 MILLION / ELEVATION 1397M

Biblical clues point to the Ajichay River flowing out of the Garden of Eden, which places Tabriz at the gates of paradise. Long a buffer between empires, Tabriz' historical heritage and Silk Road pedigree is no more evident than in its thriving bazaar, one of the world's best. This sprawling city, rich in Azeri culture, with its famous carpets, teahouse *hammams*, love of music and excellent transport links, makes a perfect introduction to Iran. Situated on a high plateau between Lake Orumiyeh and lofty Mt Sahand, and bounded by stark, eroded hills, Tabriz has milder summers than cities further east, though its winters can be formidable.

History

Tabriz was a Sassanian-period trade hub and came to eclipse Maraqeh as a later Ilkhanid Mongol capital of Azerbaijan.

BUSES FROM ORUMIYEH

DESTINATION	FARE	DURATION	DEPARTURES
Ardabil	IR250,000 VIP	5hr	frequent
Esfahan	IR532,000 VIP	16hr	3.30pm
Sanadaj	IR310,000 VIP	7½hr	7am, 10am, 11am
Maku	IR 275,000 *mahmooly*	4½hr	6am, 8am, 10am,1pm, 3pm
Tehran (western terminal)	IR330,000 VIP	10hr	10am, 6-9pm
Tabriz	IR95,000 VIP	2½hr	frequent

LAKE ORUMIYEH

Like the Dead Sea, huge Lake Orumiyeh (6000 sq km) is so super salty that you just can't sink. A Unesco Biosphere Reserve since 1976, it's become increasingly shallow (with a maximum seasonal depth of 16m) since the Zarrinehrud, a major feeder river, was diverted to slake Tabriz' growing thirst. Some worry that the lake will soon be as dead as the Aral Sea. Currently the only life form it supports directly is the very primitive, virtually transparent *Artemia* shrimp. But that's enough to attract plenty of seasonal migratory birds, notably flamingos (in spring). And the shrimp are commercially harvested for fishmeal.

With a continuing downturn in precipitation, the lake is now around 10% of its former size, which has sparked environmental protests as authorities seem baffled as to how to reverse its shrinking. Crazy plans like diverting water from the Aras River (rejected by Iran's neighbours) or relocating the population from the western shore (rejected by the inhabitants) have been put forward. A new dam at Silveh on the Lavin River hopes to channel water back into the Orumiyeh Basin. A bridge linking the eastern and western shores that carries the main highway between Orumiyeh and Tabriz effectively cuts the lake in two.

The lake's hard-to-access, though very photogenic, eastern coastline is starkly barren; the vivid blue waters contrast with jagged, sun-blasted rocks and parched mud-flat islands. The western coast is slightly greener, but the orchards stop well short of the shore. Several travel agencies in Tabriz organise lake trips, including to **Kabudi Island**, the last resting place of Hulagu Khan, Genghis' grandson. But there is no reason to make a special trip to the lake, as you'll get excellent views of it from a Tabriz-bound bus.

It recovered remarkably rapidly from Tamerlane's 1392 ravages and, while the rest of Iran was vassal to the Timurids, Tabriz became the capital of a local Turkmen Qareh Koyunlu (Black Sheep) dynasty. That dynasty's greatest monarch was Jahan Shah (no, *not* the Taj Mahal's Shah Jahan), under whose rule (1439–67) the city saw a remarkable flowering of arts and architecture, culminating in the fabulous Blue Mosque.

Shah Ismail, the first Safavid ruler, briefly made Tabriz Persia's national capital. However, after the battle of Chaldoran against the advancing Ottomans, Tabriz suddenly seemed far too vulnerable to Ottoman attack, so Ismail's successor, Tahmasp (1524–75), moved his capital to safer Qazvin. Fought over by Persians, Ottomans and (later) Russians, Tabriz went into a lengthy decline, exacerbated by disease and one of the world's worst ever earthquakes, which killed 77,000 Tabrizis in November 1727.

The city recovered its prosperity during the 19th century. Shahgoli (now Elgoli) on Tabriz' southeastern outskirts became the residence of the Qajar crown prince, but heavy-handed Qajar attempts to Persianise the Azeri region caused resentment. The 1906 constitutional revolution briefly allowed Azeri Turkish speakers to regain their linguistic rights (schools, newspapers etc) and Tabriz held out valiantly in 1908 when the liberal constitution was promptly revoked again. For its pains it was brutally besieged by Russian troops.

Russians popped up again during both world wars and built a railway line to Jolfa (then the Soviet border) before withdrawing in 1945. This left Tabriz as capital of Pisheveri's short-lived separatist provincial government (of autonomous south Azerbaijan), which tried to barter threats of secession for better Azeri rights within Iran. The provincial government was crushed in December 1946 and, far from encouraging the Azeris, the shah did the opposite, restricting the use of their mother tongue. Reaction against this discrimination put Tabriz at the forefront of the 1979 revolution well before the anti-shah struggle was railroaded by more fundamentalist Muslim clerics.

○ Sights

◎ Central Tabriz

★ **Tabriz Bazaar** BAZAAR
(بازار تبریز; Map p88; ⊘ roughly 8am-9pm Sat-Thu) The magnificent, labyrinthine, Unesco-listed Tabriz bazaar covers some 7

sq km, with 24 caravanserais (sets of rooms arrranged around a courtyard) and 22 impressive *timches* (domed halls). Construction began over a millennium ago, though much of the fine brick vaulting dates to the 15th century. Hidden behind innocuous shopfronts, it's surprisingly easy to miss, but the open Ferdosi mall is a good entry point. Take a GPS waypoint below the tourist information office (p92), then abandon yourself to the closest laneway.

There are several *mozaffareih* (**carpet** (Map p88) sections) according to **knot size** (Map p88) and type. The **Amir bazaar,** (Jewellery Bazaar; Map p88) with gold and jewellery, is immediately behind the tourist information office. The **spice bazaar** (Map p88) has a few shops selling herbal remedies, henna and natural perfumes. A couple of hat shops (in the **Kolahdozan bazaar** (Hat Bazaar; Map p88)) sell traditional *papakh* (Azeri hats) made of tight-curled astrakhan wool. Other quarters specialise in **leather** (Deri Bazaar; Map p88), silver and **copper** (Saffar Bazaar, Bakir Bazaar; Map p88), general household goods and **fruit** (Safi Bazaar; Map p88) and **vegetables** (Sabz Bazaar; Map p88).

Masjed-e Jameh   MOSQUE
(Friday Mosque; Map p88) At the bazaar's western end an exit passage hidden by a curtain leads to Tabriz' impressive Seljuk-era Masjed-e Jameh, with a magnificent brick-vaulted interior and twin, multiturreted minarets.

Blue Mosque   MOSQUE
(Masjed-e Kabud, مسجد کبود; Map p88; Imam Khomeini St; IR150,000; ⊘ 8am-5.30pm Sat-Thu) When constructed for ruler Jahan Shah in 1465, the Blue Mosque with its intricate turquoise mosaics was one of the most famous buildings of its era. Unfortunately, it was badly damaged in an earthquake in 1773, leaving only the main *iwan* (entrance hall) and Jahan Shah's tomb intact. Restoration has been slow, and though the main structure is complete again, the once-brilliant external mosaics are only visible on the original *iwan*.

Once the mosque was built, artists took a further 25 years to cover every surface with the blue majolica tiles and intricate calligraphy for which it was nicknamed. The interior is also blue, and missing patterns have been laboriously painted onto many lower sections around the few remaining patches of original tiles. A smaller domed chamber away from the entrance once served as a private mosque for the Qareh Koyunlu shahs.

Azarbaijan Museum   MUSEUM
(موزه آذربایجان; Map p88; ☑ 041-3526 1696; Imam Khomeini St; IR200,000; ⊘ 8am-5.30pm Tue-Sun) This museum's entrance is a great brick portal with big wooden doors guarded by two stone rams. Ground-floor exhibits include finds from Hasanlu (an Iron Age town that developed into a citadel over 4000 years), a superb 3000-year-old copper helmet and curious stone 'handbags' from the 3rd millennium BC. Found near Kerman, these are understood to be symbols of wealth once carried by provincial treasurers.

The basement features Ahad Hossein's powerful and disturbing sculptural allegories of life and war. The top floor displays a re-weave of the famous 'Ardebil' carpet, reckoned to be one of the best ever made; the original is beautifully displayed in London's Victoria & Albert Museum.

Arg-e Tabriz   HISTORIC BUILDING
(ارگ تبریز; Map p88) This huge brick edifice off Imam Khomeini St is a chunky remnant of Tabriz' early-14th-century citadel (known as 'the Ark'). Criminals were once executed by being hurled from the top of the citadel walls. The Russians used it as a command post during their 1911 invasion. Unfortunately, it's being dwarfed by the even more humongous **Imam Khomeini Mosalla** (Map p88; Imam St) being built next door and the whole area is presently closed off.

Municipal Hall   HISTORIC BUILDING
(City Museum; Map p88; ☑ 041-3553 9198; www.tabriz.ir; Sa'at Sq; ⊘ 8am-6pm Sat-Thu, to 1pm Fri; ◪) FREE The iconic 1930s German-designed Municipal Hall, still the bastion of city power, dominates Sa'at Sq. There's a museum in the basement with various city-related collections, such as old maps, photos, carpets and even antique vehicles.

Qajar Museum   MUSEUM
(Amir Nezam House; Map p88; ☑ 041-3523 6568; Farhang St, Sheshgelan; IR150,000; ⊘ 8am-6pm Tue-Sun) The elegant Qajar Museum is within the palatial 1881 Amir Nezam House, Tabriz' most impressive Qajar mansion, with a split-level façade.

Architecture Faculty,
Islamic Arts University   HISTORIC BUILDING
(Map p88; Walman St; tours IR50,000) A trio of impressive 230-year-old mansions with

ARMENIAN MONASTIC ENSEMBLES OF IRAN

Three ancient churches scattered across the northern Azerbaijan province – **Qareh Kalisa** (p80), **St Stephanos** (p96) and **Dzor Dzor Chapel** (p80) – constitute the Armenian Monastic Ensembles of Iran Unesco site. Armenian tradition says that two of the biblical 12 apostles – St Thaddeus (or Jude) and St Bartholomew – brought Christianity to the area in the 1st century. The earliest remains of the current churches date from the 7th century, though each has been partly rebuilt a number of times over the intervening years due to damage caused by earthquakes and various warring factions. They are important pilgrimage sites for members of the Armenian church.

Each photogenic church is in a remote, starkly beautiful setting and the journey alone is reward for the effort of tracking them down.

two-storey colonnades, inner courtyards and decorative ponds makes up the Architecture Faculty of the Islamic Arts University. You might be lucky enough to find someone willing to show you around, but be prepared to tip them.

Shahriyar House Museum   MUSEUM
(Map p88; 041-3555 8847; Maqsoudieh Alley, off Tabazan St; IR80,000; ⊙7.30am-7.30pm Sat-Thu, to 1pm Fri) Enter a time warp to late-'70s Tabriz in the preserved house of much-loved poet Ostad Shahriyar (1906–88). Surrounded by his everyday belongings, you almost expect the late poet to wander out of the bedroom. He is buried in the Poets' Mausoleum.

St Mary's Church   CHURCH
(Kalisa-ye Maryam-e Moqaddas; Map p88) Dating from the 12th century, St Mary's is a still-functioning Armenian church that was mentioned by Marco Polo. It was once the seat of the regional archbishop. Ring the bell if you want to look inside.

⊙ Outer Tabriz

Poets' Mausoleum   MAUSOLEUM
(Maghbarat al-Shoara, Maqbar al-Shoara; Map p88; Seyid Hamzeh St) Poet Ostad Shahriyar is ostentatiously commemorated by the strikingly modernist Poets' Mausoleum. Its angular, interlocking concrete arches are best viewed across the reflecting pool from the south. The complex also commemorates more than 400 other scholars whose tombs were lost in the city's various earthquakes. Take bus 116.

Elgoli Park   PARK
(Shahgoli; Ⓜ Elgoli) Elgoli Park, 8km southeast of the centre, is popular with summer strollers and courting couples. Its

fairground surrounds an artificial lake, in the middle of which a photogenic **restaurant-pavilion** (041-3380 5263; meals US$5) occupies the reconstruction of a Qajar-era palace. The park can be reached by metro line 1.

🏃 Activities

Mt Sahand   TREKKING
(Kamal Dag) Mt Sahand (3707m) is the gigantic volcanic lump south of Tabriz; Kamal is its highest peak. Access is via Sahand Ski Resort, about 60km by road from downtown Tabriz. You should be able to see the summit from the resort: it's 5km and a 900m ascent along a well-defined ridge. BYO taxi.

🧭 Tours

Nasser Khan   TOURS
(Map p88; 0914 116 0149; amicodelmondo@yahoo.com) A legendary polyglot pillar of the tourist information office, Nasser often takes small groups on people-watching trips and cultural experiences. He can often get you into officially closed buildings, such as churches and *zurkhaneh* (traditional body-building, wrestling and martial-arts gyms).

ALP Tours & Travel Agency   TOURS
(041-3331 0340; www.facebook.com/alptour; Karimkhan Sq, Valiasr; ⊙8am-5pm Sat-Thu) Dependent on numbers, this outfit can arrange Friday sightseeing trips around the province, and skiing or snowboarding trips to Mt Sahand. It's a good contact for climbing guides.

Hossein Ravanyar   TOURS
(0935-299 2296; www.iranoverland.com) Eccentric fixer Hossein has been organising tours and helping overlanders with their

Central Tabriz

N

500 m
0.25 miles
0

Khosh Zaban Kalleh Pacheh (1.3km)

Abresan (700m); Abdi (800m); Tabriz
International Hotel (1.3km); Delestan (1.6km);
Vali'asr District (2.5km); Eloqli District (6km)

Meydan-e Qotb

Aref St
Farhang St
Seshgelan (Vahidi) St
Saqqa-tol-Eslam St
Mehran River
Alameh Tabatayi St
Daneshsara St
Shiraziyen St
Modarres St
Daneshsara Sq
Daneshsara St
Shahid Beheshti St
Shahid Beheshti Sq
Shahid Beheshti
Yaniqin Borju
Khaqani Park
Khaqani St
Imam Khomeini St
Varesh St
Javolmasjid Alley
Bazaar
Meydan-e Sa'at
Molavi St
Madani St
Shohada-Shohada St Sq
Artesh St
Artesh St
Tabzari St
Azadi St
Walman St
Talaqani St
Tabriz Bazaar
Jomhuri-e Eslami St
Tarbiat St
Panahi Alley
Yushari Alley
Ardabili Alley
Namaz Sq
Ferdosi St
Imam Khomeini St
Shari'ati St
Motahhari St
Mohaqqeqi St
Qal'a Beygi Alley
Ark St
Shari'ati St
Anglican Church
Passport Office (700m)
Behboud Apartments (400m);
Main Post Office (1.4km)
Feleshin St
Nasseh alley
Termina Sq
Ahrab St
Baroun Avak St
Sarkis Church
Tohid St
Mahmudzadeh St
Bahrami St
Qareh Dash St
Qods St
Bahar St
Nuri Hava'i St
Golestan Gardens
Fajr Sq
Qonaqa Sq
Shahri St
22 Bahman St
Khayyam St
Molla Alakbar St
Kucheh Bagh
(4km)
22 Bahman St

Central Tabriz

WESTERN IRAN TABRIZ

vehicle paperwork for years. He routinely drops off the grid, but he's just as likely to bob up again.

🛌 Sleeping

Summer camping is possible at designated sites, such as in Elgoli Park and near Tabriz University. Tabriz has a wealth of hotels; most of the cheapies are near the bazaar on Ferdosi St, while the Fajr Sq end of Imam Khomeini St has some good mid-range options. The top-end hotels dominate the Abresan district.

Khorshid Guesthouse　　　　HOTEL $
(Map p88; ☏041-3553 9981; Ferdosi St; s/tw IR690,000/870,000; 🛜) Cheap and cheerful Khorshid has clean, basic rooms on busy Fedorsi St, a block from the bazaar.

Ramsar Guesthouse　　　　　HOTEL $
(Map p88; ☏041-3551 2417; Imam Khomeini St; s/tw IR690,000/870,000; ❄🛜) Clean, simple rooms come in a range of sizes at this cheerful cheapie down the Farj Sq end of Imam Khomeini St. Cheaper rooms without bathroom are also available.

Darya Guesthouse　　　　GUESTHOUSE $
(Map p88; ☏041-3554 0008; www.darya-guesthouse.com; Mohaqqeqi St; s/tw/tr IR690,000/870,000/1,210,000; 🅿🛜) A favourite budget-traveller's dosser, Darya has a variety of clean, basic, thin-walled rooms. It can be chaotic, but the friendly English-savvy owner pulls it all together. There's a useful travellers' tip book. The rooms without bathroom are cheaper still. Don't confuse it with the totally unrelated Darya Hotel.

Mashhad Guesthouse HOSTEL $
(Mosaferkhaneh Mashhad; Map p88; ☑ 041-3555
8255; Ferdosi St; dm/s/tw without bathroom
IR250,000/350,000/520,000) Rooms (including five-bed dorms), set above and below a
restaurant, are reasonable, with washbasin
and flat-screen TV. Bathroom standards
vary according to time of day and showers
cost a little extra. It's ideally central, and
the rooftop terrace has a good view.

Kosar Hotel HOTEL $
(Map p88; ☑ 041-3553 7691; info@kosarhotel.com; Imam Khomeini St; s/tw
IR600,000/900,000; ✴ @ 🛜) Centrally located on Imam Khomeini St, the Kosar has a
variety of basic rooms; cheaper ones without bathroom are also available. Cleanliness can be iffy and service a bit random,
but if you've been travelling a while you
probably won't care.

Hotel Sahand HOTEL $$
(Map p88; ☑ 041-3555 2545; www.hotelsahand.
com; Imam Khomeini St; s/d US$43/65; P ✴ 🛜)
Centrally located, the Sahand has spacious,
clean, comfortable tiled rooms, some overlooking the mosque opposite. Staff members are friendly. It's worth bargaining for
a multiday discount.

Hotel Sina HOTEL $$
(Map p88; ☑ 041-3551 6211; Fajr Sq; s/tw
IR1,100,000/1,500,000; P ✴ 🛜) Calm yet
central, this relatively plush option has
bright corridors with strip carpets over
clean tiled floors. Rooms are neat and fully
equipped. Enter from Felestin St. Parking
is limited.

Morvarid Hotel HOTEL $$
(Map p88; ☑ 041-3551 3336; www.hotel
morvarid.com; Fajr Sq; s/tw/tr IR860,000/
1,200,000/1,500,000; ✴ 🛜) Right on Fajr Sq,
opposite Golestan Gardens, the historic,
central Morvarid has been serving travellers for decades, with tidy rooms, dependable bathrooms and smiling service.

Behboud Apartments APARTMENT $$
(☑ 041-3557 6647; http://behboudhotel.com/;
Shoar St; 4-person apt IR4,200,000; P ✴ 🛜)
These swish two-bedroom, four-berth
apartments in a newish block off Artesh St
near the stadium in the southern part of
the city are perfect for families or groups.
The apartments are huge, and there's an
on-site restaurant and coffee shop. Buffet
brekkie included.

Tabriz International Hotel BUSINESS HOTEL $$$
(☑ 041-3334 1081; www.tabrizhotel.ir; Daneshgah
Sq, Imam Khomeini St, Abresan Crossing; s/d/tr
$82/116/148; P ✴ 🛜 ⊠; M Daneshgah) The
rooms are large, comfy and well appointed, the staff courteous and helpful, and the
restaurant pretty good, as you'd expect in
this price range. Share taxis pass right by
to get you into the centre, though the subway to Sa'at Sq may have opened by the
time you visit.

Pars Elgoli Hotel HOTEL $$$
(☑ 041-3380 7820; www.pars-hotels.com; Elgoli Park; s/d/ste US$81/118/217; P ✴ @ 🛜 ⊠;
M Elgoli) Three convex walls of gleaming
blue glass overlook the city's favourite park,
8km from the centre. It has everything
you'd expect from a top business hotel, except for alcohol in the minibar beers. The
atrium is airy and there's a **revolving restaurant** (meals IR250,000-500,000; ⊙ 7.30-
11pm) on top. It's only a 500m dawdle from
the Elgoli metro station.

✖ Eating

On winter evenings, sweet potatoes are sold
roasted or boiled from carts along Imam
Khomeini St, as well as *baghla* (boiled
broad beans), which are eaten as a snack
with vinegar and paprika. Imam St has
loads of juice bars and fast-food options,
mostly between Shari'ati St and the Tarbiat St pedestrian mall. Try the *dizi* in the
historically atmospheric Nobar Hammam,
now called Shahriar Restaurant (p91).

✖ Central Tabriz

Rahnama Dairy SWEETS $
(Map p88; Ferdosi St; snacks from IR30,000;
⊙ 7am-9pm Sat-Thu, to 2pm Fri) This simple
dairy-cafe at the main bazaar entrance
serves unbeatable breakfasts of *must-asal* (yogurt and honey) and *khame-asal*
(cream and honeycomb).

Emarat Restaurant IRANIAN $
(Map p88; Shari'ati St; meals IR190,000) Carpeted booths in a wide, airy space, English
menus and a plaster waterfall complete
with monkeys and goats complement the
excellent traditional Iranian food here.
Service is friendly; the English-speaking
manager sits behind a pirate galleon. From
the street, ignore the stairs that lead up to
the cafe and head straight through to the
restaurant.

Koran Restaurant IRANIAN $
(Qurani Chelokababi; Map p88; meals from IR180,000; ⊙11am-late Sat-Thu) This Tabriz institution opposite the bazaar has the best *kababs* in town, according to locals.

Haji Mahid FAST FOOD $
(Map p88; Tarbiat St; meals IR100,000; ⊙11am-10pm; ⊞) Don't bother looking for a menu – there isn't one; just say *chelo murgh* or point at anybody else's plate, as the only dish here is chicken and rice. It's upstairs and the window seats have a good view of the pedestrian mall.

Tabriz Modern Restaurant IRANIAN $$
(Map p88; ☑ 041-3556 3841; Imam Khomeini St; full-service meals IR240,000-400,000; ⊙noon-11pm; ☎) Go the excellent fried trout (IR270,000) at this friendly, rather ornate basement dining hall. Prices include 'full service': salad bar, *mast* (yogurt), soft drink and delicious barley-and-barberry soup. And, of course, there are *kababs* too.

✖ Abresan Crossing & Valiasr District

En route to the Valiasr or Elgoli Districts you'll usually need to change shared taxis at Abresan Crossing, where there are fast-food options around the junction. Valiasr's latest fad is coffee and cake, ice cream or an outrageous dessert. New cafes pop up every day; wander and try a few out, or consult http://foursquare.com.

Abdi PIZZA $
(☑ 041-3336 6245; 29 Bahman St, Abresan Crossing; pizza IR120,000-180,000; ⊙5-10.30pm) These guys have been churning out pizza forever. Check out the black decor and real flames over the doorway.

KhoshZaban Kalleh Pacheh BREAKFAST $
(Azadi St, Abresan Crossing; meals IR50,000; ⊙early) Locals rate the *kalleh pache* ('head and hoof' soup) here as the best in Tabriz. The soup is a traditional winter heart-starter and is made by boiling up an entire sheep's head (brain intact) and hooves. You've been warned.

Delestan AZERBAIJANI $$
(☑ 041-1333 8507; www.delestanfoods.com; Daneshgah Sq, 29 Bahman St, Abresan Crossing; mains from IR220,000; ⊙11am-11pm; Ⓜ Daneshgah) In Daneshgah, east of the centre near the uni entrance, this is a tale of two restaurants. The scary day-glo fast-food section is popular with students, so head right for the calmer restaurant area, notable for Azerbaijani and Persian dishes. Each dish has a handy photo on the website.

🍷 Drinking & Nightlife

★ Shahriar Restaurant TEAHOUSE
(Nobar Hammam; Map p88; ☑ 041-3554 0057; Imam Khomeini St; chay IR50,000) There are several interesting rooms in this converted subterranean 19th-century bathhouse, though the *qalyan*-wafting *chaykhaneh* (teahouse) is the most exotic. The other,

---

ⓘ BORDER CROSSINGS

Two border crossings from western Iran lead to Van in Turkey.

Sero–Esendere Through buses operate daily from Orumiyeh's terminal to Van and take around eight hours. Or you can take a savari to Sero ($US10, 45 minutes), skip the bus border queues, then either pick up the regular Yüksekova–Esendere *dolmuş* (minibus) or the hourly Vangölü Turizm (p84) Esendere–Van service (TTL30, 4½ hours). Taxi drivers, bless them, will deny the *dolmuş* exists. Yüksekova, 40km away, offers the closest accommodation on the Turkish side. Vangölü Turizm also runs hourly Yüksekova–Van buses (TTL20, 3½ hours) between 7am and 6pm, passing the magnificent ruins of Hoşap Castle in Güzelsu village (64km before Van).

Razi–Kapiköy This crossing follows the route of the Tabriz–Van rail link and is popular with travellers in their own vehicles. Through buses run from Khoy to Van ($US20, four hours), or you could string together minibuses. Take a savari from Khoy to Razi (about US$10, 30 minutes), another to Kapiköy (or walk the road between border posts) and then a *dolmuş* on to Van ($10, 1½ to two hours). From Khoy you can also head to Tabriz, Tehran or anywhere else in Iran.

Both crossings are only open 8am to 6pm local time. Iran is 1½ hours ahead of Turkey, so you need to cross out of Turkey by 4pm (allowing 30 minutes for paperwork). Heading the other way, you shouldn't exit Razi before 9.30am Iranian time.

larger room, popular with groups, is a restaurant (meals from IR200,000) with tables and chairs as well as carpeted booths; it does very good *dizi* and kababs.

Radio Cafe
CAFE

(☑ 0914 412 6645; Valiasr; coffee/cake from IR100,000/80,000; ⊙ 11am-11pm) The coffee's first class and the light meals are very moreish, but it's the signature red-velvet cake that really draws the crowds at weekends. It's at the western end of Valiasr, past the evil flyover.

Gr8 Cafe
CAFE

(Mokhaberat Blvd, Valiasr; coffee/cake from IR80,000/80,000; ⊙ 10am-11pm) One of the hippest new caffeine fuelling stations along the Valiasr strip, Gr8 has tasteful wooden panelling, herbal teas and cakes to die for. Oh, and awesome coffee!

Emarat Cafe
CAFE

(Map p88; Shari'ati St; coffee/cake IR80,000/80,000; ⊙ 11am-midnight) Turn south into Shari'ati St from Imam Khomeini St and immediately follow the coffee sign upstairs. The boys do a deft espresso and chocolate-ripple cake in the smoke haze.

ℹ Information

CONSULATES

Azerbaijani Consulate (p342) Citizens of most countries can now get an e-visa (US$23, valid for 30 days) online in three working days.

Turkish Consulate (☑ 041-3327 18 82; http://tebriz.bk.mfa.gov.tr; Homafar Sq, Valiasr; ⊙ 9.30am-noon Sun-Thu)

MEDICAL SERVICES

Nasr Clinic (Map p88; ☑ 041-3553 8701; Artesh St; ⊙ 24hr) This clinic is next to Behboud Hospital.

MONEY

Hitvan Hivan (Map p88; Imam Khomeini St; ⊙ 8am-8pm Sat-Thu), near Tarbiat St, offers quick and easy exchanges. Otherwise, try these two, both in the jewellery bazaar (they can be hard to find, so ask around or get the nearby **tourist office** to guide you):

Mahmud Abidan Exchange (Map p88; ☑ 523 1077; araye Amir, Timche Amirno 11; ⊙ 9am-6pm Sat-Wed, to 3pm Thu) Good rates and no queue (but no sign).

Ramin Exchange (Map p88; ☑ 041-3526 2016; ramin.chalani@hotmail.co.uk; 69 Saraie Amir, Passage Farsh; ⊙ 9am-6pm Sat-Thu) Reliable exchange office with decent rates.

POST

Main Post Office (Artesh St) Helpful for shipping parcels.

TOURIST INFORMATION

Armenian Prelacy Office (Map p88; ☑ 041-3555 3532; archtab@itm.co.ir) Contact the prelacy for the dates of services at **Qareh Kalisa** (p80) and other Armenian churches in the Azerbaijan provinces.

Information Office (⊙ 7am-8pm) These guys know all the schedules. The office is inside the main bus terminal.

Tourist Information Office (Map p88; ☑ 041-3524 6235; www.tabriz.ir; Ferdosi St; ⊙ 9am-2pm & 4-7pm Sat-Thu) Nasser Khan has excellent free maps and is a mine of information on Tabriz and the surrounding area. He'll create bespoke tours to whatever you want to see. It's upstairs in a building on the eastern side of the the main bazaar entrance, and signposted.

TRAVEL AGENCIES

A number of agencies have English-speaking staff and offer train and plane bookings.

Afagh Seir Tabriz (Map p88; ☑ 041-3554 8080; afaghseirtabriz@yahoo.com; Imam Khomeini St; ⊙ 8.30am-8.30pm Sat-Thu)

Azar Parand Gasht Travel (Map p88; ☑ 041-3551 1730; azar-parand@yahoo.com; Imam Khomeini St; ⊙ 9am-6pm Sat-Thu)

Mahnavard Travel (Map p88; ☑ 041-3553 9444; www.mahnavard.com; West Tarbiat St; ⊙ 8.30am-6pm Sat-Thu)

Mihan Safar (Map p88; ☑ 041-5534 4488; Imam Khomeini St; ⊙ 9am-8pm Sat-Thu, to noon Fri)

VISA EXTENSIONS

Passport Office (☑ 041-3477 6666; Saeb St; ⊙ 8am-1.30pm Sat-Wed, to 11.30pm Thu) Visa extensions currently cost IR375,000. No English is spoken, and they may want you to pay with an Iranian credit card, so you might need to find an agreeable Iranian and pay them back.

ℹ Getting There & Away

AIR

Istanbul US$183, daily with **Turkish Airlines** (☑ 041-1329 6353; www.turkishairlines.com; 57 Nasim St, Valiasr; ⊙ 9am-5pm Sat-Wed, to 1pm Thu).

Dubai US$125, weekly in summer with **Kish** (www.kishairlines.ir) and **Caspian Airlines** (www.caspian.aero).

Tehran IR1,766,000, almost hourly between 7am and midnight with local airline **ATA** (p83) and at least daily with Caspian, Kish, **Iran Air** (☑ 041-3655 4002) and **Qeshm** (p83).

Mashhad IR1,880,000, daily with ATA and **Iran Air Tour** (☑ 021-8931 7711; www.iat.aero), Tuesday and Friday to Sunday with **Meraj** (Ascension; ☑ 021-63 266; http://merajairlines.ir/en) and Sunday with Iran Air.

Esfahan IR1,9250,000, Monday, Wednesday and Saturday with **Mahan Air.** (www.mahan.aero)

Bandar Abbas IR3,444,000, Monday with Iran Air Tour and Tuesday with Qeshm.

BUS, MINIBUS & SAVARI

A couple of bus companies have offices on Imam Khomeini St. Agency **Mihan Safar** (p92) pre-sells tickets for many domestic long-distance bus companies.

Most long-distance buses depart from the huge, modern **main bus terminal**, 3km south of the centre. There's a handy **information office** (p92) inside.

Between 10pm and midnight cheaper buses to Tehran (IR280,000) leave from near the train station.

Savaris to most destinations (but not Ahar or Marand) depart from the terminal's northwestern corner. Prepay at one of two ticket booths.

Other Terminals

Use the **Rahahan terminal** (Rahahan Sq) near the railway station for Osku and thence Kandovan. Out towards the airport, the **Marand terminal** (Azerbaijan Sq) serves Marand and Hadiyshahr (for Jolfa). Buses to Ahar depart from the **Ahar Terminal** (East Terminal; 29 Bahman St).

International Buses

Bus services to Yerevan (Armenia; US$48, 15 hours), and with **Aram Safar** (Map p88; ☑ 041-3556 0597; Imam Khomeini St) for İstanbul (IR1,400,000, 30 hours) and Baku (Azerbaijan; IR800,000IR, 13 to 17 hours) all typically leave around 10pm from outside the relevant ticket offices on Imam Khomeini Ave.

Services sometimes leave from the train-station concourse, so double-check.

TRAIN

Overnight trains to Tehran (12 hours) depart at 4.40pm (from IR442,500) and 6pm (from IR372,500), running via Maraqeh (2¼ hours), Zanjan (8½ hours, arriving antisocially early) and Qazvin. There's also at least one daily train to Mashhad (IR920,000, 24 hours), leaving at 12.25pm, which could be used for Zanjan and Qazvin. The **train station** (☑ 041-3444 4419; Rahahan Sq) is 4.5km west of Farj Sq. Shuttle taxis and city bus 111 drop off at the junction of Mellat Blvd and 22 Bahman St.

The 8.20am local train to Jolfa (IR25,000, three hours) operates Tuesday, Thursday and Sunday only.

The only international train service currently running is Tabriz to Nakhchivan twice a week.

🛈 Getting Around

TO/FROM THE AIRPORT

Tabriz International Airport Airport bus **136** (Map p88) runs from Motahhari St every 40 minutes. Taxis (with blue stripe) should cost IR60,000.

BUS & MINIBUS

City buses are relatively infrequent. Pre-buy IR10,000 tickets. Useful routes from the major

WESTERN IRAN TABRIZ

BUSES FROM TABRIZ

DESTINATION	FARE (IR)	DURATION (HR)	DEPARTURES
Ahvaz	540,000	15	1.30pm, 4pm
Ardabil	220,000	4	twice hourly 5am-6pm
Esfahan	520,000	12	4-5.30pm
Kermanshah	370,000	10	6pm
Maku	80,000	3	daily
Qazvin	290,000*	6	use Tehran (west) bus
Rasht	335,000	7	8.30pm
Shiraz	950,000	22	1.30-2pm
Tehran (west)	330,000*	8	frequent till 10pm
Tehran (south)	350,000	8½	8.30am, 11am
Zanjan	250,000*	3	10am, 3pm

* signifies VIP

city-bus terminal include **bus 160** (Map p88) to the main bus terminal and **bus 110** (Map p88) to Valiasr. Several services run the length of 22 Bahman St (for the train station), including **bus 111** (Map p88). Buses **136** (p93), to the airport, and **115** (Map p88), to the Marand terminal, leave from the western side of the bazaar. Bus 101 runs to Elgoli from near Saat Sq.

SHUTTLE TAXI

A key route runs along Imam Khomeini St from Fajr Sq to Abresan Crossing (IR20,000) but on returning diverts onto Jomhuri-e Eslami St when passing the bazaar. At Abresan Crossing, walk under the flyover to continue to Valiasr (IR10,000) or go to Rahnamae (IR10,000), where you'll change again for Elgoli (IR10,000), though you're better off taking the metro. For the train station, start from Qonaga Sq (IR10,000). To the bus terminal, shuttle taxis take **Shari'ati St** (Map p88) southbound, returning via Taleqani St. *Dar bast* to/from the terminal will cost IR60,000.

TRAM & METRO

Metro line 1 is open from Elgoli to Ostad Shahriar and will soon be extended to Sa'at Sq. Three more lines (and a commuter rail line) are planned. Line 3 will link the airport to the bus terminals, and line 4 will loop around the older core of Tabriz. See http://tabrizmetro.ir/ for updates.

CAR & MOTORCYCLE

Europcar (☑ 041-3260 1565; Tabriz International Airport) has rental cars for hire at Tabriz Airport from US$60 per day.

Kandovan   کندوان

☑ 041 / POPULATION 740 / ELEVATION 1575M

Channelling Turkey's Cappadocia and looking like the cover of a fantasy novel, Kandovan's curious troglodyte cliff dwellings have been carved into eroded volcanic lahar pillars. These cones sit above a newer, lower village, which has spread extensively around their base. Beat the incessant crowds by coming late in the day, when the light is soft and the rocks have a warm glow. The village has an admission fee of IR30,000. The area also has interesting hiking possibilities.

Beyond Kandovan, smooth, steep foothills mask a full view of Mt Sahand, whose hidden volcanic summit rises to 3707m. David Rohl's book *Legend* suggests that Sahand was the Bible's 'Mountain of God'. If true, that would place Kandovan slap bang in the original Garden of Eden.

🛏 Sleeping & Eating

In Kandovan, several homes and shops at the village base offer very basic **rooms to rent** (IR300,000), mostly May to September only. You'll usually get an unfurnished room with a carpeted floor, so consider bringing a sleeping bag. Standards vary.

Jamshid   HOMESTAY **$**
(☑ 041-3323 0016; r IR350,000) Has slightly tatty rooms but offers a hot-water shower and indoor squat toilet.

⭐ **Kandovan Laleh Rocky Hotel**   BOUTIQUE HOTEL **$$$**
(☑ 041-3323 0191; http://kandovan.lalehhotels. com; r without/with Jacuzzi US$118/145, ste US$188-252; P 🐀) The Laleh's 10 remarkable rooms have been carved out of 'fairy chimney' rock knolls. Inside they're luxurious affairs, with stylish lighting, futon beds, underfloor heating and (in many) deep-stepped Jacuzzis as well as fully equipped bathrooms.

The hotel's restaurant is the best option for a meal while in town.

ℹ Getting There & Away

Minibuses from central Tabriz run regularly to Osku (IR30,000, 50 minutes) till around 6pm. From Osku to Kandovan (25km) taxis charge US$10 return, plus US$3 per hour of waiting time. Minibuses are extremely rare. A private taxi from Tabriz to Kandovan costs around US$22 return.

Jolfa   جلفا

☑ 041 / POPULATION 7500 / ELEVATION 723M

The original Jolfa was once a major Armenian settlement famous for its skilled artisans. They were so skilled, in fact, that in 1604 Shah Abbas kidnapped the entire population, whisking them off to build him a new capital at Esfahan, where their descendants still live. Jolfa is now a busy little border town centred on Ashura Sq, a sizeable roundabout directly south of the Azerbaijan immigration post.

There's little to see in town, but it makes a good budget base for crossing into Armenia or visiting the Unesco-listed Church of St Stephanos (p96) on a wooded hill above the Aras River, 17km west of Jolfa. The church's well-preserved exterior reliefs include Armenian crosses, saints and angels. The interior is still under restoration. A taxi

ℹ️ IRAN-AZERBAIJAN BORDER CROSSING

Culfa, in Azerbaijan's disconnected Nakhchivan exclave, is a short walk across the Aras River from central Jolfa. Use up your rials or exchange them for Azerbaijani manats (AZN1 equals US$1.30) before leaving Iran. Note that in Azerbaijan 'one shirvan' confusingly means AZN2.

Be aware that Culfa's police tend to be extremely suspicious of travellers. Jump into a taxi or minibus to Nakhchivan city (about 35 minutes away), which is contrastingly relaxed and cosmopolitan. From Nakhchivan city there are direct buses to İstanbul (five daily, around 30 hours via Iğdır).

The exclave is separated from the rest of Azerbaijan by firmly closed Armenian borders. You'd have to fly to reach Baku (five daily) or Gəncə (three weekly), but tickets often sell out a week ahead.

A new train service linking Nakhchivan to Mashhad (via Jolfa, Tabriz and Tehran) leaves Nakhchivan Sunday and Thursday.

from Jolfa (25 minutes) to St Stephanos costs around IR500,000 return with stops. Bring your passport with you, as there's a checkpoint just as you leave Jolfa and you may be stopped.

Other reasons to hang around including exploring the sublime Aras River Valley or the enclave of Nakhchivan.

Recommended hotels include the budget **Hotel Durna** (☎041-4302 3812; Vilaete-Fagih St; tw/tr/q without bathroom IR350,000/430,000/510,000) and the super friendly **Jolfa Tourist Inn** (Mehmansara Jahangardi; ☎041-4202 2220; www.ittic.com; Shahid Beheshti Sq, Imam St; tw IR1,090,000; 🅿❄🤖), Jolfa's nicest option with a good restaurant. The atmospheric **Fanous Aras Traditional Restaurant** (meals from IR220,000) is another good place for a meal.

ℹ️ Getting There & Away

Savaris gather just north of Ashura Sq for Marand (IR80,000, one hour), Hadiyshahr (Alamdar; IR20,000, 15 minutes) and occasionally Tabriz (IR400,000, 2½ hours). Minibuses to Marand (IR40,000, 1½ hours) run from Hadiyshahr, but not from Jolfa itself.

Some traffic uses the new sealed, very scenic, direct road to Khoy, but you'll probably need a private hire. If you're heading for Maku, jump out at the motorway 25km before Khoy; there's an obvious pickup spot.

A taxi charter along the stunning Aras River road to Kaleybar will take three to four hours ($40), which includes a couple of short stops. A full-day tour costs $80.

A train leaves at 4.20pm (IR25,000, three hours) for Tabriz on Sunday, Tuesday and Thursday. There's also a train twice a week between Nakhchivan and Mashhad that stops here, but tickets may be scarce.

Aras River Valley

A taxi trip from either Jolfa or Kaleybar through the sublime mountain scenery of the Aras River Valley should not be missed. Rarely in the world can you travel along such a sensitive international frontier so steeped in history and riven by geology.

The Aras River is the Bible's River Gihon. For millennia its valley formed a thoroughfare for traders, armies and holy men. Only with the treaties of 1813 and 1828 did Russia and Persia turn it into a border line, and mud fortifications remain from the 18th-century conflicts that led to its division.

But today the tension is east–west, not north–south. Clearly visible on the Aras' northern bank are ruined villages, sad signs of the still-unresolved 1989–94 Armenia–Azerbaijan war. What a difference 50m makes: it's fine to drive along the southern (ie Iranian) riverbank as a casual tourist (though taking photos isn't advised), but travelling along the parallel northern bank's now severed train line would be unthinkable folly. That line crosses two globally forgotten front lines: from Nakhchivan (Azerbaijan) to its mortal enemy Armenia, on through Karabagh (Armenian-occupied Azeri territory), and then back through minefields to Azerbaijan again. There's not been active fighting for over a decade, but the guard posts, bombed-out trains and barricaded tunnels add a considerable geopolitical frisson to the valley's great natural beauty.

West of Jolfa

On the Azerbaijani riverbank 7km west of Jolfa, a truncated tomb stub and broken bridge are all that mark the original site of ancient Jolfa (view it across the Aras from near a police 'fort'; leave the camera in the taxi). About 1km further west, just before the police checkpoint where the dual highway ends, is the restored **Cara-vanserai Khaje Nazar,** which overlooks the Aras beautifully. Just after the checkpoint, as you enter a spectacular red-rock canyon, you'll see the tiny **Chupan Chape** (P)l above you on the left. Ten kilometres further on you'll come to the turnoff for **St Stephanos church** (Kalisa Darreh Sham; IR150,000; ⊙8am-5pm; P).

Jolfa to Kaleybar

Travelling east from Jolfa, the horizon is a tableau of eroded red cliffs backed by snow-streaked Armenian peaks. In the middle distance is the rocky cleft of Nakhchivan's abrupt **Ilan Dağ** (Snake Mountain), through which Noah's Ark supposedly crashed en route to Ararat. Just beyond attractive **Marazad**, the sinuous mud wall of **Javer Castle** rises on a craggy shoulder. Four kilometres further, take a short detour to the picturesque stacked village of **Ahmadabad**, on a rise overlooking the Aras. Another 2.5km along the main road, a turning east leads steeply up to the popular **Asiyab Khurabe** (Xaraba Dəyirman) spring and picnic area. The side trip is justified mainly by the valley views as you drive back down.

Siyah Rud's farmers produce the raw silk for Tabriz's weaving villages of Khanemu and Osku. Locals are usually happy to show you the cocoon-extraction process if you're passing through during May or June. Further east, the road passes through canyons with glimpses of spiky,

crested ridges leading up to **Kuh-e Kamtal** (Chamtal Dagh, Tiger Mountain).

Sixty kilometres from Jolfa, the canyon widens slightly at **Norduz**, the modern Iranian–Armenian border post.

Four kilometres east of Norduz, picturesque **Duzal** village rises on a hillock dominated by a distinctive octagonal tomb tower and imamzadeh-ye (shrine or mausoleum to a descendant of an imam). Behind the next rocky bluff the road passes through the gate towers and sturdy mud-topped stone walls of the once huge **Abbas Mirza Castel** (Kordasht Castle). When viewed from the east, the walls frame an impressive spire of eroded rock on the Armenian side. One kilometre further east is a large, lovingly renovated **historic hammam** (Kordasht) with newly marbled floors and attractive ceiling patterns. Two kilometres further, at the end of Kordasht village, look west for a particularly inspiring view of saw-toothed craggy ridges.

After another 25km, a side road rises steeply to the south beside a police post. This leads to **Ushtebin** (Oshtabin, Oshtobeyin) village (entry IR30,000) after 5km. This photogenic stacked huddle of mud and stone homes, in a 'secret valley' known for its white pomegranates, has been touted as a 'new Masuleh', yet it remains virtually unvisited.

The main road continues via the photogenically stepped village of **Qarachilar** (7km from Ushtebin junction) to a road junction at Junanlu (88km). The right turn climbs steeply away from the Aras, following a narrow gorge up through orchards and nomad summer pastures to Kaleybar. Instead of turning, if you continue straight past the fork for another 10km you will see

ⓘ IRAN-ARMENIA BORDER CROSSING

The Norduz (Iran) customs yards occupy an otherwise unpopulated sweep of rural valley. Moneychangers on the Iranian side buy and sell Armenian dram (US$1 equals 390 dram) as well as dollars and rials for around 5% below bank rates. One or two taxis usually wait outside the Iranian border compound asking US$10 to Jolfa. From within the compound you'll pay US$5 more.

Walking distance from customs on the Armenian side is Agarak village. Armenian 14-day tourist visas (US$50) or three-day transit visas (US$40) are available at the border, but the process might take a while – annoying if you're on one of the through buses (Yerevan–Tehran via Tabriz). Hopefully, the bus driver will wait for you. On the Armenian side **Aries Travel** (Aries Liber; ☑+374 10-26 39 73; www.bedandbreakfast.am) coordinates pleasant homestays in **Meghri**, a 15-minute, 4000-dram taxi ride away. From Hotel Meghri, near central Meghri, there's a 9am minibus to Yerevan (9000 dram, nine to 11 hours) and a 7.30am bus to Kapan (2000 dram, two hours).

a crumbling **Khodaafarin Bridge** crossing the Aras to a bombed-out village. Photography is forbidden.

The drive between Jolfa and Kaleybar takes around 3½ hours with minimum stops – six to eight hours with side trips and lunch – and costs around US$40 for a private taxi. Expect to pay US$80 for a full-day excursion. The trip is equally stunning in either direction.

Kaleybar كليبر

📋 041 / POPULATION 12,000 / ELEVATION 1314M

Set attractively in a wide, steep-sided mountain valley, modest Kaleybar makes a great starting point for random hikes and visiting nomad camps en route to the upper Aras River Valley. But by far its biggest draw is the breathtaking crag-top ruin of **Qal'eh Babak** (Babak Castle; IR150,000). This extensive fortress, the lair of 9th-century Azeri hero Babak Khorramdin, looms above a desperately sheer chasm as you edge through a narrow cleft to the final traverse. The ascent will take one to two hours.

Beware of visiting Kaleybar during Babak's controversial 'birthday celebrations' (in the last week of June). While it's a culturally fascinating time, all accommodation will be packed and authorities might suspect you of being involved in stirring up political unrest among Azeri nationalists.

The nicest place to stay in Kaleybar is **Hotel Anza** (📋041-4444 4202; www.anzahotel.com; off Farmandari St; d US$40; ❄️🛜). The restaurant (when open) does excellent local and Western dishes. Manager Manouchc can organise tours of the surrounding villages (US$80) and transport for the Arras Valley trip to Jolfa. **Chelokababi** (Farmandari St; meals from IR120,000; ⊘noon-10pm) serves up tasty, fresh, no-frills kababs.

ℹ️ Getting There & Away

There are direct buses to Tabriz (IR200,000, three hours) at 8am and 11.30pm. A taxi to Jolfa along the Aras River will cost from US$40 and take 3½ hours with minimum stops. For Ardabil, take a savari (IR50,000) to Ahar, then change for Meshgin Shahr (IR60,000) and then travel on to Ardabil (IR80,000).

Taxis to the Babak Hotel for the start of the normal route to Babak Castle charge IR70,000; for transport to the nomad camp, much closer to the castle, expect to pay a lot more.

Ardabil اردبيل

📋 045 / POPULATION 490,000 / ELEVATION 1374M

Long a gateway to the historic cities and dry mountains of eastern Azerbaijan from the low-lying, fecund Caspian, Ardabil makes for an interesting stopover. The Unesco-listed Sheikh Safi-od-Din Mausoleum is by far its greatest attraction, but there's a scattering of other minor sights. On crisp, clear days, Mt Sabalan's snow-topped peak rises dramatically above Ardabil's Shurabil Lake.

Ardabil sits on a high, windswept plateau. The weather is pleasantly cool in summer but can turn somewhat nasty by year's end. While snow is possible from November, white winters are becoming shorter.

History

A military outpost for millennia, Ardabil was the capital of the Sajid-dynasty Azerbaijan from 871 to 929, and it saw independence as a khanate from 1747 to 1808. However, Ardabil is best remembered for spawning two great leaders: the Safavid patriarch and great dervish–Sufi mystic Sheikh Safi-od-Din (1253–1334), and his descendant Ismail Safavi. The latter expanded the clan domains so successfully that by 1502 Ismail had become shah of all Persia. His Safavid dynasty was to rule Iran for over two centuries.

◉ Sights

⭐ **Sheikh Safi-od-Din Mausoleum**   MAUSOLEUM

(Map p98; Sheikh Safi St; IR200,000; ⊘8am-5pm Tue Sun winter, 8am-noon & 3.30-7pm summer) Western Iran's most dazzling Safavid monument, and a World Heritage Site, the Sheikh Safi-od-Din Mausoleum is relatively compact. The patriarch is buried within an iconic 1334 **Allah-Allah tower**, so named because the apparently geometrical motif in blue-glazed brick is actually the endlessly repeated name of God. Much of the area around the complex is being excavated and an attractive walled garden makes a peaceful reading refuge.

To see the beautiful wooden sarcophagi, enter a small turquoise-tiled courtyard, then the **Ghandil Khaneh** (lantern house), where the intensity of the gold and indigo decoration is quite striking. The delicate 1612 **Chini Khaneh** (China Room), off to the left, is honeycombed with vaulted gilt niches originally designed to display the

Ardabil

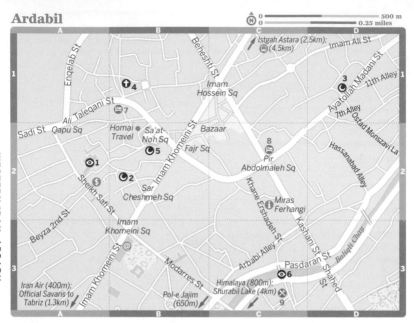

royal porcelain collection, most of which Russia took home with it after the 1828 invasion – it now resides in St Petersburg's Hermitage.

Other Sights

Ardabil has at least five restored bridges across the Baliqli Chay (Fishy River). Nicknamed Yeddi Göz (Seven Eyes), the seven-span **Pol-e Jajim** (Yeddi Göz, Seven Eyes) is the most famous, but the cute, three-arch **Pol-e Ebrahimabad** (Map p98) is more appealing.

The covered bazaar (p114) is extensive and attractive, covering the triangle between Imam Khomeini and Beheshti Sts.

Stroll the back alleys to find the handsome little **Haji Fakr Mosque** (Map p98) with its squat, Bukharan-style pepper-mill minaret and the attractively brick-vaulted **Mirza Ali Akbar Mosque** (Map p98; Sa'at-Noh Sq) decorated with a blue Kufic-tiled exterior frieze and a lighthouse-style minaret.

The **Jameh Mosque** (مسجد جامع; Map p98; Madani St) was once a truly gigantic brick edifice. It's built on the site of a Sassanian fire temple, while the **Maryam Church** (Maryam Moghadas; Map p98) has an unusual old stone pyramid as its central dome.

At Khalkhoran, a village-suburb 3km northeast of the centre, is the mildly attractive 16th-century **Sheik Jebra'il Shrine**.

Activities

Mt Sabalan TREKKING
At 4811m, Mt Sabalan is Iran's third-highest mountain and, apart from in winter, can be climbed by any experienced walker. The northeastern ridge route departs from the village of **Shabil**. Turn off the Meshgin Shahr Rd to **Lahrood** (Lahroud) and continue to Shabil. From there you can take an early 4WD up to a shelter at 3660m, then start walking.

Iran Climbing Guide CLIMBING
(0912 344 5298; www.iranclimbingguide. com) This outfit's website has good info on climbing Mt Sabalan, and it can also put together climbing packages.

Alvares Ski Resort SKIING, TREKKING
A ski lift operates in the winter months at Alvares, but the area makes a good base for trekking outside this time. Alvares is about 25km from the hot-springs resort of **Sar'eyn** (Sarein, سرعین), which is served by frequent savaris from Ardabil (IR25,000). A private taxi from Sar'eyn will cost

Ardabil

Top Sights
1 Sheikh Safi-od-Din Mausoleum A2

Sights
2 Haji Fakr Mosque B2
3 Jameh Mosque (Masjed-e Jameh) D1
4 Maryam Church B1
5 Mirza Ali Akbar Mosque B2
6 Pol-e Ebrahimabad C3

Sleeping
7 Hotel Negin B1
8 Mosaferkhaneh Ideal C2

Eating
9 Shah Abbas Restaurant C3

around US$8 to US$12 return, depending on waiting time.

Sleeping

Most of Ardabil's inner cheapies are pretty dire.

Mosaferkhaneh Ideal HOSTEL **$**
(Ideal Hotel; Map p98; ☎045-3336 8508; cnr Madani & Kashani Sts, Pir Abdolmaleh Sq; s/tw/tr IR520,000/820,000/1,060,000; ❄📶) On a busy intersection behind the bazaar.

★ **Hotel Shorabil** HOTEL **$$**
(☎045-3351 3096; www.hotelshorabil.ir; Shurabil Lakeside; s/d IR720,000/1,200,000; P❄📶) Surrounded by wasteland at the edge of an artificial lake, 4.5km southwest of the centre, this hotel might prompt you to wonder what the attraction is, but the small, modern rooms are well appointed, very comfortable and the best value in town. If you're coming from Astara, get out at the first roundabout on the ring road.

Hotel Negin HOTEL **$$**
(Map p98; ☎045-3323 5671; Taleqani St; s/tw IR950,000/1,300,000; ❄📶) Cheap, comfortable rooms in the northern end of town but still within walking distance of most sights. Staff can be hit or miss.

Eating

There are lots of pizza and other fast-food places along Moallam St between Shohada St and Pol-e Jajim.

Numerous **confectionary shops** facing the Safi-od-Din Mausoleum (p97) or along Imam Khomeini St sell *helva siyah* (black halva, or 'pest'), a rich local speciality. It costs around IR250,000 per kilogram, but a small plateful sprinkled with coconut, grated nuts and cinnamon is only IR15,000. Ardabil's famous **honey** is sold throughout the city.

Shah Abbas Restaurant TEAHOUSE **$**
(Map p98; ☎0914 351 6676; Moadi St; meals IR180,000) This hidden, tastefully renovated 640-year-old former *hammam* oozes atmosphere, with vaulted ceilings and rabbit-warren chambers. Try local *pichag qeimeh* (tender lamb, diced almonds, caramelised onions and soft-boiled egg stranded with saffron) in the restaurant area before retiring to one of the other chambers for *chay* (IR35,000) and *qalyan* (IR100,000); local women smoke quite freely here.

Shopping

Himalaya SPORTS & OUTDOORS
(☎0914 151 2871; Pasdaran St; ⏰9am-11pm Sat-Thu) Good gear shop for camping supplies.

Information

AnarNet (Map p98; Imam Khomeini Sq; per hour IR50,000; ⏰8am-midnight)

Aryana Currency Exchange (Map p98; ☎045-3323 8747; Sheikh Safi St; ⏰9am-2pm & 4-8pm)

Miras Ferhangi (Map p98; ☎045-3325 2708; Khane Ershadeh St; ⏰7.30am-2pm Sat-Thu) Excellent free maps of Ardabil, Sara'eyn and the region from a charming little brick courtyard house.

Getting There & Away

AIR

Tehran IR1,470,000, daily with **Iran Air** (☎045-3225 2040; Imam Khomeini St), weekly with **Iran Aseman** (☎045-3325 1525) and **ATA** (p83).

Mashhad IR2,020,000, several times weekly with Iran Air.

Helpful **Homai Travel** (Map p98; ☎045-3323 3233; Sa'at-Noh Sq; ⏰8.30am-7.30pm Sat-Thu, 9am-1pm Fri) sells air tickets and train tickets ex-Tabriz.

BUS & SAVARI

From the **main terminal** (Moqaddas-e-Ardabili St), 5km northeast of the centre, Tehran buses (from IR350,00,000, 10 hours) leave hourly (7am to 11pm) via Astara (IR50,000, two hours), Rasht (IR175,000, five hours) and Qazvin (IR260,000, eight hours). Buses run to Tabriz (IR220,000, four hours) via Sarab half-hourly till 6pm.

Savari services to Astara (IR80,000, 1½ hours) use **Istgah Astara** (Jam'e-Jam St), a small yard with a green sign 100m northeast of Jahad Sq. For Kaleybar, take a **savari to Meshgin Shahr** (Vahdat Sq; IR80,000, 1½ hours) from Vahdat Sq, then change for Ahar (IR60,000, one hour) and finally Kaleybar (IR60,000, 40 minutes). Savaris to Tabriz (IR250,000) leave 1.3km southwest of town.

❶ Getting Around

The airport is 1km off the Astara road, 11km northeast of Ardabil (IR300,000 by taxi). From Imam Khomeini Sq shuttle taxis run to Baho-nar Sq (for Sara'eyn minibuses) and to Besat Sq. Minibuses to Khalkhoran (for the Sheik Jebra'il Shrine) start near Imam Hossein Sq.

Khal Khal خلخال

📞 045 / POPULATION 46,000 / ELEVATION 1800M

Khal Khal's attraction is its 'three ways' location right in the centre of a haunting nomadic landscape. It makes a good base for treks and exploration of the surrounding photogenic countryside, and it's a great alternative route to Ardabil from Rasht, avoiding the overdeveloped Caspian coast. The lonely road south to Zanjan via Aqkand along the Qezel Owzan valley is incredibly scenic.

Imam St is the main drag, running northeast to southwest for about 4km. If you need a place to stay, try **Khal Khal Tourist Inn** (Mehmansara Jahangardi; 📞 045-3245 3991; www.ittic.com; Khujin Rd; s/tw/tr IR830,000/1,300,000/1,470,000; P❄🛜), 400m east of the bus terminal, just behind Valiasr Sq.

It's possible to **trek** all the way down to Asalem on the Caspian coast using a series of backcountry tracks, traversing nomadic grasslands, mountains and traditional Gilani villages. Start from Andabil, a small village a few kilometres north of Khal Khal, then just head east. Theoretically, you can camp anywhere, though you'll probably be invited for a homestay more than once.

❶ Getting There & Away

Direct savaris depart from Rasht's Pol-e Busar, leaving the coast near Asalem for the very scenic climb to Khal Khal.

Private taxis for the Qezel Owzan route via Aqkand to Zanjan (US$40-60) can be hired outside the bus terminal. Expect to pay at least US$100 to go to Takab via Mahneshan and Behestan (if you can find anyone willing to do so).

Zanjan زنجان

📞 024 / POPULATION 387,000 / ELEVATION 1653M

On a high plain, surrounded by stark, eroded hills, the modest city of Zanjan makes the perfect base for wider explorations. The architectural wonder of Soltaniyeh is nearby, while the battered hoodoos of Behestan Castle and the bizarrely striped Colourful Mountains lie further afield. Enticingly scenic roads radiate to Khal Khal and the Caspian, the subterranean delights of the Katale Khor Caves, and Takht-e Soleiman ruins.

Zanjan's moment of infamy came in 1851 with a bloody siege ordered by Persian prime minister Amir Kabir. The resulting massacre was part of the relatively successful campaign to crush the nascent Baha'i religion. Baha'ism had only broken away from Islam three years before, but it was spreading much too rapidly for Tehran's liking.

◉ Sights

◎ Central Zanjan

Zanjan Archaeology Museum MUSEUM
(Saltman Museum; Map p101; 📞 024-3333 4717; Zeinabieh St, cnr Taleqani St; IR150,000; ⊙ 9am-1pm & 3.30-8pm Tue-Sun) The archaeology museum is home to four of the fascinating 'Saltmen' mummies discovered over the years in the **Chehrabad Salt Mine** (now an archaeological site). The effect of the salt and the extremely dry air of the mine has preserved whole corpses, some with skin, hair and various organs intact. Three are on display in sealed glass cases on the museum's 2nd floor, where a guide will share their story.

Zanjan Bazaar BAZAAR
(Map p101) This intriguing long, narrow, mostly brick-vaulted bazaar hides abandoned caravanserai, subterranean *chaykhanehs* (teahouses), historic mosques and just about every homeware and personal accoutrement you can think of. The eastern end is wilder.

Hosseiniyeh Mosque MOSQUE
(Map p101) This beautiful mosque dedicated to Hossein catches the setting sun perfectly from its western face. It's off Ferdosi St.

Masjed-e Jameh MOSQUE
(Friday Mosque; Map p101) Madraseh cells line the inner courtyard of this sizeable 1826

mosque, accessed through a spired portal on Imam St.

Seyyed Ibrahim Shrine ISLAMIC SHRINE
(Imamzadeh Seyid Ibrahim; Map p101) A delicate shrine to Seyyed Ibrahim set inside peaceful grounds right in the centre of the city.

Soravardi's Bust STATUE
(Map p101; Sa'di St) Philosopher Soravardi's bust can be seen on a library wall. The 1851 Baha'i massacres were perpetrated in lanes behind the wall.

Rakhatshor-Khaneh MUSEUM
(Laundry House, Zanjan Anthropological Museum.; Map p101; ☑ 024-3332 6020; Rakhatshorkhaneh Alley; IR150,000; ☺8am-5.30pm Tue-Sun) A traditional Qajar subterranean wash house full of female mannequins, in the clothing of the era, showing how it used to be done. There's also a small garden courtyard and an above-ground workshop where people make elf shoes.

Khanum Mosque MOSQUE
(Women's Mosque; Map p101) Hidden in a back lane, this cute mosque has a pair of pepper-grinder-like turrets. To find it, head north up Ferdosi St from Sabz Sq, then turn left into the car park and head up the laneway. A few more turns and you're there.

Rasul-Ullah Mosque MOSQUE
(Mosque of the Prophet Mohammad; Map p101) Grandly tiled, the mosque's dome and minaret appear best at dawn and dusk, when they're framed by the giant revolutionary 'organ-pipes' monument of Enqelab Sq.

Mir Baha-e Din Bridge BRIDGE
This attractive three-arched Qajar bridge over the Zanjan Rud river is visible west of the road to Bijar, southwest of the railway station.

👁 Around Zanjan

Katale Khor Caves CAVE
(Ghar Katalehkhor; ☑ 024-2482 2188; info@katalekhourcave.com; IR150,000; ☺8.30am-7.30pm, last entry 6pm; ℗) The extensive Katale Khor cave system, rated by locals as the best in western Iran, is 150km south of Zanjan, off the Soltaniyeh–Hamadan road near Garmab. Less touristed than the more famous Ali Sadr caves (p131), which it is thought to eventually join, Katale Khor has 3km open to the public and another 4km

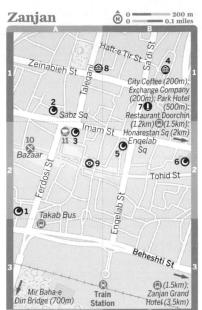

Zanjan

👁 Sights

available for experienced cavers. There are six recorded levels and a visit takes one to two hours. There's no public transport to the site; hire a taxi.

Colourful Mountains MOUNTAIN
(Aladargh) Similar to the 'painted deserts' of outback Australia and badlands America, but on a much larger scale, these incredibly coloured hills are visible to anyone

travelling between Tabriz and Zanjan in daylight. Banded in red, white and various shades of ochre, the fantastically alien-looking shapes loom up either side of Hwy 2 around the Zanjan 125km mark and extend for about 20km.

Behestan Castle   CASTLE

(Demon's Throne, Qal'eh Behestan; [P]) This wild-looking, incredibly eroded, cave-ridden mesa soars above (or, more accurately, falls into) the Qezel Owzan river in the ribbed and riven badlands 120km northwest of Zanjan. Reduced to a collection of tottering hollow hoodoos, the mesa's human-made caves were part of a Sassanid-era fortress. You'll need a full day's car hire from Zanjan to explore the area properly. The closest town is Mahneshan, 14km to the north.

🛏 Sleeping

Amir Kabir Hotel   HOSTEL $

(Map p101; 🖉 024-3332 4922; Sabz Sq, Imam St; s/d/tr IR600,000/950,000/1,350,000; ❄ 🛜) Centrally located cheapie with basic rooms (some with bathrooms).

Park Hotel   HOTEL $$

(🖉 024-3333 3533; www.parkhotel-zanjan.com; Imam St; s/tw/tr US$50/70/90; ❄ 🛜) Light, comfortable and overpriced rooms here are complemented by friendly, English-speaking staff and a good breakfast spread. The restaurant has quality meals (IR450,000), real coffee and a 25% surcharge. The wifi works downstairs and in the hallways, but not in the rooms. It's probably the best compromise you'll get in terms of comfort, location and price.

Zanjan Grand Hotel   HOTEL $$$

(Hotel Bozorg Zanjan; 🖉 024-3378 8190; http://zanjangrandhotel.com; Basij Sq; s/tw/ste US$75/115/150; [P]❄🛜) At the edge of the city by a busy roundabout, Zanjan's top option has stylishly spacious business-standard rooms with bathrooms you could sleep in. Staff try hard to please, but the noisy location is inconvenient if you're not driving.

🍴 Eating

Haji Dadash   IRANIAN $

(Map p101; 🖉 024-3322 2020; meals from IR50,000; ⊘10am-11pm) This family-oriented tea cavern overflows with character, especially in its carpet-draped front cellar. The good *dizi sangi* (stew of lamb, chickpeas and potato) comes with a plate of fresh

herbs to fine-tune the flavour, but tea and *qalyan* for four costs a hefty IR280,000. Enter opposite the portal of Mirza Mehdi mosque within the main bazaar.

★ Restaurant Doorchin   MODERN IRANIAN $$

(🖉024-3336 2783; Azardi Sq, Imam St; meals IR225,000) Nice and airy, the Doorchin has a delicious modern take on Iranian favourites. The soup is elegantly spiced, the yogurt fresh and piquant, and the service friendly. Try the *khoresht gheymeh* (lamb stew with yellow split peas and preserved lemon).

Restaurant Golrizan   IRANIAN $$

(🖉 024-3377 9262; Imam St; meals IR270,000; 🖢) Near Honarestan Sq, the family-oriented Golrizan offers an extensive salad bar to complement all your Iranian favourites. Staff are friendly and there's not a surcharge in sight.

🍷 Drinking & Nightlife

City Coffee   CAFE

(Imam St; ⊘noon-10pm Sat-Thu) Espresso-lover's nirvana.

Eloğlu Teahouse   TEAHOUSE

(Map p101; Ferdosi St; chai/qalyan IR20,000/40,000; ⊘8am-9.30pm) Old-school subterranean teahouse. Look for chai signs and a down staircase not far from the corner of Imam St.

ℹ Information

Exchange Company (🖉 024-3333 8682; unit 8, basement, Noor Bldg, Imam St; ⊘11am-11pm Sat-Thu) If you can get past the dude out the front with the machine gun, these guys are in the basement of the Noor shopping centre.

Miras Farhangi (Cultural Heritage, Handicraft & Tourism Organization; 🖉 024-3378 5010; www.miraszanjan.ir; Honarestan, Imam St; ⊘8am-4pm) You might be able to score a free city map and some brochures here.

ℹ Getting There & Away

Buses to Esfahan (IR350,000, 6.30pm), Rasht (IR250,000, 8.30am) and Tehran (IR250,000, frequent) use the big, empty **terminal**, five minutes' walk south of Shilat Sq.

Savaris and some buses for Tehran, Qazvin and Tabriz pick up at the Behesti (Khayyam)/Ferdosi St junction. If arriving on a Tehran–Tabriz bus that's bypassing Zanjan on the motorway, ask to get off at the tollgate just before the Bijar junction (NOT at the 'Zanjan' exit, which is 10km further east). There are plenty of waiting taxis (IR100,000), which are a better option than legging it 4km into town.

Savaris (IR30,000) and occasional minibuses (IR20,000) to Soltaniyeh leave from Honarestan Sq.

The direct **bus** (Map p101; ☑ 0914 482 4011) to Takab (IR120,000, 3½ hours) leaves at 10.30am daily from the small yard on Behesti St near the corner of Ferdosi St and goes via Qam Cheqay. You can hire savaris outside for the run from Takab to the Tahkt-e Soleiman ruins.

The **train station** is beyond a Dali-esque gateway of winged wheels. The best-timed departures for Tehran (IR128,000 to IR200,000, four hours) via Qazvin (two hours) are at 6.20am and 8.06am, though there are several afternoon trains as well. Buy tickets the day before for the 8.57pm and 10.33pm sleepers to Tabriz (IR375,000, eight hours) via Maraqeh (five hours).

🛈 Getting Around

Useful shuttle taxis run from Enqelab Sq to Honarestan Sq, passing near the bus terminal. Others go from Sabz Sq to Esteqlal Sq.

Soltaniyeh سلطانیه

☑ 024 / POPULATION 6000 / ELEVATION 1803M

Soltaniyeh ('Town of the Sultans') was purpose built by the Ilkhanid Mongols as their Persian capital from 1302. But less than a century later, in 1384, it was largely destroyed by Mongol invader Tamerlane. Today, the tiny town hosts day-tripping tourists eager to glimpse the Unesco-listed **Oljeitu Mausoleum** (Gonbad-e Soltaniyeh; ☑ 024-3582 2850; http://soltaniyeh.ir; IR200,000; ⊙8am-5pm), rising dramatically 48m above the surrounding dusty archaeological digs and crumbling city walls. This eight-towered octagonal building, built for a Mongol sultan, supports a brilliant turquoise-brick dome, one of the world's largest. The interior is full of scaffolding, but spiral stairs lead up through thick walls to airy terraces with exceptional views, beautiful vaulted ceilings and fine mosaics.

Oljeitu was a Mongol ruler who, after dabbling in various religions, adopted the Shia name Mohammed Khodabandeh. He had planned to rehouse in his mausoleum the remains of Imam Ali, son-in-law of the Prophet Mohammed. That would have made the mausoleum Shiite Islam's holiest pilgrimage site outside Mecca (instead of Najaf, Iraq). However, Oljeitu couldn't persuade the Najaf ulema (religious leaders) to give him Ali's relics, and eventually he was buried here himself in 1317.

Around the main site also look for the **Chalapi Oghli Mausoleum** (Sheikh Boraq; Hamadan Hwy; ⊙8am-5pm) FREE an unadorned Ilkhanid Mongol–period brick shrine to Sufi mystic Sheikh Boraq, surrounded by the courtyard of a *khanqah* (dervish monastery); and the turquoise-topped tomb of **Mullah Hasan Kashi** FREE, a 14th-century mystic whose recasting of Islam's historical sagas as Persian-language poetic epics unwittingly had a vast influence over Shia Islam's future direction.

Near the village of Vier (Viyar) lies **Dashkasan Temple** (Dragon Temple, Stone Carved Temple; IR150,000; ⊙8am-5pm), a curious collection of 'stone quarry' inscriptions, the most renowned being those of two 3.5m facing dragons. Take a taxi from Soltaniyeh (IR200,000 return) to see them.

🛈 Getting There & Away

Soltaniyeh is 5km south of the old Zanjan–Qazvin road. It's easily visited as a half-day trip from Zanjan's Honarestan Sq: direct savaris (IR30,000, 30 minutes) and irregular minibuses (IR20,000, 40 minutes) drop you an obvious 10-minute stroll north of Oljeitu Mausoleum.

It's possible to combine Soltaniyeh with a visit to **Katale Khor Caves** (p101), 150km south of Zanjan, and then continue on to Hamedan (or return to Zanjan) in one long day. Private taxis from Zanjan start at around US$80 return, though you could try stringing savaris together, at least as far as Ghydar.

Takab تکاب

☑ 044 / POPULATION 48,000 / ELEVATION 1838M

Nestled high up among rolling hills with air untainted by motorway diesel, this modest market town makes a pleasant base to explore some interesting sights in the surrounding spectacular countryside. The main drags are Imam Khomeini St, running northwest to southwest, and Enghelab St, bisecting the town southwest to northwest.

⊙ Sights

Takht-e Soleiman Ruins   HISTORIC SITE
(Throne of Solomon; ☑ 044-4545 3311; IR200,000; ⊙8am-sunset) Sitting in a lonely bowl of mountains, ringed by 1500-year-old walls, these Unesco-listed ruins are one

of the most memorable sights of western Iran. In the 3rd century the state religion of Sassanian Persia was Zoroastrianism, and Takht-e Soleiman (then called Azergoshnasb) was its spiritual centre. Today only fragments remain: you shouldn't expect Persepolis-style carvings. Nonetheless, the site's sheer age and magnificent setting are attractions enough. Taxis (US$18 return including waiting time) can be negotiated in Takab's Ghalam Sq.

The site was perfect. Zoroastrianism had by this stage incorporated many magi-inspired elements, including the veneration of earth, wind (plenty here), water and fire. Water (albeit undrinkably poisonous) was provided in abundance by the limpidly beautiful, 'bottomless' **crater lake** that still forms the centre of the site. This pours forth 90L per second and would have been channelled through an Anahita-style water temple. Fire was provided thanks to a natural volcanic gas channelled through ceramic pipes to sustain an 'eternal flame' in the *ateshkadeh* (fire temple).

Takht-e Soleiman's name isn't based on real historical links to the Old Testament King Solomon, but was a cunning 7th-century invention by the temple's Persian guardians in the face of the Arab invasion. Realising Islam's reverence for biblical prophets, they fabricated a tale of Solomon's one-time residence here to avert the site's certain destruction. The ruse worked, the complex survived and the name stuck.

In the 13th century Takht-e Soleiman became a summer retreat for the Mongol Ilkhanid khans. The remnants of their hunting palace are now covered with a discordant modern roof forming a storeroom (often locked) for amphorae, unlabelled column fragments, photos and a couple of ceramic sections of those ancient gas pipes.

A guide is often available at the site gate, and can help you make sense of all the piles of stone if you share enough language. Alternatively, navigate on your own using a glossy bilingual Farsi and English map-brochure (US$1), which is sold at the ticket booth but not displayed – ask.

Takht-e Soleiman is 2km from Nosratabad. Archaeologists believe that beneath that mud-and-haystack village is the site of Shiz, once a Nestorian-Christian centre of Greco-Persian learning. Savaris and minibuses run sporadically to the village, but traffic is often very thin, making hitchhiking beyond it difficult. It's worth checking to see whether a rumoured guest house has opened in Nosratabad.

Karaftu Caves CAVE

(غار كرفتو; IR150,000) Set in the side of a large cliff, 42km from Takab in neighbouring Kordestan, this mixture of natural and human-made caverns was used for habitation from early Sassanid times. In one room, an ancient Greek inscription references Hercules, while other more modern scrawls pay homage to Reza and Hossein, who were both 'here'. The drive from Takab is particularly scenic. There's no public transport to the caves; a taxi will cost around US$18 return including waiting time. Ask around Takab's bazaar.

Zendan-e Soleiman MOUNTAIN

This dramatic 97m conical peak dominates the valley landscape for miles around. If you're reasonably fit, climbing to the crater's edge should take less than 15 minutes. The path is muddy but obvious, zigzagging up from the Takab road about 4km south of the main Takht-e Soleiman ruins (p103).

Tours

Ayob Jahani TOURS

(0935 726 8851) Ayob speaks great English and is a font of local knowledge. He knows all the attractions, and how to get there and be back in time for a departing bus. You'll usually find him at the Hotel Ranji.

Sleeping

Hotel Ranji HOTEL $

(044-4552 3179; ayobjahani_90@yahoo.com; Englelab St N; d IR1,340,000;) Takab's only decent hotel has friendly staff, adequate rooms, working wi-fi, hot water and a reasonable restaurant (meals around IR240,000). Effusive, knowledgeable Ayob speaks excellent English and can arrange transport to the Takht-e Soleiman ruins and the Karaftu Caves (each US$20 return). The hotel's on top of the hill; the direct bus from Zanjan will drop you at its door.

Getting There & Away

Buses and minibuses leave from the **terminal** (Resalt Sq) at the northeastern edge of town. There's a 4am direct bus to Zanjan (IR120,000, 3½ hours, 0914 487 4011) via Qom Cheqay, which departs Zanjan at 10.30am for the return. The 10am Tehran bus (IR400,000, eight hours) goes via Bijar and drops off outside

ℹ VISITING TAKHT-E SOLEIMAN

An interesting, if expensive, way to visit the **Takht-e Soleiman ruins** (p103) is by chartering a taxi from Zanjan (US$80 for a full day with stops) and asking to be dropped off in Takab or Bijar. Once past the mining town of Dandy, the route passes some truly timeless villages. **Shikhlar**, 20km from Dandy, is dramatically backed by the pyramidal peak of **Tozludagh** (Dusty Mountain). **Qaravolkhana**, 20km further (10km before Takht-e Soleiman), has particularly picturesque mud-brick homes rising between spindly trees and a green, igloo-shaped shrine at its southern end. Rolling grasslands offer great hikes and the possible ascent of **Mt Belqeis**, topped by the fragmentary ruins of a Sassanid line-of-sight fortress.

A cheaper option is to take the direct Zanjan–Takab bus (10.30am), which uses the Qam Cheqay road to arrive in Takab in time to hire a taxi to Takht-e Soleiman ($18 return).

Zanjan (IR150,000, four hours) and Qazvin (IR250,000, six hours).

There are hourly morning minibuses to Bijar (for Sanandaj) and Shahin Dezh (for Miyando'ab and points further north). Savaris for Bijar (IR30,000, one hour) and Shahin Dezh (IR40,000, 1¼ hours) leave from opposite ends of Imam Khomeini St.

Rasht رامسر

🎵 013 / POPULATION 680,000 / ELEVATION 4M

Sophisticated Rasht, capital of Gilan province, has long been a weekend escape for Tehranis looking to sample the famous local cuisine (p108) and hoping for some pluvial action – it's the largest, and wettest, town in the Shomal region. Travellers use it as a base to explore the amazing Qal'eh Rudkhan and photogenic Masulch, but if they linger they'll discover a vibrancy among its young population that's quite infectious.

The rapidly expanding town has embarked on a bold urban-planning experiment, the first in Iran, called 'My Rasht': the streets surrounding Shohoda Sq have been blocked off, creating an amazing people-filled space that has reinvigorated the city centre. Small electric vehicles transfer the less agile between the road ends. Eventually the pedestrian malls will stretch 7km.

Rasht has had extended periods of independence, and the lispy local Gilaki dialect remains noticeably distinct from Farsi – its reversed adjective-noun order causes other Iranians much amusement.

History

Rasht (previously Resht) developed in the 14th century, but the population was massacred in 1668 by the forces of Cossack brigand Stepan 'Stenka' Razin, who also sank Persia's entire Caspian navy. The Russians, a constant in the region thereafter, were back in 1723 clearing space in the then-impenetrable forest to allow Resht's growth. In 1899 a Russian company cut the road to Qazvin, diminishing Gilan's isolation from the rest of Iran. By WWI the town boasted 60,000 inhabitants and four international consulates.

From 1917 Rasht was the centre of Kuchuk Khan's Jangali ('Forest') Movement, an Islamic, Robin Hood–style rebellion. Among its grievances with collapsing Qajar Iran was the shah's perceived sell-out to oil-hungry Britain. Courting the Bolsheviks who'd just taken control of Russia, Kuchuk Khan joined forces with communist agitators and, on 4 June 1920, set up Gilan as the 'Soviet Socialist Republic of Iran'. However, radical leftists and land-owning Muslim nationalists made very prickly bedfellows. Once Kuchuk Khan had ejected the infidel communists from his 'government', his Russian backers slipped away, leaving Gilan prey to the efficient new regime of Reza Khan (later Shah Reza Pahlavi), who'd taken over Persia in a February 1921 coup. Reza Khan dealt first with temporarily independent Tabriz/Azerbaijan, and then he attacked Gilan. Most of Rasht's pretty wooden houses were burnt and Kuchuk Khan was executed – his severed head was brought to Tehran for public display.

These days any enemy of the Pahlavis has become a friend of the current Islamic republic. Thus Kuchuk Khan has ridden back into favour on many a horseback statue across Gilan.

Rasht

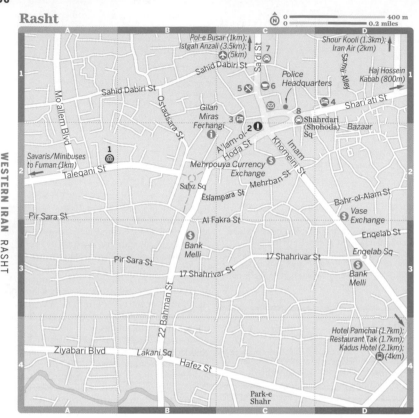

Sights

Gilan Rural Heritage Museum MUSEUM
(☎013-3369 0970; http://gecomuseum.com;
Fuman-Saravan Rd; IR150,000; ⊙9am-6pm;
P♿) Many traditional Gilani cottages
have been reassembled in the grounds
of this fascinating open-air museum that
strives to represent the different cultural
and architectural areas of Gilan. On 45
hectares within the Saravan Forest Park,
18km south of Rasht (2km off the Qazvin
highway), seven full villages have so far
been reconstructed. Events showcasing
past traditions are held during the year.
You can tuck into some traditions yourself
at the museum's cafe.

Shahrdari MONUMENT
(Map p106; Municipality Bldg, Shahrdari Sq)
Rasht's most identifiable landmark sits at
the western end of the vast, central Shohoda Sq. The Shahrdari's colonial style is

tempered by a token mini dome topping
a severe block-like clock tower. The whole
area is floodlit at night and the square is a
popular people-watching viewpoint.

Rasht Museum MUSEUM
(Map p106; Taleqani St; IR80,000; ⊙8am-
5.30pm Tue-Sun, 9am-1pm Fri) While small,
this museum is well presented in a 1930s
house. Its mannequin displays illustrate
the Gilaki lifestyle, amid a selection of
3000-year-old terracotta *riton* drinking
horns in the shape of bulls, rams and deer.
It was believed that supping from such vessels endowed the drinker with the powers
and skills of the animal depicted.

Tours

Fatimeh Norouzi TOURS
(☎0911 833 0142; faatima_ice@hotmail.com; full
day with/without car $150/80) Fatima speaks
good English and is very knowledgeable

Rasht

about the Gilan area, including Masuleh. She can also help with accommodation.

Hassan Mohit   OUTDOORS
(☑ 0911 136 7796; www.aryantour.com; daily with/ without car US$150/80) Affable, knowledgeable, English-speaking Hassan is a good choice for a driver-guide. He can also provide accommodation and meals at his homestay, Titi ('blossom') Cottage, in the semi-rural village of Ebrahim Sara, 25km east of Rasht.

🛏 Sleeping

There are many accommodation options, but occupancy is high in the peak summer season (May to September), when overwhelming humidity makes air-con virtually essential. Most of the inner cheaper hotels are signposted in English from the pedestrian mall. More expensive rooms are found in the concrete monoliths out by the ring road to the south. There's also a campground northeast of town.

Mehmanpazir Kenareh   HOSTEL $
(Map p106; ☑ 013-3322 2412; Ferdosi Alley, off Shari'ati St; s/tw/tr without bathroom IR400,000/600,000/750,000; 🛜) The most appealing of the central cheapies, with clean, basic rooms and friendly staff who speak no English. There's no breakfast, but the wi-fi works. It's opposite the bazaar; there's an English sign pointing the way.

Hotel Ordibehesht   HOTEL $$
(Map p106; ☑ 013-3322 9210; d IR1,290,000; P ❄) The nicest central option, set back

from Shohoda Sq, the Ordibehesht has comfortable, quiet, clean rooms, proper hot water and staff who are friendly and helpful. Breakfast is extra.

Hotel Pamchal   HOTEL $$
(☑ 013-3366 3822; Mosalla Sq; d/ste US$62/80; ❄) The large, comfy rooms, clean linen and friendly smiles are nice, but the hotel's 3.5km down Imam Khomeini St from the centre, by the ring road.

Kadus Hotel   HOTEL $$$
(☑ 013-3336 5075; www.kadus-hotel.ir; Azadi Blvd; d/tr IR3,750,000/4,700,000; P ❄ 🛜 ☒) Very nice rooms are well appointed, and the management speaks good English, but it's hard to justify the price, especially so far from the action.

🍴 Eating

There are stalls around the bazaar selling desserts, nuts and snacks. Many cheap kabab barbecues appear at night on Imam Khomeini St and Toshiba Sq. Most of the trendy cafes and restaurants are in blinged-up Golsar, 2.5km north of Shohoda Sq.

★**Kourosh**   IRANIAN $$
(Map p106; ☑ 013-3322 8299; Gilantur Lane; meals IR380,000; ⊙ 11am-4pm & 7.30-11pm) The easiest place to sample the delights of Gilani cuisine is the centrally located Kourosh. Start with the murky-looking but very tasty *zeitun parvardeh* (olives in walnut paste) and share some *mirza ghasemi* (dip-like pureed charcoal eggplant with garlic and tomato) before hoeing into a *torche kebab* (lamb and/or chicken coated in a sour marinade). Then waddle home.

Haj Hossein Kabab   IRANIAN $$
(☑ 013-3333 2860; Keivani St; meals from IR220,000) Don't even think about ordering the stew: you come here to go to kabab heaven via its signature *torche* (sour) kabab. (Just eat salad for a week afterwards.) It's in a laneway off Shariati St to the right just before you cross the river.

Shour Kooli   IRANIAN $$
(☑ 013-3311 7871; cnr 78th St & Golsar Blvd, Golsar; ⊙ noon-4pm & 7.30pm-midnight Sat-Thu, to 4pm Fri) A local Golsar favourite, and a good place to sample Gilani cuisine, Shour Kooli specialises in sour stews and fish.

WESTERN IRAN RASHT

LOCAL KNOWLEDGE

GILAN CUISINE

The Caspian Sea produces 95% of the world's caviar. But don't count on seeing any. Iran's caviar is virtually all for export. In fact, Gilan's cuisine largely ignores the sea and focusses on the local wealth of fruit, nuts, olives and vegetables. Typical dishes are packed with garlic and turmeric, which can be rather shocking for the sensitive taste buds of central Iranian tourists. *Sirabi* is essentially fried garlic leaves with egg, *shami Rashti* are deep-fried lentil-and-meat patties, *baghilah qotoq* are dill-and-garlic-flavoured broad beans, while *anarbij* (meatballs in walnut and pomegranate sauce) are a variant of *fesenjun* (chicken with walnuts). *Torche* (sour) kabab is another favourite. Easier to find than any of the above is *mirza ghasemi*, a vegetarian marvel of mashed aubergine, squash, garlic and egg. Although often listed as a starter, it makes a delicious meal when served with rice or bread.

Restaurant Tak IRANIAN **$$**
(☑ 013-3333 2147; Azadi Blvd, Manzarieh; meals from IR280,000; ⊘ 11.30am-4pm & 7-10.30pm) Three floors of smart Gilani dining present such options as *torshe tareh* (a citrusy dish of local sorrel and egg) and amazing oven-baked sardines.

Pizza Pizza PIZZA **$$**
(Gilan Blvd, at 149th St, Golsar; pizzas from IR250,000; ⊘ 6.30pm-midnight; 🖬) This family-friendly establishment is unusual for its female waitstaff and children's play area. The pizzas are typically Iranian style, with lots of cheese. Order downstairs; the menu is in English. It's 3km north of Shohoda Sq.

Razeghi IRANIAN **$$$**
(☑ 013-3372 3322; 123 St, cnr Sameyeh, Golsar; meals from IR350,000) At the Paris end of Golsar, this swanky diner is a good place to sample Gilani dishes, fish in particular. There's a live piano player, so go ahead and dress up.

🍷 Drinking & Nightlife

Cafe Negative CAFE
(Map p106; upstairs, Sa'di St Mall; coffee IR100,000; ⊘ noon-midnight) In this funkytown smoke haze women can light up and not get hassled. Negative also does cakes and good, strong coffee.

Babak CAFE
(Golsar Ave, at 102nd St, Golsar; coffee from IR100,000; ⊘ 10am-midnight) A stylish green, cream and chrome coffee bar serving sundaes and shakes. It's 2km north of Shohoda Sq.

ℹ️ Information

MONEY
Mehrpouya Currency Exchange (Map p106; ☑ 0939 131 0026; Sa'di Alley; ⊘ 9am-8pm

Sat-Wed, to 1pm Thu) In an alley off pedestrian Imam near Shohoda Sq.
Vase Exchange (Map p106; ☑ 013-3324 0597; 1st fl, Moravid Close; ⊘ 9.30am-8pm Sat-Wed, to 1.30pm Thu) Free chockies while you change money. Good rates.

Bank Melli has branches on **22 Bahman St** (Map p106) and **17 Shahrivar St** (Map p106) that are mostly useful for deposits.

If you need to change money and the exchange offices are closed, head for the jewellery section of the bazaar and ask around.

POST
There's a **central post office** (Map p106) on Shohoda Sq, but for parcel service use the main post office in Golsar, on Bentolhoda St just off Golsar Ave.

TOURIST INFORMATION
Gilan Miras Ferhangi (Map p106; ☑ 013-3775 4664; Ehtesab Alley, off Sabz Sq; ⊘ 8am-2pm Sat-Thu) A historic brick building and attractive garden host the tourist-information office.

VISA EXTENSIONS
Police Headquarters (Map p106; ☑ 013-218 3481; room 8, 1st fl, Shohada Sq; ⊘ 8am-1.30pm Sat-Thu) To extend your visa, apply before 10am. Previously you had to deposit IR375,000 to the specified Bank Melli branch (either **22 Bahman St** or **17 Shahrivar St**), return with the receipt and pay a further US$1 to a uniformed officer. However, you may now be requested to pay up front with an Iranian credit card, in which case you will need to enlist an obliging Iranian to help you.

ℹ️ Getting There & Away

AIR
Mashhad IR2,080,000, at least one daily flight on **Caspian** (www.caspian.aero), **Iran Air** (☑ 013-3311 2125; Golsar Ave, nr 97th St;

⊙7.30am-7pm Sat-Thu, 9am-1pm Fri), **Taban** (☑061-3338 6269; http://taban.aero/en) or **Kish** (http://en.kishairlines.ir/).

Tehran IR1,490,000, daily flights on Iran Air and **Iran Aseman** (☑013-3375 6353; Rasht airport).

Ahvaz IR2,500,000, several flights weekly on **Naft** (☑021-4469 1083; www.naftairline.com).

Shiraz (IR2,5000,000, Tuesday, Thursday and Saturday) on Iran Aseman.

Bandar Abbas (IR2,920,000, Tuesday, Friday and Sunday) on Iran Aseman.

BUS, MINIBUS & SAVARI

The main bus **terminal** is 2km south of 'Toshiba' (Mosallah) Sq, near Gil Sq. Several bus companies have handy central booking offices.

Savaris to Tehran leave from five points along Imam Khomeini St. Informal Tehran and Qazvin savaris pick up at Toshiba and Gil Sqs, southeast of the city centre.

Savaris to Bandar-e Anzali (Map p106) The Anzali touts stand at the corner of Nehest St (from the Ordibehest Hotel) and Shahrdari Sq, then lead you to the savari outside the pedestrian precinct.

Many buses to Ardabil (IR300,000-450,000, five hours) via Astara start from Tehran and pick up at **Istgah Anzali** (Valiasr Sq).

Savaris to Astara (IR210,000, 2½ hours), Asalem and Khal Khal (IR150,000, two hours) start at **Pol-e Busar**, just over the bridge on Sa'di St, an easy 15-minute walk from Shohoda Sq.

For Fuman, and thence Masuleh, savaris/minibuses (IR60,000/40,000) depart from Yakhsazi Sq (Shohaday Gomnam Sq).

Informal Lahijan savaris pick up on **Shari'ati St** (Map p106), but the official Lahijan terminal is 500m east of Janbazan Sq, hidden opposite a Saipa showroom. Minibus/savari fares to Lahijan are IR50,000/30,000, to Chalus IR150,000/60,000; durations vary widely according to traffic conditions.

🛈 Getting Around

With the centre of town now blocked off, traffic grinds to a halt daily on the outer roads. Shuttle taxis still run on the main routes but terminate at the pedestrian-precinct barriers. Free electric buses carry the less mobile around the central pedestrian precinct.

Many shuttle-taxi routes run the length of Imam Khomeini St from Shohada Sq, or along Shohada St to the Lahijan terminal. Northbound, many shuttle taxis go up Sa'di St via Shahid Ansari Sq, where some swing left up to **Golsar** (Map p106) and others continue to Valiasr Sq (Istgah Anzali). These return southbound down Takhti St.

Around Rasht

Lahijan لاهیجان

☑014 / POPULATION 83,000 / ELEVATION 5M

Famed for its tea, Lahijan is one of Gilan's oldest towns, with a tree-lined charm to its main streets and some interesting roundabout statues.

Several minor sights, including the **Masjed-e Jameh** (Friday Mosque), pierced by a blue-tipped brick minaret, and the Qajar-era **Akbariyeh Mosque** (4th West Kashef Alley) with a two-storey octagonal tower, are found around Vahdat Sq. **Chahar Padeshah Mosque** (Four Kings; Vahdat Sq) is rumoured to be the resting place of four Gilani kings, although its famous carved wooden doors are now on display in Tehran's National Museum.

Visible from the Ramsar motorway, 2.5km from Lahijan's Golestan Sq, is the beautiful **Sheikh Zahed Mausoleum** (Boq'eh Sheikh Zahed Gilani; admission by donation). Dedicated to a Sufi mystic, Sheikh Zahed Gilani (1236–1301), the mausoleum,

BUSES FROM RASHT

DESTINATION	FARE (IR, VIP/ MAHMOOLY)	DURATION (HR)	DEPARTURES
Ahvaz	545,000	15	11am, 2.30pm
Esfahan	420,000	9	6pm
Gorgan	380,000/275,000	8	hourly 7am-2pm & 7-10pm
Hamadan	350,000	7	9am, 11am, 6pm
Mashhad	750,000/600,000	16	2.30pm
Tabriz	550,000	9	4-8pm
Tehran	300,000-450,000	4	frequent

with its distinctive blue, pyramidal roof, is an important pilgrimage site.

The easternmost 800m of Kashef St climbs **Sheitan Kuh** (Satan's Mountain), a tree-covered ridge fringed with tea gardens. It's crowded on Friday with local tourists enjoying fine views over Lahijan's lake. The **telecabine** (IR200,000; ☺9am–dusk) here takes you across to another, slightly higher hill.

Near the village of Soustan (Sistan), 4km southeast of Lahijan, a **lagoon** is an important habitat for migratory birds, and is most attractive in the late-afternoon light, when the nearby peaks are mirrored in its waters.

Of several attractive villages in the appealing semi-alpine mountain hinterland, the best known is **Deilaman**, 60km away.

🛏 Sleeping & Eating

Tourist Inn   HOTEL $$
(Mehmansara Jahangardi; 📞013-4223 3051; www.ittic.com; off Sepah Sq; tw US$45; 🅿 ✳ 🛜) Comfortable, well-equipped rooms with a perfect central location and a restaurant that offers good food and a lovely ambience right on the lake.

Arash Hotel   HOTEL $$
(📞013-4234 3383; http://arashhotel.com/; Shohoda Sq; tw IR1,100,000, 1-/2-bed apt IR2,150,000/2,870,000; 🅿🛜) Comfortable twin rooms and great-value, fully kitted-out apartments are offered at the humble Arash, just north of Shohoda Sq. Walk up Shohoda St north from the square, then take the next right.

PERSIAN TEA

Gilan province produces 90% of Iran's tea. The deep-green manicured tea bushes are now so emblematic that it's hard to believe they were introduced only a century ago. In fact, tea didn't reach Persia until the 17th century, when it became an expensive luxury. Qajar-period attempts to grow the stuff were unsuccessful until Kashef-ol-Saltaneh, an Iranian consul in India, managed to learn the secret art. Around 1900 he slipped home to Lahijan with some 4000 tea plants and the rest is history. Strangely, it's not that easy to find a glass of the fair Persian brew either: most of the *chay* in cafes and restaurants (and even in souvenir shops) is cheaper black leaves from Ceylon.

Mahtab   IRANIAN $$
(Imam St; meals from IR250,000; ☺noon–4.30pm & 7.30-11pm) Great traditional Iranian restaurant doing Gilani cuisine. Try the fish or the wonderfully sour *torche* kabab. Just east of Golestan Sq, it's the place with the big sculpture of a jar of roses.

❶ Getting There & Away

Savaris from Rasht (IR40,000, 45 minutes) arrive at Vahdat Sq and leave (unofficially) from near Shohoda Sq. Minibuses (IR20,000) and official savaris use Entezam Sq, about 1.5km further west. For Ramsar and Chalus, transport leaves from near Basij Sq, a junction 200m northeast of the Tourist Inn.

Masuleh   ماسوله

📷 013 / POPULATION 850 / ELEVATION 1051M

At least a millennium old, Masuleh is one of Iran's most famous villages – and hence one of its most touristed. Picture-postcard perfect, the earth-coloured houses are stacked photogenically on top of one another like giant Lego blocks, clinging to a mountainside so steep that the roof of one house forms the pathway for the next. In summer, local and foreign tourists swarm like ants across the village's rooftops and through its narrow passageways. To avoid the coach-tour hordes, stay overnight, hike the surrounding mountains, or visit in winter when few others come. Note that there is an IR30,0000 'tax' to enter the village.

🛏 Sleeping & Eating

Almost every villager rents out a room (IR700,000–1,000,000), and quality can vary dramatically. Look around and bargain hard, as you may not even be dealing with the owner. Prices are cheaper midweek.

Abbas Bamdad   APARTMENT $
(📞0911 332 5227; ste weekday/weekend IR700,000/900,000) These renovated suites are worth the climb, with Western bathrooms and views to die for. It's hard to find, so ring first.

Mehran Hotel   HOTEL $
(Mehran Suites; 📞013-2757 2096; apt IR800,000) The Mehran has definitely seen better days, and if you like everything to work, then turn back now. But the rooms are clean, with kitchenettes (though not necessarily hot water), up to six beds, and terraces with excellent village views. The owner is friendly and speaks good English.

DON'T MISS

QAL'EH RUDKHAN

The incredible Seljuk-era walled fortress of **Qal'eh Rudkhan** (قلعه رودخان; village/fortress IR40,000/150,000; ⊙8am-5pm; P) defends a steep, wooded spur of the Alborz Mountains some 50km south of Rasht and makes a lovely day trip, especially when coupled with a visit to nearby Masuleh. From spring to autumn, the winding, vertiginous ascent through lush forests, moss-clad streams and evenly spaced teahouses should take about an hour. Start early in peak season, as the fortress is popular with locals and foreigners alike.

In winter the views of the snow-capped towers and intact ramparts are even more stunning, but be aware that the steep, icy steps can turn quite treacherous, so take your time. When passing through Fuman on the way, look out for its signature cookie, *klucheh fuman*, filled with walnut paste, available hot from bakeries all over town.

Expect to pay from $US50 for a private taxi return from Rasht (including waiting time). By savari, head first to Fuman (IR60,000), cross town to where the Masuleh and Qal'eh Rudkhan roads fork, then grab another savari (IR60,000, 20 minutes) to Qal'eh Rudhkan village; the final 7km to the Qal'eh Daneh trailhead will cost another IR60,000. Don't leave your return too late as you may get stuck in Fuman.

There's no breakfast. Head towards the back of the village.

Mehmanpazir Navid HOTEL **$$**
(☑0936 168 1977, 0911 239 6459; apt from IR1,250,000) This place has surprisingly sizeable studio apartments with fold-out couches and kitchenette.

Khaneh Mo'allem Restaurant IRANIAN **$$**
(☑013-2757 2122; meals from IR200,000; ⊙12.30-3.30pm & 7.30-9.30pm) On sunny days, the nicest places for *mirza ghasemi* (dip-like pureed charcoal eggplant with garlic and tomato) or *torche* kabab (lamb and/or chicken coated in a sour marinade) are the terraces here.

ⓘ Transport

From Rasht, head first to Fuman (savari IR60,000), then cross town to the Masuleh road where minibuses/savaris (IR22,000/37,000, 45 minutes) depart regularly in summer, less often in winter. A private **taxi** (half-/full-day hire US$40/80) charter from Rasht could include a side trip to **Qal'eh Rudkhan fortress**.

Ramsar رامسر

☑011 / POPULATION 34,500 / ELEVATION -15M

Possibly the most scenic spot on the Caspian coast and a nice place to kick back for a few days, Ramsar is where the jungle-clad lower ridges of the snow-topped Alborz tumble into the sea. It's a verdant, photogenic area, lush with orange groves, and there are walking trails into the nearby hills.

The **Ramsar Telecabine** (www.telecabinramsar.com; IR300,000; 🚡) provides a short, steep ride up the side of a hill and over the highway, amusement parks and orange groves. There are incredible views of the Caspian, and the top beckons with lookouts, cafes and walking trails.

Ramsar Palace Museum (☑011-5522 5374; Rajaei St; IR150,000; ⊙8am-6pm) is an ornately furnished 1937 building, set in a walled garden, that was once the summer palace of Reza Shah. Gilded, over-the-top rooms mix guillotine-era French furniture with distinctly Persian motifs of cheetahs and fine carpets. This is where the Ramsar Convention, an international treaty for the protection and conservation of the world's wetlands, was signed in 1971.

☞ Tours

Mr Mahdi TOURS
(☑0911 144 1442; infl20290@gmail.com) A safe, reliable driver-guide with very good English, Mr Mahdi knows Mazandaran and Gilan provinces really well.

🛏 Sleeping

★ **Gileboom Eco Lodge** GUESTHOUSE **$$**
(☑0919 639 6185; www.gileboom.ir; 69 Sand Rd, Ghasemabad; B&B without bathroom per person IR750,000; �📶🍽) 🌱 Brainchild of young Tehrani adventurers, this lodge nestled in the verdant Ramsar hinterland provides cultural, musical, gastronomic and adventure activities for all ages. Run on sound environmental principles, Gileboom offers

WORTH A TRIP

JAVAHERDEH

High in the hills above Ramsar lies the picturesque mountain village of **Javaherdeh** (جواهرده) which makes for a pleasant day trip or a good base for further exploration. The views are stunning, and, at around 2000m, the air is deliciously cool in summer. It's frozen but quite clear the rest of the time: in winter you'll need crampons just to traverse the vertiginous main street.

Apart from the two decent hotels – **Motel Javaher** (Jewel Motel; ☑ 011-5533 2031; www.en.ramsarjavaherhotel.ir; cabins from IR1,200,000; ℗ ⊛) and **Hotel Mahtab** (Moonlight Hotel; ☑ 011-5533 4000; tw/tr IR1,300,000/1,600,00; ℗ ⊛) – there are usually homestays available, but check in Ramsar before coming up. Your taxi driver should be able to find one. There's food at the hotels, but self-catering might be your best option. A bakery hidden in a back alley produces beautiful *zataar* (herb)–dusted flat bread. Ask at the small tea shop–grocer on the main street for directions – and buy some *halva* (a sweetmeat made from sesame flour and honey) to go with your bread!

Take a private taxi from Ramsar's Imam Sq (from IR600,000, 90 minutes) and enjoy the stunning views from the crazily switchbacked road. You'll pay considerably more for a day excursion.

traditional guesthouse accommodation (on roll-up mattresses) as well as a separate self-contained cottage. Look for the Shohada St turnoff from the Caspian Hwy about 16km northwest of Ramsar, just past Chaboksar.

The lodge is a fantastic place to sample the deliciously varied and seasonal Gilan cuisine. Tours (from IR300,000) include farm visits, fruit and tea picking, peak bagging, overnight treks and swimming in the Caspian.

Bam-e Sabz CABIN $$
(Ramsar Forest Resort; ☑ 011-5526 6519; www.telecabinramsar.com; Ramsar Telecabine; cabins from IR1,950,000; ⊛@⊛) For something a bit different, try these modern, comfy, hexagonal cabins atop a mountain you can only approach by *telecabine* (cable car). There are plenty of nearby forest paths to explore, Caspian views without the humidity and, in winter, snow-lathered peaks. Cabins fit two to four people. The attached restaurant (meals from IR250,000) is adequate if rather bland.

Ramsar Grand Hotel HOTEL $$$
(Parsian Azadi Ramsar; ☑ 0192-522 3592; Rajael St; new wing s/d/ste US$75/90/120; ℗⊛⊛) Sitting aloof on the hill above Ramsar, the Grand is an oasis of luxury away from the exhausts of Rte 22. Surrounded by gardens and orange groves, the older wing drips with Pahlavi-era opulence, while the newer modern rooms are just the place to unwind after a trek across the Alborz. The attached

restaurant is excellent and breakfasts are sumptuous.

Try to get a room with a Caspian view, and don't miss the sculptured rear garden. If the old wing is closed, ask the staff if you can sneak a look at the lobby. Be sure to ask for a discount.

❶ Getting There & Away

Iran Aseman (☑ 011-5522 4525) flies daily to Tehran (IR1,490,000).

Westbound savaris use Imam Khomeini Sq. Eastbound (from Basij Sq) you'll usually have to change savaris in Tonekabon (aka Shahsavar) for Chalus via Abbasabad, where a forest road shortcuts to Kelardasht.

Kelardasht کلاردشت

☑ 011 / POPULATION 14,000 / ELEVATION 1248M
Cupped between towering, broad-shouldered peaks, Kelardasht is nicknamed the 'Paradise of Iran' – it's probably the most popular Caspian-area getaway for nature-loving Tehranis. Surrounding areas offer trout fishing, cross-country skiing, trekking, mountain climbing and plenty of cool, fresh summer air. The panorama as you approach Kelardasht from Marzanabad is particularly impressive, with several spectacular views of snow-toothed Alam Kuh soaring behind the town. At **Kaleno** an 11km part-paved road leads up to **Valasht Mountain Lake**.

Kelardasht's commercial centre is **Hasankeif**, where most of the shops, banks and an internet cafe are clustered close to Hasankeif Sq. More traditional **Rudbarak** starts around 5km south of Hasankeif. It's closer to the mountains and is the starting point for most hikes, though it has fewer direct views. Here, amid the holiday homes, you can still find a few old **log-framed barns** and houses with slate or wood-slat roofs anchored with rocks.

🏃 Activities

Mountaineering Federation   CLIMBING
(Federasion-e-Kuh Navardi; ☑ 011-3264 2626, 0935 486 4066; http://msfi.ir/; Tohid St, Rud-barak) Staff here can show you climbing maps and help arrange mules and guides. The office also sells a great set of postcards with suggested routes marked onto photos of various peaks. Check in here before climbing Alam Kuh (p115); it's 7.4km from Hasankeif Sq. Pay your IR1,000,000 peak fees here. Call ahead for opening hours.

🛏 Sleeping & Eating

Kelardasht Ghasr
Apartment Hotel   HOTEL $$
(☑ 0911 391 8795; www.kelarhotel.com; opposite Khondan St, Mahestan; d IR1,600,000; 🅿✳) Fully decked-out suites have separate bedrooms, balconies and bathrooms and would suit self-caterers. It's a 15-minute hike south up the small street coming off Hasankeif Sq. Veer left where there's an obvious choice, turn right at the end and keep going uphill.

Hotel Maral   HOTEL $$
(☑ 011-5262 1130; Kelardasht-Rudbarak Rd; d from IR2,000,000; 🅿✳🛜🏊) New and totally blinged up, the Maral offers balconied rooms and well-appointed suites a 300m stroll west of Hassankeif Sq. There's a pool, a billiards room and a sheesha bar. Bear in mind that this is also the disco wedding venue of choice.

Arash Restaurant   IRANIAN $
(☑ 011-3262 8312; Hasankeif Sq; meals US$3-7; ⊙11am-3.30pm & 7.30-10pm) This bright, clean, pine-ceilinged restaurant offers Iranian and Caspian favourites right on Hasankeif Sq.

❶ Getting There & Away

Savaris to Chalus (IR80,000, one hour) and Tehran (IR520,000, four hours) leave from a **hidden yard** 3km east of Hasankeif Sq. Shuttle taxis from the square to the terminal cost

IR10,000. Buses (IR320,000, five hours) to Tehran's western terminal depart nearby (at 8am and 2pm in both directions).

If you're heading north, consider hiring a taxi (IR450,000) for the very scenic 'jungle' road to Abbasabad, bypassing the traffic snarls of Chalus altogether.

Transport within Kelardasht usually requires chartering a taxi at IR300,000 to IR400,000 per hour.

Qazvin   قزوین

☑ 028 / POPULATION 395,000 / ELEVATION 1301M

Qazvin is a pleasant city with a wonderfully restored caravanserai-turned-arts precinct, some quirky museums and a handful of decent eating options. Famed for carpets and seedless grapes, it was once the capital of all Iran, but for most foreign travellers it's primarily the staging point for excursions to the famous Castles of the Assassins and trekking in the sensational Alamut Valley. The city centre is Azadi Sq, widely known as Sabz Meydan. The bazaar and alleys to its southeast are the most atmospheric areas for random strolling.

History

Founded by the Sassanian king Shapur I in the 3rd century, Qazvin prospered under the Seljuk rulers, who erected many fine buildings. It had a second, much later burst of prominence when the second Safavid shah, Tahmasp I (r 1524–76), transferred the Persian capital here from Tabriz. A great patron of the arts, his ambitious architectural plan for Qazvin proved to be only a dress rehearsal for Esfahan, where his successor, Shah Abbas I, set up court in 1598.

◉ Sights

★ **Sa'd-al Saltaneh Caravanserai**   BAZAAR
(Map p116; ⊙8am-10pm) This huge, beautifully restored Qajar-era caravanserai is now the design centre of Qazvin. The long, vaulted passages house independent artists showcasing exquisitely crafted wares (jewellery, paintings, ceramics, carpets etc) as well as galleries, coffee shops, restaurants and quiet, hidden courtyards perfect for relaxing. Vazir Laneway is now the bazaar's western corridor.

Chehel Sotun   MUSEUM
(چهل ستون; Map p116; ☑ 028-3323 3320; Azadi Sq; IR80,000; ⊙9am-5.30pm) When Qazvin took

its turn as Iran's capital, this attractive, colonnaded cube was Shah Tahmasp's **royal palace**. Built in 1510, it was greatly remodelled in the Qajar era. Set in the town's central park, it looks especially photogenic at night, with its delicate balustrades floodlit and its back-lit coloured-glass windows glowing through the foliage. It now serves as a **calligraphy museum**.

Anthropolgy Museum   MUSEUM
(Qajar Bath; Map p116; ☎ 028-3323 3155; Obeyd-e Zarani St; IR50,000; ☺ 8am-6pm) In a beautifully restored, multichambered subterranean bathhouse dating from the Sassanian period, lifelike mannequins document the different cultural traditions of the province.

Covered Bazaar   BAZAAR
(Old Bazaar; Map p116; ☺ 9am-10pm) Now that the Sa'd-al Saltaneh caravanserai (p113) has been transformed into a modern arts-and-crafts precinct, the remains of Qazvin's original covered bazaar deals mainly in clothes, jewellery, textiles, homewares and wet, dead things. It's still worth a wander, especially in its furthest reaches.

Nabi Mosque   MOSQUE
(Shah Mosque; Map p116; Imam Khomeini St) This Qajar-era mosque has a distinctive long, narrow courtyard that acts as the demarcation line between the old bazaar and the renovated Sa'd-al Saltaneh caravanserai (p113). The mogul-style dome catches the evening light perfectly.

Masjed-e Jameh   MOSQUE
(Jameh Mosque; Map p116) Built in 1115, but extensively remodelled in the early 17th century, the Masjed-e Jameh has huge *iwans* (vaulted three-walled halls) and a fine marble *mihrab* (wall niche indicating the direction of Mecca).

Imamzadeh-ye Hossein   ISLAMIC SHRINE
(Map p116) This large, well-proportioned shrine has a Qajar facade, a 16th-century blue dome and plenty of mirror tiling. Set in a big, fountained courtyard surrounded by coloured-brick alcoves, it commemorates Hossein, son of Imam Reza. Behind are a martyrs' graveyard and an aged fighter plane on a pole.

Aminiha Hosseiniyeh   HISTORIC BUILDING
(Map p116; Molavi St, at Amin Deadend; IR50,000; ☺ 9am-1pm & 4-6pm) Behind an unassuming brick wall is this well-preserved Qajar mansion built by a rich merchant in 1773. The courtyard garden is a pleasant place to linger after being dazzled by the mirrored, glittery interior, with its coloured glass windows and vaulted basement.

Qazvin Museum   MUSEUM
(Map p116; ☎ 028-3324 7898; Helel-e-Ahmar St; IR150,000; ☺ 9am-12.30pm & 4-6.30pm winter, 9am-12.30pm & 5-7.30pm summer, closed Mon) This spacious modern museum predominantly features 19th-century decorative arts, but the bottom floor has some 3000-year-old bronzes and ceramics from the Alamut Valley.

Kantur Church   CHURCH
(Borj-e-Naghus; Map p116; Daraee Lane) The 20th-century Kantur Church has a blue-brick belfry dome and sits in a tiny Russian graveyard.

Ali Qapu   HISTORIC BUILDING
(Map p116; Helel-e-Ahmar St) The massive Ali Qapu was originally a 16th-century gateway to the royal precinct, a kind of forbidden inner city. Today it's a police post, so don't take photographs.

👁 Cisterns

Qazvin has some of Iran's best-preserved domed cisterns, where water was stored underground and cooled by wind towers. Sadly, getting in is rarely possible, so don't make a special trip, but if you're passing the most impressive from outside are the Sardar cisterns **Kuchak** (Map p116), and especially **Bozorg** (Map p116), and the **Haji Kazem Cistern** with its well-preserved wind tower.

👁 Gates

Tehran Gate (Darvazeh-e-Qadim-e-Tehran; Map p116; Tehran Ghadim Sq) and **Darbe Khoushk Gate** (Naderi St) are two scattered Qajar decorative remnants of Qazvin's once-vast city walls.

Tourist maps mark dozens of historic buildings, but few are visually exciting. Even the fine 14th-century **Amineh Khatun shrine** (Map p116; off Malekabad St) seems forlorn amid a warren of modern backstreets.

🏃 Activities

Qazvin is a good place to prepare for hikes in the Alamut area.

Mehdi Babayi HIKING
(☑ 0912 682 3228) Mehdi Babayi is an experienced trekking and climbing guide and driver who, despite his advancing years, displays an enviable level of fitness.

Safa Hammam BATHHOUSE
(Map p116; Molavi St, at Taqavi Alley; bath IR50,000; ☺ 7am-7pm Sat-Thu, to 2pm Fri) Safa Hammam is the best known of Qazvin's traditional subterranean bathhouses to remain active. The domed central rest area is attractive.

☞ Tours

★ Yousef Shariyat TOURS
(☑ 0919 180 7076; yousef.sh.khoo@gmail.com; day trip with 2/3/4 passengers $US60/70/80) Yousef's in-depth knowledge of the Alamut Valley, excellent English, intelligent, eclectic conversation and safe, relaxed driving make him the first choice for guided day trips in the region. He can also organise Alamut camping treks; the cost is the same per day as that of his day trips. Book several days in advance if possible.

🛌 Sleeping

Mosaferkhaneh Abrisham MOSAFERKHANEH $
(Abrisham Guesthouse; Map p116; ☑ 028-3357 8181; Molavi St, off Montazeri Sq; tw/tr without bathroom IR610,000/800,000; ❄ 🛜) This friendly guesthouse offers clean, budget-savvy rooms with shared bathrooms above a supermarket. The staff can help arrange Alamut trips.

Miremad Hotel HOTEL $
(☑ 028-3356 0610; www.mehotel.ir; Asadabadi Blvd; d IR900,000; 🛜) With good, cheap rooms and friendly staff, the Miremad is situated on the busy inner ring rd. It's around a 25-minute hike to the centre, though there are plenty of taxis.

WESTERN IRAN QAZVIN

CLIMBING IN THE ALBORZ MOUNTAINS

The Alborz offers climbers a selection of 4000m-plus peaks plus routes to suit trekkers and climbers of all capabilities. Many routes are documented on summitpost.org including the following. If you're looking for guides consider contacting the Tehran-based **Iranian Mountain Guides** (☑ 0912 190 2326, 021-4487 0132; http://mountainguide.ir/).

Alam Kuh

This 4850m mountain is Iran's second tallest and its most technical. An 800m near-vertical granite wall makes the mountain's north face a special challenge for climbers, though there are much easier alternative routes to the top. Ascents start 20km from Rudbarak (which is just south of Kelardasht). Before starting you should sign in (and pay IR1,000,000 in peak fees) at the **Mountaineering Federation** (p113) in Kelardasht.

For Alam Kuh, it takes at least a day to trek to one of two base-camp huts. Hesarchal offers the easier summit approach. For the wall, use the climbers' hut at Sarchal (3900m) and continue to a cwm called Alamchal (4150m). Climbing the wall itself is a very serious undertaking even for highly experienced mountaineers.

Mt Takht-e Soleiman

From Sarchal it's also possible to climb Mt Takht-e Soleiman, at the other end of the main knife-edge ridge, but there's a lot of boulder-jumping on the glacier and plenty of slippery scree. Note: this is the peak that Freya Stark wandered up almost by mistake, as described in her book *Castles of the Assassins*. It is *not* the Takht-e Soleiman citadel near Takab.

Shah Alborz

Shah (King) Alborz (4125m) is the highest peak in the western Alborz range and can be climbed in two (long) or three (shorter) days by a number of routes, the most popular via the easy southern flanks from the Taleqani Valley north of Karaj. The route isn't obvious, so consider taking a guide. The climb starts above Hasan Jun hamlet.

The southern slopes of the Alborz are undulating and covered with soft soil or grass, while the northern slopes are steeper, rockier and glaciated. A northern approach from Garmarud in the Alamut Valley would be epic indeed, though the gentler western ridge from Aveh looks more trekking friendly. A tent is essential regardless. Watch out for bears, cheetahs and sheepdogs.

Qazvin

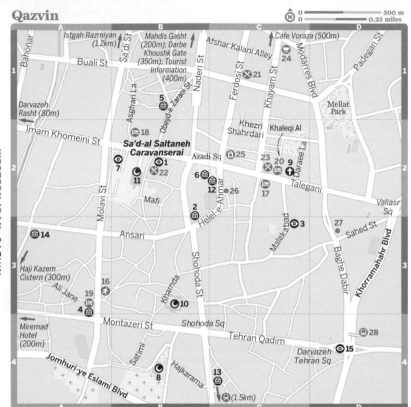

Taleghani Inn HOSTEL $
(Map p116; ☎028-3322 4239; Khaleqi Alley, off Taleqani St; d IR600,000; 🖥) Safe, cheap and central, this renovated guesthouse up an alley (the one past Yas Alley) presents basic, clean rooms. Some English is spoken and staff can organise Alamut trips.

Alborz Hotel BUSINESS HOTEL $$
(Map p116; ☎028-3323 6631; info@alborzhotel. com; Talegani St; tw US$60; 🅿🌐@🖥) It's in a great central location, but the clean, comfortable rooms are fairly expensive given that the hallways are worn out and the wifi's patchy (it works best in the coffee shop). Friendly staff speak good English and can organise Alamut trips (for a premium).

Behrouzi Traditional Hotel HISTORIC HOTEL $$$
(Khane Sonatti Behrouzi; Map p116; Ashgari Lane; s/d/tr $US48/95/145; 🖥) You'll never want to leave this exquisitely restored Qajar-era traditional house, right in the centre of the old town opposite the covered bazaar. The rooms, graceful yet sumptuous, are arranged around a central courtyard. The beds are so huge you'll need to take a GPS with you. There's also a fantastic private *hammam*. It's the perfect après-trek reward.

It's in the sixth dead end off Ashgari Lane.

✖ Eating

Qazvin's speciality is *qimeh nasar* (also spelt *gheymeh nasser*), a tangy lamb stew made with diced pistachios.

Sib Restaurant IRANIAN $$
(Map p116; Sa'd-al Saltaneh caravanserai; meals IR250,000; ⊘11am-10pm) Come to this bright new place in a hidden courtyard towards the back of Sa'd-al Saltaneh caravanserai for the airy ambience and the tasty Persian favourites.

Qazvin

Nemooneh   IRANIAN **$$**
(Map p116; ☎ 028-3332 8448; cnr Buali & Ferdosi Sts; meals from IR280,000; ⊙noon-3.30pm & 7-10.30pm; ✳) Locals rate this the best feed in Qazvin, and it's hard to argue. The handy picture menu helps visitors explore beyond kababs and try some Iranian specialties, such as *khoresht fesenjan* (chicken and walnut stew) or the succulent butter-fried salmon. It's down the glittering stairs

on the northeastern corner of Buali and Ferdosi Sts.

Yas   IRANIAN **$$**
(Map p116; ☎ 028-3322 2853; Yas Alley, off Taleqani St; IR230,000; ⊙noon-3pm & 7.30-10pm) In the alley of the same name, the Yas is cheap and cheerful and does a fine rendition of the local *qimeh nimeh* (succulent stewed lamb on rice).

🍷 Drinking & Nightlife

★**Negarossaltaneh**   CAFE
(Map p116; 34 Vazir Bazaar; coffee & snacks from IR50,000; ⊙10am-10pm Sat-Thu, 5-10pm Fri) Deep within the Sa'd-al Saltaneh caravanserai is this hipster favourite. An English menu reveals heart-starting espressos and lattes, exotic teas and trippy herbal concoctions, deliciously wicked petit fours and even breakfast eggs, all in a relaxing, intimate space. Try the *nan charie* (cardamom-flavoured biscuits shaped like Christmas trees) and *zamin megar* (a drink made from honey, condensed milk and saffron).

Cafe Voraza   CAFE
(Map p116; ☎ 028-3333 3001; http://coffeeshopvozara.com/; Khayyam St, cnr Adl Blvd; ⊙10am-late) Locals and tourists alike cram this tiny hole-in-the-wall cafe at the northern end of Khayyam St for its eclectic range of coffees (included iced), cakes and ice creams (the chocolate ice-cream cake is the best!).

🛍 Shopping

Nakhajir Camping Shop   SPORTS & OUTDOORS
(Map p116; ☎ 028-3222 4551; Ferdosi St; ⊙8am-1pm & 4-9pm Sat-Thu) Tool up here for your Alborz trek.

ℹ️ Information

TOURIST INFORMATION

Tourist Information (☎ 028-3335 4708; http://qazvin.ir; Naderi St; ⊙9am-6pm) The helpful staff at this office facing the historic Darbe Khoushk Gate dispense great free maps and useful brochures and are only too happy to design a walking tour taking in all the major sights.

Tourist Information Booth (Map p116; ☎ 0912 282 9049; www.qazvin.ir; Sa'd-al Saltaneh caravanserai; ⊙theoretically 8am-12.30pm & 5-7pm Sat-Thu) Should you find it open, you might be able to grab a map or two from this office at the Imam St entrance to the Sa'd-al Saltaneh caravanserai.

TRAVEL AGENCIES

Arash Safar Travel (Map p116; ☑ 028-3322 2260; arashsafarqazvin@yahoo.com; Helel-e-Ahmar St; ☺ 8am-1pm & 4-8pm Sat-Thu) Can book train tickets and sells air tickets ex-Tehran.

Kandovan Travel (Map p116; ☑ 028-1222 3614; Kashani Blvd)

Mahdis Gasht (☑ 028-3336 1891; North Naderi; ☺ 8am-8pm) Friendly and professional help to book flights and trains. Some English spoken.

Meraj (Map p116; ☑ 028-3322 1111; Yas Lane; ☺ 9am-7pm) This agency has friendly clerks, but they don't speak much English. Trains and planes only.

ℹ Getting There & Away

BUS, MINIBUS & SAVARI

A number of handy services run from the **main bus terminal** (Map p116; Darvazeh Sq), which has a **Golden ticket agent** (Golden; Map p116; ☑ 028-3356 1117; www.safartalaei.ir; Main Bus Terminal).

Official Tehran savaris (IR200,000) leave from the front car park. Unofficial ones pick up at Valiasr Sq.

Buses run to Hir (via Razmiyan) around 11am and to Mo'allem Kalayeh (IR80,000, 2½ hours) around 1.30pm (not Friday).

However, for these Alamut Valley destinations, savaris are vastly better. **Mo'allem Kalayeh** savaris (US$10, 1¾ hours) depart from Qarib Kosh (Minudar) Sq, with the gigantic Silk Road monument, 3km east of Valiasr Sq. **Razmiyan** savaris (IR200,000, 1¼ hours) depart occasionally from **Istgah Razmiyan** (Helalabad Sq, off Sa'di St): to get there take a shuttle taxi up Naderi St to Sardaran Sq, walk a block west along Beheshti St, then 300m southwest down Shahid Fayazbakhsh St.

For Rasht, savaris depart from **Darvazeh Rasht** (22 Bahman Sq), where some through buses also pick up/drop off.

TRAIN

The best-timed trains to Tehran (IR50,000, 2½ hours) depart at 8am and 9.56am. For Zanjan (IR66,000-120,000, 2½ hours), useful trains leave at 8am, 8.48am,10.49am, 4.04pm and 5.13pm. Sleeper trains run to Tabriz at 7.53pm (IR352,000, 11 hours) and to Mashhad (IR1,012,000, 14 hours) at 8pm; book them early if you can.

ℹ Getting Around

City buses run both ways along the main drag (Imam Khomeini St/Taleqani Blvd), but cars and shuttle taxis can only use it eastbound, returning from Valiasr Sq to central Azadi Sq (Sabz Meydan) via Shahrdari or Buali Sts. Going from the centre to the bus terminal, change at Valiasr Sq. Services from the terminal to Azadi Sq loop around via the bazaar. *Dar bast* anywhere inside the ring road will cost IR50,000.

Alamut Valley الموت

ELEVATION 1400M

Few places in Iran offer a more tempting invitation to hike, explore and reflect than the fabled Alamut and Shahrud Valleys. Beneath soaring Alborz peaks, the landscapes are both inspirational and amazingly varied, a wild melange of Patagonia, Switzerland and Outback Australia, all spiced by a uniquely fascinating medieval history. Nestled almost invisibly on widely spaced rocky knolls and pinnacles are the shattered remnants of more than 50 fortresses. Shrouded in fabulous myths, they were the heavily fortified lairs of the medieval world's most feared religious cult, and are collectively known as the Castles of the Assassins (p122). The most interesting are at Gazor Khan (Alamut Castle) and Razmiyan (Lamiasar Castle). Note that Alamut

BUSES FROM QAZVIN TERMINAL

DESTINATION	FARE	DURATION	DEPARTURES
Esfahan	IR220,000	6hr	1pm
Hamadan (VIP)	IR180,000	4hr	11.30am
Hamadan	IR140,000	4hr	2pm
Kermanshah	IR220,000	7hr	2pm
Sanandaj (VIP)	IR300,000	8hr	11.30am
Rasht	IR50,000	3hr	7.30am, 7.45am, 2.45pm, 3pm
Tehran	IR50,000	2½hr	frequent

Castle is not in Alamut town (aka Mo'allem Kalayeh).

Hiking

Caspian Trek (Farzin Malaki; ☑ 0911 291 0700; www.caspiantrek.com) can organise tailored multiday hikes to just about anywhere in the Alborz, and summitpost.org has good details of numerous routes. The trek from Garmarud to Yuj is popular, but there are lots of other, some would say better, options. You need to be totally self-sufficient and experienced for these hikes, and a guide is strongly recommended. Check the information book at the Navizar Hotel (p121) in Garmarud for ideas.

➡ Climbing majestic **Shah Alborz** (4125m) in two days from Garmarud (and optionally continuing on to the Taleqani Valley near Karaj, completing a north–south traverse of the range, which would take another one to two days).

➡ Traversing the wilderness from **Evan Lake to Tonekabon** via the Dohezar Valley (five to six days).

➡ Garmarud to Kelardasht via **Alam Kuh** (4850m; Iran's second-highest mountain), which takes between five and eight days.

Garmarud گرمارود

☑ 028 / POPULATION 380 / ELEVATION 1800M

Garmarud is where the sealed road (currently) ends, and it's the nicest place in the Alamut Valley to base yourself. You can spend your time here exploring the mountains on day (or longer) hikes. In winter the town can get cut off from the rest of the valley.

Trekking Towards the Caspian: Garmarud to Yuj

Crossing the Alborz on foot from the Alamut Valley to the Caspian hinterland is geographically compelling, scenically stunning and culturally fascinating. You'll be traversing country rarely seen by outsiders, but development is coming: roads are relentlessly pushing into all corners of the Alborz, and the mule trains that were once the mainstay of mountain transport are rapidly disappearing.

A road now covers the route described below and, though you can avoid parts of it by keeping to the old footpaths (which are almost impossible to find without a guide), it's not quite the wilderness experience some expect. In fact, you can easily hitchhike from Garmarud to Yuj and on to Tonekabon on the coast in a day.

Check the local conditions and route at the Navizar Hotel (p121) in Garmarud before you head out. Staff may suggest some better options.

Be prepared for snow on the high sections between October and June. The walk isn't especially arduous, and it's most pleasant to allow three days, though two days or even fewer is quite possible if you're in some inexplicable hurry. (In midsummer you could flag down a lift to Salajanbar.)

The hike starts in pretty, canyon-framed **Garmarud** village, 18km east of the Gazor Khan turning, where the Alamut Valley road's asphalt ends. Whether you walk or drive, the route goes via picturesque **Pichebon** hamlet and across the 3200m **Salambar Pass** beside the small, partly renovated (but deserted) **Pichebon Caravanserai** (six hours' walk from Garmarud). There are fabulous views here. From the caravanserai it's another three hours to Salajanbar, descending very slowly through pretty thorn shrubs and fields of yellow iris. If you follow the road instead of the walking path, take the right-hand fork in the pass – if you can find it.

Wonderfully picturesque **Maran** is three hours on from Salajanbar and requires fording a stream twice. While it's not that hard, it's potentially dangerous when the water's high: slip and you'll be washed over a waterfall to certain doom – unless, of course, you're still on the road. After Maran, the scenery becomes less interesting as recent road construction has scarred the landscape and most trekkers opt to take transport from here. If you keep walking it's another three hours downhill to pretty **Yuj** village, set in flower-filled meadows. The road is sealed all the way to Tonekabon.

You can camp anywhere, but if you're near a village, always ask permission. Pichebon has especially attractive soft, grassy meadows, and there are homestays in Maran (p121) and Yuj. While it's best to bring all your own food, there are simple grocery shops in the villages along the route.

Alamut Valley

N

0   0
10 miles
20 km

Dohezar Valley

Yuj
Qazimahaleh
Maran
Kulumlar
Pichebon
Carpanserai
Salajanbar
Salambar Pass
Pichebon
Mt Nargiz
Alam Kuh (8km)
Garmarud
Avarik
Shah Alborz (4125m)
Zavarak
Khoshkhal
Alamut Castle
Kuchenan
Andej
Gazor
Shuta
Khan
Gazor Khan
Canyon
Canyon
Canyon
Shahrak
Evan Lake
Mo'allem Kelayeh (Alamut Town)
Rajayi Dasht
Hir
Lamasar Castle
Razmiyan
Bahramabad
Falak
Razjero
Zereshk
Rasht-e Qun
Sutehkesh
Savari Stand for Mo'allem Kelayeh
Qarib Kosh
(Minader) Sq
Qazvin Train Station
Qazvin

🛏 Sleeping

Navizar Hotel   HOTEL **$$**
(📞028-5839 4206, 0912 459 6078; www.
navizarhotel.com; d IR1,200,000) Destined to be
a travellers' classic, this small, family-run
hotel offers clean, basic rooms, home-
cooked food and a wealth of information
about trekking in the area. It also organises
treks and guides.

Nematullah Mansukia   HOMESTAY
(📞0912 282 140; Maran; r per person US$10)
In Maran village, Nematullah Mansukla
can provide a simple homestay with great
home-cooked meals (around US$4). By
arrangement he can also organise mules
from Yuj (around US$12) or even Gar-
marud (around US$30). The village has a
tiny, super-rustic *hammam*.

ℹ Getting There & Away

To reach Garmarud, a *dar bast* savari costs
US$10 from Mo'allem Kelayeh or US$30 from
Qazvin.

Gazor Khan & Alamut Castle

📞028 / ELEVATION 2062M
Several tempting mountain hikes start in
the unpretentious little cherry-growing vil-
lage Gazor Khan or in Khoshkchal village,
a steep, 15-minute 4WD ride beyond. Ask
around for route options (or check sum-
mitpost.org before you arrive). The village
itself isn't that interesting (or even inviting)
and most people try to head to Garmarud
instead.

The region's greatest attraction is the
fabled ruin of **Alamut Castle,** (قلعه الموت;
IR150,000; ☺ dawn-dusk; 🅿) Hasan-e Sabbah's
famous fortress rising abruptly above Gazor
Khan. The access path starts about 700m be-
yond the village square and requires a steep
25-minute climb via an obvious stairway. The
archaeological workings on top are shielded
by somewhat unsightly corrugated-metal
sheeting, but the phenomenal views from
the ramparts are unmissable.

Hotel Farhangian (📞028-3377 3446; ste
IR600,000), based in a converted school, is
the best of the area's two accommodation
options.

ℹ Getting There & Away

Your bargaining position is not strong: you're
stuck there and the taxi driver knows it. To Qa-
zvin you might manage to pay just IR400,000
(2½ hours), or you can take the school bus to

Mo'allem Kalayeh (school days only, IR50,000,
45 minutes) and try your luck from there.
Both leave from the village square at 7am. To
Garmarud you'll have to deal with the same
driver; pick a number you think reasonable,
then multiply it by three. Look around for other
travellers to share the 25km trip.

Mo'allem Kalayeh   معلم کلایه

📞028 / POPULATION 3420 / ELEVATION 1652M
Sometimes called Alamut town, Mo'allem
Kalayeh is the Alamut Valley's one-street
district centre. It's a useful transport stag-
ing post for the region but not a sight in
itself. If you get stuck here, **Haddodi Res-
taurant** (📞028-3321 6362, 0936 457 7241; tw
IR800,000), on the main street 50m east of
the eagle statue, offers several twin rooms
and a couple of larger apartments. There's
also a **campground** on the right as you
first enter Mo'allem Kalayeh.

The 8km road spur to 1587m **Andej** (اندج)
passes alongside three truly awesome red-
rock side canyons, where you can cross the
river on a rickety bridge and explore. The
turnoff is just northwest of **Shahrak**, which
has a prominent (but not assassin-related)
castle ruin. After the canyons, fork left up
the hill in Andej village and double back
around towards Mo'allem for a magnificent
perspective from above.

ℹ Getting There & Away

Rare buses and savaris loiter in the town
centre, 650m east of the eagle statue. Savaris
to Qazvin (IR400,000) are an hour quicker
than the dreadfully slow bus (IR100,000,
daily except Friday) that departs once feeder
buses from outlying villages have arrived. For
Gazor Khan, taxi charters cost IR250,000, or
IR400,000 including a side trip to Andej. Or
take the returning school bus (school days
only, IR50,000, 45 minutes) around 11.45am.

Razmiyan   راز میان

📞028 / POPULATION 1800 / ELEVATION 1684M
Central Razmiyan is a strangely soulless
place, though the winding descent into
town from Qazvin passes some timeless
mud hamlets and gives wonderful views
over the Shahrud Valley's rice terraces.

The town's main attraction is **Lamiasar
Castle**. From Razmiyan, follow the Hir
road for 2.5km to the castle access path. A
20-minute stroll leads to the top edge of
the 'castle', where a hint of round bastion
and some other wall chunks remain. The

CASTLES OF THE ASSASSINS

In the 12th century, a network of incredibly well-fortified Alborz mountain castles sheltered the followers of Hasan-e Sabbah (1070–1124), spiritual leader of Islam's heretical Ismaili sect. In popular myth, Sabbah led a bizarre, much-feared mercenary organisation whose members were dispatched to murder or kidnap leading political and religious figures of the day. They believed that their actions would transport them to paradise. Supposedly Sabbah cunningly cultivated such beliefs by getting his followers stoned on hashish (unbeknown to them) and then showing them beautiful secret gardens filled with enticing young maidens. This gave the sect its popular name 'Hashish-iyun', root of the modern English term 'assassin'. Or so the story goes. Peter Willey's book, *Eagle's Nest,* gives an altogether more sympathetic version, portraying Sabbah as a champion of the free-thinking, pro-science Islamic tradition and suggesting that the hashish tales were exaggerations designed to denigrate Ismaili Islam.

Whatever the truth, most of the impregnable Ismaili castles were captured by Mongol ruler Hulagu Khan in 1256 using diplomatic trickery, having earlier forced the surrender of the Ismailis' spiritual leader (Sabbah's successor). Only two fortresses, Girdkuh and **Lamiasar** (p121), decided to put up a fight. Thanks to their sophisticated water cisterns and vast food reserves, they could hold out for years – 17 years, in the case of Girdkuh! Before moving on, the Mongols systematically destroyed the castles' fortifications to avoid future difficulties. That means that today it's history and brilliant scenery, rather than the scanty rubble, that draw the few travellers who make it here.

The crushing of **Alamut Castle** (p121) was effectively the end of the Ismailis for generations, though believers resurfaced centuries later and now Ismaili Islam is the predominant faith in parts of Tajikistan and northern Pakistan (though not at all in Iran).

The castles were forgotten and only returned to public consciousness with the publication of Freya Stark's 1930s travel diary *Valleys of the Assassins*. A copy of that recently reprinted volume makes a great companion for the trip.

site sweeps down to outer-wall remnants that drop vertically into the valley below. Allow at least an hour to seek out the various degraded fortifications. Bring a hat and sunscreen as there's minimal shade. A taxi from the village costs IR300,000 with waiting time, though it's just as easy to walk.

A **taxi** (☏ 028-3322 2828) to Mo'allem Kalayeh costs US$12, or US$15 if you tack on an 8km detour to **Evan Lake** (Ovan Lake; دریاچه اوان; IR50,000), a small, photogenic mountain-backed tarn that's not quite worth the added expense.

Sanandaj سنندج

☑ 087 / POPULATION 390,000 / ELEVATION 1502M

Even by Iran's super-hospitable standards, Sanandaj is a remarkably friendly city. It's the capital of Kordestan province, a good base for visits to Marivan, and a great place to learn more about Kurdish history and culture. You'll see plenty of men wearing traditional cummerbunds and baggy Kurdish trousers. Yet it's a modern, noticeably prosperous city with a large, fashionable population of students keen to try out their English. In Sanandaj's Sorani-Kurdish language, *ju-an* means beautiful and *deso hoshbe* means thank you.

Busily commercial Ferdosi St links the twin centres of Enqelab Sq and Azadi Sq. From the latter, Abidar St slopes up into the folds of a rocky ridge that was the city's historic defence and is today the pleasant Abidar mountain park.

History

Originally known as Senna (as it still is to local Kurds), the city was of major importance in the Middle Ages but withered to nothing in the chaotic post-Chaldoran era. A *dej* (fortress) was built here in the early 18th century and Senna-dej slowly developed into Sanandaj. From here the powerful Ardalan emirs came to rule the last autonomous principality of Iranian Kurdistan until 1867. Under the Ardalans the town acquired many fine 19th-century buildings, though most have since been lost to rapacious 20th-century development.

⊙ Sights

Asef Mansion   MUSEUM
(Asif Diwan, Kurdish Anthropology Museum; Map p124; Imam St; IR80,000; ⊙8am-6pm Tue-Sun) A fascinating museum of Kurdish culture awaits in a restored two-storey mansion dating back to the Safavids, complete with subterranean *hammam*. Mannequins are dressed in the distinctive tribal costumes still worn in valleys around Kordestan province. One room features Sanandaj's wood-inlay crafts; another has busts of prominent Kurds. The inner courtyard with its pond is a pleasant place to escape the traffic. A side courtyard leads through to a vaulted gallery that has sporadic art exhibitions.

Lotfolla Sheik-al-Islam Mansion   MUSEUM
(Sanandaj Museum, Salar Seyyed; Map p124; Habibi Lane; IR150,000; ⊙9am-noon & 4-7pm Tue-Sun, shorter hours low season) The well-renovated Qajar Lotfolla Sheikh-al-Islam Mansion houses the regional museum, whose *orosi* (multicoloured windows) – said to have 42,000 pieces of stained glass – were designed for practicality as well as beauty: supposedly they disorient mosquitoes. Exhibits include some extraordinarily old pottery and metalwork treasures, and the odd skeleton.

Moshir Divan   HISTORIC SITE
(Map p124; Shohoda St) This iconic Qajar mansion, one of several historic buildings in town that are undergoing excruciatingly slow renovations, hides seven courtyards behind its formidable entrance off Shohoda St. Buzz if the doors are closed.

Khan Hammam   HISTORIC BUILDING
(Pir Zahiri, Khan Bath; Map p124; IR150,000; ⊙9am-1pm & 3-7pm Tue-Sun) One of several historic *hammams* of Sanandaj, the unusual 1805 Khan Hammam has grey-and-white floral and bird motifs, attractive tiling and remarkably lifelike 'bathers'. The easily missed door has a brass 'fist' knocker: enter the bazaar just north of Engelab Sq and go about 100m, then start asking.

Khosroabad Mansion   HISTORIC SITE
(Khosroabad St; ⊙10am-dusk) FREE This formerly grand mansion was once the palace of Amonulla Khan. It has an impressive central courtyard with reflecting pools but is otherwise now in a fairly parlous state. Find it at the western end of the park behind the hospital on Keshavarz St.

Masjed-e Jameh   MOSQUE, MUSEUM
(مسجد جامع, Darol Eshan Mosque, Friday Mosque; Map p124; Imam St) This Qajar-era mosque was built for Amonulla Khan, with tiled twin minarets, 32 interior domes and two verandas.

🛏 Sleeping

Hotel Kaj   HOTEL $
(Map p124; ☑087-3329 1997; Ferdosi St; s/tw from IR700,000/1,000,000) Right in the heart of things, the Kaj is the budget hotel of choice, with comfortable, basic rooms.

Hotel Hedayat   HOTEL $
(Map p124; ☑087-3316 7117; Ferdosi St; s/tw/tr IR540,000/800,000/1,000,000; ☎) Centrally located, these basic though comfortable rooms right above busy Ferdosi St can be noisy.

Shadi Hotel   HOTEL $$$
(☑087-3362 5112; shadi_hotel@yahoo.com; Pasdaran St extension; tw/tr IR1,800,000/2,430,330; P❋☎) The most comfortable rooms in Sanandaj are a long way from the centre in this schmicked-up, multistorey warren of restaurants and coffee shops that's perched above a furiously busy freeway. Share taxis to Azadi Sq (IR10,000) stop right at the entrance. (Thankfully, there's a pedestrian overpass to lower the risk of death on your return.)

The 5th-floor buffet (meals IR435,000) is the best place to enjoy the views of the surrounding mountains, especially when the air is crisp and clear. While the food is good, you can expect those views to come with a hefty surcharge. The hotel can arrange agency taxis to Palangan (p126).

Tourist Inn   HOTEL $$$
(Hotel Jahangardi, ☑087-3362 3676; http://en.it-tic.com; Pasadan St extension; s/d US$55/75; P❋☎) Quiet, elegant rooms are tastefully finished in this nondescript brick bunker that sees a lot of groups. South of the centre, it's on its own hill above the freeway. The restaurant is reasonable and there's a kids' playground.

✕ Eating & Drinking

Jahannama   IRANIAN $
(Map p124; ☑087-3316 4212; Taleqani St; meals IR160,000; ⊙8am-4pm & 7-10pm) Looking for all the world like a basement bric-a-brac shop, with ancient radios and crazy wooden statues, Jahannama serves up delicious

WESTERN IRAN SANANDAJ

Sanandaj

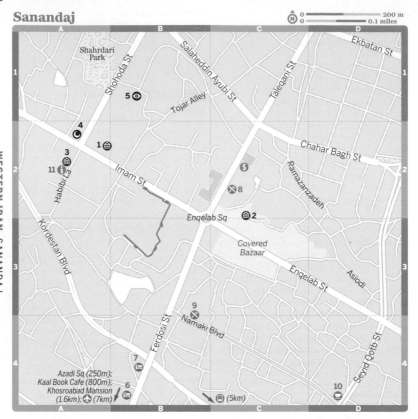

WESTERN IRAN SANANDAJ

Sanandaj

food, especially the house *khoresht sabzi* (vegetable, meat and bean stew). Other dishes to try include *juje pofaki* (marinated chicken bits) and the tangy *tahchin agusht* (a rice-cake stack of meat, raisins and barberries).

Morvarid Restaurant   IRANIAN $$
(Map p124; ☑087-3323 8444; Namaki Blvd; meals IR230,000; ⊙noon-4pm & 7.30-10pm) Just off crowded Ferdosi St is the reliable Morvarid with its eye-searingly red interior. Try the Kurdish *kofte* (meatballs).

Kaal Book Cafe   CAFE
(☑087-3371 7375; coffee/cake from IR80,000/50,000; ⊙10am-10pm) A grungy, narrow doorway leads to a refined, intimate courtyard that's perfect for a coffee or exotic *chay* and cake fix on the way back from Abidar Park. It's behind Molavi Sq.

Toranj Book Cafe CAFE
(Map p124; Seyid Qotb St; coffee/cake from
IR100,000/100,000) Shut off the outside
world and relax in the intimacy of this restored traditional Sanandaj Jewish house,
where you wish you could read the books.
It's near Namaki Blvd.

Shopping

Sanandaj is known for its wood-inlay work,
so be sure to check out the workshops near
Asef Mansion (p123).

Information

**Cultural Heritage Organisation of Kord-
estan** (Map p124; ☑ 087-3328 5725; http://
kurdistan.ichto.ir/; Habibi Lane; ⊙ 8am-2pm
Sat-Thu) This helpful, multilingual tourist
office dispenses maps and brochures from
an inner section of the restored mansion that
houses the **regional museum** (p123).
Bank Melli (Map p124; Taleqani St) To change
money use this branch, not the big branch on
Azadi Sq.

Getting There & Away

Iran Aseman (☑ 087-3323 3301) and **Qeshm**
(p83) fly to Tehran daily (IR1,480,000) from
Sanandaj's **airport** (☑ 087-3377 4052).
Savaris to Kamyaran (IR80,000, one hour),
Kermanshah (IR150,000, two hours), Qorveh
(IR100,000) and Hamadan (IR200,000) wait
in neat, well-organised queues in the **main bus
terminal** (☑ 087-3352 0341; Janbazan Blvd) area,
4km east of the centre. Minibuses leave from behind and long distance buses from a half-hidden
section to the left. Several bus companies have
handy central ticket offices around Enqelab Sq.

Getting Around

Fast-filling shuttle taxis (IR10,000 per standard hop) from Enqelab Sq run east to the main
terminal and north along Taleqani Sq to the
Marivan terminal. From Azadi Sq they run down
Pasdaran St and up Abidar St.

For Abidar mountain park, things are made
complicated by the one-way system: some cars
up Keshavarz St divert and continue up Abidar
St past JimJim, leaving you to walk the last
15 minutes or so. A taxi *dar bast* to the upper
hairpin sections of Abidar Park costs around
IR250,000.

Howraman هورامان
☑ 087 / ELEVATION 1536M

Caught at the intersection of powerful empires, the Kurds had their homes destroyed
so regularly in medieval history that, by
the 18th century, a sizeable part of Kurdish
society had forgone villages altogether and
resorted to nomadism and brigandry. An
important exception, thanks to its impen-
etrable mountain-hemmed position, was
the Howraman (Orumanat) Valley, which
remains one of Iran's least known and
most spectacular areas. In colder months
you'll still see Howraman men wearing
kolobal (brown-felt jackets with distinctive
shoulder 'horns'). There is plenty of age-
old stone terracing, and the villages are
stacked like the Caspian's famous Masuleh, with one house's roof forming the next
one's yard.

Although it now has a green-domed
Muslim prayer room, the real interest of
the **Pir Shaliar Shrine** (Howraman-at-Takht)
lies in the animistic rocks and trees behind
it, which are draped Buddhist style with
votive rag strips. A **Mithraic midwinter
festival** is reportedly still held here on
the Friday nearest to 4 February. Some
suggest that this is a cultural relic from
pre-Zoroastrian 'angel' worship, albeit
with an Islamic overlay.

The Flintstones-esque **Stone Hotel**
(Hotel-e Sangi; ☑ 087-5388 3535; Howraman-at-Takht; tw IR500,000; ☎) is mostly
constructed of small rocks. In peak season

BUSES FROM SANANDAJ

DESTINATION	FARE (IR)	DURATION (HR)	DEPARTURES
Ahvaz	475,000	10	6pm (several)
Esfahan	290-380,000	9	7pm, 9pm
Orumiyeh	300,000	6	9am, 7.45pm
Rasht	400,000	9	6pm via Hamadan (2hr), Qazvin (IR300,000, 7hr)
Tabriz	370,000	8	8pm
Tehran (western)	300-450,000	6	frequent

WESTERN IRAN HOWRAMAN

WORTH A TRIP

PALANGAN

In postcard-perfect Palangan (پلنگان; population 900), brightly dressed Kurdish children drive donkeys up the near-vertical pathways while old men in baggy black trousers sit and chew the (goat) fat outside the village hall. Women spread grains out to dry on the flat roofs of the haphazardly stacked stone houses, which tumble down both sides of a rocky cleft, ceasing just above the dark waters running in between. Unlike the more tour-isted villages of Masuleh and Kandovan, Palangan feels refreshingly authentic. Everybody is smiling. Nobody is in a hurry.

There's no official hotel, but ask around, as somebody may have a room to rent. While there are a couple of simple grocery shops, you're better off bringing your own food.

The easiest way to get to Palangan is by private taxi from Sanandaj (US$34 return). Otherwise, take a savari to Kamyaran, halfway between Sanandaj (IR80,000) and Kermanshah (IR70,000); savaris for Palangan (IR50,000) start from Kamyaran's Sala-haddin St (2km southwest of the main bus terminal), but expect to pay *dar bast* (US$15 return, plus waiting time). The asphalted 45km road passes some other interesting mud-and-stone Kurdish villages en route, and you'll usually get a lift in either direction. Getting out of Kamyaran to a city late in the day or on holidays could be a problem. If you're heading to Paveh, take a savari directly to Ravansar (IR50,000, 35km) and you can avoid Kermanshah altogether.

it fills with Iranian tourists. There's also a restaurant.

ℹ Getting There & Away

Snow allowing, Howraman-at-Takht makes a relatively easy day trip by taxi from Marivan (or even Sanandaj). There are also shared 4WDs between Biyakara and Howraman-at-Takht (IR300,000, 1¾ hours, 50km), but you can't be sure of finding a ride back again the same day. A great idea is to engage a taxi or 4WD at Biyakara or Marivan and continue all the way to Paveh. *Dar bast,* expect to pay US$90 via Belbär. Shar-ing a ride, prices will vary enormously according to vehicle, driver and the co-passengers you can find for intermediate points.

Paveh پاوه

ℐ 083 / POPULATION 24,500 / ELEVATION 1564M

Strung along narrow terraces above a pic-turesque valley, rapidly developing and Hurami-speaking Paveh (Pawa in Kurdish) makes an accessible introduction and gate-way to the Howraman region.

Paveh runs long and thin from a small bazaar and bus station in the south, wind-ing through the town centre (Maolavi Sq) in the valley 'elbow' before petering out in the north below the Eram Hotel. Several higher roads mirror the route and offer fine viewpoints.

Only the first 400m of **Quri Qaleh Cave** (IR45,000; ⊙ dawn-dusk; P), 25km east of Paveh, is open to the public, but there are still

some nice features. Beyond the locked gate, the system extends for at least another 2.7km.

On a hill above the northern edge of town, **Eram Hotel** (ℐ 083-4612 4695; tw IR1,750,000; P ✳ ☎) has adequate rooms and fine views of the surrounding moun-tains. It's a 4km slog from the bus terminal, but if you're coming in from Howraman, ask to be dropped at the first mosque.

The traditional-style **Restaurant Sonatti** (meals IR250,000) has views of the whole valley – reach it from the upper road above the town centre, via a zigzag staircase.

ℹ Getting There & Away

From the main **terminal**, 2.5km south of Moalavi Sq, minibuses and savaris depart for Kermanshah (IR200,000, 1¾ hours) and Ra-vansar (IR100,000). For Sanandaj, change at Ravansar for a Kamyaran-bound savari.

For Marivan and Howraman, shared Toyota (pronounced 'tweeter') pickups gather outside a trio of orange container huts 1km north of Shohoda Sq. Departure times are highly unpredictable, typically before dawn to How-raman-at-Takht (US$10, five hours), if at all. To allow plenty of photo stops, consider renting a taxi *dar bast* to Marivan from **Kurd Taxi Agen-cy** (Janbazan Blvd) via Howraman-at-Takht (IR2,600,000, along a very rough road that's passable in perfectly dry weather only). Note that the sealed road via Nosud close to the Iraqi Kurdistan border is not recommended and should be avoided.

Kermanshah کرمانشاه

📖 083 / POPULATION 887,500 / ELEVATION 1330M

Kermanshah developed in the 4th century AD under the patronage of Sassanian kings. The city squats astride the former Royal Rd to Baghdad, and such strategic positioning has brought both prosperity and attack: Kermanshah suffered brutal damage during the Iran–Iraq War. Briefly renamed Bakhtaran in the 1980s, the city is a melting pot of Kurds, Lori and other Iranians, many on pilgrimage west to the holy cities of Najaf (Iraq) and Kerbala.

Large, sprawling and often bewildering, Kermanshah can be a hard city to love. The centre, if there is one, feels strangely empty of people, yet traffic snarls along its main arteries. The city's proximity to the Achaemanid and Sassanid carvings of Bisotun (p130) and Taq-e Bustanis is the main tourist drawcard.

👁 Sights

The main street changes names (Ashrafti to Kashani to Modarres to Beheshti to Sheikh Shiroodi) as it stretches over 10km from the busy commercial centre (the southern third) to the foot of the magnificent rocky Parom massif. Here the Taq-e Bustan carvings, ringed by parks and outdoor restaurants, form the city's foremost attraction.

Taq-e Bustan HISTORIC SITE
(IR200,000; 🚗) Inscribed into the base of a towering cliff, these extraordinary Sassanian bas-reliefs of ancient victorious kings divide opinions. Some travellers feel disappointed by the Taq-e Bustan experience, as there's a relatively high admission price for a few stone carvings and a duck pond, both of which are viewed easily from outside the fence. For Iranians, a visit is a joyous celebration of their incredible Persian heritage. Whether you immerse yourself or crank up the zoom lens is up to you.

Taq-e Bustan was originally the site of a Parthian royal hunting garden, but the Sassanians later added their own regal stamp. The biggest alcove features elephant-mounted hunting scenes on the side walls and highlights the coronation of Khosrow II (r 590–628), beneath which the king rides off in full armour and chain mail (half a millennium before the European Black Prince made it fashionable). The second niche shows kings Shapur III and his Roman-stomping grandfather Shapur II. To the right of the niches is a fine tableau again showing Shapur II (r 379–383), in which he is depicted trampling over the Roman emperor Julian the Apostate (whom he defeated in 363) and receiving a crown of blessings from the Zoroastrian god Mithras.

Late afternoon is the best time to visit, as the cliff turns a brilliant orange in the setting sun, which then dies poetically on the far side of the duck pond. The surrounding open-air restaurants rock out till late in the evening, and the carvings are warmly floodlit. The site is 10km north of Kermanshah's city centre.

Takieh Mo'aven ol-Molk ISLAMIC SHRINE
(Map p129; Hadad Abil St; IR150,000; ⏰10am-noon & 4-7.30pm Sat-Thu) The Takieh Mo'aven ol-Molk is Iran's finest *Hosseinieh*, a distinctively Shiite shrine where plays are acted out during the Islamic month of Moharram to commemorate the martyrdom in 680 of Imam Hossein at Karbala. Enter downstairs, through a courtyard and a domed central chamber decorated with grisly scenes from the Karbala battle.

The shrine remains very much active, with pilgrims kissing the doors and being genuinely moved by the footprint of Ali (Hossein's father) on the wall of the second courtyard. This is set amid tiles depicting a wild gamut of images, from Quranic scenes to pre-Islamic motifs including Shahnameh kings, European villages and local notables in 19th-century costumes.

The building to the right is now an ethnographic museum displaying regional costumes.

HURAMI KURDISH LANGUAGE

The Hurami Kurdish language is quite distinct from Sorani Kurdish, which replaced it in Sanandaj, though Hurami was once the dialect of choice for regional Kurdish poets. Knowing even a few words will flabbergast and delight the locals you meet. *Fere-washa* and *zarif* mean beautiful, *wazhmaze* means delicious, *deset wazhbu* (literally 'hand good') means thank you, to which one replies *sarat wazhbu* ('head good'), which means you're welcome.

Biglar Beigi Tekyeh   ISLAMIC SHRINE

(Map p129; ☑ 083-3372 6597; IR80,000; ☺8am-7pm Sat-Thu) **FREE** The Biglar Beigi Tekyeh *Hosseinieh* is worth visiting for its dazzling mirror-tiled central dome room. It also houses a fairly cursory calligraphy museum. Go down the lane opposite the fine **Masjed-e Jameh** (Friday Mosque; Map p129; Modarres St), then take the first alley left.

Covered Bazaar   MARKET

(Map p129) The extensive, much-restored covered bazaar slopes up from Modarres St. With a couple of dilapidated old caravanserai courtyards at the western end, it's well worth exploring.

☞ Tours

Mohammad Puurr   TOURS

(☑ 0918 855 6840) A very safe, reliable driver in Kermanshah, Mohammad will take you wherever you want to go, including Bisotun, Paveh, Palangan and further afield.

Shapur Ataee   TOURS

(☑ 0918 856 6220; shapurataee@yahoo.com; per day plus tips US$25) Shapur is an extremely learned and interesting guide with good English and decent French.

🛌 Sleeping

Most of the cheap dossers lie around Azadi Sq, many marked only in Farsi. The further from the square, the quieter it will be; look for hidden stairways.

Shahed Park Campground   CAMPGROUND

(Shahed Park, Beheshti Blvd) **FREE** You can camp in Shahed Park, near the Kharkeh River and with views of the oil refinery.

Meraj Hotel   HOTEL $

(Map p129; ☑ 083-3823 3288; Modarres St; s/tw/tr IR460,000/610,000/760,000; ❄🛜) This hotel's right in the centre above Azadi Sq. Don't expect much and you won't be disappointed.

Resalat Hotel   HOTEL $$

(☑ 083-3724 6365; Ferdosi Sq; s/tw/tr IR1,030,000/1,400,000/1,700,000; ❄🛜) A reasonable traveller's option in the south of the city, close to Laleh Park. The rooms are adequate; the wi-fi mostly works in the lobby.

Hotel Khourosh   BUSINESS HOTEL $$

(Cyrus Apartments; ☑ 083-3839 0417; http://hotel kourosh.com/; Golrizan St; s/tw/tr IR1,530,000/ 1,830,000/2,260,000, apt from IR3,050,000; P❄🛜) The Khourosh is an island-tower of single rooms and multibedroom apartments in the city's northeast.

Hotel-Apartment Lizhan   APARTMENT $$

(Map p129; ☑ 083-3721 0102; Motahhari Blvd; apt US$78; ❄) Great for self-catering families, these apartments (with kitchens) sleep up to six in two bedrooms. It's conveniently located within walking distance of the bazaar, but nearby parking is limited.

Parsian Kermanshah   HOTEL $$$

(☑ 083-3421 9151; www.parsianhotels.com; Shahid Keshavari Blvd; s/d IR2,590,000/2,820,000; P❄🛜) The most comfortable rooms in town are in this Parsian tower 8km from the centre and walking distance to Taq-e Bustan (p127). The 6th-floor restaurant, with its expansive views and local specialities, makes for a pleasant lunch spot (meals IR280,000). Staff will organise agency taxis for Bisotun, Palangan and Khorramabad. The hotel's next to a mind-numbingly convoluted flyover near Velayat Bridge.

Jamshid Hotel   HOTEL $$$

(☑ 083-3429 6002; Kuhnavand Sq; tw/tr IR2,400,000/2,950,000; P❄🛜) Next door to Taq-e Bustan (p127), the Jamshid has an eccentric white-stone castle facade that could easily be mistaken for the entrance to an amusement park. The basement restaurant (meals from IR350,000) does nothing to dispel this impression, with wacky 'river cave' and mini–Taq-e Bustan features. The rooms are large and comfortable, but they're overpriced and showing their age.

There are plenty of other (cheaper) food options in the surrounding area, which is lucky because you're a long way from the rest of town.

🍴 Eating

Around Azadi Sq and on Motahhari Blvd at the junction of Kaangar Blvd there are snack stalls and confectioners selling Kermanshah's archetypal *nan berenji* cookies (literally 'bread-rice'; a round semi-sweet confection that's usually yellow and flavoured with saffron). There's a great concentration of *kabab* cafes and open-air teahouses near the Taq-e Bustan (p127) carvings and several restaurants around Kashani Sq.

Homa IRANIAN **$**
(Map p129; ☑ 083-3723 4246; Kashani St; meals IR180,000) At this downstairs eatery, the friendly staff churn out tasty kababs and a reasonable *khoresht khalal* (lamb stew with almonds), though it's not the sort of place to dress up for or even to linger in.

Arg IRANIAN **$$**
(Map p129; ☑ 083-3729 9410; Kashani Sq; meals from IR250,000; ☻noon-11pm) A favourite special night out for the locals, the Arg is up an elevator from Kashani Sq (above the shopping centre) and has great views of the surrounding hills. Try the *khoresht khalal*.

❶ Information

Cultural Heritage Office of Kermanshah
(☑ 083-3838 0045; ☻7.30am-2.30pm Sun-Wed, to 1pm Thu) Hard to find, this office is north on Beheshti near Shahed Park. It produces a useful city map (in Farsi only) that the better hotels will stock.
Khadivi House (Map p129; ☑ 083-3721 2696; Ma'adem St; ☻8am-3pm Sat-Thu) This more conveniently located outlet of the Cultural Heritage Office info centre operates at a beautifully restored Qajar mansion and garden used as an occasional exhibition place.
Sepehr Exchange Co (Map p129; Bank Sepah Bldg, Kashani Sq) Changes money, unlike the big Bank Melli on Azadi Sq.

❶ Getting There & Away

AIR
Tehran IR1,330,000 to IR2,000,000, daily with **Iran Air** (☑ 083-3824 8814; Beheshti St; ☻7.30am-2.30pm Sat-Thu, to 1pm Fri) and **Iran Aseman** (☑ 083-3431 0650), several times weekly with **Qeshm** (p83), **Meraj** (p93) and **Caspian** (p92).
Mashhad IR2,230,000, Wednesday, Thursday and Sunday with **Meraj** (p93).

Tickets are sold by **Setareh Soheil** (Map p129; ☑ 083-3727 1115; Kashani St; ☻9.30am-7pm Sat-Thu) and other travel agencies.

BUS, MINIBUS & SAVARI
The huge **Kaviyani Terminal** (Keshvari Blvd), 7km northeast of Azadi Sq (within walking distance of the Parsian Hotel), handles most transport – take a savari or bus 2 from Azadi Sq. Several offices sell advance tickets, including **Iran Peyma** (Map p129; Jahad Sq) and very handy **Pars Peyma** (Map p129; Modarres St) beside Hotel Nobovat, which offers tickets to almost anywhere. Savaris to Sanandaj (IR150,000, 1½ hours) and Hamadan (IR200,000) depart from this terminal.

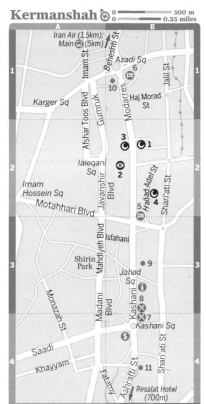

Kermanshah

⊚ Sights
1	Biglar Beigi Tekyeh	B2
2	Covered Bazaar	B2
3	Masjed-e Jameh	B2
4	Takieh Mo'aven ol-Molk	B2

🛏 Sleeping
5	Hotel-Apartment Lizhan	B2
6	Meraj Hotel	B1

✴ Eating
7	Arg	B4
8	Homa	B3

❶ Transport
9	Iran Peyma	B3
10	Pars Peyma	B1
11	Setareh Soheil	B4

Savaris to Paveh (IR150,000, *dar bast* IR600,000) depart from Gumruk St close to Azadi Sq. Savaris to Bisotun (IR30,000, 25 minutes) start from Imam Sq near the airport.

WESTERN IRAN KERMANSHAH

BUSES FROM KERMANSHAH

DESTINATION	FARE (IR)	DURATION (HR)	DEPARTURES
Ahvaz	430,000	8	8am, 9pm via Andimeshk
Esfahan	450,000	9	5pm
Orumiyeh	477,000	10	5pm
Qazvin	220,000	7	2pm
Tabriz	435,000	10	6am, 6-10pm
Tehran (western)	250,000	8	frequent

The highway to Khorramabad is especially scenic as you climb over the **Zagros mountains**. You can savari hop via Harsin (IR60,000, 45 minutes) and Nurabad (IR50,000, 40 minutes), where a final savari (IR80,000, 1¼ hours) will take you to Khorramabad. Or make the most of photo stops and take a private taxi (via Bisotun if you like) for IR1,200,000.

TRAIN

A new railway is planned, which will link Tehran to Baghdad (Iraq) via Kermanshah and Qasr-e-Shirin, but construction will take years.

❶ Getting Around

Kermanshah is spread out and has a one-way system that does nothing to alleviate traffic snarls.

Bisotun-bound shuttle taxis from 15 Khordat Sq pass the airport gates. Shuttle taxis from Azadi Sq head in all directions, most usefully to the terminals and to Mo'allem Sq for Taq-e Bustan. On Modarres St, city buses drive the 'wrong way' (northbound), but northbound shuttle taxis have to wind around the one-way system until 8.30pm.

A 12-station monorail is currently under construction...and has been for years.

Bisotun   بیستون
📞 083 / POPULATION 2800 / ELEVATION 1350M

Bisotun sits on the old Royal Rd that once linked Babylon to Medea (ie Hamadan), in the shadow of its 2500m namesake peak. Huge eroded cliffs line the northern flank of the road and look especially stunning when you approach from Sahneh.

Bas-Relief Carvings

Carved into the side of Kuh-e Bisotun (Mt Bisotun) is a series of bas-reliefs and cuneiform inscriptions (IR200,000) dating from 521 BC. The inscriptions, written in three 'lost' languages (Elamite, Akkadian and Old Persian) provided a key for decrypting cuneiform scripts, just as the Rosetta Stone did for Egyptian hieroglyphics. Unfortunately, the inscriptions and the key figure of Darius remain hidden behind scaffolding. However, the site is quite scenic to explore, with other scattered carvings, a crumbling caravanserai and the extremely cutesy teahouse **Bisotun Sherbet Khane**.

From the entrance gate you'll pass a club-wielding little **Hercules statue** from 148 BC (albeit with recently replaced head). A little further is a very eroded **Parthian relief of Mithrades II**, partly overwritten by a 17th-century Arabic inscription by Sheikh Alikhan. The main relief (which you aren't able to see) is 100m up the cliff and has Darius holding his bow and standing on the chest of a vanquished figure. Other bound figures are on his right and a farohar – a winged Zoroastrian 'angel' denoting purity – hovers overhead. The cuneiform inscriptions surround the Darius figure and detail the history of his conquests.

In 1835, eccentric British Army officer Henry Rawlinson bemused locals by dangling for months over the abyss to make papier-mâché casts of the cuneiform. It was these casts that allowed the eventual breakthrough in deciphering the inscriptions. Unesco recognised the importance of the texts by listing Bisotun in 2006.

Farhad Tarash

Some 200m past the main bas-relief site is Farhad Tarash (p339), a 1200m vertical limestone wall that's home to some of Iran's most epic climbs. With more than 100 sport and trad multipitch routes, there's a grade here for everyone, and there are three shelters perched high on ledges if you want to stay overnight.

🛏 Sleeping

Laleh Bistoon Hotel   BOUTIQUE HOTEL $$$
(📞 083-4538 3812; http://kermanshah.laleh hotels.com/; d €161) Beautifully exotic, this modern-day caravanserai, set against the

imposing backdrop of Kuh-e Bisotun (Mt Bisotun), perfectly conjures the ambience of *The Thousand and One Nights* Persia. The thick-walled, brick-vaulted rooms are simply but luxuriously decorated, with large beds and larger carpets.

ℹ Getting There & Away

The savari stop for Kermanshah and for Sahneh (and thence Hamadan) is a 10-minute walk east through Bisotun, just beyond Bank Keshvari.

Hamadan   همدان

📞 081 / POPULATION 580,000 / ELEVATION 1860M

Known in classical times as Ecbatana, Hamadan was one of the ancient world's greatest cities. Pitifully little remains from antiquity, but significant parts of the city centre are given over to excavations, and there's a scattering of historical curiosities. Sitting on a high plain, Hamadan is graciously cool in August but snow prone and freezing from December to March. In summer the air is often hazy, but on a rare, clear spring day there are impressive glimpses of snow-capped **Alvand Kuh** (3580m), sitting aloof above the ragged neocolonial cupolas of Imam Khomeini Sq.

History

According to ancient Greek historians, Median king Deiokes fortified a palace here in 728 BC, and over succeeding decades the Median capital of Ecbatana grew into an opulent city. Its massive walls were said to have had seven layers, the inner two coated in gold and silver, the outer one as long as that of classical Athens. By 550 BC it had fallen to the Achaemenid Persians, and King Cyrus was using it for his summer court.

The Medes retook the city in 521 BC but were kicked out again within six months by Darius, who was so pleased with himself that he recorded his achievements in stone beside the Royal Rd at Bisotun (p130).

After centuries of pre-eminence and wealth under Parthian and Sassanian dynasties alike, Ecbatana/Hamadan faded somewhat after the Arab conquest in the mid-7th century, but it became the regional capital under the Seljuks for some 60 years in the late 12th century. Known as Hegmataneh (Meeting Place) in Old Persian, Hamadan suffered devastation by the Mongols in 1220 and again in 1386 (by Tamerlane), but it only hit a major decline in the 18th century following a Turkish invasion.

The city began to recover in the mid-19th century and was redesigned to a modern city plan in 1929 by German engineer Karl Frisch; Frisch's master plan is a cartwheel design with six avenues radiating from Imam Khomeini Sq, referred to simply as 'meydan'. The wheel distorts to the northeast around the hill of Tappeh-ye Mosallah and the excavation site of Hegmataneh Hill.

◉ Sights

Hegmataneh Hill   ARCHAEOLOGICAL SITE

(تپه هگمتانه ; Map p132; 📞 081-3822 4005; site incl museum IR200,000; ⊘ museum 8am-4pm Tue-Sun, to noon Mon; 📷) The view of distant mountains from the top of this low, open hill is pleasantly rewarding, especially in the late afternoon, but it's what lies below that excites archaeologists: an ancient Median and Achaemenid city. Small sections have been excavated over the last century, most extensively in the 1990s. You can wander above several shed-covered trenches on wobbly plank scaffolding. There's a smart

---

ALI SADR CAVES

Ali Sadr Caves (4440 📞 081-3544 ; غار علیصدر ; www.alisadr.com; Gol Tappeh; IR700,000; ⊘ 8am-4pm winter, to 9pm summer; 🅿 📷) This massive river-cave system 70km north of Hamadan is normally visited as a day trip. It's popular with Iranian tourists, but foreigners usually have mixed feelings, most stemming from the cost (10 times what locals pay) and the perceived commercialisation. However, traversing darkened caverns by paddle boat and walking across subterranean islands is pretty special. Treat it as a cultural experience as well as a scenic one. A tour takes 45 to 90 minutes. Avoid (crowded) weekends and tip your guide.

Ignore the sign saying '$25' and insist on paying in rial – it will work out more cheaply. Ask for the (free) map in your language. The caves are a constant 16°C, so bring more than one layer. The caverns are up to 40m high and the river 14m deep; the system is thought to connect to the **Katale Khor system** (p101) in Zanjan province. There's a **Tourist Inn** (p134) nearby if you feel like staying on and exploring the surrounding area.

Hamadan

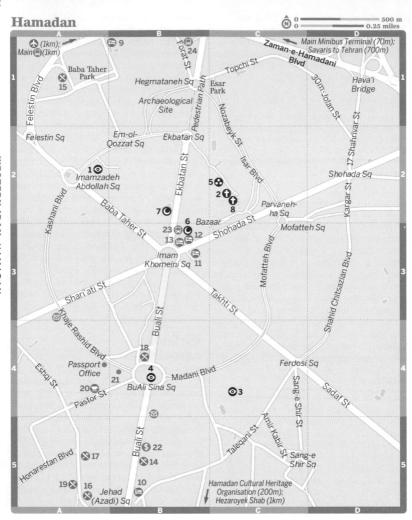

museum nearby, as well as two Armenian churches, now part of Hamadan University.

The ancient walls' gold and silver coatings are long gone and it's hard to envisage the lumpy remnants as having once constituted one of the world's great cities. The museum tries to fill the mental gap, showcasing archaeological finds such as large amphorae, Seljuk fountains, Achaemenid pillar bases and Parthian coffins. The main site entrance is to the north, but there's a handy 'back-door' staircase from the city bus terminal behind the bazaar that climbs directly to the churches.

BuAli Sina Mausoleum   MAUSOLEUM, MUSEUM
(Aramgah-e Buali Sina; Avicenna Tomb; Map p132; ☑ 081-3826 1008; Buali Sina Sq; IR200,000; ⏱ 9am-5pm) Hamadan's iconic 1954 BuAli Sina (Avicenna) Mausoleum dominates his namesake square and resembles a concrete crayon pointing to the heavens. It was loosely modelled on Qabus' 1000-year-old tower in Gonbad-e Kavus. Only aficionados will want to pay the entry fee, which gives you access to a single-room museum of Avicenna memorabilia, his tombstone, a small library and a display on medicinal herbs. Entry is from the east.

Hamadan

Alaviyan Dome   MAUSOLEUM
(Gonbad-e Alaviyan; Map p132; Shahdad Lane; IR150,000, ☺8am-7pm) The 12th-century green dome, immortalised by a reference to it in the poet Khaqani's work, has long since been removed, but the untopped brick tower remains famous for the whirling floral stucco added in the Ilkhanid Mongol era; this ornamentation is described by an enraptured Robert Byron in *Road to Oxiana*. In the crypt (steps down from the rear interior) is the plain-blue-tiled Alaviyan family tomb, covered with votive Islamic embroidery.

St Stephanos Gregorian Church   CHURCH
(Map p132; Tappeh Hegmataneh) A church dedicated to Armenian saints Stephen and Gregory has existed on this site since the 1600s, though this latest incarnation dates from the early 20th century.

Armenian Evangelical Church   CHURCH, MUSEUM
(Map p132; Tappeh Hegmataneh) Squatter and slightly older than St Stephanos Gregorian church next door, the Armenian Evangelical Church was built in 1886 and now serves as a museum of Armenian migration.

Masjed-e Jameh   MOSQUE
(Jameh Mosque; Map p132; Imam Sq) FREE A vaulted passage of the bazaar leads into the courtyard of the large Qajar-era Masjed-e Jameh. The disused south *iwan* (entrance) leads into a hall over which there's an impressively large brick dome. The north *iwan* is lavished with patterned blue tile work that continues on four of the mosque's six minarets. Some areas are restricted to men only.

Borj-e Qorban   TOMB
(Map p132) In a back alley surrounded by apartment blocks sits this 13th-century classic 12-sided, pyramid-roofed tomb tower that was once used to defend the city.

Imamzadeh-ye Hossein   ISLAMIC SHRINE
(Map p132) Worth a look is the Qajar-era Imamzadeh-ye Hossein, tucked behind Hotel Yass in a little courtyard with an ancient mulberry tree.

🏃 Activities

Alvand Kuh   TREKKING
(Mt Alvand) In good weather, Alvand Kuh (3580m) makes an excellent day walk. From Ganjnameh (p137), 8km from Hamadan, head above the river (or take the telecabine!) to Mishin Plateau (1¼ hours), where there are two shelters. From there it's another hour to Takhteh Nader Plateau, an alpine meadow with a spring, probably snow covered. The summit is a further hour through a boulder field.

Paragliding   PARAGLIDING
(www.facebook.com/hamedanparagliding) Get some altitude with the local wing crew at Shahrestaneh, 4km on from the **Tarik Dare ski resort** (☺Thu & Fri winter) along the Tuyserkan road, on the other side of Ganjnameh Pass – the views are incredible!

🛏 Sleeping

Farshchi Guest House   HOSTEL $
(Mosaferkhaneh-ye Farsi; Map p132; ☎081-3252 4895; Shohada St; dm without bathroom from IR250,000) By *mosaferkhaneh* (lodging house) standards the Farshchi is a cosy, friendly place with something of a family

atmosphere. Most of the rooms are large, with four to five beds and no bathrooms, but there are some smaller twins and triples with bathrooms.

Ordibesht Hotel   HOSTEL $
(Map p132; ☑ 081-3252 2056; Shohada St; s/tw IR500,000/800,000; ☎) At ground zero next to the bazaar, this cheap and cheerful *mosaferkhaneh* has clean, comfortable, noisy rooms.

Yas Hotel   HOSTEL $$
(Map p132; ☑ 081-3252 3464; Shohada St, Imam Sq; s/tw IR1,300,00/1,490,000) This overlander's favourite has seen better days, but the adequate, affordable rooms are where the action is.

Ali Sadr Tourist Inn   HOTEL $$
(Hotel Jahangardi; ☑ 081-3544 4312; Ali Sadr, Kabudarahang; tw/tr/q IR1,830,000/2,300,000/2,8 00,000; P ✳ ☎) A short walk from the Ali Sadr caves (p131) is this reliable inn, with comfortable rooms, functional bathrooms, restaurant with a view and opportune wallpaper. The quads are good value for groups planning to explore the local hills.

Buali Hotel   HOTEL $$$
(Parsian Buali; Map p132; ☑ 081-3825 2822; Buali St; s/d US$58/88; ✳ ✸) The excellent rooms here are fully appointed, and the complimentary breakfast includes a wide selection of hot and cold fare, including freshly baked naan straight from the hotel's own tandoor. There's a ground-level cafe doing real espresso, and a downstairs restaurant with a good selection of traditional and international dishes. The only blemish is annoying disconnecting wi-fi.

Baba Taher Hotel   HOTEL $$$
(Map p132; ☑ 081-3422 6517; babataher_hotel@ yahoo.com; Baba Taher Sq; s/tw US$105/137; P ✳) Lavishly overpriced business-class rooms are compensated for by friendly, English-speaking staff, though watch for the Hamadan up-sell. Ask for a discount and you'll usually get at least 25%. The restaurant is reasonable, though expect surcharges. The hotel's in the city's north, next door to the park housing its namesake's wacky mausoleum.

✖ Eating

Aria'ian Teahouse   IRANIAN $
(Home of the Aryans; Map p132; ☑ 081-3253 1779; Buali St; dizi from IR180,000; ☺ noon-4pm)

With caravanserai-style vaulted ceilings, mood lighting and lovingly prepared fresh *dizi*, why would you go anywhere else for lunch? It's opposite Melli Bank.

Falafel Bros   FELAFEL $
(Map p132; Eshqi St; IR25,000; ☺ noon-11pm) If you've overdone the kababs, the cheeky Bros have just the remedy: a foot-long bread-roll felafel-fest! These puppies are the best in town.

Naghshe Jahan Restaurant   IRANIAN $
(Map p132; Eshqi St; meals from IR120,000) This cheap and cheerful small restaurant does tasty takes on the usual kababs, stews and rice dishes.

Kaktus   IRANIAN $
(Map p132; Buali Sina Sq; meals from IR180,000; ☺ noon-3pm & 7-10.30pm) Down easy-to-miss stairs, Kaktus, with its clean, modern decor, remains one of Hamadan's most popular *kabab* restaurants.

Dareta Sardashi   IRANIAN $$
(Map p132; ☑ 081-3423 6740; Baba Taher Sq; ☺ meals from IR200,000; ☑) This tiny two-storey cafe pays homage to the humble *bademjan* (eggplant) with a variety of dishes, mostly stews and roasts. Service can be a bit hit and miss, and for some reason a lot of dishes come out unnaturally square. There's a cafe (aka smoking room) upstairs.

Delta Restaurant   IRANIAN $$
(Map p132; ☑ 081-3826 1813; Eshqi St; meals IR220,000-400,000; ☺ 7-10pm) Relocated from its old location on Pastor St, the Delta is in a hard-to-find new basement opposite Saidiyeh St (look for the food picture; there's no English sign). Carpeted platforms ring chair-and-table seating, though the vibe is strangely subdued. Both kababs and stews are tasty and the local *kashka bademjan* (eggplant dip) makes a fine starter.

Hezaroyek Shab   IRANIAN $$
(1001 Nights; ☑ 081-3821 4545; Farhang St; meals from IR200,000; ☺ noon-3pm & 7.30-11pm) Almost out on the ring road, this cosy restaurant has a wide selection of Iranian and Western favourites. Owner Pari Bakhtiyari speaks fluent English, so call ahead to check if it's open. A taxi *dar bast* should be IR50,000.

BUALI SINA MAUSOLEUM

Had you studied advanced medicine in 17th-century Europe, your 'textbook' would have been the great medical encyclopaedia *Canon Medicinae*. Incredibly, this book was written 600 years earlier. Its author, remembered in the West as Avicenna, was in fact the great Iranian philosopher, physicist and poet Abu Ali Ibn Sina (980–1037), 'BuAli' Sina for short. If you're a fan of aromatherapy you can thank BuAli for the development of steam distillation, with which essential oils are extracted. His ideas on momentum and inertia were centuries ahead of Newton's. And (following al-Kindi and al-Farabi), his blending of Aristotle's ideas with Persian philosophy helped inspire a golden age of Islamic scholarship. However, this philosophy rapidly led to a polarisation of views about the man whose ego was reputedly as great as his intellect.

Born in what is today Uzbekistan, BuAli studied medicine in Bukhara, where his sharp mind and photographic memory had him running rings around his teachers. Political intrigues in Bukhara meant BuAli fled westwards to Gonbad-e Kavus, only to arrive as Qabus, his illustrious prospective sponsor, dropped dead. Initially BuAli proved luckier in Hamadan, where he successfully treated the ailments of the ruling emir and was promoted to vizier. However, when his patron died, BuAli was thrown into prison for corresponding with Abu Jafar, a rival ruler based in Esfahan. Four months later the Esfahanis stormed Hamadan, releasing BuAli, who went on to work with Abu Jafar for the rest of his life, coincidentally dying while on a return trip to Hamadan some 14 years later.

Drinking & Nightlife

★ **Kaghazi Coffee** CAFE
(Map p132; ☑ 081-3825 3870; Pastor St; coffee/cake IR80,000/80,000; ⊙10am-10pm) Funky laid-back meeting place bedecked with Pink Floyd lyrics and local hipsters listening to '70s Western rock. Yes, you're still in Iran.

🔒 Shopping

Hamadan province is famous for its leatherwork, wooden-inlay work, ceramics and carpets. Several shops sell colourful, locally famous pottery from Lalejin. The pedestrian-only section of Buali St leading into Imam Khomeini Sq is destined to become a major shopping strip.

ℹ Information

MONEY

Daghoughi Exchange (Map p132; ☑ 081-3827 7424; safir_exchange@yahoo.com; Buali St; ⊙9.30am-9.30pm) Fast and easy exchange office on Buali St.

TOURIST INFORMATION

Ali Sadr Travel Agency (Map p132; ☑ 091-3828 2001; hamedan_alisadr@yahoo.com; Khaje Rashid Blvd; ⊙9am-1pm & 4-7.30pm Sat-Thu, 10am-noon Fri) Although it's a commercial agency, the English-speaking staff are super friendly and happy to answer general questions.

Hamadan Cultural Heritage Organisation (Sazemane Jahangardi; ☑ 081-3827 4771; www.hamedan.ichto.ir; Gagh-e Nazari, Aref Qazvini St; ⊙8.30am-noon & 2-5pm Sat-Thu, 8-11am Fri) Staff members speak minimal English but merrily load up visitors with beautiful books and pamphlets as though it were Christmas. It's located in a delightful Qajar mansion with gardens.

VISA EXTENSIONS

Passport Office (Edareh Gozannameh; Map p132; ☑ 081-3826 2025; 1st fl, Khaje Rashid Blvd; ⊙8.30am-2.30pm Sat-Thu) Walk past the young, bored, machine-gun-toting guards into the concrete bunker with your fingers crossed. Extensions (IR375,000) should now be granted routinely, though not if you have more than just a few days left on your current visa. Good luck!

ℹ Getting There & Away

AIR

Kish Air (p92) flies to Tehran (IR1,292,000, twice weekly). **ATA** (p83) flies to Mashhad (IR2,020,000). Tickets are sold by **Ali Sadr Travel Agency**.

BUS

All long-distance bus services start from the **Tehran terminal** (Enqelab Blvd), but some companies have city-centre **ticket offices** (generally open 7am to noon and 3pm to 7pm) near Imam Khomeini Sq: **Seiro Safar** (Map p132; ☑ 081-3252 2860; Shohada St) is next to the Ordibesht Hotel, **Iran Alvand** (Map p132;

📞 0831-3252 5763; Ekbatan St) around the corner.

Tehran buses take the expressway via Takestan or the more direct road via Saveh, but few go via Qazvin. Expect delays after fresh snow.

MINIBUS & SAVARI

There are two minibus terminals. Use the **Main Minibus Terminal** (Zaman-e-Hamadani Blvd), northeast of the centre, for Kermanshah, Sanandaj (maybe changing in Qorveh), Bijar (at 11am and noon via Qorveh) and the Ali Sadr caves (several daily). Use **Terminal Qadim** (Map p132; Ekbatan St) for hourly minibuses to Tuyserkan, more frequent services to Malayer (and thence Nahavand or Borujerd and on to Khorramabad), and to Asadabad (for Kangavar). Savaris to Malayer wait outside.

Savaris to Kermanshah (IR200,000), Sanandaj (IR200,000) and Tehran (IR700,000) leave from relevant points near Sepah Sq. The Tehran savaris are well organised by a sign-up **booth** (📞 081-3423 8669).

Savaris for Ali Sadr (IR150,00) are harder to come by midweek, so, unless you like crowds, you might have to go *dar bast* (IR1,000,000 return including waiting time).

GETTING AROUND

Shuttle taxis run along the spokes of Hamadan's cartographic wheel for IR10,000 to IR20,0000 or IR80,000 (*dar bast)*. Shuttle taxis to the bus and minibus terminals leave from Ekbatan St.

Bijar بیجار

📞 087 / POPULATION 53,000 / ELEVATION 1947M

As a destination, Bijar makes an interesting alternative to Takab, though while the scenery and size are similar, Bijar has more transport options.

The town is dominated by crumbling Nesar Kuh (Mt Nesar), at whose base a small **ski resort** (📞 0901 103 5303) runs in winter. You can also grass-ski here in summer and all gear can be hired on site.

Bijar also makes a good base for visiting Katale Khor Caves (p101) and the crumbling ruins of the ancient Median fortress **Qam Cheqay**; their location, high above a hairpin bend of the Shahan River (a tributary of the Qezel Owzan), is magnificent. The direct Zanjan–Takab bus passes right through the village of Qam Cheqay, though private taxis can also be arranged from Bijar (45km) or Takab (76km). The ruins are 5km west of the village.

⭐ Festivals & Events

Ashura Mud Ritual   RELIGIOUS

Ashura for Shiites is a time of intense mourning and of re-enactment of Imam Hossein's massacre. Self-flagellation and animal blood sacrifices are common, but in Bijar Shiites cover themselves in mud to represent their insignificance in relation to God. Emotions run high, so if you witness this (the timing varies with Ashura itself) be respectful and keep a low profile.

🛏 Sleeping & Eating

Hotel Bam   HOTEL $

(📞 087-3823 3160; Imam Sq; tw IR640,000; 🅿🛜) This big brick and blue-glass place has clean, comfortable rooms that are the best in Bijar. It's about 3km from the centre, at the roundabout marking the junction of the Takab and Sanandaj roads.

Mosaferkhaneh Moqadam   HOSTEL $

(Ardalon St; tw without bathroom IR620,000) Basic rooms are attached to the restaurant of the same name. It's near the bazaar; ask around, as it's hard to find.

BUSES FROM HAMADAN

DESTINATION	FARE (IR)	DURATION (HR)	DEPARTURES
Ahvaz	520,000	11	6-7pm
Esfahan	440,000	8	8am, 10.30am, 9pm, 10pm
Mashhad	950,000	21	9.30am
Orumiyeh	350,000	9	1.30pm
Qazvin	140,000	3½	2pm
Rasht	240,000	7	9.15am
Tehran	220,000	5	frequent
Zanjan	150,000	4	3.30pm

WORTH A TRIP

GANJNAMEH

Ganjnameh (گنج نامه; literally 'Treasure Book'), 8km from Hamadan's centre, is so named because its cuneiform rock carvings were once thought to be cryptic clues leading to caches of Median treasure. These days it's selfie central as groups of locals pose next to the inscriptions or in front of a nearby waterfall. Take a savari (IR30,000) from Shari'ati St; *dar bast* will cost IR150,000.

Belatedly translated, the texts are in fact a hubris-laden suck-up to the Zoroastrian god Ahura Mazda from the Achaemenid monarch Xerxes (r 486–466 BC) for making him such a stellar king. To emphasise the point, the message is repeated in three languages (Old Persian, Elamite and neo-Babylonian) on rock faces some 2m high. A second panel similarly commemorates his father, Darius. All this is rather ironic considering the modern-day fetish for social-media immortality.

The 9m-high waterfall nearby becomes a popular ice-climbing spot in winter. At weekends the site gets crowded, but escape is possible on the hiking trails towards Alvand Kuh, whose 3580m summit can be reached as a day trip in summer. A narrow lane continues 4km from the car park to the **Tarik Dare ski slopes** (p133) and in summer a scenic road winds right across Alvand Kuh's lower slopes to Oshtoran near Tuyserkan.

Moqadam Restaurant IRANIAN $
(Ardalon St; meals from IR80,000) Better-than-average rice and kabab dishes from the restaurant below the *mosaferkhaneh* (lodging house) near the bazaar.

ℹ Getting There & Away
The main bus terminal is on the Zanjan road, 3km northeast of the centre, and handles all transport to Zanjan (plenty) and Hamadan (rarer).

Savaris to Takab (IR60,000, one hour) and Sanandaj (IR100,000, 1¾ hours) leave from outside Hotel Bam.

Marivan مریوان
📞 087 / POPULATION 115,000 / ELEVATION 1305M
Pretty Marivan, perched at the edge of the beautiful **Lake Zarivar**, makes a pleasant place to kick back for a couple of days or to use as a base camp for further exploration, particularly to Howraman. The lake is an important habitat for local and migratory birds and local fauna.

🛏 Sleeping
Teachers Hotel HOTEL $
(Hotel Ostad; s/tw/tr IR500,000/750,000/900,000; P ❄) This tiny, unsignposted gem has simple, clean rooms. Head west down 23 Tir Blvd from Imam St and turn left at the first alley (there's a small shop run by brothers on the corner). The hotel is 100m

down the alley on the left, just past a cross lane. Look for the building with zigzag brickwork inside a small courtyard.

The wonderfully friendly staff members have not a word of English.

Hotel Zarivar HOTEL $$
(📞 087-3454 0777; www.zarivarhotel.com; tw/tr/4-bed ste IR1,800,000/2,500,000/4,500,000; P ❄ 🌐) This hotel is beautifully situated overlooking the eastern shore of Lake Zarivar, and it's worth bargaining hard for a room with a view. Only the four-bed suites have balconies. The restaurant is OK; otherwise it's a pleasant 2km stroll to the bazaar.

Tourism Hotel MOTEL $$
(Hotel Jahangardi; 📞 087-3453 2020; http://en.ittic.com; 3-/4-person bungalows from US$45/60; P ❄ 🌐 🅿) Too far out of town unless you have your own wheels, these '70s-era, free-standing brick bungalows sit right above Lake Zarivar and would suit families and groups. The restaurant has nice water views, and the sunsets are stunning when there's no haze. It's 4km from Marivan's bazaar, just off the road to Bashmaq.

🍴 Eating
⭐ Fish Restaurant SEAFOOD $
(cnr 23 Tir Blvd & Shahrdari St; whole fish IR200,000; ⏰ noon-5pm & 7-10pm) Fresh whole fish are chargrilled over a small footpath brazier outside a tiny, no-name

restaurant. The smell of succulent roasting fish will lead you straight to it.

Jazireh Pizza PIZZA $

(Shahrdari St; pizza & drink from IR115,000) This cheerful, clean and modern fast-food place is in an area where there's not much choice. The pizzas, though small, come quick, cheap and tasty. It's near the corner of 23 Tir Blvd.

❶ Getting There & Away

Buses and savaris for Sanandaj (*dar bast* IR30,000) leave from the terminal south of town.

Dorud دورود

📞 066 / POPULATION 180,000 / ELEVATION 1448M

Most travellers arrive in the industrial city of Dorud (also spelled Dorood) to hike the remotely beautiful Oshtoran Kuh Range to the exquisite alpine **Lake Gahar**, nestling under the southern wall of the range in a protected nature reserve. Beginning at the ranger hut and car park at Haft Cheshmeh, 23km from Dorud, the walk in skirts the mountain flanks and takes four hours. Bring all supplies, including a tent. The track can sometimes close for any reason. There is talk that a permit and/or guide is now required from the **Department of Environment** (DOE; 📞 066-3343 9195; www.doe. ir; Street Alley, Shariati Judge Abad I). Check the situation before heading out.

At 4150m **Oshtoran Kuh** (San Boran) is the highest peak of the range of the same name. In summer it can be climbed without technical gear, but, as the area is remote and in a protected zone, a guide is a good idea. The eastern approach is usually the easiest.

Even if you don't hike, great views justify the car journey as far as **Darb-e-Astaneh**, a mud-house village 18km from Dorud.

The other reason that you may end up in the area is by riding the incredibly scenic **Dorud–Andimeshk railway** through the rugged Zagros mountains.

There's little other reason to linger in Dorud, but if you are stuck, **Mehmansara Shahrdari** (📞 066-4422 0020; Beheshti Blvd; tw/tr IR1,200,000/1,450,000) has spacious, very comfortable rooms and a decent restaurant featuring great photos of local beauty spots.

❶ Getting There & Away

Minibuses and faster savaris run from the bus station to Khorramabad and Borujerd. Esfahan-bound buses pick up passengers around midnight from the Taavoni bus company offices on Beheshti Blvd.

Dorud is on the main Tehran–Ahvaz railway and sees several trains a day in both directions, plus the **sightseeing train to Andimeshk**. All trains are met at the station by savaris for both Khorramabad and Borujerd.

The Dorud–Andimeshk Railway

This super-scenic railway traverses remote valleys, skirting Lorestan's peaks and navigating dozens of tunnels. Most trains run in the evening, but a day service departs Andimeshk at 5.30am, returning from Dorud at 2pm. The journey is a cultural experience but also an endurance test, with the train often overcrowded to the point of mayhem and the timetabled 5¼-hour trip taking nearer seven hours.

Bisheh Waterfalls

The tiny village of **Bisheh** (Bishehpuran) hides one of Iran's prettiest **waterfalls**. It cascades in 30m chutes off a tree-topped gully, then trickles in rivulets into the river below. In summer many local tourists make the scenic day trip from Dorud (train only at 2pm, 30 minutes) or Khorramabad (new road, no public transport). By autumn only their litter remains and you'll have the village to yourself, with the entire population of children following you Pied Piper style. The best waterfall views are from across the river using a new footbridge at the northern edge of the village. The day train offers fabulous glimpses of ziggurat-shaped **Mt Parvis** en route. If the trains are on time, you'll have an ample 4½ hours in Bisheh before the 7pm Tehran-bound train arrives to take you back to Dorud.

Sepid Dasht

The railway does a switchback at **Sepid Dasht**, the biggest village along the way. Sepid Dasht itself isn't architecturally attractive, but its mountain backdrop is spectacularly spiky. Rare savaris bump their way to Khorramabad on a scenic road that passes close to the **Gerit Falls**.

Talezang

Of anywhere along the line, isolated **Talezang**, three hours north of Andimeshk, is the most tempting hop-off point for trekking into the mountain wilderness. One hiking challenge is to make for **Shevi Waterfall**, which emerges directly as a spring from a cliff, then falls around 100m in a wide sweep. The waterfall is reportedly around five hours' walk from Talezang with some climbing involved. You can camp here; bring food and a tent.

Andimeshk   اندیمشك

AREA 061 / POPULATION 134,000 / ELEVATION 176M

Flat, uninteresting Andimeshk has useful transport connections to Shush, Dezful and Shushtar. You'll need to sleep here if you're taking the scenic day train to Dorud. The best choice is the centrally located and friendly **Hotel Rostan** (☑061-4264 1818; Imam St; s/tw/tr IR700,000/800,000/900,000; ☜), while for a meal **Pars Restaurant** (☑061-4262 6121; Beheshti Sq; meals from IR250,000) does all your favourite kababs and stews in blinged-up old Persian surrounds.

❶ Getting There & Away

AIR

The airport in neighbouring **Dezful** is actually closer to Andimeshk.

Tehran IR1,810,000, daily with **Iran Aseman** (☑061-4424 2491) and **Caspian** (p92).

Less regular flights travel to Esfahan and Mashhad.

BUS, MINIBUS & SAVARI

Almost any service from Ahvaz can also be booked ex Andimeshk at the new **main bus terminal** (Azadegan Sq), 1.5km south of Beheshti Sq on the southern ring road. Iran Peyma runs two morning and three late-night services to Esfahan (IR540,000). Tehran (IR700,000) buses leave in the evening, but you're better off catching the train. There are also overnight Volvos to Tabriz (IR420,000, 2.30pm) and Shiraz (4pm).

Savaris to Dezful (IR20,000, 15 minutes) leave frequently from Beheshti Sq. Savaris for Ahvaz depart from Beheshti Sq. **Minibuses** (Imam St) for Shush (IR40,000, 45 minutes)

use a hidden yard off a lane directly west of Beheshti Sq.

For Khorramabad, direct savaris (IR200,000, 1¾ hours) depart from Enqelab St, 2km north of the centre, and zoom up into the Zagros mountains on a new, very scenic motorway in no time at all. Make sure you don't take the much longer old route via **Pol-e Dokhtar** (Virgin Bridge), unless you dig crumbling brickwork. A single remaining arch of the 3rd-century bridge spans the windy road north of town.

TRAIN

The central **train station** (Taleqani St) is one short block west of Sa'at Sq. Beheshti Sq is one big block south of Sa'at. Arrive way before the 5.30am departure time if you want a seat on the brilliantly scenic but appallingly overcrowded day train to Dorud via Bisheh. A handy 3.50am train originating in Andimeshk runs overnight to Tehran (IR465,500, 12 hours).

Shush   شوش

☑061 / POPULATION 53,000 / ELEVATION 72M

Susa was among the greatest cities of ancient Persia. Built on its embers, modern-day Shush is modestly small and relaxed, home to a vast Unesco-listed archaeological site, a compact museum, a crowning castle and the enigmatic Tomb of Daniel. An afternoon is usually enough to see all the sights.

History

An important Elamite city from about the middle of the 3rd millennium BC, Susa was burnt by the Assyrian king Ashurbanipal around 640 BC but regained prominence in 521 BC when Darius I set it up as the Achaemenids' fortified winter capital. At that time it was probably similar in grandeur to Persepolis.

The palace survived the city's fall to Alexander the Great in 331 BC, and indeed Alexander married one of Darius III's daughters here. Still prosperous in the Seleucid and Parthian eras, Susa re-emerged as a Sassanian capital. During Shapur II's long reign (AD 310–379), it regained renown as a Jewish pilgrimage site and became a centre of Nestorian Christian study. Evacuated in the face of Mongol raids, Shush disappeared into the sands of time, only re-emerging after 1852, when British archaeologist WK Loftus became the first to survey the site. His work was continued by the French Archaeological Service from 1891 more or less continuously until the Islamic Revolution of 1979.

◉ Sights

Susa
ARCHAEOLOGICAL SITE

(Ancient Shush; incl museum IR350,000; ⊙ 8am-7pm, closes after heavy rain) On the hill behind the Susa Museum, ancient Persia is unearthed at this fascinating Unesco-listed archaeological site occupying the whole southern flank of modern Shush. Originally similar in scale to Persepolis, the city saw countless invasions and sackings (the Mongols were particularly thorough), and little upright evidence remains of Darius the Great's once grand capital (p139). The site is over 6000 years old. Take plenty of sunscreen.

Exit the Susa Museum gardens via the left gate and ascend the ramp. Dominating the landscape on the right is the fortress-like **Chateau de Morgan** (Shush Castle), built on the bones of an **Elamite acropolis** by the French in the early 20th century to protect their loot from marauding tribesmen. It's not open to the public, but there are fine views from the path around the base, including a view of the Tomb of Daniel from the southern side.

To the left of the entrance ramp, follow the self-guided signage past date palms into the excavation site of the 521 BC **Palace of Darius**. Old Darius loved his **apadanas** (open columned halls), and the one here had six by six 22m-high columns in the inner section, ringed by three 12-columned verandas. All the columns were topped with animal figures, such as flying bulls. Now only the bases and the odd earthbound animal remain.

To the east lies the **Royal City**, an area of deep excavations through 15 strata; south of the castle is an eroded earthen watchtower overlooking teenagers riding dirt bikes.

Susa Museum
MUSEUM

(Susa Park, Imam Khomeini St; incl archaeological site IR350,000; ⊙ 7.30am-1pm & 3.30-7pm Tue-Sun) This gem of a small museum displays ancient stone and pottery from archaeological sites in the region. Highlights include a giant double-headed bull capital from Susa's *apadana* (open columned hall), a

lion-hugging Hercules from Masjid-i Soleiman (home of Iran's first commercial oil well) and some spooky clay death masks from Haft Tappeh. The replica mosaics (the originals are in the Louvre) are colourful and poignant. The manager speaks English.

Tomb of Daniel
TOMB

(Aramgah-e Danyal; Imam Khomeini St; ⊙ dawn-late) While several cities lay claim to the biblical Daniel's last resting place, within Iran both Jews and Muslims agree that this ornate Khuzestani *ourchin* dome (pine-cone-shaped tower) marks the spot. Pilgrims come from across the country to kiss the *zarih* (mesh grate) inside the gilded interior of what is a traditionally mosaic-clad *imamzadeh* (shrine). The current structure dates from 1871, though the tradition surrounding Daniel's relics is over 1000 years old.

In the Bible, Daniel's claim to fame was surviving the lions' den in Babylon, though there's no mention of his burial. The first accounts placing his remains in Susa (Shush) pop up around the 12th century, and proximity to the relics was thought to bring health and good fortune. With an influx of lucrative pilgrims, this caused jealousy on the part of the less fortunate on the other side of the river, so the grave was shunted back and forth between two sides on alternate years. Eventually someone decided to lash it to the bridge in between.

Haft Tappeh Archaeological Site & Museum
ARCHAEOLOGICAL SITE

(www.mpr-khuz.ir; museum IR150,000; ⊙ museum 8am-5pm Sat-Thu; ℗) You need to be a tomb junkie or have an animated guide to get the most out of this dusty, partially excavated Elamite burial site. In stark contrast, the nearby, tiny Unesco-sponsored museum, sitting oasis-like among palms and tended gardens, is definitely worth a look, and not only for its delicious air-con. The small room contains interesting artefacts, local fertility figurines, skeletons in 'burial muffins', and a model of Choqa Zanbil (p142), with detailed documentation of its discovery and subsequent restoration.

Haft Tappeh is 3km off the Ahvaz–Andimeshk Hwy, and 18km south of Shush. It's usually the first stop when heading to the more visually stimulating Choqa

Zanbil. Beyond the museum, cross the Ahvaz–Andimeshk train tracks, then turn right and follow the 1km short cut south to the Choqa Zanbil road. Or jump on a train back to Shush (15 minutes).

☞ Tours

Mahmood Kasir TOURS
(✆ 0916 342 3962; kasirmahmood60@yahoo.com; half-day tours IR1,200,000) Recommended local guide and driver with very good English who can do the Shush–Haft Tappeh–Choqa Zanbil–Shushtar run in half a day.

🛏 Sleeping & Eating

Apadana Hotel HOTEL $$
(✆ 061-4251 3131; s/tw IR1,020,000/1,417,000; P ❄) Central, though rather soulless, the Apadana is within easy walking distance of most of the sights, and the downstairs restaurant is reliable. Staff can organise a driver-guide for Haft Tappeh and Choqa Zanbil (p142). It's on the canal between two bridges.

★ Paradisa Ahura Daniel IRANIAN $
(✆ 0913 136 6315; meals from IR160,000) Delicious traditional food served on carpeted platforms makes this relaxed, modern caravanserai the best eating option in town. There's also a limited number of rooms (from IR800,000; outside bathroom only) around the perimeter. Look for the English sign in the alley directly opposite the museum (p140) entrance gate.

ℹ Getting There & Away

Long-distance buses to Ahvaz drop passengers on the highway 2km east of town, usually at insanely-early o'clock when you'll struggle to find a taxi. A better option is to take a savari from Khorramabad to Andimeshk, then get your driver to continue on to Shush *dar bast* (IR200,000, 1½ hours). Heading out of Shush, you'll need to go first to Andimeshk, Dezful or Ahvaz.

Minibuses to Ahvaz depart frequently from Khomeini Blvd, 800m northeast of the archaeological site. For Andimeshk (IR20,000, 38km) and Dezful they use small, separate yards across the road.

Shush's train station is 6km east of the centre, and theoretically you could book a ticket from here to Tehran. Haft Tappeh also has a station, and you could take a train from Ahvaz (IR44,500, 1¾ hours), see the site, then either

jump back on the next train to Shush (15 minutes) or walk the 1km to the highway and flag down a savari.

ℹ Getting Around

The **Apadana Hotel** can arrange agency taxis from Shush to Shushtar via Haft Tappeh and **Choqa Zanbi** (p142) for US$35-40. There's no public transport, though the road is hitchable.

Shushtar شوشتر

✆ 061 / POPULATION 198,000 / ELEVATION 65M

Out on the baking plains of southern Khuzestan lies the deeply historic oasis of Shushtar, strategically located on the Karun River, where fascinating ancient hydraulic engineering provided water for surrounding irrigation and industry. Exploring the bridges, dams, canals and watermills that compose the Unesco-listed system make for an intriguing stay, and there's also a smattering of *imamzadehs* (shrines) and lovely restored Qajar buildings if you get sick of all the water action. The town centre is 17 Shahrivar Sq.

History

The ancient inhabitants of proto-Iran attached great religious importance to mountains. Where they had no mountains, they made their own. This was the origin of distinctive pyramidal, tiered temples known as ziggurats. Choqa Zanbil's ziggurat was the raison d'être of the town of Dur Untash, founded by King Untash Gal in the mid-13th century BC. Dur Untash bloomed especially in the early 12th century BC, when it had a large number of temples and priests. The town was eventually sacked by Ashurbanipal around 640 BC and, incredibly, remained 'lost' for more than 2500 years. It was accidentally rediscovered during a 1935 aerial survey by the Anglo-Iranian Oil Company, the forerunner of BP.

Some of Shushtar's then state-of-the-art irrigation systems, now designated a Unesco World Heritage Site, were built using Roman technology and labour: legionnaires defeated at the 259 battle of Edessa (today's Şanlıurfa in Turkey). Their leader, vanquished Valerian, became the only Roman emperor ever to be captured alive.

Sassanian king Shahpur I was so proud of his victory over the Romans that he recorded the event with boastful carved reliefs at Naqsh-e Rostam and Bishapur. Stories vary as to Valerian's fate, but Shushtaris insist that he was imprisoned in Qal'eh Salosel. In some versions he was systematically insulted and then brutally killed by being force fed a 'soup' of molten gold.

◉ Sights

★ Choqa Zanbil Ziggurat   RUINS
(چغازنبیل; IR200,000; ⊙ 7am-6pm, guarded 24hr) Choqa Zanbil's magnificent, Unesco-listed brick ziggurat is the world's best surviving example of Elamite architecture. Even if you're not a fan of ancient ruins, the great bulk and splendid semi-desert isolation of the site can't fail to impress. Try to catch it in the soft, golden light of late afternoon rather than the harsh midday sun. A private taxi tour from Shush to Shushtar via Haft Tappeh will cost $US35. The ziggurat is floodlit at night – and closed.

The ziggurat was dedicated to Inshushinak, the chief god of the Elamite pantheon and patron of Shush. In those days the area was fertile and forested, and the ziggurat was built on a slightly raised base to guard against flooding. It has a square plan with sides measuring 105m. The original five storeys were erected vertically from the foundation level as a series of concentric towers, not one on top of another as was the custom in neighbouring Mesopotamia. At the summit (now lost) was a temple accessible only to the highest elite of Elamite society. Even now the taboo remains and you're not allowed to climb the remnant stairways that rise on each of the four sides.

The structure is made of red bricks so well preserved that an observer could believe they're brand new. However, if you look very closely, a brick-wide strip at eye level is intricately inscribed with cuneiform, the world's first alphabet, which looks like a spilt box of tin tacks. The inscriptions are not easy to make out unless you cross the rope cordon, which every guide tells you he alone has permission to do (which means he's tipped the caretaker). Look for the sacrifice stones (halfway along the northwestern side) and an ancient sundial (facing the southwestern central stairway) and, beside it, the strangely moving

footprint of an Elamite child, accidentally preserved for three millennia.

The ziggurat was surrounded by a paved courtyard protected by a wall. At the foot of the northeastern steps would once have been the Gate of Untash Gal: two rows of seven columns where supplicants would seek the pleasure of the king. Around the wall was originally a complex of tomb chambers, tunnels and *qanat* channels. Once the site's climate became drier, *qanats* brought water an incredible 45km from ancient rivers. Vestiges are still visible. Outside were the living quarters of the town and 11 temples dedicated to various Elamite gods and goddesses. Little of this remains.

★ Shushtar Historical Hydraulic System   HISTORIC SITE
(Abshari Sika; IR200,000; ⊙ 8am-10pm) Listed by Unesco as a 'masterpiece of creative genius', the Shushtar Historical Hydraulic System has been diverting water for irrigation from the Karun River for over a millennium. The system comprises bridges, weirs, canals and tunnels, but the most impressive component is a series of ancient watermills powered by human-made waterfalls. The mills are situated in a tight ravine and the cascading waterfalls, sluices and millpond are floodlit at night. The entrance is down steps just before the Shari'ati St bridge.

You can see the waterfalls almost as well from the Shari'ati St bridge (300m southeast of 17 Shahrivar Sq) or, even better, by climbing the hill on the downstream right; follow signs to Marashi House (☑ 061-3622 3484; ⊙ loosely 8am-9pm) FREE. However, nothing beats getting up close to fully appreciate the force of the water and the skill of the ancient engineers.

The hill is a prime cafe perch, so keep your eyes peeled for a *chay* with a view.

Pol-e Shadorvan   BRIDGE
(Band-e Kaisar, Valerian's Bridge, پل شادروان) Running parallel to the modern Azadegan Bridge connecting historic Shushtar to the New Town are the substantial remains of this Sassanid-era bridge and weir. Thought to have been designed and built by captured Roman engineers (p141), this bridge, along with the Band-e-Mizan weir, raised the level of the Karun River by 2m,

providing the necessary waters for the hydraulic system (p142).

The bridge originally contained 45 arches and only fell into disrepair at the end of the 19th century. According to some Khuzestani historians, it was then deliberately dynamited by British agents, the idea being to break Shushtar's trade connections and encourage locals to seek alternative work at the new (British-owned) oilfields of Masjid-i Soleiman. Less conspiratorial theories blame rebellions and floods for the bridge's deterioration.

Qal'eh Salosel RUINS

(قلعه سلاسل, Salosel Castle; tours IR150,000; P) Set on a prominent cliff overlooking the river, historic Salosel Castle is no longer much to look at above ground. However, the caretaker will gladly show you the impressive Sassanian-era subterranean rooms and water channels. The tour also includes the stables (now a small museum) and a women's weaving workshop. Look for the English sign on Shari'ati St, about 500m northwest of Shahrivar Sq, before Bateni Sq.

Salosel Castle is where Shapur I is said to have imprisoned Roman emperor Valerian. It's also here that Persians held out for two years against the invading Arab Muslim armies until secret tunnels were revealed to the attackers by a traitor. For centuries Khuzestan was governed from a palace ('Kushk') on this site, and an impressive three-storey pyramidal building stood here until the 1920s.

Imamzadeh Abdullah ISLAMIC SHRINE

(Shrine of Abdullah) On the southern edge of town, this shrine is topped by a photogenic Khuzestani ourchin dome similar to that of Daniel's tomb in Shush, though this one deploys the rarer **star base**. A gory local tale records a woman beheading her own son to swap his head for the skull of a long-dead holy man, which is now enshrined here as a sacred relic.

At its foot is **Band-e Lashkar**, a small but impressive 13-arched Sassanid bridge.

Kolah Farangi Tower TOWER

This crumbling 7.5m octagonal tower at the river's edge was most likely a Sassanid navigational aid, though local lore has Shahpur's slave driver watching the king's

Roman prisoners from here as they worked on the nearby Band-e Mizan weir.

Islamic Shrines

About 2km east of the canal, the brilliant **Sahib-al Zaman Shrine** is graced by blue mosaics. Devotees are said to have made sightings of the Mahdi (last imam) here, hence the 'empty seat' shrine box. **Sheikh Allama Shushtari Shrine** entombs 20th-century religious scholar Mohammad Taqi 'Allama' Shushtari, one of Shushtar's favourite sons.

Sleeping

Mehmanpazir Shushtar HOSTEL $

(Hotel Shushtar; ☎ 061-3622 3288; Sherafat St; s/d/tr IR520,000/600,000/710,000) Basic but good-value cheapie.

★ Shushtar Traditional Hotel HOTEL $$

(☎ 0916 613 3212; www.shushtar-hotel.com; Abdollah Banoo St; s/d IR810,000/1,305,000; 🛜) Soon to be a traveller's favourite, the Shushtar offers traditional-styled rooms that open onto a private palm-fringed courtyard. Breakfast is served in a courtyard alcove. The friendly staff can organise agency taxis to Shush and Andimeshk. Enter from a small alley behind Abdollah Banoo shrine halfway along Abdollah Banoo St; you'll see the signs if you look up.

Hotel Jahangardi HOTEL $$

(Shushtar Tourism Hotel; ☎ 061-3622 1690; Sherafat Blvd; s/tw/tr IR870,000/1,100,000/1,380,000; P ✳ 🛜) Overlooking the canal that feeds the waterfalls, the Jahangardi has clean, comfortable rooms that are a bit of a hike from Shushtar's main attractions (though if you've got your own wheels, the off-street parking could be a clincher). The restaurant is reasonable.

Afzal Traditional Residency HOTEL $$$

(☎ 061-3621 0908; www.afzalhouse.ir; r IR2,400,000; 🛜) This exquisitely restored Qajar house near Imam Khomeini St has ornate rooms surrounding an intricate brick courtyard.

Eating & Drinking

★ Mostofi
Restaurant & Museum IRANIAN $$

(☎ 061-3621 0909; http://itsh.ir; meals from IR220,000; ⏰ 8am-late; 🛜) Take your shoes off and relax under the palms as you soak up the view of Shadorvan Bridge (p142) from the airy courtyard dining platforms of this restored Qajar house. It's definitely the nicest eating experience in Shushtar. Enter from the last alley heading north before the bridge.

Khosh & Besh CAFE
(Abdollah Banoo St; ⊙noon-10pm) Get your caffeine and nicotine fixes here. It's next to the CTO building.

❶ Information

HenDooneh Coffeenet (🖀 061-3622 5653; Abdollah Banoo St; per hour IR50,000; ⊙10am-late) Near the CTO building.

Tourist Information Office (🖀 061-3621 0909; http://itsh.ir; Mostofi House; ⊙8am-3pm) The small tourist-information office in Mostofi House, near Bateni Sq, provides useful brochures and maps.

❶ Getting There & Away

Shushtar's handy central bus **terminal** (Sheikh Allama Shoshtari Blvd) is just south of Imam Khomeini St. Regular buses run to Ahvaz (IR50,000, 1½ hours) and Dezful (IR50,000, one hour), where you can transfer for Shush or Andimeshk. Savaris to both destinations leave from outside the terminal. There's no public transport to Shush (90km away), but a good asphalt road exists, passing within 5km of Choqa Zanbil and emerging near Haft Tappeh.

The **train station** (Imam Hussein Blvd) is on the northern side of the river in Shushtar New Town. There's a sporadic service to Andimeshk, but a savari is infinitely easier.

Ahvaz اهواز

🖀 061 / POPULATION 1.2 MILLION / ELEVATION 17M

Ahvaz is vast, sprawling and industrial, and its temperatures are usually life-threatening. It suffered large-scale destruction in the Iran–Iraq War. There's little of interest to tourists here other than good transport connections.

Oxin Hotel (🖀 061-3447 4720; Pasdaran Hwy; s/tw/d IR1,640,000/2,500,000/3,190,000; P ❋ 🖀) is just 2km from the airport, if you do need to stay over.

❶ Transport

AIR

Istanbul (Turkey) US$183, Monday and Thursday with **Turkish Airlines** (p92).

Dubai (UAE) US$137, Wednesday, Friday and Sunday with FlyDubai and **Naft** (www.naftair-line.com/en).

Kuwait City (Kuwait) US$125, Monday and Thursday with **Iran Air** (🖀 061-3336 5684).

Tehran from IR1,330,000, frequent with all airlines.

Shiraz IR1,434,000, daily with **Iran Aseman** (🖀 061-3445 5056; www.iaa.ir), twice weekly with **Mahan Air** (p93).

Esfahan IR1,750,000, Wednesday and Friday with Iran Air.

Mashhad IR2,080,000, daily with **Taban Air** (p109), four times weekly with **Iran Aseman** (🖀 061-3445 5056; www.iaa.ir), weekly with **Caspian** (p92), **IAT** (p93) and Iran Air.

BUS & SAVARI

The main **bus terminal** (Enqelab Sq) is 5km west of the centre up Enqelab St. You can get to Shush (IR100,000, two hours) and virtually anywhere else in Iran.

Andimeshk savaris/minibuses (IR160,000/80,000) depart from a hidden yard 200m further north. Dezful buses (IR80,000, 1¾ hours) use a different yard 100m southeast of the main terminal across Enqelab St.

Buses for Shushtar (IR50,000, 1½ hours) use **Istgah Shushtar** (Zagros Terminal; Pasdaran Blvd; Ⓜ Naft) way across town, 4km northeast of the centre (halfway to the airport).

TRAIN

The main **train station** (Ⓜ Medan-e Sa'at) is west of the river, on the far side of Hejrat Park beyond Sa'at Sq. Several trains a day leave for Tehran via Andimeshk and Dorud. There's a handy local train to Shush (IR44,500, noon, two hours) that goes all the way to Tehran (IR275,000, 16 hours) – useful in summer, as you see all of the scenic section from Andimeshk to Dorud in daylight. Other Tehran trains leave at 1.53pm, 5.15pm and 7.40pm, but these cost more (IR555,000) and have fewer stops than the noon train.

Khorramabad خرم‌آباد

🖀 066 / POPULATION 351,000 / ELEVATION 1223M

Most travellers try to pass straight through Khorramabad, but this historic city is scenically located among the sharp, jagged tors of the Zagros mountains, a rockhound's nirvana: check out **Yafteh Wall** rated in Iran's top three climbing areas.

The superbly picturesque **Falak-Ol-Aflak** (🖀 066-3333 3333; IR150,000; ⊙8am-6pm, to 8pm summer) fortress overlooks the city centre and is now a museum. Enjoy the cooler air: it's all downhill from here to Khuzestan.

Most travellers seem to end up **Shardari Hotel** (Shari'ati Park; s/d IR1,250,000/1,492,000; P ❄ 🛜) offering basic, clean, comfortable rooms; its terrace has good views of a nearby jagged tor. Other recommended places to stay are budget **Karoon Hotel** (Shari'ati St; s/d IR750,000/1,010,000; 🛜), and the **Tourist Hotel** (Sarabkiu; 🕿 066-3323 8142; www.ittic.com; d US$56; P ❄ 🛜), which has a dependable restaurant.

❶ Transport

There are daily flights to Tehran (IR1,310,000) on **Mahan Air** (🕿 021-4838 4838; www.mahan.aero/en) or **Taban** (p109). The airport is 5km southwest of the city.

Savaris (IR200,000, two hours) and minibuses (IR140,000, 3½ hours) to Andimeshk can be found in a small **yard** off Baharestan Blvd, 3km southwest of Shariati Park.

Central Iran ايران مركزى

Best Places to Eat

➜ Abbasi Teahouse & Traditional Restaurant (p172)

➜ Bastani Traditional Restaurant (p171)

➜ Shahrzad (p172)

➜ Ghavam (p205)

➜ Talar Yazd (p190)

Best Places to Sleep

➜ Abbasi Hotel (p171)

➜ Barandaz Lodge (p181)

➜ Saraye Ameriha Boutique Hotel (p155)

➜ Niayesh Boutique Hotel (p202)

➜ Fahadan Museum Hotel (p189)

Why Go?

Central Iran, encompassing the magnificent cities of Esfahan, Yazd and Shiraz, is the cultural *tour-de-force* of Iran. Wedged between the Zagros Mountains to the west and the Dasht-e Kavir to the east, it offers the quintessential Persian experience and it's no coincidence that it attracts the most visitors. But in an age that celebrates getting off the beaten track, this is one destination where this is a redundant quest: for centuries people have crossed this land, following in the footsteps of ancient empire builders, their journeys commemorated in the artistic wonders at Persepolis.

You can continue that journey today, tracing the silk route along desert byways, through city bazaars and across mountain passes – in much the same manner as the region's famous nomads. Many of the caravanserai and *khans* that dot these routes have been restored and overnighting in one of these hospitable lodgings serves as an appointment with history.

When to Go

Visit in the spring when Persian gardens are in bud, mountain orchards are full of flowers and the rose fields around Kashan are at their fragrant best.

Although there is some difference in climate from region to region, generally travelling in the extreme heat of summer when temperatures can reach 50°C or more is not much fun between June to September.

January and February can be equally challenging, not just in the Zagros Mountains, but across the whole region as locals hunker down against the freezing cold of midwinter.

Qom قم

📖 025 / POPULATION 1,250,000 / ELEVATION 933M

Iran's second-holiest city after Mashhad, Qom (Ghom) is home to both the magnificent Hazrat-e Masumeh shrine and the hardline clerics who have ruled the country since 1979. Shiite scholars and students come from across the world to study in its *madrasehs* (schools) and browse in its famous religious bookshops, pilgrims pay homage at the shrine and locals are conspicuously pious. Travellers need to be mindful of the city's religious nature when visiting and dress conservatively. Discreet behaviour is particularly appreciated around the Hazrat-e Masumeh shrine.

Qom is one of Iran's fastest-growing cities (the population has doubled since the revolution) and the outskirts are being transformed by a sprawl of apartment blocks. While the new infrastructure is rather unattractive, the population growth has at least brought new life to the old centre. Qom can be visited in an easy day trip from Tehran or en route to Kashan.

◉ Sights

★ Hazrat-e Masumeh   SHRINE
(حضرت معصومه; Map p150; Astane Sq; ⊙24hr) The physical and spiritual centre of Qom, this magnificent shrine is the burial place of Imam Reza's sister Fatemeh, who died here in the 9th century. Reza was the eighth of the 12 imams who descended from Prophet Mohammed, as the only one of the 12 to be buried in Iran (in Mashhad), his sister's burial site has a special resonance as a place of pilgrimage. Non-Muslims are allowed into the courtyards but not the shrine itself.

Much of what can be seen today was built under Shah Abbas I and the other Safavid kings in the 16th century. Anxious to establish their Shiite credentials and prove they could match the sect's shrines at Karbala and Najaf (in modern-day Iraq), they lavished the site with courtyards of brilliant tile work. For visitors, however, it is the great golden cupola that distinguishes Hazrat-e Masumeh; this was an embellishment added by the Qajar ruler Fath Ali Shah in the early 19th century. Not to be outdone by their predecessors, successive rulers have lavished various embellishments on the shrine complex over the years with the latest addition – the construction of a grand plaza next to Astane Sq – being contributed by today's Ayatollahs of Qom.

Visits by non-Muslims should officially be in groups accompanied by a guide approved by the shrine stewards (who are incidentally a mine of information about the features of the complex); in practice, however, an element of discretion is exercised in permitting entry to individual travellers. Women must wear a chador, available free of charge at entrance No 1. Discreet photography by mobile phone was permitted during our visit but large cameras were discouraged.

Old Bazar   BAZAAR
(Map p150; ⊙9am-8pm Sat-Thu) This lovely old bazaar in the heart of Qom, a short stroll from Astane Sq, is worth a visit as one of the most authentic covered markets in Iran. With a small *khan* in the middle, and the usual labyrinth of alleyways, it is distinguished from other such trading places by representing 'business as usual' for the local citizens of Qom, with little if no concession to modernity or visitors. A great place to sense the continuity of trade over centuries.

Astane Square   SQUARE
(Map p150) The city's main square is paved with marble and pedestrianised, offering a grand vista of the Hazrat-e Masumeh. The square takes on a carnivalesque quality in the evening when robed clerics hurry by while pilgrims and scholars congregate to enjoy the open space, stroll the length of the square between the shrine and the glorious blue-domed **Imam Hassan Mosque** (Map p150), and browse among the Islamic bookshops. Catering to more worldly appetites, the souvenir shops flanking the square sell delicious local sweets.

A favourite confection of Qom is *sohun*, a sinfully sweet brittle made with pistachio, almond, saffron and cardamom. Buying a tin of these from one of the shops (IR100,000) and a glass of tea from the square's tea stand is part of the local experience.

Astane Sq spills into a neighbouring pedestrianised plaza in front of the Imam Hassan Mosque. A huge multistorey underground car park under this plaza is handy for those driving to Qom.

🛏 Sleeping & Eating

During religious festivals and on Fridays Qom is packed – be sure to book ahead if you plan to stop over. The best place to stay is **Qom International Hotel** (Map p150; 📞025-1771 9208; www.qomhotel.com; Helal Ahmar St; s/d/tr IR1,890,000/3,060,000/3,920,000; ❄🛜),

CENTRAL IRAN QOM

Central Iran Highlights

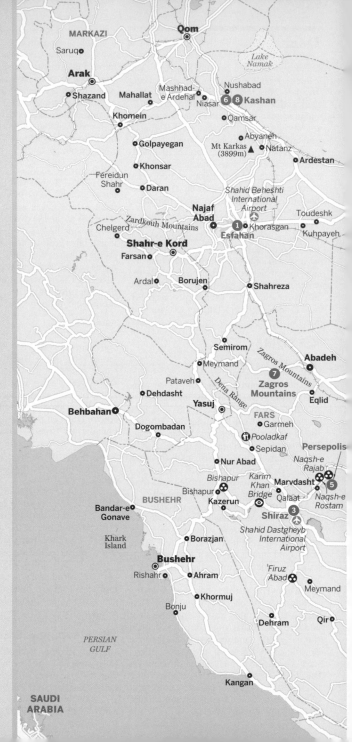

1 Esfahan (p158) Watching a master at work in this cultured capital of handicrafts.

2 Yazd (p182) Deciphering the calligraphy of the magnificent Masjed-e Jameh (Jameh Mosque).

3 Shiraz (p198) Scooping up the coloured light of a morning visit to the Masjed-e Nasir-al-Molk (Pink Mosque).

4 Dasht-e Kavir (p178) Learning the importance of water in the parched oasis towns of Mesr and Garmeh.

5 Persepolis (p207) Joining the pageant of nations in visiting the ancient Apadana Palace with its famous decorative staircase.

6 Kashan (p151) Waking up to the music of fountains in a traditional-house hotel in this city of wind catchers.

7 Zagros Mountains (p176) Hiking among herders as they migrate to their summer pastures.

8 Bagh-e Fin (p153) Enjoying the poetic delight of this classic Persian garden in spring.

9 Bavanat (p211) Slipping into the rhythm of life under the walnut trees of this rural valley.

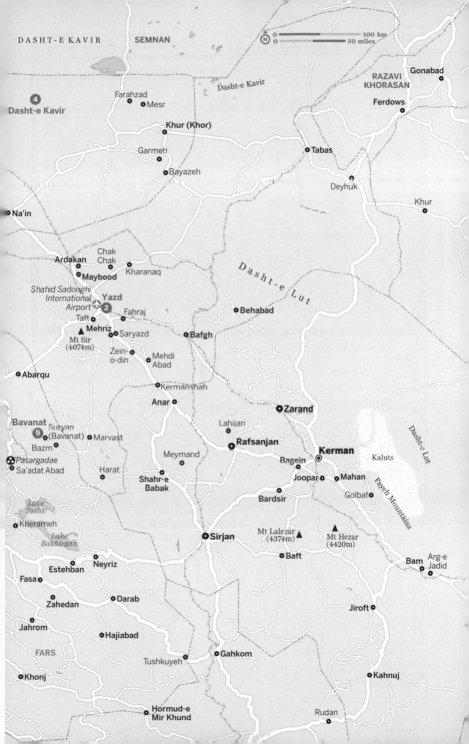

Qom

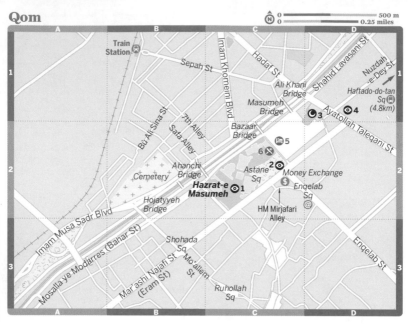

N 0 — 500 m
0 — 0.25 miles

Qom

⊚ Top Sights
1 Hazrat-e Masumeh.............................C2

⊚ Sights
2 Astane Square.......................................C2
3 Imam Hassan Mosque D1
4 Old Bazar D1

🛏 Sleeping
5 Qom International Hotel C2

🍴 Eating
6 Restaurant...C2

which also has a restaurant serving Iranian cuisine and a modern coffee shop. Alternatively fill up on the tasty kababs at the **restaurant** (Map p150; ☎ 0938 174 0328; kebab meal IR80,000; ⊙ 6am-11pm) opposite the hotel and next to the bakery.

🛈 Information

Cafenet Saeid (Map p150; cnr MR Sabori Alley & Enqelab St; per hr IR40,000; ⊙ 8am-11pm) Located near Astane Sq.

Money Exchange (Map p150; Mar'ashi Najafi St; ⊙ 9am-8pm Sat-Thu)

🛈 Getting There & Away

Transport to Qom is very crowded on Fridays and during religious holidays.

BUS & TAXI

Intercity buses and savaris leave from Haftado-do-tan Sq, a big roundabout 5km north of the shrine. Savari touts pester potential passengers here as they wait for the dozens of buses passing through en route to or from Tehran.

Buses to Tehran (VIP IR120,000, 1½ to two hours) stop here several times an hour. Southbound services to major destinations are frequent, including Esfahan (VIP IR230,000), but seats need to be prebooked.

Buses to Kashan (VIP IR100,000, 1¼ hours) or savari (IR200,000) leave from Haftado-do-tan Sq (a taxi dar bast to Kashan costs IR800,000).

TRAIN

From Qom's **train station** (Astane Sq), five trains run between Tehran and Qom daily (IR80,000, 2½ hours).

🛈 Getting Around

A taxi from Haftado-do-tan Sq or the bus terminal to Astane Sq (train station) costs around IR120,000.

Kashan کاشان

♫ 031 / POPULATION 272,359 / ELEVATION 946M

Many travellers opt to bypass Kashan on their journeys between Tehran, Esfahan and Yazd, but this delightful oasis city on the edge of the Dasht-e Kavir is one of Iran's most alluring destinations. It not only boasts a cluster of architectural wonders, an atmospheric covered bazaar and a Unesco recognised garden, but it also offers some of central Iran's best traditional hotels.

Shah Abbas I was so enamoured with Kashan that he insisted on being buried here rather than in Esfahan. Other historical figures of note who are associated with the town include Abu Musa al-Ashari, a soldier and companion of the Prophet Mohammed whose army took the town in the 7th century AD. Legend has it that his troops tossed thousands of scorpions from the surrounding desert over the city walls causing the terrified Kashanis to capitulate.

During the Seljuk period (AD 1051–1220) Kashan became famous for its textiles, pottery and tiles, reaching high levels of accomplishment in each of these cottage industries. Currently local textile artisans are enjoying something of a renaissance of interest in their work, but mechanisation has largely led to the demise of this ancient craft. Today the town is more widely known as a major centre for the production of rose water, which is sold at outlets around the main tourist attractions and at dedicated stores in the bazaar.

A visit is April is rewarded not only with a perfect climate but with an air redolent with the fragrance of roses, grown in the surrounding fields.

◉ Sights

Most of Kashan's sights are located in the old quarter, clustered around Alavi St and within walking distance of the bazaar. A few sights, such as Bagh-e Fin, the underground city of Nushabad and the ancient ruins at Seyalk, are scattered around the outskirts. At least a day and a half is needed to do all the sights justice and to relax into the town's peaceful ambience.

◎ Bazaar & Around

★ **Bazaar** BAZAAR
(بازار; Map p152; ⊘ 9am-noon & 4.30-8pm Sat-Thu) Kashan's historic bazaar is one of the best in Iran. Busy but not manic, traditional but with a nod at modern goods, large enough to surprise but not to get lost in, it's a great place to wander for a couple of hours, especially in the late afternoon when the lanes are full of shoppers. The multi-domed roof of the bazaar dates from the 19th century, but the site has been the centre of trade in Kashan for almost 800 years.

Two main alleys lead through the bazaar, one known as the 'Main Line', and the other as the 'Copper Line', which lives up to its name for at least part of its length. Step off either of these two thoroughfares, and there's a wealth of caravanserais, mosques, madrasehs and *hammams* (public bathhouses) to explore. Chief among the attractions is the fine Amin al-Dowleh Timche, a caravanserai with a soaring, beautifully decorated dome. Dating from 1868, the caravanserai has recently been restored by the Kashani Culture & Heritage Office and is home to carpet sellers and the odd curiosity shop. There's a tea stand at one of its entrances where you can sit and watch a steady stream of shoppers pass by. An equally popular tea stop is the cosy 19th-century **Hammam-e Khan** (Map p152; ♫ 031-5545 2572; admission IR20,000, incl tea & Kashan cookies IR100,000; ⊘ 9am-9pm), where three generations of *hammami* tend to the well-being of their customers – replacing the tea and towels of former times with the tea and talk of today.

Other notable features of the bazaar include the Seljuk-era Masjed-e Soltani (Soltani Mosque), located on the Main Line and open only to men, and the 800-year-old Mir Emad Mosque, along the Copper Line.

Of course, a bazaar ought to be shopped in. If the hardware shops hold little attraction and the textiles fail to bring out your inner seamstress, there is at least rose water of the highest quality midway along Main Line or boxes of Kashani biscuits from one of the bazaar's many patisseries – the *nargili* (coconut macaroons) are particularly delicious.

Masjed-e Agha Borzog MOSQUE
(مسجد و مدرسه آقا بزرگ, Agha Bozorg Mosque & Madraseh; Map p152; ⊘ 8am-8pm) FREE Comprising four storeys, including a large sunken courtyard with ablutions pool, an austere dome, tiled minarets and unusually lofty *badgirs* (windtowers), this decommissioned 19th-century mosque complex is famous for the symmetry of its design. The wooden front door is said to have as many studs as there are verses in the Quran,

Kashan

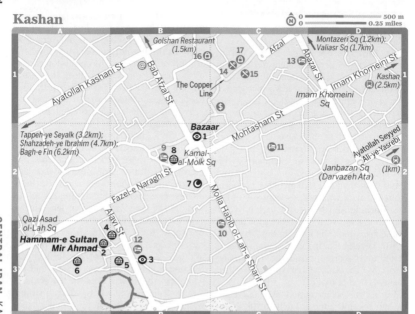

and the mud-brick walls are covered with Quranic inscriptions and mosaics. A fine portal and mihrab (niche indicating the direction of Mecca) at the rear is particularly noteworthy.

Sheibani's Museum of Fine Arts   MUSEUM
(Kaj Historical House; Map p152; ☑ 031-5544 7070; www.kajhouse.com; Ehsan Alley, off Fazel-e Naraghi St; IR50,000; ☉9am-1pm & 5-9pm) This beautifully restored old house, with a courtyard cut deep into the basement, houses the work of a popular Iranian painter, Manuchehr Sheibani. Credited as being a pioneer of the contemporary arts revolution in Iran, this 20th-century painter was also a poet. Aside from the exhibition of his work, the house encompasses a cosy coffee shop and a small library, and makes a pleasantly cultured spot to engage with Kashan's literati.

◉ Alavi St & Around

Khan-e Boroujerdi   HISTORIC BUILDING
(خانه بروجردی ها; Map p152; off Alavi St; US$0.50; ☉8am-sunset) Legend has it that when Sayyed Jafar Natanzi, a samovar merchant known as Boroujerdi, met with carpet merchant Sayyed Jafar Tabatabaei to discuss taking his daughter's hand in marriage, Mr Tabatabaei set one condition: his daughter

must be able to live in a home at least as lovely as his own. The result – finished some 18 years later – was the Khan-e Boroujerdi. Made distinctive by its six-sided, domed *badgirs,* the house boasts frescoes painted by Kamal al-Molk, the foremost Iranian artist of the time.

Khan-e Tabatabaei   HISTORIC BUILDING
(خانه طباطبایی; Map p152; ☑ 031-5422 0032; off Alavi St; ,IR350,000; ☉8am-sunset) Built around 1880, Seyyed Jafar Tabatabei's house is renowned for its intricate stone reliefs, including finely carved cypress trees, delicate stucco, and striking mirror and glass work. The seven elaborate windows of the main courtyard (most houses sport only three or five) are a particular wonder, designed to illustrate the high social status of the owner. The house is arranged around four courtyards, the largest of which boasts a large pond with fountains, helping to keep the courtyard cool. From mid-afternoon (depending on the month), sunlight and stained glass combine to bathe some rooms in brilliant colour.

To find this house, walk south past the Khan-e Borujerdi towards a distinctive blue conical tower. The tower belongs to a shrine that neighbours the Hammam-e Sultan Mir Ahmad. Turn right after the tower and the entrance to the *khan* is on the left.

Kashan

Khan-e Abbasian   HISTORIC BUILDING
(خانه عباسیان; Map p152; off Alavi St; IR150,000;
☺8am-sunset) Built by a wealthy glass merchant, this handsome set of six buildings
(signposted from the *hammam*) is spread
over several levels. The numerous courtyards,
which are subterranean – excavated from the
soil, not built on top of it – are designed to
enhance the sense of space by increasing in
size and depth as the complex unfolds. As a
result and despite illusion, the multistorey
buildings are no higher than neighbouring
properties in the old district.

★**Hammam-e**
Sultan Mir Ahmad   HISTORIC BUILDING
(حمام سلطان میراحمد; Map p152; off Alavi St;
IR150,000; ☺8am-5pm, to 7pm summer) This
500-year-old *hammam* is a superb example
of an Iranian bathhouse. A recent restoration has stripped away 17 layers of plaster
(note the wall inside the second room) to
reveal the original *sarough,* a type of plaster made of milk, egg white, soy flour and

lime that is said to be stronger than cement.
Richly coloured tiles and delicate painting
feature throughout, and a further highlight
is the panorama of the town's minarets and
badgirs viewed from the roof.

◉ Outer Kashan

★**Bagh-e Fin**   GARDENS
(باغ تاریخی فین, Fin Garden; Amir Kabir Rd; garden
IR200,000; museum IR80,000; ☺9am-sunset)
Designed for Shah Abbas I in the 16th century, this delightful garden with its symmetrical proportions, old cedars, spring-fed
pools and fountains is renowned as being
the very epitome of the Persian garden and
its evocation of heaven. Given its influence
in the planning of gardens as far afield as
India and Spain, Fin Garden, which lies in
the suburb of Fin, 9km southwest of central
Kashan, has justly earned a place on the
Unesco World Heritage list.

In contrast to the arid location, the garden flows with crystal-clear warm water
channelled from a natural spring through a
series of turquoise-tiled pools and fountains
and continuing along the main road in *jubs*
(canals, pronounced 'joobs'). The evergreen
trees inside the garden are up to 500 years
old, and the profusion of complementary
deciduous trees contributes to a garden that
works to please year-round.

The highlights of the garden are two pa-
vilions: the *shotor gelou,* a two-storey pool
house with water running through the middle of the ground floor, and a recreational
pavilion at the rear of the garden. Built in
the later Qajar period, this delightful building sports an elaborate painted dome of
outdoor vignettes (including a semi-naked
beauty being surprised in the act of bath-
ing). In the adjoining rooms, stalactite
ceilings and coloured glass windows play a
role in keeping visitors content with blue,
white and green glass chosen to be cool
and soothing and to make the room look
bigger; in contrast, red, orange and yellow
glass has the opposite effect, making the
room seem warmer in winter. Interestingly,
red and blue combined apparently confus-
es insects and wards off mosquitoes.

Many Iranians head to the *hammam*
complex along one side of the garden, famous as the place where the nationalist
Mirza Taqi Khan, more commonly known
as Amir Kabir, was murdered. Amir Kabir
served as prime minister under Nasir od-Din
Shah from 1848 to 1851. He was a moderniser

DON'T MISS

KASHAN'S TRADITIONAL HOUSES

Hiding behind high mud-brick walls are hundreds of large traditional houses built by wealthy merchants, monuments to the importance of Kashan as a Qajar-era commercial hub. Dating from the 19th century, most have long since been divided into smaller homes and many are literally turning to dust. A few, however, have been restored and are open to the public as museums or as Kashan's most desirable places to stay.

While each house has its own distinct features (the tallest wind catcher, the best plaster work, the most courtyards), they all share a common principle of design. The house is arranged around a series of interlinked courtyards, each with a separate function: the *andaruni* served as the internal area where family members lived; the *biruni* acted as an external area used for entertaining and housing guests and conducting business; and the *khadameh* (servants' quarters). Designed to be plain and modest from the outside, with no house exceeding the height of any other, the doorways show little hint of the wonders within. Even the receiving area is concealed from the courtyard by angled corridors, perhaps to ensure privacy, or perhaps to increase the impact of stepping into the first courtyard. High thresholds and low door frames into each room were built partly to keep scorpions at bay, and partly to enforce a bow on entry.

Each courtyard is arranged around a central garden with a water feature (usually a rectangular pool with fountains) and includes a warm south-facing seating area that catches the winter sun, and an opposing north-facing area for warmer months. Lofty *badgirs* channel the prevailing winds into a basement used for escaping the summer heat. The houses are full of aesthetic wonders, including elaborate stucco work, stalactite ceilings, painted murals, and gorgeous coloured glass and wood panelling.

who instituted significant change, especially in the fields of education and administration, but his popularity was not appreciated in the royal court and the shah's mother eventually persuaded her son that he had to go. Amir Kabir was imprisoned in Fin Garden and eventually murdered in the bathhouse, though some say he slashed his own wrists. Inside, mannequins posed in scenes from the drama form the backdrop of many a selfie taken by those coming to pay homage to a hero.

With extra time to spare, the modest **Kashani National Museum** (IR80,000; ☉9am-sunset), which occupies a small pavilion in the grounds, is worth a quick visit. It showcases some fine examples of Kashani velvet and brocade, and has some ceramics and calligraphy. A scale model of the garden helps to show its perfect proportions from an aerial perspective.

Don't leave the garden without pausing at the Fin Garden teahouse, which is set within its own enchanted little garden. Located near the source of the spring, the current is thick with warm-water-loving fish and shaded with aged trees. The teahouse speciality is Kashan barley soup (IR50,000) in winter and rose-water ice cream in summer.

Fin Garden is at the end of Amir Kabir Rd, which can be reached by shuttle taxi (IR60,000) from Kamal al-Molk Sq or by taxi *dar bast* (closed door; IR180,000). Alternatively, you can hop on the green bus that travels from the corner of Ayatollah Kashani and Baba Afzal Sts in central Kashan with a pre-purchased card (IR60,000) from the bus terminal. During the journey, keep an eye open for the elaborate modern Italianate houses that line the road near the garden, evidence that the location continues to attract fashionable Kashanis.

Nushabad 'Underground City' TUNNEL
(☑031-5482 5850; IR200,000; ☉9am-4.30pm) This remarkable complex of tunnels, 8km north of Kashan, originally grew up around a freshwater spring, credited with supplying delicious, crystal-clear water. Only part of the tunnel system is open to visitors today, and those parts are often subject to flooding (note the two-colour tone of the walls showing the flood level), but even a quick descent to the first level gives an idea of the complexity of this ancient engineering project.

♐ Tours

Kashan has several licensed driver-guides who specialise in bringing the old quarter and city environs to life for visitors. Most also cover half-day trips to Abyaneh or the nearby towns of Niasar and Qamsar. Their rates, which are largely set by government agencies, tend to be around US$30 for a half-day tour and US$50 for a full-day tour. These guides not only have a thorough knowledge of history and heritage, they also offer practical services such as booking onward tickets.

★**Mostafa Ramezanpoor** HISTORY
(☑0913 039 9198; m.ramezanpoor@yahoo.com; half-/full-day tour US$30/50) This excellent and personable licensed guide is a mine of information, not just about his home town of Kashan, but of the entire central region of Iran.

Leila Sabbaghi OUTDOORS
(☑0913 260 8839; sabbaghil@yahoo.com; half-/full-day tour US$30/60) An enthusiastic and knowledgeable guide with good English and basic French.

Fatima Araghi HISTORY
(☑0913 129 7196; f.araghi.d@gmail.com; half-/full-day tour US$30/50) A newly licensed tour guide with excellent English and an enthusiastic dedication to the task. She also offers a free bus and train booking service.

🛏 Sleeping

Ehsan Historical Guest House HOTEL $
(Map p152; ☑031-5545 3030; www.ehsanhouse.com; off Fazel-e Navaghi St; d/tr IR2,106,600/2,700,000; without bathroom IR1,500,000/1,800,000; ✳@🛜) 🏊 Rooms come in many shapes in this traditional house, one of the first of its kind in Kashan. Most are arranged around a pretty courtyard with a large decorative pool – a good setting for dinner (meals around IR200,000). The hotel uses profits to help fund its NGO, which promotes the arts and is linked with the neighbouring Taj House Art Gallery.

Sayyah Hotel HOTEL $
(Map p152; ☑031-5544 4535; Abazar St; d/tr 1,400,000/2,000,000; P✳🛜) If you didn't book your accommodation in a traditional-house hotel in advance and everywhere is full, this centrally located basic hotel by the bazaar offers a simple room with newly replaced toilets. The smell of smoking may be off-putting, but the view across old Kashan is an unexpected bonus. Two hours of free wi-fi is available in the lobby.

★**Manouchehri House** HOTEL $$
(Map p152; ☑031-5524 2617; www.manouchehrihouse.com; 49 7th Emerat Alley, off Sabat Alley

& Mohtasham St; d/tr/q from IR2,650,000/3,500,000/4,700,000; ✳@🛜) Opened in 2011 after a three-year restoration project, this traditional house is a joy to behold with a stunning central courtyard featuring an *iwan* overlooking a huge decorative pool. The hotel has nine comfortable rooms, the amenities are excellent (restaurant, in-house cinema) and the service is exemplary. Book well in advance at this Kashan favourite.

Breakfast includes fresh juice and good coffee (Nespresso).

Kamalalmolk Traditional Guesthouse TRADITIONAL HOTEL $$
(Map p152; ☑031-5522 5593; www.kamalalmolk-house.com; Tile 9, Allah Parast Alley, Molla Habibollah Sharif St; d/tr IR1,450,000/1,650,000, s/d/tr without bathroom IR900,00/1,000,000/1,250,000) This newly opened hotel, in a traditional house constructed nearly two centuries ago, sports a fine wind-catcher. With little characterful mid-range accommodation in Kashan to choose from, it is set to be a winner with guests. The welcoming and friendly management complements the emphasis on homely facilities, offered without pretension.

★**Saraye Ameriha Boutique Hotel** BOUTIQUE HOTEL $$$
(خانه عامری ها; Map p152; ☑031-5524 0220; www.sarayeameriha.com; Alavi St; s/d/ste US$82/115/180; ⊙9am-6pm; ✳@🛜) This is the jewel in the crown of Kashan's accommodation. Set within the most impressive of Kashan's restored mansions, guests dine under a twinkling dome of mirrors, sip tea to the sound of splashing fountains, soak in a tub the size of a fish pond and wake up to coloured light dancing on luxury linen. A range of rooms are available.

🍴 Eating

The restaurants in each of the traditional house hotels make for atmospheric places to dine; they serve good Iranian food and welcome nonguests. The garden restaurants lining the road to Bagh-e Fin are also popular with locals on summer evenings. There are plenty of places scattered near the bazaar for cheap eats, and rose-water-infused ice cream is a local speciality.

Bastani Saraye Firuzeh ICE CREAM $
(Map p152; ☑031-5544 4126; Copper Line, Bazaar; ice cream from IR20,000; ⊙9am-noon & 4.30-8pm) Forget rocky road and chocolate chip,

the defining flavours of this unimposing ice-cream cafe are pomegranate, saffron, vanilla and (given that this is Kashan and the home of rose-growing) a delicately aromatic, pink-tinged rose water. A steady stream of locals pauses during the hot work of haggling with shop owners to sample its famed delights.

Nabatrie Ghanadilpati PATISSERIE $
(Map p152; Copper Line, Bazaar; box of Kashan cookies from IR80,000; ⊘ 9am-noon & 4.30-8pm Sat-Thu) One of the best shops in Kashan to buy the town's signature biscuits and melt-in-the-mouth macaroons.

Abbasi Teahouse & Traditional Restaurant IRANIAN $$
(Map p152; Khan-e Abbasian, off Alavi St; meals IR200,000; ⊘ 11am-midnight) Occupying the basement *khadameh* of the Khan-e Abbasian, this family-run restaurant is justly popular with visitors. Traditional seating is arranged around a fountain and the menu features equally traditional dishes, including *dizi* (lamb and vegetable stew pounded to a paste at the table), *turshi* (pickles) and delicious *kashke bademjan* (roasted eggplant topped with fermented cheese). The entrance is opposite the ticket office.

Manouchehri House IRANIAN $$
(Map p152; ☑ 031-5524 5531, 031-5524 2617; www.manouchehrihouse.com; 49 7th Emerat Alley, off Sabat Alley & Mohtasham St; lunch IR300,000; ⊘ 7-10am, noon-3.30pm & 7-11pm; ✐) This beautifully restored mansion provides the perfect setting for lunch. Book ahead for a meal featuring Kashani specialities, such as *gusht lubia* (lamb and kidney-bean stew) and *polo shevid* (rice with lima beans and dill).

Golshan Restaurant IRANIAN $$
(Shahid Motahari Blvd; mains IR500,000; ⊘ noon-3.30pm & 7.30-11pm) A favourite with Kashanis celebrating weddings, birthdays and other big occasions, this brightly lit restaurant in the modern part of town serves fish dishes, *zereshk polo* (roast chicken with rice and barberries) and the full complement of kababs.

 Mirrors Restaurant IRANIAN $$$
(Saraye Ameriha Boutique Hotel Restaurant; Map p152; ☑ 031-5524 0220; www.sarayeameriha.com; Alavi St; mains IR450,000; ⊘ noon-3.30pm & 7-11pm) It is worth dining in this fabulous little restaurant for the sheer pleasure of sitting in pools of coloured light by day and under a canopy of mirrored stars at night. Ask for the daily stew and relax in the company of Kashanis enjoying a special occasion. The stone-floored antechamber lacks the dazzle of the main room's mirror work so book ahead.

🔒 **Shopping**

Kashani Traditional Millstone MARKET
(Map p152; Copper Line, Bazaar; ⊘ 9am-noon & 4.30-8pm Sat-Thu) The huge millstone in this shop has been in use for over 300 years and still grinds spices for local cooks each day. You can observe copper pots being decorated and pounded into shape at nearby stores.

Rose Water Shop PERFUME
(Map p152; ☑ 031-5544 2992; Copper Line, Bazaar; rose water from IR40,000; ⊘ 9am-noon & 4.30-8pm Sat-Thu) Run by an elderly gentleman knowledgeable in the arts of Kashani rose-water production, this shop in the middle of the bazaar stocks a range of rose-water products. The strength of aroma depends on the point at which the distillation is captured and several qualities are on offer.

ℹ **Information**

Caffenet Soroush (Map p152; cnr Bab Afzal & Amir Kabir Sts; per hr IR30,000; ⊘ 8am-midnight) One of the few *coffeenets* for checking internet still remaining in Kashan.

Beheshti Hospital (☑ 031-5554 0026; Qotb-e Ravandi Blvd) A vast medical complex at the northern end of town.

Mohtasham Exchange (Map p152; ☑ 031-5545 0444; ex.mohtasham@yahoo.com; Main Line, Bazaar; ⊘ 8.30am-12.30pm & 4.30-8.30pm Sat-Thu) A new exchange with good rates.

ℹ **Getting There & Away**

Kashan is well connected by train and bus services. There are also savaris to Tehran leaving from Valiasr Sq and costing IR350,000 (front seat) and IR300,000 (back seat); these are cheaper via Qom. Savaris to Esfahan leave from Montazeri Sq and cost IR250,000. It's possible to board (and alight) the Tehran and Esfahan bus at Montazeri Sq to save travelling out to Kashan bus terminal.

BUS

The main **Kashan bus terminal** (off Persian Gulf Blvd) is on the northern edge of the city. Buses from this terminal leave regularly to Tehran (VIP IR160,000, 3½ hours) via Qom (IR100,000, 1¼ hours), to Esfahan (VIP/ *mahmooly* IR115,000/80,000, 2½ hours) and to Shiraz (VIP IR450,000, 10 hours).

The bus from Yazd does not enter Kashan but it is possible to alight at the highway; taxis (IR80,000) wait at the junction to ferry passengers into town.

Buses depart from the terminal; boarding is also possible at Montazeri Sq (buy a ticket on the bus or purchase in advance).

TRAIN

The **train station** (end of Ayatollah Yasrebi St) is about 2km northeast of the city centre and a taxi into town costs around IR80,000.

There are four trains a day between Kashan and Tehran (IR165,000, 3½ hours) between 2pm and 7pm. There are also daily trains to Esfahan (IR220,000, 4½ hours).

❶ Getting Around

A taxi *dar bast* within town usually costs IR100,000. From Kashan bus terminal it costs IR160,000 (IR20,000 extra at night).

Around Kashan

If the mountainous landscape looming above the mud-brick houses of Kashan beckons, there are a couple of half-day trips to villages that give a reason for exploring beyond the city suburbs. Most visitors head for the picturesque pink-tinged village of Abyaneh, but for those longing to get off the beaten track, there are a couple of other options. **Niasar** offers a fine waterfall that's a popular picnic site for much of the year, as well as a well-preserved Sassanian-era fire temple. **Qamsar,** surrounded by fields of roses, is well worth a visit, particularly during late spring (May to early June) when the annual harvest of rose petals attracts visitors from across Iran.

Abyaneh   ابیانه

☑ 031 / POPULATION 305 / ELEVATION 2235M
Serenely situated at the foot of Mt Karkas (3899m), the ancient village of Abyaneh is a warren of steep, twisting lanes and crumbling red mud-brick houses with lattice windows and fragile wooden balconies. It's testament to both the age and isolation of Abyaneh that the elderly residents speak Middle Persian, an earlier incarnation of

CENTRAL IRAN AROUND KASHAN

KASHANI TEXTILES

Kashan has been an important centre for textile production since the Safavid era, but in recent decades the artisanal trade has suffered from a proliferation of cheap, factory-made textiles flooding the market. It is becoming increasingly hard to make a living producing traditional Kashani textiles such as embossed velvet and *zarbaft* (silk brocade) on hand looms, and as a result few young people are learning the trade.

Fortunately, there has been a recent revival of interest in this complex craft and students from Tehran are posted to study the intricacies of looming at a dedicated textile **Handicraft Workshop** (Kargahe Sanaye Daste; Map p152; Alavi St; ⊗ 8am-2pm Sat-Wed) **FREE** in the middle of town. It's possible to visit the working looms, which, with their hanging bags weighing down the colourful strands of the warp and the weft, make for a contemporary art installation in their own right. The industry has received further promotion through the owners of the **Manouchehri House** (p155) traditional hotel, which is contributing to the preservation of age-old skills through their support of artisans who produce these labour-intensive works of art. The setting up of the loom for velvet or brocade takes many hours and if a thread breaks, it involves an elaborate process of identifying and patching the rogue strand: sourcing fine quality cotton and silk thread is therefore a challenge in an era that favours cheap-quality imports. It is worth visiting the weavers' workshops to gain an understanding of the extreme skill required to produce these world-class textiles.

Nonguests can visit the hotel's shop where it's possible to purchase handwoven silk fabric (US$30 to US$100 per metre), cotton fabric (US$15 per metre) or museum-grade *zarbaft* produced using patterns from the Cultural Heritage Foundation in Tehran (US$6000 per metre); the shop can even organise made-to-order clothes in your choice of fabric.

WORTH A TRIP

NATANZ نطنز

Between Kashan and Esfahan it's worth considering a brief detour in Natanz, on the lower slopes of Mt Karkas. This tree-lined town has two attractions: the four-*iwan* central mosque **Masjed-e Jameh** (Jameh Mosque; Malek-e Ashtar; IR100,000; ⊙9am-sunset Tue-Sun), one of the best preserved of all Ilkhanid-era buildings, dating from the early 14th century; and **Sheikh Abd ol-Samad** (Malek-e Ashtar; admission incl in ticket for Masjed-e Jameh; ⊙9am-sunset Tue-Sun; 🚻), the tomb of a renowned local Sufi mystic of the 11th century The town is also associated with pottery making and tile production. **Charsooq Restaurant** (☑031-5422 1301; Malek-e Ashtar, next to Masjed-e Jameh; meals IR200,000; ⊙8am-4pm & 6-10.30pm) makes a comfortable rest stop before exploring the nearby pottery workshop or proceeding on your journey.

The greater area of Natanz has a further claim to fame as the country's major underground uranium enrichment plant. Visitors to the town *must not under any circumstances take photographs* of this site, or even the fence around the site, en route into town.

Buses between Kashan (IR110,000, 1¼ hours) and Esfahan (IR160,000, two hours) pass the Natanz junction but do not enter the town itself. The bus stop is on the roundabout on the main highway and the complex is a good 2km walk (down the hill, turn left at the first roundabout and pass two further roundabouts). It is easier to take a shared taxi if coming from Kashan (IR160,000). A taxi *dar bast* from Esfahan to Natanz costs IR1,200,000.

Farsi that largely disappeared some centuries ago, and many men still dress in the traditional wide-bottomed trousers and black waistcoats. Women's clothing features hejabs that cover the shoulders and are traditionally strewn with printed or embroidered red flowers.

There is an entry fee (IR50,000 per person) to visit the town with a checkpoint about a kilometre before the descent through a tree-lined avenue into town. This is to help manage the tourist influx during peak seasons.

Abyaneh is best appreciated by just meandering along the lanes and chancing upon the 14th-century **Imamzadeh Yahya** with its conical, blue-tiled roof, or the **Zeyaratgah shrine** with a pool overhung by grape vines. The views from the valley looking back at the village are some of the most iconic in central Iran.

🍴 Sleeping & Eating

Other than snacking on dried apples, apricots and plums, or sampling fresh walnuts, all of which are sold by the local women in the centre of the village, there is nowhere to eat without prearrangement in Abyaneh except at the hotel restaurant.

Harpak Traditional Residence GUESTHOUSE $
(☑031-5428 2526; standard/rooftop r IR100,000/120,000, breakfast IR5000; 🛜) Billed as the oldest apartments in Iran, the cosy

but basic little rooms in this Abyaneh house give a feeling for life in earlier times in this historical village. The views from the rooftop terrace across the village and the valley beyond make up for the minimal nature of the facilities on offer.

Abyaneh Hotel HOTEL $$
(☑031-5428 2223; www.hotelabyaneh.com; d/tr IR2,200,000/3,440,000; 🅿🌀) Located on a hill above Abyaneh, this cared-for hotel with its kind and amiable management offers the most comfortable place to stay in town. It also offers an excellent coffee bar in the foyer among a collection of keepsakes, offering a port in the storm on cold mountain visits. Some rooms have panoramic views

❶ Getting There & Away

Abyaneh is 82km from Kashan and is not serviced by public transport. With a wait of two or three hours the return trip from Kashan costs US$50 with a driver-guide or US$30 by taxi. Alternatively, a driver-guide can detour here en route to Esfahan via Natanz for US$80, or US$50 by taxi.

Esfahan اصفهان

☑031 / POPULATION 1,760,000 / ELEVATION 1571M
Esfahan is Iran's top tourist destination for good reason. Its profusion of tree-lined boulevards, Persian gardens and important Islamic buildings gives it a visual appeal

unmatched by any other Iranian city, and the many artisans working here underpin its reputation as a living museum of traditional culture. Walking through the historic bazaar, over the picturesque bridges and across the Unesco-listed central square are sure to be highlights of a holiday.

As the country's third-largest city, Esfahan is home to some heavy industry, including steel factories and a much-discussed nuclear facility in the outskirts of town. Inevitably, then, traffic jams are a regular occurrence. Despite these modern realities, the inner core of the city remains a priceless gem.

History

Little is known of Esfahan's ancient history, but the Ateshkadeh-ye Esfahan (Esfahan Fire Temple) and pillars of the Pol-e Shahrestan (Shahrestan Bridge), both of which date from the Sassanid period (224–636), attest to its longevity. By the late 10th century the walled city of Esfahan was home to dozens of mosques and hundreds of wealthy homes, and in 1047 the Seljuks made it their capital. During the next 180 years it was adorned with magnificent buildings that favoured a symmetrical style of architecture, several prominent examples of which remain.

The city declined after the Mongol invasion, but regained its former glory under the reign of Shah Abbas the Great. In 1587 it became the capital of his Safavid empire and there followed a period of grand civic projects, such as the building of the incomparable Naqsh-e Jahan (Imam) Sq. The arts flourished and crafts such as carpet weaving were the envy of the world. Esfahan's heyday was short-lived, however, and little more than a century after Abbas' death the capital was transferred to Shiraz by the succeeding dynasty.

⊙ Sights

◉ Naqsh-e Jahan (Imam) Square

A spectacle in its own right. **Naqsh-e Jahan (Imam) Square** (میدان نقش جهان/میدان امام; Map p164; horse-drawn carriage ride IR80,000, up to 3 people) is one of the largest public plazas in the world, earning a listing as a Unesco World Heritage Site. The 512m-long and 163m-wide square was laid out in 1602 under the reign of the Safavid ruler, Shah Abbas the Great, to signal the importance of Esfahan as a capital of a powerful empire.

The name means 'pattern of the world' and it was designed to showcase the finest jewels of the Safavid empire – the incomparable Masjed-e Shah, the elegant Masjed-e Sheikh Lotfollah and the lavishly decorated Kakh-e Ali Qapu and Qeysarieh Portal. It is has changed little since it was built, and at each end the goal posts used in regular polo games 400 years ago are still in place (these polo matches are depicted on miniatures for sale around the square). The only modern additions are the fountains, which were added by the Pahlavis, and the souvenir and craft shops, which occupy the spaces on either side of the arched arcades.

Recent civic administrations have restored the square to its full glory by making the entire space a pedestrian zone. Horse-drawn carriages, a few electric carts and Shank's pony are now the only transport in the square, allowing visitors to enjoy the majesty of the view untroubled by traffic.

The square is at its best in late afternoon when the blue-tiled minarets and domes are lit up by the last rays of the sun and the mountains beyond turn red. This is the time when local families congregate for a promenade around the perimeter, the fountains are turned on and the light softens, illuminating the truly splendid architecture.

★ Masjed-e Shah   MOSQUE

(مسجد امام شاه Masjed-e Imam; Map p164; Naqsh-e Jahan (Imam) Sq; IR200,000; ⊙9-11.30am & 1-4.15pm Sat-Thu, 1-4.15pm Fri) This elegant mosque, with its iconic blue-tiled mosaics and its perfect proportions, forms a visually stunning monument at the head of Esfahan's main square. Unblemished since its construction 400 years ago, it stands as a monument to the vision of Shah Abbas I and the accomplishments of the Safavid dynasty. The mosque's crowning dome was completed in 1629, the last year of the reign of Shah Abbas.

Although each of the mosque's parts is a masterpiece, it is the unity of the overall design that leaves a lasting impression, and the positioning of the much-photographed **entrance portal** is a case in point as it has more to do with its location on the square than with the mosque's spiritual aims. The portal's function was primarily ornamental, providing a counterpoint to the Qeysarieh Portal at the entrance to the Bazar-e Bozorg. The foundation stones are white marble from Ardestan and the portal itself, some 30m tall, is decorated with magnificent

Masjed-e Shah (Masjed-e Imam)

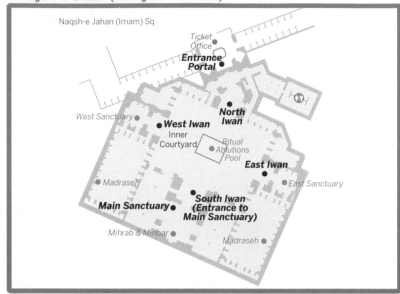

Naqsh-e Jahan (Imam) Sq

Ticket Office

Entrance Portal

West Sanctuary

West Iwan

North Iwan

Inner Courtyard

Ritual Ablutions Pool

East Iwan

Madraseh

East Sanctuary

Main Sanctuary

South Iwan (Entrance to Main Sanctuary)

Mihrab & Minbar

Madraseh

moarraq kashi (mosaics featuring geometric designs, floral motifs and calligraphy) by the most skilled artists of the age. The splendid niches contain complex stalactite mouldings in a honeycomb pattern; each panel has its own intricate design. Work began on this magnificent monument in 1611 and took four years to complete; deliberate mismatches in its apparent symmetry reflect the artist's humility in the face of Allah.

Although the portal was built to face the square, the mosque is oriented towards Mecca, so a short, angled corridor was constructed to connect the square and the **inner courtyard**, thereby negating any aesthetic qualms about this misalignment. Inside the courtyard, there is a pool for ritual ablutions and four imposing **iwans**. The walls of the courtyard contain the most exquisite sunken porches, framed by *haft rangi* (painted tiles) of deep blue and yellow. Each *iwan* leads into a vaulted sanctuary. The **east** and **west sanctuaries** are covered with particularly fine floral motifs on a blue background.

The **main sanctuary** is entered via the **south iwan**. It is worth finding a quiet corner here to sit and contemplate the richness of the domed ceiling, with its golden rose pattern (the flower basket) surrounded by concentric circles of busy mosaics on a deep blue background. The interior ceiling is 36.3m high, but the exterior reaches up to 51m due to the double layering used in construction. The hollow space in between is responsible for the loud echoes heard when you stamp your foot on the black paving stones under the centre of the dome. Although scientists have measured up to 49 echoes, only about 12 are audible to the human ear – more than enough for a speaker to be heard throughout the mosque. The marble **mihrab** and **minbar** (pulpit of a mosque) are also beautifully crafted.

The main sanctuary provides wonderful views of the two turquoise **minarets** above the entrance portal. Each is encircled by projecting balconies and white geometric calligraphy in which the names of Mohammed and Ali are repeated almost ad infinitum. To the east and west of the main sanctuary are the courtyards of two madrasehs. Both provide good views of the main **dome** with its glorious profusion of turquoise-shaded tiles.

★**Bazar-e Bozorg**　　　　BAZAAR
(بازار بزرگ; Map p164; ⊙ around 9am-8pm Sat-Thu) One of Iran's most historic and fascinating bazaars, this sprawling covered market links Naqsh-e Jahan (Imam) Sq with the Masjed-e Jameh. At its busiest in the

mornings, the bazaar's arched passageways are topped by a series of small perforated domes, each spilling shafts of light onto the commerce below. While the oldest parts of the bazaar (those around the mosque) are more than a thousand years old, most of what can be seen today was built during Shah Abbas' ambitious expansions of the early 1600s.

The bazaar is a maze of lanes, madrasehs, *khans* (caravanserais) and *timchehs* (domed halls or arcaded centres of a single trade, such as carpet vendors or coppersmiths). It can be entered at dozens of points, but the main entrance is via the **Qeysarieh Portal** (Map p164) at the northern end of Naqsh-e Jahan (Imam) Sq.

Cool in summer and warm in winter, it's easy to lose half a day wandering the bustling lanes of the bazaar, sniffing the heaps of layered spices and dishes of dried dates, watching shoppers finger coloured lengths of material, and pausing to admire the rows of red and white teapots in the many crockery shops. Teahouses help punctuate the walk and a *beryani* restaurant is the perfect place for lunch.

Masjed-e Sheikh Lotfollah
MOSQUE

(مسجد شیخ لطف الله, Sheikh Lotfollah Mosque; Map p164; Naqsh-e Jahan (Imam) Sq; IR200,000; ☺9-11.30am & 1-4pm 22 Sep-21 Mar, 9am-12.30pm & 2-6pm 22 Mar-21 Sep) Punctuating the middle of the arcades that hem Esfahan's largest square, this study in harmonious understatement complements the overwhelming richness of the larger mosque, Masjed-e Shah, at the head of the square. Built between 1602 and 1619 during the reign of Shah Abbas I, it was dedicated to the ruler's father-in-law,

Sheikh Lotfollah, a revered Lebanese scholar of Islam who was invited to Esfahan to oversee the king's mosque (now the Masjed-e Shah) and theological school.

The dome makes extensive use of delicate cream-coloured tiles that change colour throughout the day from cream to pink (sunset is usually the best time to witness this). The signature blue-and-turquoise tiles of Esfahan are evident only around the dome's summit.

The pale tones of the cupola stand in contrast to those around the **portal**, which displays some of the best surviving Safavid-era mosaics. The exterior panels contain wonderful arabesques and other intricate floral designs that have become a signature motif of Esfahan; especially fine are those displaying a vase framed by the tails of two peacocks. The portal itself contains some particularly fine *muqarnas* (stalactite-type stone carving used to decorate doorways and window recesses) with rich concentrations of blue and yellow motifs.

The mosque is unusual because it has neither a minaret nor a courtyard, and because steps lead up to the entrance. This was probably because the mosque was never intended for public use, but rather served as the worship place for the women of the shah's harem. The **sanctuary** or prayer hall is reached via a twisting **hallway** where the eyes become accustomed to the darkness as subtle shifts of light play across deep blue tilework. This hallway is integral to both the design and function of the mosque because it takes the worshipper from the grand square outside into a prayer hall facing Mecca, on a completely different axis.

CENTRAL IRAN ESFAHAN

BUILDING MASJED-E SHAH

When the Masjed-e Shah was begun, Shah Abbas the Great probably didn't think it would be 25 years before the last of the artisans left the building. He was already 52 when work began, and as he grew older he grew ever more impatient to see his greatest architectural endeavour completed.

Legend has it that the shah repeatedly demanded that corners be cut to hasten progress, even insisting work on the walls be started despite the foundations having not yet set. His architect, Ali Akbar Esfahani, was having none of it. He flatly defied his boss before making himself scarce until the shah calmed down (sensible, as Abbas was notoriously insecure and had killed two of his sons and blinded another). The architect eventually returned to the court where, because the wisdom of his decision had been demonstrated, he was welcomed back with a royal pardon.

Some of the time-saving techniques used were quite innovative: rather than covering the entire complex with millions of individual mosaic tiles, larger prefabricated patterned tiles called *haft rangi* were created – they've been standard ever since.

Inside the sanctuary, the complexity of the mosaics that adorn the walls and the extraordinarily beautiful ceiling, with its shrinking, yellow motifs, is a masterpiece of design. The shafts of sunlight that filter in through the few high, latticed windows produce a constantly changing interplay of light and shadow that enrich the space and give a tangible quality to empty air. The mihrab is one of the finest in Iran and has an unusually high niche; a calligraphic montage names the architect and the date 1028 AH.

Photography is allowed but using a flash is not.

Kakh-e Ali Qapu   PALACE

(کاخ عالی قاپو, Ali Qapu Palace; Map p164; Naqsh-e Jahan Sq; admission IR200,000, audio tour IR15,000; ⊙9am-4pm winter, to 6pm summer) Built at the very end of the 16th century as a residence for Shah Abbas I, this six-storey palace also served as a monumental gateway to the royal palaces that lay in the parklands beyond (Ali Qapu means 'Gate of Ali'). Named after Abbas' hero, the Imam Ali, it was built to make an impression, and at six storeys and 38m tall, with its impressive elevated terrace featuring 18 slender columns, it dominates one side of Naqsh-e Jahan (Imam) Sq.

The terrace affords a wonderful perspective over the square and one of the best views of the Masjed-e Shah and the mountains beyond. The attractive wooden ceiling with intricate inlay work and exposed beams has been painstakingly restored and now attention is turning towards the walls. Peer behind the scaffolding and watch the artisans at work and it's easy to understand why the project is taking so long.

Many of the paintings and mosaics that once decorated the 52 small rooms, corridors and stairways were destroyed during the Qajar period and after the 1979 revolution. Fortunately, a few fine examples remain in the throne room off the terrace, but the highlight of the palace is the music room on the upper floor. The stucco ceiling is stencilled with the shapes of vases and rose-water shakers to enhance the acoustics. This distinctive craftsmanship, considered by some to be one of the finest examples of secular Persian art, extends to the walls creating a mosaic of shadows.

⊙ Central Esfahan

★**Masjed-e Jameh**   MOSQUE

(مسجد جامع; Map p164; Allameh Majlesi St; IR200,000; ⊙9-11am & 1.15-4.30pm) The Jameh complex is a veritable museum of Islamic architecture while still functioning as a busy place of worship. Showcasing the best that nine centuries of artistic and religious endeavour has achieved, from the geometric elegance of the Seljuks to the more florid refinements of the Safavid era, a visit repays time spent examining the details – a finely carved column, delicate mosaics, perfect brickwork. Covering more than 20,000 sq metres, this is the biggest mosque in Iran.

Religious activity on this site is believed to date back to the Sassanid Zoroastrians, with the first sizeable mosque being built over temple foundations by the Seljuks in the 11th century. The two large domes (north and south) have survived intact from this era but the rest of the mosque was destroyed by fire in the 12th century and rebuilt in 1121. Embellishments were added throughout the centuries.

In the centre of the main courtyard, which is surrounded by four contrasting *iwans,* is an **ablutions fountain** designed to imitate the Kaaba at Mecca. Would-be pilgrims once used the fountain to practise the appropriate rituals prior to undertaking the hajj. The two-storey porches around the courtyard's perimeter were constructed in the late 15th century.

The **south iwan** is highly elaborate, with Mongol-era stalactite mouldings, some splendid 15th-century mosaics on the side walls and two minarets. Behind it is the grand **Nezam al-Molk Dome**, which is flanked by Seljuk-era prayer halls.

The **north iwan** is noteworthy for its monumental porch with the Seljuks' customary Kufic inscriptions and austere brick pillars in the sanctuary. Behind it (entered through a door next to the *iwan*) is a prayer hall featuring a forest of pillars. The bricks of each of these pillars is decorated with the craftsman's signature trademark. At the rear of the north *iwan* is the exquisite **Taj al-Molk Dome**, widely considered to be the finest brick dome in Persia. While relatively small, it is said to be mathematically perfect, and has survived dozens of earthquakes without a blemish for more than 900 years.

The **west iwan** was originally built by the Seljuks but later decorated by the Safavids. The mosaics are more geometric in style here than those of the southern hall. The courtyard is topped by a *maazeneh,* a small raised platform with a conical roof from where the faithful used to be called to prayer.

The **Room of Sultan Uljeitu** (a 14th-century Shiite convert) next to the west *iwan* is home to one of the mosque's greatest treasures – an exquisite stucco mihrab with dense Quranic inscriptions and floral designs. Next to this is the Timurid-era **Winter Hall** (Beit al-Shata), built in 1448 and lit by alabaster skylights.

Kakh-e Chehel Sotun   PALACE

(کاخ چهل ستون, Chehel Sotun Palace; Map p164; Ostandari St; IR200,000, ☺ 9am-4pm) Built as a pleasure pavilion and reception hall, using the Achaemenid-inspired *talar* (columnar porch) style, this beautifully proportioned palace is entered via an elegant terrace that perfectly bridges the transition between the Persian love of gardens and interior splendour. The 20 slender, ribbed wooden pillars of the palace rise to a superb wooden ceiling with crossbeams and exquisite inlay work.

Chehel Sotun means '40 pillars' – the number reflected in the long pool in front of the palace.

The only surviving palace on the royal precinct that stretched between Naqsh-e Jahan (Imam) Sq and Chahar Bagh Abbasi St, this Safavid-era complex is reputed to date from 1614; an inscription uncovered in 1949, however, says it was completed in 1647 under the watch of Shah Abbas II. Either way, the palace on this site today was rebuilt after a fire in 1706.

The **Great Hall** (Throne Hall) is a gem, richly decorated with frescoes, miniatures and ceramics. The upper walls are dominated by historical frescoes on a grand scale, sumptuously portraying court life and some of the great battles of the Safavid era – the two middle frescoes (Nos 114 and 115) date from the Qajar period but the other four are original. From right to left, above the entrance door, the armies of Shah Ismail do battle with the Uzbeks; Nader Shah battles

Masjed-e Jameh

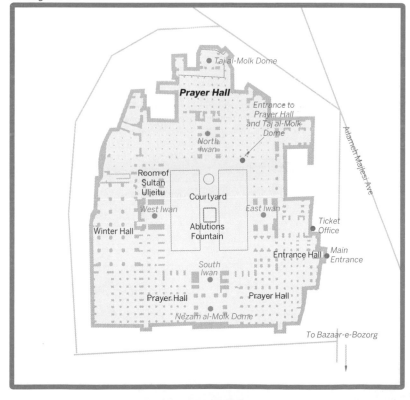

Central Esfahan

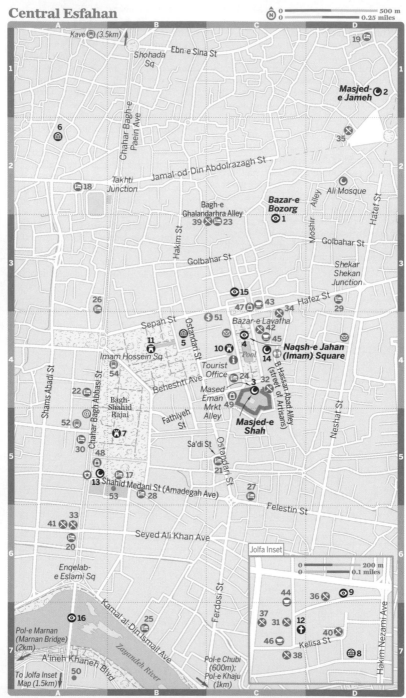

N 0 — 500 m
0 — 0.25 miles

Kave (3.5km)
Shohada Sq
Ebn-e Sina St
19
Masjed-e Jameh 2
35
Chahar Bagh-e Paein Ave
6
Takhti Junction
Jamal-od-Din Abdolrazagh St
18
Bazar-e Bozorg 1
Ali Mosque
Bagh-e Ghalandarhra Alley
39 23
Moshir Alley
Golbahar St
Hafez St
Hakim St
Golbahar St
Shekar Shekan Junction
26
15
47 43
34
29
Sepah St
51
Bazar-e Lavafha 42
Ostandari St
5
10 4 45
Hater St
Neshat St
Imam Hossein Sq
11
14 Naqsh-e Jahan (Imam) Square
Tourist Office
Beheshti Ave
24 32
3
B Hassan Abad Alley (street of Artisans)
54
22
Mased Eman Mrkt Alley
49
Masjed-e Shah
Shams Abadi St
Bagh-e Shahid Rajai
Fathiyeh St
Chahar Bagh Abbasi St
52
30
48
7
Sa'di St
13 Shahid Medani St (Amadegah Ave)
17
53
28
21
27
Felestin St
41 33
20
Seyed Ali Khan Ave
Engelab-e Eslami Sq
16
25
Kamal al-Din Ismail Ave
Ferdosi St
Pol-e Marnan (Marnan Bridge) (2km)
A'ineh Khaneh Blvd
Zayandeh River
Pol-e Chubi (600m); Pol-e Khaju (1km)
To Jolfa Inset Map (1.5km)
50

Jolfa Inset
0 — 200 m
0 — 0.1 miles
44
36 9
37
31 12
40
46
38
8
Kelisa St
Hakim Nezami Ave

Central Esfahan

CENTRAL IRAN ESFAHAN

Sultan Mohammed (astride a white elephant) on an Indian battleground; and Shah Abbas II welcomes King Nader Khan of Turkestan with musicians and dancing girls.

On the wall opposite the door, also from right to left, Shah Abbas I presides over an ostentatious banquet; Shah Ismail battles the janissaries (infantrymen) of Sultan Selim; and Shah Tahmasp receives Humayun, the Indian prince who fled to Persia in 1543. These extraordinary works survived the 18th-century invasion by the Afghans, who whitewashed the paintings to show their disapproval of such extravagance. Other items, including Safavid forebear Safi od-Din's hat, are kept in a small museum.

The palace's garden, **Bagh-e Chehel Sotun**, is an excellent example of the classic Persian garden form and was recently added to Unesco's World Heritage list. An ancient fallen pine resting on a plinth gives a sense of the great age of the garden. The polished noses of the lions on the standing water spouts at the head of the decorative pool hint at this being a favourite spot for a photograph of the garden's perfect symmetry. Art students have set up a calico shop at the garden's entrance selling Iran's popular printed fabric.

Madraseh-ye Chahar Bagh ISLAMIC SITE
(مدرسه چهارباغ, Madraseh-ye Mazadar-e Shah, Theological School of the Shah's Mother; Map p164; cnr Chahar Bagh Abbasi & Shahid Medani Sts) Built between 1704 and 1714 as part of an expansive complex that included a caravanserai (now the Abbasi Hotel) and the Bazar-e Honar, this madraseh is one of the most architecturally important buildings in Esfahan. It is

unfortunately closed to the public for most of the year (except during No Ruz), but it is possible to enjoy its attractive blue-tiled dome and Safavid-era minarets – two of the finest in Esfahan.

Hammam-e Ali Gholi Agha   HISTORIC BUILDING
(حمام علیقلی آقا, Ali Gholi Agha Bathhouse; Map p164; Ali Gholi Agha Alley, off Masjed-e Sayyed St; IR150,000; ☺8.30am-2.30pm & 3.30-6pm 21 Mar-22 Sep, 8.30am-1.30pm & 2.30-5pm Sat-Thu, 9am-1pm Fri 23 Sep-20 Mar; 🅿) Located in the historic district of Bid Abad, this beautifully restored museum of *hammams* sports a set of costumed mannequins that help to demonstrate the purpose of each part of the bathhouse. There are some wonderful details to admire, including a hunting scene interpreted in tiles, a duck-headed water spout above the main bathtub and beautiful rich marble flooring. The complex is some way from the town centre and hard to find so it's best to take a taxi.

Decorative Arts Museum of Iran   MUSEUM
(Muze-ye Honarha-ye Tazeini; Map p164; Ostandari St; IR150,000; ☺8am-1.30pm Sat-Wed, to 1pm Thu) Housed in a building that once served as stables and warehouse to Safavid kings, this small museum contains a fine collection from the Safavid and Qajar periods, including miniatures, glassware, lacquerwork, ancient Qurans, calligraphy, ceramics, woodcarvings, traditional costumes, weapons and horse tackle. Among the stars of the show are a fish divination mirror with enamel cartouches, some exquisite beadwork and priceless inlaid boxes. There's also a display of locks: locksmithing is an ancient trade in Esfahan.

Ali Mosque   MOSQUE
(Map p164; off Moshir Alley) This mosque, next to the Bazar-e Bozorg, has one distinguishing feature: it has an enormous brick minaret that looms over the adjacent square. It may not sport the extravagant tiles of neighbouring minarets, but on closer inspection the brickwork is very fine with elaborate patterns traced into the surface. If nothing else, it makes an excellent landmark while trying to navigate the bazaar, especially as it glows like a beacon at sunset.

The surrounding area is full of aged houses with wooden balconies, through which there is an alternative route back to Naqsh-e Jahan (Imam) Sq from the Jameh Mosque.

Hasht Behesht Palace   PALACE
(Kakh-e Hasht Behesht; Map p164; IR150,000; ☺9am-4pm) Once the most luxuriously decorated palace in Esfahan, the interior of the small Hasht Behesht Palace has been extensively damaged over the years, but it retains some spectacular details, including a superb stalactite ceiling with delicate painting. The same keyhole plasterwork seen in the Kakh-e Ali Qapu is featured on a small scale here too. The soaring wooden columns on the palace's open-sided terrace are almost as tall as those still growing in the parkland that frames it. A popular meeting place for retired Esfahani men, the park has a seductive tranquillity that offers the promise of peace in a city of pace.

👁 Zayandeh River & Bridges

There are few better ways to spend an afternoon than strolling along the Zayandeh River, crossing back and forth on the river's 11 bridges – or even meandering along the often empty riverbed itself. Such a stroll is especially pleasant at sunset and in the early evening when most of the bridges, five of which date back to the Safavid era, are brilliantly lit and many Esfahanis gather here to relax and socialise.

Pol-e Khaju   BRIDGE
(پل خواجو, Khaju Bridge) Arguably the finest of Esfahan's bridges, with traces of the original paintings and tiles that decorated its double arcade still visible, Pol-e Khaju was built by Shah Abbas II in about 1650, but a bridge is believed to have crossed the waters here since the time of Tamerlane. The bridge is as much a meeting place as a bearer of traffic and at nighttime Esfahanis gather under the arches to sing: those with the most convincing voices (or indeed songs) attract sizeable crowds.

Si-o-Seh Pol   BRIDGE
(سی و سه پل, Si-o-Seh Bridge, Bridge of 33 Arches; Map p164; Pol-e Allahverdi) The 298m-long Si-o-Seh Bridge was built by Allahverdi Khan, a favourite general of Shah Abbas I, between 1599 and 1602. It served as both bridge and dam, and is still used to hold water today. It is a popular meeting place when people gather to watch the sunset and catch a romantic moment under the arches.

ESFAHAN IN ...

Two Days

Begin in the **Bazar-e Bozorg** (p160) to get a feel for the beating heart of Esfahan. After lunching on *beryani*, head to **Masjed-e Jameh** (p162), one of Iran's most magnificent mosques. Follow strolling lovers over the **Si-o-Seh Pol** (p166) and trace the dry river bed along manicured pathways. Dinner has to be *shashlik* – the famed dish of choice at **Shahrzad** (p172). Complete the evening with a twist of *gaz* (nougat) from **Fereni Hafez** (p172) in glorious Naqsh-e Jahan (Imam) Sq.

On day two, visit **Masjed-e Shah** (p159), **Masjed-e Sheikh Lotfollah** (p161) and **Chehel Sotun Palace** (p163) with its Unesco-listed garden. In the evening join locals in an *ash-e reshte* (noodle and bean soup) at **Abbasi Traditional Restaurant** (p172).

Four Days

On day three visit the Armenian Quarter and admire the **Kelisa-ye Vank** frescoes. Lunch at a fashionable nearby restaurant then head to **Ateshkadeh-ye Esfahan** (p168) with its fine hilltop view of the city.

On day four, visit **Nazhvan Park** (p168) for a picnic by the river or wander round the aviary, aquarium or sea shell museum. Return to the fray and buy a carpet! Or at least, sit and have tea in a carpet shop and let the colours and designs work their magic while the vendor explains the complex art of knotting.

Pol-e Shahrestan   BRIDGE

(پل شهرستان) This is the oldest of Esfahan's bridges. Most of its 11-arched stone and brick structure is believed to date from the 12th century, although the pillars themselves remain from a much earlier Sassanian bridge. Although it's almost 4km east of Pol-e Khaju, it's a pleasant walk.

Pol-e Chubi   BRIDGE

(پل چوبی, Chubi Bridge) Nearly 150m long, and with 21 arches, Chubi Bridge was built by Shah Abbas II in 1665, primarily to help irrigate palace gardens in the area. The bridge and its two interior parlours were for the exclusive use of the shah and his courtiers.

◉ Jolfa and Greater Esfahan

The Armenian quarter of Esfahan dates from the time of Shah Abbas I, who transported a colony of Christians from the town of Jolfa (now on Iran's northern border) en masse, and named the village 'New Jolfa'. Abbas sought their skills as merchants, entrepreneurs and artists, and he ensured that their religious freedom was respected – albeit at a distance from the city's Islamic centre. At one time over 42,000 Armenian Christians lived here.

Today Kelisa-ye Vank (Vank Cathedral) forms the centre of this fashionable area. There are also a number of Armenian churches here and an old cemetery, serving a Christian community of approximately 6000. Many visitors visit in the afternoon and stay on in Jolfa to enjoy dinner in the relatively liberal village atmosphere.

Kelisa-ye Vank   CATHEDRAL

(کلیسای وانک, Vank Cathedral, Church of St Joseph of Arimathea; Map p164; Kelisa St; IR200,000; ⊙8.30am-5.30pm Sat-Thu, to 12.30pm Fri) Built between 1648 and 1655 with the encouragement of the Safavid rulers, Kelisa-ye Vank in the Armenian neighbourhood of Jolfa is the historic focal point of the Armenian Church in Iran. The sumptuous interior is richly decorated with restored wall paintings full of life and colour, including gruesome martyrdoms and pantomime demons. The highlight of the museum (separate admission IR80,000) is a fabulous collection of illustrated gospels and Bibles, some dating back as far as the 10th century.

Isfahan Music Museum   MUSEUM

(Map p164; ☑031-3625 6912; www.isfahanmusicmuseum.com; Mehrdad St (Shahid Ghandi); IR300,000; ⊙9am-1pm & 3.30-9pm) This beautiful new museum in the Armenian Quarter in Jolfa houses a fine collection of traditional Persian instruments. A labour of love for the private collector who assembled these national and folk instruments, the museum regularly hosts live performances by renowned folk musicians. For those with an interest in music, or simply with a love of finely crafted objects, it is well worth the relatively steep admission fee.

Jolfa Square
SQUARE

(Map p164) At the centre of the Armenian Quarter, a short walk from Vank Cathedral, this delightful square is a good place to sit and watch the world go by. Other than an arcade of ordinary shops propped up by brick pillars and an elaborate sundial, there's not much to see or do except sit on the wall and enjoy this little haven in common with the locals.

Pigeon Towers
HISTORIC BUILDING

(کبوتر خانه) For centuries Esfahan relied on pigeons to supply guano as fertiliser for the city's famous fields of watermelons. The guano was collected in almost 3000 squat, circular pigeon towers, each able to house about 14,000 birds. Today they are unused, made redundant by chemical fertiliser, but more than 700 of the mud-brick towers remain in the city's environs. The best place to see them is along the Zayandeh River south of the Ateshkadeh-ye Esfahan (Fire Temple).

Ateshkadeh-ye Esfahan
TEMPLE

(اتشکده اصفهان), Esfahan Fire Temple, Marbin Fortress; Saremiyeh St; IR150,000; ⊙8.30am-4.30pm, to 6.30pm summer) Dating from Sassanian times, the crumbling mud bricks of the Ateshkadeh-ye Esfahan stand on a hill above Zayandeh River on the city's outskirts. There's not much to see of the old fire temple and adjoining fortress, but the 20-minute scramble uphill is worth the effort on a clear day for the view. Sensible shoes are needed as the top part of the path is steep and slippery. A taxi to the site costs around IR280,000; it is included on driver-guide itineraries.

★Nazhvan Cultural & Recreational Resort
PARK

(Nazhvan Park; ☑031-3784 0034; www.nazhvanpark.ir; free park admission, average IR180,000 per attraction; discount for child under 5yr; ⊙8am-sunset) FREE This huge park on the outskirts of Esfahan encompasses a large complex of attractions that makes a pleasant contrast to Esfahan's intense city experience. The park includes the **Birds Garden** (IR180,000), the **Esfahan Aquarium** (IR500,000), a **Sea Shell Museum** (IR150,000), a **Reptile House** (IR150,000) and a **Butterfly Collection** (IR80,000). Each attraction is charged separately and there is no combined ticket.

With a picnic, the wooded park makes a pleasant day's outing, particularly in autumn when the leaves change colour. Other attractions inside the park include a small **chairlift** over the river, horse-drawn carriages, a miniature train and a **water park** for kids. A **Ladies Garden** (8am to sunset) gives a bit of respite for women wanting to avoid unwanted attention, kiosks sell limited snacks, there's a restaurant in the Birds Park and the grounds are serviced with clean toilet facilities. A taxi to the park costs around IR160,000 from the centre of town.

☞ Tours

Licensed guides bring a wealth of knowledge to a city whose treasures can be hard to uncover alone. They charge US$55 to US$65 for full- or half-day walking tours in Esfahan. A driver-guide costs US$80 to US$90.

We Go Persia
OUTDOORS

(☑0903 209 7700; www.wegopersia.com) Guide and tour operator Mojtaba Salsali knows Esfahan like the palm of his hand and revels in uncovering the hidden secrets of the city for his guests. Offering a range of tours around Iran, including bird-watching, he can also help with hotel bookings.

Maryam Nekoie
OUTDOORS

An English teacher with over 10 years of experience in guiding. Specialises in walking tours of Esfahan.

Azade Kazemi
OUTDOORS

(☑0913 327 9626; azadekazemi@hotmail.com) Highly professional English- and Spanish-speaking guide.

Maryam Shafiei
OUTDOORS

(☑0913 326 6127; marie13572002@yahoo.fr) A French- and English-speaking guide.

Mohammad Shahsavandi
OUTDOORS

(☑0913 313 1974; Mohammad_Shahsavandi@yahoo.com) Knowledgeable, with excellent English.

🛏 Sleeping

Finding decent and affordable accommodation in Esfahan can be difficult, especially from mid-March until the end of August. Booking ahead is essential at that time and advisable year-round as there are a surprisingly small number of rooms available across the city, despite this being the country's most popular destination for both domestic and

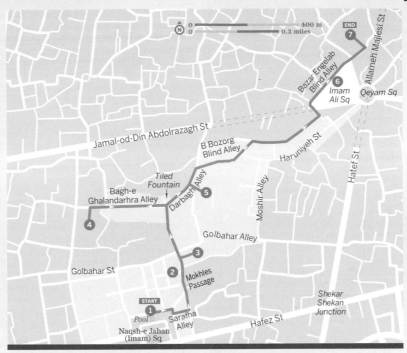

Walking Tour
Bazar-e Bozorg

START QEYSARIEH PORTAL
END MASJED-E JAMEH
LENGTH 1.1KM; TWO HOURS

Start at the ornamental pool in front of the imposing ① **Qeysarieh Portal** (p161) at the northern end of Naqsh-e Jahan (Imam) Sq. Rather than walking through the portal, head into Sarafha Alley on the right (east) side of the pool and turn left at the T-intersection at its end. Walk straight ahead, passing spectacular ② **Malek Timcheh**, a Qajar-era building with three vaulted spaces, on the left and then the ③ **M S Khan**, an old caravanserai, on the right. Continue until you come to a forked intersection with a tiled fountain straight ahead. Take the left fork (west) and walk along Bagh-e Ghalandarha Alley until you reach ④ **Masjed-e Hakim** (Hakim Mosque) on your left. Built about 1000 years ago, this is Esfahan's oldest mosque, but only the beautiful portal beside this northern entrance has survived.

Backtrack to the tiled fountain and take the east fork, signed Darbagh Alley. A few steps along on the right, some steps lead into a modern *khan* (caravanserai). It may be unattractive but it's an undeniably authentic ⑤ **teahouse** full of *bazaris* (shopkeepers in the bazaar) enjoying tea, *qalyans* (water pipes) and cheap bowls of *dizi* (lamb and vegetable stew pounded to a paste at the table). To find the caravanserai look for a signboard illustrating a water pipe. Back on Darbagh Alley, veer right after a few metres into B Bozorg Blind Alley, one of the bazaar's busiest and oldest thoroughfares.

Take a break from the jostling crowds of shoppers to walk through ⑥ **Imam Ali Sq**, with a fine view of the enormous brick minaret of Ali Mosque, ducking back into the alley at the end of the square. Note the vaulted ceiling along the alleyways, adorned with star- and hexagon-shaped apertures. The serpentine B Bozorg Blind Alley leads past a hugely popular *beryani* restaurant en route to your last stop on this tour, the magnificent ⑦ **Masjed-e Jameh** (p162). If you don't manage to reach the mosque before it closes for lunch at 11am, join the queue for *beryani* instead.

international tourists. Low-season discounts of 20% are common.

Central Esfahan

★ Iran Hotel   HOTEL $
(Map p164; ☑ 031-3220 2740; www.iranhotel.biz; Chahar Bagh Abbasi St; s/d/tr/q US$26/42/54/66; ❄️ 🛜) On a quiet lane in an excellent location, this modest hotel with its stylish foyer offers comfortable rooms with low beds, Persian rugs and a fridge. The welcoming, helpful, English-speaking management make this a top choice and the newspaper cuttings they post by the lift for the benefit of visitors shows they're willing to go the extra mile.

Azady Hotel   HOTEL $
(Map p164; ☑ 031-3220 4056; www.azadi-hotel.com; Masjed-e Sayyed St; d/tr US$41/70; ❄️ 🛜) Well run, comfortable with a spruced-up foyer supporting small craft workshops, the Azady is a good choice despite being located on one of Esfahan's busiest streets. Front room windows are double-glazed, but a room at the rear of the building is more conducive to a good night's sleep. No low-season discounts.

Naghshe Jahan Hotel   HOTEL $
(Map p164; ☑ 031-3221 9619; Chahar Bagh Abbasi St; s/d US$30/45, extra bed US$11; @🛜) A reliable midrange choice on Esfahan's major thoroughfare (request a room at the rear), the Naghshe Jahan offers recently refurbished rooms off spruced-up corridors. There's a basement restaurant serving breakfast. A shoe-shine and a collection of Esfahani enamel work nudge this otherwise nondescript hotel into a midrange bracket.

★ Isfahan Traditional Hotel   HOTEL $$
(Samaeian Historical House; Map p164; ☑ 031-3223 6677; www.ethotel.ir; Bagh-e Ghalandarha Alley, off Hakim St; s/d/tr IR1,530,000/2,610,000/4,250,000; ❄️🛜) Located in the bazaar near the ancient Masjed-e Hakim (Hakim Mosque), this hotel is set around two courtyards in adjoining Safavid- and Qajar-period homes. The characterful rooms are clean and comfortable, with satellite TV and private modern bathrooms. The cavernous restaurant here is a popular lunch spot with tour groups.

Ebnesina Traditional Hotel   TRADITIONAL HOUSE $$
(Map p164; ☑ 0913 408 2557; hoseinomidzad@gmail.com; off Ebnesina St, behind Masjed-e Jameh; d/tr IR1,950,000/2,550,000) This lovely old house, with a dazzling set of murals in the foyer and copious mirror work, is something of a treat in a city lacking in characterful accommodation. With good views from the rooftop coffee shop (open in summer), the 60 rooms each sport a hand-painted door with roses and paisley patterns. Management is friendly, though not much English is spoken.

A small workshop at the entrance supports artisans who work with *minakari* (enamel work). This ancient Esfahani craft fires (usually blue and white) enamel onto copper in meticulously fine designs.

Jaam Firouzeh Hotel   HOTEL $$
(Map p164; ☑ 031-3224 5215; www.firouzehhotel.com; Saadi St, off Ostandari St, near Naqsh-e Jahan (Imam) Sq; d/tr US$50/65) If this hotel was any closer to Esfahan's iconic square, guests would be taking up residence in Ali Qapu Palace. Aside from the perfect location, this new hotel offers friendly service, a stylish seating area in the foyer and spotless rooms. A minor downside is the absence of views – the windows are very small and some have no windows at all.

Safir Hotel   HOTEL $$
(Map p164; ☑ 031-3222 2640; www.safirhotel.net; Shahid Medani St; r from US$120; 🅿️❄️@🛜🏊) Owner-manager Mr Bagherian is extremely proud of his hotel, and no wonder. In an excellent location in the centre of town, its 60 spacious rooms have tiled floors, double-glazed windows and bathrooms with tubs. There's a top-floor restaurant and a smart modern internet cafe in the lobby.

★ Hasht Behesht Apartment Hotel APARTMENT $$
(Map p164; ☑ 031-3221 4869; www.hbahotel.com; cnr Ostandari St & Aghili Alley; d/tr/q apt US$54/69/84; ❄️🛜) It may be a bit short on style, but the centrally located Hasht Behesht, run by a delightful family, is one of the best accommodation options in town, offering clean and well-maintained apartments with comfortable beds, equipped kitchenettes and satellite TV. Enter off Aghili Alley. Transfers from the airport are available and there's a ticket-booking service. Breakfast available for IR200,000.

Sheykh Bahaei Hotel   HOTEL $$
(Map p164; ☑ 031-3220 7714; www.sheykhbahaeihotel.com; 4 Sheykh Bahaei St; d/tr US$100/129; 🅿️❄️🛜) Set back from busy Sheykh Bahaei St (the entrance is disconcertingly beside a

busy parking ramp), this modern hotel has quiet rooms with smart bathrooms and enjoys an excellent central location. The rooftop restaurant and teahouse (summer only) have views towards the mountains.

Safavi Hotel HOTEL **$$**
(Map p164; 031-3220 8600; www.safavihotel.ir; Felestin St; r from US$90; ✱@🛜) This attractively decorated hotel is in a great location between Naqsh-e Jahan (Imam) Sq and the Zayandeh River. Murals and mirror work in the common areas spice up the experience and rooms, though more functional, are comfortable with satellite TV and good-sized bathrooms. The hotel is set back from Felestin St, minimising noise.

Esfahan Tourist Hotel HOTEL **$$**
(Map p164; 031-3220 4437; www.etouristhotel. com; Abbas Abad St; s/d/tr US$60/65/70; ✱🛜) Helpful English-speaking management ensures that this establishment keeps its reputation as a reliable, midrange option. Rooms have recently been given a thorough makeover and the foyer sports some delightful new murals featuring sparrows.

Melal Hotel HOTEL **$$**
(Map p164; 031-3221 8347; www.hotelmelal.net; Kamal al-Din Ismail Ave; s/d/tr US$50/85/110, extra bed US$23; P✱@🛜) Overlooking the river east of Si-o-Seh Pol, this multistorey business-oriented hotel is professionally managed with cheerful staff. Request a room overlooking the river or enjoy the view from the top-floor restaurant. In the lobby, 200MB of free wi-fi is available.

Setareh Hotel HOTEL **$$**
(Map p164; 031-3220 7060; www.setarehhotel.ir; Hafez St; s/d IR1,540,000/2,610,000; P✱@🛜) Close proximity to Naqsh-e Jahan (Imam) Sq, professional management, uniformed receptionists and features such as satellite TV and modern bathrooms make this a good-value hotel. The rooftop restaurant is delightful (summer only). The one remaining lotus pillar and spangled doorway makes it easy to find from the street.

★ Abbasi Hotel HOTEL **$$$**
(Map p164; 031-3222 6010; www.abbasihotel.ir; Shahid Medani St; r/deluxe from US$150/200, ste from US$260; P✱@🛜🏊) The Abbasi's main building was once the caravanserai of the Madraseh-ye Chahar Bagh; arranged around a huge garden of ponds and towering cedars, and with a view of the madraseh's lovely dome beyond, this is a very special place to stay. Unfortunately, the same can't be said for the characterless new building on the eastern side of the central garden courtyard.

Hotel facilities include a cosy traditional restaurant, a welcoming coffee shop, a business centre, craft shops, and an indoor pool, sauna and gym. Breakfast is served on the galley floor of the main restaurant, ringed about with gorgeous murals, while dinner is served in the main mirrored hall below. With a sweeping staircase, extravagant chandeliers and piano music, you can almost forgive the average food. No low-season discounts offered.

✖ Eating

There are dozens of wonderful places to snack or dine in and around the Naqsh-e Jahan (Imam) Sq.

Esfahan has three local specialities: *beryani* (minced mutton and offal cooked over coals and sprinkled with cinnamon, served wrapped in flat bread), *khoresht-e mast* (a strange concoction of lamb, yoghurt, egg, saffron, sugar and orange peel, often eaten as a dessert) and *gaz* (nougat mixed with saffron, chopped pistachios or almonds).

Central Esfahan

★ Bastani Traditional Restaurant IRANIAN **$**
(Map p164; 031-3220 0374; www.bastanitradition alrestaurant.ir; Chaharsogh Maghsod Bazar, Naqsh-e Jahan (Imam) Sq; mains from IR250,000; ⊙11.30am-10pm;) Esfahan's most atmospheric restaurant is located in the shadow of the Masjed-e Shah and features an internal courtyard with fountain, tiled walls and painted vaulted ceilings with mirror inlay – truly gorgeous. Dishes such as *khoresh-e beh* (stewed lamb and quince) and *khoresh-e alu* (stewed chicken and plum) are consistently delicious. There's a cover charge for tea, worth paying just to enjoy the delightful interior.

★ Haj Mahmood Beryani IRANIAN **$**
(Map p164; www.beryaniazam.com; Bazar Engelab Blind Alley; beryani IR140,000; ⊙9am-3pm Sat-Thu) Famous for its *beryani* (which is served with a glass of *dugh;* churned sour milk or yoghurt mixed with water), Azam has several branches. This one inside the bazaar is a recommended lunch option – the queuing, the shunting into seats, the quick turn-around and the chomping on whole onions is all part of this fun experience.

Fast Food Restaurant
FELAFEL $

(Map p164; cnr Chahar Bagh-e Abbasi & Abbas Abad Sts; felafel sandwich IR50,000) Near the Si-o-Seh Pol, this modest venue offers reputedly the best fast food in town – it certainly does a roaring trade. The felafel is particularly delicious.

Fereni Hafez
SWEETS $

(Icecream Hafez; Map p164; Hafez St; bowl of fereni IR20,000; ⊙8am-midnight) Locals congregate around this humble shopfront to buy an afternoon snack of *fereni* – a tapioca-like dessert served with honey. Some pause to eat it standing, others perch on the plastic stalls on the pavement, others take it home in tubs to share with the family. One mouthful, and you'll immediately realise why it's worth the queue.

★ Malek Soltan Jarchi Bashi
IRANIAN $$

(Map p164; ☑031-3220 7453; www.jarchibashi. com; Bagh-e Ghalandarha Alley, Hakim St; mains IR450,000; ⊙noon-3.30pm & 7.30-10.30pm) This sumptuous renovation of a 400-year-old bathhouse is a highly romantic venue for dinner, especially on Wednesday and Saturday nights (or on Thursday and Friday at noon) when live music adds to the atmosphere. The vaulted interior has been beautifully restored with fountains and splendid murals. The food is not the best but it's worth having something just to enjoy the ambience.

★ Abbasi Teahouse & Traditional Restaurant
IRANIAN $$

(Map p164; www.abbasihotel.ir; Abbasi Hotel, Shahid Medani St; noodle soup IR200,000; ⊙4-10.30pm; 🛜) Set into a flank of the Abbasi Hotel's elegant main courtyard, this delightful little restaurant (not to be confused with the hotel's main restaurant) attract legions of locals in the early evening. The signature dish is *ash-e reshte* (noodle soup with beans and vegetables; IR200,000) and big bowls of this wholesome soup fly out of the kitchen in record numbers when it's cold.

★ Shahrzad
IRANIAN $$

(Map p164; ☑031-1220 4490; www.shahrzad-restaurant.com; Abbas Abad St; mains IR500,000; ⊙11.30am-10.30pm) Opulent Qajar-style wall paintings, stained-glass windows and battalions of black-suited waiters contribute to the Shahrzad's reputation as the best restaurant in Esfahan. House specialities include lamb cutlets, and *chelo fesenjan* (pomegranate and walnut stew). At the end of the meal complimentary pieces of *gaz* flavoured with almond and rose water complete the meal. Booking isn't encouraged so queues are common.

Chehel Sotun Restaurant
IRANIAN $$

(Map p164; www.abbasihotel.ir; Abbasi Hotel, Shahid Medani St; mains IR450,000; ⊙7-10.30pm) It's probably fair to say that the food in this beautiful restaurant is not the best, but if this isn't the prime concern, then it's worth a night out here to enjoy the company of Esfahanis celebrating a special occasion in surroundings fit for a shah. The sweeping staircase, mirror work and elaborate murals are a visual feast.

Traditional Banquet Hall
IRANIAN $$

(Map p164; ☑031-3220 0729; Naqsh-e Jahan (Imam) Sq; mains IR400,000; ⊙noon-4pm & 7-10.15pm) Just off Naqsh-e Jahan (Imam) Sq, this restaurant uses stained glass, colourful tiles and *takhts* (daybeds) to create a Qajar-era ambience. It's a pretty place to sit, popular with Iranians and foreign visitors alike, and the staff are friendly. It's located upstairs in one of the squares immediately north of the Masjed-e Sheikh Lotfollah.

✗ Jolfa

Romanos
IRANIAN $

(Map p164; ☑031-3624 0094; off Jolfa Sq; mains IR250,000; ⊙11am-midnight; 🛜) This attractively restored bathhouse just off Jolfa Sq (down the vaulted alley) has a teahouse and restaurant section, both relaxing, romantic spaces. The food includes tasty fish options, and there's a salad buffet.

Honey Restaurant
BUFFET $

(Map p164; ☑031-3627 1227; Hakim Nezami Ave; buffet with soup IR100,000; ⊙12-3.30pm & 6.30-11pm) Close to the Kelisa-ye Vank, this no-nonsense local favourite is housed in a cheery basement of pine furniture, illuminated dioramas and plastic flowers and is chiefly known for its daily buffets. Offering a wide selection of tasty Iranian favourites and hearty soups, there's no chance of leaving hungry.

Arc A
CAFE $$

(Map p164; ☑031-3629 0920; Vank Church Alley, Kalissa St; mains IR450,000; ⊙9am-midnight) This elegant establishment in the heart of the Armenian Quarter is arranged around a spacious courtyard, with modern decking and furnishings bringing a contemporary style to the traditional design. Menu options are far broader than the term 'cafe' suggests, with modern dishes using ancient influences such as tamarind and pomegranate. It's virtually opposite the entrance to the Kelisa-ye Vank.

Khan Gostar Restaurant IRANIAN $$
(Map p164; ☑031-1627 8989; Ground fl, Julfa Hotel, off Hakim Nezami Ave, Jolfa; mains IR500,000; ☺noon-3.30pm & 7.30-10.30pm) Located in the Armenian Quarter, this cafeteria-style restaurant serves enormous plates of food. There's a large self-service salad bar and several *tah-hin* (crunchy rice) dishes on offer: the *tahchin barreh* (rice cake with slow-cooked lamb shank garnished with barberries and nuts) is particularly recommended. There's also a downstairs restaurant with traditional seating (same opening hours and prices).

Hermes CAFE $$$
(Map p164; ☑031-3555 5555; www.hermescafe. ir; Jolfa Alley; mains IR650,000; ☺11am-11.30pm; ☎) This bright, modern designer cafe offers a fashionable dining experience in the heart of the Amenian Quarter. Food focuses on Western-style diner fare, including burgers and pizzas, but with a local twist.

🍸 Drinking & Nightlife

While there are lots of delightful teahouses around the old city, perhaps the most relaxed venues for a sociable night out are in the Armenian quarter where every other doorway seems to open into a fashionable coffee shop or restaurant. All around town, live traditional music is usually played as an accompaniment at dinner.

Marseille Cafe CAFE
(Map p164; ☑031-3628 0252; Kalissa St; coffee IR200,000; ☺9.30am-2pm & 5-11pm Sat-Thu) This friendly, family-run little coffee shop is devoted to coffee in a country devoted to tea. Most of the beans are sourced from Brazil, and a range of beans, blends and barista equipment is on sale. A slice of the daily cake makes a good match for the delicious brews.

Sharbat Khan Bahar Nareng CAFE
(Sour Orange Cafe; Map p164; ☑031-3627 5269; Kalissa St, off Hakim Nezami Ave, opposite Julfa Hotel; ☺8am-10pm) Round the corner from the Kelisa-ye Vank, this magnificently painted one-room coffee shop is like an Esfahani miniature, with its exquisite patterned ceiling and murals on the wall. Providing

the perfect venue for a cup of coffee while touring the Armenian Quarter, it also offers a tasty breakfast (IR10,000; from 8am to 11am) for those fed up with normal hotel fare.

Roozegar CAFE
(Map p164; ☑031-3223 4357; Espadana Inn, off Naqsh-e Jahan (Imam) Sq; ☺10am-10.45pm; ☎) After a few laps of the square, this little cafe is a lovely spot to pause and relax. Soothing music, rich honey cake, good coffee and herbal teas served with *nabat* (crystallised sugar) help restore energy levels. The cafe is in a small courtyard north of the Masjed-e Sheikh Lotfollah and is a sociable spot for meeting fellow travellers.

Azadegan Teahouse TEAHOUSE
(Chaykhaneh-ye Azadegan; Map p164; off Naqsh-e Jahan (Imam) Sq; ☺7am-midnight) In a lane off the northeastern corner of Naqsh-e Jahan (Imam) Sq, this popular teahouse sports an enormous collection of bric-a-brac hanging from its walls and ceiling. Enter down the passageway lined with scooters, lamps and old radios.

🛍 Shopping

Esfahan has a long history of artistic achievement and arts and crafts continue to thrive in the city to this day. There are many places to see artisans at work, including B Hassan Abbad Alley, off the southeast corner of Naqsh-e Jahan (Imam) Sq and in the many *khans* (caravanserais) of the Bazar-e Bozorg. Peer through one shop window and someone is painting miniatures with a single hair brush, look through another and they're printing on calico; in parts of the bazaar, the tap, tap, tap of hammer on metal is as memorable as the dazzling display of copper dishes beaten into shape.

The city, then, with its emporiums of handcrafted goods rubbing shoulders with shops offering cheaper souvenirs, is an exciting place to shop. Offering the widest selection of handicrafts in Iran in the most enjoyable setting, the shop owners can be forgiven for charging higher prices for some of their goods than in Tehran or Shiraz, especially as they compensate with cups of *chay* (tea) and (mostly) good-natured haggling. The best buys are carpets, hand-painted miniatures on camel bone, intricate metalwork and enamelware, all of which are available in the bazaar and under the arcades around Naqsh-e Jahan (Imam)

Sq. Competition between vendors is fierce and it's best to ignore what one shop owner says about competitors in their bid to seal the deal.

Certain crafts are concentrated in particular areas. For jewellery, for example, the **Bazar-e Honar** (Map p164; Chahar Bagh Abbasi St; ⊙8.30am-1pm & 4-9pm Sat-Thu) is a honeypot of gold bangles, extravagent necklaces and gem pendants in antique designs. Posht Matbakh St, off Naqsh-e Jahan (Imam) Sq, is home to the miniaturist arts, including Fallahi Miniatures, Photo Vat Miniatures and Unique Gallery (enamelware). The arcades near the Masjed-e Shah house some of the most established carpet and Iranian textile shops, and the copper trade is plied in the alleys beside Chehel Sotun Palace.

If a carpet is too big for the suitcase, then *gaz* (Esfahan's traditional Persian nougat), in one of the elaborate presentation boxes, may make a more portable souvenir. Most locals think that the best brand is Kermani Gaz, which can be bought pretty much everywhere, but especially in confectionery shops along Chahar Bagh Abbasi St and around Naqsh-e Jahan (Imam) Sq.

Hossein Fallahi   ARTS & CRAFTS
(Miniature Art Gallery and Workshop; Map p164; ☑031-3220 4613; www.miniatureart.org; Posht Matbak St, off Naqsh-e Jahan (Imam) Sq; minature painted box from US$25; ⊙9am-9pm) In this studio it's possible to watch the master at work, peering through a magnifying glass as he applies tiny brushstrokes of paint, applied with a cat's hair and pigeon feather, to a miniature painting or a box made of bone. Using a single line to create a wealth of expression, this is art and craft at its most accomplished.

Paradise Handicrafts   CARPETS
(Map p164; ☑031-3220 4860; paradisecarpets@yahoo.com; 19 Afarinesh Bazaar, Naqsh-e Jahan (Imam) Sq; ⊙9am-1pm & 3-7pm Sat-Thu) This friendly father-and-son team specialise in nomadic carpets from all over Iran. High-quality pieces are available and postage can be arranged.

Aladdin Carpets   CARPETS
(Map p164; ☑031-3221 1461; aladdin_shop@yahoo.com; 160 Naqsh-e Jahan (Imam) Sq; ⊙9am-1pm & 3-7pm Sat-Thu) This small shop has an interesting range of carpets and experienced salesmen.

❶ Information

EMERGENCY
Call and request **Tourist Police** (Map p164; ☑110; Chahar Bagh Abbasi St; ⊙24hr) and an English-speaking operator will assist. English-speaking officers can also be found at a booth in the middle of the street outside the Madraseh-ye Chahar Bagh.

INTERNET
There are **coffeenets** (Map p164; per hour IR40,000; ⊙8am-10pm) along Chahar Bagh Abbasi St.

MEDICAL SERVICES
Al-Zahra Hospital (☑031-3620 2020; Soffeh St) Best hospital in Esfahan. English-speaking doctors.

MONEY
Sepah St off Naqsh-e Jahan (Imam) Sq has several exchange agencies.
Jahan-e Arz Money Changer (Map p164; Sepah St; ⊙8.30am-3pm Sat-Thu) Offers good rates.

POST
Main Post Office (Map p164; www.post.ir; Neshat St) East of Naqsh-e Jahan (Imam) Sq; for posting anything big – like a carpet.
Post Office (Map p164; www.post.ir; Naqsh-e Jahan (Imam) Sq; ⊙8am-6pm) For postcards and letters.

TOURIST INFORMATION
Tourist Office (Map p164; ☑031-3221 6831; Naqsh-e Jahan (Imam) Sq; ⊙7.30am-2pm Sat-Thu) Under the Ali Qapu Palace; the English-speaking staff hand out maps and

FLIGHTS FROM ESFAHAN

DESTINATION	FARE (US$)	FREQUENCY	CARRIER
Ahvaz	$75	10 per week	Iran Air, Aseman
Bandar Abbas	$87	2 weekly	Iran Air, Aseman
Kish	$96	5 weekly	Iran Air, Taban
Mashhad	$84	daily	Iran Air, Taban, Kish
Shiraz	$50	2 weekly	Iran Air
Tehran	$80	daily	Iran Air, Taban, Qeshm

brochures about the city and the surrounding area.

TRAVEL AGENCIES

Donyaye Parvaz Tour & Travel Agency (Map p164; ☎ 031-3667 3101; donyayeparvaz@aol.com; 8 Chahar Bagh-e Bala St; ⊗ 8.30am-5pm Sun-Thu) Located at the southern end of the Si-o-Seh Pol, this professional outfit can arrange tours and visas, book accommodation, and organise train, air and ferry tickets. Staff member Mr Morshedi speaks excellent English and is extremely helpful.

Iran Travel & Tourism (Map p164; ☎ 031-3222 3010; irantravel1904@yahoo.com; Shahid Medani St; ⊗ 8.30am-7pm Sat-Thu) Opposite Abbasi Hotel; can book plane, train and even ferry tickets.

VISA EXTENSIONS

The **Department of Aliens Affairs** (Rudaki St; ⊗ 8am-2pm Sat-Thu) is in a large, drab-looking government building. Passports must be shown at the gate and paperwork picked up from the office in the courtyard. Same-day service (three to four hours) is possible if the application is lodged early. Women applicants must wear *hejab* in the required photographs. Showing proof of a prebooked onward plane/bus ticket helps.

ⓘ Getting There & Away

AIR

Esfahan international airport (http://enisfahan.airport.ir/) is about 25km northeast of town and there is no airport bus service. A taxi *dar bast* costs around US$9.

The office of **Iran Air** (Map p164; ☎ 222 8200; www.iranair.com; Shahid Medani St) is in the shopping complex opposite the Abbasi Hotel.

BUS

Esfahan has a few bus terminals. **Kave bus terminal** (Kave Blvd) in the north is the busiest and most commonly used by travellers. It services Tehran, Kashan and Yazd. Most passengers buy their tickets at the ticket desks inside the terminal building just before they depart, but during

holiday periods it's wise to purchase tickets one or two days ahead through a travel agent. A taxi *dar bast* to Kave from the centre of town should cost around IR160,000.

Buses to destinations closer to Esfahan leave from two smaller bus terminals:

Zayandeh Rud bus terminal (☎ 031-3775 9182) Has services to Shahr-e Kord (VIP IR130,000), with departures every hour or so between 6am to 9pm. To get here from the centre of town, take a shuttle taxi west from Nazar St (East), just south of Si-o-Seh Pol (IR160,000).

Joy bus terminal (Jey St) Offers hourly departures to Yazd between 6am and 1am (VIP IR260,000, six hours) and Na'in (minibus IR60,000, three to four hours). To get here, take a shuttle taxi from Takhti Junction (IR20,000).

TRAIN

The train station *(istgah-e ghatah)* is on the southern edge of the city. It can be reached by bus from a stop outside Kowsar International Hotel, although the wait and the journey can take over an hour. A taxi costs IR300,000. Train tickets must be booked (most easily through a travel agent) well in advance, particularly on weekends or in holiday periods.

ⓘ Getting Around

Esfahan's ambitious metro-building project has been underway for many years now and unfortunately shows no sign of being completed in the near future. This means that some parts of the central city, including Takhti Junction, are huge construction sites.

BUS & MINIBUS

Local buses and minibuses leave the **bus terminal** (Map p164) near Chehel Sotun Palace every few minutes. Just ask – and keep asking – for one heading your way. Elsewhere in town ask at a bus stop and you will be pointed to the correct conveyance. Buses to Ateshkadeh-ye Esfahan (Esfahan Fire Temple) leave from the **terminal** (Map p164) on Sheykh Bahaei St.

TRAINS FROM ESFAHAN

DESTINATION	FARE (IR; NORMAL)	DURATION (HR)	DEPARTURES
Bandar Abbas	600,000	15	1st week – Sun, Tue & Thu; 2nd week – Mon, Wed, Fri & Sat
Kashan	220,000	4½	1st week – Sun, Tue & Thu; 2nd week – Mon, Wed, Fri & Sat
Mashhad	100,000	18	daily
Tehran	370,000	7½	daily

Rides cost US$0.40 to US$0.90 and you buy books of tickets at booths along the routes.

TAXI

Depending on the distance – not to mention negotiating skills – a fare in a private taxi around inner Esfahan costs anything from IR120,000 to IR320,000. Taxi drivers outside the main tourist sites, such as Naqsh-e Jahan (Imam) Sq and Kelisa-ye Vank (Vank Cathedral), inevitably charge more than those cruising around the suburbs.

The long Chahar Bagh Abbasi St is the city's main thoroughfare, and every couple of seconds a shuttle taxi goes *mostaghim* (straight ahead) for about IR500 per kilometre.

To outlying destinations such as the transport terminals, taxis lead from the following landmarks: Takhti Junction, Laleh, Qods and Ahmad Abad Sqs (for anywhere to the east); Imam Hossein and Shohada Sqs (for the north); and the southern end of Si-o-Seh Pol and Azadi Sq (for the south and west).

Zagros Mountains

A driving tour through the barren ridges of the Zagros Mountains offers an interesting alternative to the direct bus or flight between Esfahan and Shiraz. The mountains are home to Persians, Loris and Kurds as well as to a large number of nomads (primarily Bakhtiari and Qashqa'i). Nomadic traditions weave in and out of the daily rhythms of mountain culture, making it a fascinating place to observe the differences between the cultivated uplands and the interspersed desert plains.

Few people speak English, public transport is infrequent or nonexistent, and accommodation is basic in this part of Iran, qualifying the region as genuinely 'off the beaten track'. The best time to travel here is from April to November, when the nomads set up camp across the mountain slopes. In winter they move to the valleys south of Shiraz and many of the high mountain roads can be impassable with snow.

Shahr-e Kord   شهر کرد

📋 038 / POPULATION 380,312 / ELEVATION 2070M

A 30-minute drive from Esfahan, Shahr-e Kord is the sleepy capital of Chahar Mahal va Bakhtiari province. Known as the 'roof of Iran' on account of its high altitude, this is primarily a working, agricultural town, although it's becoming less of a staging post and more of a destination as the nearby villages recognise their potential for outdoor activities.

Shahr-e Kord itself has a couple of attractions: a modest **museum** (📋 038-3333 1245; Valiasr St, north of Valiasr Junction; IR150,000; ⏲10am-4pm Sat-Thu) occupying a beautifully-restored old *hammam*; and the **Ferdosi Soffrekhaneh** (📋 038-3225 4355; Ferdosi Sq; chay IR20,000; ⏲8am-10pm) one of Iran's most atmospheric, original teahouses. Also look

BUSES FROM ESFAHAN (KAVE)

DESTINATION	FARE (IR; VIP/ MAHMOOLY)	DURATION (HR)	DEPARTURES
Bandar Abbas	600,000 (VIP)	12	4.30pm & 6.30pm
Hamadan	400,000 (*mahmooly*)	7	1.15pm & 10.45pm
Kashan	115,000/80,000	3	frequent 5am-7pm
Kermanshah	470,000 (*mahmooly*)	10	8.45am & 9.45am
Khorramabad	335,000 (*mahmooly*)	6	2.15pm & 11.55pm
Mashhad	780,000/515,000	16	5 daily 3.30-7.30pm
Orumiyeh	750,000 (VIP)	17	2.30pm
Sanandaj	340,000 (*mahmooly*)	10	9pm
Shiraz	360,000 (*mahmooly*)	6	frequent 24hr
Tabriz	650,000 (VIP)	12	5 daily 6-7.30pm
Tehran	330,000 (VIP)	6	frequent 24hr
Tehran Airport (Imam Khomeini International Airport)	350,000 (VIP)	5	3 daily 8-10pm
Yazd	260,000 (*mahmooly*)	5	frequent 1am-7pm

for the **Wool Merchant** (Ferdosi Sq; ⊘8am-6pm) selling the local traditional goat-haired jackets worn by men. Black and white, knee-length and without arms, these jackets provide a surprisingly windproof layer against the winter cold.

It's also worth making time to visit the nearby village of **Chaleshtar** (چالشتر), where the chief attraction is the **castle** (IR80,000; ⊘8am-4pm). This magnificent little museum is housed in the residence of a former *khan*, who provided equally for his two sons by building each a sumptuous wing of the house, arranged around courtyards. Look for the ancient tombstones provided with two holes for water and grain for the benefit of birds.

In the surrounding countryside there are opportunities for hiking, rafting (without rapids) and horse riding, all of which can be organised through Chaleshtar's good local guesthouse **Khan-e Mosafer** (☑0913 106 5637; r up to 5 people IR1,600,000, breakfast IR80,000).

There are frequent buses to Shahr-e Kord and from Esfahan (IR80,000); taxis cost IR1,200,000 for the same journey. Local taxi is the best way to reach Chaleshtar from Shahr-e Kord (IR20,000).

Chelgerd   چلگرد

☑038 / POPULATION 2708 / ELEVATION 2319M

Chelgerd is the home of skiing in this part of the Zagros range. The **Koohrang Ski Resort** offers a single 800m-long T-bar running up a slope near the Koohrang Tunnel; the snow is generally skiable between late December and late February and the slopes are often empty on weekdays.

South of Chelgerd, the **Zardkuh Glaciers**, at an altitude of 4050m, are beginning to appear on the occasional tour itinerary, although facilities at present are not in place to do more than admire the formations from a safe distance. Discovered only in 1933, the largest glacier is 500m wide and 150m long and forms an unusual feature in the heart of a predominantly tropical (as opposed to polar) desert region.

The town makes a good base for climbing some of the many surrounding peaks that rise to nearly 4000m. There are also some unique attractions in and around this tiny village, including seasonal visits to local nomadic communities.

The remarkable old flat-top village of **Sar Aqa Seyyed**, 25km along a dirt track

from Chelgerd, is a popular local destination. Layered down the hillside, the roof of each house forms a walking platform for the house above. During some winter months, the village is cut off from the lower valleys by snow. Locals are ambivalent about visitors, and the village is best approached with a guide.

Koohrang Hotel (☑0912 114 4030, 038-3362 2302; www.koohranghotel.com; d/tr/q IR2,00 0,000/2,700,000/3,332,000; ❄) is in a pretty valley near a river and makes up for any lack of exterior charm by the warmth of its welcome. With a range of activities available, the English-speaking managers are a mine of information about the whole region.

There is a minibus between Chelgerd and Shahr-e Kord (IR120,000, 1½ hours) once daily most days of the week.

A taxi *dar bast* costs IR800,000 to/from Shahr-e Kord and IR160,000 to/from Esfahan.

Sepidan   سپیدان

☑071 / POPULATION 87,801 / ELEVATION 2250M (ARDAKAN), 2818M (POOLADKAF)

The county of Sepidan, around 80km and a one-hour drive from either Shiraz or Yasuj, is an area popular for outdoor activities, most of which are best organised from Shiraz. The staging post for this activity is the traditional town of **Ardakan** on the edge of the Zagros Mountains where supplies for hiking and camping can be bought. Many of the women in town wear the heavy velvet-pleated skirts of the region, decorated with dazzling beadwork or lace, and the bazaar is frequented with nomads in summer.

Most people pass through Ardakan en route for **Pooladkaf Hotel** (☑0917 601 5053, 071-3625 8025; www.pooladkafhotel.com; r IR3,000,000 incl breakfast; Ⓟ❄🛜), a ski resort about 15km uphill from the village. The resort boasts a ski lift of 2100m in length, below a peak of 3400m. In Ardakan you could stop over at the simple and characterful **Partaknah Motel** (☑0917 100 6319; Ardakan–Pooladkaf Rd; IR800,000 per person;).

Mr Raeisi from Shiraz-based **Iran Sightseeing** (☑071-1235 5939, 0917 313 2926; www.iransightseeing.com) can arrange downhill and cross-country skiing in winter, and trekking and mountain biking during the rest of the year. He also has excellent contacts with the nomads and can customise trips to visit and stay in their camps.

❶ Getting There & Away

Reaching the Sepidan region by public transport is problematic, but a taxi for the one-hour drive from Shiraz to Ardakan costs around IR500,000, and from Ardakan to to Pooladkaf the 15km drive will cost around IR100,000.

Qalaat

📞 071 / POPULATION 2613 / ELEVATION 1956M

In the foothills of the Zagros Mountains, just 15km northwest of Shiraz, the crumbling old village Qalaat (aka Ghalat) is slowly coming back to life as visitors from Shiraz head out this way to enjoy a taste of the rural life. Many of the stone and adobe houses are slowly being restored and some have been converted into restaurants such as the delightful **Kooch Traditional Restaurant** (📞 0917 116 7028, 071-3670 6907; meals IR400,000).

It's worth climbing to the upper reaches of the village, marked by the tiled minaret of an aged mosque, for the attractive views across the surrounding mountains. As to be expected of a region of orchards, it's particularly pretty in spring.

For the visitor, Qalaat makes for a pleasant afternoon or evening jaunt from Shiraz or a leg stretch and tea stop en route to Ardakan in the Sepidan region. There's no public transport to Qalaat; a return taxi from Shiraz (35km) costs around IR400,000 including waiting time. It's quite a steep haul up to the upper reaches of town, making it worth requesting to be dropped near the top of the old quarter, rather than the bottom!

Dasht-e Kavir   دشت کویر

The Dasht-e Kavir, one of two deserts dominating the region's landscape, is a mix of sand and salt as blinding in its whiteness as it is deafening in its silence. Against the odds, oases exist within these desolate environs, home to villages that are sustained by the wells of sweet water that have been part of desert mythology for centuries.

The desert nips at the ankles of all the roads east of Esfahan, luring some travellers 400km into the heart of the Dasht-e Kavir in and around the main town of Khur. To enjoy the desert without committing to the long journey into empty space, the small towns of Kuhpayeh, Toudeshk and Na'in offer caravanserai, picture-perfect adobe houses and inspiring landscapes en route between Esfahan and Yazd.

Few choose to stay long in the desert in summer, as temperatures regularly reach 50°C and air-conditioning is yet to become routine.

Kuhpayeh & Toudeshk   کوهپایه تودشک

📞 031 / POPULATION 4587 (KUHPAYEH), 3940 (TOUDESHK) / ELEVATION 2200M

East of Esfahan, along the main road to Na'in, two small villages invite travellers to break their journey en route to Yazd in two outstandingly hospitable places to stay.

🛏 Sleeping

⭐ **Tak-Taku Guesthouse**   HOMESTAY $

(📞 0913 365 4420, 031-4643 2586; www.taktaku. com; B&B in dm US$15, full board per person US$35; @ 🛜) English-speaking owner Mohammad Jalali and his family offer guests an authentic experience of Iranian hospitality with great charm and warmth. Their traditional house has rooms set around a courtyard and guests eat and sleep the Iranian way (ie on the floor). Eating the home-cooked dishes here is one of the culinary highlights of a visit to central Iran.

An interesting free walking tour around the village, and the use of bicycles, is included in the cost of accommodation, or guests can visit the local *hammam* (Thursday and Friday only). Also on offer are day trips to a salt lake (US$45) and camping expeditions to the sand dunes of the Varzaneh Desert (US$30 or US$65 for equipment, dinner and breakfast). Camel-riding trips at sunset and stargazing trips are other popular excursions.

⭐ **Kuhpayeh Caravansary Hotel**   CARAVANSERAI $$

(📞 0913 411 5632, 031-4642 4791; www.koupa hotel.ir; Khojaste Bakht St; s/d/VIP IR1,500,000/ 1,750,000/3,200,000) With two impressive portals at either end of a large central courtyard, this old caravanserai has been sensitively restored to suggest a continuity of lodging between the old mud walls. Big rooms, some with beds and modern, tiled bathrooms, a grand dining hall with traditional and modern seating, and a garden of gnarled willows single this out as a top choice.

❶ Getting There & Away

From Esfahan's Jey bus terminal, buses to Yazd and Na'in pass through Toudeshk (VIP/*mahmooly* IR90,000/70,000, one hour). There is also an occasional minibus service to Toudeshk (IR35,000). A taxi *dar bast* costs IR850,000.

From Yazd, buses to Esfahan pass through Toudeshk (*mahmooly* IR260,000, 3½ hours).

From Toudeshk, taxis *dar bast* cost IR450,000 to Na'in, IR850,000 to Esfahan and IR1,900,000 to Yazd.

Na'in نائين

📱 031 / POPULATION 25,329 / ELEVATION 1545M

Well regarded for its handicrafts, the town of Na'in (aka Naein, Naeen) dates back 2000 years, making it one of the oldest continuously settled towns in Iran. Located at the junction of the desert road to Tabas and Mashhad, it has been an important crossroad on converging trade routes since Sassanid times. In the past it was known for its ceramics and textiles; today it's primarily known for fine hand-knotted carpets and for hand-loomed camel-wool cloaks, which are produced in the neighbouring village of **Mohamadieh** and sold in Yazd.

◎ Sights

A newly laid walking path leads from the Masjed-e Jameh's entrance to the ruined Narej Fortress, the town's oldest structure, passing a *hosseniah* (building used during the rituals to commemorate the death of Imam Hossein), underground cisterns and wind catchers. Together these aged structures make for an attractive ensemble, especially in the golden light of late afternoon.

Masjed-e Jameh MOSQUE
(مسجد جامع, Jameh Mosque; junction Naini & Dr Taba Sts; IR100,000; ⊙9am-sunset Tue-Sun, closed for Fri prayers in summer) The town's Friday mosque is the highlight of a visit to Na'in. Constructed between the 10th and 11th centuries, it was one of the first mosques built in Iran and is unusual in that it doesn't conform to the usual four-*iwan* plan of its time (eg the Masjed-e Jameh in Esfahan). The exterior facade and minaret are austerely beautiful and many parts of the interior (including the mihrab) are decorated with finely detailed stucco work.

Kavir Ethnology Museum MUSEUM
(Pirnia Mansion; www.naeinsun.ir/info; opposite Masjed-e Jameh, junction Naini & Dr Taba Sts; IR100,000; ⊙9am-sunset) With a few interesting artefacts, including hand looms and wool-spinning equipment, this small museum is housed in a grand old mansion that belongs to the Safavid period. The plaster work and painted ceilings (of peacocks and delicate leaf motifs) steal the show.

☞ Tours

Mahmood Mohammadipour HISTORY
(📱0939 863 6090; www.naeinsun.ir; city tours from US$25, treks from US$23) This licensed guide is the official oracle on Na'in and his tours come highly recommended. He offers two tours: a two-hour city tour of Na'in (US$25) and a three-hour tour that includes neighbouring Mohamadieh (US$30). He also organises trekking and camping, including a four-hour trip to Iran's highest (62m) sand dunes (US$35). Discount available for groups of two, three or four people.

🛏 Sleeping

Campers can pitch their tents in the open ground near the *hosseinieh,* located close to the Masjed-e Jameh. The nearby public toilets are open 24 hours.

Naein Tourist Hotel HOTEL $
(Jahangardi Inn; 📱031-4625 3081; fax 031-4625 3665; Ahmar Shahid Rajaie St; d IR1,640,000, extra bed IR500,000; 🅿❄) A cut above the average travellers' inn, this Pahlavi-era hotel makes an overnight stay in Na'in rather inviting. There are eight split-level suites arranged around an attractive courtyard and the hotel restaurant (meals from IR250,000, open noon to 3pm and 6.30pm to 9.30pm), with its neat tablecloths and attractive wall hangings, is a favourite with locals and tourists alike.

ℹ WHEN TO VISIT

Many visitors come to the middle of the Dasht-e Kavir to experience the peace and quiet that the desert has to offer, but for a time that seclusion was under threat by an unlikely source: parties of fashionable youngsters from Tehran used to head out this way to let their hair down. Behaving in ways that some thought inappropriate to cultural norms brought their activities to the attention of the authorities and now the so-called 'boom box' safaris have largely come to an end. That said, visitors seeking only the sound of the wind whistling over the dunes or the occasional bellowing camel may prefer to avoid public holidays and weekends.

The hotel is 150m southwest of Naqsh-e Jahan (Imam) Sq.

Mosaferkhaneh Gholami　　HOSTEL $
(Gholami Hostel; ☏ 0913 223 4667; Imam Khomeini Ave; s/d IR600,000/700,000) Mr Gholami's cheap and cheerful guesthouse is about 300m east of Naqsh-e Jahan (Imam) Sq above an ice-cream shop. The simple rooms have hard beds and shared bathrooms, and there's a kitchen that guests can use. No breakfast and no English spoken.

🛍 Shopping

Aba Bafi　　CLOTHING
(Mohamadieh Caves; kilims from US$25; ☉ sunrise-1.30pm & 2.30pm-sunset) Heavy sheep-and-camel woollen cloaks (famous among Arab customers) are made in underground wool-weaving workshops in this suburb of Na'in. They cost around US$80 depending on size, or more portable striped kilims cost US$25.

The openings of the man-made caves all face the rising sun and are thought to have been constructed by Zoroastrians who traditionally respect the sources of light. Nowadays the caves support a cottage industry that is over 700 years old.

ℹ Getting There & Away

Buses and minibuses run every 30 minutes between Na'in and Esfahan's Jey bus terminal (minibus IR60,000, two to 2½ hours) between 6am and 4pm. A shared taxi between Na'in and Esfahan costs IR130,000.

Three buses travel daily to Tehran (VIP/ mahmooly IR430,000/260,000; six hours) via Kashan. Two of these travel between Na'in and Jonub and one between Na'in and Beihaghi (Arjantin).

Some Yazd-bound buses from Esfahan stop in Na'in. To reach Yazd from Na'in on this service it costs VIP/mahmooly IR430,000/260,000 and takes three hours.

Garmeh　　گرمه

☏ 031 / POPULATION 244 / ELEVATION 889M

Surrounded by date palms clustered around a small warm-water spring clouded with fish, Garmeh is the classic desert oasis. The 1500-year-old mud-brick village at the heart of the oasis is currently enjoying something of a renaissance, driven by enterprising locals who have understood the village's attraction for tourists. There is a pleasant walk through the date palms and

orchards (although locals are beginning to wall their properties against the incursion of fruit-picking tourists), and camel treks, hikes to hot-water springs and mountain-village visits are also possible to arrange. During summer it gets ridiculously hot here, but this at least offers the authentic desert experience.

A cluster of traditional-style hotels (and a nearby atelier) have sprung up in Garmeh, thanks largely to the visionary efforts of the landlord of the highly popular guesthouse and hostel **Ateshooni** (☏ 0935 422 4748; www. ateshooni.com; full board in guesthouse per person US$35, hostel per person US$15, apt rates by request; ❀ 🛜). Artist and musician Maziar Ale Davoud has almost single-handedly saved Garmeh from the fate of many small desert communities, restoring a number of its mud-brick buildings as homes for members of his family and running a highly successful guesthouse, backpacker hostel and 12-bed holiday apartment. In the process he has provided employment for locals and brought much-needed income and infrastructure to the village, stemming the migration of youth to the big cities.

ℹ Getting There & Away

From Tehran's Terminal-e Jonub buses to Tabas or Birjand leave frequently between 1.30pm and 5.30pm and stop en route in Khur, 28km to the north of Garmeh on the Na'in to Tabas road (VIP/ mahmooly IR720,000/540,000, nine/10 hours).

From Esfahan's Kave bus terminal buses to Khur leave at 1pm (IR220,000, seven hours). The return service departs Khur at 1pm.

From Yazd, a mahmooly service to Khur leaves at 1pm. The return service to Yazd departs at 7.30am (IR150,000, five hours).

From Khur, the Ateshoonia can organise a transfer service to Garmeh for IR220,000.

The Ateshooni can also organise private transport from main cities costing IR3,200,000 from Esfahan, IR2,600,000 from Yazd and IR1,800,000 from Na'in.

Khur

☏ 031 / POPULATION 6126 / ELEVATION 1045M

There are so few settlements and villages in Dasht-e Kavir that the existence of the bustling town of Khur (also spelt Khor) comes as some surprise. While there's not much to see in this desert outpost itself, the town forms the main transport hub of the region. It also offers excellent accommodation in the grand, traditional-style **Bali Desert Hotel**

BAYAZEH

The half-forgotten village of **Bayazeh**, best visited en route between Khur (or Garmeh) and Yazd as part of a desert loop with driver-guide, would be hardly worth a mention but for an enormous mud-brick castle **Narin Ghale** (Bayazeh Castle; off Hwy 81; IR50,000; ☺ by appointment, call telephone number at entrance) dating from the Sassanid era. This crumbling warren of over 700 rooms makes a dramatic backdrop to the tiny village sheltering beneath it.

There is another excellent reason to venture out this way: **Yata Traditional Hotel** (☑ 031-4634 6189, 0912 219 6216; www.yatahotel.ir; Hwy 81, Bayazeh; s/d/extra bed IR1,100,00/1,500,000/400,000; P ✳ 🛜) offers a cool sunken courtyard, a fine wind catcher and gorgeous rooms with beds and private bathroom. Even with no intention to stay, the aroma of home-cooked *fesenjan* stew with beef meatballs makes lunch or dinner (from IR150,000) here compelling.

(☑ 0913 125 4828; www.hotelbali.ir; Fatemi Sq; d/tr IR1,850,000/2,550,000, breakfast IR20,000; P ✳ 🛜), an attractive stopover en route to destinations deeper in the desert.

Nearby, along the road from Khur to Tabas, there is a huge salt lake used for the harvesting of phosphates. The vast pock-marked disc spreads out across the desert and makes an interesting photo opportunity early and late in the day when the shadows are at their longest.

🛈 Getting There & Away

A daily bus to Khur leaves both Esfahan (Kave bus terminal) and Yazd (Homafar Sq) at 1pm and takes seven hours. Buses from Tehran (nine hours) leave the Terminal-e Jonub (Southern terminal) for Tabas, passing through Khur. There's no public transport from Khur to Mesr or Farahzad but taxis make the 60km journey in about an hour (IR720,000).

Mesr & Farahzad   مصر

☑ 031 / POPULATION 200 / ELEVATION 853M

The small town of Mesr, 425km from Esfahan, is an oasis located amid sand dunes in the Dasht-e Kavir. Just a couple of kilometres further into the desert, along a sandy track, lies an even smaller settlement called Farahzad. The residents of both are all members of one extended family who make a living from agriculture and by operating various lodges and tours into the desert.

Both settlements, which originated over 150 years ago, give access to a magnificent portion of the Dasht-e Kavir. With dunes, a 3km-long flowing river arising out of the sands, patches of reeds, salt pans, weathered escarpments and eroded sandstone features, a 4WD, camel or hiking excursion to explore this remarkable landscape is

highly recommended and easily organised through one of the guesthouses.

👉 Tours

Mojtaba Heidari   OUTDOORS
(☑ 0935 066 2366; www.mesrvillage.ir) This guide is an expert of this portion of the Dasht-e Kavir and his website gives information on tours and services dedicated to making the most of the desert region.

🛏 Sleeping

★ Barandaz Lodge   GUESTHOUSE $
(☑ 0913 323 4188; www.mesr.info; Rd End, Farahzad; B&B per person US$15; P 🛜) 🥢 In the tiny outpost of Farahzad, neighbouring Mesr, this 11-room guesthouse occupies two beautifully restored mud-brick houses. The simple rooms with traditional bedding, hydronic heating and clean bathrooms are arranged around a tiny courtyard, while home-prepared meals (dinner US$10) using locally sourced ingredients are served in the carpeted *iwan*.

Afzal Ecotourism Residence   GUESTHOUSE $
(☑ 0910 302 0465; mesrafzalhouse@gmail.com; Main St, Mesr; r with inside bathroom US$14) This large and attractive mud-and-thatch property with a fountain pool in the garden is run by a pair of hospitable brothers and is a notch above others in the facilities it offers. Some rooms have air-con, some fans and most have internal bathrooms. Meals featuring 'naughty camel' kebabs (US$5) are a culinary highlight of a visit to Mesr.

Shenzar II Resort   GUESTHOUSE $
(☑ 0912 399 7252; www.persiantourismservice. com; Mesr Rd, Mesr; full board per person US$27) The largest of the mud-brick houses in Mesr, this well-run establishment offers tradition-

al rooms around a courtyard (sleeping on the roof is permitted in summer) and has a cosy indoor communal dining area. It also runs a range of desert activities, including a four-hour visit to the nearby villages of Aroosan and Korgaz (US$88).

Teeda Hotel   HOTEL $$
(☑ 031-3220 6970, 0912 467 1237; www. teeda-hotel.com; Rd End, Farahzad; d/tr IR2,350,000/3,350,000; P❉🛜) Lacking some of the charm of the old traditional-style accommodation, this hotel with its comfortable beds, crisp linen and air-con allows for a visit in summer when other guesthouses can be swelteringly hot. The restaurant (dinner per person from IR25,000) and coffee shop is housed in a mud *ab anbar* (water reservoir).

❶ Getting There & Away

The 60km-taxi journey from the main town of Khur to Mesr costs around IR720,000. Farahzad is a few kilometres further along an off-road track from Mesr.

Yazd   یزد

☑ 035 / POPULATION 1,110,000 / ELEVATION 1229M
With its winding lanes, forest of *badgirs,* mud-brick houses and delightful places to stay, Yazd is a 'don't miss' destination. On a flat plain ringed by mountains, the city is wedged between the northern Dasht-e Kavir and southern Dasht-e Lut and is every inch a city of the desert. It may not have the big-ticket sights of Esfahan or Shiraz, but, with its atmospheric alleyways and centuries of history, it exceeds both in its capacity to enchant. Yazd warrants a lazy approach – rambling around the maze of historic lanes (referred to locally as Yazd's 'historical texture'), popping into random teahouses or pausing to work out calligraphic puzzles in the city's exquisite tilework.

Originally settled 5000 years ago, Yazd has an interesting mix of people, 10% of whom follow the ancient religion of Zoroastrianism. An elegant *ateshkadeh* (fire temple) near the city centre shelters an eternal flame and visitors are welcome.

History

Yazd has a long and important history as a trading post. When Marco Polo passed this way in the 13th century he described Yazd as 'a very fine and splendid city and a

centre of commerce'. It was spared destruction by Genghis Khan and Tamerlane, and flourished in the 14th and 15th centuries, with silk, textile and carpet production as main home-grown industries. Like most of Iran, Yazd fell into decline when the Safavids were defeated and remained little more than a provincial outpost until the railway line from Tehran was extended here by the last shah. Today, it is a thriving city of over a million inhabitants.

⦿ Sights

◉ Old City

Yazd's historic centre emerges like a phoenix from the desert with an **old city** (بافت قدیم; Map p184) that, according to Unesco, is one of the most ancient settlements on earth. It is the perfect place to get a feel for the region's rich history as just about everything here – including 2000 Qajar-era houses – is made from sun-dried mud bricks. The resulting tan-coloured, high-baked skyline is dominated by tall *badgirs* (windtowers) on almost every rooftop – a reminder of the extreme heat of summer. The residential quarters appear almost deserted because of the high walls, which shield the houses from the narrow and labyrinthine *kuches* (lanes) that criss-cross the town.

By following a walking tour or just wandering around, it's easy to stumble across treasures of urban architecture – a covered walkway, a simple courtyard, an ornate wooden door, a shaft of light on a tiled surface. However captivating the experience at ground level, though, the real highlight is the view over the rooftops: in late afternoon the sun melts across the adobe skyline and floods the desert beyond.

Expect to get lost wandering the lanes – it's part of the old quarter's appeal.

★ Masjed-e Jameh   MOSQUE
(مسجد جامع, Jameh Mosque; Map p184; Masjed-e Jameh St; IR80,000; ⊙ 8am-8pm, museum 8-11am) FREE Soaring above the old city, this magnificent building is graced with a tiled entrance portal (one of the tallest in Iran), flanked by two 48m-high minarets and adorned with inscriptions from the 15th century. The exquisite mosaics on the dome and mihrab, and the tiles above the main western entrance to the courtyard are masterpieces of calligraphy, evoking sacred names in infinitely complex patterns.

Built for Sayyed Roknaddin in the 15th century, the mosque is built on 12th-century foundations over a former fire temple and with access to the Zarch Qanat (a stairwell leads down to part of this ancient water channel but is closed to the public).

The Jameh Mosque is particularly notable for the prevalence of faience – a form of tiling that, like mosaic, is formed of different coloured pieces that are sandwiched together to create the design. These predate later uniform tiling, which feature painted designs. The *gardoneh mehr* (swastika symbol) used on some tiles symbolises infinity, timelessness, birth and death, and can be found on Iranian buildings dating back as early as 5000 BC.

This is one sight where having a guide (and ideally a rudimentary knowledge of Arabic script) can transform the experience of a visit as it is impossible to guess at the calligraphic conundrums involved in the design without expert interpretation.

The most revered object in the small museum, which is only open in the mornings, is a piece of hand-loomed cloth that once adorned the Kabbah in Mecca.

★ **Amir Chakhmaq**
Mosque Complex   NOTABLE BUILDING
(مجموعه امیر چخماق; Map p184; Amir Chakhmaq Sq) The stunning three-storey facade of this Hosseinieh is one of the largest such structures in Iran. The rows of perfectly proportioned sunken alcoves are at their best and most photogenic in late afternoon, when the copper-coloured sunlight is captured within each alcove and the towering exterior appears to glow against the darkening sky. New two-storey arcades hem the pedestrianised square and illuminated fountains lend an attractive foreground to the splendid vista at night. Only the 1st floor of the structure is accessible.

A huge wooden palm *nakhl* (cypress tree-shaped wooden structure) is parked under the Amir Chakhmaq. An important centrepiece for the observance of Shiite Ashura commemorations, this *nakhl* is over 200 years old and is no longer moved. During Ashura, it is draped in a black cover for a day or two around the celebrations to represent the coffin of Imam Hossein. Illusions to cypress trees, and by association the *nakhl* (which in fact means date palm), predate Islam and signify immortality, resistance and freedom – qualities that have come also to be associated with the Shiite imam, Imam Hossein.

Underneath the complex is a bazaar where *kababis* specialise in *jigar* (grilled liver).

★ **Saheb A Zaman**
Zurkhaneh   CULTURAL CENTRE
(زور خانه صاحب الزمان; Map p184; off Amir Chakhmaq Sq; IR200,000; ⊙ reservoir 6am-9pm, workouts 7-8pm Sat-Thu) The cavernous *ab anbar* (water reservoir), built around 1580, resembles a 29m-high standing egg from the inside. Crowned with five burly *badgirs,* this impressive piece of architecture stored water for much of the city until modern irrigation made it redundant. The building has found a new purpose as a *zurkhaneh* (house of strength) in which *javan mard* (gentlemen) exercise using heavy wooden clubs to build muscle. The practitioners of this ancient sport are expected to display chivalrous values and embrace high integrity.

★ **Yazd Water Museum**   MUSEUM
(Map p184; Amir Chakhmaq Sq; IR150,000; ⊙ 8am-2.30pm & 3.30-7pm) Yazd is famous for its *qanats* (underground aqueducts) and this museum, one of the best of its kind, is devoted to the brave men who built them. Located in a restored mansion with a visible *qanat* running underneath, the museum offers, through a series of photographs, exhibits and architectural drawings, a fascinating glimpse into the hidden world of waterways that have allowed life to flourish in the desert.

The uniform of the *qanat* builders shows an early form of Personal Protective Equipment (PPE), with padded cotton hats and white-coloured clothing that was both luminous in the dark and would act as a shroud in the event of a fatal accident.

The museum, which charts the 2000 years that Iran's unique irrigation system has been in operation, describes the drilling of mother wells (which can reach a depth of 300m, such as the *qanat* near Mashad) and the use of water distribution clocks. These clocks (basically a bowl with a hole in the bottom) helped to mark out the 15- or 20-minute shares of water purchasable by householder or farmer.

Qanats run through many of the wealthy old houses in Yazd, collecting in pools in basements known as *sardob*. As the coolest part of the house, these rooms were often beautifully decorated and several fine examples exist in Yazd's old traditional hotels today.

Yazd

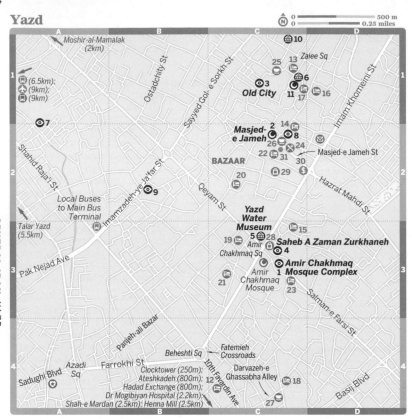

The *qanats* (there are many running through each town) are the reason why the wealthiest districts are always closest to the mountains – to be closest to the freshest water.

Khan-e Lari
HISTORIC BUILDING

(خانه لاری; Map p184; near Zaiee Sq; IR80,000; ☺8am-8pm) This 150-year-old building is one of the best-preserved Qajar-era houses in Yazd. The *badgirs,* traditional doors, stained-glass windows, elegant archways and alcoves distinguish it as one of the city's grandest homes. It is worth noting the particularly delicate white-and-cream plaster work, traced with slivers of mirror, that decorate the courtyard *iwans.* The merchant family who built the mansion have long gone, and it's now home to a set of archives. It's signposted west of Zaiee Sq.

The son of the owner of this house had a penchant for Western women and the walls and ceiling of one of the rooms is dedicated to their demure (and not so demure) por-traits. Another interesting feature of the house is the sitting platform with all four legs in the water to avoid the harassment of scorpions – a reminder that the desert is only just kept at bay in this desert city.

Ateshkadeh
TEMPLE

(آتشکده, Sacred Eternal Flame; Kashani St; IR80,000; ☺8-11.45am & 4-6.45pm, to 7.45pm in summer) Often referred to as the Zoroas-trian Fire Temple, this elegant neoclassical building, reflected in an oval pool in the garden courtyard, houses a flame that is said to have been burning since about AD 470. Visible through a window from the entrance hall, the flame was transferred to Ardakan in 1174, to Yazd in 1474 and to its present site in 1940. It is cherished (not worshipped) by the followers of the Zo-roastrian faith – the oldest of the world's monotheistic religions.

Yazd

Bagh-e Dolat Abad   PAVILION, GARDENS

(باغ دولت آباد; Map p184; ☑ 035-3627 0781; Shahid Raja'i St; IR150,000; ⊙ 7am-11pm) Once a residence of Persian regent Karim Khan Zand, this small pavilion set amid Unesco-listed gardens was built around 1750. The interior of the pavilion is superb, with intricate latticework and exquisite stained-glass windows. The pavilion also boasts Iran's loftiest *badgir;* standing over 33m tall, it was rebuilt in the 1960s. The pretty garden, built on the traditional Persian garden principle of symmetrical design, is planted with soaring evergreens and dotted with sour orange and pomegranates.

Bogheh-ye Sayyed Roknaddin   SHRINE

(بقعه سید رکن الدین, Mausolem of Sayyed Roknaddin; Map p184; off Masjed-e Jameh St; ⊙ 8am-1pm & 4-8pm Sat-Thu, 10am-noon Fri) **FREE** The beautiful blue-tiled dome of the tomb of local Islamic notable Sayyed Roknaddin Mohammed Qazi is visible from any elevated point in the city. Built 700 years ago, the dome (currently under repair) is an impressive piece of architecture and the stuccoed interior is also worth a visit.

Imam Zadeh Jafar   SHRINE

(Map p184; ⊙ 8am-8pm) **FREE** This magnificent modern shrine is best experienced at night when the lighting is inspirational, both from the courtyard outside and from within the elaborately mirrored inner sanctum that houses the tomb. Women must wear chador (available at the entrance gate) and enter through the specified door.

◉ Outer Yazd

Mirror & Lighting Museum   MUSEUM

(Kashani St; IR80,000; ⊙ 8am-8pm) This elegant 20th-century mansion, dating from the 1940s, was confiscated after the 1978 revolution and has been converted into a quirky and fun museum celebrating the wonder of reflection. Some fine examples of mirrors and lamps are on display, and a photo booth, featuring opposing mirrors, provides for the ultimate selfie. Despite its name, the museum's highlight is neither mirror nor lamp but a superb piece of plaster work in the shape of a curtain. It took the 46-year-old master craftsman four years to complete.

Henna Mill

(Mazari-ha Alley) FREE The lanes off Kashani St, near the Mirror & Lighting Museum, are home to a number of henna mills. With their huge grinding stones, rotated against a flat plate on a brick plinth, these mills have been grinding down henna for well over a hundred years. A few are still in operation and make for an interesting quick visit en route to lunch in one of the renovated mills now serving as restaurants.

MILL

Dakhmeh-ye Zartoshtiyun

(برج خاموشی, Towers of Silence; IR80,000; ☉7am-2pm winter, 8am-noon summer) Abandoned in the 1960s, these evocative Zoroastrian Towers of Silence are set on two lonely, barren hilltops on the southern outskirts of Yazd. Several buildings used for the ceremonial preparation of bodies dot the site, while the modern Zoroastrian cemetery is nearby. An elderly man at the entrance is often on hand to pose for a photograph: he is the last remaining porter of bodies, whose responsibility it once was to transport the deceased up the steep path to their final resting place.

TOWER

The easiest way to reach the towers from central Yazd is by taxi *dar bast* (one way/return with waiting time IR100,000/350,000). It takes around 45 minutes to climb to the top of the towers and back.

Hidden Desert

VIEWPOINT

Within 30 minutes (15km) drive of Yazd city centre, this belt of rippling sand dunes is a popular spot to watch the sun set across the desert landscape. As the colours of the pink-hued mountains beyond intensify with the last of the sun's rays, the shadows of the dunes are thrown into sharp relief, making for the perfect photo opportunity. While a taxi may be persuaded to the edge of the sands, it is better to take a licensed driver-guide who can navigate the soft terrain.

Tours

A full-day tour of Yazd costs US$70. Some sample popular excursions from Yazd include the loop around Meybod, Chak Chak and Kharanaq (US$70 to $80) and the loop around Zein-o-din, Saryazd and Fahraj (US$65). A tour from Yazd to Shiraz via Persepolis and Naqsh-e Rostam and Naqsh-e don't Rajab costs US$135. Prices generally don't include meals and entrance fees. Guides pay their own meals and don't have to pay entrance fees.

Although some hotels offer tours, these are not licensed operations and they encroach on the business of licensed guides and driver-guides. Bona fide guides must carry a license (with photo ID and hologram with the date of expiry clearly displayed).

Mojtaba Heidari

TOURS

(☑0935 066 2366; www.mojirantrip.com) With detailed knowledge about Yazd and the whole central Iran region, and a willingness to share a wealth of cultural insights, this excellent driver-guide is fluent in English and treats each of his commissions as a personal crusade. It's fair to say that he's not without

---

THE BADGIRS OF YAZD

Any summer visitor to Yazd will understand immediately why the city's roofscape is a forest of *badgirs* (windtowers or ventilation shafts). These ancient systems of natural air-conditioning are designed to catch even the lightest breeze and direct it to the rooms below. To appreciate the effect, just stand beneath one.

Iranian *badgirs* are divided into three common types: Ardakani, which capture wind from only one direction; Kermani, which capture wind from two directions; and Yazdi, which capture wind from four directions. Other variations can capture wind from up to eight directions. All have a structure that contains the shafts, air shelves that are used to catch some of the hot air and stop it entering the house, flaps to redirect the circulation of the wind and a roof covering. The currents that enter the house often do so above a pool of cool water, thereby cooling the air, while the warm air continues its circular path, redirected upwards and out of the house through a different shaft. Genius!

In case you're wondering, the horizontal wooden poles that stick out either side of the ventilation shafts have several functions. Primarily they are used as a scaffolding and hoist point for maintenance, but they also function as a pigeon roost, useful for the collection of guano for fertiliser. Equally, they are also part of the aesthetics of the structure, helping to give character, balance and distinction to each tower.

a quirk or two, but these make for an endearing personality – and an unforgettable trip!

Experienced in giving help with obtaining visa codes.

Mazieh Mandegari   HIKING
(☑ 0913 453 3833; maziehmandegari@yahoo. com; same-day or 24hr mountain ascent per person US$100, up to 6 people) This licensed, trained and highly experienced mountain guide operating out of Yazd offers hikes up Shirkouh at any time of year, although she recommends spring and autumn as the best time to see wildflowers and for the climate. At 4074m the ascent is hard-going but poses no technical difficulties, and can be summited in trainers (boots needed in winter).

Mohsen Hajisaeid   OUTDOORS
(☑ 035-3622 7828, 0913 351 4460; www.iranpe rsiatour.com) Mohsen has the well-deserved reputation as being one of the best licensed guides in Iran. Based here in Yazd, he's also an executive of the Yazd Tourism Associations Council. He is unparalleled as a fixer, and is a mine of cultural and practical knowledge. Check the website for a full list of his tours in Yazd and around the country.

Mehran Toosizadeh   TOURS
(☑ 0913 359 7003; www.mehran-2c.blogfa.com) Friendly and helpful, Mehran speaks good English and is an engaging licensed guide for interesting city and local tours in the Yazd area.

Pegah Latifi   OUTDOORS
(☑ 0935 935 7079; traveltoyazd@gmail.com; half-/ full-day city tour incl transport US$45/80) Pegah is a safe driver and enthusiastic guide who specialises in tours for women travellers, but is happy to guide anyone. She works in Yazd and the surrounding areas.

🛏 Sleeping

For many visitors, a highlight of Yazd is sleeping in one of the many restored traditional houses that have been converted into hotels. This experience is not for everyone, however, and Yazd offers a few modern accommodation options for those who prefer a fuller range of amenities, and fewer stairs, lifts and windows. In the low season, most midrange and top-end hotels offer a 20% to 40% discount.

★ Narenjestan
Traditional House   HOMESTAY $
(Map p184; ☑ 035-3627 3231, 0913 455 6598; www. narenjestanhouse.com; Shahid Sadoughi Alley, off Imam Khomeini St; r from US$35) This licensed homestay, in the heart of the old city, is a real find. The couple who run it speak excellent English (the husband gained his PhD in New Zealand) and have committed their time and energies both to restoring the 200-year-old family home with a flair for interior design, and to perfecting the art of hospitality.

Yazd Backpack Hostel   HOSTEL $
(Map p184; ☑ 0913 520 5100, 035-3627 2458; www.yazdbackpacker.com; Amir Chakhmaq Sq; s/d US$15/25, s without bathroom US$10) For clean, private rooms for the price of a dorm, this hostel is a great choice. Opened in 2017 by a lively, youthful crew, most of the eight rooms are compact and essentially windowless but with brand-new beds and neatly tiled floors. There's a communal kitchen and the rooftop panorama is spectacular. Low-season discounts available.

Kourosh Traditional Hotel   HOTEL, HOSTEL $
(Map p184; ☑ 035-3620 3560; www.yazd hotelkourosh.com; off Imam Khomeini St, near Alexander's Prison, Fahadan district; s/d IR1,050,000/1,350,000; ❄ 🛜) Buried deep in the old city, this cordial and relaxed hotel surrounds a pretty garden courtyard giving a pleasant, shady spot to while away the heat of the day or to sunbathe in winter. The simple rooms are traditional in style with some offering a little more comfort than others.

Kohan Traditional Hotel   HOTEL $
(Kohan Kashaneh; Map p184; ☑ 035-3621 2485; www.kohanhotel.ir; Alley 40, off Imam Khomeini St, Fahadan district; dm/s/d/tr IR480,000/900,000/ 1,300,000/1,800,000; ❄ @ 🛜) Stencilled signs point the way to this historic family home with its warm welcome and home-cooked food. The 18 unadorned but comfortable rooms are set around a very beautiful garden planted with banana, sour orange and sprays of bougainvillea. While the upstairs 17-bed dorm (only one shower and one toilet) is dark and dingy, the rooms around the courtyard are good value.

Orient Hotel   HOSTEL, HOTEL $
(Hotel Shargh; Map p184; ☑ 035-5626 7783; www. orienthotel.ir; 6th Alley, off Masjed-e Jameh St; dm/ s/d/VIP US$15/25/45/70; ❄ @ 🛜) Owned and operated by the crew from the Silk Road Hotel, the Orient is set around two high-sided

Walking Tour
The Old City

START AMIR CHAKHMAQ MOSQUE COMPLEX
END FAHADAN MUSEUM HOTEL
LENGTH 3KM; TWO TO THREE HOURS

Starting from the pretty pedestrian area in front of ① **Amir Chakhmaq Mosque Complex** (p183), stock up on sustenance in the form of traditional Yazdi sweets at ② **Haj Khalifeh Ali Rahbar** (p192), on the northeast corner of Amir Chakhmaq Sq. Suitably fortified, head along Imam Khomeini St and turn left up Masjed-e Jameh St, pausing to admire the beautiful vista ahead. Before reaching the imposing mosque that gives this street its name, turn down the lane to the right to admire the stunning portal of the turquoise-domed ③ **Bogheh-ye Sayyed Roknaddin** (p185). Continue into the ④ **Masjed-e Jameh** (p182) and enjoy the sensory overload of its magnificent architectural details.

Exit the mosque complex through the northeastern door (near the *qanat*), turn right, then left, and keep straight for about 75m until a junction with several arches and open ceilings. Turn left here and the lane leads into an open space with a playground; a doorway opens into a library and curio shop at the edge of the square. Veer right at this shop and follow the lane (tending northeast). After about 250m on Fazel St, a small lane leads off to the right where an ⑤ **ab anbar (water reservoir)** surrounded by four *badgirs* (windtowers) stands next to a park.

Continue left (northeast), pass Kohan Traditional Hotel and continue another 100m or so until you come to Mirzazadeh St. Heading left (northwest), walk past Ziaee Sq and keep straight for about 150m. Turn right down an alley to the ⑥ **Khan-e Lari** (p184), a stunning traditional house. Head back to Ziaee Sq and turn right. Ahead is the dome of ⑦ **Alexander's Prison** and just beyond is the ⑧ **Tomb of the 12 Imams**. The neighbouring shops offer an interesting collection of old tiles and new ceramics.

The tour ends at ⑨ **Fahadan Museum Hotel** (p189) opposite the tomb. With its lovely courtyard teahouse and fine internal details, it is very much a destination in its own right. The views from the roof defy every sense of the route followed to reach here!

courtyards and offers a range of rooms and a reasonable six-bed dorm with shared bathroom. The rooftop Marco Polo Restaurant (p191) has a great view over the Masjed-e Jameh.

★ Fahadan Museum Hotel   HOTEL $$
(Map p184; ☑035-3630 0600; www.mehrchain hotels.com; Fahadan St; s/d/tr IR2,120,000/3,1 60,000/4,000,000; ❋ 🛜) Arranged around delicately painted courtyards, this beautiful little establishment is more museum than hotel and some of the rooms are exquisite. With a flamboyant, moustachioed manager, a location in the heart of the old city, a popular teahouse in the main courtyard and a rooftop with spectacular views, this is one hotel that's well worth booking in advance.

For honeymooners, there are romantic VIP rooms with four-poster beds, mirror-work and painted murals – some rooms even have their own *badgirs*. On a hot day those in the know escape to a tiled basement room through which runs one of the city's *qanats*, keeping the room cool even in mid-summer.

Hotel Vali   HOTEL $$
(Map p184; ☑035-3622 8050; www.valihotel. com; off Imam Khomeini St; s/d/tr US$58/70/94; P ❋ 🛜) This restored caravanserai attracts large crowds of travellers from around the country, congregating over *chay* from the samovar in the canvas-covered courtyard. There's a bewildering range of rooms, some with exterior bathroom, and with sizes ranging from spacious to compact, but the gem of this antique establishment is the upholstered basement room with a pool fed by the *qanat*.

Silk Road Hotel   HOSTEL, HOTEL $$
(Map p184; ☑035-3625 2730, 091 3151 6361; www.silkroadhotel.net; 5 Tal-e Khakestary Alley, off Masjed-e Jameh St; dm/s/d/tr US$10/35/60/70; ❋ @ 🛜) Two minutes' walk from the Masjed-e Jameh, the Silk Road's traditional courtyard setting, delicious Indian-style food and sociable atmosphere attracts a steady stream of backpackers. The standard rooms aren't the the major draw here: it's the ambience that counts and there is no doubting that this is one of the most convivial places to stay in town. Beware overbooking.

Yazd Traditional Hotel   HOTEL $$
(Hotel Sonnati; Map p184; ☑035-3622 8500; www.yazdhotel.com; Amir Chakhmaq Sq; d/tr IR1,830,000/2,300,000; ❋ @ 🛜) Rooms at this 200-year-old mansion opposite the Amir

Chakhmaq Mosque Complex are set around two large courtyards and retain their aged charm with stained-glass windows and low doorways – charming enough to be used as a recent film set for local TV. Recently refurbished and with delightful painted murals in each room, this is a good-value, well-located, friendly choice.

Mehr Traditional Hotel   HOTEL $$
(Map p184; ☑035-3622 7400; www.mehrhotel.ir; Labe Khandaq Alley, off Qeyam St; d/tr US$95/120; P ❋ @ 🛜) A traditional property belonging to the high-standard Mehr chain, the 250-year-old Khan-e Zargar-e Yazdi has been beautifully restored. With large, well-equipped rooms, delicious food and expansive rooftop views, this is a good midrange choice.

Fazeli Hotel   HOTEL $$
(Map p184; ☑035-3620 8955; fazelihotel@yahoo. com; off Masjed-e Jameh St; s/d/tr/VIP IR1,750, 000/2,680,000/3,225,000/4,960,000) Occupying a purpose-built modern building but emulating a traditional style, this attractive midrange hotel in the heart of town has all the amenities that are often missing from converted establishments, such as accessible en-suite bathrooms and easy-to-climb stairs. This new, welcoming and attractive establishment seems set to become a future top choice.

Moshir-al-Mamalak   HOTEL $$
(Moshir Gardens; ☑035-3523 9760; www.hotel gardenmoshir.com; Enqelab Ave; s/d/tr IR2,250, 000/3,470,000/4,650,000; P ❋ 🛜) The hotel may be faux-traditional, the piped music irritating and the greeting from the bewhiskered, fancy-dressed doorman somewhat routine, but there's nothing fake about the good intentions of this fashionable hotel. A good choice in summer as the high-standard rooms are set around an expansive, tree-filled garden with fountains and pools. The location (4km northwest of Amir Chaqhmaq Sq) is somewhat inconvenient.

Dad Hotel   HOTEL $$
(Map p184; ☑035-3622 9438; www.dadhotel.com; 214 10th Favardin Ave; s/d US$71/110; P ❋ @ 🛜 ✹) The 54 spacious but slightly dark rooms of this attractive hotel are set around a grand central courtyard and offer comfortable beds, satellite TV and good bathrooms. Facilities are excellent – there's an in-house travel agency and a leisure centre with pool, spa, sauna and table tennis.

CENTRAL IRAN YAZD

Laleh Hotel
HOTEL $$

(Map p184; ☑ 035-5622 5048; www.yazdlaleh hotel.com; Basij Blvd, off Darvazeh-e Ghassabha Alley; r from US$90; P ✳ @ 🛜) The grand Laleh is undoubtedly one of the most impressive of Yazd's restored homes, with 40 rooms set around three expansive courtyards. It may lack some of the cosy character of its more central rivals, but the helpful staff and attractive restaurant and teahouse help compensate.

★ Malek-o Tojjar
HOTEL $$$

(Map p184; ☑ 035-3622 4060; www.mehrchain hotels.com; Panjeh-ali Bazar, Qeyam St; d/tr/VIP IR3,530,000/4,470,000/8,400,000; P ✳ 🛜) Hidden along a narrow, lamp-lit passage from the Panjeh-ali Bazar lies Yazd's original traditional hotel. The small sign above a modest door gives no hint of the treasure trove of exquisite details that are a feature of this Qajar-era house. For those on honeymoon or celebrating a special occasion, the VIP rooms are something very special with superbly painted ceilings, extravagant mirror work and bathrooms with Jacuzzi.

✗ Eating

The courtyards of most of the traditional hotels function as restaurants, all of which offer Iranian cuisine in a delightful setting. In winter the courtyards are covered over with tarpaulin creating a cosy if not exactly warm interior space.

Camel-meat kababs are a local favourite, best tried at the *kababi* opposite the mosque on Kashani St.

Silk Road Hotel Restaurant
INDIAN $

(Map p184; ☑ 035-3625 2730; www.silkroadhotel. ir; 5 Tal-e Khakestary Alley, off Masjed-e Jameh St; mains from IR150,000; ⊘ 7am-10.30pm) While the Iranian food here is very good, the delicious subcontinental curries are the most popular dishes among travellers, particularly those who've run out of patience with kababs. The sociable courtyard atmosphere makes for a pleasant evening. A wide choice of teas and fresh juices makes this a good place to pause while on a walking tour.

★ Talar Yazd
IRANIAN $$

(☑ 035-3522 6661; www.talareyazd.ir; Ghandehaeri Alley, off Jomhuri-e Eslami Blvd; mains IR250,000; ⊘ noon-4.30pm & 7-11pm) Elegant but uncomplicated, the Talar, with its prim white tablecloths and waiters wheeling trolleys, has a 1950s appeal. Its short menu of classic Iranian dishes, including slow-roast lamb, is delicious and the kababs are perfect. It's an 8km ride from central Yazd (IR150,000 in a cab) but worth it to spend time in the company of Yazdis out for lunch at the weekend.

Malek-o Tojjar
IRANIAN $$

(Map p184; ☑ 035-3622 4060; www.mehrchain hotels.com; Panjeh-ali Bazar, off Qeyam St; buffets from IR450,000; ⊘ breakfast 7.30-9.30am, lunch noon-3pm, dinner 7-10pm) The highly decorated main hall of this classic Iranian restaurant makes for a romantic setting for a special evening. The menu is complemented with several regional variations, including *kufteh Yazdi* (Yazdi meatballs).

Shah-e Mardan
IRANIAN $$

(☑ 035-3824 4039; cnr Mazari-ha & Kashani St; 3-person tray IR510,000; ⊘ 11am-4pm lunch & 7-11pm dinner) Offering delicious 'tray food' of traditional mixed grills (kababs and vegetables), this restaurant is housed in the henna district of Yazd in a former henna mill.

TRADITIONAL HOUSE ACCOMMODATION

More than 20 *khan-e sonnati* (traditional houses) have been transformed into hotels in Yazd, offering some of the most attractive and characterful accommodation in the country. Staying in one of these old mansions is a full cultural immersion where guests wander around the alleyways of this historic city by day, and sit on *takhts* (daybed-style tables), sip tea and eat local food as Iranians have for centuries in their hotel at night.

As to be expected from buildings designed over 100 years ago, there are some drawbacks. These include shared toilets or steep stairs down to en-suite bathrooms, a lack of windows or rooms opening directly into the social space of the courtyard, noisy neighbours or late-night tea-drinking sessions.

For most guests, these are minor inconveniences that are more than compensated for by the beauty of the interior design, the charm of fountains tickling fish in the courtyard pools, and the general conviviality of a *khan* that has been receiving guests with traditional Persian hospitality since the days when Yazd was a rest stop on the ancient silk route.

NARTITEE ECOLODGE

For a rewarding experience, spending a night at the charming licensed homestay **Nartitee Ecolodge** (Pomegranate Flower Ecolodge; ☑ 0919 405 7118, 035-3262 2853; www.nartitee.ir; Khayam Alley, off Rahatabad St, Taft; per person US$15, incl tea & fresh fruit from garden, dinner IR200,000; ℗ ❄ 🛜) 🍃 is highly recommended. Located close to Yazd in the village of **Taft**, the ecolodge is housed in a 100-year-old adobe building, painstakingly restored by the grandchildren of the original Zoroastrian owners. Staying here, therefore, is more than just a night's sleep, it's a cultural experience.

To reach Taft by public transport, take a bus (every 20 minutes) from Imam Ali Sq in Yazd (IR150,000) to Kokabiye St. The hosts guide guests from there.

The homestay has its own orchard in which guests can walk. It also rents bicycles (IR80,000 per hour) with a map for those with the time to explore – and there's much to commend the area, including a museum, old watermill and an ancient cypress tree in the neighbouring all-Zoroastrian town of Cham.

Marco Polo Restaurant RESTAURANT $$
(Map p184; ☑ 035-5626 7783; Orient Hotel, 6th Alley, off Masjed-e Jameh St; mains around IR150,000; ⏱ 11am-11pm) Set like a crown atop the Orient Hotel, this popular glass-sided restaurant, with its grand views of the Masjed-e Jameh and surrounding blue-tiled domes, serves delicious Iranian food in a romantic venue.

Caesar ITALIAN, IRANIAN $$
(☑ 035-5826 5600; Sonbol Alley, 140 Saderat Bank St, off Abuzar Sq; mains IR250,000; ⏱ 11.30am-3.30pm & 7.30-11.30pm) Caesar, in vogue with a fashionable crowd, is a world away from Yazd's old city. Decent attempts at classic Italian dishes are worthwhile; while the Iranian dishes are also tasty. Try the delicious fresh lemonade, and the coffee is also tops. The upstairs seating is quieter. It's quite a way southeast; a taxi ride from central Yazd costs IR150,000.

🍷 Drinking & Nightlife

★ Art Center TEAHOUSE
(House of Mehdi Malek Zadeh; Map p184; next to Chehel Mehrab Mosque, Fahadan district; ⏱ 8am-9pm) This tiny, friendly rooftop teahouse is the perfect place to enjoy soup, or an uncomplicated tea and cake (IR160,000) with one of the best views in town. There's a craft shop and workshop downstairs.

Fooka Cafe CAFE
(Map p184; ☑ 035-3620 8520; Masjed Jameh St; ⏱ 8am-midnight) As a refreshingly modern alternative to the traditional teahouses of old Yazd, this stylish cafe, with its installation of hanging coffee cups, is a popular meeting place for Yazd's younger in-crowd. A full menu of traditional favourites (mains from IR150,000) is available and there's rooftop seating.

Laleh Teahouse Restaurant TEAHOUSE
(Map p184; www.yazdlalehhotel.com; opposite Abanbar Golshan, off Basij Ave; ⏱ 7-11pm) Persian music, courtyard fountains and a gentle breeze are good companions at this tranquil teahouse restaurant. Sit in the courtyard or in the attractive main hall to enjoy tea and sweets (IR400,000).

☆ Entertainment

Traditional Persian Night LIVE MUSIC
(Map p184; ☑ 0935 935 7123; www.tpersiannight.com; Kohan Traditional Hotel, Alley 40, off Imam Khomeini St, Fahadan district; child/adult IR550,000/690,000; ⏱ 7-10pm, seasonal) The Kohan Traditional Hotel offers an evening of classical entertainments over a Persian dinner in the fine setting of its beautiful courtyard garden. The price includes live sitar music, story-telling, a three-course meal, including Yazd cake with bitter orange blossom tea. Reservations are required. The evening is subject to sufficient bookings.

🛍 Shopping

Marco Polo passed through Yazd in 1272 and remarked on its silk production. This heritage is maintained today and the bazaars are full of beautiful brocades that remind visitors of Yazd's location on the crossroads of history, including *ejrami* (handwoven cotton cloth), *termeh* (a textile made from silk, cotton and wool), *daraie* (a soft silk fabric) and *zilu* (light carpet).

Yazd is also known for its sweets, which are presented in exotic collections of jellies and *baghlavas* featuring almond, pistachio and coconut. They can be purchased at hundreds of shops throughout the city.

Haj Khalifeh Ali Rahbar CONFECTIONER
(Map p184; www.hajkhalifehalirahbar.com; cnr Amir Chakhmaq Sq & Imam Khomeini St; ☺9am-1pm & 5-9pm Sat-Thu) The best and most famous of Yazd famous sweets can be found in this centenarian-old store. Customers survey the samples, write down what they want on the form provided, take it to the counter for boxing, pay at the cashier and then collect the sweets on the way out.

Khan Bazaar MARKET
(Map p184; entrance on Imam Khomeini St; 9am-1pm & 3.30-8pm Sat-Thu) The alleyways of this covered bazaar extend back to the 9th century and make for a diverting hour or so's meander. Many stores sell various grades of cloth that have been handwoven in Yazd for centuries.

ℹ Information

DANGERS & ANNOYANCES

Yazd and the surrounding desert areas are backpacker hubs, and there is a small number of dubious and irresponsible operators focussing particularly on this segment of the tourism market. The problems include the offering of cheap but unlicensed (and therefore illegal) homestay accommodation; the selling of tours from hotels with unlicensed guides; the heavy promotion of some establishments over others without merit; the swapping of less characterful accommodation for the one made during booking; and the misrepresentation of some services as being Lonely Planet–approved.

It might sound like a saving or an adventure to be offered cheap hostels in Tehran, Shiraz and Yazd with alcohol and even drugs sold into the bargain, but needless to say, those caught in an illegal homestay where there is alcohol and/or drugs present during a police raid face serious trouble. Put simply, however cheap the deal, it's not worth the risk.

It is important to be wary of over-friendly strangers, and even fellow foreigners, and to insist on seeing a guide's license. To be bona fide, this must include a photograph, hologram and expiry date.

EMERGENCY

Police Headquarters (Map p184)
Tourist Police Office (📞110; Kashani St, near Abuzar Sq; ☺8am-2pm Sat-Wed, to noon Thu)

MEDICAL SERVICES

Dr Mogibiyan Hospital (📞035-5624 0061; Kashani St) For emergency treatment.

MONEY

Hadad Exchange (📞035-3624 7220; Kashani St; ☺9.30am-2pm & 4-7pm Sat-Wed, 9.30am-2pm Thu) On the 2nd floor of a building opposite the *ateshkadeh* (fire temple)..
Khaki Exchange (Map p184; Imam Khomeini St) Good rates.

POST

Post Office (Map p184; Imam Khomeini St) Near Bank Melli.

TOURIST INFORMATION

For virtual tours of the city's main monuments, go to the website (mostly in Farsi) of the **Yazd Cultural Heritage, Handicrafts and Tourism Organization** (www.yazdchto.ir).

There are two privately operated tourism information offices in the old city. Don't believe claims that one is more official than the other. Both have English-speaking staff.

Tourist Office (Map p184; Amir Chakhmaq Sq; ☺5-8pm Sat-Thu high season only; 🛜) Located in the Amir Chakhmaq Mosque Complex, this office supplies maps and advice, makes hotel bookings, books desert tours and offers free wi-fi.
Yazd Tourist Information Office (Map p184; 📞035-621 6542; Ziaee Sq; ☺8.30am-7pm, to 8pm summer) Stocks a few maps and brochures, but is mainly dedicated to selling tours. It also rents bikes for IR60,000 per hour.

TRAVEL AGENCIES

Persian Odyssey (Shirdal Airya Travel & Tours; Map p184; 📞0912 427 9943, 035-3627 1620; www.persianodyssey.com; 6th Alley, Masjed-e Jameh St) This excellent, award-winning travel

TRAINS FROM YAZD

DESTINATION	FARE (IR; NORMAL)	DURATION (HR)	DEPARTURES
Bandar Abbas	360,000	11	3 daily 8am-11.30pm
Kerman	220,000	7	2 daily
Mashhad	900,000	14	every 2nd day
Tehran via Kashan & Qom	310,000	8	frequent

agency is run by a dynamic team of young entrepreneurs with many years of experience in licensed-tour guiding. Interesting cultural tours on offer include an Iranian religious life tour, a Zoroastrian tour and visits to local villages, including Fahraj, Saryazd and Zein-o-din. They also organise transfers to Shiraz, Esfahan and Kerman punctuated with interesting stops en route.

Starsland Tour & Travel (Map p184; ☑ 035-1827 0091; starsland91@yahoo.com; Masjed-e Jameh St; ⊘9am-2.30pm & 3.30-6pm) This little upstairs office is very helpful for arranging tours and onward travel on trains, planes or buses.

VISA EXTENSIONS

A visa can be extended in Yazd in under an hour. The **Tourist Police Office** (p192), close to Abuzar Sq, processes same-day applications.

ℹ Getting There & Away

AIR

Located to the west of Yazd city centre, **Shahid Sadooghi International Airport** (Yazd Airport; ☑ 035-3721 4444; www.yazd.airport.ir; Azadegan St) offers a couple of useful services. Iran Air and ATA fly to Tehran (from US$62, 70 minutes, twice daily), Bandar Abbas (from US$75, 80 minutes, every Tuesday) and Mashad (from US$75, 80 minutes, four times weekly). Aseman offers weekly flights to Bandar Abas from US$75.

BUS

Most buses leave from the **main bus terminal** (Shahrak-e Sanati) about 10km west of the old city of Yazd (IR150,000, 20 minutes by taxi *dar bast*). It is accessible by shuttle taxi from Beheshti and Azadi Sqs.

Other bus stops include **Fahraj Bus Stop** (Shohadaye Mehrab Sq). **Buses to Bazm** (Imam Ali Sq), near Bavanat, leave daily except Friday at noon (IR160,000).

TRAIN

In the south of the city, the **train station** (Rah Ahan) offers limited services. Train tickets are more easily purchased at travel agencies.

GETTING AROUND

Taxis *dar bast* start at about IR100,000 for short trips, and cost IR150,000 to IR200,000 from the airport or main bus terminal to the city centre. Taxis are more expensive at night.

Local buses (IR30,000) travel between the main bus terminal and the **bus stand** (Map p184) near the corner of Imamzadeh-ye Ja'far and Shahid Raja'i Sts near the old city.

Around Yazd

There are two popular local excursions from Yazd: the long Kharanaq, Chak Chak and Meybod loop (whole day) to the northeast of the city, and the shorter Zein-o-din, Saryazd and Fahraj loop (around half a day) to the southeast. Both are most rewarding as part of a tour or with a private driver-guide.

Kharanaq

خرانق

The all-but deserted mud-brick village of Kharanaq (Kharanagh) is crumbling back into the valley out of which it emerged over 1000 years ago. What remains in this ghost town, 70km north of Yazd, is a Qajar-era **mosque**, a cylindrical 17th-century **shaking minaret** and a **caravanserai** (closed at the time of research), near the entrance of the village. Although these structures have been restored, many of the surrounding buildings are in various states of ruin so it's helpful to have a guide who can navigate a safe pathway to the highlights.

From the heart of the old quarter, there's a beautiful view across the valley (which is

CENTRAL IRAN AROUND YAZD

BUSES FROM YAZD

DESTINATION	FARE (IR; VIP/ MAHMOOLY)	DURATION (HR)	DEPARTURES
Bandar Abbas	295,000 (*mahmooly*)	9	3 daily 8-8.30pm
Esfahan	260,000 (*mahmooly*)	5	frequent 1am-7.30pm
Kashan	500,000/300,000	5	frequent 8.30am-11pm (stops on hwy)
Kerman	200,000/160,000	5	4 daily 7.45am-2.30pm
Mashhad	600,000/410,000	12	8 daily 4-8pm
Shiraz	360,000/200,000	6	frequent 24hr
Tabriz	800,000 (VIP)	14	1 daily 6pm
Tehran	490,000/295,000	7	frequent 8.30am-11pm

still farmed) towards the mountains. It looks particularly harmonious at sunset when the aged adobe appears to dissolve into dust with the sinking sun.

Chak Chak   چک چک

📱 035 / POPULATION 156

High above the desert floor, under a cliff with a venerable old tree, this sacred site has great significance for Zoroastrians. Legend has it that after the Arab invasion in AD 637, the Sassanian princess Nikbanuh fled to this site. Short of water, she threw her staff at the cliff and water began to flow – *chak, chak* means 'drip, drip'.

The **Pir-e-Sabz Fire Temple** (IR50,000; ⊘ 7.30am-sunset) forms the main focus of interest. Reached via 230 steps, it is worth making the ascent to appreciate the isolation that marks this spot. The entrance of the cave, where an eternal flame is kept alight, is decorated with a brass door embossed with the likeness of Zoroaster.

The whole site is off limits during an annual festival held between 14 and 18 June when thousands of pilgrims come to pay their respects.

Meybod   میبد

📱 035 / POPULATION 58,295 / ELEVATION 1070M

About 52km north of Yazd, Meybod is a sprawling mud-brick town that is at least 1800 years old. Several sites of interest are dotted around the town centre, chief of which is the town's ancient fortress. Those on a whirlwind tour are rushed round the sights in under an hour but the characterful town deserves a more leisurely visit.

🔘 Sights

Narin Castle   CASTLE
(Rashiddadin Ave; IR150,000; ⊘ 8am-sunset) In the centre of Meybod, crumbling Narin castle rises imposingly above the town that has grown up around it. Revealing three layers of construction, the oldest foundations suggest some kind of settlement was built here as early as 4000 BC. Legend has it that the castle belonged to King Solomon and was built by *jinns* (spirits), but whatever the original provenance of the castle's foundations, most of what can be seen today dates from the Sassanian era.

Meybod Yakhchal   HISTORIC BUILDING
(Icehouse; IR100,000; ⊘ 8.30am-sunset) Recently restored, this magnificent 400-year-old

structure (one of the most impressive icehouses in Iran) dominates the north-facing part of the street, opposite the former posthouse and caravanserai. The enormous, meticulously built mud and brick structure consists of two shallow icing ponds where water freezes in winter, tall 2m-thick walls that prevent the sun reaching the icing ponds, a pit for the storage of the ice from the ponds and a dome to shelter the ice from summer heat.

Pigeon Tower   TOWER
(Kaboutar Khaneh Tower; IR50,000; ⊘ 8am-sunset) Despite first impressions, this beautifully restored tower was not military in purpose but dedicated to something altogether more prosaic: it is a pigeon house, a giant roost for the collection of guano. Used for fertiliser, the guano was a precious commodity before the introduction of chemical equivalents, so the more pigeons that could be induced to take up residence the better. This particular example, with its fine brick work, is around 200 years old and provided nesting space for 4000 birds.

Zeilo Museum   MUSEUM
(IR80,000 incl coffee; ⊘ 9.30am-sunset) Housed within Meybod's old caravanserai, the Zeilo Museum is dedicated to the hand-looming of prayer rugs. Some fine examples date back to the 16th century and it is possible to see how they are made in the workshops occupying some of the former caravanserai lodgings. The cotton kilims are double-sided and many feature the cypress tree. Only a dozen *zeilo* masters still work at this ancient craft and prices for each piece (from around US$40) vary according to the complexity of the design.

Zein-o-din   زین الدین

The sole reason for travelling out this lonesome spot is to visit the 400-year-old **Caravanserai Zein-o-din** (📱 0912 306 0441; half board per person IR1,680,000, admission & dinner only IR380,000, admission for visit only IR100,000; 🅿 ☀) built on the orders of Shah Abbas I. Located two days' camel ride south of Yazd (around 60km) on the main road to Kerman in an otherwise vacant desert plain, the caravanserai was part of a network of 999 such hostels built to promote trade.

After a three-year renovation, during which 13,000 pumice stones were used to scour centuries of grime from the walls, this simple accommodation has been pared back almost to its original state. The carpeted platforms that function as rooms are screened from the corridor by curtains. The welcome is somewhat hit-or-miss but the food is good, with hot and cold buffets. Reservations are *essential.*

Zein-o-din's claim to fame is that it is one of only two circular caravanserais (the other, near Esfahan, is largely destroyed). It continues to function as a traveller's lodge, and for those with the imagination to muster days of yore with camels grumbling outside the door, a night's stay here offers a haunting glimpse of a caravan traders' life on the Silk Road.

The caravanserai's isolated location also ensures minimal light pollution at night, allowing for crystal-clear **stargazing.** Taking advantage of the clarity, enthusiastic amateur astronomer Reza Tamehri conducts two-hour astronomy sessions on the caravanserai's roof. The price includes transport from Yazd and guided use of equipment. Bookings – through **Mohsen Hajisaeid** ([📱]0913 351 4460, 035-3622 7828; www.iranpersiatour.com) in Yazd – are essential. The skies are clearest in winter but it's freezing

Saryazd سریزد

[📄] 035 / POPULATION 421

Around 6km east of Hwy 71, Saryazd, meaning 'head of Yazd', once formed the last rest stop before reaching the city on the famous Silk Road from the east. Today it is hard to imagine that anything other than the wind passed this way, but a collection of impressive old buildings, including a castle, two caravanserais and a fine reservoir, prove otherwise.

The wonderful old **Saryazd Fortress** (IR100,000; ⊙ 9am-sunset) was once used as a giant safety deposit box for the protection of grains, jewellery and other valuables. The fortifications are elaborate with two main concentric walls, high towers and a moat (now empty).

The **Gate of Farafar** is of disputed origin. Estimated to be at least 1000 years old, it may represent the only remaining wall of a domed mausoleum or it may have been constructed as a gateway to the town. Either way, it makes for a good photographic opportunity as it frames a modern sculpture of **Arash the Archer**, a figure drawn from Persian mythology, that sits in the field nearby.

A wealthy benefactor who hailed from the village has spent a fortune in restoring Saryazd's aged landmarks, turning one of the caravanserai into a restaurant. Some local ceramics are on sale here too.

Fahraj

[📄] 035 / POPULATION 2700 / ELEVATION 1272M

On the edge of the Dasht-e Lut, this agricultural village 35km southeast of Yazd offers a few sights of interest, including a well-restored historic centre and the **Masjed-e Jameh** (Jameh Mosque; ⊙ 24hr) [FREE], possibly Iran's oldest purpose-built mosque. The mosque's internal courtyard, vaulted sanctuary and arcades date from the Sassanid period, although its cylindrical clay minaret is more recent – built as a lighthouse for caravans around 400 years ago. In the surrounding area is a ruined castle, a *hammam* and an *ab anbar* (water reservoir) with four *badgirs*.

There's nothing specifically to do in town other than wander around the mud-brick lanes, but there is a small traditional lodging here for those with the urge to stay.

Local buses to Fahraj leave Yazd on the hour between 6am and 8pm from Shohadaye Mehrab Sq (IR20,000, 50 minutes). A taxi *dar bast* (closed door) costs IR300,000.

Shiraz شیراز

[📄] 071 / POPULATION 1,460,665 / ELEVATION 1506M

Celebrated as the heartland of Persian culture for over 2000 years, Shiraz has become synonymous with education, nightingales, poetry and wine. It was one of the most important cities in the medieval Islamic world and was the Iranian capital during the Zand dynasty (AD 1747–79), when many of its most beautiful buildings were built or restored.

A city of poets, Shiraz is home to the graves of Hafez and Sa'di, both major pilgrimage sites for Iranians. It's also home to splendid gardens, exquisite mosques and whispered echoes of ancient sophistication that reward those who linger beyond the customary excursion to nearby Persepolis – the area's major tourist destination.

There are the usual Iranian traffic issues, but the city's agreeable climate, set in a fertile valley once famed for its vineyards, makes it a pleasant place to visit (except at the humid height of summer or the freezing depths of winter).

History

Shiraz is mentioned in Elamite inscriptions from around 2000 BC and was an important regional centre under the Sassanians and has enjoyed its fair share of mixed fortunes. It became the provincial capital in about AD 693, following the Arab conquest of Estakhr, the last of the Sassanian capitals (8km northeast of Persepolis, but now completely destroyed). By 1044 Shiraz was said to rival Baghdad in importance and it grew further under the Atabaks of Fars in the 12th century, when it became an important centre of the arts.

Shiraz was spared destruction by Tamerlane and the rampaging Mongols because the city's rulers wisely decided that paying tribute was preferable to mass slaughter. Having avoided calamity, Shiraz thrived during the Mongol and Timurid periods and developed rapidly. The encouragement of enlightened rulers and the presence of Hafez, Sa'di and many other brilliant artists and scholars helped make it one of the greatest cities in the Islamic world throughout the 13th and 14th centuries.

Shiraz remained a provincial capital during the Safavid period, when European traders settled here to export the region's famous wine, but by the mid-17th century it entered a long period of decline. Several earthquakes, the Afghan raids of the early 18th century and an uprising led by Shiraz's governor in 1744, which was put down in typically ruthless fashion after a siege by Nader Shah, all contributed to the city's misfortunes. At the time of Nader Shah's murder in 1747, Shiraz was a squalid place with a shrunken population of just 50,000, a quarter of the number 200 years earlier.

Shiraz's fortunes were briefly reversed by the enlightened Karim Khan, the first ruler of the short-lived Zand dynasty, who made Shiraz his national capital in 1750 and was determined to invest it with the kind of splendour enjoyed by Esfahan under Shah Abbas I. Despite being master of most of Persia, the modest Karim Khan refused to assume a higher title than *vakil* (regent) – hence the name of many of the city's monuments. He founded a royal district in the area of the Arg-e Karim Khan and commissioned many fine buildings, including the best bazaar at the time in Persia. After Karim Khan's death, the Qajars, his long-time enemies, attacked and destroyed the city's fortifications and by 1789 the national capital – and the remains of Karim Khan – moved to Tehran.

Despite being stripped of its capital status, Shiraz remained prosperous for a while due to its position on the trade route to Bushehr, but this role was greatly diminished with the opening of the trans-Iranian railway in the 1930s. Much of the architectural inheritance of Shiraz, and especially the royal district of the Zands, was either neglected or destroyed as a result of irresponsible town planning under the Pahlavi dynasty. Lacking any great industrial, religious or strategic importance, the city is now largely an administrative centre, famous for its universities and for the souls of the poets who rest here.

◉ Sights

Most of the city's old-quarter sights, hotels, the bazaar and the major mosques and shrines are within walking distance of the Arg-e Karim Khan fortress in the middle of Shohada Sq, widely considered as the city centre. The square intersects the city's major thoroughfare, Karim Khan-e Zand Blvd (usually referred to as Zand Blvd). To the north is the Khoshk River, and north of the river lie the tombs of Hafez and Sa'di and the modern landmark, Darvazeh-ye Quran (Quran Gateway).

◉ Around Shohada Square

★**Bagh-e Nazar**   GARDENS
(باغ نظر; Eye-catching Garden; Map p198; Karim Khan-e Zand Blvd; ⊙8.30am-1.30pm & 2.30-5.30pm) This formal garden encompasses an octagonal pavilion, which is now home to the **Pars Museum** (موزه پارس; Map p198; IR150,000; ⊙8.30am-1.30pm & 2.30-5.30pm). Karim Khan once received foreign dignitaries in the pavilion, which, with its stunning stalactite ceiling and delightful murals of lovers courting, scholars reading and horsemen hunting, is a highlight in its own right. Exhibits include Karim Khan Zand's sword and some interesting old ceramics.

Bazar-e Vakil   BAZAAR
(بازار وکیل; Map p198; off Karim Khan-e Zand Blvd; ⊙8am-9pm Sat-Thu) The city's ancient trading district is home to several bazaars dating from different periods. The finest and most famous of these is the Bazar-e Vakil, a cruciform structure commissioned by Karim Khan as part of his plan to make Shiraz into a great trading centre. The wide vaulted brick avenues are masterpieces of Zand

architecture, with the design ensuring the interior remains cool in summer and warm in winter. Today the bazaar is home to almost 200 stores selling carpets, handicrafts, spices and clothes.

The bazaar is best explored by wandering without concern for time or direction, and heading at whim along the atmospheric maze of lanes that lead off the main thoroughfares. With any luck, a ramble will lead to the tribal handicraft arcade of Shamshirgarha Bazaar (p205), the Seray-e Moshir (p205; a restored caravanserai) and the nearby Seray-e Mehr Teahouse (p204) – an atmospheric little place to pause for lunch.

Bazar-e Vakil continues on the north side of Karim Khan-e Zand Blvd but is of less immediate interest.

Masjed-e Vakil   MOSQUE
(مسجد وکیل, Regent's Mosque; Map p198; off Karim Khan-e Zand Blvd; IR150,000; ⊘8am-8pm) Begun in Karim Khan's time, this mosque next to the tribal arts arcade in the Bazar-e Vakil has an impressive tiled portal, a recessed entrance decorated with Shirazi rose-pink tiles, two vast *iwans,* a magnificent inner courtyard surrounded by beautifully tiled alcoves and porches, and a pleasingly proportioned 75m-by-36m vaulted prayer hall. The distinguishing feature of the mosque, however, is the forest of 48 diagonally fluted columns that support the prayer hall, displaying a hypnotic rhythm of verticals and arabesques.

Hammam-e Vakil   HISTORIC BUILDING
(حمام وکیل, Regent's Bath; Map p198; off Taleqani St; IR150,000; ⊘7.30am-8pm Sat-Thu) The vaulted central chamber of this Zand-era bathhouse features some fine plasterwork and candy-twist columns. A series of costumed mannequins illustrate how Shirazis would have relaxed by the fountain after taking a bath in the handsome heat room, which has a vaulted ceiling, pillars and a small (empty) pool.

Arg-e Karim Khan   FORTRESS
(ارگ کریمخان, Citadel of Karim Khan; Map p198; Shohada Sq; IR200,000; ⊘7.30am-9pm summer, 8am-8pm winter) Dominating the city centre, this burly fortress was built in the early Zand period and formed part of the royal court that Karim Khan hoped would rival Esfahan. The high walls feature ornamental brickwork and are punctuated by four attractive 14m-high circular towers. The southeastern tower has a noticeable lean,

having subsided into the underground cistern that served as the Arg's bathhouse.

Museum of Iranian Fine Arts   MUSEUM
(Map p198; Namazi Junction, Dastgheib St; IR200,000; ⊘8.30am-noon & 3.30-8pm) Set within a delightful old house around a warren of courtyards, corridors and painted rooms, this museum is home to both permanent and temporary fine-art exhibitions. The collection of old photographs may not mean much to foreign visitors but the house itself, with its lovingly restored details, makes a visit worthwhile.

◉ Around Ahmadi Square

★Bagh-e Naranjestan   PALACE
(Citrus Garden; Map p198; Lotf Ali Khan Blvd; IR200,000; ⊘8am-7pm) Named after the bitter oranges that line the central courtyard, this is Shiraz's smallest but most lovely garden. Enclosing the delightful **Naranjestan-e Ghavam Pavilion** (Map p198) it was laid out as part of a complex owned by one of Shiraz's wealthiest Qajar-era families. The pavilion's mirrored entrance hall opens onto rooms covered in a myriad of intricate tiles, inlaid wooden panels and stained-glass windows. Particularly noteworthy are the ceilings of the upstairs rooms, painted with European-style motifs, including Alpine churches and busty German frauleins.

Built for the wealthy and powerful Mohammad Ali Khan Qavam al-Molk between 1879 and 1886 as the *buruni* (public reception area) of his family home, the pavilion is connected to the **Khan-e Zinat ol-Molk** (Zinat-ol Molk Museum; Map p198; ☑071-1224 0035; off Lotf Ali Khan Blvd; IR150,000; ⊘8am-7pm) ✍, which housed the family's *andaruni* (private quarters), by an underground passage (not open to the public).

The basement of the pavilion houses an archaeological collection put together by Arthur Upham Pope, an American scholar who taught at the Asia Institute in Shiraz between 1969 and 1979. There is also an excellent selection of handicrafts for sale in the basement, including miniatures painted on camel bone and tiles inspired by antique designs.

Those looking to take part in the current craze for dressing up in Qajar-era costume can do so at the booth in the corner of the courtyard. Receiving the last rays of the day's sun, the teahouse here is a good spot to enjoy the light fading over the garden wall;

Shiraz

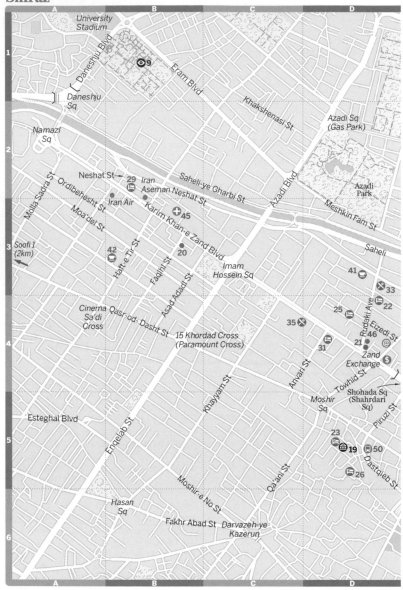

it also sells delicate tinctures of rose- and pomegranate-flavoured jellies.

★ **Masjed-e Nasir-al-Molk**　　MOSQUE
(مسجد نصیرالملک), Nasir-al-Molk Mosque, Pink Mosque; Map p198; off Lotf Ali Khan Blvd;

IR150,000; ⊙ 7.30-11.30am & 2.30-5pm) One of the most elegant and most photographed pieces of architecture in southern Iran, the Pink Mosque was built at the end of the 19th century and its coloured tiling (an unusually deep shade of blue) is exquisite. There

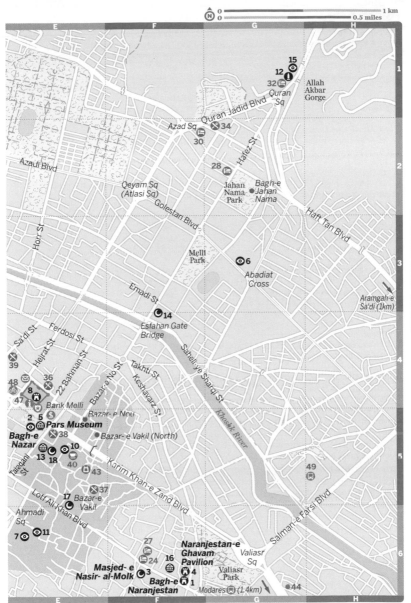

are some particularly fine *muqarnas* in the small outer portal and in the northern *iwan*, but it is the stained glass, carved pillars and polychrome faience of the winter prayer hall that dazzle the eye when the sun streams in.

The mosque attracts most visitors early in the morning (9am to 11am is best) when the hall and its Persian carpets are illuminated with a kaleidoscope of patterned flecks of light. It makes for a magical experience – and an irresistible photograph.

Shiraz

A museum in the opposite prayer hall opens into the Gav Cha (Cow Well), where cows were used to raise water from the underground *qanat*. The structure has survived numerous earthquakes, due in part to its construction using flexible wood as struts within the walls – look for the wooden bricks in the *iwan* columns. The rose-pink floral tiles are a signature feature of Shiraz.

Aramgah-e Shah-e Cheragh   SHRINE
(ارامگاه شاهچراغ), Mausoleum of Sayyed Mir Mohammad; Map p198; Ahmadi Sq; ⊙ variable, often 24hr) FREE Sayyed Mir Ahmad, one of Imam Reza's 17 brothers, was hunted down and killed by the caliphate on this site in AD 835 and his remains are housed in a dazzling shrine of mirrored tiles. A mausoleum was first erected over the tomb during the 12th century, but the courtyard and tile work represent relatively modern embellishments from the late-Qajar period and the Islamic

Republic. The blue-tiled dome and dazzling gold-tipped minarets form a magnificent context for the Shiite rituals at this revered centre of pilgrimage.

The museum in the northwestern corner of the courtyard, next to the shrine, houses an interesting collection of shrine-related objects, including some highly prized old Qurans upstairs and an exquisite door decorated with silver, gold and lapis lazuli downstairs.

In the southeastern corner of the courtyard, the **Bogh'e-ye Sayyed Mir Moham-med** (Mausoleum of Sayyed Mir Mohammad; Map p198) houses the tombs of two brothers of Mir Ahmad. The shrine has the typical Shirazi bulbous dome, intricate mirror work and four slender wooden pillars that boast near perfect proportions.

Visitors are welcome to enter the courtyard in the middle of the complex and to take discreet photographs (no large cameras or tripods), but entrance to the shrines was not permitted to non-Muslims at the time of writing. Women must wear chador within the whole shrine complex (available for free at the women's entrance).

Madraseh-ye Khan ISLAMIC SITE

(مدرسه خان; Map p198; Dastqeib St, off Lotf Ali Khan Blvd; ☺ knock on the door; tip appreciated) Imam Gholi Khan, governor of Fars, founded this serene theological college for around 100 students in 1615. Over the years the building has been extensively damaged by earthquakes, but thankfully the impressive portal at the entrance remains intact. With its unusual *muqarnas* inside the outer arch and some intricate mosaic tiling, it is a masterpiece of early design. The college (still in use) has a fine stone-walled inner courtyard decorated with the typical pink-and-yellow floral tiles of Shiraz.

◉ North of the River

Aramgah-e Hafez MAUSOLEUM

(آرامگاه حافظ; Tomb of Hafez; Map p198; Golestan Blvd; IR200,000; ☺ 7.30am-10pm, to 10.30pm summer) There is no better place to understand Hafez's place in the nation's psyche than at his tomb and the memorial garden within which it is set. Iranians have a saying that every home must have two things: first the Quran, then a collection of the works of Hafez. This 14th-century Iranian folk hero is loved and revered and almost every Iranian can quote his work, bending it to whichever social or political persuasion they subscribe.

Hafez died in middle age in 1389 and his tomb was placed here by Karim Khan in 1773. The marble is engraved with a long verse from the poet, and in 1935 the site was embellished with an octagonal pavilion, supported by eight stone columns beneath a tiled dome. Sunset is the most popular time of day for Iranians to gather at the garden to pay their respects; some come to perform the *faal-e Hafez*, a popular ritual in which a volume of Hafez's works is opened randomly and the future interpreted therein. There's a teahouse in the grounds where admirers sit to enjoy the recitations broadcast around the garden over a bowl of *ash* (noodle soup) or *faludeh* (a frozen sorbet made with thin starch noodles and rose water). The tomb is 2km from the town centre (IR80,000 by taxi).

Aramgah-e Sa'di MAUSOLEUM

(آرامگاه سعدی; Tomb of Sa'di; Bustan Blvd; IR200,000; ☺ 7.30am-10pm, to 10.30pm summer) One of Shiraz's several shrines, housed in an open-sided colonnade built during the Pahlavi era, is dedicated to Sheikh Mohammed Shams-ed-Din, simply known as Sa'di – a poet who lived and died between 1207 and 1291. Set amid generous gardens of evergreens, bitter orange and roses, appropriate to a man who wrote so extensively of flowers, it is a tranquil place that makes a pleasant respite from the noise of the surrounding city.

The tomb is easily reached from the shrine of a fellow poet, Hafez. From Golestan Blvd, shuttle taxis travel southeast (IR15,000) to Sa'di Sq, then walk about 1.3km uphill to the tomb.

Imamzadeh-ye Ali Ebn-e Hamze ISLAMIC TOMB

(امامزاده على ابن حمزه; Map p198; ☎ 071-1222 3353; Hafez St, near Hamzeh Bridge; ☺ dawn-dusk) Built in the 19th century over the tomb of Emir Ali, a nephew of Shah Cheragh who also died here while en route to Khorasan to help Imam Reza, this shrine is the latest of several earlier incarnations destroyed by earthquakes. Highlights include the Shirazi dome, dazzling Venetian mirror work, stained-glass windows and an intricate wooden door. Visitors are welcome (chadors for women are loaned at the door) and photography is permitted.

Bagh-e Eram GARDENS

(باغ ارم; Garden of Paradise, Eram Garden; Map p198; Eram Blvd; IR200,000; ☺ 8am-sunset) Famous for its tall cypress trees, this Unesco-listed garden, designed to complement a Qajar-era pool and palace (closed to the public), incorporates elements from an earlier Seljuk landscape. There's a small museum of mineralogy in the grounds, but mostly the garden is known for its secret assignations among the rose buses. The gardens are easy enough to reach by taking any shuttle taxi (IR15,000) along Karim Khan-e Zand Blvd, alighting at Namazi Sq and then walking north across the river.

Darvazeh-ye Quran MONUMENT

(Quran Gateway; Map p198; Quran Sq) The modern assembly of arches that form Shiraz's ceremonial gateway until recently housed a revered antique Quran (since moved to the Pars Museum opposite the fort in the centre of town) that travellers traditionally passed beneath before undertaking a journey. Now the main reason for visiting the gateway is to enjoy **Khaju Garden** (Map p198; above Darvazeh-ye Quran; IR115,000; ☺ 7.30am-midnight) and its teahouse, or to climb up to the city viewpoints on either side of the road.

☞ Tours

Tours, which can be arranged through most hotels in town, cover Shiraz and nearby destinations such as Persepolis and Bishapur. Licensed guides generally charge standard tour prices set by the Tourist Guide Union. These are US$35 to US$40 for a half-day tour and US$75 to US$90 for a full-day tour with a driver-guide.

Shahram Rafie   OUTDOORS
(☑ 0939 625 0511; www.steptoiran.com) An expert on Persepolis and the Shiraz region, but also greatly knowledgeable about the whole of Iran, Shahram is a refreshingly calm yet endlessly obliging licensed driver-guide whose manner as much as his knowledge recommends him.

Iran Travel Service   TOURS
(☑ 0917 300 3249; www.irantravelservice.com) Run by Mojtaba Rahmanian, who has excellent English and is a mine of information on the country, this agency organises tours around Shiraz as well as month-long tailor-made itineraries.

Pars Tours Agency   TOURS
(Map p198; ☑ 071-3223 2428; www.key2persia. com; Karim Khan-e Zand Blvd; ☺ 9am-9pm Sat-Thu, to 1pm Fri) Offers a large range of cultural, adventure and ecofriendly tours (check website for details), this agency is particularly recommended for its popular half-day group trips to Persepolis for US$30 per person, leaving daily at 8am.

Bahman Mardanloo   OUTDOORS
(☑ 0917 910 0943; b_mardanloo@yahoo.com; half-board tours staying 1 night in nomad tent per person US$95, 4 people or more US$55) The son of nomadic parents, this licensed guide is an expert in organising tours for those seeking sensitive cultural interaction with nomadic groups.

MTB2R Mountainbiking in Iran   CYCLING
(☑ 0913 951 6835; www.mtb2r.com) With 12 years of experience, the keen mountain-bike tour guide Yaghoob Afshariani organises hiking and cycling trips into the Zagros Mountains.

Iran Sightseeing Tours   ADVENTURE
(Map p198; ☑ 071-3235 5939; www.iransightseeing. com; 3 Alley, Sooratgar Ave, off Karim Khan-e Zand Blvd; ☺ 9am-9pm Sat-Thu, to 1pm Fri) Specialises in skiing, mountaineering, trekking, mountain-biking, rock-climbing and horse-riding tours. It has its own horses, ski lodge and equipment. Also offers nomad tours.

Nadia Badiee   OUTDOORS
(☑ 0917 307 4682; nadiabadiee@ymail.com) English-speaking guide, focused on Shiraz.

Azadeh Khademi   OUTDOORS
(☑ 0917 105 2191; tbs-azadehkhademi@hotmail.com) Knowledgeable French- and English-speaking female guide.

Maryam Zare   OUTDOORS
(☑ 0936 022 1513; zare.maryam1368@yahoo.com) Good English-speaking guide with a degree in English translation.

Farkhondeh Zareie   OUTDOORS
(☑ 0917 715 5850; farkhondeh_yas_zareie@yahoo. com) Experienced guide and driver who specialises in food and nomad tours.

🛏 Sleeping

Shiraz has a huge number of hotels, most located in streets leading off Karim Khan-e Zand Blvd and within a short walk of the main sights. Competition is keen so most managers will be happy to offer low-season discounts. There are one or two hotels in traditional houses but most largely occupy uninspiring modern concrete blocks.

★Forough Hotel   BOUTIQUE HOTEL $
(Map p198; ☑ 071-3222 5877; foroughhotel@ gmail.com; Namazi Junction, Dastghieb St; d/tr US$45/65; 图🖂) This newly restored old house, in the heart of the old quarter, is arranged around two courtyards and immediately conveys a sense of hospitality. A peaceful retreat in the bustling bazaar area, the beautifully decorated hotel offers homely rooms that come with pristine duvets and freshly laundered towels. The hotel offers half-price entrance to the delightful little Museum of Iranian Fine Arts next door.

★Niayesh Boutique Hotel   BOUTIQUE HOTEL $
(Map p198; ☑ 071-3223 3622; www.niayeshhotels.com; 10 Shahzadeh Jamaili Lane; s/d/tr/q US$35/50/68/85; P图🖂) One of only a handful of traditional hotels in Shiraz, this delightful, sociable hotel in the heart of the old quarter is a firm backpacker favourite.

The most characterful rooms are arranged around the central courtyard of the original house; others are housed in a purpose-built annexe at the front of the building.

Parhami Traditional House   HOTEL $
(Map p198; ☎ 071-3223 2015; www.parhamihouse. com; off Lotf Ali Khan Zand Blvd; s/d US$30/35; ☎) This attractive hotel, run by an enterprising family who has renovated the surrounding lanes over the past five years, is located in a traditional house wrapped around a citrus-filled courtyard with a blue pool. Homely rooms are decorated with rugs, and the home cooking attracts local youngsters into the courtyard restaurant. Request the family's help in finding the hotel from the main road.

Golshan Hostel   HOSTEL, HOTEL $
(Map p198; ☎ 071-3222 0715; www.golshanhostel. com; Alley 38, Lotf Ali Khan Blvd; dm/d/tr/q US$15/45/55/65; ☎) Set around a courtyard in the vicinity of the bazaar, Golshan Hostel has a characterful location and is handy for exploring the old quarter. As with most traditional-style accommodation, the dorm and rooms echo with courtyard noise, but they are comfortable enough, making it a pleasant and sociable retreat.

Sasan Hotel   HOTEL $
(Map p198; ☎ 071-3230 2028; www.sasan-hotel. com; Anvari St; s/d/tr US$35/50/64; ✳@☎) This is an especially well-maintained hotel with a friendly manager who likes a chat. More budget than the price suggests, the location near the city centre, the carpeted corridors and the stylish little restaurant are worth paying slightly over the odds for.

★Shiraz Hotel   HOTEL $$
(Map p198; ☎ 071-3227 4820; www.shiraz-hotel. com; Quran Sq; r from US$95) This is currently Shiraz's most desired residence, attracting international visitors to its conference facilities and well-heeled Iranian travellers in town for business. The rooms are luxurious and spacious, with panoramic views of the city, and a number of eating options, including a revolving restaurant. The midrange prices are a bargain: in other locations this would be considered a top-end hotel.

★Karim Khan Hotel   HOTEL $$
(Map p198; ☎ 071-3223 5001; www.karimkhanho-tel.com; Rudaki Ave; d US$63; P✳@☎) This centrally located hotel with its stained-glass windows casting lozenges of light across the foyer in a modern take on an ancient theme

is a characterful choice in a city with few outstanding hotels. The rooms don't quite live up to the promise of the lobby and are made dark by the same stained-glass motifs – but this is a minor criticism. Breakfast is served in its sister hotel a few paces along the road.

Royal Shiraz Hotel   HOTEL $$
(Map p198; ☎ 071-3227 4356; www.royalshiraz hotel.com; Quran Jadid Blvd; d/ste/extra bed IR2,870,000/7,325,000/760,000; P✳@☎✈) With a popular restaurant on the 6th floor, a sports complex including an attractive pool, sauna and Jacuzzi, this new and stylish hotel is giving the larger upper-end options a run for their money. Located by the Quran Gateway, there are impressive views over the city and fashionable eating options near by.

Chamran Grand Hotel   HOTEL $$
(☎ 071-3626 2000; www.hotelchamran.com; Chamran Blvd; s/d/ste IR3,520,000/4,956,000/7,263,760; P✳@☎✈) There are good city views from the rooms and upper-floor restaurant of this five-star hotel, but the location, next to the tree-lined Ghasr-e Dasht Gardens, is a long way from central Shiraz. A taxi to the city centre costs around IR300,000. The hotel makes up for the inconvenience with an impressive health club and close proximity to some of the city's best restaurants.

Aryo Barzan Hotel   HOTEL $$
(Map p198; ☎ 071-3224 7182; www.aryohotel.com; Rudaki Ave; s/d US$65/105; ✳@☎) The centrally located Aryo is a favourite among business travellers thanks to the excellent service, the rather grand entrance and a wide range of Persian favourites at the breakfast buffet. The rooms are small but well provisioned. The Aroyo Travel Agent inside the lobby (open 8.30am to 4pm Saturday to Thursday) can book tickets and organise tours.

Park Saadi Hotel   HOTEL $$
(Map p198; ☎ 071-3227 4901; www.parksaadihotel. com; Hafez St; s/d US$63/105; P✳@☎) The Saadi is in a quiet location opposite lovely Bagh-e Jahan Nama. With large, bright rooms, a decent restaurant and experienced management, this is a no-nonsense hotel that makes up for being slightly out of the city centre by its location next to a peaceful Persian garden.

Jaam-e-Jam Apartment Hotel   HOTEL $$
(Map p198; ☎ 071-3231 6607; www.jaamejamho-tel.com; Eizedi St; s/d/tr IR1,700,000/2,870,000/

3,620,000; P ✳ @ 🛜) Rooms in this dark, Persepolis-inspired hotel, with its cavernous maroon-coloured foyer, are nicely presented. On a quiet street in a central location, the hotel also offers serviced apartments. Friendly and professional management make up for any unusual choices in the interior design!

Pars International Hotel HOTEL $$$
(Map p198; ☑ 071-3233 2255; www.parsinternationalhotel.com; Karim Khan-e Zand Blvd; s/d/extra bed IR2,810,000/4,570,000/1,270,000; P ✳ @ 🛜 ⚄) This stylish hotel, with a pianola trotting out tunes in the marble foyer, is one of the few upmarket hotels in Shiraz. A little further from the city centre than other options, it is nonetheless conveniently located on the city's main thoroughfare. Rooms are characterless but well equipped, and the hotel boasts four restaurants, a travel agent and a carpet shop.

 Eating

Shiraz is noted as a culinary capital but in recent years Shirazis have embraced Western-style fast food with apparent relish. Chamran Blvd and Sattar Khan Blvd, in the upmarket suburbs northwest of central Shiraz, are where many of these outlets are located. Some more characterful options are dotted around the city centre, including one or two highly popular local-style restaurants.

★**Seray-e Mehr Teahouse** TEAHOUSE $
(Map p198; Seray-e Mehr, just off Rouhollah Bazaar, Bazar-e Vakil; meals from IR250,000, tea IR40,000; ⏱9.30am-9.30pm) This serendipitous little jewel in the middle of the Bazar-e Vakil is hidden behind a small door next to the Seray-e Moshir caravanserai. Decorated with painted panels and antiques on the wall, this split-level teahouse has a small menu of tasty favourites (think *dizi, kubideh, zereshk polo*) and a delightfully relaxed atmosphere in which to sit, eat and sip tea.

Mahdi Faludeh SWEETS $
(Map p198; Naser Khosrow St; per cup IR40,000; ⏱2-10pm Sat-Thu) Opposite the Arg-e Karim Khan, Mahdi is the most famous *faludeh* shop in Shiraz. It also sells delicious *bastani* (Persian ice cream).

Niayesh Restaurat & Coffee Shop IRANIAN $
(Map p198; 10 Shahzadeh Jamaili Lane; meals from IR150,000; ⏱9am-midnight) The tranquil internal courtyard of the Niayesh Boutique Hotel is a pleasant place to escape the crowds and relax over a tea, espresso coffee or meal. There's a limited menu of tasty home-style dishes, all of which are well priced. The hotel can be difficult to find – head to the Imamzadeh Bibi Dokhtar and then follow the signs.

Haji Baba Restaurant IRANIAN $
(Map p198; ☑ 071-1233 2563; Karim Khan-e Zand Blvd; roulette kabab IR200,000; ⏱7am-10pm) The friendly waiters at this tiny, attractively decorated restaurant in a busy part of town certainly earn their wages, rushing upstairs to serve a constant stream of customers. The *khoresht-e mast* (a strange concoction of lamb, yoghurt, egg, saffron, sugar and orange peel, often eaten as a dessert) is a favourite with locals – men sit downstairs, women and families upstairs.

★**Shater Abbas** IRANIAN $$
(Map p198; ☑ 071-3227 1617; Sa'di St; mains US$4-13; ⏱7am-midnight; 🛜) This restaurant is housed in a vast dining hall with giant murals on the wall and canteen-style salad bars. Hot bread is made near the entrance, luring potential diners in, and the lamb preparations – *shandiz lary kabab* (spiced lamb) or *kubideh* (minced lamb kabab) – are signature dishes. Fish dishes are available for non-meat eaters.

Soofi 1 IRANIAN $$
(☑ 071-3649 0000; www.soofirestaurant.com; Sattar Khan St; meals from IR400,000; ⏱noon-midnight) Out in the suburbs, the Soofi is where middle-class Shirazi families come to celebrate big occasions and it can be loads of fun on weekends when live music is played. Kababs are the order of choice, particularly the famous 'Special Kabab', which is served in a theatrical manner. A taxi between here and Shohada Sq costs around IR160,000.

Sharzeh Traditional Restaurant IRANIAN $$
(Map p198; ☑ 071-3224 1963; Vakil St, off Karim Khan-e Zand Blvd; meals US$5-13; ⏱noon-3pm & 8-11pm) Near Masjed-e Vakil, this hugely popular restaurant is in the basement of an arcade with galley-style seating around the upper of the two floors. It's best for lunch, when *bazaris* (shopkeepers) flock here to eat hearty local dishes, such as *baghela mahicheh* (rice with broad beans, mutton and dill) and *kalam polo Shirazi* (beef meatballs). There's usually live music.

★ **Haft Khan**   IRANIAN $$$
(Map p198; ☑ 071-3227 0000; www.haftkhanco.
com; cnr 17th Alley & Quran Jadid Blvd; buffet
IR750,000, à la carte mains from IR250,000;
⊙10am-midnight; P ⊛ 🎧 🍴) Wildly popular
with fashionable Shirazis, this enormous
restaurant complex near Quran Gateway
offers four types of dining experience:
there's a generous buffet on the ground
floor, a fast-food court on the 2nd floor, an
à la carte restaurant on the 3rd floor serv-
ing Iranian barbeque and a teahouse on the
roof.

★ **Ghavam**   IRANIAN
(Map p198; ☑ 071-3235 9271; Rudaki Ave; dizi
IR210,000; ⊙6.30am-1.30pm & 4.30-11pm;
⊛🍴) This tiny restaurant, more shop than
diner, is an absolute favourite with locals,
foreign expats and the odd tour group
whose guide is in the know. Would-be din-
ers queue up on the street to find a place
at the tightly packed tables, drawn to the
delicious home-cooked fare. The aubergine
dishes will delight vegetarians.

🍸 Drinking & Nightlife

Hedayat Cafe   CAFE
(Map p198; ☑ 071-3234 9152; Hedayat St; coffee
& cake of the day IR80,000; ⊙9am-midnight; 🎧)
This trendy spot near the commercial cen-
tre of town attracts young Shirazis looking
for an international coffee-shop vibe. The
technically accurate 'chemical mix' coffees
are heated to the exact temperature for the
bean.

Ferdowsi Cafe   CAFE
(Map p198; Ferdosi St; ⊙9am-11pm; 🎧) Attract-
ing a loyal local crowd of liberally minded
young Shirazis, overseen by a genial boss,
this cafe does a range of brilliant flavoured
teas – the sour one is a particular assault on
the tastebuds.

Bazar Cafe   CAFE
(Map p198; Seray-e Fil, Bazar-e Vakil; coffee
IR40,000; ⊙9am-7pm Sat-Thu; 🎧) This casual
coffee shop in the middle of an old cara-
vanserai offers a surprisingly peaceful open
space in the middle of the busy bazaar in
which to take a break and check your email
(wi-fi free). Just off Shamshirgarha Bazaar,
the tribal handicraft arcade, the cafe is sur-
rounded by some colourful carpet shops
selling tribal rugs.

🛍 Shopping

Good buys in the Bazar-e Vakil include
metalwork and printed cottons, especially
calico tablecloths and rugs woven by Fars
nomads.

Shamshirgarha Bazaar   ARTS & CRAFTS
(Map p198; Bazar-e Vakil; ⊙8am-9pm Sat-Thu) For
foreign visitors, one of the most interesting
parts of the covered alleyways of Bazar-e
Vakil is coming across the Shamshirgarha
Bazaar. Housed under an arcade off the
bazaar's main thoroughfare, it is dedicated
to a host of tribal handicrafts. The kilims,
rugs and camel bags for sale are in predom-
inantly primary hues and make for a riot of
colour.

Seray-e Moshir   ARTS & CRAFTS
(Map p198; just off Rouhollah Bazaar, Bazar-e Vakil;
⊙8am-9pm Sat-Thu) This tastefully restored
two-storey caravanserai, set around an at-
tractive tree-filled courtyard with a pool and
fountains, has become a meeting place for
locals, pausing in the important business of
shopping. A cluster of souvenir and jewel-
lery shops occupies the former rooms of the
khan, shaded by bright coloured awnings.

ⓘ Information

EMERGENCIES
Tourist Police Booth (Map p198; Karim Khan-e
Zand Blvd) Outside the Arg-e Karim Khan but is
rarely open outside peak season.

INTERNET
There are a shrinking number of **coffeenets**
(Map p198; per hour IR40,000) on Sa'adi St, off
Karim Khan-e Zand Blvd.

MEDICAL SERVICES
Dena Hospital (☑ 628 0418, 628 0411; www.
denahospital.com; Dena Alley, Motahari Blvd)
Best in Shiraz. It's west of the city centre.
Dr Faghihi Hospital (Map p198; ☑ 071-1235
2220; Karim Khan-e Zand Blvd) The most
central hospital; public.

MONEY
There are two excellent money exchanges on
Karim Khan-e Zand Blvd:
Bank Melli (Map p198) Located on Shohada
Sq, next to the Arg-e Karim Khan. Exchange on
1st floor.
Zand Exchange (Map p198; ☑ 071-3222 2854;
⊙8am-1pm & 4-7pm Sat-Wed, 8am-1pm Thu)
Good rates, no commission, fast, and longer
hours than most.

POST

Post Office (Map p198; 071-3726 9070; Modarres Blvd) The nearest post office to the city centre.

TOURIST INFORMATION

Tourist Office (Map p198; 071-3224 1985; Karim Khan-e Zand Blvd; 9.30am-4.30pm Sat-Thu) Located in a booth outside the Arg-e Karim Khan. Reasonably helpful but staff seem to work to an unpredictable timetable. They can supply a free map and/or directions, and give updates on the opening hours and prices of all sights.

TRAVEL AGENCIES

Pars Tourist Agency (Map p198; 071-3222 2428; www.key2persia.com; Karim Khan-e Zand Blvd; 9am-9pm Sat-Thu, to 1pm Fri) As well as organising tours, the multilingual team covers the booking of air, bus and train tickets.

VISA EXTENSIONS

Department of Aliens Affairs (Map p198; 57 St, off Modares Blvd; 8am-1pm Sat-Wed, 8-11am Thu) Extension requests take a minimum of two hours to process and cost IR340,000. The payment must be deposited at Bank Melli (Shohada Sq). To reach the Department of Aliens Affairs, bus 70 from Karim Khan-e Zand Blvd goes to Valiasr Sq, from where it is an easy walk; the office is on the 3rd floor.

🚗 Getting There & Away

AIR

It's easy to start or finish a trip to Iran in Shiraz because several airlines operate direct flights from **Shiraz International Airport** (flight info 071-3711 8890; www.shiraz.airport.ir) to gulf cities and İstanbul.

Fly Dubai has flights between Shiraz and Dubai (one way US$100); Turkish Airlines flies to İstanbul (one way US$260); Air Arabia flies to Sharjah (one way US$95) and Qatar Airways flies to

Doha (one way US$330). Check schedules with a travel agent.

Reliable domestic carriers, including **Iran Air** (Map p198; 071-3233 0040; www.iranair.com; 7.30am-2.30pm), **Iran Aseman** (Map p198; 071-3722 6009; www.iaa.ir; Karim Khan-e Zand Blvd; 7.30am-8pm Sat-Thu), Kish Airlines, Naft, Caspian Tabar and Mohan, connect Shiraz with other major destinations in Iran, including the capital Tehran and Mashhad in the east.

BUS

Shiraz is well connected with other main cities in Iran by both VIP and normal buses from the relatively central **Karandish bus terminal** (Terminal-e Bozorg; Map p198; Salman-e Farsi Blvd).

Amir Kabir bus terminal (Amir Kabir Blvd), located on the southern outskirts, is used for destinations west and southwest of Shiraz.

Minibuses (IR80,000) and taxis *dar bast* (IR1,000,000) to Firuz Abad leave from **Modares bus terminal** (Modares Blvd).

SAVARI

The most useful use of savari from Shiraz is for Marvdasht, near Persepolis, as there is no bus to this destination. They leave from the southern edge of Karandish bus terminal on a semi-regular basis and cost around IR80,000. Taking a taxi *dar bast* costs IR400,000. Better still book a driver-guide and make a comfortable and informed day of it.

🚗 Getting Around

Most people get around town by shuttle taxis, which ply the streets for around IR20,000 per trip. A typical short-hop taxi *dar bast* in the centre of town costs around IR100,000.

A taxi *dar bast* between the airport and the city centre costs around IR250,000.

Short-hop journeys around the city originate from the **local bus terminal** (Map p198) and trips cost around IR10,000.

FLIGHTS FROM SHIRAZ

DESTINATION	FARE	FLIGHTS	CARRIER
Bandar Abbas	from US$75	daily	Iran Air, Iran Aseman
Bandar-e Lengeh	from US$50	3 weekly	Iran Air
Esfahan	from US$35	2 weekly	Iran Air, Naft
Kish	from US$60	4 weekly	Iran Aseman, Kish Airlines
Mashhad	from US$70	2 weekly	Iran Aseman, Caspian Tabar, Iran Air
Tehran	from US$82	daily	Iran Aseman, Iran Air, Kish Airlines, Mohan

BUSES FROM SHIRAZ

DESTINATION	FARE (IR; VIP/ MAHMOOLY)	DURATION (HR)	DEPARTURES
Bandar Abbas	440,000/240,000	11	frequent 8am-11pm
Esfahan	300,000/200,000	8	frequent
Hamadan	515,000 (VIP)	15	2pm
Kashan	450,000 (VIP)	10	7pm
Kazerun (for Bishapur)	80,000 (mahmooly)	2½	hourly 9.30am-8.30pm
Kerman	360,000/210,000	10	6 daily 6.30am-9.20pm
Kermanshah	650,000 (VIP)	16	1.30pm & 2.30pm
Mashhad	790,000/470,000	20	4 daily 2.30pm-4pm
Rasht	655,000 (VIP)	16	2pm
Sanandaj	600,000 (mahmooly)	19	1.30pm
Tabriz	790,000 (VIP)	20	2 daily 2pm & 2.30pm
Tehran	570,000/350,000	13	frequent 1-11pm
Yazd	300,000/200,000	6½	frequent 7.30am-11.55pm

A **bike station** (Map p198; Karim Khan-e Zand Blvd; per hr IR60,000; ⊙7.30am-8pm) just west of Shohada Sq hires out bikes for those brave enough to chance their luck with the traffic. A passport or other documentation is required as a deposit. Available in the high season only.

The **Shiraz Urban Railway** (www.shirazmetro.ir) is still under construction and will eventually include three lines, 40 stations and 47km of track. Line 1 will run from southeast to northwest, including a stretch along Zand Ave between Valiasr Sq (good for visa extensions) and Imam Hossein Sq.

Persepolis   پرسپولیس

🕗071 / ELEVATION 1634M

One of the great wonders of the ancient world, **Persepolis** (Takht-e Jamshid; admission IR200,000, parking IR80,000; ⊙8am-5pm Nov-Mar, to 7pm Apr-Oct) embodies not just a grand architectural scheme but also a grand idea. It was conceived by Darius the Great who, in 520 BC, inherited the responsibility for ruling the world's first known empire founded by his predecessor, Cyrus the Great. Embracing tenets such as cultural tolerance and fair treatment of all subjects, Darius sought to reflect these concepts in the design of the magnificent palace complex at Persepolis, inviting architects from the furthest corner of the Persian Empire to contribute to its construction. The result is an eclectic set of structures, including monumental staircases, exquisite reliefs and imposing gateways, that testified to the expanse of Darius' domain.

History

Built on the slopes of Mt Rahmat (Mount of Mercy) Persepolis was intended as a showcase of the Achaemenid empire, designed to awe visitors with its scale and beauty. It served this ceremonial function most particularly during the annual No Ruz (New Year) celebration, when subjects came from across the empire to pay homage and tribute – to their rulers. Some suggest that at other times the administrative business of the empire returned to the city of Shush.

Over a period of 150 years, the city was embellished with the additions of subsequent kings, including Xerxes I and II, and Artaxerxes I, II and III. By the 4th century BC Persepolis was an elaborate project of palaces, treasuries and necropolis, illustrating unsurpassed artistic excellence.

Inevitably, the city attracted the envy of powerful rivals and in 330 BC it was all but razed to the ground by the armies of Alexander the Great. Although the main buildings were constructed of stone walls, their ceilings are believed to have been supported by timber beams, which caught fire and melted the iron and lead clamps that held the stone structures together.

While the ruins seen today merely hint at Persepolis' former glory, excavations in the 1930s have helped restore some of the features to their original splendour. In recognition of its historical significance, its scale and the artistic mastery shown in the stone

Persepolis

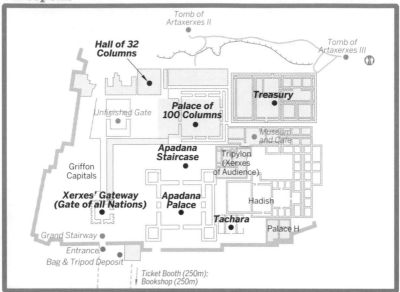

reliefs, Persepolis has been awarded the coveted status of Unesco World Heritage Site.

For an idea of how the city may have looked in its former glory, **Persepolis3D. com** (www.persepolis3d.com) gives a convincing computer simulation of the site.

◉ Sights

To do justice to the site, it is worth dedicating half a day to explore the ruins; this allows time to examine some of the fine details, visit the museum, climb up to the rock tombs above the treasury, and to simply sit and enjoy the spectacle of towering pillars against the blue sky. Even better, a night's stay at the hotel during high season allows for enjoyment of the sound and light show in the evening and a leisurely amble around the ruins in the early morning before the tour groups arrive.

While it's fun to wander around the site and discover the parts of Persepolis that are personal highlights – such as a beaked bird capital that was never used but is now the emblem of an airline, the leading of camels across the frieze on the staircase, the connection of the rock-hewn tombs to those of the Nabataean culture in Jordan and Arabia – this is one site that repays engaging the services of an enthusiastic expert. Licensed,

English-speaking guides (US$15 for 1½ hours) are available from the entrance gate.

There is little shade at Persepolis and from May until early October it can be intensely hot. Bringing water and a hat are useful precautions against heat exhaustion.

★ Xerxes' Gateway   GATE
The bronze trumpets that once heralded the arrival of important foreign delegations (a fragment of which is on display in the museum) may now be silent, but it is still possible to capture the sense of awe on approaching the colossal main gateway. Built during the reign of Xerxes I, who called this his Gate of All Nations, the pillared entrance is guarded by bearded and hoofed mythical figures in the style of Assyrian gate-guards.

The gateway bears a cuneiform inscription in Old Persian, Neo-Babylonian and Elamite languages declaring, among other things, that Xerxes is responsible for the construction of this and many beautiful wonders in Parsa. Centuries of graffitists have also left their mark, including explorer Henry Morton Stanley.

★ Apadana Staircase   RUINS
The stairs, which are guarded by stone soldiers, are decorated by an exceptionally finely crafted frieze in three panels. Each

panel is divided into several tiers depicting the reception of various visitors to Persepolis and these can be read, by those with the expertise, almost like a history text book. As such, this is one sight that really repays the engagement of a tour guide.

★ Apadana Palace   PALACE
Constructed on a stone terrace by Xerxes I, the Apadana Palace lies largely in ruins. It's thought that this is where foreign delegations would have been received by the king and the splendour accompanying their audience is captured in the bas-reliefs on the northern wall. It's the exquisite reliefs of the Apadana Staircase on the eastern wall, however, that are the star attraction. A virtual log of visitors to Persepolis from across the Achaemenid Empire, they continue to draw people from around the world today.

Tomb of Artaxerxes II   TOMB
On the hill above the Treasury are two rock-hewn tombs. The larger and more elaborate of the two belongs to Artaxerxes II, and clambering up to this remarkable structure allows something of an aerial perspective on Persepolis and a better appreciation of its scale.

Private Palaces   PALACE
The palaces in the southwestern corner of the site are believed to have been constructed during the reigns of Darius and Xerxes. The Tachara is easily the most striking, with many of its monolithic doorjambs still standing and covered in bas-reliefs and cuneiform inscriptions. The stairs on the southern side bear highly skilled reliefs and are some of the most photogenic. The palace opens onto a royal courtyard flanked by two palaces.

To the east is the Hadish, a palace completed by Xerxes and reached via another monumental staircase. Some scholars speculate that its wooden columns on stone bases might have served as kindling for Alexander's great fire – especially as it had been Xerxes who had put Athens to the torch. To the south of the square are the remains of an unfinished palace known as Palace H.

Palace of 100 Columns   PALACE
With an extravagant hall measuring almost 70 sq metres and supported by 100 stone columns, this palace formed one of two principal reception areas in Persepolis. Built during the reigns of Xerxes and Artaxerxes I, some believe it was used to receive the military elite upon whom the empire's security rested. Today, enough of the broken columns remain to give an idea of the palace's former grandeur, and fine reliefs show a king, soldiers and representatives of 28 subject nations.

Little remains of the adjacent Hall of 32 Columns, built at the end of the Achaemenid period. The arrival of Alexander and his armies brought an end to work on a larger version of the Xerxes' Gateway (Gate of All Nations) in the wide courtyard in front of the Palace of 100 Columns; the unfinished gate still stands – a commentary on the city's sudden demise.

Grand Stairway   GATE
Persepolis sits on top of a great plinth of stone blocks and today, as in ancient times, visitors seeking entry to the city must approach this elevated complex of wonders from a tree-lined avenue across the plain, before ascending to the entrance via the monumental Grand Staircase. The stairs were carved from massive blocks of stone, but each step was shallow so that Persians in long elegant robes could ascend the 111 steps gracefully.

Treasury   RUINS
The southeastern corner of the site is dominated by Darius' Treasury, one of the earliest structures at Persepolis. Archaeologists have found stone tablets in Elamite and Akkadian languages detailing the wages of thousands of workers. When Alexander looted the Treasury, it's reported he needed 3000 camels to cart off the contents. The foundations of walls and the bases of 250 columns are all that remain.

Tomb of Artaxerxes III   TOMB
Few visitors wander up to the smaller of the two tombs above the Treasury but it has its own charms, not least for a commanding view across the plain. It's not possible to enter this tomb but the frieze above the lintel is in good condition and a bas-relief depiction of the winged Fravashi (guardian spirit) graces the upper part of the rock face.

Persepolis Museum   MUSEUM
(IR200,000; ⊙8am-5.30pm) Restored in the 1930s, what was perhaps once the royal harem now houses the museum and administrative offices. The museum contains a stone foundation tablet and a range of artefacts discovered during excavations: alabaster vessels, cedar wood, lances and arrow tips.

CENTRAL IRAN PERSEPOLIS

☞ Tours

Just about every hotel in Shiraz organises tours to Persepolis, and prices are usually based on the rates set by the local cultural heritage and tourism office. Accredited guides generally have foreign-language skills and must carry a badge with a hologram, photograph and expiry date, and many drive their own vehicle. Their expertise obviously entitles them to charge more than a non-accredited driver.

A driver-guide usually charges US$60 (for up to three people) for a half-day tour of Persepolis, Naqsh-e Rostam and Naqsh-e Rajab. A full-day tour including Pasargadae costs US$85.

Pars Tourist Agency (p206) in Shiraz operates a daily half-day group bus tour with guide for US$30 per person, including entry fees (US$55 for day-trip including Pasargadae).

Some travellers opt for a driver who speaks English to ferry them around for a half-day (IR800,000 plus IR160,000 for each extra hour). The driver usually won't enter any of the sites but our information at least gives context for further reading. A taxi from Persepolis to Pasargadae and back costs IR2,300,000.

🛏 Sleeping

Hotel Persepolis   HOTEL $$
(☑071-4334 1550; www.persepolis-apadana-hotel.com; s/d US$43/74, d with view of Persepolis US$96; 🅿❄) Guests at this gracious hotel, with its attractive porch and fine garden, can enjoy the perfect shaded view of the ruins of Persepolis while sipping tea from white china. Rooms are comfortable and the service charming. There's also a rather grand restaurant with a menu of Persian favourites, such as a daily stew with rice (IR250,000).

❶ Getting There & Away

While tours, especially with licensed driver-guides, offer the most rewarding way of visiting Persepolis, it is possible to visit the ruins by other means. A return taxi costs IR400,000 from Shiraz, including an hour's waiting time. Minibuses from Karandish bus terminal in Shiraz to Marvdasht cost IR40,000, from where a taxi *dar bast* to Persepolis should cost IR160,000, although local taxi drivers tend to charge foreigners a premium.

Taxis wait outside the entrance gate to Persepolis for the return trip to Shiraz and are usually willing to add in quick stops at Naqsh-e Rostam and Naqsh-e Rajab for IR800,000.

There's no public transport linking Persepolis with Pasargadae, 84km to the northeast.

Naqsh-e Rostam & Naqsh-e Rajab

In the cliffs neighbouring Persepolis are two ancient sites featuring rock-hewn tombs that are well worth a visit and are usually included in a guided tour to Persepolis from Shiraz.

The must-see one is **Naqsh-e Rostam** (Marv Dasht–Sarooie Rd; IR200,000; ⊗8am-6pm winter, 7.30am-8pm summer) where the four tombs are believed to be those of Darius II, Artaxerxes I, Darius I and Xerxes I (from left to right facing the cliff), although historians are still debating this. The seven Sassanian stone reliefs cut into the cliff depict vivid scenes of imperial conquests and royal ceremonies; signboards below each relief give a detailed description in English.

The reliefs above the openings to the funerary chambers are similar to those at Persepolis, with the kings standing on thrones supported by figures representing the subject nations below.

Facing the cliff is the **Bun Khanak** (Central Home). This was long thought to be an Achaemenid fire temple, but scholars now argue that it might have been a treasury. The walls later marked with inscriptions cataloguing later Sassanian victories.

The **Naqsh-e Rajab** (off Marv Dasht–Sarooie Rd; IR80,000; ⊗8am-6pm winter, 7.30am-8pm summer) rock carvings could easily escape notice if it weren't for the sign and the entry kiosk. Four fine Sassanian bas-reliefs are hidden here from the road by the folds of a rocky hill and depict various scenes from the reigns of Ardashir I and Shapur the Great.

It's feasible to walk the 6km from Persepolis to Naqsh-e Rostam, stopping off at Naqsh-e Rajab en route in winter, but this is not an option in the heat of summer. Taxis waiting outside the entrance gate to Persepolis for the return trip to Shiraz can be persuaded to make a detour at Naqsh-e Rostam and Naqsh-e Rajab with a brief stop at each for IR800,000.

Pasargadae   پاسارگاد

☑071 / POPULATION 400 / ELEVATION 1847M
Begun under Cyrus the Great in about 546 BC, the ruins of **Pasargadae** (Pasargad Rd, off Hwy 65; IR200,000; ⊗8am-5pm) are located

near the village of the same name, lying some 60km north of Persepolis on a windswept plain surrounded by arid mountains .

Marked by an austere beauty, these ruins of empire will enthral historians and those with a detective interest in piecing together the clues of an ancient civilisation. It has to be said, there are not that many clues to go on, but enough to suggest that the ancients were sophisticated in their tastes and grand in their design.

Proud and alone on the Morghab Plain, the **Tomb of Cyrus** is the first of the monuments encountered on entering the site of Pasargadae. The tomb consists of a modest rectangular burial chamber perched on six tiered plinths. Its unique architecture is a totem of conquest, combining elements of all the major civilisations captured by Cyrus.

'I am Cyrus, the Achaemenid King' reads the cunieform inscription on a pillar of **Cyrus' palace complex**. The minimal ruins of what must have been a grand set of structures lie about 1km north of the king's tomb. Archaeologists note the unusual plan of the palace with its central hall of 30 columns (the stumps of which remain) and its two great opposing verandahs, but it takes a bit of imagination to reassemble the fallen masonry.

About 250m to the southeast is the rectangular **Audience Palace**, which once had an 18m-high hypostyle hall surrounded by smaller balconies. One of the eight white limestone columns has been reconstructed on a rare black limestone plinth.

Around 500m north of Cyrus' Private Palace are the remains of the **Prison of Solomon** (Zendan-e Soleiman), variously thought to be a fire temple, tomb, sundial or store. On the hill beyond is the **Tall-e Takht** – a monumental 6000-sq-metre citadel used from Cyrus' time until the late Sassanian period. Local historians believe the references to Solomon date from the Arab conquest, when the inhabitants of Pasargadae renamed the sites with Islamic names to prevent their destruction.

Finally, the hard-to-discern remnants of **Darius' garden**, added to the World Heritage list as part of a joint entry under Persian gardens, display a sophisticated irrigation system. The water channels, punctuated by square pools, run along the perimeter of the garden giving a good indication of the enormous scale of the palace project.

ℹ Getting There & Away

The easiest way to reach Pasargadae by public transport is to board a bus between Shiraz and Yazd or Esfahan (or vice versa) along Hwy 65 and alight at the Pasargadae junction. From here taxis cover the 5.5km along Pasargad Rd to the ruins (IR100,000). More conveniently, it is easy to find a taxi from Shiraz for the 84km round trip (around IR2,400,000, with a one-hour wait).

Bavanat بوانات

☑ 071 / POPULATION 45,000

The beautiful Bavanat region, 230km northeast of Shiraz, encompasses a 20km-long walnut-growing valley between the Zagros Mountains in the south and the arid deserts to the north. The main town is Suryan, aka Bavanat, but most visitors head for **Shah Hamzeh Bazm** (or just Bazm) 18km further east. The mountains near Bazm are home to Khamseh nomads, a confederation of five groups of Arabic, Turkish and Farsi-speaking people. From about April until October they pitch their tents in the hills and survive with few of the 'luxuries' you might see in the tents of Qashqa'i nomads north of Shiraz.

An enterprising resident of the village, Abbas Barzegar, who is himself part Khamseh, and his family run a great **homestay** (☑ 0917 317 3597, 071-4441 2357; www.bavanattravel.com; half-board package IR2,000,000, incl museum entry & mountain/nomad walk; ℗ 🐾 🏊) 🅿 comprised of a range of 35 traditional or modern rooms, some with private bathroom, set in 8 hectares of garden and orchard growing pumpkins, peaches, walnuts and grapes. Reservations are essential.

Abbas Barzegar's fluent English-speaking daughter acts as the tour guide around their one-of-a-kind family **museum** (IR200,000, open from 9am to sunset) that showcases rural life in the region. The family also arranges guided tours of the village and offers overnight packages that include accommodation, delicious home-cooked meals and a walk or nomad visit. Between April and October, they can organise camping with the nomads, some 25km (30 minutes' drive) from Bavanat, in the family's goat-hair tents.

Bavanat can be reached from Yazd by taking a bus from Imam Ali Sq to Bazm at noon daily except Friday (IR160,000, four hours). From Shiraz (IR120,000, three hours), buses leave Karandish bus terminal at noon, 7pm and 8pm daily. From Bazm, call Bavanat Homestay to be collected.

Firuz Abad

فیروز آباد

📞 071 / POPULATION 64,969 / ELEVATION 1329M

The monumental Sassanian-era sites around modern Firuz Abad are the remains of structures originally built by the founder of the Sassanian empire, Ardashir Babakan, in the 3rd century BC. Firuz Abad was once an important stop on the Sassanid roadway between Shiraz and the ancient port of Shiraf. Today it's mainly a Qashqa'i farming town.

Coming from Shiraz, the first site is **Qal'eh-e Doktar** a three-tiered palace atop a steep hill that's a 20-minute climb above the footbridge that crosses the road. Made of rock and gypsum, it was Ardashir's first attempt at creating a palace, and its position and fortification reflect the lingering Parthian threat of the time. While crumbling, it's not difficult to imagine the palace's original layout.

Very close to Firuz Abad, a dirt road fords the Tang Ab River to reach **Ardashir's Palace**. This much grander 1800-year-old structure, with its domes, high *iwans* and clean stable lines, it is one of the earliest examples of classic Sassanian architecture. In winter the Tang Ab is impassable requiring a lengthy detour through Firuz Abad by taxi.

The nearby site of **Gur** is worth a quick stop en route to the palace: this settlement, an ambitious piece of town planning, was laid out in equal sectors separated by high walls. It requires some imagination, however, to make sense of the ruins.

❶ Getting There & Away

Minibuses (IR80,000, 2½ hours) and taxis *dar bast* (IR1,000,000, 2¼ hours) run from Shiraz's Modares bus terminal (near the Visa Extension Office) to Firuz Abad. Returning, the last services leave in the early evening. A driver-guide from Shiraz charges US$75 to US$80 for a half-day visit.

Kazerun & Bishapur

📞 071 / POPULATION 889,685 / ELEVATION 860M

Just off the ancient royal road between Shiraz and Bushehr lies the modern town of Kazerun. Set among fertile fields in the southern foothills of the rugged Zagros Mountains, the surrounding area is particularly beautiful in spring when sweet-smelling narcissus is grown across the plain and carpets of wild poppies bloom beneath the region's famous oak trees. Nearby **Parishan Lake**, 12km from the town, attracts flamingoes, ducks, pelicans, geese and cranes, and is home to four endemic species of fish.

As lovely as the landscape around here is, visitors normally venture to Kazerun from Shiraz to see the monuments associated with the ancient city of **Bishapur** (site IR200,000, museum IR80,000; ☺ 7.30am-6pm). Around 20km to the north of Kazerun, the ruins extend over a wide area and include six Sassanian-era bas-reliefs along the walls of **Chogan Gorge**.

The highlight is the 7m-high **Statue of Shapur I** in a cave high above the valley floor. The Sassanian-era image, weighing about 30 tonnes, is carved from a single limestone block, with the ball of the crown chiselled from the cave roof. Damaged, probably during an earthquake, the statue was re-erected in 1958 and reinforced somewhat unsympathetically with concrete.

The cave is reached by tracing the road through Chogan Gorge and crossing the dry river bed in the village of Shapur (6km from the ruins at Bishapur). From here it's a rough ride (or 30-minute walk) to the beginning of the ascent and a further 1½-hour hike up the steep path (there are a few fixed steel ladders at the end) to the cave. Walking shoes, a hat, water and an early start in summer are advisable as there are no facilities.

❶ Getting There & Away

The full-day trip to Bishapur is easiest with a driver-guide (US$115 to US$130), but public transport is viable with a very early start. A bus (*mahmooly* IR80,000, 2½ hours, frequent) to Kazerun leaves from the Amir Kabir bus terminal in Shiraz. From Kazerun, a taxi *dar bast* (IR1,200,000) can be engaged for a couple of hours to cover the sights of Bishapur.

From Shiraz, keep an eye out en route for the 15-arch Karim Khan Bridge, a Zand-era bridge about 40km west of Shiraz.

Persian Gulf خليج فارس

Best Places to Eat

➜ Bandar (p221)

➜ Fanoos (p220)

➜ Kolbeh Darvish (p217)

➜ Mir Mohanna (p218)

➜ Shabhaye Talai – Golden Nights Beach Restaurant (p226)

➜ Kaleng (p226)

Best Places to Sleep

➜ Atilar Hotel (p220)

➜ Mr Amini's House (p225)

➜ Mrs Fattahi's House (p225)

➜ Toranj Marine Hotel (p217)

➜ Ecotourism Hotel (p219)

Why Go?

Quick – turn around: there's an entire travel experience that you probably haven't even considered. While you've been planning your Iranian sojourn around the jewels of the country's rich history (Esfahan, Shiraz, Yazd), to the southeast the Persian Gulf is equally deserving. Explore the magnetic islands of Kish, Qeshm and Hormoz, which are absurdly easy to combine and are altogether different. While Kish is unashamedly glam and glitzy, Qeshm and Hormoz are refreshingly void of large-scale development and offer a chance to glimpse a more traditional way of life – not to mention an array of geological wonders. Along the coast, soak up the vibes of lively Bandar Abbas and make a beeline for the delightful town of Kong, whose historical centre is peppered with charming old houses and monuments. Thus, you'll have the full monty.

When to Go

The gulf is hotter than Hades between April and November, with temperatures averaging 35°C and occasionally climbing as high as 50°C. Not surprisingly, life adjusts accordingly – most businesses start early and then shut up shop from about noon to 5pm.

During No Ruz (Iranian New Year; 21 March to 3 April) the entire coast is inundated by swarms of domestic tourists and most hotels are full – avoid travelling here at this time. Try to visit during winter, when the temperature averages between 18°C and 25°C, humidity is relatively low and crowds are nonexistent.

Kish Island جزیره کیش

📻 076 / POPULATION 27,000

Welcome to Iran's Sunshine Coast, or Iran's Costa del Sol. However you label it, say hello to this attractive island that, since the 1970s, has become a beach resort where visitors can swim, shop and sample a laid-back and relatively liberated local lifestyle. Iran's most hedonistic spot, Kish is booming. Hotels, apartment blocks and retail complexes (it enjoys free-trade-zone status) dominate the once-empty desert landscape and domestic tourist numbers are on the rise, especially in winter, when it's freezing cold on the mainland. Kish is largely ignored by foreign tourists, though. That's a shame, because a visit here is a great way to experience Iran from an altogether different perspective. Leave the sight-laden cities of the mainland and come here to enjoy sea, sand and sun in a relaxed atmosphere.

History

Kish Island is first recorded in the memoirs of Nearchus, the Greek sailor commissioned by Alexander the Great to explore the Persian Gulf in 325 BC. In the Middle Ages Kish became an important trading centre under its own powerful Arab dynasty and at one time supported a population of 40,000. The main town was Harireh, which is believed to be the town referred to by the poet Sa'di in his famous work *Golestan* (Rose Garden).

Kish was known for the quality of its pearls; when Marco Polo was visiting the imperial court in China, he remarked on the beauty of the pearls worn by one of the emperor's wives and was told they had come from Kish. In the 14th century Kish fell into decline and it remained obscure until the 1970s, when it was developed as a semi-private retreat for the shah and his guests – complete with international airport, luxury hotels and a casino.

PERSIAN GULF KISH ISLAND

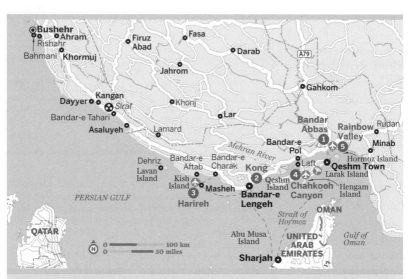

Persian Gulf Highlights

1 Bandar Abbas (p219) Soaking up local vibes while wandering through the animated streets of this city and visiting its fish market.

2 Kong (p219) Immersing yourself in a traditional port town blessed with plenty of historical buildings and houses.

3 Harireh (p215; Kish Island) Exploring this splendid old city that comprises the remains of a large house and an old port.

4 Chahkooh Canyon (p224) Marvelling at this sculptural canyon, one of many geological wonders on Qeshm Island.

5 Rainbow Valley (p227) Wandering in a Martian landscape on Hormoz Island.

◉ Sights

An easy bicycle ride west of the port is **Harireh** (Historical City & Seaport; Map p216; ⊘24hr; **FREE**), a splendid archaeological site comprises the remains of a large house with private *qanat* (underground water channel), a public *hammam* and a congregational mosque. It was originally positioned next to a busy commercial port; across the road, you can still see access stairs cut into the rocky cliff, as well as rock-cut wells and channels that were part of workshops producing date nectar, once one of the island's major exports.

Next to the tennis stadium is **Kariz-e-Kish** (Kish Underground City; Map p216; IR500,000; ⊘8.30am-10.30pm), a subterranean network of stone passageways built around a historic *qanat*. It's said to have been built some 2500 years ago to collect, purify and store water for the inhabitants of Harireh; given the arid climate, water was, unsurprisingly, a precious commodity.

🏃 Activities

🏃 Cycling

Kish is only 15km long and 8km wide, rising just 45m at its highest point. This means that cycling the flat, purpose-built bicycle path that follows the entire 40km of coastline is a popular way to spend a day. Bikes can be hired for around IR50,000 per hour from various stands around town.

🏊 Diving

Although it cannot compare with, say, the Red Sea, Kish Island offers the best diving in Iran, with a series of healthy reefs that are well stocked with fish. You'll find a smattering of dive centres on the island. Standards are fairly good, but check out the equipment before signing up for a dive. Also note that local instructors don't always speak English. Women must wear a special wetsuit (provided) that covers the head.

Kish Diving Center   DIVING
(Map p216; ☑0912 854 3246; www.kishdiving.com; ⊘7am-6pm) Found on the beach outside Shayan Hotel, Kish's oldest diving centre charges about IR2,300,000 for a one-hour dive including equipment hire and IR12,500,000 for a four-day PADI open-water course. It also offers various water sports.

🏊 Swimming & Watersports

Kish is one of the very few places in Iran where swimming is actively encouraged. There are sandy, uncrowded beaches around most of the coast, but women must use the **Ladies' Beach** behind the Kish Free Trade Organization Building. The official **Gentlemen's Beach and Beach Volleyball Sports Complex** is near Twins Park, though in reality men can swim anywhere other than at the Ladies' Beach.

Ocean Water Park   WATER PARK
(Map p216; www.oceanwaterpark.com; off Jahan Rd; adult/child IR1,400,000/500,000; ⊘10am-4pm) Adrenaline rushes are guaranteed at this water park, which opened in early 2017 on Kish's southern coast. The centrepiece is a 28m-high tower with several slides. Food and drinks are available. Note that there are days for women and days for men – ring ahead.

Aquacom Cable Park   WATER SPORTS
(Map p216; off Ferdosi Blvd; per 30min/hour US$30/40; ⊘11am-6pm) Located near the Grand Recreational Pier, Aquacom offers water-ski and wakeboard rides on the main beach. The cableway is 860m long and 160m wide and operates at a speed of up to 62km/h (novices can request a slower speed of 28km/h). Both men and women can participate, but women must wear an Islamic-style wetsuit.

🛏 Sleeping

There is a huge array of hotels, resorts and holiday apartments to choose from on Kish, but virtually nothing for budgeteers. Prices are significantly higher than they are elsewhere in Iran but can vary wildly by season; whatever you do, avoid visiting during No Ruz, when rates skyrocket. At non-peak times the hotel desk at the airport offers good midrange deals.

Prices usually include airport or port transfers.

Jam-e-Jam Kish Hotel   HOTEL $$
(Map p216; ☑076-4442 4801; jamejamkishhotel@yahoo.com; off Amir Kabir Sq; d incl breakfast IR2,600,000; P❄🗟) An attractive, low-slung building in a quiet area, Jam-e-Jam is one of Kish's best-value hotels. There's no great luxury involved and some of the furnishings have seen better days, but the rooms are well appointed, light filled and clean as a whistle.

PERSIAN GULF KISH ISLAND

Kish Island

Persian Gulf

Speedboats to Bandar-e Charak; Catamarans to Bandar-e Lengeh

Grand Recreational Pier

Sanaee Blvd

Darya Beach Park

Gentlemen's Beach

Marjan Beach Park

Dariush Sq

Molavi St

Marjan St

Siri Sq

Dolphin Park

Ladies' Beach

Ferdosi Blvd

Sanaee Sq

Sahel Sq

Andisheh St

Morvarid Blvd

Qeshm Sq

Lavan Sq

Ashena Sq

Sadaf Sq

Sadaf Blvd

Kish Hospital

Hormoz Sq

Olympic Blvd

Olympic Sq

Harireh

Sports Complex

Imam Sq

Jahan Rd

Faroor Sq

Khatam Blvd

MIR MOHANNA

Mir Mohanna Blvd

Mir Mohanna Recreational Pier

Ghorub St

Khark Sq

Jask Sq

16

20
17
18

1
9
3
4

8
19
13
6
7
15
11

1
2

10
12
14
5

Kish Island

★ **Toranj Marine Hotel**   RESORT $$$
(Map p216; 📞076-4445 0601; www.toranj-hotel.
com; d incl breakfast from US$330; P ❄ 🛜)
Iran's first (and only) over-water hotel, the
Toranj is one of Kish's best resorts. The 100
bungalows are built on stilts and come with
the requisite glass floor panels for viewing
fish and decks with gorgeous lagoon views.
Amenities include five restaurants (one of
them on stilts over the water), a kids' club,
a gym and free kayaks.

Maryam Sorinet Hotel   HOTEL $$$
(Map p216; 📞076-4446 7511; www.sorinethotels.
com/en; off Amir Kabir Sq; d incl breakfast US$310-
350; P ❄ 🛜) This genteel hotel with a boutique feel has an atmosphere and class of its
own, partly engendered by the plush interi-
or and top-quality restaurant. Retire to chic
and understated rooms styled in soothing
earth tones.

Shayan Hotel   HOTEL $$$
(Map p216; 📞076-4442 2771; shayan@pars-hotels.
com; Sahel Sq; d incl breakfast IR6,700,000-7,500,000;
P ❄ 🛜 🏊) When it opened as the shah's
beachfront casino-hotel in 1973, this was the
most glamorous shack on the gulf. It hasn't
changed much, and the angular architecture,
perspex furniture and sprayed-concrete detail-
ing are certainly retro cool. Rooms, most with
balcony, are comfortable and have excellent
bathrooms. Another draw is its excellent loca-
tion close to the beach.

The sea-view rooms are well worth the
extra cash.

Dariush Grand Hotel   RESORT $$$
(Map p216; 📞076-4444 4995; www.dariushgrand-
hotel.com; Dariush Sq; d incl breakfast US$490-
590; P ❄ @ 🛜 🏊) This Achaemenid-inspired
monument in marble is often described as
Iran's best hotel, though its Vegas-style os-
tentation won't please everyone. Rooms are
comfortable and well equipped, but their
decor is starting to date and the bathrooms
are petite. There's a good gym, an outdoor
pool (men only), two restaurants and a coffee shop. It's close to the beach.

✕ Eating

Be sure to enjoy a tea, cold drink or ice
cream at one of the beach cafes south of the
Grand Recreational Pier – they're fabulous
people-watching spots. You'll also find plenty of fast-food joints on Morvarid Blvd. Most
hotels also have restaurants if you don't fancy
venturing out.

★ **Kolbeh Darvish**   IRANIAN $$
(Map p216; 📞0913 325 3338; Jahan Rd;
mains IR150,000-320,000; ⏱2pm-1am) This
much-lauded eatery specialising in tradi-
tional Iranian food is the perfect place to
try out *kubide kabab* (minced mutton,
breadcrumbs and onion, served with rice) or
ghorme sabzi (diced meat with beans, veg-
etables and rice). Vegetarians could try the
mirza ghasemi (mashed eggplant, squash,
tomato and egg). Yummy! Another draw is
the location – it's right on the seashore.

Burger House   BURGERS $$
(Map p216; 📞076-4445 8411; Morvarid Blvd; mains
IR180,000-310,000; ⏱noon-midnight) If you're
at the stage of screaming when presented
with yet another meat dish with rice, this
sleek fast-food joint may well be for you,
with a wide array of delectable burgers and
sandwiches and average pizzas.

★ **Mir Mohanna** SEAFOOD $$$
(Map p216; ☑ 076-4442 2855; off Ferdosi Blvd;
mains IR550,000-900,000; ☉ noon-3pm &
8.30pm-midnight) This perennial fave, with
large windows overlooking the beach, serves
exciting fish dishes and shrimp as well as
excellent salads. The food is super fresh and
well cooked, the decor is cheerful and the
service is attentive. It's without a doubt the
best eating option on the island.

Shandiz Safdari Saheli IRANIAN $$$
(Map p216; ☑ 0934 769 1460; Jahan Rd; mains
IR630,000-890,000; ☉ noon-4pm & 8pm-mid-
night) Shandiz Safari isn't just a restaurant
– it's an experience, especially at dinner. This
huge venture overlooking the seashore is the
venue of choice for cashed-up Iranian tourists, who come to devour well-presented fish
and meat dishes and entertain themselves
(it usually stages live music and comedy
shows from 9pm). The restaurant offers free
pick-up from your hotel.

ℹ Information

Bank Melli (Map p216; Sanaee Blvd; ☉ 7.30am-
1.30pm) Changes currency.
Kish Hospital (Map p216; ☑ 076-4442 3711;
Hormoz Sq) A well-equipped hospital in the
island's northeast.
**Ministry of Foreign Affairs Kish Island
Mission** (Map p216; ☑ 076-4445 5670; Sanaee Blvd; ☉ 7.30am-2pm Sat-Thu) Kish (with
Qeshm) is the only place in Iran that foreigners
can visit without needing a visa. If you're
arriving by air or boat from outside Iran, you
get a free one-month 'Kish visa' on arrival.
Once on Kish, the ministry can supposedly

issue normal tourist visas for those who want
to continue into Iran, but it's better to organise
your Iranian visa before you arrive or get it
on arrival at an international airport in Iran if
you're eligible.
Tourist Information (Map p216; ☑ 076-4442
5768; http://tourism.kish.ir/en; Kish Free Zone
Organization Bldg, Sanaee Blvd; ☉ 8am-2pm
Sat-Thu) The helpful English-speaking PR staff
at the Kish Free Zone Organization can help
with tourist information and supply maps and
brochures. Its office is on the building's ground
floor; entry is via the rear of the building rather
than the front staircase.

ℹ Getting There & Away

AIR
To Tehran there are at least three daily flights
(about IR4,000,000) on at least three airlines:
Kish Airlines (Map p216; ☑ 076-4445 5729;
http://en.kishairlines.ir; Sanaee Sq; ☉ 8am-7pm
Sat-Thu, 9am-noon Fri), **Iran Air** (Map p216;
☑ 076-4445 5683; www.iranair.com; Sanaee
Sq; ☉ 8am-2.30pm Sat-Thu, 9am-noon Fri) and
Mahan Air (Map p216; ☑ 076-4444 2930; www.
mahan.aero/en; Ferdosi Blvd). There are also
several daily flights to Esfahan (IR3,700,000)
and Bandar Abbas (IR2,300,000) as well as a
few weekly connections to Shiraz (IR2,300,000)
and Mashhad (IR4,400,000).

Kish Airlines also has daily flights to Dubai
(one way IR5,700,000, 30 minutes).

BOAT
In calm conditions, passenger ferries travel to/
from Bandar-e Charak (one way IR220,000,
about 1½ hours). From Kish's port, these leave
between 8am and 4pm depending on weather
conditions and passenger numbers.

IRAN'S BANDARI

About 3% of Iranians are Arab and most of these live in Bushehr, Khuzestan and Hormozgan provinces, near or on the Persian Gulf coast. They have traditionally lived in the gulf
ports (known as *bandars*) and are often called Bandari. Arabs in Khuzestan are mostly
Shiite, many having arrived from Iraq during the Iran–Iraq War, while those along the
Persian Gulf are mainly Sunni.

These Iranian Arabs speak a dialect of Arabic and usually have darker skin than other
Iranians. They also dress differently – women's clothes are refreshingly colourful and
some women wear the *burqa,* a sometimes-metal, sometimes-fabric mask that can
differ in design from village to village, town to town. *Burqas* are not very common these
days but can still be seen in Bandar Abbas, on Qeshm Island and in the southeastern
town of Minab. Men wear the *abba*, a long, sleeveless tunic, usually in white, with sandals
and perhaps an Arabic turban. Elsewhere you will see men in a *dishdasha* (the traditional
floor-length shirt-dress) and a *gutra* (long headscarf).

Iranian Arabs have their own music, characterised by the *ney ammbooni* (a sort of
bagpipe) and a strong, fast beat, often accompanied by a shimmying dance similar to
belly dancing.

KONG بندر کنگ

How is it possible that the utterly picturesque port town of Kong (pop 5500) a mere 5km east of Bandar-e Lengeh, has remained so far off the tourist radar? Culture aficionados and seekers of the offbeat will love exploring its maze of alleyways flanked by historical buildings and old traditional houses with elaborately carved wooden doors – not to mention more than 300 *badgirs* (wind towers), a small maritime museum and a handicrafts centre.

Accommodation options are limited, but there's the delightful **Ecotourism Hotel** (☑ 0917 993 6542; kongtourismnetwork@gmail.com; Kong; s/d incl breakfast IR700,000/1,100,000; ✱ 🛜), right in the middle of the old town. This well-run guesthouse is an opportunity to stay in a traditional home brimful of local charm. Rooms are super clean and well organised; most have private facilities. Your host, Mohammad, can organise various tours and will happily pick you up at the savari station in Kong if you give him a call.

You'll find a few cafeterias and modest eateries on the seafront and near the market. Meals can also be had at the Ecotourism Hotel.

All savaris between Bandar Abbas and Bandar-e Lengeh can drop you in Kong (IR200,000 per person, 2¼ hours). A taxi ride to Bandar-e Lengeh costs IR20,000. Find inspiration at www.kongtourism.com.

Valfajr Shipping Co (Map p216; ☑ 076-1542 5120; http://valfajr.ir; Kish Shipping Bldg, Sanaee St) operates catamarans linking Kish with Bandar-e Lengeh (one way IR900,000, four hours) – but only when Kish is busy enough to warrant it, which usually means during No Ruz only. When they operate, catamarans leave in the morning (returning from Bandar-e Lengeh at 1pm).

❶ Getting Around

Midrange and top-end hotels provide free airport transfers for their guests. Otherwise, a taxi from the airport to most parts of the island will cost IR190,000.

Excellent air-con minibuses (IR20,000) cruise the northern and eastern roads between Mir Mohanna and Marjan Mall; just flag one down, hop on and pay the driver when you get off. From the boat terminal, you can crowd onto a local minibus or take a private taxi. A short taxi trip costs IR115,000.

You can also rent bikes (IR50,000 per hour) and cycle around the island on a purpose-built path.

Bandar-e Lengeh   بندر لنگه

☑ 076 / POPULATION 27,000

Bandar-e Lengeh is useful as a transit point for travellers aiming for the nearby picturesque port town of Kong, or waiting for a ferry to Kish or Dubai.

Assuming that the seas aren't too rough, it's usually much quicker to take a **ferry** (one way IR230,000, about 1½ hours) from **Bandar-e Charak** (89km west of Bandar-e Lengeh) to Kish. To do this, take a savari from Lengeh to Charak, where it will drop

you at the ferry terminal. There are four to five ferry services per day between Bandar-e Charak and Kish.

Valfajr Shipping Co (☑076-4222 0252; http://valfajr.ir; Imam Khomeini Blvd; ☉ 8am-2.30pm Sat-Thu) also operates catamaran services to Dubai in the UAE. These usually leave on Saturday and Wednesday; tickets cost IR2,200,000 one way (four hours). Contact the office or an accredited ticket agency to book and purchase tickets.

Lengeh's **bus terminal** is about 2km east of town on the gulf side of the main highway. Buses to/from Bandar Abbas (*mahmooly* IR200,000, three hours, three daily) stop here en route to/from Bushehr (IR350,000, 8½ hours) but only usually run in the afternoon. Savaris are a better option.

Savaris to Bandar Abbas (IR200,000 per person, 2¼ hours) leave regularly between 6am and 8pm from outside the bus terminal. Savaris to Bandar-e Charak (IR120,000 per person, 80 minutes) leave from outside the petrol station situated about 1.8km west of the port, where you'll also find the **Diplomat Hotel** (☑076-4424 5526; Diplomat_Hotel@yahoo.com; Janbazan Blvd; d incl breakfast IR1,850,000; ℗✱🛜), offering clean rooms, Western toilets and sea views.

Bandar Abbas   بندر عباس

☑ 076 / POPULATION 445,000

Strategically positioned overlooking the Strait of Hormoz and the entrance to the Persian Gulf, Bandar Abbas, known to most Iranians simply as 'Bandar', is the capital of Hormozgan province and home to Iran's busiest port. Although Bandar isn't blessed with many must-see sights, it's much more than a transport hub for Qeshm or Hormoz Islands. It's a lively city with a great bazaar, an appealing fish market, and plenty of atmosphere.

History

The rise, fall and rise again of Bandar Abbas over the last five centuries has been directly linked to the role of European powers. Once a tiny fishing village called Gamerun, it was chosen as Persia's main southern port and naval dockyard after Shah Abbas I defeated the Portuguese on nearby Hormoz Island in 1622. The British East India Company was granted a trading concession, as were Dutch and French traders, and by the 18th century Bandar had become the chief Persian port and main outlet for the trade in Kermani carpets.

The port went into decline following the end of the Safavid dynasty and the withdrawal in 1759 of the British East India Company. The Sultan of Oman took control of Bandar in 1793 and held sway until 1868. The city's role remained peripheral until the Iran–Iraq War, when Iran's established ports at Bushehr, Bandar-e Imam Khomeini and Khorramshahr were either captured or became too dangerous for regular shipping. With the help of road and railway links to Tehran and central Asia, Bandar Abbas hasn't looked back.

◉ Sights

Bandar Abbas has a vibrant fishing industry, and its lively **fish market** (Map p221; Sayyadan St; ☺ 7am-8pm Sat-Thu, to 11am Fri) is a sight to behold. Early morning is the best time to come, when fishmongers display an astonishing variety of seafood, from barracuda to groupers. It's an incredibly photogenic place, full of charismatic old salts happy to pose for pictures with their catch.

The bustling **bazaar** (Map p221; Taleqani Blvd; ☺ 8am-8pm) rambles its way in a blaze of colour across two blocks just back from the seafront. In contrast, is the modest **Indian Temple** (Map p221; Imam Khomeini St; ☺ 8am-5pm) FREE. Set back from the main drag, this small stone building with a conical dome was built in the late 19th century to serve the Hindu community working for the British East India Company.

🛏 Sleeping

Hotel Darya HOTEL $
(Map p221; ☏ 076-3224 1942; Eskele St; s/d without bathroom IR700,000/1,000,000; 🕸 🛜) Set back from 17 Shahrivar St behind a car park, the Darya is probably the pick of the town's budget places. Though they don't live up to the promise of the swish foyer, rooms have comfortable beds and the shared bathrooms (squat toilets only) are clean. Some English is spoken at reception.

Naz Hotel 2 HOTEL $$
(Map p221; ☏ 076-3222 6969; s/d incl breakfast IR2,000,000/2,500,000; 🕸 🛜) Secreted at the end of Haleh Alley, off Imam Khomeini St (and therefore quiet), this discreet number is a solid middle-of-the-road option with efficient staff and good facilities. Rooms are practical with no flouncy embellishments – just good lighting, strong air-con, back-friendly mattresses and salubrious bathrooms. There's an on-site restaurant.

★**Atilar Hotel** HOTEL $$$
(Map p221; ☏ 076-3222 7420; off 17 Shahrivar St; d incl breakfast IR3,700,000; 🕸 🛜) The professionally run Atilar is a great place to drop anchor in the centre. Expect efficient service, spacious rooms, excellent bedding, sparkling bathrooms, a good restaurant and very helpful English-speaking staff. Its central location is ideal if you want to immerse yourself in Bandar. Rooms on the upper floors are blessed with sea views.

🍴 Eating

Sajjad KEBAB $
(Map p221; ☏ 076-3223 0576; Imam Khomeini St; IR80,000-160,000; ☺ 8am-4pm & 7-10pm Sat-Thu, 8am-2pm Fri) Considered locally to offer the best kababs in town, this humming venue on the main drag has a well-priced menu and efficient waiters. Try the *barg* kabab, a copious (and delicious) concoction of beef (or lamb) fillet, onions and olive oil.

★**Fanoos** IRANIAN $$
(Map p221; ☏ 076-3225 4501; Imam Khomeini St; mains IR100,000-320,000; ☺ 11am-11pm) This trendy institution with colourful tables offers a wide choice of savoury appetisers and mains at very palatable prices. For a quick bite, opt for a well-prepared salad or a sandwich. It's right in the centre, opposite the City Center Shopping Center building. The menu is in Farsi only.

Bandar Abbas

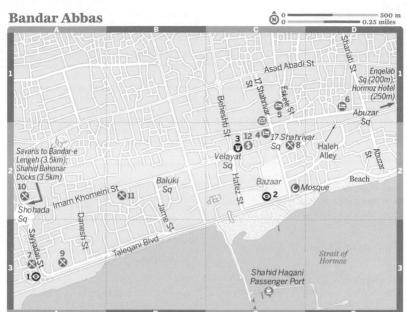

Qasr Honar
Traditional Restaurant IRANIAN $$
(Map p221; ☑ 076-3223 7475; Shohada Sq; mains IR300,000-400,000; ⊙11.30am-4pm & 7-11pm) After something extra-special? At this long-standing favourite you'll go giddy over the ever-so-slightly-OTT interior, with faux waterfalls, vines and stones that create a lush ambience. The kitsch decor will be forgiven the minute you taste the toothsome fish and meat dishes on offer. The wide-ranging menu (in English) includes vegetarian options.

Bandar SEAFOOD $$
(Map p221; ☑ 076-3355 2530; Sayyadan St; mains IR160,000-400,000; ⊙noon-2pm & 8-10pm Sat-Thu, noon-2pm Fri) If pressed, locals in the know will 'fess up and say that this discreet restaurant close to the bustling fish market is their favourite place to sample seafood in Bandar. The menu (in Farsi) features grouper, barracuda and shrimp, among others.

Fast Food Kavooki FAST FOOD $$
(Map p221; Taleqani Blvd, next to 15 Moj Alley; mains IR160,000-350,000; ⊙6-11.30pm) A great location on the seaside promenade and offerings that are a cut above the competition make this wildly popular place worth a vis-

Bandar Abbas

◉ **Top Sights**
1 Fish Market..................................A3

◉ **Sights**
2 Bazaar...C2
3 Indian Temple.............................C2

🛏 **Sleeping**
4 Atilar Hotel..................................C2
5 Hotel Darya.................................C1
6 Naz Hotel 2.................................D1

🍴 **Eating**
7 Bandar..A3
8 Fanoos..C2
9 Fast Food Kavooki.......................A3
10 Qasr Honar Traditional
    Restaurant................................A2
11 Sajjad..B2

ℹ **Information**
Atilar Safar Tour & Travel
    Agency...................................(see 4)
12 Darya Money Exchange..............C2
Morvarid Money Exchange........(see 12)

it. Tuck into well-made hamburgers, pizzas or fried chicken. Eat inside the castle-like building or claim a table on the terrace, which overlooks the sea.

ℹ Information

Atilar Safar Tour & Travel Agency (Map p221;
📱 076-3224 4033; atilar_safar@yahoo.com;
Atilar Hotel, off 17 Shahrivar St; ⊕ 8am-8pm
Sat-Thu, to noon Fri) Located in the foyer of
the Atilar Hotel, this extremely efficient agency
with English-speaking staff can organise tours
and book air, train and ferry tickets.

Darya Money Exchange (Map p221; Imam
Khomeini St; ⊕ 9am-2pm & 5-7.30pm Sat-Thu)
Located in an arcade beside the Indian Temple,
this place offers good rates.

Morvarid Money Exchange (Map p221; Imam
Khomeini St; ⊕ 8am-1.30pm & 4-8.30pm Sat-
Thu, 4-8.30pm Fri) Good rates and no hassle.
In an arcade beside the Indian Temple.

Main Post Office (Map p221; 17 Shahrivar St;
⊕ 8am-2pm Sat-Thu) About 50m north of 17
Shahrivar Sq.

ℹ Getting There & Away

AIR

If you need to purchase air tickets in Bandar, do
so at the **Atilar Safar Tour & Travel Agency**.

Domestic Flights

Iran Air, Aseman, Mahan Air and Kish Airlines
all fly in and out of Bandar. There are about five
weekly flights to Esfahan (one way IR2,900,000)
and Mashhad (one way IR3,500,000), two
daily flights to Shiraz (one way IR2,270,000),
four to six daily services to Tehran (one way
IR3,700,000) and two weekly flights to Yazd
(one way IR2,700,000).

International Flights

For the 30-minute hop to Dubai, you can fly Iran
Air (Thursday and Saturday), Kish Air (twice a
week) or FlyDubai (Monday, Wednesday, Friday
and Sunday). Flights cost from US$100 one way.

BOAT
Domestic Services

Ferries from Bandar to the nearby islands of
Hormoz (IR80,000, 40 minutes) and Qeshm

(IR150,000, 45 minutes) leave from the **Shahid
Haqani Passenger Port,** (Map p221; Taleqani
Blvd) near the bazaar.

International Services

Valfajr Shipping Co (📱 076-3342 5034;
http://valfajr.ir; IRISL Bldg, Eskeleh Shahid
Bahonnar Blvd, near Jahangardi Crossroads)
operates a thrice-weekly catamaran service
to Sharjah in the UAE. A one-way ticket in
economy class costs IR2,900,000; contact the
office or an accredited ticket agency to book
and purchase your ticket. It also has plans to
launch a weekly service to Dubai.

BUS

Buses leave Bandar for almost every city in Iran.
Tickets can be bought at the bus station, which
lies about 4km east of the centre.

SAVARI

Savaris for Bandar-e Lengeh (IR200,000 per
person, 2¼ hours) leave from a stand about
4km west of the centre.

Train

The train station is 8km northwest of the centre;
a taxi into the centre of town costs IR200,000.

You'll need to book well in advance for all train
trips, particularly if you want to travel at weekends or in holiday periods – use a travel agent.

GETTING AROUND

It's easy enough to get around Bandar on foot.
Taking taxis makes good sense in summer - a
trip within the city in a private taxi will cost about
IR100,000 while a taxi from the airport to the
town centre costs IR200,000.

Qeshm Island   جزیره قشم

📱 076 / POPULATION 117,000

The largest island in the Persian Gulf, Qeshm
is fringed with biologically diverse mangrove
forests, attractive beaches and 60 Bandari
villages. Its sun-scorched interior features
geologically significant canyons, hills, caves

BUSES FROM BANDAR ABBAS

DESTINATION	FARE (VIP/MAHMOOLY)	DURATION (HR)	DEPARTURES
Bushehr	IR550,000 (*mahmooly*)	8-12	3 daily, afternoons
Esfahan	IR700,000/520,000	14-16	5 daily, afternoons
Kerman	IR460,000/300,000	7-8	9 daily
Shiraz	IR350,000 (*mahmooly*)	11	frequent
Sirjan	IR230,000 (*mahmooly*)	4½	9 daily (Kerman service)
Tehran	IR650,000 (*mahmooly*)	14-17	frequent
Yazd	IR350,000 (*mahmooly*)	11	1-2 daily

and valleys, most of which are protected as part of the Unesco-recognised Qeshm Island Geopark – bliss for nature-lovers.

Qeshm is a duty-free zone, but in a gulf increasingly full of gleaming skyscrapers it remains refreshingly attached to the age-old Bandari way of life. If you're after an authentic island experience, Qeshm won't disappoint. Here, locals wear traditional dress, live in houses cooled by *badgirs* (wind towers) and work in boat-building yards turning out *lenges*, the large wooden cargo boats that have criss-crossed the gulf for centuries.

The island has an abundance of wildlife, including birds, reptiles, dolphins and turtles.

◉ Sights & Activities

◉ Queshm Town شهر قشم

Qeshm's main settlement lies on the far-eastern tip of the island. Many Iranians come here to shop in one of the numerous duty-free malls dotted around the centre. The main attractions include the crumbling **Ghal'e-ye Portoghaliha** (Portuguese Castle; Qeshm Town; IR20,000; ☉ 7am-3pm), the extensive **Bazar-e Bozorg** (off Pasdaran Sq, Qeshm Town; ☉ 8am-10pm), which extends along the main drag, and the family-friendly **Zeytoun Park**, a patch of greenery that overlooks a large beach.

◉ Laft لافت

This fishing village on the northern coast of Qeshm Island is the best place in Iran to encounter the fast-disappearing traditional culture of the Persian Gulf. Perched on a rocky slope overlooking the Khoran Strait, Laft has a wonderfully photogenic roofscape of *badgirs* and minarets. Views are best from the hill near the ruins of the

Portuguese-built **Naderi Fort**. From this vantage point you'll also see dozens of ancient wells and a white-domed *ab anbar* (water cistern).

◉ Hara Sea Forest حرا جنگل دریا

In the local dialect, *harra* is the word for grey mangrove, and this protected area is the Persian Gulf's largest mangrove forest – a definite must-see for nature-lovers. During spring, more than 150 species of migrating bird can be found here, including the great egret and the western reef heron. The finless porpoise, humpback dolphin, common dolphin and endangered green turtle are also regularly spotted. Boat tours are easily organised from Tabl or Laft.

◉ Qeshm Island Geopark پارک زمین شناسی قشم

In 2006 the 300-sq-km mountainous area on the western half of Qeshm Island was gazetted as the Qeshm Island Geopark, Iran's first member of the Unesco-listed Global Geopark Network (to be a member, parks must have a geological heritage of international significance and must use that heritage to promote the sustainable development of the local communities who live there). Whether you're driving through this area or looking at it on a Google Earth image, the geological significance is easy to see. Nature has carved steep-sided stone canyons, eroded flat-topped hills into sandy dunes and dramatic organ-pipe ridge lines, and dug deep into the island to form caves including **Khare Namaki** (Namakdan Cave), which at 6.8km is the longest known salt-cave system on earth.

The park is operated by a small but extremely motivated team that works with

PERSIAN GULF QESHM ISLAND

TRAINS FROM BANDAR ABBAS

DESTINATION	FARE (GHAZAL/NORMAL)	DURATION (HR)	DEPARTURES
Esfahan	IR616,000 (normal)	15½	1st week Sat, Mon, Wed & Fri, 2nd week Sun, Tue & Thu
Mashhad	IR1,168,000 (*ghazal*)	22	daily
Sirjan	IR357,000/259,000	5	daily (Tehran service)
Tehran	IR1,135,000/681,000	19	daily
Yazd	IR649,000/454,000	9	daily (Tehran service)

Qeshm Island

the Qeshm Free Zone Organization, Unesco, NGOs, ecotourism operators, Iranian naturalists and the local community to preserve the island's unique geology and heritage. Its programs include a project to create employment and socialisation opportunities for local women, the responsible aquaculture of pearls by the people of Berkeh Khalaf village and the propagation of native plants and mangroves by the people of Shibderaz and Dayrestan villages. For more information about the park stop by its **headquarters** (☑ 076-3525 2237; www.qeshmgeopark.ir/en; Imam Gholi Khan Sq, Qeshm Town; ☺8am-3pm Sat-Thu).

A highlight of the park is the sinuous **Chahkooh Canyon** (near Chahkooh village; IR20,000; ☺8am-7pm) seemingly carved into the earth by a master builder. The exposed rock and lack of plant life are quite startling and invoke a quiet sense of awe. The canyon's rounded edges and sharp corners create a symphony in stone of imposing proportions. You can climb up to the intersection of two narrow vertical canyons and drink from a *chah* (well) that has been used by shepherds for centuries.

One of the park's projects is the onshore preservation of the hawksbill and green turtles through community participation, which you can see in action in the picturesque village of **Shibderaz**. On the long beach here, where the turtles lay their eggs between April and July, locals work in shifts through the night to protect the eggs from predators.

○ Hengam Island جزیره هنگام

This lovely island off the southern coast of Qeshm is surrounded by impressive soft-coral reefs that offer great diving. Hengam is also known for its wildlife, including birds, gazelles and dolphins. The beaches are pristine, but only men are allowed to swim. The small fishing village overlooking the main beach features a row of simple eateries selling seafood. Get there by boat from the village of Shibderaz.

Hengam is also a dependable location to spot pods of dolphins, which usually congregate off the island's northeastern coast and can be seen frolicking around boats – a magical experience. From Shibderaz, local boatmen can arrange one-hour dolphin-watching excursions, taking in Hengam Island too. It costs IR1,560,000 per boatload (up to 10 people).

○ Other Sights

Valley of Stars   CANYON
(IR20,000; ☺8am-7pm) One of the most spectacular natural sites on Qeshm Island, the Valley of Stars features a series of majestic gorges and canyons that were formed over centuries by erosion. Wandering amid the valley is a magical experience – it's like stepping into a Dalí painting.

Naz Islands Beach   BEACH
This 3km-long golden strand caressed by clear, shallow and mostly calm waters is easily the most popular beach on Qeshm Island. In high season it's full of holidaying Iranian families. There are no amenities, but you

can enjoy paramotoring and camel riding along the beach. At low tide, it's possible to walk to the three tiny Naz Islands, which lie just offshore.

Khorbas Caves CAVE

(IR60,000; ⊙8am-7pm) In Qeshm Island's southeast you'll find this almost vertical limestone cliff pockmarked with caves. They are said to have sheltered local villagers seeking refuge from pirates and bandits raiding the island in the past centuries.

🏃 Activities & Tours

Sea Forest Tours BOATING

(Tabl; per boat IR700,000; ⊙7am-sunset Sat-Thu, to noon Fri) From the village of Tabl, south of Laft, local boatmen offer 45-minute tours of the sea forest in their motorised dinghies. Note that operation times can change with the season. Each boat can take six passengers.

🛏 Sleeping

Most lodging options are in Qeshm Town. They consist of low-key resorts, characterless midrange hotels and a few luxurious options. Outside Qeshm Town, accommodation options are virtually nonexistent bar a smattering of homestays that offer a window into a more traditional way of life. A recommended option for travellers, these family-run ventures offer basic bedding and bathroom facilities but are impeccably clean, extend warm welcomes and serve delicious food.

⭐**Mrs Fattahi's House** HOMESTAY $

(📱0936 783 9692, 0936 077 3467; Shibderaz; per person with half board IR700,000; ❄) This pleasing homestay is in Shibderaz village, a short stroll from the beach where turtles lay their eggs between April and July. Bedding is laid out in the lounge room in the evening, and the shared shower and squat toilet off the entrance hall get all the proper scrubbing. For more privacy, choose the room with private facilities in the courtyard.

The owner, Leila Fattahi, will happily arrange for you to watch local women making handicrafts or have them give you a Bandari henna tattoo. Various tours around the island can also be organised, as well as transfers to/from the jetty in Qeshm Town.

⭐**Mr Amini's House** HOMESTAY $

(📱0917 767 7601; Tabl; per person with half board IR900,000; ❄) Esmael Amini and his family welcome travellers into their attractive home in Tabl near the Harra Sea Forest and

are great hosts. Bedding is laid out on the floor at night in one of the 10 spotless rooms that are arrayed around a courtyard. Shared facilities (squat and Western-style toilets) are in top nick and the homemade meals are delicious.

Transfers from Qeshm Town (IR500,000 per car) as well as various tours can be organised.

Shabhaye Talai – Golden Nights Beach Restaurant CABIN $

(📱0933 597 9673, 0936 397 4103; www.shabhayetalai.com; Zeytoun Park, Qeshm Town; d with shared bathroom IR850,000-1,100,000; P❄🛜) No language barrier at this quirky venture: it's run by Annelie, from Germany, and her husband, Ali Reza, who both speak fluent English and go to great lengths to help travellers. They've set up four rooms in two trailers behind their renowned restaurant (p226). Rooms feel a tad boxy but are exceedingly neat and fit the bill if you're counting your rials.

There are plans to build cottages too. Annelie runs reputable tours and day trips around the island.

Alvand 2 HOTEL $$

(📱076-3522 8906; info@hotelalvand.com; Barg-e Sabz St, Qeshm Town; d incl breakfast IR2,800,000; ❄🛜) Opened in early 2017, this impeccably maintained hotel has a flashy lobby and carpeted rooms that are far classier than you usually get for this price in Iran. The buffet breakfast is excellent. Another draw is the on-site cafeteria. It's off a busy roundabout north of the centre – there's a bit of street noise, but nothing to lose sleep over.

Golden Beach Hotel RESORT $$

(📱0902 534 2900; www.goldenbeachhotel.ir; d IR2,750,000-3,500,000; P❄🛜) Right on an appealing beach (with a women's section) about 15km southwest of Qeshm Town, this low-key but well-kept resort with a family atmosphere is a great place to chill out for a few days. The 56 rooms aren't fancy, but they're functional and have sea views, and renovations are under way. The restaurant serves simple Iranian food.

Geopark Hotel HOTEL $$

(📱076-3522 1630; Eskele St, Qeshm Town; d incl breakfast IR2,500,000-3,000,000; ❄🛜) Conveniently located near the centre and the jetty, this old favourite has been given a thorough makeover and now flaunts bright rooms with scrupulously clean bathrooms

GOLABTOUN DOUZI SEWING

The women of Qeshm Island are known throughout Iran for their expertise in *go-labtoun douzi*, the sewing of colourful designs onto fabric, sometimes as embroidery and sometimes as an appliqué of sequins and/or hand-woven piping. These designs often incorporate images of flowers or local marine life such as turtles and starfish.

Traditionally, women have worked on *golabtoun douzi* at home and rarely left their houses, leading to their social isolation and total economic dependence on men. All this changed in 2003, when a group of women from Shibderaz and Berkeh Khalaf villages were given assistance from the UN Small Grants Program and a Tehran-based ecotourism outfit, the Avaye Tabiate Paydar Institute, to gather together and produce clothing and accessories featuring *golabtoun douzi*. The project was called 'Art for Conservation' and the products were sold to tourists, with the profits shared between the women and local conservation projects.

The program has been so successful that the women have now opened several shops and have significantly contributed to the funding of conservation efforts on the island. They now have the opportunity to become financially independent (with the collapse of the local fishing and boat-building industries, many have become the main breadwinners in their households) and they also leave their homes for part of each day to work with other women and operate the shops, giving them a hitherto unimaginable freedom of movement as well as opportunities to socialise and communicate outside their immediate families.

One of the shops is located in a handicraft booth at the entrance to Shibderaz village and two are in Berkeh Khalaf village (one next to the Khalij supermarket and another at the entrance to the village near the school). All three are open from 9am to 8pm daily, though they usually close for a few hours at lunchtime. The shops sell hand-decorated shawls, bags, headbands, hair clips and clothes.

and excellent bedding, pleasing earth and beige tones, and an attached quality restaurant. Opt for a room with a sea view.

✕ Eating

There are plenty of restaurants and cheap eateries in Qeshm Town. Around the island, eating options are much more limited and it's not a bad idea to bring some supplies. All homestays serve meals to their guests.

Nansito   BAKERY $
(☑ 076-3522 2592; Barg-e Sabz St, Qeshm Town; pastries from IR30,000; ⊙ 8am-11pm) Hands down the best bakery–pastry shop in Qeshm Town, Nansito has a tantalising array of doughnuts, muffins and breads. It's across the road from Alvand 2 hotel (p225) (look for the '30' sign).

★ Shabhaye Talai – Golden Nights
Beach Restaurant   SEAFOOD $$
(☑ 0936 397 4103; www.shabhayetalai.com; Zeytoun Park, Qeshm Town; mains IR170,000-380,000; ⊙ noon-4pm & 5pm-midnight; 🐾) Conveniently located at the edge of Zeytoun Park and benefitting from top-notch views of the beach, Shabhaye Talai is easily the most atmospheric

restaurant in Qeshm Town. It specialises in seafood, including lobster (from Larak Island) and shrimp, salads and burgers, all prepared to perfection. Vegetarian dishes are available, and the menu is in English.

It's also a fantastic place for a drink, and there's a happening buzz in the evening.

★ Kaleng   SEAFOOD $$
(Hengam Island; mains IR15,000-350,000; ⊙ 8am-5pm) Feel the sand between your toes at this casual family-run shack soothingly positioned right on the beach on Hengam Island. It serves only fresh fish and shellfish, as well as unforgettable *naan temoshi* (flat bread with minced fish and spices) and *sambouseh* (samosas) made to order.

Ghaleh Restaurant   SEAFOOD $$
(Qeshm Town; mains IR200,000-260,000; ⊙ 7-11pm) This simple place on the waterfront opposite the Ghal'e-ye Portoghaliha (p223) (*ghaleh* means 'castle' in Farsi) serves delicious Arabic seafood in the cool of evening. There's no printed menu – be sure to sample the famous *morakab* (octopus) if it's on offer. The terrace has great sea views.

ℹ Information

There's no shortage of banks in Qeshm Town. Private exchange shops, which offer the best rates, are harder to come by. You'll find one on Valiasr Blvd across the road from Qeshm Ferdosi Complex (look for the sign 'Exchange') and one inside Qeshm Ferdosi Complex.

ℹ Getting There & Away

AIR

Qeshm International Airport is in Dayrestan, about 43km southwest of Qeshm Town. Various domestic airlines, including Iran Air, Qeshm Airlines and Mahan Air, operate daily flights to/from Tehran Mehrabad (one way from IR3,100,000, 2¼ hours).

Qeshm Air and Mahan Air operate a few weekly flights to and from Dubai.

BOAT

Regular ferries (IR150,000, 45 minutes) run between Bandar Abbas' Shahid Haqani Passenger Port and Qeshm's Bahman Dock. There are also twice-daily ferries (IR90,000) between Hormoz Island and Qeshm Town.

A car ferry (IR100,000 return for one car and two passengers, seven minutes) crosses from Bandar-e Pol, 89km west of Bandar Abbas, to Laft-e Kohneh, near the village of Laft. The service operates 24 hours and ferries leave when full.

ℹ Getting Around

This is one place where it really helps to have a car. Consider hiring one at Bandar Abbas airport and bringing it to the island on the car ferry from Bandar-e Pol.

There is no public transport on Qeshm, and the only way of exploring or getting from one place to another without private transport is to hire a taxi for between IR3,300,000 and IR4,800,000 per day. Another option is to book a tour of the island with **Shabhaye Talai – Golden Nights Beach Restaurant** (p225).

Hormoz Island   جزیره هرمز

♪ 076 / POPULATION 6000

This little charmer of an island packs a big punch. What it lacks in size it more than makes up for in beauty and atmosphere. There's only one road and virtually no cars, just motorbikes and tuk-tuks; there are no showy resorts, just a smattering of simple homestays. Most of its visitors are day trippers from Bandar Abbas or Qeshm, so even the only settlement, Hormoz, is a sleepy little village that kicks off its shoes each evening and relaxes into mellow contemplation of the setting sun. The rest of the 42-sq-km island is virtually uninhabited. The rugged interior is a scenic geological wonderland of different-coloured volcanic rocks and soils, while the coastline is a stunning mix of golden beaches and awesome bluffs.

History

Until the 14th century the island was called Jarun Island – Hormoz was the name of a long-established commercial town on the mainland. That changed when repeated, bloody Mongol raids prompted the 15th emir of Hormoz to seek a home where his head had a greater likelihood of remaining on his shoulders. He and many of his subjects moved first to Kish Island but finally settled on Jarun.

Standing sentinel over the narrow entrance to the Persian Gulf, this new Hormoz soon became a grand emporium that attracted immigrants from the mainland and traders from as far away as India and Africa. Visitors to Hormoz described it as heavily fortified, bustling and opulent. European traders arrived and before long the Portuguese took over.

The Portuguese were eventually kicked out in the early 17th century and Shah Abbas I relocated the trading hub to the mainland fishing village of Gamerun, which he promptly named after himself (it's now Bandar Abbas). Without commerce the power of Hormoz was shattered and its people reverted to a traditional fishing lifestyle. These days the fishing industry on the island has collapsed, and the local economy has been crippled as a result.

⊙ Sights

★ Rainbow Valley   CANYON
(Hormoz) Rainbow Valley is a geologist's dream and an inspiration for artists and nature enthusiasts. Imagine a narrow valley with multi-hued earth and sand and colourful mountains in shades of red, purple, yellow, ochre and blue – the result of the uneven cooling of molten rock. On all sides, patches of colour form geometric patterns. This awesomely photogenic natural site is at its best in the late afternoon.

Valley of the Statues   LANDMARK
(Hormoz) This stunningly beautiful natural site is called 'Valley of the Statues' because here tall rocks have been sculpted into

PERSIAN GULF HORMOZ ISLAND

THE PORTUGUESE ON HORMOZ

In 1507 talented Portuguese admiral and empire builder Afonso de Albuquerque (also known as Afonso the Great) besieged and conquered Hormoz as part of his plan to expand Portuguese power into Asia. The sea fortress of Hormoz, which he ordered to be built in the same year, was completed in 1515.

With Hormoz Island as their fortified base, the Portuguese quickly became the major power on the waters of the Persian Gulf. Virtually all trade with India, the Far East, Muscat (Oman) and the gulf ports was funnelled through Hormoz, to which the Portuguese, through an administration known for its justice and religious tolerance, brought great prosperity for over a century.

But Portugal's stranglehold over vital international trading routes could hardly fail to arouse the resentment of Persia and the other rising imperial powers. In 1550 Ottoman forces besieged the fortress of Hormoz for a month but failed to take the island. In the early 1600s Shah Abbas I granted the British East India Company trading rights with Persia through the mainland port of Jask, thus breaking the Portuguese monopoly. In 1622 the shah, who had no naval power with which to challenge the Portuguese, cunningly detained the company's silk purchase until the English agreed to send a force to help liberate Hormoz. The Portuguese put up a brave defence but ultimately were forced off the island.

strange shapes by the elements. With a bit of imagination you can see a dragon, birds and mythical creatures. The site is located on a bluff that affords fantastic vistas of the coastline.

Ghal'e-ye Portoghaliha — FORTRESS

(قلعه پرتغاليها; Hormoz; IR50,000; ⊙8am-6pm) Some 750m north of the harbour is the famous Portuguese sea fort, probably the most impressive and ambitious colonial fortress built in Iran. Centuries of neglect have seen much of the original structure crumble into the sea, but the thick, muscular-looking walls and rusting cannons give it a haunting beauty. From the port, walk along the waterfront until you reach the fort's walls, then continue to walk with them on your left.

The archway opens onto a wide courtyard facing the sea. On the right as you enter is the ancient armoury. In the middle of the courtyard is a subterranean church that has some splendid vaulted ceilings. Before following the path marked by stones up onto the ramparts, you can visit the ground-floor room of the watchtower if the door is open. Higher up is another door to the submerged 'water supply', a surprisingly deep and impressive cistern encircled by an elevated interior walkway. The crumbling upper levels of the castle offer fine views back over the village to the starkly beautiful mountains, all surrounded by the blue gulf waters; it's a nice spot to sit, soak up the silence and let your mind wander back a few hundred years.

Salt Cascades — LANDMARK

(Hormoz) FREE One of Hormoz Island's star attractions, these multicoloured geological formations that consist of cliffs and towers of petrified salt combined with various types of rock have a Tolkienesque appeal. The site is inland but can easily be reached from the main road.

Snowy Mountains — LANDMARK

(Hormoz) It's hard not to be enthralled by the eerie lunar landscape in Hormoz Island's southwest, where a series of hills is covered with endless fields of salt crystals. And yes, they do look like 'snowy mountains'!

Mofanegh Beach — BAY

(Hormoz) This scalloped sandy bay south of the island is blessed with a gorgeous stretch of golden sand.

Museum & Art Gallery of Ahmad Nadalian — MUSEUM

(☑076-3532 3187; www.riverart.net/hormoz/; Hormoz Village; IR20,000) This quirky and very colourful museum – it occupies a brightly painted house smack dab in the village – shows the works of local artist Ahmad Nadalian. Artworks include sand paintings and dolls made of recycled materials. There's a video in English that explains his involvement with local communities.

🛏 Sleeping & Eating

There's no formal accommodation on the island, but you can easily arrange a homestay with the locals – count on IR950,000 per person, including breakfast. Ask at the ferry port or contact one of the tuk-tuk drivers at the jetty. You can also bring a tent and camp on a beach or in a valley, but there are no facilities – bring your own supplies.

ℹ Information

There are no exchange offices on the island. Bring enough rials.

ℹ Getting There & Around

The only way to get to Hormoz is by ferry (one way IR80,000, about 40 minutes) from the Shahid Haqani Passenger Port in Bandar Abbas.

There are usually four daily services. The last boats tend to return to Bandar between 4pm and 6pm, but to be safe you should aim to return much earlier than this. There are also twice-daily ferries (IR90,000, about 1½ hours) between Hormoz Island and Qeshm Town.

The winds around the island are notoriously changeable and boat services can be cancelled at any time. Be sure to check a local weather forecast before you leave Bandar Abbas.

Your boat will probably be met by a motorised cart (the local equivalent of a Thai tuk-tuk). You'll need to bargain with the tuk-tuk driver if you want him to take you to the castle and around the island – count on IR800,000 for a 90-minute tour, including Rainbow Valley.

Southeastern Iran
جنوب شرقی ایران

Best Places to Eat

➡ Hamam-e Vakil Chaykhaneh (p237)

➡ Shamsol Emare (p244)

➡ Keykhosro (p237)

➡ Shah Nematollah Sofrakhane (p240)

➡ Sofrakhane Sonati Qaleh (p243)

Best Places to Sleep

➡ Motevibashi Hotel (p240)

➡ Keykhosro (p236)

➡ Kashkiloo Lodge (p242)

➡ Parvin Homestay (p241)

Why Go?

While central Iran's gem cities are deservedly a far bigger draw, the southeast offers cave-houses, classic gardens, fortresses, deserted villages, oases and fabulous erosion patterns all set in scenery that intersperses great expanses of desert with chains of high mountains. Especially if you're mobile, this is a thrilling region in which to feel like a real-life explorer discovering timeless ancient sites...and enjoying them all on your own.

If planning a multiday loop, do it clockwise: Birjand and Kerman seem far more delightful if you've yet to see Yazd and Esfahan. And crossing the Dasht-e Lut westbound provides a scenic crescendo that reaches a glorious climax at the Kaluts.

When to Go

The best seasons to visit are typically early spring and late autumn. In Kerman city (around 1750m) and surrounding towns, elevation tempers the heat but summers are impossibly hot in the Lut desert. If you're there from June to August, arrive before dawn and be out by 9am.

In winter, desert temperatures are pleasant by day but can plunge to -10°C at night (when even oasis village homestays need heaters). Reaching the desert from Kerman involves crossing the mountains through a tunnel at nearly 2700m, which can be temporarily blocked by winter blizzards.

Meymand

ميمند

📞 034 / POPULATION 50 / ELEVATION 2220M

Continuously occupied for millennia – the lowest estimate is 2000 years – Meymand is a unique troglodyte village of *kiche* (cave-houses) burrowed into gently sloping composite rocks and backed by a wild-west scenic skyline of eroded crags and mesa-like rock formations. Set around a small stream-fed orchard, this Unesco site makes a memorable stop between Kerman and Yazd (or Shiraz).

Meymand Guesthouse (📞0913 392 6199; www.maymand.ir; Meymand; per person without bathroom foreigner/Iranian from

Southeastern Iran Highlights

① The Kaluts (p240) Watching the desert sun setting over extraordinary wind-eroded 'statues' before sleeping beneath the stars.

② Rayen (p242) Delving deeper into one of Iran's most appealing small towns, beyond its fabulous Arg.

③ Meymand (p231) Sleeping in a troglodyte cave house while learning about traditional shepherd lifestyles.

④ Old Deyhuk (p242) Seeking out a whole series of abandoned ghost villages around appealing Boshrooyeh.

⑤ Hamam-e Vakil Chaykhaneh (p237) Lunching with traditional music in a converted old bathouse within Kerman's historic bazaar.

⑥ Qa'en Castle Peak (p244) Descending from mountaintop fortifications as a muezzin calls to sunset prayers and the lights start to glow on the Bozorgmehr tomb.

IR500,000/280,000) provides the chance to sleep in a semi-restored ancient *kiche*. Its cave-rooms have been equipped with clean bedding, tree-branch shelving, heater and lamps for overnight stays. Yet with carpets on uneven floors and smoke-blackened rock ceilings it's easy to be transported to another time. The communal village toilets are nearby (with a sit-down toilet in the women's).

Tours often include Meymand as a stop between Kerman and Yazd, also incorporating Caravanserai Zein-o-din (p194) and Saryazd (p195). Some such tours might also add in the impressive, recently-discovered **Rageh Canyon** (www.rageh.ir), near Rafsanjan, or the eccentric **Bagh-e Sangi** (Stone Garden; near Balvard). Possibly Iran's most mind-blowing work of contemporary art this 'stone garden' was haphazardly created over decades by deaf/non-verbal shepherd Darvish Khan Esfandiarpur, who hung a square patch of some 150 dead fruit trees with a series of dangling rocks – some weighing as much as 30kg apiece. Later famed as the subject of Parviz Kimiavi's classic film *Garden of Stones*, Khan died in 2007. His lonely creation, in semi-desert, 6km east of Balvand, is still maintained by his son.

ⓘ Getting There & Away

From Shahr-e Babak's small **bus terminal** (☑ 034-3412 0557; Mehr Park Rd) there are buses to Yazd (IR110,000, 4½ hours) at 7.30am and 1pm and to Kerman (IR110,000, four hours) at 5am, 7am, 1pm and 2.15pm. For Shiraz or Bandar Abbas start with a savari to Sirjan (front seat/back seat/vehicle IR140,000/120,000/500,000, 1½ hours), organised through **Kiar Safar** (☑ 034-3412 0217; Mehr Park Rd), near the Shahr-e Babak terminal.

Taxis to Meymand from Yazd or Kerman charge around IR2,000,000. To save money head first by bus to Shahr-e Babak, then hire a taxi *dar bast* (private hire; around IR250,000, or IR300,000 after dark) for the 35km trip to Meymand.

Kerman   کرمان

☑034 / POPULATION 621,000 / ELEVATION 1760M

Big, sprawling Kerman is something of a cultural melting pot, blending Persians with the more subcontinental Baluchis, who dominate areas east of here. This mix is most evident in the long, ancient covered bazaar, which is the city's entrancing main highlight. Otherwise the region's main attractions – notably Mahan, Rayen and the Kaluts – are well out of town. All three can be seen on a long day trip from Kerman, but each now have their own decent accommodation if you'd prefer to escape the city bustle.

◉ Sights

Kerman is a large, somewhat formless city. The centre is roughly defined as the 3km stretch of Shari'ati/Beheshti streets between Azadi and Shohada Sqs (the latter is nearer the bazaar).

★**Bazar-e Sartasari**   MARKET
(بازار سرتاسري, Grand Bazaar; Map p234; Tohid Sq) Kerman's magnificent 'Sartasari' ('end-to-end') Bazaar is one of the oldest and most memorable trading centres in Iran. Its main thoroughfare stretches 1200m from Tohid Sq to Shohada Sq, the majority covered with classic vaulting and with several caravanserai courtyards off to the north. Within are several museums, bathhouses and religious structures, while the vivacity of the whole experience is enough in itself to keep visitors interested for at least an hour or two, especially in the morning and late afternoon.

ⓘ TRAVEL CAREFULLY

➡ Be prepared for infrequent buses and almost no English spoken beyond Kerman.

➡ Kerman (and the region east of it) is considered less secure than the rest of Iran due to petty crime, opium smuggling and the increased police/army presence. Things have much improved in the last decade, but the road from Bam to Zahedan – and especially from Zahedan to the Pakistan border – is still a concern.

➡ Currently several foreign embassies advise against travel to Bam and the region further east of it. Ignoring this advice could negate your insurance, so it's important to check the latest situation carefully. Read the **Thorn Tree** (www.lonelyplanet.com/thorntree) for recent traveller reports.

To explore, start from Tohid Sq. At the first *charsoq* (12-sided passage junction) you'll find lawn-filled **Ganj Ali Khan Sq.** Its colonnades have much of interest to peruse, including a **bathhouse museum** (Map p234; ☑ 034-3222 5577; Ganj Ali Khan Sq; foreigner/Iranian IR150,000/25,000; ⊙ 9am-1pm & 3-6pm), **coppercrafts bazaar** (Coppersmiths' Market; Map p234; Ganj Ali Khan Sq), the unusual little **Ganj Ali Khan Mosque** (Map p234; Ganj Ali Khan Sq; ⊙ 9am-1pm & 3-6pm Tue-Sun) FREE and a **money museum** (Mint Museum; Map p234; Ganj Ali Khan Sq; foreigner/Iranian IR150,000/20,000; ⊙ 9am-1pm & 3-6pm Tue-Sun), more interesting for its tall wind tower than the coin collection within. Behind, jewellers of the **gold bazaar** (Gold Bazar; Map p234) spill into a couple of old caravanserai yards.

A great place for lunch, tea or just to admire is the Hamam-e Vakil Chaykhaneh (p237), from which the vaulted main bazaar continues some 600m before reaching a more down-market section of open-air stalls. From there you can cut through **Masjed-e Jameh** (مسجد جامع, Jameh Mosque; Map p234; off Shohada Sq; ⊙ approx 7.30am-7.30pm) to reach Shohada Sq.

Museum of the Holy Defence   MUSEUM
(موزه دفاع مقدس; Map p234; Felestin St; foreigner/Iranian IR150,000/25,000; ⊙ 7am-12.30pm & 4.30-6pm) The Museum of the Holy Defence remembers the eight-year Iran–Iraq War through maps, gruesome photos, weapons, letters and intelligence documents from the war. There are brief summaries in English, but you'll need a guide to really interpret what you're seeing in any depth. That's not the case outside, however, where tanks and missile launchers overlook a mock battlefield complete with bunkers, minefield and pontoon-bridges across a waterway.

Moshtari-ye Moshtaq Ali Shah   MAUSOLEUM
(مشتری مشتاق علی شاه; Map p234; Shohada Sq; ⊙ 8am-1pm & 4-6pm) With prominent blue-and-white-tiled roofs dating from the late Qajar period, this attractive mausoleum is the last resting place of several Kerman notables, but it's remembered particularly (and named) for the 18th-century minstrel and dervish Moshtaq Ali Shah.

Masjed-e Imam   MOSQUE
(مسجد امام; Imam Mosque; Map p234; Imam Khomeini St, cnr 14th Alley; ⊙ 10.30am-1hr after sunset) The expansive Imam Mosque court-yard covers 6000sqm with tiled *iwans* (barrel-vaulted halls) on three sides. But it's the main southwest *iwan* that's the attraction here, a massive Seljuk structure in mostly uncoloured 10th-century brick. Small remnant sections of original Kufic plasterwork remain. Renovation has added back the missing majority, but in a new style easily differentiated from the original.

Muzeh Sanati   GALLERY
(موزه صنعتی هنرهای معاصر, Sanati Museum of Contemporary Art; Map p234; ☑ 034-3222 1882; Dr Beheshti St, btwn 18th & 20th Alleys; foreigner/Iranian IR80,000/30,000; ⊙ 9am-2pm & 4-6pm Tue-Sun winter, 9am-2pm & 5-7pm summer) The 'contemporary' section of this wide-ranging gallery is a selection of thought-provoking photographic and illustrative social commentary in the rear halls. There's also an intriguing modern section, including a grasping hand sculpture (credited somewhat questionably to August Rodin), two Béla Kádár watercolours and a small Kandinsky landscape. Some of the Iranian works are more compelling, notably Mohammad Javadipour's semi-cubist rural scene and Rajbali's classic Persian-style rendering of Shah Nematollah Vali.

Yakkchal Moayedi   HISTORIC BUILDING
(یخچال معایدی, Moayedi Ice House; Map p234; Kamyab St) This Safavid-era ice house has preserved not just the stepped, conical adobe dome but also the tall mud walls that created winter shade over what would have been shallow ice-making pools. When frozen, chunks of ice would be stacked between layers of straw deep within the *yakkchal* (ice pit) for use in warmer months.

Kerman National Library   HISTORIC BUILDING
(کتابخانه ملی کرمان; Map p234; Shahid Qarani St; ⊙ 7am-9pm Sat-Wed, to 3pm Thu) FREE The hushed Kerman National Library has modestly billed itself as Iran's 'greatest informatic research centre', but for non-Farsi speakers it's the architecture that appeals, a harmonious variation on late Qajar-era design with a forest of interior columns supporting vaulted bare-brick ceilings. Originally a wool-spinning factory, it was constructed between 1929 and 1934.

Gonbad-e Jabaliye   HISTORIC BUILDING
(گنبد جبلیه, Tower of Stone; Shohada St, Km3; foreigner/Iranian IR100,000/20,000; ⊙ 8am-12.30pm & 3-6pm Tue-Sun) Where Shohada St approaches the arid crags that abruptly mark the city's eastern edge sits this hefty

Kerman

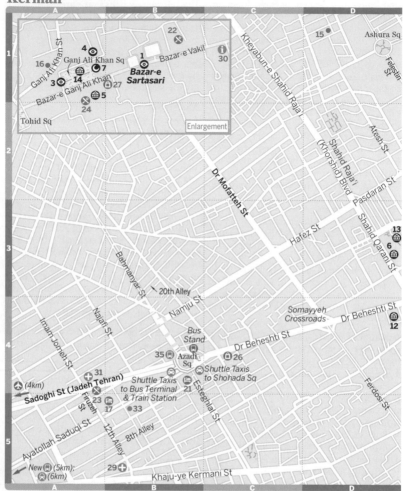

SOUTHEASTERN IRAN KERMAN

octagonal structure of mysterious provenance. Some scholars date it to the 2nd century AD and think it may have been an observatory; others say it was a tomb. Whatever its function, it's unusual hereabouts for being constructed mostly of stone – though the double-layered dome, added 150 years ago, is brick.

Today it houses a **museum of old gravestones**. (Be careful not to photograph the neighbouring army base!) Across the ring road from the tower, Shohada St continues east through a large park towards the eye-catching new **Saheb Zaman Mosque**.

Shuttle taxis from Shohada Sq head this way.

☞ Tours

Most hotels can arrange a taxi for daytours – notably combining Mahan, Rayen and the Kaluts. Akhavan Hotel (p236) offered us a taxi-only deal for €40/43 for a group of three/four people.

If you want to book an English-speaking guide yourself, reliable choices include **Iraj Rahmani** (☎ 0913 341 7865; www.tour guide.blogfa.com) and **Jalal Mehdizadeh** (Map p234; ☎ 034-3271 0185, 0913 142 3174;

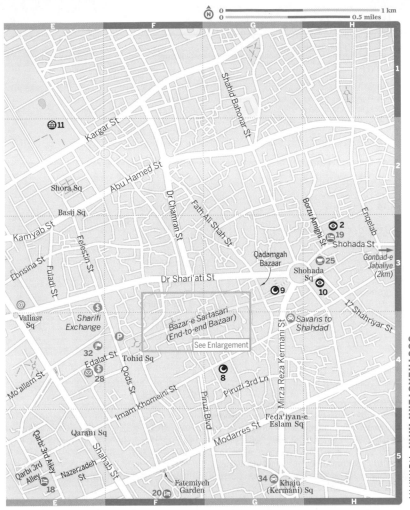

jalalguesthouse@yahoo.de; Jalal Guesthouse, 11 Gharbi 3rd St, near Ashura Sq) – both offer overnight Kaluts trips that include Shafiabad homestay accommodation (around US$150 per car) – while Kalut trips with **Vatani Caravan** (Map p234; ☎0913 343 5265; www.vatancaravan.com; Pasazh Ganj Ali Khan, Ganj Ali Khan St; ⊙call ahead) offer desert camping. Photographer **Amir Mahani** ('Saba'; ☎0913 342 5815; www.instagram.com/mahani59) offers many intriguing alternative trip ideas, too. Dozens more are members of the **Kerman Tour Guides Association** (Map p234; ☎034-3223 2855; Ganj Ali Khan Caravanserai).

🛏 Sleeping

Omid Guesthouse
HOTEL $

(Map p234; ☎034-3244 7488; Esteghlal Lane No 2, near Azadi Sq; s/tw/tr without bathroom IR350,000/460,000/550,000; 🅿) Female-run Omid is cleaner than most ultra-budget guesthouses; the simple rooms have a TV and fridge – and rock-hard beds – and guests can use the kitchen. The shared squat toilets and surprisingly good showers are in a corrugated hut partly shaded by grape-vines in the central yard.

The small reception room is through the fifth door to the right as you walk along

Kerman

2nd Alley from Estaghlal St. For cars, access is via Saduqi 1st Alley.

⭐ **Keykhosro**   HERITAGE HOTEL **$$**
(Map p234; ☑ 034-3312 7264; www.keykhosro house.com/default.aspx; Borzu Amighi St; dm IR60,000-80,000, s/d/tr IR1,000,000/2,000,00 0/3,000,000; ✳🔊) Built around a century ago to accommodate the priest of the nearby (and still active) **Zoroastrian temple** (Fire Temple; Map p234; Borzu Amighi 1st Alley; ⏱8am-noon & 3-6pm) FREE, this delightfully quirky place has two spacious guestrooms with beds attached to a beautiful, traditional-style restaurant–coffeeshop (p237). Or you can pay 'dorm' price and sleep on floor mats in the niches that are used as dining areas (available from 11pm).

Khane Pedari   GUESTHOUSE **$$**
(Map p234; ☑ 0913 142 3174; jalalguesthouse@ yahoo.de; Shahab 3rd Alley; dm/s/d €10/20/40) German-speaking tour guide Jalal has poured his heart into restoring his classically styled ancestral home to create an appealing little guesthouse. The two bigger rooms have 80cm-thick walls but others are tucked into curious recesses; the 'dormitory' means

a pair of domed cellar pod-rooms. There's a pleasant courtyard with twin pines, a shared kitchen and several sparkling new bathrooms.

Hezar Hotel   BOUTIQUE HOTEL **$$**
(Map p234; www.hezarhotel.ir; Qarbi 3rd Alley/ Neshat 5th Alley; d/tr/q IR2,300,000/3,500,00 0/4,000,000; ✳🔊) Barely signed in a residential yet reasonably central location, this low-profile hotel has a 1960s-retro minimalist style. There's a large, rectilinear lounge area and basement restaurant facing a small water feature. Rooms have excellent mattresses and decent bathrooms in two tones of brown marble. Triple and quad rooms are mini apartments (albeit with the kitchenette in the second bedroom).

Akhavan Hotel   HOTEL **$$**
(Map p234; ☑ 034-3244 1411; akhavanhotel@yahoo.com; Ayatollah Saduqi St; d/tr IR1,950,000/2,470,000; 🅿✳🔊) Faux Corinthian columns and King Kurosh (Cyrus) reliefs give a sense of slightly kitschy grandeur, while warmly decorated rooms are comfortable if slightly ageing. But the main attraction is

the chance to meet other travellers attracted by the gregarious, English-speaking Akhavan brothers, who make this Kerman's unofficial information booth for foreign tourists and organise popular day trips to regional sights.

✖ Eating

The city has several appealing traditional-style teahouse restaurants and some local specialities of its own, notably *boz ghormeh* (a minty mush of meat, beans and reconstituted dried whey) and *qotoq* (meatballs and potato in a zireh-flavoured roux) – add chunks of bread to it before eating.

★ **Hamam-e Vakil Chaykhaneh** TEAHOUSE $
(Map p234; ✆ 034-3222 5989; Bazar-e Vakil; mains IR150,000; ☺ 9am-6pm Sat-Thu, to 2pm Fri) Architecturally magnificent, this elegantly arched subterranean teahouse was built as a bathhouse in 1820. Live music – typically a singer accompanied by *santur* (dulcimer-like instrument) – plays throughout the day; meals are available from 1pm to 4pm. At other times, you can drink a variety of herbal or fruit teas or even smoke a *qalyan* (IR120,000). Note that there's a small admission fee (foreigner/Iranian IR30,000/10,000).

**Keykhosro Restaurant &
Coffeeshop** IRANIAN $
(Map p234; www.keykhosro.com; Borzu Amighi St; mains IR110,000-250,000, coffee IR70,000; ☺ cafe 6am-11pm, main meals 1pm-10pm) Keykhosro serves traditional Kermani specialities *qotoq* and *boz ghormeh* – as well as more standard Iranian favourites – in a lovely garden or in carpeted floor-seating niches that double as sleeping spaces for the co-managed boutique guesthouse (p236).

Max IRANIAN, PIZZA $$
(Map p234; ✆ pizzeria 034-3245 5595, restaurant 034-3245 8004; Jomhuri-ye Eslami Blvd; mains IR100,000-240,000; ☺ pizzeria 5pm-midnight, restaurant 11am-11pm) Max's large, contemporary fast-food place serves unusually good Iranian pizza in the vividly yellow-green upstairs section. Easily missed in the basement below is the atmospheric traditional Iranian restaurant, where the friendly English-speaking owners help you understand the fair-priced menu, which includes the local speciality *boz ghormeh* (mutton-whey mush).

Sofrakhane Zirebazarche IRANIAN $$
(Map p234; ✆ 0913 191 2169; Zirebazarche Alley; mains IR100,000-250,000, shishlik IR385,000, qalyan IR100,000; ☺ 9am-8.30pm mid-Mar–Sep, to 6pm Oct–mid-Mar) If you can find it, this brick-domed subterranean cavern makes an appealingly untouristy alternative to the larger Hamam-e Vakil teahouse. It's not quite as atmospheric but food is served for longer hours and at prices that are slightly lower.

Walking from Tohid Sq, turn right at the first *charsoq* (12-sided passage junction), then turn left at the first alley and look for 'Traditional Restaurant' banners.

🍷 Drinking & Nightlife

Sonati Kohan TEAHOUSE
(Map p234; Shohada St, cnr 2nd Alley; qalyan/tea IR100,000/70,000; ☺ 10.30am-11pm) At the rear of a preserved semi-historic building, this tea garden throws together an intriguing, stylistic mishmash of palm-frond shelters, old niche-style rooms and plastic-tarp shelters to house smokers, who can choose from a menu of 27 flavours for their water pipes.

Paeiz Cafe COFFFF
(www.instagram.com/paeiiz_cafe; Hamze Blvd, cnr 26th Alley; coffee IR80,000-120,000; ☺ 9am-11.30pm Sat-Thu, 5pm-11.30pm Fri) Great caffeine fixes provided by baristas whose beards are more Hackney hipster than Mashhad mullah. Tables are old cable spools, a bicycle hangs from the wall and female customers seem unusually relaxed, wearing jeans and allowing glimpses of hairlines.

🛍 Shopping

As well as carpets, Kerman is known for a local craft called *pate* squares or diamonds of cloth intricately embroidered with brightly coloured designs. *Kolompeh* (date-stuffed biscuits), sold at Novin (Map p234; Bazar-e Sartasari; ☺ 9am-8.30pm), and local style *gaz* (nougat with pistachios) make popular edible souvenirs.

Iran Handicrafts Organisation ARTS & CRAFTS
(Map p234; Dr Beheshti St, btwn 2nd & 4th Alleys; ☺ 9am-1pm & 4.30-8.30pm Sat-Thu) Government craft emporium proffering a high-quality, fixed-priced selection of beautiful enamelware, Hamadan pottery, leatherwork and glassware. *Khatam* (intricate inlay-work) boxes cost from IR120,000.

❶ Information

DANGERS & ANNOYANCES

➜ Kerman is reasonably safe but the number of drug addicts makes it worth taking extra care at night.

➜ Iranians joke that drivers here are particularly devil-may-care in their attitudes to road safety. If you've got your own wheels, drive carefully.

➜ For years, overpass construction has turned Azadi Sq into a chaotic traffic bottleneck forcing vehicles to take vast detours just to get across the street.

INTERNET ACCESS

Signal (Map p234; Valiasr Sq, Atlas Shopping Centre; per hr IR70,000; ⏱8.30am-2.30pm & 4-9pm) is one of two *coffeenets* (internet cafe) in the shopping centre on the northeast side of Valiasr Sq. There are several more close to the Hotel Omid.

MEDICAL SERVICES

Emam Reza Pharmacy (Map p234; Imam Jameh 1st Alley; ⏱24hr) Located downstairs beneath a dress shop.

Darmangah-e Amir Almomenin (Map p234; ☎034-3252 0668; Firuze St, btwn 12th & 14th Alleys; ⏱24hrs)

MONEY

Sharifi Exchange (Map p234; ☎0913 341 6474, 034-3222 3502; Qods St, cnr 1st Alley; ⏱9am-1pm & 3-6pm) One of three exchange shops near the bazaar's western end.

POST

Post Office (Map p234; Edalat St; ⏱8am-2pm Sat-Thu)

TOURIST INFORMATION

Behind a beautifully moulded entrance, the so-called **Econo Museum** (Map p234; Kerman Bazaar; ⏱9am-1pm & 3.30-6pm) is actually a series of craft shops and workshops off hidden courtyards – but the ticket desk doubles as a tourist info office of sorts, with free city maps if you ask for them.

TRAVEL AGENCIES

Parse Owj (Map p234; ☎034-3244 6003; www.parseowj.com; Ayatollah Saduqi St, cnr 7th Alley; ⏱8am-7.30pm Mon-Thu, 9am-12.30pm Fri) Reliable agency selling air, train and bus tickets.

VISA EXTENSIONS

Management of Foreigners Affairs Office (Map p234; ☎034-3218 3269; Mo'allem St; ⏱8am-1.30pm Sat-Thu) For visa extensions. Arrive as early as possible; once your application has been received, pay the fee around the corner at a poorly marked branch of **Bank Melli** (Map p234; Adalat St; ⏱7.30am-1.30pm Sat-Wed). If all goes well you might have the extension the same day.

❶ Getting There & Away

AIR

The airport is on the western edge of the city. There's no airport bus; a taxi to the city centre costs around IR150,000.

Flight destinations include:

Tehran (IR1,500,000 to IR3,500,000) At least twice daily

Esfahan (IR1,980,000) Monday, Wednesday, Friday and Saturday

Mashhad (IR1,880,000) Wednesday and Sunday

BUSES FROM KERMAN TERMINAL

DESTINATION	FARE IN IR (VIP/MAHMOOLY)	DURATION (HR)	DEPARTURES
Bandar Abbas	370,000/250,000	7–8	10.15am, 11.30am, 2.30pm, 9–11pm
Birjand	–/250,000	10	8.30pm
Esfahan	490,000/280,000	9–11	noon, 5pm, 9–10.30pm
Mashhad	690,000/420,000	13–15	2pm–8.30pm
Shahr-e Babak	–/110,000	3–4	8.30am, 12.30pm, 2pm, 5pm
Shiraz	490,000/215,000	8	6.15am, 7.15am, 8.30pm, 9.30pm
Tehran	690,000/420,000	14–16	frequent 2.30pm–10pm
Yazd	280,000/160,000	4–5	regular 5am–5pm

Shiraz (IR1,500,000) Tuesday, Thursday, Friday and Sunday

BUS, MINIBUS & SAVARI

The **new bus terminal** (Terminal Adine Kariman) is well out of the centre in the southwest of Kerman, but some major bus companies have offices around Azadi Sq, including **Taavoni 7** (Map p234; www.adlt7.ir; Behmanyar St; ⊘8.30am-8.30pm Sat-Thu, 9am-noon Fri) and **Seiro Safar** (Map p234; Behmanyar St; ⊘7.30am-1pm & 4-8.30pm). Travel agencies such as **Parse Owj** (p238) can also book buses on your behalf.

For Shahr-e Babak, either take a direct bus from the main bus terminal or go via Sirjan in savari hops, starting from Azadi Sq.

To Shahdad (for the Kaluts) a handful of **savaris** (Map p234; ☑ 0913 398 1708; Mirza Reza Kermani St, cnr 5th Alley; front/back seat IR120,000/100,000, 1¾ hours) wait on a small patch of ground behind the Torse'e Ta'avoni Bank building (near the Imam Khomeini junction). Continue south down Mirza Reza Kermani St to Khaju Sq to find **savaris to Mahan** (Map p234; Khaju (Kermani) Sq; per person/car IR40,000/160,000, 40 minutes). Or cross the street and take a city bus for the 5km ride out to Sarasiyab Sq, where you'll find transport to Rayen (bus/savari IR60,000/120,000 1¼/1½ hours).

TRAIN

Trains to Tehran leave daily at 3pm (IR503,000, arrives 5am) and some days at either 4pm (IR930,000, arrives 7am) or 11.45pm (IR429,000, arrives 2.20pm). The 3pm and 11.45pm services stop at Yazd (IR215,000, 6¼ hours) but not Esfahan.

To Mashhad (IR640,000 to 810,000) trains depart at 1.10pm on Mondays, Tuesdays, Fridays and Sundays, arriving at 4.40am.

Buying tickets from a travel agency saves a long trip to the **train station** (☑ 034-3211 0762) which is 8km southwest of town (it's IR80,000 by private taxi from Azadi Sq).

ⓘ Getting Around

Taxis wait at key points around Azadi Sq. **Shuttle taxis for the bus and train stations** (Map p234; Ayatollah Saduqi St, Jadeh Tehran) stop directly west of the square on the north side of Saduqi (Tehran) St but finding a shared ride can take a while as most people seem happy enough to pay IR80,000 to go *dar bast* ('closed door', meaning a private hire).

For the bazaar, **shuttle taxis towards Shohada Sq** (Map p234) pick up briefly at the southern side of Azadi Sq, while buses start from that square's otherwise closed-off northeast quadrant. (This may change in a year or two when the Azadi Sq roadworks are finished.)

Around Kerman

Mahan   ماهان

☑034 / POPULATION 19,600 / ELEVATION 1905M

Picturesque Mahan, 35km southeast of Kerman, is a low-key town that's widely famed for its shrine and Unesco-listed Persian garden. With a superb little heritage hotel and a fine (and unpretentious) teahouse at the shrine-area, it's worth considering Mahan as an alternative place to stay in the Kerman region.

⊙ Sights

**Aramgah-e Shah
Ne'matollah Vali**   MAUSOLEUM

(آرامگاه شاه نعمت الله ولی; Imam Khomeini St, opp 18th Alley; ⊘8am-10pm) FREE The physical and spiritual heart of Mahan is filled by the impressive mausoleum complex of dervish-mystic and poet Shah Ne'matollah Vali, who died in 1431 (aged more than 100!). Built five years after his death by an Indian king who followed his teachings, the complex has received many additions, most notably the **Abbasid blue cupola** and **Qajar-era twin minarets**. The two charming, pond-filled courtyards have roosting birds in the trees who are all a-twitter at dusk.

The main tomb lies beneath a 17m dome surrounded by carpets incorporating pentagram symbols, some with elements of backward mirror writing. An easily missed highlight is a tiny **prayer chamber** whose walls and ceiling are covered with calligraphy in a spiral pattern.

There is a small **museum** (ticket required) but it was under reconstruction at time of research. To access the rear Abbasid courtyard you might need to ask a guardian to open the heavy doors behind the main shrine room (a donation is appropriate).

Bagh-e Shahzde   GARDENS

(باغ شازده, Shah Zadeh Garden; foreigner/Iranian/parking IR300,000/200,000/30,000; ⊘9am-10pm) Arriving at these handsome gardens is like being beamed onto a different planet. One second you're in the arid semidesert, the next it's all flowing mountain water and tall green trees. Built in 1873, the garden rises to a small villa that was once the residence of Abdul Hamid Mirza, one of the last princes of the Qajar dynasty. It now houses a handicraft shop, restaurant (p240) and teahouse. In the early evening it looks charming when floodlit.

The gardens are well outside Mahan, 1.2km south of the southern ring road and 5km from the mausoleum. There's a small taxi stand in the car park; it'll cost IR50,000/300,000/600,000 to Mahan/Kerman/Rayen.

Sleeping

Mahan Tourist Inn   HOTEL $
(Hotel Jahangardi; ☑034-3377 2700; aminhotel @yahoo.com; Qarani Sq; s/d/ste IR650,000/890,000/1,420,000; P⭐@) Designed throughout with pointed arch effects for a sense of local style, this hotel offers reliable midrange quality at very affordable prices. It's on a roundabout 800m north of the Aramgah, up Imam Khomeini St.

★**Motevibashi Hotel**   HERITAGE HOTEL $$
(☑034-3377 8613; www.motevibashi.ir; Mahan Aramgah; d/tr/q IR1,600,000/2,400,000/3,200,000) The classic, 180-year-old house of Aramgah's one-time *motevibashi* (caretaker) has been tastefully converted into an eight-room boutique hotel using traditional fabrics and earthenware decoration, with full mod cons and breakfast served on the grand porch facing the shrine. Most rooms are triples; the one double is a little small but adorably appointed.

Eating & Drinking

Sofrekhane Shah Zadeh   IRANIAN $$$
(☑0913 664 8213; Bagh-e Sharzde; mains IR138,000-497,000; ☺noon-4pm & 6-9pm) Within the upper section of the Shahzde gardens (p239), this restaurant offers private courtyard niches and two multidomed dining rooms, one cosier but darker, with lamplit tables. As well as typical kabab meals the menu includes minty *boz ghormeh*, a meat/bean mush with *kashk* (reconstituted whey) – delicious (if somewhat small portions). There's an additional 15% service/tax not included in menu prices.

★**Shah Nematollah Sofrekhane** TEAHOUSE
(☺9am-10pm Sat-Thu, noon-10pm Fri) Hidden within the Aramgah complex, this brick-domed teahouse offers spiritual music and a short menu of well-made Iranian favourites, including a minty *kashke bademjan* (mashed eggplant with whey; IR70,000). Enter between the first and second courtyard gardens through the doorway opposite the small museum.

ℹ Getting There & Away

Savaris to Kerman (Imam Khomeini St; per person/car IR40,000/160,000) start 600m north of the Aramgah shrine. The spot is outside a shop marked 'Apple Mobile', some 200m south of the Tourist Inn. Across the road, the little office marked 'VIP Scania' is a travel agency where you can buy onward tickets for bus services departing from Kerman.

To Rayen, taxis want around IR800,000 return, including waiting time while you visit the Arg.

A taxi one-way to the Bagh-e Shahzde costs IR50,000/300,000 from central Mahan/Kerman. There's no need to have it wait – there are usually a couple of cars waiting for returning passengers, at least till around 8pm.

The Kaluts (Lut Desert)

With dramatic eroded mesas reminiscent of Monument Valley, towering sand dunes to challenge those of Arabia and a claim to being the world's hottest desert, it's not hard to see why the Dasht-e Lut is considered one of Iran's most exciting adventure destinations.

You can get a good glimpse of the region's magnificence by driving the Nehbandan-Shahdad road, by taking a day trip excursion from Kerman, or by renting a taxi from Shahdad. But to reach the dunes you'll need to do a tour with a 4WD and experienced guide. Don't attempt to visit by day in summer, when midday ground-temperatures can rise to an almost unimaginable 65°C.

An area of around 30 oasis villages – known as the Takhab – stretches a green swathe of date palms around 25km from the large but sleepy town of Shahdad to the twin villages of Shafiabad–Dehseif. Here you'll find a mud-walled 'caravanserai', actually a **citadel** (Dehseif), with shattered remnants of many former buildings surviving within atmospherically crumbling earthen walls. The nearby **adobe houses** are similarly fascinating for their rustic simplicity.

North of that the desert starts. The most impressive part of the landscape here are five- to 10-storey high *yardangs* ('sand castles') with vertical or stepped sides. They are especially spectacular at dawn and sunset when light and shadows turn the scene into a shimmering canvas of gold and brown.

'Kaluts' actually applies more accurately as the general term for a series of different erosion patterns – the most dramatic are fortress-like vertical towers and stepped mesas. The best examples are near a parking area signed 'Kalout'. Further east are *tokhmemorghi* (egg-shaped muddy hillocks) and essentially similar *merikhi* (rounded on one side but sharply cut into verticals on the other).

Amid all the mirages, water really does flow through the desert: at **Rud Shur bridge** you'll cross a real, if tiny, meandering stream. Another 30km east, the erosion pattern becomes a series of vertically serrated cliffs.

The desert has a whole palate of other erosion patterns, visible for over 80km along the Birjand–Kalout–Kerman road – a route that's more satisfying driven east to west so that the Kaluts come as a grand finale. If you're driving this way **Deh Salm** (Nehbandan–Shahdad Rd, Km80) oasis village is a delightful discovery, and with a well-organised 4WD tour (and advanced paperwork) you can experience the vast **Rigi Yalan sand dunes.**

Activities

Kalut Bike & Camel Rides ADVENTURE SPORTS
(Kalout; per ride IR100,000; ☉ Thu & Fri Oct-Mar) All day on Thursdays and to sunset on Fridays during the cooler months, freelancers appear at the small area of stable desert known as Kalout proffering five-minute rides on quad bikes, trail bikes or camels to tourists and weekenders. It's not long enough to get beyond the nearest *yardang* ('sand castle') but there's a certain exhilaration in the experience.

Tours

Guided tours (p234) are available from Kerman that take in the Kaluts as well as Rayen and Mahan. You can take a day trip or else opt for a night's stay in Shafiabad – or even camp overnight in the open desert.

If you're starting from Birjand, Asia Parvaz (p244) does multiday Lut Desert tours. **Mojtaba Heidari** (www.mojirantrip.com) has an appealing itinerary combining the Kaluts as part of a longer desert-loop tour.

Sleeping

A great part of the Kalut desert experience used to be sleeping outside under the night sky in what was dubbed the 'million-star hotel'. These days such camping is considered dangerous by some locals (thanks

partially to poisonous spiders), but Hossein Vatani (p235) is one guide who still offers the full outdoors experience.

The so-called **Shahdad Desert Camp** (Desert Camp Rd, Km8, Shafiabad; per person IR100,000), 8km from Shafiabad, while cheap and akin to camping, provides covered but semi-exposed sleeping places – though floodlights and paved areas mean you won't really get to drown in that magical sea of starlight.

★ **Parvin Homestay** HOMESTAY $
(☑ Zahra Parvin 0915 740 0872; Deh Salm; per person with breakfast IR500,000) This ultra-simple, 40-year-old adobe house has just two thick-walled rooms, one adorned with embroidery on old rice sacks and the other with decor ingeniously fashioned from recycled plastic bottles. You'll sleep on clean floor mats; the toilet is across the classic, desert-style courtyard. A two-minute walk takes you past ruined buildings into the beautiful date-palm groves.

Kalut Ecolodge HOMESTAY $
(☑ 0913 764 8279; Shafiabad; per person with half-board IR500,000) Kalut Ecolodge is marginally the most charming of half a dozen closely grouped homestays in Shafiabad village, thanks in part to friendly hostess Sekina Hajiabadi, who can speak a few words of English. There's a small, tree-shaded yard, a large communal sitting area around the kitchen and bedrooms are cleaner than average, though don't expect too much.

Yadegar Ecolodge HOMESTAY $
(☑ 0913 396 6839; 3rd Alley, Dehseif; per person incl half-board IR500,000) Yadegar is the only homestay within the intriguingly timeless settlement of Dehseif, tucked behind

SOUTHEASTERN IRAN THE KALUTS (LUT DESERT)

that village's ruined caravanserai/citadel ruin. It's just 800m north of the Shafiabad junction, but it's often empty as it's a little harder to find than the alternatives in Shafiabad.

★ **Kashkiloo Lodge** BOUTIQUE HOTEL **$$**
(☏ 0913 744 4614, 034-3375 0110; www.kash-kiloo.ir; Shafa St, cnr 7th Alley, Shahdad; d/tr IR1,200,000/1,700,000; **P ✳ 🛜**) By far the most comfortable logings in the Kaluts region, Kashkiloo is a very professional six-room mini hotel combining stylishly modernised traditional elements and backing onto a walled palm garden that is colourfully lit at night. Air-con makes it a great choice for visits closer to the summer season. A wide variety of excursions are organised here, too.

❶ Getting There & Away

There is no public transport to the Kaluts. The nearest access point with a savari link is Shah-dad, 24km south of Shafiabad, to which savaris (front/back seat IR120,000/100,000) run from Kerman's **Chahara Imam** (p239). In Shah-dad, the savaris start from the easily missed office of **Golestan va Dustan** (☏ 034-3375 0022; Qavam St; ⊙ 5am-4pm), 300m east of the main traffic circle. From here a return taxi to Rud Shur bridge with a stop at Kalout shouldn't cost more than IR800,000.

Rayen راين

☏ 034 / POPULATION 11,000 / ELEVATION 2200M

The highlight of this charming small town, 100km southeast of Kerman, is **Arg-e Rayen** (Valiasr 2nd Alley; foreigner/Iranian IR150,000/25,000; ⊙ 8am-sunset), one of Iran's most impressive fortress-citadels. The Arg's vast adobe walls top a gentle slope directly south of central Rayen. Inside is a castle within a castle. Some sections are very ruinous but, wandering through the extensively restored governor's quarters, you can easily imagine the trepidation that supplicants must have once felt approaching the powerful local ruler through dark passages and hidden inner courtyards.

Superb views from the battlements above the gatehouse reveal a backdrop of **Mt Hezar** (4420m).

In Rayen, at the eastern end of 17 Shahri-var St (turn off Imam St at the mountaineer statue) you'll find six-domed **traditional houses**, along with a little maze of mud-walled footpaths between pomegranate orchards.

Five beautifully appointed modern apartments are available at **Shabhayeh Rayen** (☏ Ruhollah 0913 298 6516; Imam St, cnr 11th Alley; d/q IR1,450,000/2,000,000; ✳), three minutes walk from the Arg. For budget travellers there's the far less appealing

KHORASAN'S GHOST VILLAGES

With more sanitary housing being provided for rural populations, some villages have been essentially abandoned, with a new settlement either built next to it, or possibly a kilometre or two further away. In many cases the old houses are now used as animal pens, or have simply been left to crumble – either way they offer a remarkable sense of discovery for visitors who stumble upon them.

In the Boshrooyeh area, the 17-family hamlet **Haogand** (off Boshrooyeh–Raqeh Rd) is a good example, with the added bonus of a mud-walled fortress used as a barn and a view of the **Qaleh Dokhtar** castle on the horizon. At bigger **Eresk** (Deyhuk–Raqeh Rd, Km 51), old and new areas are somewhat intermingled, with many domed mud houses still used and each built – almost on top of the next – around a trio of rock-top watchtowers. Easily accessed just 1km from the Kerman–Mashhad highway, **Old Deyhuk** has a wonderful photogenic integrity set around a low, rocky ridge with a single round tower. Further south the villages of **Marghoob** (off Kerman–Mashhad Hwy) – pretty but very decrepit – and especially **Esfandiar** (off Kerman–Mashhad Hwy) – with ruins up to three storeys high – are set high on mountain foothill slopes, fronted with terraced gardens and far enough from their respective newer incarnations to create a real sense of wonder.

There are yet more discoveries to be made around Qa'en (p244) – where **Afin** (Effin) is touted as a potential 'tourist village' – but we prefer the smaller and easier-to-reach **Khonik Sofla** (off Qa'en–Taybad Rd) for its low-rise domed integrity, and the crumbling 'palace tower' at nearby **Khonik Olya**.

Hotel Tala Arg (☑ 034-3376 1578; Modarres St, cnr 8th Alley; s/tw IR350,000/450,000; ❄), amid mechanics' workshops 300m north of Azadi Sq, or the seasonal option of bedding down in the tea cottages at **Shahriyar** (☑ 0913 841 5846; Qarbi St; qalyan & tea set IR100,000; ☺ Mar-Sep).

Several fast-food and sandwich shops are dotted along Imam St and around Azadi Sq. **Khansalar** (Imam St, Imamzadeh Sq; mains IR80,000-190,000; ☺ noon-4pm & 7.30-11pm) serves excellent-value kabab meals in a pleasant environment, while other garden restaurants open from March to September.

Getting There & Away

Rayen is 22km off of the Kerman–Bam highway, just beyond a major police checkpost (carry your passport).

Savaris to Kerman (IR120,000, 1¼ hours) leave from Azadi Sq, 1km north of Rayen's Arg. Around 30m up Modarres Blvd from the savari point, **Peykis Savar** (☑ 0913 197 6950) has buses to Kerman (IR60,000, 1½ hours), leaving roughly hourly.

Birjand بیرجند

☑ 056 / POPULATION 184,000 / ELEVATION 1530M

A logical stop if you're making the long cross-desert drive between Mashhad and Kerman via the Kaluts, Birjand is the capital of South Khorasan province, known for saffron, barberries and especially annab (jujube fruit, considered a herbal remedy for coughs and colds). In winter, snowtopped mountains give Birjand's southern flank an impressive backdrop, while to the north, assorted ridges and triangular geological protuberances create a contrasting desert feel.

The sprawling city hasn't done a great job at preserving its once fascinating old mud-brick buildings, but the **Qaleh Tarikhi** (Burg; Imam Hossein Sq, Jomhuri-e Eslami Blvd; IR10,000; ☺ 8am-noon & 3.30pm-11pm) fortress has been restored, and looks particularly impressive at night when glowing with the lights of the teahouse-restaurant that occupies its ground floor. There are a few notable historic buildings and the **Akhbarieh Garden** (Valiasr Sq; ☺ 9am-1pm & 4-7pm Tue-Sun, closed Fri mornings) FREE is Unesco-listed (though once you visit you might ask why).

Birjand is also a possible launch-point for visits to Forg, Boshrooyeh and the towering sand dunes of Rigi Yalan (tour only).

Sleeping

Hotel Ghaem HOTEL $
(☑ 056-3221 1244; Jomhuri 15th S, Imam Khomeini Sq; s/d/tr IR670,000/966,000/1,290,000; ❄ ☎) In a bland, new, grey-white stone building set back from Imam Khomeini Sq, the Ghaem's location is excellent and rooms are good value: unfussy but comfortable enough, with wi-fi and en suite bathrooms, plus settees in better versions. Toilets are sit-down style in two of the suites.

Birjand Mountain Grand Hotel RESORT $$
(☑ 056-5832 3368; www.bmgh.ir; Band Amir Shah; s/d/tr without view IR1,374,000/1,810,000/2,224,500, with view IR1,526,000/2,125,000/2,616,000; ℗ ☎) Tucked into ruggedly contoured hills in a sharp stream valley around 4km southwest of Birjan's southern ring road, this upper-market layered hotel has plenty of fashionable notes. The charming setting is ideal for strolling between the colourful little teahouses nearby, as long as you don't mind being a 20-minute drive from the centre.

Birjand Tourist Hotel HOTEL $$
(Hotel Jahandardi Birjand; ☑ 056-3222 2320; www.jahangardi-birjand.ir; Artesh St; s/d/tr IR1,650,000/2,354,000/2,940,000; ❄ ☎) Recently refurbished with a pleasant restaurant and coffeeshop. Some rooms have rather busy decor with whole-wall picture wallpaper, but many have sit-down toilets en suite; you also get a basket of toiletries and there's at least one English-speaking receptionist. The location isn't ideal but with discounts as much as 40% it's worth considering in the low seasons.

Eating & Drinking

⭐ **Sofrakhane Sonati Qaleh** IRANIAN $$
(Birjand Fortress; mains IR120,000-220,000; ☺ 8.30am-1pm mid-Mar–Sept, 4pm-midnight Oct–mid-Mar) Although the menu is somewhat standard Iranian fare, dining in small alcove rooms within Birjand's restored castle makes for a memorable experience – especially at night, when the interior is bathed in a golden light. Alternatively, just come to puff on a qalyan (with tea set IR250,000).

Pie   ITALIAN **$$**
(Modarres Blvd, cnr 50th Alley; mains IR180,000-230,000) Sparsely decorated with old plates and potted plants in an attractive single room, this calm, couple-y restaurant serves interesting twists on Italian classics: the garlic-rich pesto pasta, for example, comes with chicken, walnut and pepper.

★**Shamsol Emare**   IRANIAN **$$$**
(☑056-3244 4720; Valiasr Sq, Akhbarieh Garden; mains IR145,000-490,000; ⊙noon-3pm & 7-10.30pm) A series of private dining spaces with carpeted floor-seating, elbow cushions and fireplaces for winter evenings are ranged around a pretty fountain yard, with globe lamps, traditional music and artificial streams. A kabab speciality is *juje kabab ba ostefan* (on-the-bone chicken); small, deep-fried trout come filleted with a sesame crust and the *mirza ghasemi* (garlic-smoked eggplant mush) is divine.

Caffe Chi   COFFEE
(Modarres Blvd, cnr 66th Alley; coffee from IR40,000, cake IR60,000; ⊙9.30am-1pm Sat-Thu & 5-11.30pm daily) Excellent coffee from a Wega machine in a mood-lit, female-friendly cafe displaying pipes, coffee paraphernalia and B&W photos of film stars.

🛍 Shopping

The bazaar area lacks any kind of architectural elegance but fascinating shops like **Yas Saffron** (Jomhuri 12th Alley, Birjand Bazar; ⊙8.30am-1pm & 4-8pm Sat-Thu) are good for buying Birjand's archetypal products: saffron, barberries and jujube.

Birjand also has a good reputation for carpets. Bulk dealers, liable to be cheaper than the glamorous boutiques, are tucked away on Ghaem St, along with a couple of carpet repair workshops.

ℹ Information

Asia Parvaz (☑056-3223 3090, Ahmad Kashani 0912 870 1726; http://en.asiaparvaz. com; Sayyad Shirazi Blvd; ⊙8am-2.30pm & 5-8pm Sat-Thu) Useful Birjand-based contact for regional exploration offering October saffron-field tours and a range of Lut Desert explorations, complete with quad-biking on the dunes.

ℹ Getting There & Away

Active since 1933, Birjand's small airport (XBJ) has daily flights (from IR2,300,000, 1 hour 40 minutes) to Tehran-Mehrabad. It's just beyond the northeast ring road, 1km east of the bus terminal.

The big **bus terminal** (Mostafer Blvd), 4km southeast of the city centre, deals with all major destinations, including:

Boshrooyeh (IR130,000, four hours, 1.30pm)
Kerman (IR250,000, eight hours, 8.30pm & 9pm) Or use the 2.30pm Hamsafar bus bound eventually for Bandar Abbas
Mashhad (via Qa'en; IR348,000, seven hours, hourly 8am to 11.30pm)
Tehran (via Tabas; *mahmooly*/VIP IR480,000/810,000, 15 hours, 2.30pm to 4.30pm)
Yazd (IR350,000, 11 hours, 7pm)

Just outside the terminal exit (turning left, ie away from the city centre), **Sarina Safar** (☑056-3231 9392; Mosafer Blvd; per km IR5500; ⊙6am-9pm) is a long-distance taxi company with very good rates.

ℹ Getting Around

Birjand is pretty spread out. By day, streams of city buses run on a plethora of routes – but without route numbers, so they can be hard for foreigners to use. Fortunately taxis are remarkably reasonable, charging only IR40,000 to cross the city. Call ☑133 for a cab or use the handily central **Aboozar Sq rank** (www. taxibirjand.ir; Aboozar Sq).

Qa'en   قائن

☑056 / POPULATION 64,800 / ELEVATION 1440M
Variously Romanised as Ghayen, Ghaen and Qayen, Qa'en is one of the larger desert towns on the Mashhad–Zahedan corridor. Like Birjand it has a reputation for fine felt, carpets and saffron. Come in September/October to see purple crocuses in the saffron fields and the plains towards Afin blushing red with barberries.

At the southeastern edge of town, rugged, dry mountains are topped by the attractive ruins of **Qa'en Castle** (قلعه کوه قائن; Abouzar Park; ⊙24hr) **FREE**, fortified by Uzbek occupiers in the 16th-century. The ancient and beautifully restored **tomb** of 6th-century vizier-philosopher Bozojomahr (Bozorgmehr) overlooks the scene. Time your time descent from the castle to coincide with sunset, when the lights of the tomb are coming on and the muezzin is calling mellifluously to prayer.

Qa'en also has an unusual 9th-century **Jameh Mosque** (Imam Khomeini St) **FREE**: the hollow, central, summer section is decorated in chequered white-and-sepia detail; the mihrab, added later, was angled to compensate for the discovery that the builders had misaligned the mosque several degrees away from the true direction of Mecca.

🛏 Sleeping & Eating

There's only one simple hotel in town, the **Mehmanpazir Saeed** (☑056-3252 3735, 0915 561 8831; Mahdiyeh 1st Alley; s/tw IR290,000/400,000; ❄).

The pick of the town's limited dining choices are **Sofrakhane Sonati Hezardastan** (Sahel St, Enghelab Park, near Taleghani Sq; mains IR50,000-90,000; ◷6am-3pm Mon-Sun & 6-10pm Sat-Thu), a semi-traditional, domed teahouse in Enghelab Park; and the reliable

Sahel (☑054-3253 2002; Gendarmerie Bridge, Beheshti St; mains IR90,000-220,000; ◷7am-1am) for high-quality kababs. Teahouse **Bozajomehr** (Abouzar Park; mains IR150,000-200,000; ◷7pm-11pm Mon-Sun & noon-3pm Fri) serves basic meals and you can get decent cakes and inexpensive, yet remarkably good coffee, at **Coffeeshop Fenjoon** (Rajai-i St; ◷3pm-midnight).

❶ Getting There & Away

Buses to Mashhad (via Gonabad; IR90,000, 5½ hours) depart at 7am, 9.30am, 2.30pm, 10.30pm and 11pm from the small, relatively central main **terminal** (Mobarezan St), 500m west of Imam Khomeini Sq. **Savaris to Birjand** (Western Ring Road; IR90,000, 1¼ hours) start 200m further west, from the ring road.

Northeastern Iran
شمال شرقی ایران

Best Places to Eat

➡ Cafe Sonati Tadaion (p253)

➡ Babaghodrat (p264)

➡ Dehnamak Caravanserai (p254)

➡ Flamingo (p255)

➡ Zendegi (p253)

➡ Bagh-e Salar (p269)

Best Places to Sleep

➡ Setar-e Kavir (p254)

➡ Radkan Arg Ecolodge (p269)

➡ Javad Hotel (p262)

➡ Vesal Homestay (p271)

➡ Vali's Non-Smoking Homestay (p260)

Why Go?

The Northeast's primary attraction is Mashhad's extraordinarily grand Haram-e Razavi complex – the shrine of Imam Reza – which attracts pilgrims in their millions. The main highway to Mashhad from Tehran parallels the classic silk route via a series of former caravanserai villages and towns edging round the vast desert emptiness of the Dasht-e Kavir. An alternative route crosses the Alborz Mountains, descends to the highly developed Caspian coast then passes through Turkmensahra (an area that's culturally Turkmen), skirting the ancient Hyrcanian oak forests of the Golestan (Paradise) National Park, mountain home to a small population of leopards.

There's much to discover here – and you'll need to come this way if travelling overland to Turkmenistan – but foreign tourists remain extremely rare throughout the region. Cities like Semnan, Shahrud, Gorgan and Mashhad are vibrant and increasingly modern, but don't expect to find many English speakers or even any Latin script on most signs.

When to Go

April to May is beautiful, with steppe and mountains mantled in technicolour flowers. Come on spring or autumn weekends (Thursday to Friday) to see horse-racing at Gonbad-e Kavus. In December temperatures can occasionally dip to -20°C, but more likely hover around 0°C. Winter snows block some minor roads (eg Kordkuy–Radkan) but can make spotting elusive leopard tracks in the Golestan National Park a bit easier.

Avoid Mashhad around No Ruz (Iranian New Year) in late March and during religious holidays – innumerable pilgrim crowds turn the city into pandemonium. July and August are blisteringly hot and the Caspian region's infamous humidity peaks.

History

Historically, the northeast developed as Khorasan ('Where the [Iranian] Sun Rises') and Tabarestan/Mazandaran (the southeastern Caspian littoral). Millennia of culture reached a zenith here around 1000 years ago, producing many of the era's great scientists and poet-philosophers. But the 13th- and 14th-century ravages of the Mongols and Tamerlane were so complete that Tabarestan's settled civilisation was virtually wiped out in many places; even now the sites of several once-prosperous cities are mere undulations in the steppe. A few marvellous, lonely towers, most astonishingly at Radkan and Gonbad-e Kavus, are the last witnesses of former glories.

The 16th-century Safavid regime's move towards formal state Shiite Islam was a major factor in the growth of Mashhad from a shrine-village to the region's foremost city.

Sari   ساری

📋 011 / POPULATION 299,000

The sprawling capital of Mazandaran is an infuriating, traffic-snarled place not really worth a big detour. However, it's a key connecting point if you're trying to reach Badab-e Surt by public transport, and the place you're likely to arrive if you've travelled the impressive Trans-Alborz Railway, which switchbacks down steep valley sides from the central plateau to the low-lying Caspian coast.

The best places to stay are **Hotel Badeleh** (📋 011-3388 4497; www.hotelbadeleh.ir; Sari–Gorgan Hwy Km10; tw/ste IR2,834,000/3,924,000; P❄❄) and **Hotel Asram** (📋 011-3325 5090; asramco@gmail.com; Valiasr Hwy; s/tw/tr/ste foreigners €40/55/80/100, Iranians IR997,000/1,635,0 00/2,087,000/2,152,000; P❄🖥❄) which has a good restaurant-teahouse on its top floor.

ℹ️ Getting There & Away

Sari Airport (📋 011-3372 2133; http://sari.airport.ir; off Sari–Gorgan hwy, Km11) is 14km east of the city. By train, arriving in Sari from Tehran or Garmsar is the one way of travelling the **Trans-Alborz Railway** (www.rai.ir) in daylight (IR140,000, five hours, departs Garmsar 10.40am).

Most long-distance buses use the big **Dolat Terminal** (Valiasr Hwy). However, for Bardab-e Surt, the 8am Orost minibus leaves from the **Mazandaran–Semnan Savari Stand** (Terminal Rahband; 📋 011-3323 1661; Keshavarz Blvd), a small, easily missed garage, around 800m from the train station, on the west side of Keshavarz Blvd. Savaris and twice-daily buses to Damghan (IR250,000, four hours) also start there, making a rest stop at Telma Dareh (95km).

Savaris for Gorgan (front/back seat IR150,000/140,000) and Gonbad-e Kavuz (IR250,000/235,000) start on the Gorgan Hwy, 2km east of Golha Sq/Hotel Asram.

Gorgan   گرگان

📋 017 / POPULATION 343,000 / ELEVATION 135M

This appealing, rapidly expanding city has a lively vibe and a colourful character, thanks to an ethnically mixed population and an attractive location where the green Alborz Mountains stoop to meet the northeastern steppe.

Gorgan was the birthplace of 'eunuch-king' Aga Mohammad, who founded the expansionist Qajar dynasty (1779–1925). Its architectural heritage is relatively limited but Gorgan makes a fine base for visiting the Turkmen steppes and Golestan's forested mountains.

👁 Sights

Gorgan Tower   TOWER
(Borj-e Basij; Basij Sq; IR50,000; ⏰8am-midnight) The three-legged giant folly of a tower that sits on Basij Sq like a child's fantasy spacecraft is actually a jerkily revolving restaurant-coffeeshop that spins once in 45 minutes (if you persuade the barista to set it moving). Upstairs there's also a ring of open-air seating. Grab a coffee (IR80,000) to take advantage of the free customer wi-fi.

It's a fun novelty if you're driving by but getting here is a pain without a car: you'll need to find the **pedestrian access tunnel** (Basij Sq) from the road that runs parallel to the Sari Hwy, a block north of Basij Sq.

Taqavi House   HISTORIC BUILDING
(Map p250; Imamzadeh Nur Alley; ⏰8am-2pm) **FREE** This magnificent complex of historic buildings houses the Golestan Miras (p251) cultural-tourist office. Ask to peep inside the 'eight-wife' harem building – it's not your average bureaucrat's photocopier cupboard.

🛏 Sleeping

In the evenings till fairly late at night you'll see what appear to be hitchhikers on the south side of Mofateh Sq, and possibly other major thoroughfares. Their boards actually read سویت ('suite' in Farsi) and they're

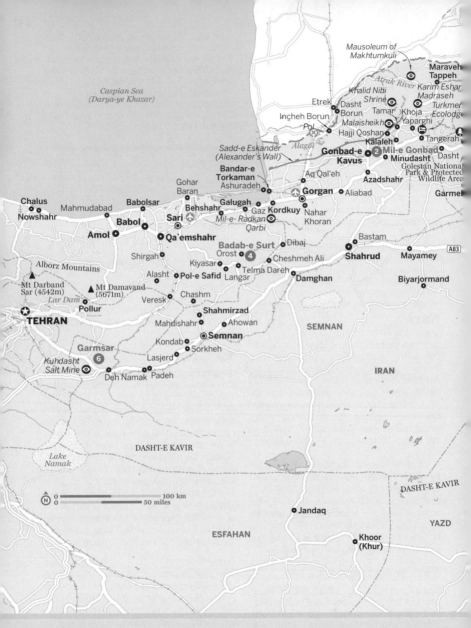

Northeastern Iran Highlights

1 Haram-e Razavi (p258)
Sharing in the emotion of countless pilgrims as you jostle closer to the heart of Mashhad's magnificent holy shrine.

2 Mil-e Gonbad (p256)
Creating surreal echoes at Gonbad-e Kavus' soaring, millennium-old tomb-tower.

3 Belqays (p271) Feeling like an old-time explorer with the

mud walls of this lonely, ruined citadel towering above you.

4 Badab-e Surt (p251)
Watching changing sky colours reflected in the terraced pools of Iran's mini Pamukkale.

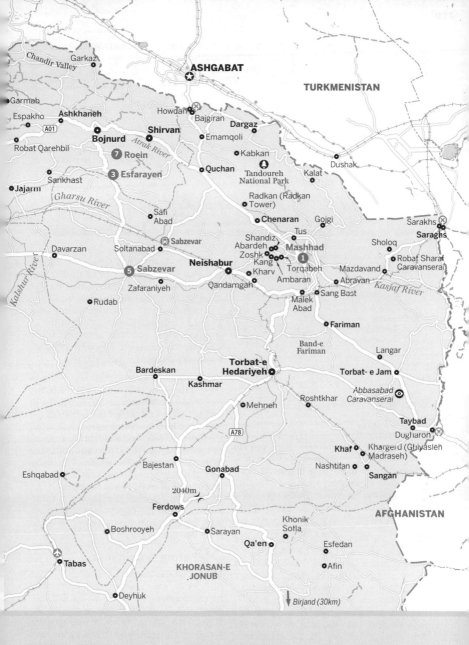

Chandir Valley

TURKMENISTAN

ASHGABAT

Garkaz
Garmab
Espakho
Ashkhaneh
A01
Robat Qarehbil
Bojnurd
7 Roein
3 Esfarayen
Jajarm
Sankhast
Gharsu River
Howdan
Bajgiran
Dargaz
Shirvan
Emamqoli
Atrak River
Quchan
Kabkan
Tandoureh
National Park
Kalat
Dushak

Safi
Abad
Radkan (Radkan
Tower)
Chenaran
Gojgi
Sarakhs
Saraghs

Davarzan
Soltanabad
Sabzevar
Kalshur River
5 Sabzevar
Zafaraniyeh
Neishabur
Qandamgah
Shandiz
Abardeh
Zoshk
Kang
Kharv
Tus
Mashhad **1**
Torqabeh
Ambaran
Sholoq
Mazdavand
Robat Sharaf
Caravanserai
Abravan
Kasjaf River

Rudab
Malek
Abad
Sang Bast

Fariman

Band-e
Fariman
Langar

Bardeskan
Torbat-e
Hedariyeh
Kashmar
Torbat- e Jam

*Abbasabad
Caravanserai*
Mehneh
Roshtkhar

A78
Taybad
Dogharon

Eshqabad
Bajestan
Gonabad
Khargerd (Ghiyasieh
Madraseh)
Khaf
Nashtifan
Sangan

2040m
Ferdows

Boshrooyeh
Sarayan
Qa'en
Khonik
Sotla
Esfedan

Tabas
Afin

Deyhuk
**KHORASAN-E
JONUB**
Birjand (30km)

AFGHANISTAN

---

5 **Zafaraniyeh** (p271)
Sleeping amid the mud-building
remnants of this forgotten little
caravanserai hamlet.

6 **Garmsar** (p254) Drinking
excellent coffee at the bottom
of a huge medieval cistern.

7 **Roein** (p271) Hiking
into the mountains from this
preserved stepped village.

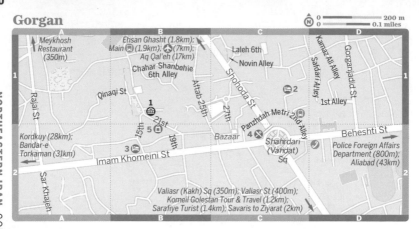

Gorgan

⊙ **Sights**

🛏 **Sleeping**

🍴 **Eating**

🛍 **Shopping**

ℹ **Information**

offering a place in a private house – typically a self-contained mini apartment. Quality is pot-luck but for around IR500,000 you'll typically get a bathroom, kitchenette and one or two beds.

Guesthouse Pars HOSTEL $
(Map p250; ☎ 017-3222 9550; off Panzhdah Metri 2nd Alley; tw/tr IR350,000/450,000/500,000; ❄) Set around a pleasant courtyard of orange trees, this clean and central – yet surprisingly peaceful – *mosaferkhaneh* (cheap hotel) lies just a minute's walk from Shahrdari Sq (take the first dead end off of Panzhdah Metri 2nd Alley). Ali, the gregarious, philosophical owner, speaks great English. Should it be full, there's another mehmanpazir across the alley.

Khayam Hotel HOTEL $$
(Map p250; ☎ 017-3225 0916; www.khayamhotel. com; 15th Aftab Alley, off Imam Khomeini St; s/d/

tr IR950,000/1,440,000/1,880,000; ☎) Adding to the great location in front of the bazaar's main produce section in the oldest part of town, Khayam has brightened the lobby and freshened up its small en suite rooms with sash curtains. However, four of the 13 are windowless, and there are a few minor faults if you look closely. Breakfast included. Enter between two pharaoh statues.

Nakar Khoran Tourist Hotel HOTEL $$
(Hotel Jahangardi; ☎ 017-3254 0034; www.ittic. com; Ziyarat Rd; tw/bungalows US$42/55; ☎) In a woodland setting behind the garden of the appealing **Telar teahouse** (open from 3pm), the Tourist Hotel's main building has renovated rooms that are better than you'd imagine from the dowdy 1970s facade. The tight-packed pastel cubes of bungalows are slightly cheaper but in need of some refreshing.

It's 200m beyond the **Nahar Khoran** roundabout in the direction of Ziyarat village, 9km from central Gorgan. Wi-fi in main building only.

🍴 Eating & Drinking

Meykhosh Restaurant INTERNATIONAL $$
(☎ 017-3243 7964; www.instagram.com/meyk-hosh.restaurant.gorgan; Resalat St, cnr 12th Alley; mains IR130,000-350,000; ⊙ noon-4pm & 7.30-11.30pm) Brightly lit but effortlessly contemporary, with clean lines, globe lamps and wooden fittings, the menu here includes pasta, steak, shrimp and a few salads as well as the usual Iranian favourites.

Eros Restaurant IRANIAN $$
(Absha Restaurant; Map p250; ☎ 017-3223 3303; Imam Khomeini St; mains IR90,000-320,000;

BADAB-E SURT باداب سورت

These photogenic series of stepped travertine (a type of limestone) **terrace pools** (near Orost) are smaller in scale than the famed ones at Pamukkale in Turkey, but more colourful and with a gloriously lonely setting on a hillock in a mountain-hemmed valley. They can be reached by minibus from Sari.

Local minibus driver **Shaaban-Ali Bagheri** (☑ 0911 776 0190; Orost Village) can arrange homestays for IR500,000 in **Orost**, the nearest village to Badab-e Surt, but ideally you should call him ahead (in Farsi). The website www.badabsoort.com advertises nearly a dozen villas for short-term rent in the village.

⊙ 8am-10.30pm) Though lacking any contemporary zest, Eros (formerly called Absha) is the neatest of many eateries around Shahrdari Sq. It's owned by a butchery company so has a reputation for fresh meat dishes, but is also a good place to try *ghorme sabzi* (mix of diced meat, beans and vegetables, served with rice).

Jersey Caffe COFFEE

(2nd fl, Surmayeh Complex, Valiasr Sq; ⊙ 10am-11pm) Stylised cityscape silhouettes are the only decorative quirks of this understated, female-friendly coffeeshop (coffees IR70,000 to IR100,000), which also serves a range of herb teas, cakes and fast food at glass tables with leaf-shaped chairs. It's up one short flight of stairs within the Surmayeh tower.

🛍 Shopping

Bagheri Complex ARTS & CRAFTS

(Gorgan Handicrafts Centre; Map p250; Aftab 19th Alley, off Imam Khomeini St; ⊙ 8am-7pm) An easily missed doorway leads into the internal courtyard of this historic, tile-roofed house where five craft shops sell woodcraft, copperwork, pottery and more.

A *sonati*-style (traditional) restaurant should open by the time you read this, and a boutique heritage hotel is planned.

ℹ Information

Sharab Coffeenet (☑ 017-3223 8298; Panzhdah Metri 2nd Alley; per hr IR25,000; ⊙ 8am-9pm) Upstairs via the yellow door beside a vacuum cleaner repair shop, on Panzhdah Metri 2nd Alley just off Beheshti St.

Payphones (Map p250; Beheshti St) There's a row of payphones outside the telecom office.

Police Foreign Affairs Department (Modairiyat Gozarnameh atbae Khareje; Behzisti 4th Alley; ⊙ 8am-2pm Sat-Thu) Offers visa extensions; apply by 9.30am for same day service. The office is two short blocks south of the big Bank Melli tower, where you'll need to go to pay the fee.

Golestan Miras (Map p250; ☑ 017-3226 1802; www.golestanchto.ir; Taqavi House, Imamzadeh Nur Alley; ⊙ 8am-2pm Sat-Thu) This cultural–tourist office occupies part of the splendidly renovated 19th-century **Taqavi House** (p247) and produces plenty of colourful brochures.

Saraflye Turist (Tourist Exchange; Valiasr St, cnr Edalal 23rd St; ⊙ 10am-1pm & 5-8pm) Currency exchange.

ℹ Getting There & Away

AIR

There are daily flights to Tehran, three weekly to Mashhad, two to Esfahan (Sunday and Wednesday) and one each to Rasht (Friday) and Kish

BUSES FROM GORGAN

DESTINATION	FARE IN IR (VIP/MAHMOOLY)	DURATION	DEPARTURES & COMPANY
Esfahan	620,000/350,000	14hr	3–5pm
Mashhad	470,000/260,000	9–10hr	7–10am & 8–11pm
Rasht	394,000/250,000	10hr	noon (Hamsafar) & 11pm (Seiro Safar)
Semnan	185,000 (*mahmooly* only)	6hr	7.30am & 3.30pm (Taavoni 8)
Tabriz	760,000 (VIP only)	15hr	1pm (Seiro Safar)
Tehran	430,000/220,000	7-8hr	frequent, 7.30am–11pm

(Tuesday). English-speaking **Komeil Golestan Tour & Travel** (☑ 017-3232 6664; Valiasr St, cnr Edalat 21st St; ☺ 8am-6.30pm Sat-Wed, to 1.30pm Thu) sells the tickets.

BUS, MINIBUS & SAVARI

Most major bus destinations are served from the big **main terminal** (Enqelab Sq), north of the centre; from nearby, **Ehsan Ghasht** (☑ 017-3268 0280; Main Bus Terminal, Enghelab Sq; ☺ 6am-8pm) organises savaris to destinations west. Many through-buses to/from Mashhad don't bother with the terminal, instead dropping off and picking up passengers at Enqelab Sq and/or just east of Mofateh Sq (west of the centre).

Savaris for Gonbad-e-Kavus (front/back seat IR90,000/80,000, 1½ hours), along with minibuses to Aliabad, are supposed to use **Istgah Gonbad** (Blvd Jorjan), a small yard on the north side of Blvd Jorgan at the eastern edge of town, but most usually grab passengers from across the road, facing the logical direction of travel.

TRAIN

Gorgan–Tehran services travel overnight in both directions, departing at either 7pm or 8.20pm from Gorgan and arriving at dawn. You can buy tickets at **Komeil Golestan Tour & Travel**.

ℹ️ Getting Around

Many **city buses** (Map p250) start from Panzhdah Metri 2nd Alley, an arc of road that parallels Shahrdari Sq's northeast side. **Buses for Nahar Khoran** (IR10,0000; ☺ 6.20am-8pm) start from Valiasr (Kakh) Sq, departing four or five times an hour from 6.20am to 8pm.

Convenient shuttle taxis run from predictable points near Shahrdari Sq. **Savaris to Ziyarat** (IR20,000) leave from the corner of Valiasr St and Edalat 47th Alley, 1.5km southeast of Valiasr Sq.

Semnan   سمنان

☑ 023 / POPULATION 163,000 / ELEVATION 1130M

Booming Semnan city is well placed to give swift access to both the Alborz Mountains and the vast Dasht-e Kavir desert, while still being an easy 240km drive by expressway from Tehran. Since Sassanian times it has been a key stop on the silk route, attracting wealth and regular destruction in equal measure.

At first glance it's a diffuse, nondescript city of low-rise modern buildings and wide boulevards. But around the appealing covered bazaar is an interesting complex of historical buildings.

◉ Sights

Semnan Bazaar   BAZAAR

Semnan's cross-shaped covered-bazaar marks the old heart of the city. While far less extensive than the great bazaars of Kerman or Tabriz, there is plenty of 19th-century vaulting and the north-south section (bisected by Imam Khomeini St) links two log-pillared *takiyeh* (three-storey tall covered halls). The southern of these, **Takiyeh Pehneh**, is an access point for most of Semnan's key historical sites and is the centre for religious mourning during Moharram.

The more northerly **Takiyeh Nasar**, dating from 1926, is arguably more attractive and would be all the more interesting if the disused *abambar* (cistern) and nearby underground *hammam* (bathhouse) were to become accessible.

Masjed-e Jameh   MOSQUE

(Jameh Mosque; Semnan Bazaar; ☺ 1hr before/after prayers) The extraordinarily high, if austere, west *iwan* of the Masjed-e Jameh dates from a 1424 rebuild, rising above a bare-brick octagonal prayer hall. But the mosque's most lovable feature is older: the gorgeous, 32m-tall patterned-brick **minaret**, which is still standing after more than a millennium, albeit leaning and a bit kinked.

Masjed Imam   MOSQUE

(Sultani Mosque; Semnan Bazaar; ☺ dawn-dusk) Founded under Fath Ali Shah in the 1820s, this mosque is a large courtyard affair with four *iwans* at the cardinal points – the higher east and west ones offer a measured use of restrained coloured brickwork. On Friday mornings the courtyard is filled with colourful carpets to prepare for lunchtime prayers.

🏃 Activities

★ **Gootkemall Water Park**   WATER PARK

(www.gootkemall.com; Daneshgah St; per 3hr session IR150,000; ☺ 5-8pm & 8-11pm, men/women on odd/even dates) Costing nearly US$20 million to build, this inventive new complex includes eight indoor water slides – one whizzes you into a rotating spinner. There are many smaller water attractions and a 'tubing stream' for floating a course around the various attractions. Admission includes use of a sauna and Turkish bath, plus lockers for your clothes. Bring your own towel.

LOCAL KNOWLEDGE

ALBORZ FOOTHILLS

A popular weekend getaway for Semnanis, **Shahmirzad** (شهميرزاد) is a quietly charming 'oasis' amid spiky rock ridges. Gushing streams and a few remnant mud-compound houses grace the upper parts of town around Naqsh-e Jahan Sq.

Between Shahmirzad and Mahdishahr, **Darband** is a somewhat scraggy picnic spot behind which a path leads to a locally famous cave in the cliff above.

Draped amid rocky folds, **Mahdishahr** (مهدي شهر) is dominated by the impressive (if mostly contemporary) blue-domed Al-Mahdi Hosseinieh. There's also a museum focused on nomad culture.

You can visit all of the above as a mildly interesting day trip from Semnan. Minibuses (IR20,000) and savaris (IR40,000) leave from Semnan's **Mo'allem Sq**, returning from Shahmirzad's Imam St (500m downhill from Naqsh-e Jahan Sq). The road is fast and wide taking, barely 15 minutes to Mahdishahr and around 30 minutes to Shahmirzad.

🛏 Sleeping

Semnan's handful of hotels cover most budgets competently enough, albeit without great pizazz. Central **Mehmanpazir Kumesh** (☑ 023-3332 3647; Imam Khomeini 18th Alley; s/tw without bathroom IR400,000/600,000) is a bare-bones cheapie; mid-range **Semnan Tourist Inn** (Mehmansara Jahangardi; ☑ 023-3344 1433; Basij Blvd; d/tr/ste IR1,664,000/2,070,000/3,500,000; P ❀ 🤶), 3km from the centre, offers spacious rooms; and guests at the comfortable **Gootkemall Hotel** (☑ 023-3333 3338; www.gootkemall.com; Daneshgah St; s/d/tr/ste IR2,200,000/3,100,000/3,800,000/4,500,000; ❀ 🤶) have free evening use of the attached water park.

When it opens after its long-term repurposing, the **Tarherian House** promises something with more heritage style.

🍴 Eating & Drinking

Darchin (Cinnamon Restaurant & Coffee; off Qods Blvd, near Mashahir Sq; ☺ 8am-midnight; 🤶), behind the Mashahir Cistern, has live music after 8pm. The **Kalantar House** (Abuzar Sq), with its distinctive tower, is soon to open as a teahouse.

★ **Cafe Sonati Tadaion**   IRANIAN $
(☑ 023-3332 1097; Tadayon House, Taleqani St; mains IR45,000-60,000, dizi IR100,000; ☺ 8am-10pm) This charming family restaurant makes delightful use of a domed cellar room off the rear courtyard of the historic **Tadayon House**, in which you'll also find a gift shop, gemstone store and cultural office Semnan Miras (p254). Delicious house-cooked specialities include *khorak-e gushk* (mince with potato) that is best ordered along with some of their divine *mirza ghasemi* (garlic aubergine paste).

★ **Zendegi**   IRANIAN $$
(☑ 0919 132 5438; www.instagram.com/zendegi_complex; Kohneh Dezh 13th Alley; kabab meals IR150,000-350,000, salads IR40,000-65,000; ☺ noon-11pm, limited menu 4-7pm) This upmarket restaurant occupies several small rooms and two open terraces in the fountain-centred **Zendegi House**, a 180-year-old miller/trader's mansion with a museum room of 20th-century oddments, a crystals shop and glass-painting workshop. (It's worth a look even if you don't stop to dine.) The menu is mostly kabab-based but also offers salads and eggplant dishes. Bookings advised on Thursdays.

Sofrakhane Kohamdezh   IRANIAN $$
(☑ 023-3333 8333; Kohneh Dezh St, mains IR125,000-350,000; ☺ 8.30am-11.30pm, breakfast only before noon) Fronted by a *badgir* (windtower), this late-Safavid house opened as an upmarket restaurant teahouse in early 2017. Specialities include fish fillets, and shrimp served with fresh-baked *tanour* bread coloured with tumeric and subtly flavoured mutton fat. Tea for two costs IR40,000, plus IR5000 each for their delicious house-made *shirini* (date pastries).

Restaurant Sonati Mashahir   IRANIAN $$
(☑ 023-3333 0463; Mashahir Sq; mains IR80,000-320,000; ☺ 9am-11pm) The facade looks bland, but inside the decor is a kitschy delight. Achaemenid figures lead down to a vaulted cavern, artificial grotto and circular dining area backed by mock-ancient portraiture in relief. On top of a standard kabab menu they serve *tahchin* (layered rice and marinated meat; IR300,000) in its Sangesar nomad version, using lamb rather than chicken.

ⓘ Information

Sadi Coffeenet (Sadi Sq; internet per hr IR40,000; ⊙10am-7pm Sat-Wed)

Semnan Miras (🖉 023-3332 1602; www.mirassemnan.ir; Tadayon House, Taleqani St, btwn 3rd & 5th Alleys; ⊙8am-2.30pm Sun-Wed, to 1.30pm Thu) Semnan's cultural information office occupies one room within a lovely Qajar-era mansion that also features Semnan's finest surviving windtower, a gift shop and a gemstone shop, along with an easily missed **traditional cafe** (p253) in the back courtyard basement.

ⓘ Getting There & Away

Semnan's airport is under construction, 6km east of the city limits. For Mashhad, trains are better than buses, which are mostly through-services from Tehran passing around the ring roads.

BUS & SAVARI

Semnan's **main terminal** (Imam Reza Expressway) is 3km west of Sa'di Sq, 100m beyond Imam Hossein Sq. Between 5am and 7pm buses leave up to every half-hour for Tehran (IR140,000, three hours) supplemented by savaris (front/back seat IR240,000/220,000, *dar bast* IR900,000) operated by four companies at the terminal, each with their own waiting room. **Mohebban** (🖉 023-3346 8585; www.mohebban.ir; ⊙24hr) also has a few daily cars to Sari (front/back seat IR310,00/270,000, *dar bast* 1,120,000, five hours). **Hedayate** (🖉 023-3346 7620; ⊙24hr) handles shared rides to Garmsar (front/back seat IR115,000/105,000, *dar bast* IR450,000, 1¼ hours) from 6am to around 5pm.

Mola-i buses (Jahadieh Blvd; ⊙7am-6pm) to Damghan (IR70,000, 1¾ hours) and Shahrud (IR100,000, 2½ hours), leave most hours on the hour from 7am to 6pm from a little terminal 200m south of Standard Sq (3km east of the centre). **Savaris** to Damghan and Shahrud start from the southeast corner of Standard Sq.

TRAIN

There are several daily trains from Tehran (three hours) and three departures to Mashhad (nine hours), stopping at 10.10am, 3.30pm and 6.30pm. The **station** (Motahari St) is 1.5km south of Imam Khomeini Sq. For more choice head first to Shahrud.

Garmsar

گرمسار

🖉 023 / POPULATION 58,000

For those driving by, or planning to connect to the Caspian coast on the Alborz Railway using the day-train to Sari, Garmsar is worth considering as a brief coffee stop thanks to the unique **Cafe Abenbar**, (Aftab Alley, Imam Khomeini Sq; ⊙9am-1pm & 3.30-10.30pm) set at the bottom of a deep, historic water cistern, hidden away behind the Jameh Mosque. The atmosphere is low-lit and female-friendly. They serve drinks, cakes and sundaes (IR65,000 to IR90,000). For full meals consider driving out to Dehnamak and eating in the 16th-century **caravanserai** (🖉 0912 611 3387, 0911 805 3814; www.dehnamak.net; Garmsar–Semnan Hwy; mains IR100,000-320,000; ⊙11am-10pm) there.

Otherwise Garmsar itself is eminently forgettable. Nearly 20km from Garmsar you could drop by the **Kuhdasht Salt Mine** (Qom–Garmsar Hwy; ⊙by arrangement) **FREE**; sometimes they let visitors drive (accompanied) along their 700m of vast tunnels, past some 70 gigantic, artificial, barely lit pillars. Before heading there, consider visiting Garmsar's **Aghvam Museum** (Baghavi House, Faisali Hossein Alley; foreigner/Iranian IR100,000/20,000; ⊙8am-4pm Tue-Sun) to get nominal 'permission'.

Likely the best reason for heading this way is to stay at **Setar-e Kavir** (🖉 023-3453 4095, 0912 531 9327, Mr Famili 0912 121 0959; www.ssdg.ir; Haji Abad, near Garmsar; per person from IR1,299,000; ❄🖉), in a small settlement on the westbound Mashhad–Tehran Hwy around 9km northeast of Garmsar. This boutique hotel offers six cosily comfortable mini-suites in a pseudo-historical architectural style but with full conveniences. There's a courtyard garden, small restaurant-teahouse in an ancient *hammam* building and a double windtower above the little gift shop.

ⓘ Getting There & Away

There's a small **terminal** (Rah-Ahan Blvd) for Tehran buses (IR60,000, hourly) 2.4km outside the centre, outside which is an informal **taxi stand** (Rah-Ahan Blvd) with savaris to Tehran (front/back seat IR120,000/110,000) and Semnan (IR110,000/100,000).

From **Garmsar station** (🖉 051-3420 0655; Taheri St; ⊙ticket office 8am-1pm daily & 4-6pm Sat-Thu), another 1.1km past bus terminal, the 10.40am train to Sari (IR140,000, five hours) is ideal for enthusiasts wanting to ride the Trans-Alborz Railway by day. An 11pm overnight train runs to Gorgan (IR380,000). For Mashhad there's a stopping service at 9am (IR380,000) and more luxurious trains (IR720,000) at 2.30pm and 5.30pm. Trains to Tehran (IR50,000, 1¼ hours) depart at 7.20am, 4.20pm, 5pm and around midnight.

Shahrud

شاهرود

☑ 023 / POPULATION 150,000 / ELEVATION 1410M

If you're bus-hopping between Semnan and Mashhad, you'll generally need to change vehicles in Shahrud, a pleasant, booming, student-centric city with leafy streets. The main sight is the **Bezayit Bastami Complex** (Taleqani St, Bastam; ☉ dawn-dusk) [FREE] a collection of mostly 13th-century historical buildings around 7km from the centre.

Half-day excursions take visitors up to **Jangali Abr**, a road winding up into forests with a European feel where the attraction is to emerge above a sea of clouds.

Places to stay include the simple guesthouse **Mehmanpazir Pars** (☑ 023-3223 3546; 22nd Bahman St, Jomhuri-e Eslami Sq; s/d/tr/q without bath IR245,000/342,000/414,000/470,000; [P]) beside the covered bazaar; the dated, comfy and centrally located **Shahrud Tourist Inn** (☑ 023-3223 1288; http://en.ittic.com; off Ferdowsi St; s/d/ste IR1,310,000/1,640,000/2,800,000; [P][✳][🛜]); and the small, functional **Bastam Tourist Hotel** (☑ 023-3252 4596; http://en.ittic. com; Motahari Park, South Shohada St, Bastam; d/tr/ste IR1,664,000/2,070,000/3,500,000; [P][✳][🛜]).

Good for kababs or a relaxed pot of tea is **Sofrakhane Sonati Emarat** (Ferdowsi St; mains IR90,000-400,000; ☉ noon-midnight). Fancier Iranian meals can be had at the suave yet understated mod-trad **Haft Khan Restaurant** (☑ 023-3107, 023-3222 2440; www.7khanco.com; Ferdowsi St; mains IR150-400,000; ☉ 7am-1am).

For more eccentric decoration, the quirky cafe-bar **Flamingo** (Pishvar St; ☉ 10am-midnight) fits the bill. There's so much detail to appreciate that you might choose to stay for dinner (burgers IR220,000, pizzas IR160,000). The castle-styled teahouse **Kahkeshan** (تفریحی کهکشان; ☑ 025-3252 5200; Gorgan Rd, Bastam; ☉ noon-midnight) has a rooftop offering appealing mountain panoramas.

❶ Getting There & Away

BUS & SAVARI

At the far western edge of town, 6km from Azadi Sq, the **Tehran Terminal** (Shahrud–Damghan Hwy) has buses to Tehran hourly in the mornings (*mahmooly* IR180,000) and every 30 minutes from 2pm to 6pm (mostly VIP IR330,000, six hours), of which five head for Tehran's Arjentin (rather than Janub) bus station. Iran Peyma has a single overnighter to Mashhad at 10pm (IR210,000, seven hours) and there's a 5pm service to Esfahan (IR430,000, 12 hours). Savaris to Semnan and Tehran start from outside.

---

❶ IRAN–TURKMENISTAN BORDER CROSSINGS

Incheh Borun

The border known as 'Incheh Borun' is actually at **Pol**, 4km off the Gorgan–Incheh Borun road, turning north 12km before Incheh Borun village. On the Iran side there's a border market where peddlers sell felt rugs; nearby lakes are popular with picnickers on Fridays, but there's no public transport. There's 1.5km of no-man's-land before the Turkmenistan post. In 2016 a new Gorgan–Balkanabat railway opened using this route; it's currently freight only, but a passenger service might be introduced in future.

Bajgiran

From Bajgiran's lower border gate, it's a steady 1.7km climb to the **immigration posts** (Bajgiran; ☉ 7.30am-3.30pm Iran time, 9am-5pm Turkmen time); taxis want IR50,000. Before crossing the border, consider changing at least US$20 into Turkmen manats, either with traders in Bajgiran village or at a shop beside the Iranian immigration building. Turkmenistan immigration is just 50m away. As at any Turkmen entry point you'll need US$12 (in US dollars) to pay for the hologrammed entry card. If arriving on a tourist visa your voucher must be with the immigration officers and the agency representative should be waiting, so be sure to synchronise your watches. (That's not required if you're on a transit visa.)

Turkmen immigration procedures can be appallingly ponderous, even when everything's in order. Beware that Howdan (*hov*-dan; the Turkmen-side upper customs post) is not a village, lacks facilities and is 25km from the Turkmen lower border gate (Berzhengi Tamozhna). Minivans charging the equivalent of US$10 per person shuttle across this no-man's land, departing once they have a handful of passengers. After further passport checks, a taxi to Ashgabat costs around US$5 from here.

Savaris to Gorgan (front/back seat IR230,000/210,000) and Azad Shahr (IR180,000/160,000) depart from outside a **minibus terminal** – signed as 'Garazh' – just beyond Imam Reza Sq, around 1km east of Azadi Sq.

TRAIN

Trains for Mashhad (IR270,000 to IR370,000) leave at 3am, 4am, 9.40am, 11.20am, 12.50pm, 1.30pm, 3.43pm, 6.30pm and 8.32pm. Most take 5½ hours but the 3.43pm is a fast 'Pardiz' service, taking just four. There are also nine daily departures to Tehran.

ℹ Getting Around

City share-taxis (22 Bahman St) to Imam Reza Sq and 'Garazh' (IR10,000) start from near Jomhuri-e Eslami Sq and Garazh. Others starting from Imam Sq head for Bastam, returning from Taleqani St, right outside the historical complex.

A taxi *dar bast* (charter) to Bastam costs IR50,000 from central Shahrud. Many city buses use a **central bus stand** (Jomhuri-e Eslami Sq) near Mehmanpazir Pars.

Gonbad-e Kavus گنبد کاووس

📞 017 / POPULATION 146,000 / ELEVATION 39M

The 53m Unesco-listed **Mil-e Gonbad tower** (www.gonbad-eqabus-whb.ir; Imam Blvd; foreigner/Iranian IR200,000/30,000; ⊙7.30am-8pm) is the unmissable attraction of what is otherwise a faceless, forgettable urban sprawl famous for Turkmen horse racing and a nationally prominent volleyball team.

The tower, which looks like a buttressed-brick spaceship with the cross-section of a 10-pointed star, is so remarkably well preserved that one can scarcely believe it's a hundred years old, let alone over a thousand. Paying the entrance fee means you can listen to echoes in the bare interior and, even more spookily, from the marked circular spot some 40 paces in front of the tower.

Back in 1006 when the tower was built, this was the thriving city of Jorjan. It was utterly obliterated by the 13th-century rampages of the Mongols, though, and the only other remains of ancient Jorjan visible today are lumpy excavations behind the huge, ornate **Imamzadeh-ye Yahya** (Imamzadeh Blvd), 4km southwest of central Gonbad-e Kavus. If you have time to kill, consider checking out the town's small but well-presented **Carpet Museum**

(📞017-3322 7769; Imam Blvd; foreigner/Iranian IR80,000/20,000; ⊙7.30am-2pm Sat-Thu).

🛏 Sleeping & Eating

There are two acceptable options around Imam Ali Sq on the ring road, 2.5km south of the centre: clean, basic **Mehmanpazir Ferdows** (📞017-3333 0364; Imam Ali Sq; d without/with bathroom IR400,000/600,000; [P][❄]) and the somewhat more comfortable **Hotel Ghaboos** (📞017-3334 5402; hotelghaboos@gmail.com; Imam Ali Sq; s/d/ste IR750,000/1,100,000/1,450,000; [P][❄][📶]). A better hotel is under construction nearby, but until that's finished head to Minudasht or Azadshahr (both around 20km away) for better options.

There are *kababis* and fast-food places along Imam St (either side of the tower area) and better options in the faceless modern Danshju district. If sleeping in the outwardly unpromising Imam Ali Sq area you're actually only 300m from **Havash Traditional Restaurant** (📞017-3172; Southeast Ring Rd; starters IR60,000-120,000, kababs IR200,000-410,000), Gonbad's best, which is off the southeast bypass road around halfway to the Havash Hypermarket.

Around the tower there's great coffee with a view at **Cafe Night Star** (2nd fl, Keykabus Shopping Centre, Qabus St; ⊙11am-midnight Sat-Thu, 4pm-midnight Fri; 📶), while less-fashion-conscious **Safa Café** (Imam Blvd; juice IR50,000-70,000; ⊙8am-midnight Sat-Thu, 9am-midnight Fri) is good for fresh-squeezed juices and ice cream.

ℹ Information

Amarken (Blvd Entezami; ⊙7.30am-2pm Sat-Wed, to noon Thu) The Mehmanpazir Ferdaws asked us to go to this rather daunting police office to register ourselves before allowing us to stay. It's through the second set of grey gates to the left as you head west from 17 Shahrivar Sq, around halfway between central Gonbad and Imam Ali Sq.

ℹ Getting There & Away

Savaris to Gorgan (front/back seat IR90,000/80,000, 1½ hours) are operated by **Qabus Safar** (📞017-3334 5008; Imam Blvd) from an almost hidden yard. **Savaris to Kalaleh** (Basij Sq) cost IR30,000, take 45 minutes and start from the southeast corner of Basij Sq, where **Akhlaghi** (📞017-3355 7770; Enghelab St, Basij Sq; ⊙8.30am-1pm & 4-6pm) sells air and train tickets for travel ex-Gorgan.

Golestan National Park

پارک ملی گلستان

East of Gonbad-e Kavus, the limited-access **Golestan National Park** includes partly cultivated steppe and thick mountain forests of oak, beech and Persian ironwood, whose leaves blaze with colour in autumn. The park's forested western end rises rapidly from around 500m to over 1600m atop the **Beyli Plateau**, which is dramatically ringed with stepped cliffs. The eastern areas are arid but better for wildlife-watching: at least 22 large leopards live within the territory.

Just beyond the park's eastern tip lies the ruined caravanserai **Robat Qarehbil** and the appealing little village **Espakho** with a Sassanid-era fire temple ruin.

To explore the park you're supposed to get official permission – which can take days or weeks to organise. A delightful (if somewhat expensive) way to visit is on hiking-, riding- or wildlife-watching tours, organised through the **Turkmen Ecolodge** (☑ 0912 720 6741; www.turkmenecolodge.com; Tootli Tamak, Golestan National Park; per person without bathroom US$29; ☺ Sep-Jun) 🖉. Charming Furukh and her gregarious husband Kamran converted a rustic, thick-walled adobe homestead into this delightful four-room ecolodge, artfully decorated with old furniture and local craftwork. Entirely unmarked, it's in a tiny Turkmen hamlet beside the park; Kamran leads various park tours in fluent English. You sleep and eat on floor mats; bathrooms are outside (bring your own towel). Prices are per person, with meals costing extra (breakfast/lunch/dinner US$10/15/15) – and there's no real alternative to eating at the lodge around here. The communal dinners are wholesome, mostly organic and accompanied by numerous local pickles but are very expensive by local standards; simple lunches inexplicably cost as much. If accommodating larger groups (maximum 20) there might be as many as six guests sleeping side-by-side in the bigger rooms. Book at least three weeks in advance.

Twice a year (May and late September), you can join group tours with **Persian Voyages** (www.persianvoyages.com) that include a five-day horseback and camping expedition in this fascinating area.

A taxi here from Gonbad costs around IR500,000. Alternatively, you can catch glimpses of the national park as you drive through between Gorgan and Bojnurd.

Bajgiran

باجگیران

☑ 051 / POPULATION 410 / ELEVATION 1630M

This small village is the main crossing point for those heading for Ashgabat, Turkmenistan's surreal capital. Consider sleeping here to get an early start. The nine-room **Hotel Bajgiran** (☑ 051-3372 3212; Bajgiran; tw IR450,000) has survivable but rather bare rooms with shared toilets; it's 800m before the lower border gate in Bajgiran. Dining choices are limited so it's worth carrying some food with you for the potentially lengthy waits at the border.

There's a larger choice of accommodation and dining options in **Quchan**, the nearest major town.

✶ Getting There & Away

A direct taxi from Mashhad to Bajgiran costs IR1,500,000. Alternatively head first to Quchan's Felestin Sq, from which savaris to Bajgiran (per person/car IR200,000/700,000, 1¼ hours) terminate at the lower border gate (p255).

Buses to Quchan run regularly from Bojnurd (IR80,000, two hours) and Mashhad's Meraj Terminal (IR80,000, 1¾ hours), arriving at either Azadi Sq or out at Quchan's **main bus terminal** (Modarres Blvd). From either point, taxis want IR50,000 to Felestin Sq.

Mashhad

مشهد

☑ 051 / POPULATION 2,965,000 / ELEVATION 975M

Mashhad is Iran's holiest and second-largest city. Its raison d'être and main sight is the beautiful, massive and ever-growing Haram (shrine complex) commemorating the AD 818 martyrdom of Shiite Islam's eighth Imam, Imam Reza. The pain of Imam Reza's death is still felt very personally well over a millennium later and more than 20 million pilgrims converge here each year to pay their respects. Witnessing their tears is a moving experience, even if you're not Muslim yourself.

Mashhad is also a good place to buy carpets, and it's a staging post for travel to Turkmenistan, Afghanistan and the little-touristed Khorasan region.

Be aware that during No Ruz and major Muslim holidays, almost all accommodation and transport will be booked out months in advance. (By contrast, at other times visiting Mashhad can prove quite a bargain.)

History

Following Imam Reza's burial here, the small village of Sanabad began to attract

Shiite pilgrims and soon became known as Mashhad ('place of martyrdom'). Nearby Tabaran (today's Tus) remained a more significant town until 1389, when Tamerlane sacked the whole area – thereafter it was Mashhad that eventually limped back to life as the new capital of Khorasan.

The shrine was enlarged in the early 15th century by Tamerlane's son, Shah Rokh, and his extraordinary wife, Gohar Shad, for whom the Haram's main mosque is named. Once the Safavids had established Shiism as the state creed, Mashhad became Iran's pre-eminent pilgrimage site and Shah Abbas I rebuilt the Holy Shrine's new core around 1612.

Politically, Mashhad reached its zenith under Nader Shah, whose empire was focused on Khorasan. Even though Nader was a Sunni of missionary zeal, he continued to sponsor the Haram, which was vastly expanded again in 1928, in the 1970s and almost nonstop since 1979. The Haram's charitable foundation, Astan-e Qods e Razavi, is now a powerful business conglomerate managing enterprises from baking to carpets and minerals to transport. But most of the Haram's money comes from donations, bequests and the selling of grave sites: to be buried near the Imam is a great honour (and suitably expensive). And if you notice a lot of young couples, that's because honeymooning here is believed to help bless a marriage.

◉ Sights

★ **Haram-e Razavi** ISLAMIC SITE
(حرم امام رضا; Map p264; www.imamrezashrine.com; ☉24hr) FREE Imam Reza's Holy Shrine (p263) is enveloped in a vast series of sacred precincts collectively known as the Haram-e Razavi, or Haram for short. This magical city-within-a-city sprouts dazzling clusters of domes and minarets in blue and pure gold behind fountain-cooled courtyards and magnificent arched arcades. It's one of the marvels of the Islamic world, and it's worth savouring its moods and glories more than once by visiting at different times of day.

Compare the orderly overload of dusk prayer-time to the fairy-tale calm of a floodlit nocturnal wander. And take time to visit the complex's trio of eclectic museums, filled with bequests and donations from the faithful.

No bags or cameras are allowed within the complex (although snapping photos with mobile phones appears to be perfectly acceptable). There are left-luggage offices near most entrances. Men and women enter through different carpet-draped portals and are politely frisked. Women must wear a chador but at most gates there is a stock to borrow for the unprepared. For either sex it's important to dress in suitably clean, conservative clothing.

Non-Muslims are allowed in most of the Haram's outer courtyards, but they're not allowed inside the complex's two holiest buildings, the Holy Shrine and the Gohar Shad Mosque, or the magnificent Enqelab and Azadi courtyards.

Haftado Tan Mosque MOSQUE
(مسجد هفتاد و دو شهید; Map p264; Andarzgu 13th Alley) Just outside the Haram complex's official limits sits this splendid 15th-century mosque, originally built as a Timurid-era tomb. It is famous for its *mo-ar-raq* tilework and beautiful tracery lamps. The two tiled **minarets** appear to have been prematurely decapitated; the taller one is inscribed with square, deep-blue cryptograms reading 'Mohammad' in four directions.

Boq'eh-ye Khajeh Rabi MAUSOLEUM
(بقعه خواجه ربیع; Map p259; Khajerabi Blvd; ☉5am-sunset; 🚍34, 38, 99) FREE This beautifully proportioned, blue-domed mausoleum commemorates an apostle of the prophet Mohammad who later exiled himself to Khorasan to avoid tensions between the prophet's then-feuding followers. Paying respects at the grave was said to have been Imam Reza's 'main consolation' in coming to Mashhad. The mausoleum took its present domed form after a 1612 rebuild, though much of the decorative tilework came later. Look for the two little dragon heads in green on the west *iwan*.

A large arcade surrounds the mausoleum, containing a cemetery paved with thousands of tombstones. Burial here costs up to IR180,000,000 – but that's still only half what you'd pay to inter a body beneath the Haram.

Get here on bus 34 from Tabarsi Blvd, bus 38 from Kuh-e Sangi (via Shohada Sq) or bus 99 from Vakilabad Metro.

Nader Shah Mausoleum MAUSOLEUM
(Map p261; cnr Shirazi & Azadi Sts; foreigner/Iranian IR150,000/25,000; ☉8am-4pm, to 6.30pm summer) Elsewhere in the Middle East, Nader Shah is considered something of a historical tyrant. But here he's a local hero for briefly returning Khorasan to the centre of a vast Central Asian empire. Nader's equestrian statue crowns his otherwise

Greater Mashhad

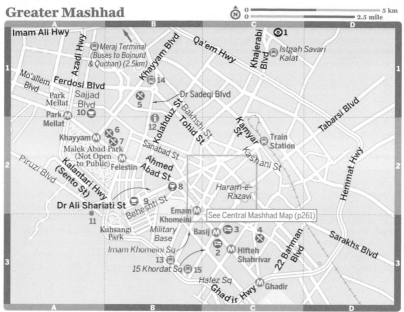

dour grey-granite mausoleum, built in 1956 to emulate the lines of a tent (Nader was reputedly born and died under canvas).

A small **museum** displays guns, a rhino-hide shield and a carpet portrait of Nader on horseback. 'Guarding' the monument is a Portuguese cannon made in the 1590s and seized 30 years later at Hormuz.

Anthropology Museum MUSEUM
(موزه انسان شناسی, Astan Quds Razavi, Mehdi Gholibek Hamam; Map p264; www.aqm.ir; Andarzgu 13th Alley, Haram Complex; IR5000; ⊙8am-2pm Mon-Thu, to 1pm Fri) The main delight of this spacious museum in a former bathhouse is the central dome's 1922 naive murals featuring anthropomorphic figures gallivanting between giant bicycles, a Russian vintage car, an early biplane and a curiously unconcerned-looking victim facing a firing squad.

Gonbad-e Sabz MAUSOLEUM
(Map p261; Akhund Khorasani St; ⊙7.30am-9pm) FREE The small, 17th-century blue-domed tomb of scholar and mystic Momen Mashhadi forms a pretty sight in the middle of a traffic circle. The last remaining Safavid monument in what was once a large *wakuf* (bequest) garden, it retains pretty multi-coloured *mo-ar-raq* (piece-by-piece) floral

Greater Mashhad

◉ Sights
1 Boq'eh-ye Khajeh Rabi......................C1

😴 Sleeping
2 Ghasr Talaee International.................C3
3 Hotel Darvishi.....................................C3

✗ Eating
4 Babaghodrat......................................C3
5 Fanous-e Abi......................................B1
6 Food Factory......................................B2
   Naseem Lebanon........................(see 3)
7 Olive Garden.....................................B2

🍷 Drinking & Nightlife
8 Malas...B2
9 The Wall...B2
10 Toranj Cafe.......................................A1

🛍 Shopping
   Bahraman Saffron.......................(see 3)

ℹ Information
11 Edareh-ye Gozarnameh....................A2
12 Miras Ferhangi Khorasan.................B2

🚍 Transport
13 Enghelab City Bus Terminal.............B3
14 Falakeh Ferdosi (Buses for Tus).........B1
15 Imam Reza Bus Terminal.................B3

THE MARTYRDOM OF IMAM REZA

Within Mashhad's Holy Shrine, pilgrims break into conspicuous, heartfelt outpourings of grief for murdered Imam Reza as though his assassination (carried out with poisoned grapes and pomegranate juice) were only yesterday. In fact it was over a millennia ago, in the year 818.

The story starts 20 years earlier with Haroun ar-Rashid, immortalised as the great caliph in *the Thousand and One Nights*. Less fictionally, Haroun ruled the Abbasid caliphate and was very influential in bringing Greek-style analytic thinking and cosmopolitan sophistication to Arab-Muslim society. His temporal power was unassailable. But he coveted the spiritual pre-eminence of Musa, the seventh Shiite Imam. Musa was eventually slapped into Haroun's Baghdad jail, then killed.

Musa's 35-year-old son Ali al-Raza (Razavi) inherited his father's pious mantle, becoming Imam Reza. Meanwhile, after Haroun's death, Haroun's sons Ma'mun and Amin slogged out a civil war to succeed their father as caliph. Ma'mun, based temporarily at Merv (in what today is Turkmenistan), emerged victorious, but needed Reza's help to calm a series of revolts. Having failed to entice the Imam to support him voluntarily in this effort, Ma'mun's agents dragged Reza forcibly across rebellious regions as a symbol of imperial power. However, the ploy appeared to backfire. The Imam's charismatic presence captivated the royal court, leaving Ma'mun worried that he would be upstaged. So out came the deadly grapes. Ma'mun disguised the crime by honouring Reza's body with burial in Sanabad (today's Mashhad), close to Ma'mun's own father – and Reza's father's nemesis – Caliph Haroun.

tiling on the four small *iwans* of its square-plan exterior.

The charming guardian often offers tea to visitors outside the mausoleum's discordantly new electronic sliding doors.

Caravanserai Azizolaof BAZAAR
(Map p264; Abbasqolikhan 6th Lane; ⊗ 8am-7pm Sat-Thu, to noon Sat) Behind heavy wooden doors, this 90-year-old caravanserai is full of underwear stalls run by Afghan merchants. It's fascinating for its cameo scenes of real local life as much as for its uncelebrated architecture.

🏃 Activities

Chalidareh BUNGEE JUMPING
(☑ 0915 009 1434; www.chalidareh.ir; Torqabeh–Kang Rd Km2; ⊗ 8.30am-2am mid-Mar–mid-Sep, to 7pm mid-Sep–mid-Mar) Accessed by either a short, rickety **funicular** (foreigner/Iranian IR70,000/35,000) or **chairlift** (IR370,000/185,000), Chalidareh is a **boating lake** ringed by a series of minor attractions, of which the most iconic will be the 38m bungee jumping tower (at time of research scheduled to open in spring 2017).

☞ Tours

Faramarz Aminian OUTDOORS
(☑ 0915 508 5420; aminian.faramarz@gmail.com) This licensed, English speaking driver-guide, originally from Torbat-e Heydarieh, offers imaginative, tailor-made itineraries, including saffron field tours in October and visits to nomad areas around Kalat in spring.

Vali Ansari Astaneh TOURS
(☑ 0915 100 1324; vali32@imamreza.net) Vali offers inexpensive, low-tech walking, cycling and public-transport-based city tours, village visits and mountain walks. He's a fascinating, ever-enthusiastic (if sometimes over-familiar) character.

Towhid Foroozanfar TOURS
(☑ 0915 313 2960; towhidfroozan@yahoo.com) Well-informed and engaging, Towhid is a certified driver-guide based in Mashhad.

🛏 Sleeping

Timing is everything for visiting Mashhad – in peak season, accommodation is jam-packed; off-season the ubiquitous apartment-hotels that might ask IR3,000,000 at No Ruz can sometimes give away suites for as little as IR500,000. The best bargains are often hidden away in forgotten smaller alleys. Major hotel prices tend to be more stable but some still offer discounts of up to 50% in the low season.

⭐ **Vali's Non-Smoking Homestay** HOSTEL $
(Map p261; ☑ 051-3851 6980, 0939 250 1447; www.valishomestay.com; 277, Malekoshoara Bahar 38th Alley; dm/s/d without bathroom IR400,000/800,000/1,000,000, breakfast/dinner

Central Mashhad

Central Mashhad

IR80,000/180,000; ⊜ 🛜; 📶 83, 86, Ⓜ Emam Khomeini) Eccentric, endlessly enthusiastic Vali is a hospitable (if full-on), English-speaking carpet merchant/guide offering a six-bed mixed dorm and double-bedded private guest room in his rug-bedecked home. In summer, some also sleep on the open-air terrace. It's Mashhad's only real backpacker option but vastly more personal and interactive than most hostels, with great home-cooked family meals and interesting regional tours available.

Prices stay the same all year. Take bus 86 from Andarzgu (p268) in the Haram area to Metro Imam Khomeini, or bus 83 from the Imam Reza Bus Terminal (p267) to (less convenient) Docharkhe Crossing.

Pars Hotel   HOTEL **$**
(Map p261; ☑ 051-3222 4030; Imam Khomeini St, 26th Alley; per person US$12; ❈ 🖳) Mashhad's oldest hotel, the Pars occupies a 1935 brick building that's somewhat gone to seed, but for the price its ageing en suite rooms are nonetheless reasonable value. Manager Hassan speaks good English and the guests-only restaurant is a vaulted *sofrakhane sonati*–style basement, with a *tanour* oven providing fresh bread to accompany meals.

Khorshid Taban Hotel   HOTEL **$$**
(Map p261; ☑ 051-3222 2263; www.khorshidtaban-hotel.com; Pasdaran Ave; s/d/tr IR1,480,000/2,560,000/3,150,000; ❈ 🖳🌊) Luxurious for the price, this nine-storey hotel has an understated grandeur to its lobby/coffeeshop area and its comfortably contemporary rooms, embellished with dark-wood veneer with red velvet panels.

Discounts of around 10% are available off-season if you forgo the breakfast. Use of the swimming pool costs IR160,000. Some English spoken.

Hotel Hejrat   HOTEL **$$**
(Map p264; ☑ 051-3222 6513; Molla Hashim Lane (Shirazi 3rd); r IR1,000,000-1,700,000; ❈ 🖳) The most appealing of several smaller hotels directly north of the Haram Complex, the clean, new Hejrat is aimed at couples, families or women (no unaccompanied male guests are accepted). Rooms are compact but very well equipped with a small kitchenette and choice of toilet type.

Kosar Ghods Hotel   HOTEL **$$**
(Map p264; www.kosaronline.com; Andarzgu St, btwn 2nd & 4th Alley; s/d IR994,000/1,520,000; ❈) With an unbeatable Haram-front location staring straight at the main entrance gates, the Kosar Ghods' compact rooms are fairly modest but bright and clean, with gleaming tiled floors.

It's between 2nd and 4th alleys, signed in Farsi and Arabic (but not in English).

Hotel Zamzam   HOTEL **$$**
(Map p264; ☑ 051-3228 2828; Zeiya Lane; tw/tr year-round US$35/40) Hidden up a seemingly

unpromising alley, this comfortable (if stylistically demented) 51-room hotel contrasts an inviting contemporary lobby-lounge with gilt-edged classicism in corridors and a touch of 1960s-retro in the impeccable rooms. Bathrooms could be bigger.

★**Ghasr Talaee International**   HOTEL **$$$**
(Map p259; ☑ 051-38038; www.ghasrtalaee.com; Imam Reza St; s IR2,790,000, d IR3,990,000-4,990,000; ⊖❈🖳🌊) A gigantic chandelier, tinkling piano music and suavely personable, English-speaking staff welcome guests into this lush five-star hotel with 650 rooms spread over 20 storeys. Rates include use of an indoor swimming pool (women 9am to 3pm, men 4pm to 10pm), Jacuzzis (separated by sex) and a glowing salt room.

★**Javad Hotel**   HOTEL **$$$**
(Map p264; ☑ 051-3222 4135; www.javadhotel.com; Imam Reza St; full season s/d IR2,200,000/3,800,000, off-season IR1,500,000/2,800,000; 🅿❈@🖳🌊) An oasis of calm, contemporary elegance, this excellent hotel has polite, English-proficient staff, a great basement coffeeshop and comfortable rooms whose golden curtains add pizazz yet stop short of excessive glitz.

Hotel Darvishi   RESORT **$$$**
(Map p259; ☑ 051-3855 4008; www.darvishihotel.com; Imam Reza St; d from IR5,000,000; 🅿❈🖳🌊) Designed to make arriving guests gape with wonder, the luxurious Darvishi's gigantic foyer feels like something from 21st-century Las Vegas, albeit without the gambling machines. A multistorey, hanging abstract sculpture looks like a hell-load of intertwined glass snakes, four tall palm trees (convincing fakes) rise within the atrium restaurant and the smaller 2nd-floor restaurant occupies a greenhouse garden.

✖ Eating

There are endless cheap eateries in (mostly subterranean) restaurants in the Haram area, but for a selection of classier options you might want to head to the western suburbs around Sajjad Blvd, to the streamside teahouse-restaurants of **Torqabeh** or to **Shandiz** for indulgent grandeur.

Sholeh Mashhadi is a locally typical home-cooked meat-and-lentil stew, albeit originally served on post-funeral mourning days.

Chahar Fasl   IRANIAN $

(Map p261; ☑ 051-3853 1010; Imam Khomeini St, 45th Alley; kabab meals IR125,000-220,000; ⊗5am-8am, 11am-4pm & 6.30pm-midnight; Ⓜ Imam Khomeini) Upstairs within this ordinary-looking, counter-service *kababi* is a pleasant stone-and-brick dining room. For breakfast (before 8am) you can get *halim* (IR85,000) – Iranian porridge.

Fanous-e Abi   AFGHANI, IRANIAN $$

(Map p259; ☑ 051-3768 0345; Ferdosi Blvd; mains IR100,000-290,000; ⊗noon-4pm & 8-11pm; 🚍12 to Aparteman Haye Mortafa) Less central or authentic but considerably more reasonably priced than Mashhad's other *sonati* (traditionally styled) dining options, Fanous serves Afghan-Uzbek and Iranian meals in a photogenic teahouse basement decked with wagon wheels, paraffin lamps, 'Old Orient' murals and even a mock well. No qalyan (officially) but excellent coffee (IR70,000 to IR100,000) is served.

It's beneath a modern building right beside a stop for the number 12 bus to the Haram.

Food Factory   INTERNATIONAL $$

(Map p259; ☑ Shahrab Nikpour 0915 504 0338; Hooshiyar St, opp 10th Alley; mains IR180,000-400,000; ⊗11am-midnight; Ⓜ Khayyam) With a ceiling of barrels, green-washed tables, frilled lamps and exposed brick walls, the main triangle of dining room is very inviting but it's the darker, glass-walled upstairs that packs in the youth crowd for mixed meat in mushroom sauce, salad, pasta or burgers. The menu is unpriced and all in Farsi but owner Shahrab speaks English.

Olive Garden   ITALIAN $$

(Map p259; Khayyam 1st Alley; mains IR150,000-340,000; ⊗6-11pm) If you want a classy meal of something other than Iranian fare, this cosy little (and much-applauded) Italian choice might be worth the ride out to Metro Khayyam.

They have another branch near Sajjad Blvd.

Naseem Lebanon   LEBANESE $$

(Map p259; Imam Reza St, cnr 24th Alley; mezze items IR50,000, kababs IR140,000-240,000; ⊗12.15-4pm & 7pm-midnight) Excellent-value

---

ⓘ VISITING THE HARAM COMPLEX

It's worth visiting the Haram several times to witness its ever-changing moods. The experience is especially powerful around sunset prayer time, but also late at night. (Note that some areas are officially out of bounds to non-Muslims.) If you want a free day-time tour of the complex, along with lots of background and a video to watch, ask at the **Foreign Pilgrims Affairs Office** (مرکز توریستی زائران خارجی; Map p264; ☑ 051-3221 3474; www.imamrezashrine.com; Jomhuri Courtyard; ⊗7am-6pm).

If you're not there on a pilgrimage yourself, a good starting point for is **Falakeh Ab**, from which you enter the vast, highly impressive **Razavi Grand Courtyard**. Especially in the evening, visitors are often permitted to continue from there into the **Imam Khomeini Ravagh** (Map p264; ⊗24hr), a covered, mixed-sex prayer hall with a dazzling interior of tree-like mirror columns and faceted ceilings. Pilgrims surge on into the **main shrine** (Map p264) to approach Imam Reza's tomb. Amid tearful prayer and meditation, the emotional climax to any Mashhad pilgrimage is touching and kissing the shrine's *zarih* (gold-latticed cage), which covers Imam Reza's tomb. Non-Muslims should not approach the *zarih* and are not usually allowed closer than the entrances of the two most glorious courtyards, **Azadi** and **Enghelab**, each connected to the inner sanctum via golden *iwans* (vaulted portals).

You might catch a glimpse of the 50m blue dome and cavernous golden portal of the classic Timurid **Azim-e Gohar Shad mosque** (Map p264), built from 1405 to 1418. Of three rather eclectic **museums**, the one displaying a fine collection of **carpets** (موزه فرش; Map p264; Kausar Courtyard; IR5000; ⊗8am-12.30pm Sat-Wed, to 11.30am Thu, to noon Fri) is arguably the best, though given the minimal entrance fees it's fun to have a look through all of them if you're not in a hurry.

Entry to the Haram precinct starts with a polite, airport-style security screening and you'll need to deposit bags, computers, power packs etc in one of the free baggage stores, at most gates and at the **main entrance**. Women who don't have their own chador can borrow one at most of the gates. Entry gates include **Tusi** (northwest), **Tabarsi** (north), **Javad** and **Hadi** (west), and **Navvab Safavi** (east).

Haram Area

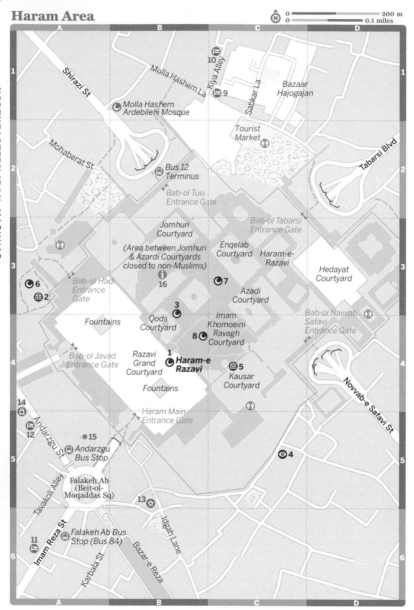

0   200 m
0   0.1 miles

Shirazi St

Molla Hashem La

Kiya Alley

10

9

Sabkar La

Bazaar Hajogajan

Molla Hashem Ardebilehi Mosque

Mohaberat St

Tourist Market

Tabarsi Blvd

Bus 12 Terminus

Bab-ol Tusi Entrance Gate

Jomhuri Courtyard

Bab-ol Tabarsi Entrance Gate

(Area between Jomhuri & Azadi Courtyards closed to non-Muslims)

Enqelab Courtyard

Haram-e Razavi

Hedayat Courtyard

16

7

Bab-ol Hadi Entrance Gate

6

2

Azadi Courtyard

Bab-ol Navvab Safavi Entrance Gate

Fountains

3

Qods Courtyard

Imam Khomoeini Ravagh Courtyard

8

Bab-ol Javad Entrance Gate

Razavi Grand Courtyard

1

Haram-e Razavi

Fountains

5

Kausar Courtyard

Novvab-e Safavi St

Haram Main Entrance Gate

14

12

Andarzgu St

15

Andarzgu Bus Stop

4

Falakeh Ab (Beit-ol-Moqaddas Sq)

13

Tavakoli Alley

Imam Reza St

Idgah Lane

Bazar-e Reza

11

Falakeh Ab Bus Stop (Bus 84)

Karbala St

Lebanese fare in a deep, high-ceilinged restaurant, with a photo menu and English translations displayed helpfully over the long barbecue-serving bar.

★ **Babaghodrat**   IRANIAN $$$
(Map p259; ☏ 051-3344 0124; www.babagh odrat.com; Sadr 16; mains IR320,000-600,000; ☺ noon-4pm & 7.30pm-midnight) Part of an impressive cultural complex, this memorable restaurant serves kababs, trout and huge

Haram Area

◎ **Top Sights**
1	Haram-e Razavi	B4

◎ **Sights**
2	Anthropology Museum	A3
3	Azim-e Gohar Shad	B3
4	Caravanserai Azizolaof	C5
5	Carpet Museum	C4
6	Haftado Tan Mosque	A3
7	Holy Shrine	C3
8	Imam Khomeini Ravagh	B4

🛌 **Sleeping**
9	Hotel Hejrat	C1
10	Hotel Zamzam	C1
11	Javad Hotel	A6
12	Kosar Ghods Hotel	A5

🍸 **Drinking & Nightlife**
	Javad Hotel Coffeeshop	(see 11)

🎭 **Entertainment**
13	Zorkhane	B5

🛍 **Shopping**
14	Saroye Saeed	A5

ℹ **Information**
15	Main Entrance Baggage Store	A5
16	Management of Foreign Pilgrims Affairs	B3

bowls of *mirza ghasemi* (IR160,000) within the spacious brick vaults of a Qajar-era caravanserai. It's around 10 minutes' walk from the southeast end of the Reza covered bazaar.

★ **Hezardestan Traditional Teahouse** IRANIAN $$$
(Map p261; ☎ 051-3222 2943; Jannat Lane; mains IR287,500-540,500; ☻11am-4pm & 6-11pm) Hezardestan is one of Iran's most beautiful teahouse-restaurants, with a museum-like basement full of of carpets, samovars, antique metalwork and countless knick-nacks around a small fountain. The menu is limited to *ghormeh*, chicken kabab, *dizi* or mashed *halim bademjan* (lamb and mashed aubergine). Beware when ordering tea: while a cup costs IR23,000 the tea 'set' costs ten times that (IR230,000).

There's live music most nights. The manager speaks some English.

🍸 **Drinking & Nightlife**

Sofrekhane-style teahouse experiences are alluring at Babaghodrat (p264) and

Hezardestan but both are pricey. Fanous-e Abi (p263) is cheaper but further out.

Hotel Javad's **coffeeshop** (Map p264; Imam Reza St, cnr 3rd Alley; ☻7am-1am; 🛜) is recommended but otherwise Mashhad's contemporary coffeehouse culture is mostly far from the main pilgrim area: try around **Kuh-e Sangi**, home to some of Mashhad's more interesting coffeeshops, which lie within a warren of otherwise mostly residential roads to the northwest of the park area; the upmarket **Sajjad Blvd** area (note the best cafes and restaurants tend to be hidden away, entered from arcades or back lanes); or near **Khayyam metro**.

The Wall COFFEE
(Map p259; Reza Blvd, cnr 40th Alley; ☻9am-11pm) The logo apes the classic Pink Floyd album, but the music played in this couple-y, mood-lit coffeeshop ranges from Persian love ballads to shoegazing. Excellent coffee (from IR90,000) and toasted sandwiches. It's around 400m northeast from Kuh-e Sangi metro station.

Toranj Cafe COFFEE
(Map p259; Sajad Blvd, at Bozorgmehr 10th St; ☻9am-midnight) Toranj's panelled ceiling and fireplace give the impression of an updated gentleman's club with African masks. Shakes, ice creams and juices supplement coffee (from IR80,000) made on a Conti machine. Staff speak a little English.

It's up a triple flight of stairs within the fourth arcade to left as you walk west along Sajad Blvd from the Bozorgmehr 10th St junction.

Malas JUICE BAR
(Map p259; Shariati Sq; ☻9am-3am; M Shariati) It's pomegranate paradise – from juice (from IR50,000) to cake to the stylised red frontage of this small, contemporary juice bar.

Vitamin Sara JUICE BAR
(Map p261; ☎051-3222 6712; Shahid Diyalemeh (Bahonar) St; ☻9am-11pm Sat-Thu, to 2pm Fri) This unpretentious juice shop serves Mashhad's best *maajun* (IR80,000-150,000), a fabulous mush of crushed walnuts, pistachios, ice cream, cream, banana and honey, all whizzed together to form one of Iran's most spectacular desserts.

☆ **Entertainment**

Zurkhaneh SPECTATOR SPORT
(Map p264; Idgah Lane; requested donation IR20,000; ☻6.30-9pm) While the chamber

is less exotic than the equivalent at Yazd, this regular *zurkhaneh* meet is a very real – and surreal – Iranian experience, with well over a dozen regulars going through a series of different displays of meditative strength and agility to the sound of insistent percussion. Rare spectators who stumble in generally receive tea (a small tip is expected).

 ## Shopping

 ### Carpets

Half-hidden through small doorways, both **Bazaar-e Farsh** (Map p261; Imam Reza St; ⊙9am-8.30pm Sat-Wed, to 1pm Thu) and **Saroye Saeed** (Map p264; Andarzgu St; ⊙8am-2pm & 4-8pm Sat-Wed, 8am-2pm Thu) are multi-unit carpet markets mostly aimed at bulk dealers, meaning prices can be excellent. Both places are architecturally bland but have interesting top-floor **repair workshops** – and remarkably there seems to be no sales pressure.

The **old carpet bazaar** (Map p261; Andarzgu 13th Alley; ⊙approx 9am-1pm & 4pm-sunset) is more atmospheric but also more commercially minded.

 ### Saffron

Cleopatra added it to her mare's-milk baths. Indian Buddhists dyed their robes with it. Romans slapped it on to cure scabies. And Alexander the Great used it to patch up his battle scars. Today saffron adds flavour and colour to Cornish saffron cake and Spanish paella as well as to *chelo* (rice) in Iran, where it remains Persia's classic spice.

Saffron comes from the delicately dried stigmas of *Crocus sativus* flowers, grown extensively in southern regions of Khorasan. But producing a kilogram of saffron requires around 200,000 flowers – no wonder it's

often so staggeringly pricey. However, there are a wide range of qualities dependent on which part of the stamen has been collected (and whether or not it's really saffron). Shops around Mashhad's Falakeh Ab sell comparatively inexpensive variants and well-reputed **Bahraman** (Map p259; Imam Reza St, cnr 8th Alley; saffron per g from IR82,000; ⊙8am-10pm Sat-Thu, 9am-2pm & 5-8pm Fri) has snazzy saffron boutiques. Some general spice shops also sell vastly cheaper *golerang* ('false saffron'), commonly used to colour rice and some breads.

 ## Information

CONSULATES

Turkmen Consulate (Map p261; ☑051-3854 7066; Do Shahid St, off Dah-e Dey Sq; ⊙8.30-noon Mon-Thu & Sat) Allow at least 10 days to get a five-day transit visa (US$55 to $85, depending on nationality). You'll need colour photocopies of your passport info page and onward visa (Uzbek, Kazakh) and will usually need to state the entry and exit points and dates by which you'll transit Turkmenistan (inflexible). To apply you'll need to knock on a tiny window-slit; some staff do speak English. Alternatively it is possible to apply here and collect the visa at the **embassy** (Map p52; ☑021-2220 6306; http://iran.tmembassy.gov.tm; 5 Barati St, off Vatanpour St; ⊙9.30-11am Sun-Thu; Ⓜ Tajrish, then taxi) in Tehran (or vice versa). Note that the visa fee is payable on collection even if you have pre-paid elsewhere (eg in a European country before leaving for Iran). Hard luck! You must apply in person. There's a handy photocopy shop 300m north of the consulate.

INTERNET ACCESS

Some upmarket coffeeshops offer free internet. **Cafenet Khayyam** (Map p261; 2nd fl, Imam Reza St, btwn 4th & 6th Alleys; internet per hr IR30,000 (downloads extra); ⊙9am-11pm) is a relatively central internet cafe, upstairs above the photography studio marked (in English) 'Hosne Yousouf Foto'.

MASHTI

Although slightly less significant than pilgrimages to Mecca, Najaf or Karbala, a pilgrimage to Mashhad remains a deeply significant expression of faith for any Shiite Muslim. After *wudu* (ablutions), the supplicant humbly enters the Holy Shrine asking 'permission' from Imam Reza through specific prayers and recitations. Following tearful meditations and Quranic readings, the pilgrimage culminates with the recitation of the *ziyarat nameh* prayer in front of the *zarih* (tomb) of Imam Reza.

In the same way that hajj pilgrims are respectfully known as *hajji*, those who have fulfilled the pilgrimage to Mashhad are entitled to attach the prefix *mashti* to their names.

MEDICAL

Imam Reza Hospital (Map p261; ☑ 051-3854 3031; www.mums.ac.ir; Ibn-e Sina St) Good, accessible hospital with 24-hour pharmacy.

MONEY

There are several money-changers on Pasdaran and Imam Khomeini streets, including **Baghoi Exchange** (Map p261; ☑ 051-3853 3438; Imam Khomeini St; ☺ 9am-2pm & 5-7pm Sat-Wed, 9am-1pm Thu). If you need to change money late at night or on Fridays, try the booth at the upmarket **Ghasr International Hotel** (Map p261; Imam Reza St, cnr 16th Alley; ☺ 24hr).

POST

Post Office (Map p261; Imam Khomeini St) After 2pm, when the main hall closes, a small booth out front will still sell stamps (until 6pm).

TOURIST INFORMATION

Miras Ferhangi Khorasan (Map p259; ☑ 051-3725 9311; www.razavichto.ir; Sadeghi Blvd; ☺ 8am-2pm Sat-Thu) Prints lavish bilingual brochures for each district in Khorasan Razavi, but unless you speak Farsi and have a specialist question, it's not really worth the trip out to their office.

TRAVEL AGENCIES

Very professional **Adibian Travel & Tours** (Map p261; ☑ 051-5513 2539; www.adibian. com; Pasdaran Ave, cnr 4th Alley; ☺ 8am-7pm Sat-Wed, to 6pm Thu, 9am-noon Fri) is an English-speaking agency that sells air and train tickets. **HGH724** (Map p261; ☑ 051-3806 9000; www.hgh724.com; Malekoshoara Bahar St; ☺ 8.30am-7pm Sat-Thu; Ⓜ Imam Khomeini) and more central Mahan Air are also reliable for air tickets.

VISA EXTENSIONS

Edareh-ye Gozarnameh (Map p259; ☑ 051-3218 3907; 45 Metri-ye Reza St, Piruzi Blvd; ☺ 8am-1pm Sat-Wed, to 10.30am Thu) Behind fortified green fencing, this inconveniently located place for visa extensions would look like a prison except that the mad crush of inmates are all trying to get in. It's not the best place to apply. Visas can also be extended at Tehran's **Foreign Intelligence Office** (p68).

🛈 Getting There & Away

During peak seasons long-distance transport can be booked up months ahead.

AIR
Domestic Services

To Tehran there are over two dozen daily flights (IR2,000,000 to IR2,800,000) on at least seven airlines. There are at least three flights daily to Ahvaz, Esfahan, Kish, Shiraz, Tabriz and Yazd,

none costing over IR3,000,000. There are a few weekly connections to Bandar Abbas, Kerman and Qeshm.

Flight frequency increases in peak seasons but demand remains very heavy around No Ruz and key religious festivals.

International Services

Iran Aseman (www.iaa.ir) has flights to Dushanbe, Tajikistan (from IR6,100,000, Thursday).

For Afghanistan there are three weekly flights to Kabul (IR6,000,000) on Mahan Air and one to Mazar-i-Sharif (IR6,000,000) on **KamAir** (www.flykamair.ca).

To go further afield, use connections with Air Arabia, Qatar Airways or Turkish Airlines via the Gulf or Istanbul. **Jazeera Airways** (www.jazeeraairways.com) has flights to Kuwait twice weekly in season.

Bus, Minibus & Savari

All of Mashhad's numerous transport terminals are well out of the centre. The huge **Imam Reza Bus Terminal** (Map p259; end of Imam Reza St; 🚌 84) handles most long-distance services. Pre-purchase tickets for most routes, but pay the driver directly for Neishabur (IR80,000, departs when full, platform 8).

For Quchan, Esfarayen and Bojnurd, buses use the **Meraj Terminal** (Meraj Sq, Toos Blvd), as do Chenaran-bound minibuses, useful for reaching Radkan.

Savaris to Bajgiran (IR1,500,000 *dar bast*), Quchan (IR100,000) and Chenaran start from the intimidatingly hassle-filled **Park Savar Shahid** (Shahed Ride Station; ☑ Tirzo Tarobar Taxis 051-3666 3101; www.mashhadterminals.ir; Azadi Expressway, at 99th Azadi Alley).

For Kalat, savaris (IR130,000) and eight daily buses (IR70,000, 2½ hours) use the small **Istgah Savari Kalat terminal** (Map p259; Khajerabi Blv, cnr 11th St), 600m south of Khajerabi Shrine.

For villages west of Mashhad, including Torqabeh and Kang, most transport starts from the **bus station** (🚌 10, Ⓜ Vakilabad) outside Vakilabad metro terminus.

Bus 202 to the Ferdosi Museum in Tus starts from **Falakeh Ferdosi** (Map p259; Toos Blvd).

Train

The train offers a wonderfully comfortable alternative to flying, especially if you pamper yourself with a 1st-class berth (comfortable beds, flatscreen TV, full meal service included). Book as far ahead as possible. Useful options:

Esfahan (IR720,000 to IR859,000) Two overnight trains both depart around 1pm, arriving 7am.

Tehran (IR440,000 to IR1,500,000) Runs 13 daily trains of various classes. Most take 11 to 12 hours, but the 7am express (IR1,100,000) zips along in just seven. The cheapest option is on the seat-only 7.20am service, arriving at 7.30pm.

Tabriz (IR1,130,000) 8.15pm alternate days, arrives 8.30pm

Yazd (IR900,000) Departs 7.30pm, arrives 9.25am

❶ Getting Around

There's a plethora of bus routes around town. The metro should become much more useful with the opening of lines 2 (2017) and 3 (possibly 2018–19).

TO/FROM THE AIRPORT

The airport, 5km east of **Imam Reza Bus Terminal** (p267), has three terminals. The metro station is at Terminal 1. Terminal 3 (International Arrivals) is around 350m to the southeast. Terminal 2 (International Departures) is 800m west.

While the metro link sounds useful, the service from the airport to the city is limited, operating at 7.58am, 8.22am, 8.46am and 9.11am, then roughly twice an hour from 3.22pm to 9.25pm.

Bus 77 leaves on the hour (6am to 8pm) from stops just west of Terminal 1 and outside Terminal 2. It returns from the **Enghelab City Terminal** (Map p259) on the half-hour.

Most travellers use taxis, which should cost around IR120,000 to the central area.

BUS

Buses cost IR5000 per hop, or IR3500 if you pay using an electronic, pre-paid MAN-card (IR50,000 deposit). Most buses stop running after 9pm.

Useful services include bus 83, which goes from the main bus terminal to the train station via central Mashhad; 84 runs a similar route in the reverse direction, giving a great view of the central sights en route and picking up southbound at **Falakeh Ab** (Map p264; Imam Reza St). Bus 86 runs to Kuh-e Sangi from Falakeh Ab.

Bus 12 (Map p264; Haram NW exit) starts near the Haram's northwest exit and makes stops at **Nader Shah Mausoleum** (Map p261; Shirazi St), Shohoda Sq, Ferdosi Sq and **Fanous-e Abi** (p263; one stop beyond the big Saba Hotel). Some crosstown buses also start from the **Andarzgu bus stop** (Map p264; Andarzgu St) south of the Haram.

METRO

The 24-station metro line 1 starts from the airport in the southeast, runs underground beneath Feda'iyen-e Eslami, Malekoshoara Bahar, Enqelab-e-Eslami and Ahmedabad Sts to Park Mellat, then overground to Vakilabad down the middle of Vakilabad Blvd (rendering that thundering highway almost uncrossable). At the time of writing, line 2 was about to open between Kuh-e Sangi and the train station via Shariati (interchange), while line 3 (also under construction) should eventually link the bus station and Haram, interchanging with line 1 at Basij.

Tickets for two/six rides cost IR20,000/40,000. Often these must be purchased from shops within the stations as the ticket machines only work with Iranian debit cards.

Note that while the line 1 metro extends to the airport, trains only actually run on the airport spur four times each morning (7.30am to 8.40pm from Imam Khomeini Station), and then again around twice an hour between 2.53pm and 8.49pm. The airport metro station is at Terminal 1 (Domestic); Terminal 2 (International Departures) is an 800m walk away.

Around Mashhad

Mashhad's inexorable growth is starting to engulf outlying villages while once quaint hamlets in the Binalud foothills are turning into strip towns of upmarket restaurants,

BUSES FROM MASHHAD'S IMAM REZA TERMINAL

DESTINATION	FARE (IR; VIP/MAHMOOLY)	DURATION (HR)	DEPARTURES & COMPANY
Birjand	350,000/205,000	7	5.30am–2pm
Boshrooyeh	180,000/–	6	3pm (Taavoni 12)
Esfahan	780,000/550,000	22	7am, 3pm, 6–8pm
Gorgan	500,000/265,000	9	5.30–10am, 2pm & 6–9pm
Kerman	643,000/405,000	14	1–8pm
Qa'en	265,000/147,000	5	5.30am–2.30pm
Tehran	685,000/420,000	12	frequent 7am–10pm
Yazd	645,000/400,000	16	3–8pm (Saadet Peyma)

most notably at **Shandiz**; the best place to eat here is **Bagh-e Salar** (☑051-3432 3866; www.baghselar.com; Mashhad–Shandiz Rd; buffet meals IR600,000, shishlik IR637,700; ☺noon-4.30pm & 6.30-11pm). Prettier teahouse-retreat **Torqabeh** remains somewhat more rustic, but to get a little further from the concrete of urban sprawl, the stepped village of Kang makes an appealing option, especially if you're hiking.

For devotees of Iran's great medieval poets, the garden-set mausoleums of **Omar Khayyam** (foreigner/Iranian IR150,000/25,000; ☺garden 8am-9pm, museum 8am-2pm Tue-Sun; ☑10) at **Neishabur** and **Ferdosi** (Blvd Shahnameh; foreigner/Iranian IR200,000/30,000; ☺8am-sunset (museum closes 30min earlier)) at **Tus** might appeal, but be aware that both were built in the 20th century.

Longer but more off-beat day trips take visitors to Nader Shah's unfinished tomb-palace at Kalat via an appealingly desolate cross-mountain road. Or buzz up the motorway to find a lonely 13th-century astronomical tower near Radkan, a village with one of the region's best-conceived little ecolodges.

Kang کنگ

☑051 / POPULATION 2300 / ELEVATION 1710M

Photogenic Kang is a contender as 'Khorasan's Masuleh', a fairly homogenous **stepped village** of stacked mud-brick homes, most with porch-balconies and earthen roofs. Stairways duck beneath overhangs while steep, slate-bottomed streams run down the middle of alleyways. To find the base of the village, fork left at the teahouse where the bus terminates. For the best viewpoint continue another 400m, cross the river and climb for about three minutes more – then look back from a small orchard garden.

A rewarding 1½-hour **hike** from Kang crosses a bald, low-mountain pass on a rough 4WD track to the Shandiz–Zoshk road. The trek is a speciality day-trip of Mashhad guide Vali Astaneh (p260), who also adds in a meal stop with a local family in Abardeh. Another option for the more energetic is climbing **Shirabad Peak** (3211m).

🛏 Sleeping & Eating

There's no hotel accommodation in Kang but village homestays (where you'll sleep on floor mats) are possible if you ask around. The easiest to find is that of **Majid Asayesh** (☑0915 908 7381; r in new/

old bldg IR800,000/600,000, peak season IR1,100,000/900,000), who lives above the little store at the base of the village. Though he has a newer (so-so) apartment for rent, it's cheaper and more atmospheric to opt for a room in his 'traditional' house in a timeless alley around the corner.

There's a basic, summer-only teahouse at the base of the village, with many more dotted along the roadside stream towards Torqabeh. All are simple, family affairs with little pretense and a genuinely rural feel. Our favourite, **Ehsan** (☑0915 643 3965; Kang–Torqabeh Rd, Km3; ☺8am-late), opens even in winter.

🛈 Getting There & Away

From the metro terminus at **Vakilabad** (p267) in Mashhad, there are three daily buses to Kang (IR15,000, 40 minutes), departing 6.50am, 10.50am and 2.50pm, and returning from Kang's unmarked **bus stop** (400m northeast of the two shops) at 9.20am, 1pm and 5pm.

Radkan رادکان

☑051 / POPULATION 2270 / ELEVATION 1190M

Around 9km off the Quchan–Mashhad Hwy, Radkan village is surrounded by a quietly fascinating scattering of old mud ruins and ancient sites, including a conical former **ice house** right in the heart of the hamlet. But much the most interesting and best preserved monument is the 13th-century **Radkan Tower**. Fenced amid fields 3km southeast, this conically spired 25m brick tower has baffled visitors for centuries. Was it a tomb? A coronation spot?

According to Iranian archaeo-astronomer Manoochehr Arian (www.jamejamshid.com), it was actually a highly sophisticated instrument for studying the stars, built in 1261 by astronomers led by Khajeh Nasir Al-Tusi (Nasruddin Tusi; 1201-74). By design, the sun shines directly through its doors and niches on solstice and equinox days. It was possibly with data collected here, and at his more famous observatory at Maraqeh, that Tusi managed to calculate the earth's diameter and explain discrepancies between Aristotle's and Ptolemy's theories of planetary movement.

With 12 sleep-on-floor rooms (two of them en suite) ranged round a central well and fountain pool, **Radkan Arg Ecolodge** (☑Dr Kazemian (owner) 0915 122 3247; www.radkanarg.ir; per person with full board IR1,200,000) is a delightful rural guesthouse. The long-ruined adobe villa of a former village 'governor', it has been lovingly restored with small wind-towers, roof-top terraces, crenellated walls and even a little aviary corner for pigeons. Book at least two days ahead as the place is not permanently staffed.

🛈 Getting There & Away

Radkan is 9km off the Mashhad–Bojnurd Hwy, with the turning 58km before Quchan (about 75km northwest of Mashhad).

Unmarked **taxis** wait where the main village road turns a right angle, 100m north of the tower-roundabout (Imam Khomeini Sq). To Chenaran they charge IR100,000 per car direct, or IR130,000 with a brief stop en route to see the tower. From Chenaran, minibuses run up to twice an hour to Mashhad's **Meraj terminal** (p267; IR15,000, 50 minutes). To central Mash-had, taxis will want IR400,000, or IR500,000 with a stop en route at Tus.

Kalat   کلات

📱 051 / POPULATION 11,600 / ELEVATION 880M

Admiring its near-vertical backdrop of moun-tain cliffs, you don't need to be a military commander to see why Kalat has historically made the ideal last holdout for rebels on the run. It was one of the only places to have re-sisted the armies of Tamerlane, and it's still widely called 'Kalat Naderi' for Nader Shah, who is said to have hidden the priceless plun-ders from his Indian campaign somewhere hereabouts.

Beyond the setting, Kalat's main at-traction is **Khorshid Palace** (Kakh-e Nad-er, Ghasr-e Khorshid; 📱051-3272 2239; Imam Khomeini St; foreigner/Iranian IR80,000/20,000; ☉ sunrise-sunset). Set in manicured lawns this isn't really a palace at all but a distinc-tively fluted, circular tomb-tower for Nader Shah. (The name Khorshid (literally 'sun') refers to one of Nader's wives, not some arcane astronomical purpose.) It was nev-er finished, hence the odd proportions and lack of a dome. The tower's interior uses gilt and ample colour (albeit partly faded) to bring life to 16 stalactite-vaulted alcoves.

Entering Kalat the main road passes through a long tunnel then crosses a bridge shortly before the savari and bus stands. If you double back on the north side of the river and follow it 500m southwest you'll see **Borg-argavan Shah**, an iconic, round mud-brick tower rising on the rocks above. Just beyond is the **Katibeh Nader**, an unfinished inscription on a smoothed section of cliff-face

praising Nader Shah with poetry in Turkish and Farsi.

Many Kurds were settled in Kalat here during the Safavid dynasty to guard against northern invaders, and some women still wear Kurdish costumes. Spring is the best time to visit, when the countryside turns emerald green and nomad tents dot the foothill grasslands, especially along the Kalat–Dargaz road.

🛏 Sleeping

Sandati House   APARTMENT **$$**

(📱 caretaker 0910 576 4458, owner in Mashhad 0915 245 6413; Shahid Alipur St, opp 17th Alley; peak season d/tr IR135,000/1,500,000, off-peak IR800,000/950,000) In the white build-ing beside the ambulance station are five spacious new suites, in which most of the space is used for kitchen and sitting areas, bedrooms seemingly an afterthought. It's on the upper road from the Khorshid Pal-ace that converges with Imam Khomeini St near the mosque. Be sure to call ahead in the off-season.

🛈 Getting There & Away

Kalat is 150km from Mashhad. En route, 35km beyond Khajerabi Sq, the route passes through **Gojgi**, a timeless, mud-built village set in arid hills and backed by a red-rock crag. The road then crosses a pass and descends between eroded hilltop spikes and minor canyons to tiny **Taherabad** (80km from Mashhad), which overlooks a sea of badlands. From here the road swings abruptly west towards **Dargaz**, running along the base of low, arid mountains.

Savaris (IR130,000, two hours) and eight daily buses (IR70,000, 2½ hours, last departure 4pm) shuttle between Kalat's **savari stand** (Imam Khomeini St) at the entrance to town and a special terminal in Mashhad, 600m south of Khajerabi Shrine (from which bus 38 connects to Kuh-e Sangi via Shohada Sq).

Bojnurd   بجنورد

📱 058 / POPULATION 207,200 / ELEVATION 1060M

North Khorasan's capital, fast-growing Bo-jnurd is mainly useful as a place to change transport en route to Esfarayen/Roein. While you're here, though, you might pop into the centre to see pretty **Aynekhane** (Mirror House; Shari'ati St; Aynekhane/museum foreigners IR100,000/150,000, Iranians IR20,000/30,000; ☉ 7am-4.30pm), a distinctive building with Qajar-tiled frontage and a notable mirror-room.

WORTH A TRIP

ZAFARANIYEH

Timeless and virtually deserted, **Zafaraniyeh** (Sabzevar–Neishabur Rd Km37.3) is a rare example of a Silk Road village that has managed to maintain not only its **caravanserai** (merchant's inn) but also a whole series of mud-domed ancillary buildings around it, including a beehive-shaped **ice house** (Ice House; Zafaraniyeh) FREE that was in use up till the 1970s, a *hammam*, a *chaparkhane* (stabling yard) and large **citadel** in which the shattered remnants of the older village lie in a fascinating state of photogenic collapse.

According to village folklore, Zafaraniyeh's caravanserai was built from bricks scavenged from two much older versions that had fallen into ruin. To bless the construction, a sack of saffron (*zafaran*) was purchased from passing traders and mixed into the mud used to cement the stones together, an act of extravagance for which the village got its name.

Zafaraniyeh makes a satisfying half-hour stop if you're driving by on the Sabzevar–Mashhad Hwy, but it's also a good place to sleep thanks to the village cooperative's bargain-value **'ecolodge'** (📞 Mr Arabkhani 0915 171 3065, Mr Fakhor 0915 707 2639; Zafaraniyeh; per person IR400,000), comprising three rooms in a tiny former school.

From Sabzevar, a daily yellow minibus (IR20,000, one hour) to Zafaraniyeh leaves from Seraheh Mosallah, near Shohoda Sq, at 1pm, returning the next morning at 7am. *Dar bast* (charter) taxis (IR300,000) start from the south side of Sarbedoran Sq.

🧭 Tours

Farhad Soleymani   OUTDOORS
(📞 0902 777 0117; FarhadSoleymani7@gmail.com) Knowledgeable Bojnurd-based guide and filmmaker Farhad has lived in many foreign countries, speaks excellent English and offers driving tours or short hiking itineraries tailored to visitor requirements.

❶ Getting There & Away

The **bus terminal** (Defa-e Moqaddes Sq) is at the southernmost point of the ring road. Buses leave to Mashhad (IR100,000, four hours) at least twice hourly from 5am to 6pm. For Gorgan, Seiro Safar has a 6.30am bus (IR170,000, six hours) or use one of the Tehran services that leave between 4pm and 7.30pm. There's a 6pm Esfahan service (IR800,000, around 18 hours) and a 1.30pm bus to Sabzevar (IR100,000, three hours).

For Esfarayen, **savaris** (Chamran Blvd; IR55,000, one hour) depart from a point 2km southwest on Chamran Blvd, where it meets with Daneshgah St; a couple of daily minibuses (IR25,000) also leave from there. **Mashhad savaris** (Mashhad Hwy; IR200,000, 3½ hours) leave from just northeast of Imam Reza Sq.

Bojnurd's airport, directly northwest of the city centre, has daily flights to Tehran.

Esfarayen   اسفراین

📞 058 / POPULATION 63,900 / ELEVATION 1180M
Distantly overshadowed to the south by the hefty peak of **Mt Shahjahan**, and snuggled against colourful, crumpled badlands to the cast, Esfarayen sits at the edge of a wide flat plateau on which you'll find the gigantic ruined citadel site of **Belqays** (Old Esfarayen) FREE. Much smaller but with more vernacular mud-building ruins is the rarely visited village **Dowlatabad** (Sabzevar Hwy, Km10).

Another village, **Roein** (Rooin; off Esfarayen–Bojnurd Hwy) retains several areas of predominantly mud-built houses stepped up the amphitheatre behind the new mosque, which is fronted by an 800-year-old *chinar* (plane tree). Another old *chinar*, once hollow, has been bricked up but was previously used as a butcher's shop. Across the road are the domes of a century-old *hammam* (bathhouse).

On a village walk with Ali, owner of **Vesal Homestay** (Eqamatgah Burngardi Vesal Roein; 📞 Ali Vesal 0915 652 7079; www.vesal-rooin.ir; Roein; 10-person apts IR1,100,000; 🛜), a highlight is drinking tea at his grandmother's house while watching a very personal demonstration of traditional towel-weaving and enjoying some of the best views of old Roein. Nearby are even better views, from a knoll with a 360-degree panorama.

Beside the Roein access lane, just 1km off the Bojnurd–Esfarayen road, the rarely visited hamlet of **Araghi** is far smaller than Roein but almost entirely untouched by new construction, and lies close to a picturesque stream.

🍴 Eating & Drinking

Parsian Restaurant   IRANIAN $$
(Valiasr St, cnr 13th Alley, Esfarayen; chicken meals IR90,000-135,000, kababs IR110,000-325,000;

⊘noon-4pm & 6.30-11pm) This understated place, decorated in two tones of dark-wood veneer, serves huge portions of *akhbar juje* (tender, slow-cooked chicken) as well as typical kababs. A barely-soup starter comes free with meal orders.

Cafe Dastan COFFEE
(🖉935 376 4821; Imam Khomeini Sq; ⊘4-11pm) Super-central yet hidden away down a tiny alley beside Bank Sepah, this well-pitched, youthful coffeehouse (coffee IR60,000 to IR110,000) is most notable for its swirling Van Gogh ceiling.

☆ Entertainment

Koshti Bachukeh SPECTATOR SPORT
(Wrestling; Godeh Zeynalkhan Amphitheatre, Imam Reza 40th Alley, Esfarayen; ⊘2 Apr) A local form of wrestling, *koshti bachukeh* is popular across the region, but every year, two weeks after Noruz, the year's championship comes to a conclusion in the gladiators' pit that is Esfarayen's Godeh Zeynalkhan Amphitheatre, with its steep-raked step-seating and curiously desolate location pressing against the nearby badlands.

❶ Getting There & Away

Esfarayen's small **bus terminal** (Ring Road, Esfarayen) handles departures to Mashhad (via Bojnurd; IR115,000) at 7am, 8am, 9am, 1.30pm and 2.30pm, plus a midnight service via Sabzevar. There are also overnight buses to Tehran (IR330,000 to IR560,000) via Sabzevar between 4.30pm and 8.30pm, stopping near Shahrud (IR175,000), Damghan (IR210,000) and Semnan (IR240,000).
Savaris to Bojnurd (Safar Seir Arya; Modarres Blvd; IR55,000) start 250m from Pahlavan Keshveri Sq. When university is in session there are also two or three minibuses, aimed mainly at students, for IR25,000. **Savaris to Sabzevar**

(Blvd Azadi; IR95,000, 90 minutes) start from nearly opposite the Sarigol Hotel at the south edge of town.

Going to Roein from Bojnurd, taxis charge around IR200,000.

Savaris from Esfarayen's **Istgah Bojnurd taxi stand** run to Roein (per person/vehicle IR25,000/100,000) from dawn to dusk.

Sabzevar سبزوار

🖉051 / POPULATION 242,000 / ELEVATION 960M
Sabzevar's a likeable place, with several notable historical structures – including an impressively tiled mausoleum and a large mosque – along its main drag, Beyhagh St; three tombs and a caravanserai are a few minutes' walk from Kargar Sq. Prices for everything from shopping to hotels to coffee are generally far lower here than elsewhere in the region.

Even if you skip Sabzevar itself, it's worth considering a drive-by stop or overnight stay in Zafaraniyeh (p271), some 40km east, to explore a little-visited caravanserai village whose numerous deteriorating mud-and-brick relics are romantically photogenic.

❶ Getting There & Away

The **bus terminal** (Sarbedaran Blvd) and savari points for Esfarayen, **Mashhad** (Sarbedoran Sq) and Shahrud are all found around or conveniently close to Sarbedaran Sq, on the city's westernmost edge.

Buses leave to Tehran (IR300,000 to IR510,000, three hours) between 7pm and 10pm. To Mashhad they're half-hourly from 6am to 6pm (IR95,000, 3½ hours), and there are Gorgan services at 8am and 8pm (IR245,000, eight hours).

There are four weekly flights to Tehran from Sabzevar Airport, which is 4km west, then 3km south from the bus terminal.

Understand
Iran

Iran Today

Modern Iran seems to be forever sitting at a crossroads between Islam and the West, between reformists and conservatives, between rogue state and responsible international citizen. Whichever of these Irans is in ascendance, the country remains one of the Middle East's most important regional powers. And just as relations between Iran and 'the Great Satan' (USA) appeared to be thawing, along came Donald Trump.

Best on Film

Taste of Cherry (1997) Abbas Kiarostami tackles the taboo subject of suicide.

The Apple (1998) Samira Makhmalbaf's stunning debut about two adolescent girls imprisoned by their father.

A Separation (2012) Asghar Farhadi's Oscar-winning movie about a marriage falling apart.

Taxi (2015) Brilliant 'docu-fiction' as Jafar Panahi gives a voice to ordinary Iranians in a Tehran taxi.

The Salesman (2016) Farhadi's second Oscar scoop looks at the effect of an assault on a marriage.

Best in Print

Shah of Shahs (Ryszard Kapuściński; 1982) Lyrical study of the Shah's hold over Iran and demise.

Mirrors of the Unseen (Jason Elliot; 2006) Perceptive and entertaining travelogue-history of Iran.

Iranian Rappers and Persian Porn: A Hitchhiker's Adventures in the New Iran (Jamie Maslin; 2013) Rollicking ride through Iran counterculture.

City of Lies (Ramita Navai; 2014) Gripping account of contemporary Iran told through a cast of Tehran characters.

Regional Meddling

Few countries hold as much power in the Middle East right now as Iran. Having taken up the mantle of defender of Shiites and their interests across the region, and having spent decades channelling funds into the coffers of friendly governments and movements, Iran now has a powerful voice in what happens in some of the world's most important conflicts. Iranian-backed Hezbollah is widely credited with propping up the Syrian government, fighting alongside government troops to turn back the march of Islamic State and other groups who would overthrow the Assad regime. In Lebanon and Iraq, both countries with Shiite majorities like Iran, Iran has advisors on the ground and provides financial support to ensure that its view of politics prevails. In this role, Iran provides a counterpoint to Saudi Arabia and the Gulf States as regional powers; Iran has also been vocal in its defence of Shiite communities in Bahrain and Saudi Arabia. Perhaps more than at any time in recent history, Iran is one of the region's most important kingmakers and policy decisions made in Tehran will play a role in determining the future of the region. Which is, of course, just the way the Iranian government likes it.

Iran & the United States

Iran's relationship with the West, particularly the United States, has long defined the image the country has of itself and which it projects onto the world stage. The flashpoints have ranged from the CIA-backed coup in 1953 to the seizing of US embassy personnel in Tehran in 1979. Since the Islamic Revolution, the relationship has had far more lows than highs and remains one of profound mutual suspicion. Things began to thaw under President Khatami and many years of tough negotiations, sanctions and brinkmanship finally culminated in a mutual victory whereby Iran's nuclear program would come under international supervision in return for the lifting of sanctions. Iran was, it seemed, finally about to come in from the cold. And then, along came Donald Trump, who made the nuclear deal one of the foreign policy platforms of his campaign, threatening to rip it up should he become president. At the time of writing, President Trump had yet to do so, but his early indications were that it remained very much on his agenda. Add to this the Trump government's aim to ban immigrants from six majority Muslim countries (including Iran) and it appears very possible that relations could once again take a turn for the worst.

The Liberal-Conservative Divide

For most of the last 100 years, power in Iran has swung like a pendulum between two very different views of the world. On one side, the liberals and reformists, those who enjoyed the social freedoms of the Shah's Iran and who supported the Green Movement of 2009. Although it is always dangerous to generalise, it is the young and the urban who most often define this stream of Iranian society. Pitted against them are the conservatives led by the clerical establishment, the guardians of the Islamic Revolution, and with a loyal rural heartland. They are the Ayatollah Khomeini's footsoliders, and those who swept (former president) Ahmadinejad to power in 2005 and kept him there until 2013. Historically, both have suffered at the hands of the other. It is Iran's eternal battle of ideas and occasional violence.

May 2017 Presidential Election

After Supreme Leader Ali Khamenei, the second most powerful person in Iran is the president. Elections in May 2017 saw incumbent president and moderate Hassan Rouhani decisively beat his main rival, the conservative cleric Ebrahim Raisi, with 57% of the 41 million votes cast.

Rouhani (born Hassan Fereydoun and whose adopted name is Farsi for 'spiritual') holds a PhD in law from Glasgow Caledonian University. Under his stewardship, Iran's economy has stablised, with growth of around 6.6% in 2016–17 and inflation down to 8% in 2016. However, unemployment is stuck at 12.5%, and is much higher for the young at around 30%.

Improving civil liberties in Iran was a key policy that gained Rouhani another four years of power. However with Khamenei still having a veto over all policies and ultimate control of the security forces, it remains to be seen how far Rouhani can lead the country down the path of liberalisation. Also unknown is who will succeed the aging Supreme Leader, who has suffered ill health for years.

POPULATION: **82.8 MILLION**

AREA: **1,648,195 SQ KM**

GDP: **US$1.459 TRILLION**

INFLATION: **8%**

UNEMPLOYMENT: **10.7%**

if Iran were 100 people

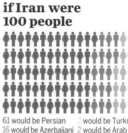

61 would be Persian
16 would be Azerbaijani
10 would be Kurds
6 would be Lur or Bakhtiari
2 would be Turkmen
2 would be Arab
2 would be Baluchi
1 would be other (including Armenians)

belief systems

(% of population)

90-95 Shiite Islam
5-10 Sunni Islam
less than 1 Zoroastrian, Christian or Jewish

population per sq km

IRAN   UK   US

≈ 32 people

History

Iran's history is one of the region's greatest stories ever told. It is, above all, a story of civilisations, ancient and great, of Islam's complicated march, and of some of the most heroic names in world history, among them Cyrus the Great, Alexander the Great and Genghis Khan. Fast-forward to the 20th and 21st centuries and Iran has again returned to centre stage and remains a key player in one of the world's most turbulent regions.

The Elamites & Medes

Elam was the lowland region in what is now Khuzestan province and the first organised settlements appeared as far back as 2600 BC. Elam was close enough to Mesopotamia and the great Sumerian civilisation to feel its influence and the two were regular opponents on the battlefield. The Elamites established their capital at Susa (Shush) and derived their strength through an enlightened federal system of government that allowed states to exchange natural resources unique to each region.

The Elamites believed in a pantheon of gods, and their most notable remaining building, the enormous ziggurat at Choqa Zanbil, was built around the 13th century BC and dedicated to the foremost of these gods. By the 12th century BC the Elamites are thought to have controlled most of what is now western Iran, the Tigris Valley and the coast of the Persian Gulf.

The Elamites' system of inheritance and power distribution was sophisticated for the time, ensuring power was passed through various family lines.

About this time Indo-European Aryan tribes began arriving from the north. These Persians eventually settled in what is now Fars province, around Shiraz, while the Medes took up residence further north, in what is today northwestern Iran. The Medes established a capital at Ecbatana, now buried under modern Hamadan, and first crop up in Assyrian records in 836 BC. Little more is heard of them until, according to Greek historian Herodotus, Cyaxares of Media expelled the Scythians in about 625 BC.

Under Cyaxares, the Medes became a formidable military force, repeatedly attacking the neighbouring Assyrians. In 612 BC, having formed an alliance with the Babylonians, the Medes sacked the Assyrian capital of Nineveh and chased the remnants of this once-mighty empire into history.

TIMELINE	3200–2100 BC	3000–2000 BC	c 1340–1250 BC
	The 150-hectare Shahr-e Sukhteh (Burnt City) thrives – and is burnt down three times – near modern Zabol before being abandoned. Some archaeologists think it was independent of ancient Mesopotamia.	Inscriptions recently uncovered near Jiroft, in southeastern Iran, are possibly the world's earliest known writing, pre-dating Mesopotamian writing.	The enormous Choqa Zanbil ziggurat is built to honour the pre-eminent Elamite god, Inshushinak. It is lost under the sands from about 640 BC until being rediscovered in 1935.

The Achaemenids & the Rise of Cyrus

In the 7th century BC the king of one of the Persian tribes, Achaemenes, created a unified state in southern Iran, giving his name to what would become the First Persian Empire, the Achaemenids. By the time his 21-year-old great-grandson Cyrus II ascended the throne in 559 BC, Persia was a state on the up. Within 20 years it would be the greatest empire the world had known up until that time.

Having rapidly built a mighty military force, Cyrus the Great (as he came to be known) ended the Median empire in 550 BC when he defeated his own grandfather – the hated king Astyages – in battle at Pasargadae. Within 11 years, Cyrus had campaigned his way across much of what is now Turkey, east into modern Pakistan, and finally defeated the Babylonians. It was in the aftermath of this victory in 539 BC that Cyrus established a reputation as a benevolent conqueror. According to Herodotus in *The Persian Wars,* Cyrus declared he would 'respect the traditions, customs and religions of the nations of my empire and never let any of my governors and subordinates look down on or insult them... I will impose my monarchy on no nation...and if any one of them rejects it, I never resolve on war to reign'.

Cyrus colonised the old Median capital at Ecbatana, redeveloped Shush and built himself a new home at Pasargadae, establishing the pattern whereby Persian rulers circulated between three different capitals. Unfortunately for him, the Scythian Massagetae from the northeast of the empire decided he was indeed imposing his monarchy on them. Cyrus fully incurred the wrath of the Massagetae queen, Tomyris, after he captured her son (who killed himself) and slaughtered many of her soldiers in a battle made especially one-sided because the Massagetae army were drunk on wine planted by the Achaemenids. Herodotus writes:

> When Tomyris heard what had befallen her son and her army, she sent a herald to Cyrus, who thus addressed the conqueror: 'Thou bloodthirsty Cyrus, pride not thyself on this poor success: it was the grape-juice...it was this poison wherewith thou didst ensnare my child, and so overcamest him, not in fair open fight. Now hearken what I advise, and be sure I advise thee for thy good. Restore my son to me and get thee from the land unharmed... Refuse, and I swear by the sun...bloodthirsty as thou art, I will give thee thy fill of blood'.

Cyrus paid no heed to Tomyris, who gathered her forces for what Herodotus described as the fiercest battle the Achaemenids had fought. Cyrus and most of his army were slain. When his body was recovered Tomyris reputedly ordered a skin filled with human blood and, making good on her threat, dunked Cyrus' head in it. Cyrus' body was eventually buried in the mausoleum that still stands at Pasargadae.

Ancient Persia (1996), by Josef Wiesehöfer, is a study of the country's origins and why it collapsed so dramatically after the Arab invasions of the 7th century.

Cyrus the Great (1850), by Jacob Abbott, tells the story of the fair-minded empire builder through the writings of Greek historian Herodotus and general Xenophenon, with extensive commentary from Abbott.

c 1125 BC	c 836 BC	625–585 BC	559 BC
The king of Babylon, Nebuchadnezzar I, invades Elam and sacks the capital Susa (Shush).	The Medes establish a capital at Ecbatana (modern Hamadan) and compete for trade and influence with Babylon, Lydia, Scythia and the Neo-Assyrian empire.	Median king Cyaxares the Great joins with Babylon to sack Nineveh and end the Neo-Assyrian empire, expanding Median control from Asia Minor in the west to Kerman in the east.	Aged 21, Cyrus II becomes king of the fast-rising Achaemenid people. His 30-year rule establishes a multi-state empire governed from Pasargadae, Babylon, Susa and Ecbatana, each with limited regional autonomy.

THE FIRST CHARTER OF HUMAN RIGHTS...OR NOT

In 1879 Assyro-British archaeologist Hormuzd Rassam unearthed a clay cylinder during a dig in the ancient Marduk temple of Babylon. What became known as the 'Cyrus Cylinder' bears a cuneiform inscription recording, among other things, that Cyrus 'strove for peace in Babylon and in all his [the god Marduk's] sacred sites' and 'abolished forced labour' for those (Jews) who had been enslaved in Babylon.

These passages have been widely interpreted as a reflection of Cyrus' respect for human rights, and many consider it the world's first charter of human rights. Indeed, a replica remains on permanent display at UN headquarters in New York (the original is in the British Museum), and in 1971 the cylinder became the symbol of the 2500th anniversary of Iranian royalty. However, not everyone agrees. Some scholars argue that Mesopotamian kings had a tradition dating back to the 3rd millennium BC of making grand and popular statements espousing social reform when they came to the throne, meaning Cyrus' declaration was neither new nor unique.

Whether the cylinder was the world's first declaration of human rights or not, it seems fair to say that Cyrus was an unusually benevolent ruler for his time, and he's well remembered across the faiths. In the Bible both Ezra and Isaiah speak of Cyrus as a benign ruler responsible for the restoration of the temple in Jerusalem. And he is the only Gentile (non-Jew) designated as a divinely appointed king, or messiah, in the Tanakh.

Cambyses & Darius

In 525 BC, Cyrus' son, Cambyses, captured most of Egypt and coastal regions well into modern Libya. It was later recorded that Cambyses had quietly arranged the assassination of his brother, Smerdis, before he left. The story goes that while Cambyses was distracted in Egypt, a minor official called Magus Gaumata, who had an uncanny resemblance to Smerdis, seized the throne. Cambyses died mysteriously in 522 BC while still in Egypt – by some reports he and his entire army marched out into the Sahara on some unknown quest and not one of their number was ever seen again. With the king dead, Darius I, a distant relative, moved quickly and soon had 'Gaumata' murdered. This 'justice' was glorified in a giant relief at Bisotun, near Hamadan, where you can see Darius' foot on Gaumata's head. What we will probably never know is whether Darius rid Persia of the so-called 'False Smerdis', or whether he murdered the real Smerdis and cooked up this story to justify his regicide.

Darius had won an empire in disarray and had to fight hard to re-establish it, dividing his sprawling inheritance into 23 satrapies to make it easier to govern. The magnificent complex at Persepolis was created to serve as the ceremonial and religious hub of an empire whose primary god was Ahura Mazda, also the subject of Zoroastrian worship. The Median

550 BC	539 BC	529–522 BC	522–486 BC
Cyrus II effectively ends the Median empire when he defeats his own grandfather – the hated king Astyages – in battle at Pasargadae. Within five years he also conquers Lydia.	The Achaemenids destroy the Babylonians at Opis. Cyrus releases Jews who had been enslaved in Babylon. Such benign policies were key to maintaining good relations with defeated subject nations.	Cyrus' son Cambyses II continues his father's empire building by conquering Egypt, Nubia and Cyrenaica during his short rule. His mysterious death in Egypt sparks a succession crisis.	Darius I (the Great) creates the first superpower through sword and organisation. He divides Persia into provinces, creates a uniform monetary system and adopts a common language.

cities of Ecbatana and Shush became administrative centres, but Persepolis was the imperial showcase, extravagantly decorated to intimidate visitors and impress with its beauty. Darius eventually expanded the empire to India and pushed as far north as the Danube River in Europe.

It was the greatest of the early civilisations. Paved roads stretched from one end of the empire to the other, with caravanserais at regular intervals to provide food and shelter to travellers. The Achaemenids introduced the world's first postal service, and it was said the network of relay horses could deliver mail to the furthest corner of the empire within 15 days.

But it wasn't all smooth sailing. When the Greek colonies of Asia Minor rebelled against their Persian overlord, Darius decided to invade mainland Greece to make an example of those states that refused to subject themselves. It didn't work. In 490 BC, Darius' armies were defeated at the famous battle at Marathon near Athens. He died in 486 BC.

The subsequent defeat of Darius' son Xerxes at Salamis in Greece in 480 BC marked the beginning of a long, slow decline that would continue, with glorious interludes, for another 150 years.

Alexander the Great & the End of Persepolis

Young and charismatic like Cyrus before him, it was Alexander the Great of Macedonia who finally ended the First Persian Empire. Having defeated the Greeks and Egyptians, Alexander saw off Persian armies at Issus in Turkey (333 BC) and Guagamela in present-day Iraq (331 BC), before sweeping aside the remaining armies of Darius III. Darius himself fled east to Bactria, only to be murdered by his cousin. In the wake of his victory, Alexander spent several months at Persepolis, before the finest symbol of Achaemenid power burned to the ground.

Alexander's empire soon stretched across Afghanistan, Pakistan and into India, but after his death in 323 BC it was divided between three squabbling dynasties, with Persia controlled by the Macedonian Seleucids. Gradually the Greek language became the lingua franca, Greeks settled new towns and Greek culture stamped itself on the older Persian one. However, ambitious satraps and feisty ethnic minorities were bucking the system, particularly the Parthians.

The Parthian Takeover

The Parthians had settled the area between the Caspian and Aral Seas many centuries before. Under their great king Mithridates (r 171–138 BC), they swallowed most of Persia and then everywhere between the Euphrates in the west and Afghanistan in the east, more or less re-creating the

Persian Fire (2005), by Tom Holland, is a page-turning history of the Persian Wars, the first battles between East and West, and the Achaemenid Empire at its most powerful. Recommended reading before visiting Shush or Persepolis.

Even today experts argue whether the burning of Persepolis was the accidental result of a drunken party or deliberate retaliation by Alexander for the destruction of Athens by Xerxes.

486–465 BC	358 BC	334–330 BC	323–162 BC
War with the Greeks dominates Xerxes I's reign. After burning Athens in 480 BC, the Persians lose control of Macedonia, Thrace and Ionia. The Apadama Palace at Persepolis is completed.	Artaxerxes III (358–338 BC) takes the throne after assassinating eight half-brothers. In 343 BC he defeats Egypt, which is again made a Persian satrapy.	Alexander the Great's Macedonians defeat Persian armies at Granicus, Issus and Guagamela. He marches on Susa and Persepolis, whose surrender in effect ends the once-mighty Achaemenid Empire.	After Alexander the Great dies in Babylon in 323 BC, infighting sees his empire divided in three, with the Seleucids ruling parts of Persia until 162 BC. Greek becomes the lingua franca.

The modern term 'parting shot' derives from the ancient 'Parthian shot'. As Parthian horsemen rode away from their enemy they would turn in their saddles and fire arrows at their pursuers. This was the 'Parthian shot'.

old Achaemenid Empire. They had two capitals, one at what is now Rey, the other at Ctesiphon, in present-day Iraq.

Expert horsemen and archers, the Parthians spent much energy fighting with Rome for control of Syria, Mesopotamia and Armenia. In 53 BC, Roman general Crassus, who had defeated Spartacus and was now one of three men controlling Rome, took on the Parthians at Carrhae, in modern-day Turkey. Crassus saw his armies decimated before being captured, having molten gold poured down his throat to mock his greed, and losing his head. Extended periods of peace followed, though the Romans and Parthians were only ever an ambitious leader away from a fight.

More enlightened than later dynasties, the Parthians oversaw significant progress in architecture and the arts, though little remains today.

The Sassanids & the Second Persian Empire

Like the Achaemenids before them, the Sassanid rise from small-time dynasty to empire was nothing short of staggering. Beginning in the province of Fars, Ardashir I (r 224–41) led a push that saw the Sassanids replace the ailing Parthians in Persia and within 40 years become a renewed threat to the Roman Empire.

Between 241 and 272 Ardashir's son, Shapur I, added Bactria to the empire and fought repeatedly with the Romans. In one of the most celebrated of all Persian victories, Shapur's armies defeated the Romans at Edessa in 260 and took the Roman emperor Valerian prisoner. You can still see the cities of Bishapur and Shushtar, where Valerian was held, and bas-reliefs depicting the victory at Naqsh-e Rostam.

The Sassanids re-formulated Zoroastrianism into a state religion incorporating elements of Greek, Mithraic and ancient animist faiths. They spoke their own language, Pahlavi, which is the root of modern Farsi, and developed the grand *iwan* (barrel-vaulted hall) that dominated much Persian architecture.

The Sassanids developed small industries, promoted urban development and encouraged trade across the Persian Gulf but eventually they, too, were weakened by seemingly never-ending conflict with Byzantium. Ironically it was in its last years that the empire was at its largest, when Khosrow II (590–628) recaptured parts of Egypt, Syria, Palestine and Turkey. However, after Khosrow was murdered by his son, at least six rulers, including Persia's only two women monarchs, came and went in the following five years. Persia was in no state to resist when the Arabs attacked in 633.

The Arabs & Islam

A crucial chapter in Persian history began when the Arabs defeated the Sassanids at Qadisirya in 637, following up with a victory at Nehavand near Hamadan that effectively ended Sassanid rule.

By the time of Mohammed's death in 632 the Arabs were firm adherents of Islam. The Persians found plenty to like in Islamic culture and

247 BC	123–88 BC	53 BC	AD 25
The Parthians, natives of the area southeast of the Caspian Sea, rebel against the Seleucids to begin the longest empire in Iranian history, lasting 471 years.	Mithridates II expands Parthian control from the borders of the Roman Empire to China and India. He establishes diplomatic and trade relations with China. Greek remains the lingua franca.	Parthian armies rout the Romans at Carrhae. Those Roman soldiers fortunate enough to survive report the Parthians fought under dazzlingly bright flags. It is Europe's first glimpse of silk.	Parthian emissaries deliver lions to the court of the Han dynasty in China. These are believed to be the inspiration for the lion dancing still seen at Chinese New Year.

religion, and readily forsook Zoroaster for the teachings of Mohammed. Only Yazd and Kerman (both of which clung to Zoroastrianism for a few centuries more) and a few isolated mountain tribes held fast to their old religions. As they rapidly spread across the Middle East, the Arabs adopted Sassanid architecture, arts and administration practices.

The Umayyad caliphs initially governed Persia from their capital in Damascus, but in 750 a Shiite rebellion led to the elevation of the Abbasid dynasty, which set up its capital near Baghdad. The Abbasid caliphs presided over a period of intellectual exuberance in which Persian culture played a major role. Persians also held many high offices at court, but the Arabic language and script became the norm for day-to-day business.

THE SILK ROAD

Silk first began moving westward from China more than 2000 years ago when the Parthians became enamoured with the soft, fine fabric. By about 100 BC the Parthians and Chinese had exchanged embassies, and silk, along with myriad other goods, was being traded along the route. Trade grew after the Romans developed a fixation with the fabric after their defeat at Carrhae in 53 BC. Eventually silk would become more valuable than gold to the Romans, who fixed the supply issue when Emperor Justinian sent teams of spies to steal silk-worm eggs in the 6th century.

It took many months to traverse the 8000km Silk Road route, which was not a single road but rather a web of caravan tracks dotted with caravanserais a day's travel apart – roughly 30km. These were fortified rest stops with accommodation for traders, their camels and goods. The network had its main eastern terminus at the Chinese capital Ch'ang-an (now Xian). Caravans entered present-day Iran anywhere between Merv (modern Turkmenistan) and Herat (Afghanistan), and passed through Mashhad, Neishabur, Damghan, Semnan, Rey, Qazvin, Tabriz and Maku, before finishing at Constantinople (now İstanbul). During winter, the trail often diverted west from Rey, passing through Hamadan to Baghdad.

Unlike the Silk Road's most famous journeyman, Marco Polo, caravanners were mostly short- and medium-distance hauliers who marketed and took on freight along a given beat. Goods heading east included gold, silver, ivory, jade and other precious stones, wool, Mediterranean coloured glass, grapes, wine, spices and – early Parthian crazes – acrobats and ostriches. Going west were silk, porcelain, spices, gems and perfumes. In the middle lay Central Asia and Iran, great clearing houses that provided the horses and Bactrian camels that kept the goods flowing.

The Silk Road gave rise to unprecedented trade, but its glory lay in the interchange of ideas. The religions alone present an astounding picture of diversity and tolerance: Manichaeism, Zoroastrianism, Buddhism, Nestorian Christianity, Judaism, Confucianism, Taoism and shamanism coexisted along the 'road' until the coming of Islam.

The Silk Road was eventually abandoned when the new European powers discovered alternative sea routes in the 15th century.

224	241–272	c 250	387
Ardashir Babakan overcomes local rivals to challenge and defeat the Parthian king Artabanus V, and seize control of Parthian territories. He establishes the Sassanid capital at Firuz Abad.	Shapur I succeeds Ardashir and expands Sassanid hegemony to include Bactria. He famously defeats the Romans at Edessa in 260, where emperor Valerian is captured on the battlefield.	The Sassanid state religion is Zoroastrianism and other faiths are not allowed. However, Shapur I is interested in the philosophy of Mani (216–276), which goes on to become Manichaeism.	The Persian and Byzantine Empires solve their long-running dispute over control of Armenia by carving it up; it was one of the first (and ultimately unsuccessful) examples of partition.

During the 9th century Abbasid power crumbled and, one by one, regional governors established their own power bases. In eastern Iran these new Iranian dynasties included the Tahirids (820–72), the Saffarrids (868–903) and the Samanids (874–999), who set up their capital at Bukhara and revived the Persian language.

The Coming of the Seljuks

Inevitably, these local dynasties could not hold onto their power and eventually were ousted by the Seljuk Turks who pushed on through Persia, capturing Esfahan in 1051 and making it their capital. Within a few years they had added eastern Turkey to their empire and, despite numerous rebellions, managed to maintain control with a large and well-paid army.

The Seljuk dynasty heralded a new era in Persian art, literature and science, distinguished by geniuses such as the mathematician and poet Omar Khayyam. Theological schools were also set up throughout Seljuk territories to propagate Sunni Islam. The geometric brickwork and elaborate Kufic inscriptions of Seljuk mosques and minarets can still be seen, particularly in Esfahan's Masjed-e Jameh (Jameh Mosque).

The death of Malek Shah in 1092 marked the end of real Seljuk supremacy, and once again a powerful empire splintered into fragments.

Genghis Khan & Tamerlane

In the early 13th century, the Seljuk empire came to a final and bloody end when the rampaging Mongols swept across the Iranian plateau on their horses, leaving a trail of cold-blooded devastation and thousands of dismembered heads in their wake.

Under the leadership first of Genghis Khan, and then his grandsons, including Hulagu, the Mongol rulers managed to seize all of Persia, as well as an empire stretching from Beijing (China) to İstanbul (Turkey). Eventually they established a capital at Tabriz (too close, as they later found out, to the Turks). It was Hulagu Khan who put an end to the stealthy power of the Assassins, destroying their castles around Alamut. After a flirtation with Christianity and Buddhism, Hulagu was forced to adopt Islam by social pressures in Persia. He called himself *il khan* (provincial khan or ruler, deputy to the great khan in Mongolia), a name later given to the entire Ilkhanid dynasty (1256–1335).

The Mongols destroyed many of the Persian cities they conquered, obliterating much of Persia's documented history. But they also became great arts patrons, leaving many fine monuments, including the wonderful Oljeitu Mausoleum at Soltaniyeh. During Mongol rule Farsi definitively replaced Arabic as the lingua franca.

Ferdosi wrote his epic poem, the *Shahnameh* (Book of Kings), between about 990 and his death in around 1020. Its 60,000 couplets are considered the foundation stone of modern Farsi, in the same way Shakespeare is considered the father of English.

529	590–628	632	661–750
One of history's first socialists, Mazdak, wins a huge following preaching that nobles should share their wealth and women with the masses. After a noble revolt he is assassinated.	Khosrow II expands the Sassanid empire to its largest, stretching from Egypt to the borders of modern China. He is murdered by his son in 628 and the empire quickly unravels.	The Prophet Mohammed dies and a year later Arab forces driven by religious zeal attack Persia. By 651 the last Sassanid king is dead and the empire is history.	The Umayyad Caliphate take control of much of the lands of the former Sassanid empire, governing from Damascus and spreading Sunni Islam.

The empire fragmented when Abu Said died without a successor, and soon succumbed to invading forces from the east led by Tamerlane (Lame Timur), who swept on to defeat the Ottoman Turks in 1402. Tamerlane came from a Turkified Mongol clan in what is now Uzbekistan and moved the capital to Qazvin. He was yet another of the great contradictions who ruled Persia over the years: an enthusiastic patron of the arts and one of history's greatest killers (after one rebellion 70,000 people are said to have been executed in Esfahan alone).

When he died in 1405, Tamerlane's empire immediately started to struggle. The Timurids in eastern Iran clung to varying degrees of power for several decades, maintaining their support of Persian art, particularly the miniaturists of Shiraz. Gohar Shad, the wife of one of the Timurid rulers, was responsible for the beautiful mosque at the heart of Mashhad's Holy Shrine to Imam Reza.

The Safavids & the Third Persian Empire

A Sufi called Sheikh Safi od-Din (d 1334) was the inspiration for and progenitor of the Safavi, a powerful sect of Shiite followers from Ardabil. Ismail Safavi, a distant descendent of Safi od-Din, eventually conquered all the old Persian imperial heartlands, from Baghdad to Herat. He ruled as Persian Shah (r 1502–24) and despite defeat to Ottoman sultan Selim the Grim at the disastrous battle of Chaldoran (which started 41 years of warring with Persia losing control of eastern Anatolia and Iraq), his Safavid dynasty ushered in a great Iranian revival.

Under Ismail's son Tahmasp (r 1524–76), the capital was moved from Tabriz to Qazvin, and European monarchs started to take an interest in Persia. The Safavids reached their peak under the brilliant Shah Abbas I (Abbas the Great; r 1587–1629), who, with military advice from English adventurer Robert Shirley, finally crushed the assorted Turkmen and Turkish factions to create what is considered the Third Persian Empire.

The Safavids enshrined Shiism as Persia's state religion, bringing it into regular conflict with the Sunni Ottoman Empire, and oversaw a renewed flowering of Persian art and architecture. Abbas moved the capital to Esfahan and promptly set about rebuilding the city around Naqsh-e Jahan (Imam) Sq.

European powers began looking on Persia as a market. English companies were given business concessions and trade increased. The Safavid empire continued for almost a century after Abbas' death, but it was a period of political infighting and internecine rivalries. In 1722 the Afghans besieged Esfahan and eventually took control of the city, slaughtering thousands but sparing the architectural wonders.

Genghis Khan took the most beautiful women from the lands he defeated and made them wives or concubines, fathering hundreds of children. A recent DNA study across Asia found that some 16 million men living today can likely trace their heritage back to the loins of the great ruler.

HISTORY THE SAFAVIDS & THE THIRD PERSIAN EMPIRE

680	749–830s	820–999	928–1140
Imam Hossein, son of Imam Ali, is killed along with 72 partisans at Karbala. This becomes the defining event in the antagonism between Sunni and Shiite Muslims.	An uprising in Khorasan casts off Ummayad rule and the Abbasid Caliphate is born. Heavily influenced by Persian customs, the Abbasids choose Baghdad as their capital, near the former Sassanid capital Ctesiphon.	As Abbasid control weakens, a series of regional dynasties takes control. The Tahirids (820–72) in Khorasan, the expansionist Saffarids (868–903) from Sistan and the Samanids (874–999), based in Bukhara.	The Persian Ziarids (928–1077) and Buyids (945–1055) are noted for their support of the arts, but their power gives way to Turkish clans, beginning with the Qaznavids in 962.

Nader Shah & Karim Khan Zand

The Safavids were briefly rescued from oblivion by a soldier of fortune, Tahmasp Qoli, who in 1729 scattered the Afghans, along with the Russian and Turkish forces that were encroaching in the north. He ruled Persia in all but name until 1736, when he grew tired of the pretence and crowned himself Nader Shah, thus ending once and for all the Safavid dynasty. To describe Nader Shah as a brilliant but war-loving mercenary is something of an understatement. History regards him as a megalomaniac who, in a show of supreme self-confidence, invaded India in 1738 and returned with loot that included the Kuh-e Nur and Darya-e Nur diamonds; see the latter diamond in Tehran's Treasury of National Jewels. His constant warring rapidly wore out the country and his assassination in 1747 brought a welcome, if temporary, end to hostilities.

A Lor from western Iran, Karim Khan Zand (r 1750–79) grabbed power. He had little interest in warfare and is instead remembered for moving the capital to Shiraz, where he built the impressive Arg-e Karim Khan and the Masjed-e Vakil (Regent's Mosque).

A steady trickle of European travellers and adventurers came, saw and wrote about Safavid Persia, most notably the French jewellers Jean-Baptiste Tavernier (1605–89) and John Chardin (1643–1713), and English buccaneers Sir Anthony Shirley (1565–1635) and Sir Robert Shirley (1581–1628), in the early 17th century.

The Qajars & the Constitutional Revolution

The Qajar dynasty was a disaster for Iran, taking just a few years to turn the country into an international laughing stock. Following Karim Khan's death in 1779, eunuch Aga Mohammad Khan united the Azeri Qajars and created a new capital in the village of Tehran. By 1795 he had wrested control of Persia from Lotf Ali Khan.

Both the Russians and British had their eyes on Iran. Russia was determined to gain access to the Persian Gulf and India, while Britain was equally determined to deny them. During the undistinguished reign of big-bearded Fath Ali Shah (r 1797–1834) Russia captured Georgia, Shirvan (today's Azerbaijan), eastern Armenia and Daghestan, all semi-independent entities previously within Persia's sphere of influence.

While responsible for a broad campaign of modernisation, Nasser al-Din Shah (r 1848–96) was generally more interested in collecting art, building museums and servicing his numerous wives. The Qajar shahs spent so much on luxuries that the treasury needed to hastily sell state assets. Foreign buyers were more than happy to pick up the bargains. In one notorious incident, Nasser al-Din tried to sell exclusive rights to exploit Iran's economic resources (including all the banks, mines and railways) for a one-off sum of UK£40,000 to be followed by payments of UK£10,000 for the next 25 years. He was made to cancel the deal once news of it leaked out.

980–1037	1051	1079	1218
Philosopher and physician BuAli Sina (Avicenna or Ibn Sina) lives primarily in Hamadan and Esfahan and publishes 250 books including the *Canon Medicinae*, used in European universities until the 17th century.	Nomad Turks from Central Asia, the Seljuks (1051–1220) sweep across Persia and create an empire reaching east to Syria, Palestine and the gates of Byzantine Constantinople.	In an observatory built by the Seljuks, mathematician and poet Omar Khayyam (1048–1123) calculates the length of the year as 365.242198 days, preceding the Gregorian calendar by almost 500 years.	Mongol leader Genghis Khan's westward advance arrives with catastrophic results. The Mongols take most Persian territories, raze cities including Tus and Nishabur and slaughter tens of thousands.

When news broke of an attempt to sell the tobacco monopoly, discontent boiled over into revolt. In 1906 the third-last Qajar shah, Muzaffar al-Din (r 1896–1907), was forced to introduce an embryo parliament, the first Majlis, and a constitution. It became known as the Constitutional Revolution.

However, the Majlis didn't appeal to ruthless new shah Mohammad Ali, who attacked it with artillery and, in 1908, introduced martial law. This led to an uprising in Tabriz in 1909. Shah Mohammad Ali was forced to abdicate in favour of his son, who was still a child.

During WWI both Britain and Russia occupied parts of Iran while the Turks ravaged the partly Christian northwest. Inspired by the new regime in Russia, Gilan (the west Caspian area) broke away in 1920 to form a Soviet republic under Kuchuk Khan. The weak Qajar shah seemed unable to respond, so Britain backed charismatic army officer Reza Khan, who swiftly retook Gilan before ousting Shah Ahmad.

The Pahlavis

Reza Khan

From the moment in 1921 that Reza Khan staged a coup d'état to, in effect, end Qajar rule, the poorly educated but wily soldier was king of Persia in all but name. Initially he installed a puppet prime minister, but in 1923 he took that role himself and in 1925 crowned himself, Napoleon-like, as the first shah of the Pahlavi line.

Reza Shah, as he became known, set himself an enormous task: to drag Iran into the 20th century in the same way his neighbour Mustafa Kemal Atatürk was modernising Turkey. Literacy, transport infrastructure, the health system, industry and agriculture had all been badly neglected. Like Atatürk, Reza Shah aimed to improve the status of women and to that end he made wearing the chador illegal. Like Atatürk, too, he insisted on the wearing of Western dress and moved to crush the power of the religious establishment.

However, Reza had little of Atatürk's subtlety and his edicts made him many enemies. Some women embraced his new dress regulations, but others found them impossible to accept. Even today, some older Iranians talk of how their mothers didn't leave home for six years: too scared of prosecution to go outside wearing a head-covering, too ashamed to leave home without one.

Despite being nominally neutral during WWII, Reza's outspoken support of the Nazis proved too much for Britain and Russia. In 1941 Reza was forced into exile in South Africa, where he died in 1944. The British arranged for his 21-year-old son, Mohammad Reza, to succeed him. In 1943 at the Tehran Conference, Britain, Russia and the USA signed the Tehran

It was the Greeks in the 5th century who first started calling this land Persia. However, Reza Shah hated the name and in 1934 changed it to Iran – derived from the Middle Persian word 'Eran' and used by natives as the name of their country since the 1st millennium BC.

1256	1271–95	1380	1502
Hulagu Khan leads a second Mongol drive into the Middle East, destroying the power of the Ishmaelite Assassins. The Ilkhanids rule from Maraghe, then Soltaniyeh, until 1335.	Marco Polo crosses Iran while travelling to and from China, stopping in Tabriz, Kashan, Yazd, Kerman, Hormoz, Bam, Tabas and Neishabur, among others.	Tamerlane, the sword-happy Tatar, brutally takes control of Persia from a series of local rulers. Governing first from Samarkand, then Herat and Qazvin, the Timurids prove great patrons of the arts.	A teenage Ismail Savafi (r 1502–24) takes Tabriz and, within 10 years, territories from Baghdad to Uzbekistan to establish the Safavid empire.

Declaration, accepting the independence of Iran. The young Mohammad Reza regained absolute power – under heavy influence from the British.

Mohammad Reza

When prime minister Ali Razmara was assassinated in 1951, 70-year-old nationalist Dr Mohammad Mossadegh, leader of the National Front Movement, swept into office on the back of promises to nationalise the hugely profitable Anglo-Iranian Oil Company (later British Petroleum). However, two years later he was removed in a coup organised by the CIA and Britain.

With Mossadegh gone, the US government encouraged the shah to press ahead with a program of social and economic modernisation dubbed the White Revolution because it was intended to take place without bloodshed. Many Iranians remember this period fondly for reforms including the further emancipation of women and improved literacy. But for a conservative, mainly rural Muslim population it was all too fast. The religious establishment, the ulema, also took exception to land reforms depriving them of rights and electoral reforms giving votes to non-Muslims.

By 1962 Ayatollah Ruhollah Khomeini, then living in Qom, had emerged as a figurehead for opposition to the shah. In 1964 the shah approved a bill giving US soldiers in Iran complete immunity from arrest. Khomeini responded by claiming the shah had 'reduced the Iranian people to a level lower than that of an American dog', because if anyone ran over a dog in America they would be prosecuted for doing so, but if an American ran over an Iranian in Iran he could do so with impunity. The shah reacted by banishing Khomeini.

In 1971 the shah organised lavish celebrations for the 2500th anniversary of the founding of the Persian Empire, hoping to fan the flames of nationalism. More than 60 international monarchs and heads of state came to the party, held in a purpose-built tent city at Persepolis. The news coverage brought Iranian culture to the world, but at home it encouraged those who saw the shah as wasteful.

Ironically, the 1974 oil price revolution also contributed to the shah's undoing. In just one year the income from oil shot from US$4 billion to US$20 billion, but the shah allowed US arms merchants to persuade him to squander much of this on weapons that then stood idle in the desert. As the world slipped into recession, oil sales slumped and several planned social reforms were cut.

The Revolution

Since the beginning of the Pahlavi dynasty, resistance had smouldered away and occasionally flared into violence. Students wanted faster reform, devout Muslims wanted reforms rolled back, and everyone attacked the Pahlavis' conspicuous consumption.

Unlike many of his predecessors, who concentrated on religious architecture, Shah Mohammad Reza Pahlavi commissioned secular buildings in strikingly modern styles. Tehran's Carpet Museum of Iran, Museum of Contemporary Art, Teatre Shahr (City Theatre) and monolithic Azadi Tower are among the best.

1514	1587	1736–47	1750
The Ottomans rout the Safavids at the battle of Chaldoran, starting 41 years of warring that sees Persia lose control of eastern Anatolia and Iraq.	Strong, paranoid Safavid Shah Abbas I (Abbas the Great; 1587–1629) moves the capital to Esfahan and embarks on a monumental building program from which Naqsh-e Jahan emerges.	Nader Shah crowns himself shah, moves the capital to Mashhad, drives the Ottomans from Georgia and Armenia and the Russians from the Caspian coast, reclaims Afghanistan and invades India for treasure.	Karim Khan Zand emerges from three years of war to claim power. He moves the capital to Shiraz and is remembered as a humble ruler who calls himself *vakil* (regent) rather than shah (king).

The opposition came from secular, worker-communist and Islamic groups whose common denominator was a desire to remove the shah. Exiled Ayatollah Khomeini was an inspirational figure, but contrary to the official Iranian portrayal much of the organising was done by unionists, communists and ordinary middle-class citizens.

As the economy faltered the opposition grew in confidence and organised massive street demonstrations and small-scale sabotage. The shah responded with brutal force and his security agency, Savak, earned a reputation for torture and killing. In November 1978, he imposed martial law and hundreds of demonstrators were killed in Tehran, Qom and Tabriz. The USA's long-standing support began to falter and in December the now-desperate shah appointed veteran opposition politician Shapur Bakhtiar as prime minister. It was too late. On 16 January 1979 (now a national holiday), Shah Mohammad Reza Pahlavi and his third wife, Farah Diba, finally fled.

MOHAMMAD MOSSADEGH & THE CIA'S FIRST COUP

Before Lumumba in Congo, Sukarno in Indonesia and Allende in Chile, Mohammad Mossadegh was the first democratically elected leader toppled by a CIA coup d'état. Mossadegh, a highly educated lawyer, paid the price for seeking a better deal for Iran from the hugely profitable oilfields run by the Anglo-Iranian Oil Company (later British Petroleum). When the British refused Iran a fairer share, he nationalised the company and expelled British diplomats, whom he rightly suspected of plotting to overthrow him. The significance of this act went far beyond the borders of Iran, and Mossadegh was named *Time* magazine's Man of the Year in 1951 for his influence in encouraging developing nations to shake off the colonial yoke.

The British were desperate to get 'their' oil back. They encouraged a worldwide boycott of Iranian oil and worked hard to muddy Mossadegh's name in Iran and internationally. After arch-colonialist Winston Churchill was re-elected in 1952, he managed to persuade the new Eisenhower administration in the USA that Mossadegh had to go. The CIA's Operation Ajax was the result. Kermit Roosevelt Jr, grandson of former president Theodore Roosevelt and one of the agency's top operatives, established a team in the basement of the US embassy in Tehran and soon won the shah's support. But that alone wasn't enough and another US$2 million was spent buying support from senior clerics, military officers, newspaper editors, *bazaris* (shopkeepers in the bazaar) and thugs.

The CIA was new at the coup game – it started badly when Mossadegh loyalists arrested the coup leaders on 16 August. The shah promptly fled to Rome, but three days later there was a second attempt and Mossadegh was toppled. The shah returned and the oil industry was denationalised, but the British monopoly was broken and for its trouble the USA claimed a 40% stake. Mossadegh spent the rest of his life under house arrest.

1795	1797–1834	1848–96	1906
After years of war, Qajar ruler Aga Mohammad Khan finally defeats the Zand. He moves the capital to Tehran before being murdered by his servants.	Fath Ali Shah presides over two disastrous wars with expansionist Russia that illustrate how Iran has fallen behind the world. Iran is forced to cede Caucusus territories (modern Azerbaijan and Armenia).	Nasser al-Din Shah attempts to modernise Iran, all the while siring hundreds of princes who take from the treasury at will. Russia and Britain assert control in domestic politics and trade.	The 'Constitutional Revolution' sees Iran get the Middle East's first constitution after public outrage at Mozaffar-e-din Shah's reckless spending threatens to boil over into revolt. A Majlis (parliament) is formed.

AYATOLLAH RUHOLLAH KHOMEINI

An earnest, ruthless and intensely committed man, Ayatollah Ruhollah Khomeini is reviled and little understood in the West but revered as a saint by many Iranians. Khomeini was a family man who lived a modest life; a religious leader who reduced the age at which 'women' could marry to nine; a war leader who sent young men to their deaths with the Iraqi as martyrs; and the man who proclaimed the infamous fatwa against Salman Rushdie.

Born in the village of Khomein in central Iran about 1902, Sayyed Ruhollah Musavi Khomeini followed in the family tradition by studying theology, philosophy and law in the holy city of Qom. By the 1920s he had earned the title of ayatollah (the highest rank of a Shiite cleric) and settled down to teach and write.

He came to public attention in 1962 when he opposed the shah's plans to reduce the clergy's property rights and emancipate women. In 1964 he was exiled to Turkey, before moving on to Iraq and, in 1978, to Paris. When the shah fled in 1979, Khomeini returned to take control of Iran through force of character, and remained leader until his death in 1989.

Today, Khomeini is officially known as Imam Khomeini, raising him to the level of saint, and almost every town in the country has a street or square named after him. His portrait is everywhere, often beside and thus legitimising that of the current leader, Ayatollah Ali Khamenei.

Khomeini's frequent broadcasts on the BBC's Persian Service had made him the spiritual leader of opposition. But at 76 years old, everyone expected that once the shah was ousted he would assume a more hands-off, statesman-like role. They were wrong. On his return to Iran on 1 February 1979, Khomeini told the exultant masses of his vision for a new Iran, free of foreign influence and true to Islam: 'From now on it is I who will name the government'.

The Aftermath of the Revolution

Ayatollah Khomeini soon set about proving the adage that 'after the revolution comes the revolution'. His intention was to set up a clergy-dominated Islamic Republic, and he achieved this with brutal efficiency.

At the urging of the new Islamic government, Iranian women had, on average, six children each during the 1980s; the population almost doubled in a decade.

Groups such as the People's Feda'iyin, the Islamic People's Mojahedin and the communist Tudah had been instrumental in undermining the shah. But once the shah was gone they were swept aside. People disappeared, executions took place after brief and arbitrary trials, and minor officials took the law into their own hands. The facts – that the revolution had been a broad-based effort – were revised and the idea of the Islamic Revolution was born.

1921	1941	1951–53	1962
Soldier Reza Khan takes control of the army in a coup. By 1925 he has crowned himself the first shah of the Pahlavi line. He sets about modernising Iran.	Reza Shah's support for Nazi Germany prompts an invasion by Soviet and British forces. Reza Shah is exiled and his 21-year-old son Mohammad Reza becomes shah.	Having arranged the nationalisation of the British-owned Anglo-Iranian Oil Company in 1951, Mohammad Mossadegh is elected prime minister, only to be overthrown in a coup orchestrated by America's CIA.	Mohammad Reza embarks on an ambitious reform agenda, known as the White Revolution, to improve education and women's rights, reform land title and erode the power of the clerics.

Following a referendum in March 1979, in which 98.2% of the population voted in favour, the world's first Islamic Republic was formed with Ayatollah Khomeini as Supreme Leader.

Almost immediately, the Islamic Republic was viewed suspiciously and accused of adopting confrontational policies designed to promote other Islamic revolutions. In November 1979, conservative university students burst into the US embassy and took 52 staff hostage, an action later blessed by Khomeini. A US special forces rescue mission failed when the helicopters supposed to carry them to safety collided in the desert near Tabas. For 444 days the siege of the US embassy dogged US president, Jimmy Carter.

The Iran–Iraq War

In 1980, hoping to take advantage of Iran's domestic chaos, Iraq's president Saddam Hussein made an opportunistic land grab on oil-rich Khuzestan province, claiming it was a historic part of Iraq. It was a catastrophic miscalculation that resulted in eight years of war.

Ironically, the invasion proved to be pivotal in solidifying support for the shaky Islamic Revolution by providing an obvious enemy to rally against and an opportunity to spread the revolution by force of arms. Iraq was better equipped and better supplied, but Iran could draw on a larger population and a sense of righteousness and religious fervour, fanned by its mullahs (Islamic clerics).

Fighting was fierce, with poison gas and trench warfare being seen for the first time since WWI. Islamic volunteers (the Basijis) as young as 13 chose to clear minefields by walking through them, confident they would go to heaven as martyrs. By July 1982 Iran had pushed the Iraqis back to the border, but rather than accept peace Iran adopted a new agenda that included occupying Najaf and Karbala, important Shiite pilgrimage sites.

The war dragged on another six years. Millions of Iranians lost their homes and jobs, and some 1.2 million fled the battle zone, many moving permanently to far-away Mashhad. A ceasefire was finally negotiated in mid-1988, though prisoners were still being exchanged in 2003.

While war was raging, different factions within Iran continued to jostle for supremacy. In June 1981 a bomb blast at the headquarters of the Islamic Republican Party killed its founder Ayatollah Beheshti and 71 others, including four cabinet ministers. A second bomb in August killed President Rajai and the new prime minister. The Islamic People's Mojahedin, once co-revolutionaries but now bitter enemies of the clerics, were blamed. Despite this, by 1983 all effective resistance to Khomeini's ideas had been squashed.

Reading Lolita in Tehran (2003), by Azar Nafisi, is nominally a work of literary criticism, but in reality Nafisi writes a moving memoir of her life in Iran after the revolution.

Iranians refer to the war as the 'Iraq-imposed war' and it remains a huge influence on the country. Pictures of martyrs can be seen in every city, and barely a day passes without TV broadcasting interviews with veterans.

HISTORY THE IRAN–IRAQ WAR

16 Jan 1979	1 Feb 1979	4 Nov 1979	1980–88
After months of demonstrations, crackdowns, funerals and more demonstrations, Mohammad Reza Shah Pahlavi and his family leave Iran. In 1980 he dies of cancer in Egypt.	Ayatollah Khomeini, now 77, returns and turns a broad-based revolutionary movement into a victory for hardline Islamic forces. In April a referendum confirms Iran as an Islamic Republic.	Conservative students storm the US embassy in Tehran and take 52 Americans hostage. They are held for 444 days and finally released on the day of Ronald Reagan's presidential inauguration.	The Iran–Iraq War begins with an opportunistic invasion by Saddam Hussein's forces. In Iran, 87 cities and nearly 3000 villages are bombed. More than 900,000 people are killed on both sides.

After Khomeini

When Ayatollah Khomeini died on 3 June 1989 his position as Supreme Leader passed to the former president, Ali Khamenei. The presidency, which had previously been a largely ceremonial post, was transformed with the election of the cleric Ali Akbar Hashemi Rafsanjani, who began a series of much-needed economic reforms. Despite being widely seen as the richest – and most corrupt – man in the country, Rafsanjani was re-elected in 1993. Social and religious conservatism remained firmly ingrained in Iranian society but domestic policy took on a more pragmatic tone. This included an aggressive campaign to curb sky-rocketing

A REVOLUTION IN STREET NAMES

Across Iran you'll find streets named after the same few martyrs of the revolution, historical figures (often poets) and revolutionary buzzwords. In many places the government has conveniently painted a huge mural or erected a mosaic likeness of the person beside the street that bears his (it's almost always a man) name. So who are these men?

Ayatollah Beheshti Founded the Islamic Republic Party (IRP) in 1979. He took part in the negotiations over the US embassy hostages but was killed a year later by a bomb planted in IRP headquarters by the Mojahedin Khalq Organisation (MKO).

Ayatollah Mahmoud Taleghani A much-admired cleric who was repeatedly exiled and later tortured by the last shah. He led the first Friday prayers after the revolution but died soon afterwards.

Amir Kabir This was the nickname of Mirza Taghi Khan, a reformist prime minister (from 1848 to 1851) who was executed on the orders of his jealous shah in Fin Gardens near Kashan.

Dr Ali Shariati Returned to Iran from France in 1964 with a doctorate in sociology from the Sorbonne. He combined radical political thought with socially conscious traditionalism and became an inspiration to many women. Barred from teaching, he went to England in 1977, but was found dead in his apartment three weeks later – allegedly a victim of the shah's secret police.

Ayatollah Morteza Motahhari Was a close confidant of Ayatollah Khomeini who railed against communism and the effect it would have on Islam. He became president of the Constitutional Council after the revolution, but was assassinated by a rival Islamic group in May 1979.

Streets named for revolutionaries and Islamic phrases include Valiasr, which means 'Prince of this Time' and is a nickname for Mahdi, the 12th imam; Azadi, which translates to 'freedom'; Jomhuri-ye Eslami, which means 'Islamic Republic'; and Enghelab, Farsi for 'revolution'. For more on these and other Iranian figures, see www.iranchamber.com and follow the links through History to Historic Personalities.

1989	1997	2003	2003
Ayatollah Ruhollah Khomeini dies on 3 June, aged 86. The leadership shuffles, with recently appointed Ayatollah Ali Khamenei becoming Supreme Leader and Ayatollah Akbar Hashemi Rafsanjani elected president.	Reformist Mohammad Khatami is elected president in a landslide. Harsh laws on dress and social interaction stop being so strictly enforced and many women start wearing make-up and tighter clothing.	On 26 December, the oasis city of Bam is devastated by an earthquake that kills more than 31,000 people and largely destroys the ancient Arg-e Bam.	Shirin Ebadi, the founder of Iran's Defenders of Human Rights Center, becomes the first Iranian to win the Nobel Peace Prize. She later moves into exile after a crackdown on government critics.

population growth through contraception and a greater effort to bring electricity, running water, telephone and sealed roads to rural areas long ignored under royal rule.

Khatami & the Reformists

In 1997 the moderate, reform-minded Hojjat-ol-Eslam Sayyed Mohammad Khatami won the presidency in a landslide; Rafsanjani may have lost power but he would remain a key figure and political power broker until his death in early 2017. Almost everyone, and especially the ruling clerics, was shocked by Khatami's victory. Khatami was a liberal by Iranian standards, but he was also an insider. He had studied theology in Qom, had held important posts during the Iran–Iraq War and served as Minister of Culture and Islamic Guidance for 10 years until he was forced to resign in 1992 – for being too liberal.

His election sent an overwhelming message of discontent to the ruling Islamic conservatives and resulted in a spontaneous, unlegislated liberalisation. Khatami promised 'change from within', a policy of avoiding confrontation with the clerics and engineering change from within the theocratic system. When reformers won a large majority in the Majlis in 2000 and Khatami was re-elected with 78% of the vote in 2001, hopes were high. But what the public wanted and what Khatami and the Majlis were able to deliver proved to be very different. Of the hundreds of pieces of legislation the Majlis passed during its four-year term, more than 35% were vetoed by the conservatives on the Guardian Council.

The conservative backlash didn't stop there. Reformist intellectuals were assassinated, students beaten for protesting, dozens of reform-minded newspapers were closed and editors imprisoned. With the reformers either unable or too scared to institute their promised reforms, the public lost faith in them and the idea of 'change from within'.

Ahmadinejad Era

With Reformists barred from running and the public disillusioned with politics, former Republican Guard member and Tehran mayor Mahmoud Ahmadinejad was unexpectedly elected president in 2005. Despite his religious conservatism, Ahmadinejad's man-of-the-people image appealed to a population frustrated and angry with the clique of clerics, military and their cronies that had become Iran's new elite.

Ahmadinejad's promises to 'put petroleum income on people's tables' went down well but in reality were not affordable. Fuel prices, inflation and unemployment rose, social crackdowns were more frequent, international sanctions over the nuclear issue became tighter and, particularly in urban areas, Ahmadinejad and his government were seen by many Iranians as incompetent. In the background, Ahmadinejad quietly

During the 1980s and early 1990s several high-profile opposition leaders were assassinated while in exile in Europe. These included Kurdish human rights activist Dr Kazem Rajavi, shot in Switzerland in 1990, and former prime minister Shapur Bakhtiar, stabbed to death in Paris in 1991.

In 2004 the Guardian Council barred more than 2000 Reformist candidates, including 82 sitting members, from Majlis elections. Many Iranians chose not to vote and conservatives were swept back into power.

2005	2006	2008	2009
Populist Tehran mayor Mahmoud Ahmadinejad is elected president, defeating regime insider, former president and wealthy businessman Ayatollah Akbar Hashemi Rafsanjani.	Iran deflects international criticism over its nuclear program and receives widespread criticism for hosting a conference on the Holocaust, a conference attended by several Holocaust deniers.	Many pro-reform candidates are disqualified from standing in parliamentary elections in which conservatives win more than two-thirds of seats. The UN Security Council strengthens sanctions against Iran.	Mahmoud Ahmadinejad wins a second term as Iran's president. Liberal reformers back the Green Movement, a popular uprising that disputed Ahmadinejad's win.

ARGO

Argo (2012) is a rollicking good (and Oscar-winning) tale that tells the story of a group of American embassy personnel who escaped from Iran during the hostage crisis that began in 1979. Most of it was based on real events and the basic premise of the movie is broadly accurate. But critics have argued that many liberties were taken with the facts. The escapees, for example, were never turned away by the New Zealand and British embassies, and the dramatic scenes at Tehran airport depicting the escape itself are pure fiction. It was also claimed that the film presented the unbalanced view that it was the CIA rather than the Canadians that was primarily responsible for getting the six out of the country.

replaced provincial governors and experienced bureaucrats with his own ex-Revolutionary Guard cronies.

In the run-up to the 2009 presidential election, opposition coalesced around Reformist candidate and former prime minister Mirhossein Mousavi. When Ahmadinejad was hastily declared the winner, the Green Movement staged massive street protests in Tehran and elsewhere, orchestrated on Twitter and by mobile phones. The ensuing crackdown claimed dozens of lives.

The Struggle for Iran

Rosewater (2014) dramatises the 2009 Green Movement and its aftermath, by telling the story of an Iranian-Canadian journalist (played by Gael García Bernal) who is detained while on assignment in Iran and accused of being a spy. It was written, produced and directed by Jon Stewart, formerly the host of *The Daily Show* in the US.

Ahmadinejad clung to power and the grinding weight of repression gradually overcame the opposition – the Green Movement dissipated or went underground. In the same year, the Iranian government confirmed international suspicions that it was building a uranium-enrichment plant close to Qom, although it insisted that its nuclear program was for entirely peaceful purposes. Whether it was the goverment's intention or not, the issue diverted attention away from the vexed questions of social and political reform to one of a beleaguered country at odds with the international community and determined to assert its sovereignty. In the years since, Iran's nuclear program and its relationship with the international community have kept the country in the headlines and on the margins of international respectability.

The Reformist movement had been severely battered and bruised by the aftermath of the Green Movement's failure to win power in 2009. Even so, the unstable faultline that ripples through modern Iranian society – liberal reformers with an urban power base pitted against conservative clerics and their rural heartland – simply won't go away and is unlikely to any time soon. In 2013, the Reformist-backed Hassan Rouhani won presidential elections as the pendulum swung back again in favour of those who would reform the Islamic Republic.

2012	2013	2015	2016
Conservatives sweep to victory in parliamentary elections boycotted by reformist candidates.	Cleric Hassan Rouhani, who is backed by the liberal reform movement, wins the presidential election with more than 50% of the vote. President Rouhani says Iran will never build nuclear weapons.	Iran reaches a landmark deal with the international community aimed at restricting Iran's nuclear activity in return for a lifting of international economic sanctions.	The 2015 nuclear deal becomes a hotly contested issue in the US elections, with president-to-be Donald Trump promising to rip up the treaty if elected.

People

Iran is one of the Middle East's most diverse countries, a crossroads of peoples in whose traditions are written the region's history, both ancient and modern. For all of these traditions that are very much a part of modern life in the country, there is a unifying Iranian identity. Forged through shared histories, centuries of constant proximity and the struggles and conflicts of recent decades, this sense of being Iranian keeps all these disparate peoples discernibly part of a bigger whole.

Persians

Persians are the descendents of the original Elamite and Aryan races who arrived in what is now Iran during the 3rd millennium BC. The Persians, or Farsis, were originally the tribes that came to establish the Achaemenid Empire and, when Gilaki and Mazandarani people are included in the number (their language is a variation on Farsi but they are still ethnically Persians), they now make up about 60% of the population. Persians are found across Iran, but Tehran, Mashhad, Esfahan, Yazd and particularly Shiraz have the highest concentrations. Farsi is the main Iranian language and Persian culture is often considered Iranian culture.

As the largest and most influential ethnic group, Persians fill most of Iran's senior government posts. However, people from most other ethnic groups (as opposed to religions) can still reach the top – Iran's Supreme Leader, Ali Khamenei, is an ethnic Azeri.

Azeris

Commonly called 'Turks' in Iran, the Azeris make up about 16% of the population. They speak Azeri Turkish, a dialect mixing Turkish with Farsi and have strong cross-border links with neighbouring Turkey and Azerbaijan. They are concentrated in northwest Iran, in the Azerbaijan provinces around Tabriz, and are predominantly Shia Muslims.

Kurds

Iran has more than seven million Kurds. The Kurds lay claim to being the oldest Iranian people in the region, descended from the Medes who ruled the region from Iran in the 7th century BC. The wider Kurdish homeland is a largely contiguous area split between southeastern Turkey (Kurds represent around 20% of Turkey's population), northeastern Syria (7% to 8%), northern Iraq (15%) and northwestern Iran. There are more than 20 million Kurds in total and they comprise the largest ethnic group without their own country. In Iran, Kurds (who are predominantly Sunni Muslims) live in the mountainous west, particularly Kordestan province near the Iraqi border.

Arabs

Arabs make up about 2% of the population and are settled mostly in Khuzestan, near the Iraqi border, and on the coast and islands of the Persian Gulf. They are often called *bandari* (*bandar* means port), because of their historical links to the sea. Their differing language (a dialect of Arabic), dress, music and faith (many are Sunni Muslims) often keep them on the margins of mainstream Iranian life.

NOMADS

About a million people still live as nomads in Iran despite repeated attempts to settle them. Most migrate between cooler mountain areas in summer and low-lying warmer regions during winter, following pasture for their livestock. Their migrations are during April and May, when they head uphill, returning during October and November.

Most of Iran's nomads belong to the Qashqa'i and Bakhtiyari tribes of Turkic origin. The Qashqa'i are based in central Iran, where they move between the summer and winter pastures of Fars province along some of the most challenging migration routes in the country. On the road for 45 days, they have become famous for their resilience – and for the production of a hand-loomed rug known as gabbeh.

It is the Bakhtiyari whom visitors to the Zagros Mountains are most likely to encounter. Concentrated in a wide area west of Esfahan and ranging near to the Iraqi border, they move their herds of sheep and goats between summer and winter pastures and speak a distinct dialect called Lori.

Other nomadic groups in Iran are comprised of Kurds, Lors, Baluchis and smaller groups, such as the Khamseh of Bavanat, but they all share skills in animal husbandry, craft production and an instinct for survival. Nomadic women are noticeable about town in their colourful layered dresses and jewellery, while men often wear sleeveless white wool coats and felt hats.

Many travel agencies offer opportunities to visit with these communities on a specialist tour. Such tours, however, are not without their critics, and engaging a specialist guide may prove a more rewarding and culturally sensitive experience.

Lors

These proud people constitute about 6% of Iran's population and are thought to be descendants of the first peoples in the region, the Kassites and Medes; they have strong historical ties to the Kurds. Many speak Lori, a mixture of Arabic and Farsi, and a significant minority remain nomadic. Whether nomadic or settled, most live in or near the mountainous western province of Lorestan.

More than 40% of Iran's population is aged under 25 years old and about 25% is under 15. Although things have improved in recent years, Iran's economy is still unable to keep up with youth unemployment at around 27% in 2016, although real figures are thought to be much higher.

Turkmen

Making up about 2% of the population, Iranian Turkmen are descended from the nomadic Turkic tribes that once ruled Iran. They live in the northeast of the country, especially around Gorgan and Gonbad-e Kavus and close to the border with Turkmenistan. They are, however, present across the north of the country and have ties to Turkmen people across the border in Iraq. They speak their own Turkic language.

Baluchis

Around 1.5 million Baluchis live mostly in Sistan va Baluchestan and (to a lesser extent) Kerman provinces. They are part of a much greater population whose traditional lands cross the Baluchestan desert deep into Afghanistan and Pakistan. A significant minority are still nomadic, living in tents and migrating in pursuit of seasonal pastures. They speak Baluchi, a language related to Pashtu, and the majority are Sunni Muslims.

Baluchis are easily recognisable for their darker skin and distinctive clothing, with women typically wearing colourful attire and men the *shalwar kameez* (long loose shirt and baggy trousers).

Daily Life

Like any people in a dynamic modern society, Iranians live a multiplicity of lives that make generalisations dangerous, especially at a time when the conservative-liberal divide that runs through Iranian society is as significant as ever – there are as many ways of being Iranian as there are Iranians. Even so, there are some mainstays – the importance of religious faith, the significance of family, and a proud attachment to local culture and traditions while generally remaining warm and welcoming to outsiders.

How Iranians Live

Life is a struggle for many Iranians and often bears little resemblance to the lives lived by their parents and grandparents. The majority of Iran's urban dwellers live in flats, and in major cities homes are rapidly being replaced with apartment blocks. Land in Tehran is as expensive as many North American and European cities, and the cost of living is increasingly prohibitive. With prices for rental properties outstripping salaries more with each passing year, the struggle to make ends meet means many Iranians work more than one job and, in the case of the middle classes, often both men and women work. Many couples live with parents for years before they can afford their own place.

The area of land that is Iran has been continuously inhabited by a single nation for longer than any other land.

Rich & Poor

The gap between rich and poor is huge. Teachers, earning not much more than US$300 a month, are the sort of middle-class state employee hardest hit by inflation rates running at more than 8% per annum (although it has hovered around 20% in recent years). On the other hand, a fortunate minority live in lavish villas or marble-and-glass

THE POWER OF THE BAZARIS

In Iran a bazaar is more than just a place to stock up on a few essential shopping items. For centuries the *bazaris*, who run the businesses in the bazaar, have held enormous economic and political power. They are usually conservative, religious people who have a long history of standing against authority – none more so than the *bazaris* of Tehran.

In an attempt to weaken their power, the last shah bulldozed new roads through parts of the bazaar, gave subsidised credit to competing supermarkets and set up state purchasing bodies to handle sugar, meat and wheat. Not surprisingly, the Tehran *bazaris* hit back during the Islamic Revolution when the closure of the bazaar wrought havoc on the economy.

While international-style shopping centres are now common in major cities, most Iranians still shop in a bazaar or a smaller store that buys wholesale from a bazaar. It has been estimated Tehran's Grand Bazaar controls one-third of Iran's entire retail and trade sector. Prices here are said to set the standard for prices across the country.

However, the power of the *bazaris* is waning. Competition from supermarkets and modern shopping malls and the time it takes for most Tehranis to reach the bazaar is inevitably bleeding money away from this traditional market, and with it the power of its merchants.

Shiites were historically persecuted by the Sunni majority and so developed a doctrine (called *taqiya*) whereby it is fine to conceal one's faith in order to escape persecution.

apartments in the wealthy northern suburbs of Tehran. It is not uncommon to spend US$100 on a meal for two at a trendy northern Tehran restaurant, an amount most Iranians could not even dream of spending. The women of such families tend not to work but instead lead lives revolving around their children, visiting parents and friends and working out with personal trainers.

In contrast a middle-class couple may leave their modest apartment together in the morning after the typical Persian breakfast of bread, cheese, jam and tea. Their children, if small, will mostly be looked after by grandparents while the couple go to work. One or the other may make it back for lunch, unless living in Tehran where distances are greater and traffic hideous. In the evening the family meal will be taken together, often with the wider family and friends. Iranians are social creatures and many visits occur after dinner.

In poorer or more traditional families it is likely that the woman will stay at home, in which case her whole day revolves around housework, providing meals for her family and shopping (in ultraconservative families the men may do the shopping).

Iranian meals take time to prepare and though supermarkets exist and some pre-packaged ingredients are available, many women spend a decent chunk of each day just buying, cleaning and chopping the herbs served with every meal. Working women generally see to these tasks in the evenings, when they may prepare the next day's lunch. Mostly it is safe to say that men's role in the home is confined to appreciating the quality of the cooking. Which they do well, Iranians being true gourmets.

Family Life

Nearly three-quarters of Iran's population live in urban areas, one of the highest rates of urbanisation in the region.

Family life is of supreme importance to Iranians and often a family will include children, parents, grandparents and other elderly relatives. As a result, Iranian society is more multigenerational than Western society, something that's most obvious on holidays and weekends when you'll see several generations walking, laughing and picnicking together.

Living alone is extremely unusual and unmarried children usually only leave home to attend university in another town or for work. Although the young people of Iran long for independence and their own space, just like their Western counterparts, there is not much cultural precedence for this. Those who do live alone – mostly men – are pitied. Women living alone are regarded with extreme suspicion. Being married and having a family is regarded as the happiest – not to mention the most natural – state of being.

For the most part, the average Iranian family is a robust unit and, despite economic and social differences, most operate in broadly the same way. They provide an essential support unit in a country with no state benefit system.

Education

Iran has more than one million drug addicts, even though drug dealing and drug use can be punishable by death. Iran also has enlightened policies for treating addiction, including methadone programs and clean needles for addicted prisoners.

Education is highly regarded; adult literacy is well above average for the region at 86.8% (91.2% for men, 82.5% for women), according to Unesco. The average years children attend school is 15 (the same for men and women), again one of the highest in the region. Many middle-class teenagers spend up to two years studying for university entrance exams, though the sheer number of entrants, ideological screening and places reserved for war veterans and their offspring make it very hard to get in. And once out of university, there is no guarantee of work.

With the sexes segregated at school and boys and girls discouraged from socialising together, trying to get to know members of the opposite sex is a huge preoccupation for Iranian teenagers. They hang around shopping malls, in cafes and parks, parade up and down boulevards and spend lots of time cruising around in cars.

Sport

Football is a national obsession and Iran has been competing internationally since 1941, winning three Asian Cups during the '60s and '70s and qualifying for four World Cups (1978, 1998, 2006 and 2014). Many Iranians of a certain generation can tell you where they were when Iran defeated Australia in dramatic fashion to qualify for the 1998 World Cup, their first appearance in two decades. The men's professional league has 18 teams in the top division and runs from August to May, with games played most Thursdays and Fridays.

You'll see kids playing football in streets and squares across Iran, but you won't see too many pitches. This is partly because religious strictures mean women should not see unrelated men in shorts, so most grounds are behind large walls. Women are barred from attending men's sporting events even though they are, conversely, free to watch them on TV; this oft-debated issue is dealt with in Jafar Panahi's film *Offside*. Wrestling, skiing, tae kwon do and archery are also popular.

Modern-day restrictions aside, Iran does have an interesting sporting history. Polo is believed to have originated in Iran and was certainly played during the reign of Darius the Great. Shah Abbas the Great also enjoyed polo, and today you can still see the burly stone goal posts at either end of Esfahan's Naqsh-e Jahan (Imam) Sq.

Iran's biggest football rivalry is between Tehran clubs Persepolis (pronounced 'Perspolis' and playing in red), known as the working-class team, and Esteghlal (blue home strip), the villainous wealthy club.

Zurkhaneh

Unique to Iran, the *zurkhaneh* literally means 'house of strength' and is a mix of sport, theatre and religion that dates back thousands of years. As it was refined through the ages, the *zurkhaneh* picked up different components of moral, ethical, philosophical and mystical values of Iranian civilisation. The *zurkhaneh* itself is a small, traditional gymnasium often decorated like a shrine, and what goes on inside incorporates the spiritual richness of Sufism, traditional rituals of Mithraism and the heroism of Iranian nationalism. Typically a group of men stand around a circular pit and perform a series of ritualised feats of strength, all to the accompaniment of a leader pounding out a frenetic drumbeat. The leader sings verses from epics such as the *Shahnameh* and recites poetry by Hafez. Most *zurkhaneh* are open to the public and it's usually free to watch. You won't see many local women, but Western women are welcomed as honorary men.

At the 2016 Rio Olympics, Kimia Alizadeh became the first Iranian woman to win an Olympic medal, taking bronze in the under-57kg tae kwon do class.

Women in Iran

Nowhere are the contradictions in Iranian society more apparent than in the position of women; some of the fiercest battles in Iran's ongoing liberal-conservative schism have been over the issues of women's rights. That said, the situation is far from black and white and is one that defies easy simplification.

Women Through the Ages

Historically, women have lived in a relatively progressive society and enjoyed more equality and freedom than their neighbours. In Iran women are able to sit in parliament, drive, vote, buy property and work. There is a long precedence for this. Archaeological evidence suggests that in pre-Islamic times, women in Iran were able to work, own, sell and lease property and that they paid taxes. Women managed work sites and held high-level military positions. But it wasn't until the Prophet Mohammed that women's rights were specifically addressed. Islam recognises men and women as having different rights and responsibilities. Men are expected to provide financially, therefore women are not seen as needing legal rights as men are there to protect and maintain them.

In reality, for Iranian women, the arrival of Islam after the Arab conquest saw a decline in their position at every level. Most of their rights evaporated, the Islamic dress code was imposed, polygamy was practised and family laws were exclusively to the advantage of the male.

Reza Shah started legislating for women in 1931 with a bill that gave women the right to seek divorce. In subsequent years the marriage age was raised to 15 for girls, girls gained access to an education equal to that of boys, women were encouraged to work outside the home and legislation was passed to abolish the veil, a move that polarised opinion among women. In 1962 Mohammad Reza Shah gave women the vote and in 1968 the most progressive family law in the Middle East was ratified. Divorce laws became stringent and polygamy was discouraged. The marriage age was raised to 18.

> According to Unesco, 96.4% of births in Iran are attended by a skilled attendant, and in 2016, the average number of children per woman was 1.83, down from around six during the early years of the Islamic Revolution.

Impact of the Iranian Revolution

Many Iranian women were active in the revolution that overthrew the shah, but it's safe to say that few foresaw how the Islamic Republic, and its adoption of a version of Sharia law, would affect their rights. Within a couple of years women were back in the hejab – and this time it was compulsory. The legal age of marriage for girls plummeted to nine (15 for boys), and society was strictly segregated. Women were not allowed to appear in public with a man who was not a husband or a direct relation, and they could be flogged for displaying 'incorrect' hejab or showing strands of hair or scraps of make-up. Travel was not possible without a husband or father's permission and a woman could be stoned to death for adultery, which, incidentally, included being raped. Family law again fell under the jurisdiction of the religious courts and it became almost impossible for a woman to divorce her husband without his agreement. In any case of divorce she was almost certain to lose custody of her children. Women holding high positions – such as Shirin Ebadi, who became a judge in 1979 and won the Nobel Peace Prize in 2003 – lost their jobs and many gave up promising careers.

However, Iranian women had tasted emancipation, and they resisted a total return to the home. There were many rights that women did not lose – such as the right to vote and the right to hold property and financial independence in marriage – putting them at a marked advantage to some Arab neighbours. In fact, the rates of education and literacy for women have shot up since the revolution for the simple reason that many traditional families finally felt safe sending their daughters to school once Iran had adopted the veil.

In 1997 reformist president Khatami was voted in by mostly women and young people, promising change. By 2001 there were 14 women in the Majlis (Iranian Parliament) and calls to improve women's rights became louder.

> Among the most prolific Islamic feminists is Faezeh Rafsanjani, the daughter of the ex-president, who herself was a member of parliament, a magazine proprietor, an academic, a mother and an Olympic horse rider.

Women Today

The Khatami period brought a series of hard-fought minor victories. The reformists managed to win the right for single women to study abroad, to raise the legal age for marriage from nine to 13 for girls (though they had proposed 15), to defeat an attempt to limit the percentage of female students entering university and to improve custody provisions for divorced mothers. Although women's importance in the

IRAN'S AGE-OLD CELEBRATION OF THE NEW YEAR

No Ruz literally means 'new day' and while the celebration is for Persian New Year, much of the traditional ceremony is about renewal and hope for the future. The roots of No Ruz stretch deep into history, with the spring equinox (usually 21 March) having been celebrated since before Achaemenid times. It's a peculiarly Persian tradition that has nothing to do with Islam – a fact many Iranians are proud of but which doesn't sit well with the Islamic theocracy.

Haft Seen

No Ruz festivities stretch for about three weeks. Apart from frenzied shopping, the outward sign of No Ruz is street-side stalls selling the *haft seen* (seven 's'es; seven, or sometimes more, symbolic items with Farsi names starting with the letter 's'). Like a Christmas tree, they are supposed to be set up at home, though you'll see them everywhere from TV news studios to taxi dashboards. Today's most commonly seen *seen*, and their symbolic meanings:

➡ *sabzi* (green grass or sprout shoots) and *samanu* (sweet wheat pudding) represent rebirth and fertility

➡ *seer* (garlic) and *sumaq* (sumac) symbolise hoped-for good health

➡ *sib* (apple) and *senjed* (a dried fruit) represent the sweetness of life

➡ *sonbol* (hyacinth) is for beauty

On many tables you'll also see *sekeh* (a gold coin, symbolising adequate income), *serkeh* (vinegar to ward off bitterness), a mirror, a Quran and candles. You'll also see sorry-looking goldfish in tiny bowls symbolising life – until they die in their millions after No Ruz.

Chahar Shanbe-soori

On the Tuesday night before the last Wednesday of the year chahar shanbe-soori, (Wednesday Fire), people sing, dance (men only) and jump over fires. The jumping symbolises the burning away of ill luck or health, to be replaced by the healthy redness of the flames. Unfortunately, actually finding a fire can be tough.

Chahar shanbe-soori is viewed as a pagan festival by the government and there is sometimes open animosity between revellers and (half-hearted) police or Basij militia men. Some towns have grudgingly 'approved' fire-sites, though visiting these can be deafening and rather hazardous due to the uncontrolled bursts of fireworks. In many cities, however, fires are banned altogether; ask locally for the situation.

No Ruz

When No Ruz finally arrives, families gather around the *haft seen* table to recite a prayer seeking happiness, good health and prosperity, before eating *sabzi polo* (rice and vegetables) and *mahi* (fish). Mothers are also expected to eat symbolic hardboiled eggs – one for every child. At the moment the sun passes the celestial equator (announced on every radio station), people kiss and hug and children are given *eidi* (presents). For the following two weeks Iranians visit relatives and friends in their home towns.

Sizdah be Dar

No Ruz celebrations finish on the 13th day of the year, *Sizdah be Dar* (usually 2 April). Everyone goes picnicking out of town, taking their *haft seen sabzi* with them. The *sabzi* is either thrown into water or, in some cases, left to blow off the roof of the car. Either way, the *sabzi* is meant to have soaked up the bad aspects of the previous year, so this ceremony symbolises getting rid of bad luck.

workforce is acknowledged – maternity leave, for example, is given for three months at 67% of salary or four months if breastfeeding – there is still widespread discrimination.

However, a woman's testimony is still only worth half that of a man's in court and in the case of the blood money that a murderer's family is obliged to pay to the family of the victim, females are estimated at half the value of a male.

Sigheh is the Islamic practice of a temporary marriage contract that allows sex outside of a normal marriage. To many Iranians, especially women, it is seen as a sort of legalised prostitution.

On the street, especially in Tehran, you will see that superficially the dress code has eased compared with the days when the black chador dominated. Despite crackdowns that ebb and flow with the political winds, women of all ages can often be seen wearing shorter, tighter, brightly coloured coats and headscarves worn far back on elaborate hairstyles. Some young women have lost their fear of being seen outside the home with unrelated men and are prepared to risk arrest to do so. Activists such as Shirin Ebadi, who now works as a lawyer and champions human rights, are insistent that within Islam are enshrined all human rights and that all that is needed is more intelligent interpretation.

Any visit to an Iranian home will leave you in no doubt as to who is really in charge of family life – which is arguably the most important institution in Iran. Many Iranian women are feisty and powerful and they continue to educate themselves. Some will tell you that the hejab is the least of their worries; what is more important is to change the institutional discrimination inherent in Iranian society and the law.

Under Ahmadinejad's presidency between 2005 and 2013, such change became more difficult to achieve. Following the Green Movement mass protests in 2009, the government was much more aggressive

TA'AROF

At the end of your first taxi trip in Iran, there's a good chance you'll ask the driver *'chand toman'* (how many tomans?) and he'll reply *'ghabeli nadari'*. His words mean 'it's nothing', but the taxi driver still expects to get paid. This is *ta'arof*, a system of formalised politeness that can seem confusing to outsiders, but is a mode of social interaction in which everyone knows their place.

Despite the apparent contradictions in the taxi, you'll soon learn that *ta'arof* is more about people being sensitive to the position of others than routine politeness. So for example, an offer of food will be repeatedly turned down before being accepted. This gives the person making the offer the chance to save face if in reality they cannot provide a meal (they will stop offering after the second or third time). A good rule is to always refuse any offer three times but, if they continue to insist, do accept. When a shopkeeper, restaurateur or (less often) a hotel manager refuses payment when asked for a bill, do remember that this is just *ta'arof* – don't leave without paying! If you accept an offer that is in fact *ta'arof*, the shocked look on the vendor's face should soon reveal your error.

Ta'arof also involves showing consideration of others in your physical actions, so try not to sit with your back to people and expect to be delayed at doorways as Iranians insist that whoever they're with goes through the door first with repeated *'befarmayid'* (please). Be prepared for small talk at the beginning of any exchange, as the health of every member of your family is enquired after. Returning this courtesy will be greatly appreciated. Also be prepared for questions considered personal in the West, such as your salary, marital status, why you don't have children and so on. This is quite normal. Steer away from politics or religion unless your Iranian host broaches the subject first.

And don't forget to pay the taxi driver...think of it this way: it would be bad form for the driver not to offer you the trip for free, and worse form for you to accept his offer.

in enforcing restrictive laws that had, in effect, been dormant during the Khatami years. Across the country, female university students were told to start wearing a *maqna'e* (nunlike headscarf or wimple) or stop coming to class. In cities, and especially in Tehran, the liberties taken for granted for a decade from 1997 were challenged by periodic high-profile crackdowns on what is perceived as bad hejab – usually too much make-up and not enough scarf. Many of the Khatami-era reforms remained, but the immediate future for women seemed less optimistic and more uncertain than it had been for almost a decade.

And then, the pendulum swung back: in 2013, reformist-backed Hassan Rouhani won the country's presidential elections. Even so, the reformist influence over legislative agendas and enforcement remains tenuous.

No matter how Iran's political landscape changes, it seems certain Iranian women will continue to assert their rights and slowly chip away at the system, be it with a defiant splash of red lipstick, making visionary movies or becoming expert at interpreting the law and winning the Nobel Peace Prize.

Women make up almost two-thirds of all university entrants, though their subsequent employment rate is below 20%.

Iranian Cuisine

Iran's food is one of the enduring highlights of any visit to the country. Mastered over three millennia, the cuisine is a reflection of the very soul of the country and its varied terrain. Think camel kabab and dates in the desert, fish on the Gulf coast and a huge variety of vegetable dishes (with meat, of course) in the fertile Caspian provinces of Gilan and Mazandaran.

Staples & Specialities

While tastes are broadening, it remains that outside Tehran restaurant menus are dominated by kababs and fast food. To enjoy the best cooking you really need to be invited into an Iranian home. There's a good chance that will happen and when it does, just say 'yes'. As a guest you will be honoured as a 'gift of God' and the fabulous food and humbling hospitality should make for a meal you'll remember for a lifetime.

New Persian Cooking: A Fresh Approach to the Classic Cuisine of Iran (2011), by Dana-Haeri and Shahrzad Ghorashian, does what its title says, adding some fresh takes on Iranian staples. *Pomegranates and Roses: My Persian Family Recipes* (2012), by Ariana Bundy, is also excellent, with an emphasis on home cooking.

Bread & Rice

Almost every meal in Iran is accompanied by *nun* (bread) and/or *berenj* (rice). *Nun* is cheap and usually fresh. There are four main varieties:
Barbari Crisp and salty and more like Turkish bread; often covered with sesame seeds.
Lavash Common for breakfast and is flat and thin; it's mouthwatering when fresh but soon turns cardboard-like.
Sangak The elite of Iranian breads, long and thick and baked on a bed of stones to give it its characteristic dimpled appearance – check carefully for rogue chunks of gravel.
Taftun Crisp with a ribbed surface.

Chelo (boiled or steamed rice) forms the base of many an Iranian meal, and especially at lunch is served in vast helpings. Rice cooked with other ingredients, such as nuts, spices or barberry (small, red berries), is called *polo* and is worth asking for specifically. *Za'feran* (saffron) is frequently used to add flavour and colour. If rice is served with a knob of butter on top, blend this in as the Iranians do. *Tahdig,* the savoury crust from the bottom of the rice pan, often including slices of potato, is a national favourite.

Kababs

Even in a restaurant with a long menu, most main-dish options will be kabab. These are served either on bread or as *chelo kabab* (on a vast mound of rice). In contrast with the greasy doner kebabs inhaled after rough nights in the West, Iranian kababs are tasty, healthy and cooked shish-style over hot charcoals. They are usually sprinkled with spicy *sumaq* (sumac) and accompanied by raw onion, grilled tomatoes and, for an extra fee, a bowl of *mast* (yoghurt).

Common kabab incarnations include:
Bakhtiyari kabab Lamb chops and chicken, the king of kababs.
Chelo kabab Any kind of kabab in this list served with *chelo* (boiled or steamed rice); the default option will be *kubide* if you don't specify.

GETTING DIZI

Known alternatively as *abgusht* (or as *piti* in Azerbaijan), *dizi* is a cheap soup-stew meal named for the earthenware pot in which it is served. It's considered by many Iranians as the food of the poor, but assuming you're neither a vegetarian nor obsessive about cholesterol, it's actually a delicious and filling dish. There is, however, an art to eating it.

First, tear some bread into bite-sized morsels, put it into your bowl and drain the soupy broth from the *dizi* over the top of the bread. Eat this then turn to the main ingredients left in the *dizi*: chickpeas, potatoes, tomatoes and soft-boiled mutton. Grind these together using the provided metal pestle; do include the inevitable chunk of fat, which while looking unappetising does add taste and texture. Eat the resulting mush with a spoon or bread. If it gets too hard, fear not, the waiter will show the way.

Juje kabab Grilled chicken pieces marinated in *sumaq*.
Kubide kabab The cheapest, most common version made of minced mutton, breadcrumbs and onion ground together.

Non-Kabab Meals

For a change from kabab it's worth asking for common stand-bys *zereshk polo ba morgh* (chicken on rice made tangy with barberries), *ghorme sabzi* (a green mix of diced meat, beans and vegetables, served with rice) or various mouthwatering vegetarian dishes made from *bademjan* (eggplant).

But it doesn't end there. Certain (usually downmarket) eateries and many *chaykhanehs* (teahouses) specialise in underrated *dizi* (a cheap soup-stew meal). Most restaurants will also serve one or another variety of *khoresht* (thick, usually meaty stew made with vegetables and chopped nuts, then served with rice and/or French fries). However, in some less popular restaurants *khoresht* can live in big pots for days before reaching the plate, so if you have a suspect stomach think twice.

Dolme (vegetables, fruit or vine leaves stuffed with a meat-and-rice mixture) make a tasty change. *Dolme bademjan* (stuffed eggplant) is especially delectable. The Persian classic *fesenjun* (sauce of pomegranate juice, walnuts, eggplant and cardamom served over roast chicken and rice) is increasingly found in restaurants, but it's rare enough to feel like a prize when you find it. Or you might get lucky and be served *fesenjun* in an Iranian home, which is quite an honour.

In western Iran, along the Persian Gulf coast and elsewhere, *chelo mahi* (fried fish on rice) is quite common in season, while on the Caspian coast (and sometimes elsewhere) it's relatively easy to find *mirza ghasemi* (mashed eggplant, squash, garlic, tomato and egg, served with bread or rice).

Aashpazi (www.aashpazi.com) has dozens of recipes for Persian dishes. There's little overarching context on the role of food in Iranian life, but the recipes are reliably outstanding. My Persian Kitchen (www.mypersiankitchen.com) is also good for recipes.

Desserts & Sweets

While after-meal dessert is often a bowl of fruit, Iran produces such a head-spinning array of freshly made *shirini* (sweets) that sweet-toothed travellers might remember the country by its regional specialities:
Esfahan *Gaz*, rose water–flavoured nougat, often with pistachio; prices vary greatly according to the percentage of pistachio, whether honey or sugar is used, and to what extent *angevin* (extract from the tree called *gaz*, hence the name) is used.
Kerman *Kolompe*, a soft, date-filled biscuit.
Orumiyeh *Noghl*, sugar-coated nuts.
Qom *Sohan*, a brittle, toffee-like concoction of pistachio and ginger.
Yazd *Baghlava*, like Turkish baklava but thicker, and *pashmak*, candyfloss made of sugar and sesame.

The Temporary Bride: A Memoir of Love and Food in Iran (2017), by Jennifer Klinec, is at once a love story and food journey, with the contradictions of modern Iran as a backdrop.

Other widely available sweets worth trying include refreshing *paludeh* or *falude* (a sorbet made of rice flour, grated fresh fruit and rose water) and *bastani* (Iranian ice cream).

Drinking

Alcohol is banned in Iran but brace yourself for gallons of tea.

Tea, More Tea & Coffee

Socialising in Iran almost inevitably involves *chay* (tea). Whether you're in a *chaykhaneh* (teahouse), carpet shop, someone's home, an office, a tent – actually, almost anywhere – chances are there will be a kettle steaming away nearby. According to the rules of Iranian hospitality, a host is honour bound to offer a guest at least one cup of tea before considering any sort of business, and the guest is expected to drink it.

Tea is drunk black and is usually served with a bowl of *ghand* (chunks of sugar). It is customary to dip the sugar into the tea and place it between the front teeth before sucking the brew through it. Dentists don't recommend this.

Like Turkey, Iran was a nation of coffee drinkers until tea was introduced by British traders in the 19th century. These days traditional Iranian *ghahve* (coffee), served strong, sweet, black and booby-trapped with a sediment of grounds, is hard to find. Instead, in the past decade there has been a rapid spread of European-style cafes and coffeehouses, especially in wealthier suburbs of major cities, where you can get an excellent espresso. Outside cities, coffee addicts should consider self-catering.

Coffeehouses are now very big. Almost always in the rich part of cities, ie well away from historic/tourist centres, they are great places to meet hip locals. Espresso machines are very impressive in many.

PERSIAN FOOD PHILOSOPHY: IT'S 'HOT' & 'COLD'

Ancient Persians believed good diet was light on fat, red meat, starch and alcohol – these transformed men into selfish brutes. Instead, fruit, vegetables, chicken and fish were encouraged as the food of gentler, more respectable people. In practice, this philosophy was governed by a classification of 'hot' and 'cold' foods, which is still widely used today.

Similar to China's Yin and Yang, the belief is that 'hot' foods 'thicken the blood' and speed metabolism, while 'cold' foods 'dilute the blood' and slow the metabolism. The philosophy extends to personalities and weather, too. Like foods, people are believed to have 'hot' and 'cold' natures. People with 'hot' natures should eat more 'cold' foods, and vice versa. And on cold days it's best to eat 'hot' foods, and vice versa.

So what's 'hot' and what's not? The classification has nothing to do with temperature, and regional variations exist, but it's generally agreed that animal fat, wheat, sugar, sweets, wine, most dried fruits and nuts, fresh herbs including mint and saffron, and most meats are 'hot' (but not beef). 'Cold' foods include fish, yoghurt and watermelon (all 'very cold'), rice, many fresh vegetables (particularly radishes) and fruits, beef, beer and other nonwine alcohol. Some foods are hotter or colder than others, and some, such as pears, feta and tea, are neutral.

As you travel, you'll see the balance in dishes such as *fesenjun* (sauce of pomegranate juice, walnuts, eggplant and cardamom served over roast chicken and rice), where the pomegranate (cold) is balanced by the walnuts (hot). On the table, *mast* (yoghurt), cheese, radishes and greens – all cold – are balanced with 'hot' kababs, chicken and sweets. Getting the balance right is what is most important. Too much 'cold' food is thought to be particularly unhealthy, so be careful of eating watermelon and *dugh* (churned sour milk or yoghurt mixed with water) with your fish meal, unless the *dugh* comes with chopped herbs to balance it out. 'Hot' foods are apparently not so dangerous: too much 'hot' and you might end up with a cold sore, if you're prone to them.

ISLAMIC BEER BUT NO SHIRAZ

While alcohol is quietly tolerated in Christian communities, it is strictly forbidden to Iranian Muslims. There is, of course, a black market – oddly enough often operated by greengrocers – and you'll occasionally hear 'whisky' whispered as you go by. But, believe us, the sickly sweet clear spirit you'll likely be sold is rocket fuel.

There are several brands of *ma'-osh-sha'ir* ('Islamic beer') proudly declaring '0.0% alcohol'. Russian-made Baltika tastes most like beer, while Delster comes in several fruit 'flavours' and is popular because it doesn't try too hard to taste like beer.

There's no chance of finding a glass of Shiraz (Syrah) in Shiraz. There are various theories on the origin of this varietal, most involving cuttings being taken from vineyards in Shiraz back to the Rhône Valley in France during the Crusades. Iranian vines were either ripped up after the 1979 revolution or now produce raisins. Today there are no (legal) wineries.

Juices, Shakes, Dugh & Soft Drinks

You'll never be too far from a delicious fresh fruit *ab* (juice) and fruit *shir* (milkshake). Both cost between US$2 and US$4. Juices are seasonal and usually come au naturel, without added sugar. Popular shakes include *shir moz* (banana), *shir peste* (pistachio) and *shir tut farangi* (strawberry). Shakes are often loaded with sugar.

Some of the more popular juice varietals include *ab anar* (pomegranate), *ab talebi* (honeydew melon), *ab hendune* (watermelon), *ab porteghal* (orange), *ab sib* (apple) and a*b havij* (carrot)

Also widely available, *dugh* (churned sour milk or yoghurt mixed with water) is a sour but refreshing drink. The best *dugh* is usually found in restaurants, comes with chopped herbs and is uncarbonated, unlike most prepacked bottles found in stores.

Tap water is drinkable almost everywhere, and bottled water is widely available. Despite the USA embargo, Coca-Cola is bottled under licence and competes with local soft drinks Zam Zam, Parsi Cola and others. Canned drinks cost multiples of the same drinks sold in bottles.

Vegetarians & Vegans

Vegetarianism is growing in popularity among educated urbanites, particularly in Tehran. But for most Iranians, it remains a foreign concept. Sure, there are a lot of good vegetarian dishes in Iranian cuisine, but most restaurants don't make them.

Solace can be found in the felafels, samosas and potatoes sold in street stalls, and in the Persian mastery of all things *bademjan* (eggplant), especially the meatless Caspian dish *mirza ghasemi*. The various *kuku* (thick omelette dishes) make great snacks, served hot or cold. Varieties include *kuku-ye sabzi* (with mixed herbs), *kuku-e-ye bademjan* (with eggplant) and *kuku-e-ye gol-e kalam* (with cauliflower). In cheaper restaurants, watch for *adas-polo* (yellow rice with lentils, sometimes cumin flavoured).

Vegans will struggle to find anything completely free from animal products; even rice is often served with butter. Fortunately, fresh and dried fruit and varieties of nut and vegetables are widely available. Cheaper hotels might let you use the kitchen.

Habits & Customs

Breakfast is a simple affair, consisting of tea served with leftover *lavash,* feta-style cheese and jam – often carrot-flavoured. Most hotels usually throw in an egg. Lunch is the main meal, eaten with mountains of rice between noon and 2pm. Dinner is usually lighter and eaten from about 7pm onwards. Many restaurants close earlier on Friday. On religious holidays, almost everywhere selling food will shut for the morning at least.

Faith in Iran

Official statistics suggest 99.4% of Iran's population are Muslim, made up of between 90% to 95% Shiite and 5% to 10% Sunni. Small communities of Baha'is, Zoroastrians, Christians and Jews make up the numbers. Aside from the Baha'i religion, the practise of which is outlawed, freedom of worship is guaranteed in the constitution. Iranians will happily accept that visitors are Christians and, in most circumstances, Jewish. But admitting to being atheist or agnostic can result in incomprehension, even among better-educated Iranians.

Islam

The Birth of Islam

Abdul Qasim Mohammed ibn Abdullah ibn Abd al-Muttalib ibn Hashim (the Prophet Mohammed) was born in 570. Mohammed's family belonged to the Quraysh tribe, a trading family with links to Syria and Yemen. By the age of six, Mohammed's parents had both died and he came into the care of his grandfather, the custodian of the Kaaba in Mecca.

At the age of 40, in 610, Mohammed retreated into the desert and began to receive divine revelations from Allah via the voice of the archangel Gabriel; the revelations would continue throughout Mohammed's life. Three years later, Mohammed began imparting Allah's message to Meccans, gathering a significant following in his campaign against idolaters. His movement appealed especially to the poorer, disenfranchised sections of society.

> All Muslims, regardless of whether Sunni or Shiite, are forbidden to drink alcohol or eat anything containing pork, blood or any meat that died in any way other than being slaughtered in the prescribed manner (halal).

Islam provided a simpler alternative to the established faiths, which had become complicated by hierarchical orders, sects and complex rituals, offering instead a direct relationship with God based only on the believer's submission to God (Islam means 'submission').

By 622, Mecca's powerful ruling families had forced Mohammed and his followers to flee north to Medina where Mohammed's supporters rapidly grew. In 630 Mohammed returned triumphantly to Mecca at the head of a 10,000-strong army to seize control of the city. Many of the surrounding tribes quickly swore allegiance to him and the new faith.

Five Pillars of Islam

In order to live a devout life, Muslims are expected to observe, as a minimum, the five pillars of Islam:

Shahada 'There is no god but Allah, and Mohammed is the Prophet of Allah', is Islam's basic tenet. This phrase forms an integral part of the call to prayer and is used at all important events in a Muslim's life.

Salat (Namaz) This is the obligation of prayer, ideally five times a day for Sunnis, though Shiites only pray three times. It's acceptable to pray at home or elsewhere, except for Friday noon prayers, which are performed at a mosque.

Zakat Muslims must give alms to the poor to the value of one-fortieth of a believer's annual income.

Sawm (Ruzeh) Ramazan, the ninth month of the Muslim calendar, commemorates the revelation of the Quran to Mohammed. As Ramazan represents a

Muslim's renewal of faith, nothing may pass their lips (food, cigarettes, drinks) and they must refrain from sex from dawn until dusk.

Hajj Every physically and financially able Muslim should perform the hajj to the holiest of cities, Mecca, at least once in their lifetime. The reward is considerable: the forgiving of all past sins.

Shiism & Sunnism

Despite the Prophet Mohammed's original intentions, Islam did not remain simple. When the Prophet Mohammed died in AD 632, he left no sons and no instructions as to who should succeed him. Competing for power were Abu Bakr, the father of Mohammed's second wife Aisha, and Ali, Mohammed's cousin and the husband of his daughter Fatima. Initially, the power was transferred to Abu Bakr, who became the first caliph, or ruler, with Ali reluctantly agreeing.

Ali was passed over three times before becoming the fourth caliph in 656, only to be assassinated five years later. The Muslim community was by now divided into two factions: the Sunnis, who followed the Umayyad Caliphate, and the Shiite (from 'Shiat Ali', meaning 'followers of Ali').

The episode that ensured Sunni and Shiites would be antagonistic to one another was the massacre of the third imam, Hossein, and his 72 followers in 680. Having set up camp at Karbala, in present-day Iraq, the group was besieged for nine days by the Umayyad caliph's troops, and on the 10th day Hossein was killed. Hossein's martyrdom is commemorated in a 10-day anniversary that culminates on Ashura. It's during Ashura that the Iranian culture of martyrdom is most evident. It's not unusual to see men flailing themselves with chains or crying genuine tears for their lost hero.

When Hossein and his supporters were slaughtered by the caliph's troops, the division became permanent and bitter. Today the representation of its imams ('leaders' or more loosely, 'saints') is one of the most visible aspects of Shiism and you'll see pictures of Imam Hossein, in particular, everywhere.

Shiism reached its greatest influence in Iran. Iranian converts to Islam were attracted by the idea of the imam as a divinely appointed leader

Traditionally, a town's most important mosque was the Masjed-e Jameh. Modern congregations have often outgrown the capacity of the old Jameh mosques so, while Jameh means Friday, the name doesn't always imply that this is where Friday prayers are actually held.

THE 12 IMAMS

Shiism has several sub-branches but the Twelvers are by far the largest group, and make up the vast majority in Iran. Twelvers believe that following the death of Mohammed the rightful spiritual leadership of the Islamic faith passed to 12 successive descendants of the prophet. These were known as imams ('leaders' or more loosely, 'saints') and apart from Ali, the first imam, they weren't recognised by the caliphate (the dynasty of the successors of the Prophet Mohammed as rulers of the Islamic world).

Devout Shiite Muslims might celebrate the death days of all 12 imams, but most concentrate on the first, Ali, the third, Hossein, and the eighth, Reza – the only one buried in Iran, in the lavish Haram-e Razavi in Mashhad.

Almost as important is the 12th imam, known as the Mahdi or Valiasr (Leader of Our Time). Mahdi is the Hidden Imam, believed to have disappeared into a cave under a mosque at Samarra in AD 874. Most Shiites believe he lives on in occultation as their divine leader. It is believed Mahdi will eventually return when, with the prophet Jesus, he will guide the world to peace and righteousness.

Shiites believe only the imams can truly interpret the Quran and the clergy act as their representatives until the Hidden Imam returns. Ayatollah Khomeini was given the honorary title imam after his death.

Martyrdom remains a powerful motivator in modern Iran. During the Iran–Iraq War thousands of men and boys quite literally sacrificed their lives (some cleared mine fields by walking through them) in the name of country and/or religion.

possibly because the Iranians possessed a long heritage of government by a divinely appointed monarch.

Sunni comes from the word *sonnat,* which means tradition and refers to the fact that the Sunnis follow the traditional line of succession after the Prophet Mohammed. Sunnism has developed into the orthodox branch of Islam.

Beyond this early dynastic rivalry, there's little doctrinal difference between Shiite Islam and Sunni Islam, but the division remains to this day. In recent years, the division has sharpened with the targeting of Shiites as apostates by fundamentalist Sunni groups such as so-called Islamic State.

Sunnis comprise some 90% of the world's Muslims, but Shiites are believed to form a majority of the population in Iraq, Lebanon and Iran. There are also Shiite minorities in almost all Arab countries.

> Muslims believe Jesus was a prophet second only to Mohammed. The concept that he is the son of God is considered heretical.

Sufism

A mystical aspect of Islam that is particularly close to Iranian hearts, *tassawof* (mysticism) is ultimately discovered in and derived from the Quranic verses. According to Sufis, God must be felt as a light that shines in the believer's heart and the heart must be pure enough to receive the light. The two are separated: man's soul is in exile from the Creator and longs to return 'home' to lose himself again in Him. Sufism has various orders and throughout Iran you can find *khanqas* (prayer and meditation houses) where people go to worship. Sufism does not conflict with Shiism or Sunnism, yet is treated with suspicion by the authorities.

Some of Iran's greatest thinkers, poets and scholars have had Sufi mystic tendencies, including Sohrevardi, Ghazali, Rumi, Hafez and Sa'di.

Other Religions

Throughout history Iranians have shown tolerance towards other people's religious beliefs (with the exception of Baha'is), and since the adoption of Islam they have been particularly tolerant of Christians and Jews, who are 'People of the Book'. Christians, Jews and Zoroastrians are all officially recognised, are exempt from military service and have guaranteed seats in the Majlis (parliament). However, they are not encouraged; conversion from Islam is punishable by death.

Baha'ism

Baha'ism originated in Iran during the 1840s as a Shiite reform movement. Baha'i doctrines are egalitarian, teaching the complete equality of men and women and the unity of all humanity. They didn't, however, impress Iran's authorities, who tried to suppress the movement by massacring followers and executing the founding prophet, The Bab, in Tabriz in 1850.

> The website www.bahai.org is a comprehensive site for and about the Baha'i religion and community with a good overview of beliefs, traditions etc.

Today they remain the most persecuted religious minority in Iran. It is illegal to practise the religion in public and followers are routinely discriminated against when it comes to jobs and education. Of the world's five million Baha'is, around 300,000 remain in Iran – the country's largest religious minority. Most are urban, but there are some Baha'i villages, especially in Fars and Mazandaran provinces.

Zoroastrianism

Until the Arab conquest introduced Islam, Zoroastrianism was the main religion across the Iranian plateau. It takes its name from its prophet Zoroaster (Zartosht or Zarathustra), who was probably born between 1000 BC and 1500 BC, possibly near present-day Lake Orumiyeh or further north in Central Asia – no one knows for sure.

Zoroastrianism was one of the first religions to postulate an omnipotent, invisible god. The supreme being, Ahura Mazda, has no symbol or icon, but according to Zoroastrian tradition, he dictated that followers should pray to him in the direction of light. The only light the ancients controlled was fire, so they created fire temples to keep the flame burning eternally.

Very little of the writings of Zoroaster have survived, though the teachings in the Avesta (sometimes referred to as the Zoroastrian bible) are attributed to him. The core lesson is dualism: the eternal battle of good and evil. Zoroaster believed in two principles – Vohu Mano (Good Mind) and Ahem Nano (Bad Mind) – which were responsible for day and night, life and death. These two opposing 'minds' coexisted within the supreme being, Ahura Mazda, and in all living things.

Since Zoroastrians respect the purity of the four so-called sacred elements (water, earth, air and fire), they historically refused to bury their dead fearing that it pollutes the earth. Cremation is similarly renounced as polluting the air. Instead, the dead were exposed in towers of silence, where their bones were picked clean by vultures. As this practice is no longer permitted in Iran, deceased Zoroastrians today are usually buried in graves lined with concrete to prevent 'contamination' of the earth.

Many Zoroastrian temples are adorned with bas-relief winged figures of a Fravashi (guardian spirit) that symbolise Fravahar, the part of the spirit that reaches Ahura Mazda after death. The Fravashi's head symbolises experience and wisdom; the right hand pointing upward symbolises admiration of god; the ring in the left hand symbolises unity; and the larger middle ring symbolises eternity and the reflection of a person's own actions. The three layers of feathers on the wings symbolise purity of thought, word and deed, while the tail feathers represent evil thoughts, evil deeds and evil words. One of the strings represents goodness and the other represents darkness and evil.

Of the 150,000 or more Zoroastrians in the world, 20,000 live in Iran, with 10,000 in Tehran and 4000 in Yazd. Zoroastrian women can be recognised by their patterned headscarves and embroidered dresses with predominant colours of white, cream or red. They don't wear chadors, but they do wear the hejab, as proscribed by national law.

Christianity

The Christian community in Iran consists mainly of Armenians who settled at Jolfa, in the north of Iran, and were then moved to New Jolfa in Esfahan in Safavid times. Others live around Orumiyeh. Today Iran's 250,000 Christians also include Roman Catholics, Adventists, Protestants, Chaldeans and about 20,000 Assyrians. Christians are allowed to consume alcohol and hold mixed-sex parties with dancing, just as long as no Muslims can see the revelry, let alone partake.

Judaism

Iran has been home to Jews since about the 8th century BC – even before Cyrus the Great famously liberated Jews enslaved at Babylon. Today about 25,000 Jews live in Iran, primarily in Tehran, Esfahan and Shiraz. More than 50,000 left Iran when life became more difficult following the revolution – most migrating to the USA. In 2007 Israel offered up to US$60,000 a family to all remaining Iranian Jews to migrate to Israel. However, the Society of Iranian Jews snubbed the offer, saying the 'identity of Iranian Jews is not tradable for any amount of money'.

Several traditions and ceremonies dating from Zoroastrian times are important in modern Iranian culture, including No Ruz (the Iranian New Year), Chahar shanbe-soori on the Wednesday before No Ruz, and Shab-e yalda, celebrated on the winter solstice.

About 10,000 Aramaic-speaking Mandaeans live around the Shatt al Arab in Khuzestan. Mandaeism is a gnostic religion some believe descends from John the Baptist.

Esther's Children: A Portrait of Iranian Jews (2002), by Houman Sarshar, is a comprehensive history of Iran's Jews from the Achaemenid Empire to the community that remains following the revolution of 1979.

FAITH IN IRAN OTHER RELIGIONS

Architecture

Architecture is one of Persia's greatest gifts, among many, to world culture. For the visitor, it can seem as if every town and village has some historic signpost to the varied peoples and dynasties that have ruled the nation during the past 3000 years. Most of the greatest buildings were built for religious purposes, with first Zoroastrianism and Islam (after AD 637) most prevalent. As such, most of what is known as Persian architecture is also called Islamic architecture.

Persian Architecture – An Overview

The defining aspects of Persian architecture are its monumental simplicity and its lavish use of surface ornamentation and colour. The ground plans of ordinary Persian buildings mix only a few standard elements: a courtyard and arcades, lofty entrance porticoes and four *iwan* (barrel-vaulted halls opening onto the courtyard).

Typical Persian mosque design consists of a dome above an entrance *iwan* that leads into a large courtyard surrounded by arched cloisters. Behind these are four inner *iwan,* one of them featuring a decorated niche indicating the direction of Mecca. In the Islamic world in general this is usually called a mihrab although in Iran this term is also used to refer to the cut-out space in the ground in front of it. Many commentators believe the four-*iwan* design can be traced to old Zoroastrian ideas about the four elements and the circulation of life.

WORLD HERITAGE SITES

Most of Iran's 21 Unesco World Heritage sites are significant architectural landmarks, listed here chronologically. For details and the full list of Iran's Unesco sites, see http://whc.unesco.org.

➡ Choqa Zanbil (p142), 13th century BC
➡ Pasargadae (p210), 6th century BC
➡ Susa (p140), 5th century BC
➡ Persepolis (p207), 5th century BC
➡ Shushtar Historical Hydraulic System (p142), primarily 3rd century BC
➡ Armenian Monastic Ensembles (p87), 7th to 14th centuries
➡ Masjed-e Jameh (p162), Esfahan, from 9th century
➡ Takht-e Soleiman (p340), primarily 13th century
➡ Oljeitu Mausoleum (p103), Soltaniyeh, 14th century
➡ Sheikh Safi-od-Din Mausoleum (p97), Ardabil, 16th to 18th centuries
➡ Naqsh-e Jahan (Imam) Square (p159), Esfahan, 17th century
➡ Tabriz Bazaar (p85), primarily 18th century
➡ Golestan Palace (p37), Tehran, 18th century

These basic features are often so densely covered with decoration that observers are led to imagine the architecture is far more complex than it actually is. The decorations are normally geometric, floral or calligraphic. A wall's decoration sometimes consists of nothing but mosaics forming the names of Allah, Mohammed and Ali, repeated countless times in highly stylised script.

Tiles

The tiled domes of Iranian mosques, reminiscent of Fabergé eggs in the vividness of their colouring, are likely to remain one of your abiding memories of Iran.

The art of Persian tile production dates back to the Elamite period, but it peaked during the Safavid era (1502–1736). Safavid-era tiles come in two main forms. The best are *moarraq kashi* (mosaics) – patterns are picked out in tiny pieces of tile rather than created in one piece. Less fine and more common are the *haft rangi* (seven-coloured) tiles, which are square with a painted surface and first appeared in the early 17th century.

In terms of colourful tiles, Qajar buildings may lack in quality, but they often make up in quantity. Standout examples include the Golestan Palace (p37) in Tehran and the walls of the wonderful Takieh Mo'aven ol-Molk (p127) in Kermanshah.

Domes & Minarets

The development of the dome was one of the greatest achievements of Persian architecture. The Sassanians (AD 224–642) were the first to discover a satisfactory way of building a dome on top of a square chamber by using two intermediate levels, or squinches – the lower octagonal and the higher 16-sided – on which the dome could rest. Later domes became progressively more sophisticated, incorporating an inner semicircular dome sheathed by an outer conical or even onion-shaped dome. Externally the domes were often encased in tiles, with patterns so elaborate they had to be worked out on models at ground level first.

The minaret started life as an entirely functional tower, from the top of which the muezzin called the faithful to prayer. However, during the Seljuk period (AD 1051–1220) minarets became tall, tapering spires, which were far more decorative than practical. Since it is feared that someone standing atop a minaret can look into the private family areas of nearby houses, Shiite mosques often have a separate hutlike structure on the roof from where the muezzin makes the call to prayer (azan; though these days it's more likely to be a tape recording). Most minarets still have a light, often green (the colour of Islam), in the uppermost gallery. Traditionally these lights and indeed the minarets themselves acted as a beacon to direct people coming to town to pray.

Pre-Islamic Architecture

The only substantial remains left from before the 7th century BC are those of the remarkable Elamite ziggurat at Choqa Zanbil (p142). The ancient inhabitants of Persia imbued their mountains with great religious symbolism and built characteristic pyramidal ziggurats to imitate them. The earliest builders used sun-dried mud bricks, but baked brick was already being used for outer surfaces by the time Choqa Zanbil was built in the 13th century BC – the bricks there look like they came out of the kiln last week.

The surviving sites from the Achaemenid era (550–330 BC) include the magnificent ceremonial palace complexes and royal tombs at Pasargadae (p210), Naqsh-e Rostam (p210), Shush (p139) and the awesome Persepolis (p207). These are decorated with bas-reliefs of kings, soldiers,

Persian architecture has strongly influenced building throughout the Islamic world, especially in Central Asia, Afghanistan, Pakistan and India. Probably the most famous building of Persian origin is India's iconic Taj Mahal, designed by Safavid-era architect Ustad Ahmad Lahouri.

Many mosques occupy sites that were once home to Zoroastrian fire temples. When Islam arrived and religious preferences changed, so too did the use and decor of the local place of worship.

ARCHITECTURE PRE-ISLAMIC ARCHITECTURE

supplicants, animals and the winged figure of the Zoroastrian deity Ahura Mazda.

The Achaemenids typically built with sun-dried brick and stone and there are links with the old ziggurats in both shape and decoration. The Achaemenid style also incorporated features taken from Egyptian and Greek architecture. They built colossal halls supported by stone and wooden columns with typically Persian bull's-head capitals.

Alexander the Great's arrival in 331 BC brought Greek and Macedonian architectural styles. The ruined Anahita Temple at Kangavar, built with Greek capitals to honour a Greek goddess, is probably the best remaining example. Under the Parthians (from 247 BC to AD 224) a few characteristically Persian features, including the *iwan*, began to appear, though little remains.

In the Sassanian period (AD 224–642), buildings became larger, heavier and more complex even while stone was used less. Ardashir's Palace (p212) at Firuz Abad is one monumental example. The four-*iwan* plan with domed, square chambers became increasingly common, with the distinctive Persian dome seen for the first time. The Sassanians built fire temples throughout their empire and the simple plan of the earliest examples was retained throughout the pre-Islamic era, even in the design of churches.

Early Persian Islamic Style

In desert cities, such as Yazd and Esfahan, minarets are quite tall because they traditionally acted as a landmark for caravans crossing the desert. In mountainous areas or places surrounded by hills, such as Shiraz, where this function was impossible, most minarets are short.

The Arab conquest didn't supplant the well-developed Sassanian style but it did introduce the Islamic element that was to have such a pervasive impact on Persian arts. Not only did the Arab period (AD 642–1051) shape the nature and basic architectural plan of religious buildings, but it also defined the type of decoration – no human representation was to be permitted, and ceremonial tombs or monuments also fell from favour. In place of palace complexes built as symbols of royal majesty came mosques designed as centres of daily life for ordinary people.

As Sassanian and Arab ingredients merged, a distinctly Persian style of Islamic architecture evolved. From the mid-9th century, under the patronage of a succession of enlightened rulers, there was a resurgence of Persian nationalism and values. Architectural innovations included the high, pointed arch, stalactites (elaborate stepped mouldings used to decorate recesses) and an emphasis on balance and scale. Calligraphy became the principal form of architectural decoration. A good example is the Masjed-e Jameh (p179) in Na'in.

The period also marks the emergence of a series of remarkable towers, more secular than religious in purpose. Built of brick and usually round, the towers show a development of ornamentation starting with little more than a single garter of calligraphy and graduating to elaborate basket-weave brickwork designed to deflect the harsh sunlight. Today these are commonly referred to as tombs, but some, such as Radkan Tower (p269), were important early astronomical observatories.

The Seljuks, Mongols & Timurids

Many of the Seljuk rulers (1051–1220) took a great personal interest in patronage of the arts. Architectural developments included the double dome, a widening of vaults, improvement of the squinch and refinement of glazed tilework. A unity of structure and decoration was attempted for the first time, based on rigorous mathematical principles. Stucco, incorporating arabesques and Persian styles of calligraphy, was increasingly used to enhance brick surfaces.

Although often seen as a dark age in Iranian history, the Mongol period (1220–1335) saw new developments in Persian architecture. The conquest by Genghis Khan's rampaging hordes was initially purely

CARAVANSERAI, YAKH DANS & BADGIRS

All along the great trade routes from east to west, caravanserais (inns or way stations for camel trains, usually consisting of rooms arranged around a courtyard) were set up to facilitate trade. Although the earliest caravanserais date to Seljuk times, many of those surviving date from the reign of Shah Abbas I who was credited with establishing a network of 999 such structures. Caravanserais were built either at regular points along trading routes (roughly every 30km, a day's camel ride), or beside the bazaar in towns and cities. It's easy to see this arrangement in Esfahan and Kerman, in particular.

In the hot southern deserts you will see the remains of *yakh dans* (mud-brick ice houses) built to store ice through the summer. Water was left outside to freeze during winter – the ice that formed was scraped off and then moved to an adjoining building, often a stepped dome. The *yakh dan* at Meybod near Yazd resembles a circular ziggurat outside and a vast hollow egg inside.

Yazd is also famous for its *badgirs* (windtowers), while Esfahan still has many curious-looking circular towers that were once used to rear pigeons for meat and manure.

destructive, and many architects fled the country, but later the Mongols, too, became patrons of the arts. The Mongol style, designed to overawe the viewer, was marked by towering entrance portals, colossal domes, and vaults reaching up into the skies. It also saw a refinement of tiling, and calligraphy, often in the formal angular Kufic script imported from Arabia. Increasing attention was paid to the interior decoration of domes.

The Timurids (1380–1502) went on to refine the Seljuk and Mongol styles. Their architecture featured exuberant colour and great harmony of structure and decoration. Even in buildings of colossal scale, they avoided the monotony of large empty surfaces by using translucent tiling. Arcaded cloisters around inner courtyards, open galleries and arches within arches were notable developments.

The Safavids

Under a succession of enlightened and cultivated rulers, most notably Shah Abbas I, came the final refinement of styles that marked the culmination of the Persian Islamic school of architecture. Its greatest expression was Abbas' royal capital of Esfahan, a supreme example of town planning with one of the most magnificent collections of buildings from one period anywhere in the world – the vast and unforgettable Naqsh-e Jahan (Imam) Square (p159).

Other fine examples of Safavid architecture are at Qazvin (p113), while the Haram-e Razavi (p258) at Mashhad gained much of its present magnificence in Safavid times.

The Qajars

The Qajar period (1795–1925) marks the rather unhappy transition between the golden age of Persian Safavid architecture and the creeping introduction of Western-inspired uniformity from the mid-19th century. Now widely regarded as tasteless, flimsy and uninspired, the often colourful Qajar style did produce some fine buildings, including the Golestan Palace (p37) in Tehran and the stately mansions in Kashan (p154).

Persian Gardens

Persians, it is rumoured, are born with green fingers – gardens are part of the national psyche and horticulture runs in the veins. Flowers, particularly roses, are celebrated in poetry, are woven into the iconography of rugs, grace the tiles of mosques and turn up as garnishes in

During the Safavid period Shah Abbas the Great ordered 999 caravanserais to be built. Of them, only two were circular, one near Esfahan and the other at Zein-o-din, south of Yazd. The latter has been restored and turned into a wonderful hotel.

Iranian cuisine. Palace and municipal gardens traditionally have tended to be quite formal, with an emphasis on straight lines, ornamental pools and rigid symmetry, but they dissolve into charming, redolent affairs in the courtyards of even the humblest homestead. For a visitor, one of the undoubted delights of central Iran is the opportunity to pick a bitter orange from a tree in winter, sniff the fragrant narcissus and roses in spring, and enjoy the shade of towering cypresses in summer.

In 2011 Unesco added a group of nine Iranian gardens to the World Heritage list, describing them as the best existing examples of the classic Persian garden form. Traditionally conceived to symbolise Paradise, these gardens are divided into four sections, symbolising the Zoroastrian elements of fire, water, earth and air.

The gardens that are included in the listing date back to different periods since the 6th century BC and include five gardens in central Iran that are easy to visit: the Bagh-e Fin (p153) in Kashan, the Bagh-e Chehel Sotun (p163) in Esfahan, the Bagh-e Dolat Abad (p185) in Yazd, the Bagh-e Eram (p201) in Shiraz and the ancient garden of Pasargadae (p210) near Persepolis.

Qanats

Persian Art & Architecture (2012), by Henri and Anne Stierlin, is a fabulous overview of Persian architecture.

If you've been wondering how it's possible for so much life to come out of the desert (irrigated towns and villages, orchards producing delicious fruit, mansions with beautiful gardens), it's largely due to a miracle of engineering. For at least 2000 years Iranians have been digging *qanats* (underground water channels) to irrigate crops and supply drinking water and this has allowed for sustainable communities in the least hospitable environments.

The first challenge in building a *qanat* is identifying an underground water source. This source could be more than 100m deep, but as the whole system is reliant on gravity, it must be higher than the final destination. The next challenge is in digging a tunnel just wide and tall enough to crawl along, so that the water can flow across an extremely shallow gradient to its destination. The mounds of soil you'll see in long lines across the desert are the tops of wells, dug to dispose of excavated soil and allow ventilation.

Because of the hazards and expense of constructing a *qanat*, complex laws govern every aspect of their use and maintenance. Iran is thought to have more than 50,000 of these waterways and while modern irrigation projects now take priority, *qanats* and other traditional methods of supplying water are still greatly respected. Hundreds of towns and villages – including Kashan and Mahan – still rely on *qanats* for water.

Carpets, Arts & Crafts

If you've never travelled in an Islamic country before, you may need to reset your artistic eye. In Iran, Islamic art (there is rarely any other kind) favours the non-representational, the derivative and the stylised over the figurative and the true to life, primarily because Islam forbids the representation of sentient beings. That doesn't mean Iran's art is not beautiful – very often it's exquisite and intricate and glorious all at once with geometric shapes and complex floral patterns especially popular.

Carpets

The best-known Iranian cultural export, the Persian carpet, is far more than just a floor covering to an Iranian. A Persian carpet is a display of wealth, an investment, an integral aspect of religious and cultural festivals, and part of everyday life.

History

The oldest surviving carpet is the 'Pazyryk' rug, believed to date from the 5th century BC and discovered in the frozen tomb of a Scythian prince in Siberia in 1948. Its exact origins are unknown, but some scholars believe it is in the style of carpets found in the Achaemenid court. Today it is in the Hermitage Museum in St Petersburg.

Early patterns were usually symmetrical, with geometric and floral motifs designed to evoke the beauty of the classical Persian garden. Stylised animal figures were also woven into carpets, and along with human figures (often royalty), became more popular in the later pre-Islamic period. After the Arab conquest, Quranic verses were incorporated into some carpet designs, and prayer mats began to be produced on a grand scale; secular carpets also became a major industry and were prized in European courts. However, little remains from before the 16th century.

During the 16th and 17th centuries, carpet-making was patronised by the shahs and a favoured designer or weaver could expect great privileges. Carpet designs were inspired by book illumination and the whole process reached a peak during the reign of Shah Abbas I (Abbas the Great; r 1587–1629). As demand for Persian carpets grew, so standards of production fell and designs became less inspired, though they still led the world in quality and design.

According to the National Iranian Carpet Center, today more than five million Iranians work in the industry and carpets are the country's largest non-fossil-fuel export by value. The trade relies on the prestige evoked by the term 'Persian carpet', but maintaining the brand is increasingly difficult with cheaper 'Persian carpets' being produced in India and Pakistan, and fewer young Iranians interested in learning to weave.

Arguably the most famous Persian carpets are the twin 'Ardabil carpets', vast rugs (10.7m x 5.34m) woven with 30 million knots in the 16th century for the Sheikh Safi-od-Din Mausoleum. They are now kept in London's Victoria & Albert Museum (www.vam.ac.uk) and the Los Angeles County Museum of Art (www.lacma.org).

Types of Carpets & Rugs

To most people (including us in this section), the words 'carpet' and 'rug' are used interchangeably. But there is a difference – a carpet is bigger than a rug. Anything longer than about 2m is considered a carpet, while anything shorter is a rug. As well as carpets, which are made using thousands or even millions of knots, you will also find kilims, which are thinner, flat-woven mats without knots and thus, no pile.

Carpets come in a huge variety of designs. Some are inspired by religion, such as those on prayer rugs, usually displaying an arch representing the main arch of the Al Haram Mosque in Mecca and perhaps a lamp symbolic of the statement in the Quran that 'Allah is the light of Heaven'. Other common motifs include amulets to avert the evil eye and other, pre-Islamic motifs, such as stylised Trees of Life. They may also be inspired by whatever surrounds the weaver, eg trees, animals and flowers, particularly the lotus, rose and chrysanthemum. Gardens are commonly depicted and, in the case of a tribal nomad, such a carpet will be the only garden the weaver will ever own.

In general, these designs are classified as either 'tribal' or 'city' carpets. Tribal designs vary greatly depending on their origin, but are typically less ornate. City carpets are the classic Persian rugs, usually highly ornate floral designs around one or more medallions.

Most Iranians aspire to own fine, formal city rugs of Tabriz, Esfahan, Kashan, Qom or Kerman. They consider tribal carpets the work of peasants, and those who cannot afford hand-woven city carpets would buy a carpet made on a machine using chemical dyes and inferior wool (or even synthetic fibres) before they'd buy a tribal carpet.

In 2006–7 some 1200 Iranians produced the world's largest hand-woven carpet for the vast Sheikh Zayed bin Sultan Al Nahyan mosque in Abu Dhabi. It measures 5627 sq metres, weighs 35 tons and includes 2,268,000,000 knots.

Weaving

Most handmade carpets are woven from hand-spun wool. Each rug is woven around a vertical (warp) and horizontal (weft) foundation, usually made of cotton – the skeleton of the rug. The best are made from sheep wool though occasionally goat or camel hair is used, usually by tribal weavers in the warps or selvedges (edge bindings) of rugs, kilims or saddle bags to give them strength. Silk carpets are magnificent but they're largely decorative, while wool and silk mixtures are more practical and look beautiful. Weavers are often, but not always, women.

Dyes

Dyeing is often done in large vats in small, old-style buildings in the older parts of towns; walk the old town streets of Kashan, in particular, to see it in action. The dyes themselves are the product of centuries of innovation and experimentation. Colours are extracted from natural, locally available sources, including plants (such as herbs, vegetables and fruit skins), insects and even shellfish.

During the Safavid period sheep were bred specifically to produce the finest wool, and vegetable plantations were tended with scientific precision to provide dyes of just the right shade.

In 1859 chemical dyes such as aniline and chrome were introduced. They caught on quickly because they were cheap and easy to use. Not everyone abandoned the old ways, however, and some weavers, notably those in the Chahar Mahal va Bakhtyari region west of Esfahan, have continued using natural dyes almost uninterrupted to the present day. Today Iranian rug producers big and small are turning back to natural dyes.

Looms

Traditionally, nomadic carpet-weavers used horizontal looms, which are lightweight and transportable. Designs were either conjured up from memory, or made up as the weaver worked. These carpets and rugs were woven for domestic use or occasional trade and were small because they had to be portable. In villages, many homes or small workshops have simple upright looms where weavers can create better designs, with more variety.

Over the last 150 years larger village workshops and city factories have begun using bigger, modern looms. Some still require people to do the

WHERE TO BUY YOUR PERSIAN RUG

Persian carpets come in almost as many different designs as there are ethnic groups and major urban centres. Usually the name of a carpet indicates where it was made or where the design originated. The bazaars are the best places to buy and the experience of shopping, haggling and eventually buying is a memorable part of travelling in Iran.

Tehran (p65) With more than 3000 carpet merchants, this labyrinthine bazaar has the biggest range, most competition and lowest prices.

Esfahan (p160) Many travellers buy here because shopping around Naqsh-e Jahan (Imam) Sq is so enjoyable. Prices are a bit higher. Plenty of Esfahani city carpets are available, and the widest selection of Bakhtiyari rugs from the nearby Zagros Mountains.

Shiraz (p196) Another pleasant place to shop, with evenings in the bazaar particularly atmospheric. Shiraz has the best range of Qashqa'i rugs, runners, kilims and saddle bags, with their distinct geometric patterns, including stylised animals and birds and floral designs in the borders, and fine gabbeh, small, thick flat-woven rugs with loose pile.

Tabriz (p85) Huge range of carpets, from fine works in silk or with silk highlights, to simpler weaves from regional villages and tribal groups.

weaving, while others are fully mechanised – producing 'machine carpets' that cost about half as much as their hand-woven equivalents.

Knots

You may come across the terms 'Persian (or *senneh*) knot' (known in Farsi as a *farsi-baf*) and 'Turkish (or *ghiordes*) knot' *(turki-baf)*. Despite the names, both are used in Iran: the Turkish knot is common in the Azerbaijan provinces and western Iran.

As a rough guide, an everyday carpet or rug will have up to 30 knots per sq cm, a medium-grade piece 30 to 50 knots per sq cm, and a fine one 50 knots or more per sq cm. A prize piece might have 500 or more knots per sq cm. The higher the number of knots, the better the quality. Nomad weavers tie around 8000 knots a day; factory weavers about 12,000 knots a day.

Buying Carpets & Rugs

Iranians have had more than 2500 years to perfect the art of carpet making – and just as long to master the art of carpet selling. If you don't know your warp from your weft, it might be worth reading up before visiting Iran, or taking an Iranian friend when you go shopping (bearing in mind that professional 'friends' who make a living from commission are a fact of life).

If you know what you're doing you might pick up a bargain, but unless you're an expert, don't buy a carpet or rug as an investment – buy it because you like it. Before buying, lie the carpet flat to check for bumps or other imperfections. Small bumps will usually flatten out with wear but big ones are probably there to stay. To check if a carpet is handmade, turn it over; on most handmade pieces the pattern will be distinct on the underside (the more distinct, the better the quality).

Tehran's Carpet Museum of Iran has a priceless collection from around the country and is the best place to see rugs without going to a bazaar.

Taking Them Home

Export regulations for carpets are notoriously changeable; ask a reputable dealer for the latest. At the time of writing there was no limit to the number of carpets you could take home. However, some larger, older and more valuable carpets cannot be exported without special permission.

CALLIGRAPHY

With the arrival of Islam, several distinctly Persian calligraphic styles emerged, some of them so elaborate that they are almost illegible, eg *nashki* and later, *thulth*. The Quran was faithfully reproduced as a whole in calligraphic form, but you're more likely to see Quranic verses, and the names of Allah and Mohammed, in tiles and deep relief stucco in mosques across the country.

By the 16th century, Shiraz and Esfahan were producing some of the finest calligraphy in the Islamic world. Some of the best examples can be seen at Tehran's Reza Abbasi Museum (p47), named for the renowned 16th-century calligrapher and painter.

Sanctions mean the customs guys in your home country might frown upon purchases from Iran. One reader reported US customs are 'quite strict' about anything bought in Iran for more than US$100 – meaning most carpets. Carpet sellers know this and will offer to give you a receipt for less than you paid, or even to indicate you bought it in Dubai.

Carrying carpets is usually cheaper than posting because you're less likely to have to pay duty if you can get them through airport customs at home. Alternatively, most carpet dealers can arrange postage and costs are not outrageous. If there are no sanctions, most countries allow you to import up to 25 sq metres of Persian carpets before they start charging you as a merchant; though you will probably still have to pay some duty.

Painting

The earliest known distinctively Persian style of painting dates back to the Seljuk period (1051–1220) and is often referred to as the Baghdad School. Early painting was mainly used to decorate Qurans and pottery, and during the Mongol period (1220–1335) all sorts of manuscripts, especially poetry books.

In the 16th century an important school of Persian art developed in Tabriz, under the guidance of Sultan Mohammed, and its distinctive designs and patterns also influenced carpet design. Persian painting reached its apex under the Safavids, when Shah Abbas I turned Esfahan into a centre for the arts. The demise of the Safavids deprived artists of their patrons, and coincided with growing influences from India and Europe. Persian artists rarely signed their works so little is known about most artists.

One of the best-loved modern Iranian artists is Sayyed Ali Akhbar Sanati, whose sculpture and paintings are on display in the Sanati Museum of Contemporary Art in Kerman.

Miniatures

The Persian miniature-painting *(minyaturha)* tradition began after the Mongol invasion, influenced by artisans brought to the royal court from China. It reached its peak during the 15th and 16th centuries. Later, artists from eastern Iran, who had studied under the great Mohammadi in Herat (now in Afghanistan), also influenced this art form.

Persian miniatures are now famous throughout the world. Favourite subjects include courting couples in traditional dress (usually figures from popular poetry), polo matches and hunting scenes. Esfahan has dozens of miniaturists and is the best place to buy.

Contemporary Art

Iran has a thriving contemporary art scene, with most of the action centred in Tehran, where a small but sophisticated community of artists produce and exhibit work in a variety of media. Their work is not always appreciated by the authorities, and several, including Tehrani artist Khosrow Hassanzadeh, have found greater acclaim internationally than at home.

Photorealist painter Afshin Pirhashemi is another name to look out for, with his paintings casting sometimes uncomfortable light upon the contradictions of modern Iranian life, particularly when it comes to women and their role in society. Farhad Moshiri somehow manages to blend pop-art and advertising influences with religious iconography and paintings of antique urns.

Of Iran's contemporary women painters, Golnaz Fathi is a renowned calligraphist who uses performance-art installations in her work. Monir Shahroudy Farmanfarmaian is a veteran of Iran's artistic scene and her style reflects Iran's journey through the 20th century – she uses deeply traditional forms such as geometric patterns and cut-glass mosaics but her work has also been deeply influenced by everything from Western expressionism to Sufi imagery; she went into exile in the US in 1979 but returned to Iran in 2004.

Despite the limited resources available to Iranian artists – there are few professional galleries and institutions capable of launching an artist's career – the restrictions themselves seem to inform their aesthetic. The art has a distinctive Iranian flavour that several experts argue is impossible to classify in terms of Western contemporary art.

Tehran Studio Works, The Art of Khosrow Hassanzadeh (2007) details some of the Tehrani painter's acclaimed work, which now hangs in galleries around the world

Crafts

Glassware

Small, translucent glass vessels dating back to the 2nd millennium BC have been found at Choqa Zanbil and by the Sassanian era Persian *shisheh alat* (glassware) had become a sought-after luxury traded as far away as Japan. By early Islamic times, two principle techniques were used: mould-blown to produce thicker items, and free-blown for more delicate articles. Glassware was usually green, lapis lazuli, light blue or clear with a tinge of yellow, and decorations were cut into the glass. The art reached its peak during the Seljuk era when the manufacture of enamelled and gilded glassware flourished.

Under the Safavids, Shiraz became an important centre of glass production, with rose-water sprinklers, long-necked wine bottles, flower vases and bowls particularly popular. By the reign of Karim Khan Zand, the famous wine from Shiraz was exported in locally crafted jugs and bottles.

Lacquer Work

Some consider this the most interesting of Iran's decorative arts; it can be traced back to early Islamic times as an independent art form. Wooden or papier-mâché objects are painted, then a transparent sandarac-based varnish is applied in successive layers from three to more than 20 coats. The result gives an impression of depth and provides great durability. Common designs are the popular Persian motif of the nightingale and the rose, flowers and classic love stories. Pen boxes are the most common form of lacquer work.

Iran Chamber (www.iran chamber.com) is a terrific resource covering Iran's peoples, as well as architecture, music, religion, literature, cinema and more.

Marquetry

One of the most intricate styles of woodwork is a form of marquetry *(moarraq)* called *khatam*. A Persian style of marquetry slowly developed through the centuries and by the 17th century *khatam* was so prestigious that several Safavid princes learned the technique.

Several different woods, including betel, walnut, cypress and pine, are used, with the inlaid pieces made from animal bones, shells, ivory, bronze, silver and gold. The final product is coated with varnish. Genuine Persian *khatam* contains no paint; the colours come from the inlaid pieces. *Khatam* can be used for furniture but visitors usually buy it in the form of ornamental boxes or picture frames. Most of what you'll see for sale in souvenir shops is not genuine, as they are often made with the use of machines.

Literature, Music & Cinema

Drawing in equal measure on the many sophistications of Ancient Persia and the dynamic cultural space that is modern Iran, the country's writers, musicians and, perhaps above all, film-makers have created bodies of work that are as popular at home as they are acclaimed by critics around the world. Wherever you get started, whether with the great poets whose works seemingly every Iranian can recite or the latest release film by a director whose films sell out for weeks, you're in for a real treat.

Literature

Iran is a nation of poets and overwhelmingly the most important form of writing is poetry. Familiarity with famous poets and their works is universal: ask and almost anyone on the street can quote you lines from Hafez or Rumi.

While writers have long been persecuted in Iran, their numbers increased dramatically during the Khatami years, particularly women novelists who regularly topped best-seller lists. Things have quietened down a lot since then, due in no small measure to the eight-year rule of the conservative Ahmadinejad government to 2013. But whichever direction the political winds are blowing, all books must be approved by government censors before publication; thousands of new and old works have been banned.

Poetry

The 9th century AD saw several poetic styles born in Persia. These include the *masnavi,* with its unique rhyming couplets, and the *ruba'i,* similar to the quatrain (a poem of four lines). Poems of more than 100 nonrhyming couplets, known as *qasideh,* were first popularised by Rudaki during the 10th century. These styles later developed into long and detailed 'epic poems', the first of which was Ferdosi's *Shahnamah.*

Moral and religious poetry became popular following the success of Sa'di's most famous poems, the *Bustan* and *Golestan.* By the 14th century, smaller *qazal* poems, which ran to about 10 nonrhyming couplets, were still being used for love stories; the most famous *qazal* poet is Hafez.

Early in the last century modernist Persian poetry changed the poetic landscape. This style is exemplified by the work of Nima Yushij. Ahmad Shamloo's *Fresh Air,* a book of poems published in 1957, marked the introduction of a lyrical style that was also political and metaphoric.

Faces of Love: Hafez and the Poets of Shiraz (Hafez and Jahan Malek Khatun; 2013) is like a greatest hits of Hafez' work, ideal for getting a taste of what all the fuss is about.

Novels

Literary fiction is a young but fast-growing art in Iran, with beginnings in the 19th century evolving with political upheavals in the 20th and 21st centuries. While writing styles have changed, the spectre of censorship has been ever-present and continues today. As such, few of the hundreds of published novelists (about half of whom are women) write completely freely, and fewer are translated into English.

Sadeq Hedayat is the best-known Iranian novelist outside Iran, and one whose influence has been most pervasive in shaping modern Persian fiction. *The Blind Owl,* published in 1937, is a dark and powerful portrayal of the decadence of a society failing to achieve its own modernity. Hedayat's uncensored works have been banned in Iran since 2005. Contemporary author Shahriar Mandanipour was also banned from publishing between 1992 and 1997 and, after years of struggle against the censor's pen, eventually moved to the USA in 2006. In 2009 he published the critically acclaimed *Censoring an Iranian Love Story.*

Recommended Iranian Reads

The Rubaiyat of Omar Khayyám (1120) Classic epic poem and arguably Iran's best-selling work ever on the international stage.

The Blind Owl (Sadeq Hedayat; 1937) An affecting tale built around a beautiful woman, an old man and a cypress tree.

THE GREAT IRANIAN POETS

Iranians venerate their great poets, who are often credited with preserving the Persian language and culture during times of occupation. Streets, squares, hotels and *chaykhanehs* (teahouses) are named after famous poets, several of whom have large mausoleums that are popular pilgrimage sites.

Ferdosi 940–1020

Hakim Abulqasim Ferdosi, first and foremost of all Iranian poets, was born near Tus outside Mashhad. He developed the *ruba'i* (quatrain) style of 'epic' historic poems and is remembered primarily for the *Shahnamah* (Book of Kings), which took 33 years to write and included almost 60,000 couplets. Ferdosi is seen as the saviour of Farsi, which he wrote in at a time when the language was under threat from Arabic. Without his writings many details of Persian history and culture might also have been lost and Ferdosi is credited with having done much to help shape the Iranian self-image.

Hafez 1325–89

Khajeh Shams-ed-Din Mohammed, or Hafez (meaning 'One Who Can Recite the Quran from Memory') as he became known, was born in Shiraz. His poetry has a strong mystical quality and regular references to wine, courtship and nightingales have been interpreted in different ways (is wine literal or a metaphor for God?). A copy of his collected works, known as the *Divan-e Hafez,* can be found in almost every home in Iran, and many of his verses are used as proverbs to this day.

Omar Khayyam 1047–1123

Omar Khayyam (Omar the Tentmaker) was born in Neishabur and is probably the best-known Iranian poet in the West because many of his poems, including the famous *Rubaiyat,* were translated into English by Edward Fitzgerald. In Iran he is more famous as a mathematician, historian and astronomer.

Rumi 1207–73

Born Jalal ad-Din Mohammad Balkhi in Balkh (in present-day Afghanistan), Rumi's family fled west before the Mongol invasions and eventually settled in Konya in present-day Turkey. There his father (and then he) retreated into meditation and a study of the divine. Rumi was inspired by a great dervish, Shams-e Tabrizi, and many of his poems of divine love are addressed to him. He is credited with founding the Maulavi Sufi order – the whirling dervishes – and is also known as Maulana ('the Master').

Sa'di 1207–91

Like Hafez, Sheikh Mohammed Shams-ed-Din (known as Sa'di), lost his father at an early age and was educated by some of the leading teachers of Shiraz. Many of his elegant verses are still commonly used in conversation. His most famous works, the *Golestan* (Rose Garden) and *Bustan* (Garden of Trees), have been translated into many languages.

Books that have been banned by Iran's censors in the past (and many remain off the bookshelves) include *The Symposium* (Plato), *Ulysses* (James Joyce), *As I Lay Dying* (William Faulkner), *The Blind Owl* (Sadeq Hedayat) and *The Da Vinci Code* (Dan Brown).

Censoring an Iranian Love Story (Shahriar Mandanipour; 2009) Story of an author who struggles to write a love story that will get past the censors.

Land of the Turquoise Mountains: Journeys Across Iran (Cyrus Massoudi; 2014) Modern Iran seen through the sympathetic, enquiring eyes of a British-born Iranian writer.

Persepolis: The Story of a Childhood (Marjane Satrapi; 2000) Autobiographical graphic novel about growing up through the Islamic Revolution.

Iran Awakening: A Memoir of Revolution (Shirin Ebadi; 2007) Enlightening and sobering self-portrait by Iran's first winner of the Nobel Prize for Peace.

Tehran, Lipstick & Loopholes (Nahal Tajadod; 2009) Kafkaesque true story of the author's journey through Iranian bureaucracy as she tries to renew her passport.

Music

Aside from traditional music, which is played in teahouses across the country, it's not easy to find musical performances in Iran. That doesn't mean there aren't any musicians. But government restrictions mean every public performance needs a licence, which is difficult to obtain for anything modern or remotely political. Women performers were banned for many years but now women-only concerts are commonplace.

Music lovers will adore the new Isfahan Music Museum (p167) with traditional Persian instruments and live performances by folk musicians.

Classical

For Iranians there is no distinction between poetry and lyrics, and traditional Persian music is poetry set to a musical accompaniment. Like epic poems, some 'epic songs' are very long and masters can spend most of their lives memorising the words.

Classical Persian music is almost always downbeat and can sound decidedly mournful or, as one young Shirazi told us, 'depressing'. Despite this, it remains hugely popular and you'll hear it in taxis and teahouses across the country. Two singers particularly worth listening out for are Shajarian and Shahram Naziri, both of whom have helped promote interest in classical Persian music internationally.

While the voice is usually central to this form of music, it is backed by several instruments that have deep roots in Persian culture. Among the most common:

Tar A six-string instrument, usually plucked

Setar Similar to the *tar* but with four strings

Nay Generic name for various types of flute

Sorna Similar to an oboe

Kamancheh A kind of four-stringed viola played like a cello

Santur Dulcimer played with delicate wooden mallets

BEST IN MUSIC

Googoosh (Googoosh; 2011) Iran's 1970s superstar-in-exile has the most wonderful voice.

Gole Aftabgardoon (The Sunflower; Arian; 2000) Debut album by this hugely popular mixed gender band.

Kherghe Biandaz (O-Hum; 2014) Combines rock music with Persian traditional lyrics and instruments.

Music of Iran (Mohammad Reza Shadjarian & Ensemble Aref; 2012) An excellent introduction to Persian classical music from the World Network label.

Living Fire (The Kâmkârs; 1995) Superstars from Kurdish Iran with hypnotic sounds.

Tombak Vase-shaped drum with a skin at the wide end
Dahol and zarb Large and small drums respectively

Folk

The most appealing and melodious traditional music is heard among ethnic minorities, such as the Turkmen in northern Iran. Azeris favour a unique style of music, often based around a love song, whereas Kurds have a distinctively rhythmic music based mainly around the lute and their own versions of epic songs, called *bards*.

Folk music employs most of the instruments mentioned above, with regional variations; along the Persian Gulf a type of bagpipe called the *demam* is popular. The music of Sistan va Baluchestan is understandably similar to that of Pakistan and typically uses instruments such as the *tamboorak* (similar to the Pakistani *tambura,* a type of harmonium).

Pop & Rock

Iranian pop music has re-emerged under the watchful eye of the Iranian authorities. Many of the most popular Iranian musicians fled after the Islamic Revolution, including '70s superstar Googosh. They now perform abroad. While their music is largely created in Los Angeles, these and more modern 'Tehrangeles pop' artists are widely available on bootleg copies in Iran.

Nine-piece Arian was the first mixed-gender band to get official approval after the revolution. Their debut album, *Gole Aftabgardoon* (The Sunflower), was released in 2000 and soon they were playing to crowds of more than 50,000. Other favourite artists include Benyamin Bahadori, Moin, Omid and current favourites Mohsen Yeganeh and Barobax.

Iran's rock and rap scene is mainly underground but a steadily growing number of bands and musicians are finding a Persian way to rock. Groups such as O-Hum set the scene with 'Persian rock', a mix of familiar and Iranian instruments and the poetic lyrics of Hafez and Rumi. The result is like '90s grunge rock with an Iranian flavour; download free tracks at www.iranian.com. Other popular rock acts include Barad, Meera, Hypernova, Niyaz and Mohsen Namjoo.

Other Genres

Iranian hip-hop is heavily influenced by US artists accessible to younger Iranians through satellite television. Those with a mainstream profile include Yas, Ho3ein, Zedbazi and Arash, while underground artists include among their ranks Hichkas, Bahram Nouraei and Reza Pishro.

Electronica is another popular musical style in Iran, but most of its artists live and work beyond Iran's shores. Popular names include Deep Dish (Ali 'Dubfire' Shirazi and Shahram Tayebi; US), DJ Aligator (Denmark) and Arsi Nami (US).

Iran's best-known jazz musician is Ardeshir Farah. In 1991 he won a Grammy as part of Strunz & Farah, and he is perhaps Iran's premier crossover artist, collaborating often with Western performers.

Cinema

Before the Islamic Revolution

Iran's love affair with cinema started in 1900 when the country's first public cinema opened in Tabriz. Though Iranian films were made earlier, Esmail Kushan's 1948 *The Tempest of Life* was the first film to be made in Iran and since then the home-grown industry has not looked back.

It was not until the 1960s, however, that the first signs of a distinctive Iranian cinematic language emerged, with poet Forough Farrokhzad's 1962 film of life in a leper colony, *The House Is Black,* and Hajir Darioush's

LITERATURE, MUSIC & CINEMA CINEMA

The Kâmkârs, a Kurdish family ensemble, have been celebrated for their concerts featuring traditional Iranian music and rousing Kurdish folk songs. They tour in Iran and worldwide. *Living Fire* (1995) is the easiest of their albums to track down.

To hear Iranian music listen to free tracks available at www. iranian.com/ music.html. To buy Persian music, and make sure your money goes to the artists, check out www.cdbaby. com.

LITERATURE, MUSIC & CINEMA CINEMA

THE MAKHMALBAF FAMILY – A CINEMA DYNASTY

Born in 1957 in Tehran, Mohsen Makhmalbaf first gained infamy when he was imprisoned for five years after fighting with a policeman. He was released during the Islamic Revolution in 1979 and started to write books before turning to film-making in 1982. Since then he has produced more than a dozen films, including *Boycott, Time for Love, Kandahar, Gabbeh* and, more provocatively, *Salaam Cinema*. Many of his films are based on taboo subjects: *Time for Love* was filmed in Turkey because it broached the topic of adultery; and *Marriage of the Blessed* was a brutal film about the casualties of the Iran–Iraq War.

Makhmalbaf has become a virtual exile from Iran because of the country's censorship. In 1997 Makhmalbaf's daughter Samira produced her first film, *The Apple*, to critical acclaim. In 2000 her second film, *Blackboards*, was a smash hit at the Cannes Film Festival; she was the youngest director ever to have shown a film there.

The Makhmalbaf movie factory continues to churn out winners. Samira's younger brother made a 'making-of' documentary about *Blackboards*; then younger sister Hana directed a feature about the shooting of Samira's film *At Five in the Afternoon*. On the strength of that film, *Joy of Madness*, Hana beat Samira to a 'youngest-ever' record by being invited to the Venice Film Festival at the age of 14. Even Mohsen Makhmalbaf's second wife (the sister of his first wife, who died tragically), Marzieh Meshkini, has directed an acclaimed film, *The Day I Became a Woman*, which examines what it is to be a woman in Iran.

Mohsen Makhmalbaf survived two assassination attempts while filming *Kandahar* in Iran, and in 2007 the whole family was attacked while on location in Afghanistan for Samira's film *The Two-Legged Horse*. A man posing as an extra threw a bomb onto the set, wounding six actors and several extras and killing the horse in the film's title.

Having moved to Paris in 2005, in 2009 Mohsen Makhmalbaf became a spokesman abroad for Green Movement leader and presidential candidate Mirhossein Mousavi. His outspoken criticism of the Ahmadinejad government left him, in effect, in exile. For more on the Makhmalbafs, see www.makhmalbaf.com.

second film *Serpent's Skin* (which was based on DH Lawrence's *Lady Chatterley's Lover*) setting the scene.

The Cow (1969), directed by Darius Mehrjui, really set Iranian cinema on the upward trajectory along which it still travels. A dark, poignant and deceptively simple tale of a man's love for his cow and the trauma he suffers when it dies, the film is set against the backdrop of Iranian village life. In its use of the simple details of daily life in Iran to subtly tell a larger story of love and loss, as well as to make nuanced social commentary on community life, it set the standard for Iranian cinema's central motif.

The first 'new wave' of Iranian cinema that followed in the 1970s captured the attention of art-house movie fans around the world: key directors apart from Mehrjui were Abbas Kiarostami (who died in 2016), Bahram Beiza'i, Khosrow Haritash and Bahram Farmanara.

> For movie trailers from the latest releases of Iran's art-house film directors, check out the Iranian Film Society (www.irfilms.com). It also has interviews and general industry news.

After the Islamic Revolution

The second 'new wave' of Iranian cinema was made up of post-revolutionary directors such as Mohsen Makhmalbaf, Rakhshan Bani Etemad, Majid Majidi (whose film *Children of Heaven* was nominated for an Oscar) and Jafar Panahi. It helped develop a reputation for Iranian cinema as art house, neorealist and poetic.

The newest generation is known as the 'third wave' and its most notable exponents are Asghar Farhadi, Bahman Ghobadi and Mani Haghighi. Whatever the number, Iranian new wave is consistent in looking at everyday life through a poetic prism that is part fictional feature, part real-life documentary – an Iranian specialty.

The strict censorship of the post-revolutionary state has encouraged the use of children, nonprofessional actors and stories that are fixated on the nitty-gritty of life, and which have proved popular overseas. The highpoint of this technique is perhaps Jafar Panahi's brilliant 2015 'docu-fiction' *Taxi* (or *Taxi Tehran* as it is sometimes known) which gives a voice to ordinary Iranians (whose identities are never revealed) in a Tehran taxi. Panahi has been banned from making films and his solution is to make a stunningly subversive work that never feels like a film. Another brilliant example is Mohsen Makhmalbaf's *Salaam Cinema* (1995), which tells the story of modern Iranian society through the would-be actors (ordinary Iranians) who turn up to audition for one of Makhmalbaf's films.

Iranians love their own cinema and flock to it in droves. But many internationally acclaimed 'art-house' films never get released at home, and are distributed on the bootleg market instead or watched online. Some Iranians feel the masters are making movies specifically for foreign markets and film festivals. Dozens of films are churned out every year for the domestic market, many of them action flicks, though the appetite for films looking at social issues is increasing.

Of these the most notable is *A Separation,* the 2012 winner of the Academy Award for best foreign language film and nominee for best original screenplay. Asghar Farhadi's masterfully told film looks at a Tehran couple's dissolving marriage and how the hiring of a carer for an ill parent complicates matters further. Farhadi bagged a second Oscar in 2017 for *The Salesman,* a fascinating study of a relationship under pressure following an assault on the wife.

Recommended Iranian Films

As well as the films listed on p274, here are five more classics of Iranian cinema:

Salaam Cinema (Mohsen Makhmalbaf; 1995) Utterly subversive docu-drama that gives ordinary Iranians a voice.

The White Balloon (Jafar Panahi; 1995) Written by Abbas Kiarostami, this is the story of a young girl who loses her money while on the way to buy a goldfish.

Children of Heaven (Majid Majidi; 1997) Oscar-nominated tale focusing on two poor children losing a pair of shoes.

Persepolis (Marjane Satrapi and Vincent Paronnaud; 2007) Compelling, funny and, ultimately, heart-rendingly sad portrayal of growing up through the Islamic Revolution.

The President (Mohsen Makhmalbaf; 2014) A story of our times, with a dictator on the run and made to look absurd and abandoned.

The Garden of Stones (1976) and *The Old Man and His Stone Garden* (2004) are classic movies directed by Parviz Kimiavi which depict a deaf-mute shepherd who devotes his life to creating a garden of withered trees and large blocks of stone.

LITERATURE, MUSIC & CINEMA CINEMA

Natural Environments

Iran is a beautiful, fragile country. Its mountains and deserts are the signature land-forms here, and the country has some real surprises when it comes to wildlife, which is remarkable considering how unprotected most of the country's national parks really are.

The Land

If you're flying into Iran, be sure to ask for a window seat – you might be surprised by what you see. Iran is a diverse land where snow-capped mountains border vast desert plateaus and cliffside villages contrast with palm-filled oases. It also has 2440km of coastline, spread between the Persian Gulf and the Caspian Sea.

Mountains

More than half of Iran is covered by mountains, with four ranges most prominent. The smaller, volcanic Sabalan and Talesh Ranges in the northwestern Azeri provinces provide fertile pastures for nomads. Near-by, the majestic Alborz Mountains skirt the Caspian Sea from the border of Azerbaijan as far as Turkmenistan, and are home to ski fields and the snowcapped Mt Damavand (5671m), the Middle East's tallest mountain. The northern slopes of the Alborz Mountains are densely forested to about 2500m and form the largest area of vegetation in the country. The forests will look familiar to Europeans (oak, ash, pine, poplar, willow, walnut, maple and elm), and the loveliest pockets are around Masuleh, in the Golestan National Park east of Minudasht, and, more accessibly, at Nahar Khoran, just south of Gorgan.

With an area of 1,648,195 sq km, Iran is more than three times larger than France; nearly one-fifth the size of the USA; and almost as big as Queensland, Australia. Iran shares borders with seven countries: Iraq, Turkey, Armenia, Azerbaijan, Turkmenistan, Afghanistan and Pakistan.

Sitting on the world's second-largest known reserve of natural gas, the immense Zagros Mountains stretch about 1500km from Turkey to the Persian Gulf, rising and falling like the ridged back of a great crocodile. There are several peaks reaching more than 4000m, though heights fall to an average of 1500m in the south.

All these mountains exist because Iran sits at the junction of three major tectonic plates – the Arabian, Eurasian and Indian – making the country highly susceptible to earthquakes.

Deserts

East of the Zagros Mountains is the central plateau and its two vast deserts, the Dasht-e Kavir (more than 200,000 sq km) in the north and the Dasht-e Lut (more than 166,000 sq km) in the southeast, accounting for almost 25% of the country. The deserts include occasional salt lakes and are dotted with luxuriant oases – a welcome sight for travellers down the ages. Here, where temperatures regularly top 50°C in summer, dozens of subtly different date palms thrive, often sharing space with hardy pomegranate trees and modest fields of cucumber and melon; Garmeh and the villages around are classic examples.

Surprisingly, it's in the deserts (often where they meet the mountains), that Iran's larger mammal species – such as the leopard and the Asiatic cheetah – survive.

EARTHQUAKES

To say that Iranians are anxious about earthquakes is quite the understatement. The country sits on dozens of seismic fault lines and every year scores of tremors rattle homes and gnaw away at nerves. When a major quake strikes, as it did in Bam in 2003 at a cost of more than 31,000 lives, Iranians everywhere start speculating about who will be next. Sadly, earthquakes, albeit on a smaller scale, are all too frequent, with earthquakes in Zarand (2005; 612 people killed), Borujerd (2006; 66), Tabriz (2012; 306) and Saravan (2013; 35) just a few of the quakes to strike in recent years.

Iran has had more than 20 major earthquakes (above 6 on the Richter scale) in the past century, and seismologists estimate that a large population centre will be hit every eight years. While the vast majority of seismic activity occurs along the Zagros Mountains, where the Eurasian and Arabian tectonic plates meet, it is in the desert regions of central Iran that the biggest movements are felt: Ferdows (1968; 7.3 on the Richter scale; up to 20,000 dead), Tabas (1978; 7.8; more than 1500 dead) and Bam (6.6) are all in this area.

However, the mountainous regions in the north are also susceptible, and Tehran reportedly has two major faults running directly beneath it. In the wake of the Bam disaster there was much speculation in Tehran about what kind of hell would be unleashed if a large quake rocks the capital. Building standards are poor (and poorly enforced) and a government report in 2004 stated that of the 15 million homes in Iran, 7.2 million are vulnerable to a major earthquake.

People of the Land

Think of Iran's mountain ranges as the foundations of a vast central plateau. Everything but the narrow coastal regions of the Persian Gulf and the Caspian Sea, and the Khuzestan plain near southern Iraq, is about 1000m above sea level or higher. This elevation, the mountains and the lack of rivers have had a direct effect on the development of Persian culture.

Unlike many ancient civilisations, such as those in Egypt and Mesopotamia, Persian settlements did not develop around major rivers. The longest and sole navigable river is the Karun (890km) in the southwest, and it's no Nile. Rather, settled areas are almost entirely confined to the foothills of mountains, where natural springs and melting snow provide sufficient water, with melted snow often channelled through ingenious underground canals called *qanats*.

Without river connections, these communities lived in relative isolation. Large towns would be the focus of trade for hundreds of surrounding villages otherwise hemmed in by mountains or desert. Further trade was done by camel caravans, which linked these population basins to each other and beyond via the silk routes and the coasts.

These environs also dictated the Iranian cuisine. With fresh vegetables hard to find, people of the deserts ate a menu heavy with protein (camel and goat meat) and hardy fruits (dates, oranges and pomegranate), while those from the wet, fertile, Alborz provinces in the north ate more vegetables (hello eggplant) and a wider variety of fruit. For a taste of these contrasting lifestyles, spend a night each in Garmeh (desert) and Masuleh (mountain).

Only about 11% of Iran is arable land; 7% is forest, 47% is natural (ie nonarable) pastures and 35% is infertile land, including desert.

Wildlife

Iran's diverse landscapes are home to a fascinating and sometimes exhilarating mix of wildlife. Seeing this fauna is not easy – casual encounters are extremely rare. But with planning, patience and good guiding, you might get lucky.

In 2015, the Iranian Cheetah Society released a camera-trap photo of a Pallas Cat, a small, stocky feline with an unusually flat forehead and wide face, from Salouk National Park in northeastern Iran.

Mammals

Iran is home to 158 species of mammal, about one-fifth of which are endemic. Large cats, including the Persian leopard and Asiatic cheetah, are the most glamorous, but a range of wild sheep, deer, gazelle and bears are just as interesting.

Indeed, Iran's seven species of wild sheep might well be the progenitors of the modern, garden variety sheep and goat. They include species such as the Transcaspian oreal, Laristan mouflon and Alborz red sheep, an ibex with a long black beard and curved horns. And, as described in Jason Elliot's book *Mirrors of the Unseen*, the origins of the modern horse come from the loins of the pint-sized and now near-extinct Caspian horse.

Notable other species include the spectacular Persian wild ass, goitered and Jebeer gazelles, maral, Asian black bear and brown bear. Most larger mammals are found in the forests of the Alborz Mountains, although large cats, wild dogs and gazelle are also found around the deserts.

Camels still roam the deserts of the eastern provinces of Kerman, Sistan va Baluchestan and Khorestan, and while they might look wild they almost certainly belong to nomadic or seminomadic communities.

Birds

Sitting at the crossroads of the European, Oriental and African faunal regions, and harbouring an amazing array of habitats from alpine tops to semitropical mangroves and intertidal sand flats, Iran is an exceptional country for birds, boasting almost 500 species, many of which are listed as globally endangered. While the jewel in the crown is the Pleske's ground jay, a bird unique to Iran and a resident of the central deserts, the country is also rich in mountain species, including Caspian snowcock, Caucasian

THE ASIATIC CHEETAH

The Asiatic cheetah is one of the most endangered cats on earth. The 50 to 100 living on the edges of Iran's Dasht-e Kavir are all that remain of a population that once ranged from India to the Mediterranean. Cheetahs were prized by ancient Persian royalty, who trained them to hunt gazelles. It is this long history, and the fact that Iran's population of Asiatic lions and Caspian tigers has been hunted into extinction, that has made the cheetah the poster cat of the country's conservation movement.

That the cheetah, the fastest land animal on earth, survives in Iran's deserts is a remarkable story – hunting in such conditions requires a high success rate and remarkable stealth. But in other ways, it makes sense – with hunting having driven the cheetah to extinction elsewhere, the uninhabited deserts of Iran's interior make an ideal refuge.

Even so, severe habitat loss during the 1980s and the resultant loss of cheetah prey, traditionally jebeer, goitered gazelles, wild sheep and goats, has made this harder, as it has forced the cats deeper into mountainous areas in search of more modest meals – such as hare and even lizards.

Since 2000 the Iranian government has worked with the United Nations Development Programme and peak cat-conservation NGO Panthera to designate land, mainly in Yazd and Semnan provinces, as parks and reserves, increase punishments for poaching and undertake an extensive tracking program. The aim was to identify exactly where the cheetah roam and try to link existing reserves to form a safe haven for the few remaining populations.

In 2015, monitoring of camera-trap facilities revealed that 'Pouyan', a male cheetah known to researchers from earlier camera-trap photos, made a remarkable journey: in nine months, he travelled from Dare-Anjir Wildlife Refuge to Naybandan Wildlife Refuge and back, a distance of 415km. Despite such exciting news, the Iranian Cheetah Society announced in 2016 that just two adult female Asiatic cheetahs were known to survive in the wild.

On the positive side, education programs have reduced poaching and the creation of protected areas is expected to help other species. The project is ongoing. For more information visit the Iranian Cheetah Society (www.wildlife.ir) or Panthera (www.panthera.org).

black grouse and Radde's accentor, as well as a large number of the expected desert birds, such as assorted sandgrouse, larks and wheatears.

A growing number of birders are coming to Iran in search of these birds, many of which are hard to find elsewhere, and to enjoy the exceptional birding along the Persian Gulf. In winter in particular, many hundreds of thousands of birds flock to the shallow waters of the Gulf, with the Bandar Abbas–Qeshm areas particularly good. Vast flocks of waders, including crab plovers and terek sandpipers, mingle with various herons, egrets and pelicans and together create one of the most important wintering areas for birds in the Middle East.

For the casual birder, some of the more prominent species include golden eagles in the northern mountains, three species of bee-eaters, the colourful pied and Smyrna kingfishers, both common in Khuzestan, plus the startling blue Indian roller in the Bandar Abbas area and its cousin, the European roller, in the north.

Endangered Species

Habitat loss and one million hunting licenses (each with free bullets from the state) have taken their toll on the wildlife. In the mountainous northwest, the lammergeier (bearded vulture) has been shot and poisoned to the brink of extinction due to a misconception among farmers that they attack sheep. In fact, this fascinating bird usually eats only what other vultures have left behind, and often breaks bones by dropping them onto rocks from a great height. They apply the same method to the unfortunate Greek spur-thighed tortoises in the area.

The Persian fallow deer remains vulnerable but is nonetheless a rare Iranian conservation success story. Thought extinct in the 1950s, a small population was discovered in Khuzestan province, and intensive breeding efforts saw numbers rise throughout the '60s and '70s. Today populations exist in Khuzestan, Mazandaran, the Arjan Protected Area and on an island in Lake Orumiyeh.

National Parks & Reserves

National parks, and the wildlife they are designed to protect, are luxuries most Iranians don't have the time, money or education to be concerned with. As a result, most national parks are terribly underfunded and understaffed, and the most accessible zones tend to be rubbish-strewn picnic sites. Unauthorised hunting is a problem, as is illegal cultivation. Attitudes are changing in cities such as Tehran and Shiraz but it could be decades before Iran's nature reserves have the status of their Western counterparts.

So what does this mean for the visitor? About 5% of Iran is protected. But in the 16 officially mandated national parks and more than 140 other protected areas there are few fences, few, if any, rangers, no maps, no guides and no facilities – you may not even realise you're in a national park. Even finding certain parks can be difficult as they don't appear on maps and there are few signs. Other parks, such as Sisingan on the Caspian, suffer the opposite problem: they are small, overused and quickly overrun by weekenders.

Hardy souls might strike out on their own, but unless time is no problem and you have some Farsi, it will be difficult. Your best bet is to employ a travel agency close to the park you want to visit. Alternatively, use a recommended specialist outdoor agency.

Relatively accessible national parks and protected areas:

Arjan Protected Area Lake and wetland area near Shiraz. Home to masked tits, waterfowl and seasonal migratory birds, plus mammals including Persian fallow deer.

Bakhtegan National Park Incorporating Lakes Bakhtegan and Tashk, this park is about 80km east of Shiraz. Flamingos and other migratory birds loiter here in winter.

Birding Online Resources

Birds of Iran (www.birdsofiran.com)

Birding Pal (www.birdingpal.org/Iran)

Ornithological Society of the Middle East (www.osme.org)

NATURAL ENVIRONMENTS NATIONAL PARKS & RESERVES

More than a thousand wetland sites around the world are protected under a 1971 agreement, signed in Ramsar, on Iran's Caspian Sea coast. Known as the Ramsar Convention, birds and their wetland habitats are the greatest beneficiaries. Iran is home to 22 wetlands that are protected by Ramsar.

Ancient Greek playwright Aechylus was killed when a tortoise landed on his bald head. This story was thought to be a myth until a bearded vulture was seen dropping a tortoise onto rocks to crack it open. It now seems a bearded vulture confused poor Aechylus' head for a stone.

Iran harbours more than 8200 species of plants, about 2000 of them endemic.

While most attention has been focused on the country's nuclear-power program, Iran is the Middle East's only producer of wind turbines and has several wind farms and a major solar-power plant in Yazd.

Bijar Protected Area About 15km north of Bijar town in Kordistan. Home to Alborz red sheep, hyenas and jackals. Best visited in spring and autumn.

Golestan National Park Forested mountains between Gorgan and the Caspian Sea. Home to wild boars, oreal rams, brown bears, wolves, leopards, goitered gazelles and assorted bird life. Best visited in spring. Permits required.

Lake Orumiyeh National Park An important wetland, this park is home to rare deer and a multitude of migratory birds. Relatively accessible from Tabriz, but increasingly threatened.

Environmental Issues

Iran faces several serious environmental challenges, most of which can be summed up as habitat loss and pollution. But it's not all bad news. Public awareness of the environment has risen significantly in recent years.

A report by the United Nations Environment Programme ranked Iran at 117th place among 133 countries in terms of environmental indexes.

Habitat Loss

When environmental historians look back at Iran, the 1980s will be seen as a disastrous decade. Upheaval following the revolution and during the Iran–Iraq War prompted rapid, uncontrolled expansion of grazing lands, often into sensitive semidesert areas, leading to overgrazing and, in some areas, desertification. Massive population growth didn't help and crops were soon being sewn in areas unsuitable for intensive agriculture.

The impacts have been dire. Official estimates suggest 80% of the forest that existed in Iran during the 1970s is now gone, resulting in flooding, erosion and desertification. Wildlife has been pushed into ever-decreasing areas and competition for prey has become critical.

These problems have been exacerbated by a land tenure act passed in the 1980s that changed millennia of land-use practice. Traditionally rangelands were grazed seasonally by nomadic tribes, but tenure over rangelands is now obtained by regular cultivation of land, regardless of its suitability. On the plus side, the government is aware of the problem and in recent years school children have planted millions of trees.

Pollution

Chronic air pollution is the environmental problem you're most likely to notice while travelling in Iran. Tehran sets the standard but growing industry and car ownership have made poisonous air a problem across the country. Iran's pollution problem is worse for having been ignored until it reached crisis point. And that day may soon be coming: according to the World Bank, deaths caused by air pollution (mostly as a result of respiratory illnesses) cost the economy an estimated US$640 million every year.

The good news is the government has taken dramatic steps to force people into realising the impact of endlessly burning fossil fuels. The most important, and controversial, has been removing subsidies and thus raising the price of all fuels (that the motivation was more economic than environmental is by the by). Until about 2007, many Iranians believed cheap fuel was their birthright. Since then the prices of *benzin* (petrol), gas and electricity have gone up by between 800 and 1000 percent each. Not surprisingly, per person consumption has fallen. In theory, market forces should bring more efficient vehicles and fuel to Iran, too. In practice, sanctions are a huge barrier.

There are other problems. The Persian Gulf has been repeatedly contaminated by leaks from oil rigs and tankers, untreated sewage and overly rapid development on the islands of Kish and Qeshm. Pollution in the Caspian Sea is a problem that now threatens the internationally recognised wetlands of the Anzali Lagoon at Bandar-e Anzali.

Survival Guide

Safe Travel

Iran is generally a very safe place to travel, so much so that many travellers describe it as the 'safest country I've ever been to', or 'much safer than travelling in Europe'. Violent crime against foreigners is extremely rare and, indeed, if you do your best to fit in with local customs, you are unlikely to be treated with anything but courtesy and friendliness – that applies to Americans, too. We have hitchhiked across deserts, stayed in the homes of strangers and left bags in restaurants and cafes without any problem.

Western embassies advise their nationals to register on arrival, especially if you will be in Iran for 10 or more days, or plan to visit remote places.

For women travellers, like anywhere, it pays to be cautious and avoid situations where you are alone with a man you don't know. Foreign women will attract unwanted suggestions and, in crowded bazaars and Metro carriages, the odd grope.

Some official paranoia does exist, and there have been instances of travellers being arrested and held until it became apparent they weren't spies. The biggest dangers are actually driving and crossing the street. For an idea of how fellow travellers found Iran, see the Thorn Tree (www.lonelyplanet.com/thorntree).

Crime

While there are few stories of assaults and thefts in Iran, it pays to take the usual precautions. It makes sense, too, that if the economic situation worsens crime will rise. Basic things to be aware of:

➡ On transport keep valuables, including your passport, money and camera, with you at all times.

➡ Hotels are quite safe but locking your bags prevents hotel staff going through them and, perhaps, 'sampling' your toiletries.

➡ There is a black market in stolen foreign passports so, unless it's with your hotel reception, keep yours strapped to your body.

➡ If you are to encounter a pickpocket, it will be in a crowded bazaar.

Kidnapping & Terror

Kidnapping and terror-related crime is extremely rare in most of Iran. That said, at the time of writing, most government travel advisory services were advising against travelling to:

➡ within 100km of the Iran–Afghanistan border

➡ within 10km of the Iran–Iraq border

➡ the province of Sistan va Baluchestan

➡ the area east of the line running from Bam to Jask, including Bam and Zahedan

Police & Security Forces

Uniformed police and military are ubiquitous but have no interest in hassling foreigners. In cities such as Esfahan, Shiraz and Mashhad you'll find helpful Tourist Police – usually including an English-speaker – in conveniently located booths.

Photographing the wrong thing is the action most likely to spark police interest. If you have unwittingly aroused the attention of police for photographing the wrong thing (eg at the border, Tehran train station etc), emphasise you are a tourist and delete the pictures. Do not argue in these situations.

Foreigners are expected to carry their passport at all times, but this can be tricky as hotels are also supposed to keep guests' passports for police inspection. Always carry several photocopies of both your passport's face page and your Iranian visa, and if you go out of town leave a photocopy at reception and take the passport. If you are stopped, show your photocopies unless you are sure the police are genuine.

On roads near borders your transport is likely to be stopped by police searching for drugs and other smuggled goods.

Road Safety

Iranian driving is unpredictable and it's on the road – or crossing it – that you're most likely to be in danger. There's little you can do to control this beyond asking your driver to slow down ('yavash tar boro!') or take a train.

Iranians will tell you with a perverse mix of horror and glee that Iran competes for the highest per-capita number of road deaths on earth – in 2014 that was more than 17,000 people, with another 300,000-plus injured.

No one pays any notice of road rules and the willingness of a car to stop at a busy intersection is directly proportional to the size of the vehicles in its path. Playing on this, some cunning motorists have fitted deafening air horns, usually found on trucks and buses, to their Paykans and Prides. A quick blast sees other traffic screech to a halt, fearing they've been outsized. Meanwhile, the modest little Paykan/Pride sails through the intersection. Size (or at least the perception that you're big) matters.

Be aware of contraflow bus lanes (along which buses hurtle in the opposite direction to the rest of the traffic), and motorbikes speeding through red lights, along footpaths and through crowded bazaars.

Vehicles never stop at pedestrian crossings so don't underestimate the possibility of dying a horrible death while crossing the road. It may be little consolation, but the law says that if a pedestrian is hit the driver is always at fault and is liable to pay blood money to the family of the victim. Until you've got your head around the traffic, perhaps the best advice comes from one pragmatic reader: 'Cross a busy street with an Iranian person, but make sure the Iranian is closest to the approaching traffic.'

Earthquakes

Earthquakes happen every day in Iran, but most travellers will never feel one. If you get unlucky, the following precautions might help.

It's most important to protect yourself from falling debris. If you're indoors, stay inside and take cover under a sturdy desk or table. Hold on to it and be prepared to move with it. Hold the position until the shaking stops and you can move outside. Stay clear of windows, appliances and freestanding furniture (such as wardrobes) that might fall over. Use a pillow to protect your head.

In a mud-brick building it's vital to create space (under a bed, perhaps) that won't be filled with dirt and dust, which could lead to suffocation.

If you're outside, stay away from buildings and power lines.

Women Travellers

Females planning a trip to Iran should consider four questions: What should I wear? How should I behave? Will I be safe? What should I take? This information aims to give practical advice, dispel preconceptions and reassure.

What Should I Wear?

Since the revolution of 1979 all women in Iran, including foreigners, have been required *by law* to wear loose-fitting clothes to disguise their figures. They must also cover their hair. This form of dressing is known as hejab, a term that refers in general to 'modest' dress, and is also used to refer specifically to the hair-covering.

Signs in public places show officially acceptable versions of hejab: the chador (literally 'tent' in Farsi), an all-encompassing, head-to-toe black garment held closed with hand or

---

GOVERNMENT TRAVEL ADVICE

The following government websites offer travel advisories and information for travellers:

Australian Department of Foreign Affairs & Trade (www.smartraveller.gov.au)

Canadian Department of Foreign Affairs & International Trade (www.voyage.gc.ca)

French Ministère des Affaires Étrangères et Européennes (www.diplomatie.gouv.fr/fr/conseils-aux-voyageurs)

Italian Ministero degli Affari Esteri (www.viaggiaresicuri.mae.aci.it)

New Zealand Ministry of Foreign Affairs & Trade (www.safetravel.govt.nz)

UK Foreign & Commonwealth Office (www.gov.uk/foreign-travel-advice)

US Department of State (www.travel.state.gov)

teeth; or a manteau (shapeless coat or coat dress) and a *rusari* (scarf) covering the hair, neck and décolletage. Girls must start to wear hejab when they reach puberty, but many start from a much earlier age (we've seen plenty of babies and toddlers sporting Islamic head coverings).

In reality the dress code is more relaxed and open to interpretation. It's not unusual to see young women in the larger cities wearing figure-hugging manteaus (often tightly belted trenchcoats), skinny jeans, high heels and colourful *rusaris* that have been arranged to offer plentiful glimpses of hair and neck. But in the smaller cities, towns and villages this rarely happens – the chador is common and those who don't wear it are clad in an ensemble of shapeless coat, black pants, sensible shoes and a *maqna'e* (nun-like head scarf, or wimple). Colour schemes are uniformly dull.

Iranian women who flout hejab can find themselves in serious trouble. Their infringements have included wearing sunglasses above the headscarf, failing to wear a coat that fully covered their bottom, wearing bright colours, wearing nail polish, wearing sandals that show the feet or ankles, and not fully covering their hair.

Fortunately, foreign women are not usually judged as harshly as Iranian women when it comes to hejab, and few Iranians will bat an eyelid if you have your fringe or a bit of neck or hair showing. It pays to look at what women around you are wearing; for example, you'll want to dress more conservatively in Qom than you would in Tehran.

HEAD COVERINGS
The biggest challenge that you'll encounter is keeping your scarf on. Silk scarves aren't much use, as they tend to slip off; the only way to make them work is

to tie them under the chin babushka-style. Wool can work, but not if it's too fine and slippery. Your best bet is textured cotton, which tends to adhere to hair more effectively and slips less. Make sure that your scarf is wide enough to cover all of your hair, and long enough to be able to throw over your shoulders as an anchoring device. Practice before you leave home.

Some travellers wear a thick elasticised headband and fasten their scarves to it with safety or bobby pins, ensuring that their scarf doesn't slip – this can work well with silk and fine cotton, so is worth considering if you are travelling here over summer and want to wear something light. Bring the band with you.

At the time of writing, local fashionistas in Tehran were wearing their scarves as high and as far back on their heads as possible. This is relatively easy to do if you have long hair (the scarf is draped over a high ponytail or bun, which anchors it), but it's impossible for those with shorter hairstyles.

MANTEAUS
The majority of manteaus are made from polyester (ghastly in summer) or cheap cotton. The trench-coat style is the most popular version for fashion-conscious Iranian women, but it can be hot and uncomfortable – remember that your manteau will need to stay on in restaurants, cinemas, shops and other interior public spaces.

Loose-fitting cardigans going down to the mid-thigh are a comfortable, alternative form of outerwear. These can be worn over T-shirts or jumpers (sweaters) but bring them from home – they're hard to source in Iran. In summer, you'll need to wear something light – long peasant blouses and tunics made with natural fibres work well, as do *shalwar kameez*,

a long shirt or tunic worn over baggy pants. If you're coming overland from India you'll have plenty of opportunities to purchase these along your journey.

All manteaus are worn over trousers; jeans are perfectly acceptable. Do not wear skirts.

CHADORS
The only times when foreign women must wear a chador are when visiting important shrines. In these instances, the chadors can almost always be borrowed on-site.

How Should I Behave?
Half-truths and stereotypes about women exist on both sides of the cultural divide: some Westerners assume that all Iranian women are black-cloaked, repressed victims, while some Iranians, influenced by foreign movies and media, see Western women as 'easy' and immoral. When in Iran, be aware that sex before marriage is uncommon (well, that's the official line) and that there may be some males who – influenced by the aforementioned stereotype – will try it on with you, particularly if you are travelling solo. The best way to prevent this happening is to be polite but not overly friendly in your dealings with local males. If you need advice or directions, approach women first. Younger ones are more likely to speak English.

Most Iranian women only travel with their fathers, brothers and husbands, so Western women travelling by themselves or with male friends may be considered as being of dubious moral standing. Be aware of this and be careful not to break the following local conventions:

➜ In restaurants and teahouses, head to the separate areas set aside for women and families where these exist.

→ If you are by yourself it's best not to enter teahouses, as men will either harass you or treat you like a leper (the only local women who would do such a thing are of very dubious moral standing).

→ On city buses, use the women's entrance in the middle of the bus and sit at the back with the other women.

→ On intercity buses you can sit in any part of the bus, but you should always try to sit next to a woman (it's OK to sit next to a Western male you are travelling with).

→ Don't shake hands with Iranian men unless they initiate this. Instead, place your hand over your heart as a greeting.

→ If you are by yourself or even with another female, don't accept an invitation into a man's house unless at least one of his female relatives will also be present.

Will I be Safe?

Violence against foreign women is almost unheard of in Iran, even if the odd grope in a savari isn't (consider yourself warned). You rarely hear about instances of sexual assault, although this has happened – if travelling solo it may be safer to use female guides, steer clear of teahouses and avoid budget hotels where Iranian or migrant workers stay (eg *mosaferkhanehs*). Some cities – Yazd is one example – have 'Women Taxis', with female drivers and for female customers only.

What Should I Take?

If you use tampons, take enough to last your whole trip. They're expensive and very hard to find. Sanitary pads are widely available. It's also handy to take some plastic bags for carrying out your toilet paper, tampons and pads from toilets that don't have rubbish bins.

Directory A–Z

Accommodation

The Ministry of Culture and Islamic Guidance categorises most hotels and decides what they can charge. Prices rise in April each year and the rates are displayed (usually in Arabic numerals) at reception.

While *otagh* (room) prices are fixed, friendly negotiation might save you a bit during quieter times, especially between mid-October and early March. But don't count on it. The reluctance to bargain is partly due to a lack of effective competition. For foreigners, midrange and top-end places will sometimes quote prices in US dollars or euros, though they accept (and are, in theory, required to be paid in) local currency.

Hotels will almost always keep your passport overnight so carry a photocopy, and get the original back if you're heading out of town. Check-out time is usually 2pm.

If you get off the beaten track and are open to it, you'll likely encounter heart-warming hospitality that sucks you into unplanned homestays. It's worth packing a few small presents from home to express your gratitude, as paying cash for such accommodation might be inappropriate.

Seasonal Swing

There are two clear tourist seasons in Iran. Low season starts in October and continues through winter until shortly before No Ruz (Iranian New Year, on 21 March) and the beginning of spring. From a few days before No Ruz, hotels in popular holiday destinations, such as Kish Island, Esfahan, the Caspian Sea coast, Shiraz and Yazd, are packed, and prices are at their highest.

No Ruz marks the beginning of daylight saving, longer opening hours and annual government-approved price increases across the economy, including hotels. After the 13-day holiday period is over you'll find room prices usually rise by about 20% from the winter (low season) rate, and stay that way until October, when they fall back a bit or can be (slightly) more easily haggled down. The whole cycle then begins again next No Ruz. There are a few exceptions. In summer, prices along the Caspian Sea coast can skyrocket, while in hot places like Yazd and Kerman prices can fall with demand.

Camping

Iranians love tents, but there are few official camping grounds. Unless you can make yourself look like a nomad, camping can draw unwanted attention from the authorities. Trekkers and mountaineers who need to camp should discuss plans with the provincial tourist information office first if not accompanied by a recognised guide. The office may be able to write a letter of introduction.

Couchsurfing

Iran has a growing couchsurfing (www.couchsurfing.org) community and making contact with its members is an easy and increasingly popular way to get 'inside' Iranian culture. Remember, though, that couchsurfing is technically

SLEEPING PRICE RANGES

Prices vary across the country, with Tehran usually the most expensive, Esfahan, Shiraz and Mashhad in the middle, and less visited centres such as Kerman, Hamadan and Bandar Abbas the cheapest.

The following prices are a rough guide for double rooms with bathroom and breakfast and include the 17% for tax and service charged by upmarket hotels.

Budget < US$40 (US$50 for Tehran & central Iran)

Midrange US$40-150 (US$50 to US$200 for Tehran & central Iran)

Top-end > US$150 (US$200 for Tehran & central Iran)

illegal in Iran, although it is widely tolerated.

Most readers who have surfed Iranian couches, or more likely carpets, have reported a memorable time for positive reasons. However, there have also been warnings that some Iranian hosts expect to accompany their guests everywhere, and if you're not up for that it's best to commit to less time with the option of extending to avoid an early and embarrassing departure. Also, ta'arof (p300) or not, do insist on paying for at least something during your stay, or take a gift from home. Be aware, however, that some hosts use the service to corral people into paying for expensive tours run by these same hosts.

Mosaferkhanehs & Mehmanpazirs

Iran's most basic accommodation is in male-dominated *mosaferkhanehs* (literally 'travellers' houses'), a dorm or basic hotel, and similar *mehmanpazirs*. Standards in these places vary but expect shared bathrooms, squat toilets and no spoken English. Some bottom-end places won't even have a communal shower. Prices start at around US$6 per bed in a noisy, grotty, male-only dorm. Simple, private rooms, perhaps with a sink, start at about twice that. Pack a towel, toilet paper and sleep sheet, as bedding can sometimes be semi-clean and/or stained.

In some cities some *mosaferkhanehs* are not allowed to accept foreigners, or require written permission from the police; this is more likely to affect women travellers. Permission is easy to organise through a 10-minute visit to the local Amaken – an arm of the police – assuming you arrive in business hours.

Hostels

Tehran has a growing number of decent backpacker-style hostels with shared dorms (usually single sex) and

communal facilities. Some have not been government approved, but are reputable places nonetheless. They're great places to meet fellow travellers. For more options see www.hihostelsiniran.com

Hotels
BUDGET

Basic one- and two-star hotels, or 'budget hotels', normally have an attached bathroom with at least a hot shower, plus air-con, heating, TV (Iranian channels), fridge and maybe a phone. Double beds are rare, breakfast will often cost extra, and cleanliness can be questionable – don't be afraid to ask for fresh sheets.

MIDRANGE

Most two-star hotels, and all three- and four-star rooms, will come with a clean private bathroom, phone, fridge and TV (sometimes with foreign channels). There might be a reasonable restaurant, and breakfast will be included. You'll find toilet paper but bath plugs are a long shot. Like a 40-something boxer, a lot of places in this range charge rates that reflect a more glorious past than the beaten-around present; try negotiating. Aside from garden-variety hotels, the midrange includes:

Traditional hotels The most charismatic midrange places are the *hotel sonnati* (traditional hotels), where old courtyard houses have been transformed into social little hotels. If you're staying in a *hotel sonnati*, you'll know you're in Iran. Yazd has many and others can be found in Kashan, Esfahan and Shiraz.

Apartment hotels In the upper midrange are a growing number of modern 'apartment hotels', which

can be good value outside the high season.

Tourist Inns Most towns of decent size have a government-run Tourist Inn *(mehmansara jahangardi)*. Standards vary considerably but they are usually fair value and often employ at least one English speaker.

TOP END

Until recently, many of Iran's top hotels pre-dated the 1979 revolution. Several accidentally maintained decor which, like the Bee Gees, became so outdated that it was almost retro-cool. However, competition from new luxury hotels and apartment hotels has seen many, though not all, of these places refitted.

In most top-end establishments, the rooms and service will not live up to Western standards, but while prices are high by Iranian standards they are not (in most cases) outrageous compared with what you'll be used to. Note that hotels with indoor pools and saunas have segregated swimming times for men and women. The generously sized outdoor pools of the disco-era hotels are purely ornamental these days.

Ecolodge

You'll increasingly encounter places known as ecolodges, which can be popular accommodation options. Some can be good places to stay, although the experience is more about traditional-style rooms with local food and possibly costumed staff rather than anything obviously ecofriendly.

Other Accommodation

Along the Caspian Sea coast and in those northwestern rural resort-villages most frequented by Iranian tourists, you'll find locals renting out rooms, bungalows and self-contained apartments ('suites') in their homes and gardens or above shops. In the low season prices can be very reasonable, but in summer prices rise by up to 400% and bookings are essential. Some suites and almost all rooms/homestays are unmarked in Farsi let alone English so it's just a case of asking around for an *otagh*. Food is generally not included.

Activities

Iran's landscapes offer up numerous opportunities to get active, with the undoubted highlights trekking, rock climbing, mountaineering and snow skiing; both diving and swimming are possible in the waters of the Persian Gulf, although these tend to be more local pursuits.

Cycling

Iran's main highways can be terrifyingly truck-dominated, but secondary routes are well-suited to cycle touring. Few locals push the pedals, but a steady stream of overlanders has long braved the traffic en route between Europe and Asia. We're not sure we'd be going any further east than central Iran right now, but that has more to do with the security situation than it does with cycling conditions.

Diving & Snorkelling

Scuba diving and snorkelling are limited to sites around Kish Island and Qeshm Island in the Persian Gulf. There are some great coral reefs and plenty of colourful critters, although it can't rival the Red Sea or other world-class diving regions. Qeshm is the better option, while **Kish Diving Center** (Map p216; ☑0912 854 3246; www.

kishdiving.com; ⊘7am-6pm) is a good operator.

Women and men don't dive together – they travel on separate boats.

Mountaineering

Iran boasts dozens of high mountains, some of them permanently snowcapped. Many can be climbed by anyone fit, without the need for special equipment, experience or a guide, but you should always check the situation before embarking on a mountain trek. Early June to late August is the climbing season.

The following are good places to get started:

Iran Mountain Zone (www.mountainzone.ir) Iranian mountaineering website with some trip logs in English, a mountain index and contacts for local climbing clubs.

Peakware (www.peakware.com) Has summit logs for 36 Iranian peaks, including Damavand and Sabalan.

Summit Post (www.summitpost.org) Search Iran for dated but detailed trip reports.

Iranian Mountain Guides (http://mountainguide.ir/) Useful for tracking down a mountaineering or trekking guide.

Mazieh Mandegari (mazieh mandegari@yahoo.com) Licensed and highly experienced female mountain guide operating out of Yazd.

WHERE TO CLIMB MOUNTAINS

The magnificent Alborz Mountains contain about 70 peaks over 4000m; those listed here are the most notable.

Mt Damavand (5671m; p74) Northeast of Tehran, Iran's highest and best-known peak has a classic Fuji-esque profile, but reaching the summit is not of great technical difficulty.

Alam Kuh (4850m; p115) Mt Alam is Iran's most technical peak with an 800m near-vertical granite wall on its most difficult northern face: a world-class challenge.

OUTDOOR & ADVENTURE AGENCIES

The following companies specialise in trekking, mountaineering and eco-tourism in Iran.

Aftab Kalout (☑021-6648 8375, 021-6648 8374; www.kalout.com) Professional Tehran-based outfit specialising in eco-tourism, desert trips, trekking and eco-cum-cultural tours.

Araz Adventure Tours (☑021-7760 9292; www.araz.org) Recommended by readers. Offers range of mountaineering, climbing, horse- and camel-trekking, plus cultural tours. Director Mohsen Aghajani speaks English. Most equipment can be provided.

Kassa Tours (☑021-7751 0464/3; www.kassatours.com) Trekking, rock-climbing, heli-skiing, desert expeditions and climbing tours to 'any mountain you want to climb'. Run by experienced, English-speaking climber Ahmad Shirmohammad.

Sepid Mountaineering Company (☑0917-313 2926, 0711-235 5939; www.iransightseeing.com) Shiraz-based Abdollah Raeesi and crew organise mountaineering, cross-country skiing, nomad and horseback tours.

Adventure Iran (☑021-2656 6026; www.adventureiran.com) Tehran-based company run by experienced trekkers and mountaineers including Reza Zarei. Can put together backpacker-specific itineraries.

Mt Sabalan (4811m) Ardabil's incredible peak (and Iran's third-highest) can be climbed in three days if you walk, or one day if you cheat and get a lift to base camp.

Oshtoran Kuh (San Boran; 4150m) Enigmatic, and that's just the access – you'll probably need a guide for this Zagros behemoth sitting high above the frozen waters of Lake Gahar.

Shah Alborz (4125m) A three-day wilderness trip brings you up the southern flank of the highest peak in the western Alborz.

Mt Sahand (Kamal Dag; 3707m) An easy 5km stroll from a ski re-sort brings you to Tabriz' famous summit. It could be a tad windy...

Alvand Kuh (Mt Alvand; 3580m) In good weather you can knock off Hamadan's pride and joy in a big day out.

Rock Climbing

Rock climbing is growing in popularity in Iran and there are several accessible and challenging climbing routes. Hiring equipment is not easy but if you are keen you'll probably be able to turn up to many walls and be invited to join the locals (on week-ends especially). You'd be wise to check with police or tourist information offices before climbing as certain innocuous-looking climbs can overlook sensitive military posts. That said, if locals are using the climb there won't be a problem.

WHERE TO GO ROCK CLIMBING

There's good climbing around Maku and Yafteh Wall near Khorrammabad. Otherwise the most appealing climbs include the following:

Band-e Yakhchal Easily accessed by hiking an hour uphill from Darband in north Tehran, there are several low walls and the 200m-high Shervin wall; there's a hut here called Shervin Hut. The lower 25m have been set up for climbing and reports are that in summer it's a difficult but not especially technical climb to the summit. It's busy on Fridays.

PRACTICALITIES

Electricity Current is 220V AC, 50Hz. Wall sockets are mainly the European, two round-pin type.

Newspapers Iran's English-language daily newspapers are the *Tehran Times* (www.tehrantimes.com) and *Iran News*, both of which cleave to the government line with exceptions from the wires. They are available only in Tehran and some other large cities. Both offer decent, if sometimes eccentric, international coverage.

Radio Frequencies for the BBC World Service (www.bbc.co.uk/worldserviceradio) include 11760Hz, 15575Hz and 1413kHz; and for VOA (www.voanews.com) 11740Hz and 15195kHz.

TV Iranian broadcasters are state-controlled. However, many Iranians get Farsi-language satellite TV from North America. On Iranian TV, channels 1 to 4 are national, 5 and 6 province-based. Most hotels have the 24-hour IRINN news channel, which has a news-ticker in English.

Weights & Measures Iran uses the metric system.

Farhad Tarash (Bisotun Wall) Cliffs around the ancient collec-tion of inscriptions at Bisotun include a particularly challenging rock face. The Kermanshah tour-ist information office can put you in touch with the local climbers club for support and equipment.

Alam Kuh (Mt Alam) The 800m-high wall here rises from an elevation of 4200m and is a major expedition. **Kassa Tours** (☎021-7751 0464/3; www.kassatours.com) offers a six-day trip, including acclimatisation time. **Iran Mountain Zone** (www.mountainzone.ir) has a thorough description of routes.

A good place to meet people who know these climbs is online at **Summit Post** (www.summitpost.org). And www.rockclimbing.com/routes/Asia/Iran lists options but adds few details.

Skiing

There are more than 20 func-tioning ski fields in Iran. The season is long, the snow is often powdery and untracked and, compared with West-ern fields, skiing in Iran is a bargain.

All the resorts have lodges, chalets and hotels. Ski lifts cost as little as US$10 a day. You can hire skis, poles and boots, but not clothes, at the resorts. The slopes are also some of the most sexually equal areas of Iran outside of the family home; skiing was banned after the revolution, and after the ban was lifted in 1988 the images were of women skiing in chadors. But with Khatami's rise to the presidency in 1997 came a considerable easing of re-strictions on the slopes. These were tightened somewhat under the Ahmadinejad presi-dency; women must still keep their heads covered, but on higher slopes there is usually plenty of hair to be seen (par-ticularly at Shemshak). Skiing is very popular among the affluent young.

WHEN TO SKI

The season in the Alborz Mountains (where most slopes are located) starts as early as November and lasts until just after No Ruz (ie early April); around Tabriz and at Dizin (close to Tehran) it can last until mid-May. The slopes are busy with Iranians on Thursdays and Fridays, and with diplomats and expats on Saturdays; other days it should be pretty quiet. Iranians don't get off-piste that much, so even on Fridays finding untouched powder is not hard.

WHERE TO SKI

Some of Iran's major ski fields:

Tehran Most accessible and with the best skiing are Dizin (p72), Darbansar (p72), Tochal (p51) and Abali (p72).

Western Iran There is also good downhill skiing available near Tabriz and ski resorts can be found nearby at Ardabil, Hamadan and Bijar.

Zagros Mountains Smaller fields at Sepidan (p177), north of Shiraz, and Chelgerd (p177), west of Esfahan.

RESOURCES

Contact or visit the very helpful **Iran Ski Federation** (☑021-2256 9595; www.skifed. ir) or check its website (in Farsi, translate in Chrome) for details of all the slopes.

Also check out www.iran-skitours.ir and www.iranski. com.

Trekking

There's plenty of good trekking in Iran, but information is hard to come by. Nader's descriptions of various routes on www.summitpost.org are probably the best place to start, even if they are more than a decade old.

Solo trekking is possible but taking a guide is a good idea as much for translation skills and friends along the route as the actual navigation. In remote regions, especially near borders, you may stumble across military/police/ security areas; in 2009, three Americans were imprisoned after straying into Iran while hiking in Iraqi Kurdistan and they were not released until 2011 – an Iranian guide or a few phrases of Farsi should hopefully smooth over any misunderstandings. Drinking water is often scarce, so take your own supplies in desert regions, and purification tablets or water filters elsewhere.

For women travellers seeking a female guide, contact

Mazieh Mandegari (mazieh mandegari@yahoo.com) who operates out of Yazd.

WHERE TO TREK

One and two-day walks are possible in many areas, particularly the northwest and around Tehran. For Tehran, nearby **Tochal** (تله کابین توچال; Map p52; ☑021-2387 5000; www.tochal.org; Yaddeh-ye Telecabin, off Velenjak Ave; one-way/return Station 2 IR100,000/150,000, Station 5 IR130,000/270,000, Station 7 IR380,000/650,000; ⊙from Station 1 8.30am-2pm Sat, Tue & Wed, to 3pm Thu, 7am-3pm Fri; Ⓜ Tajrish, then taxi) and **Darband** (دربند; Map p52; Ⓜ Tajrish, then taxi) are a good start. Further afield, Kelardasht (p112), Masuleh (p110) and **Takht-e Soleiman** (Throne of Solomon; ☑044-4545 3311; IR200,000; ⊙8am-sunset) make good launch pads for mountain walks. Day and overnight desert treks can be easily arranged from Yazd.

But perhaps the most popular and rewarding route (in spring and summer) is through the historic Alamut Valley (p118), once home to the Assassins, including a trek taking you across the Alborz Mountains and down to the Caspian.

Children

Foreign children will be the source of much amusement and curiosity, which is both a great cultural ice-breaker and, after a while, annoying. Nappies (diapers), powders, baby formula and most medications

Climate

Tehran

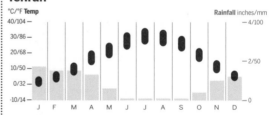

Esfahan

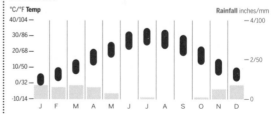

Mashhad

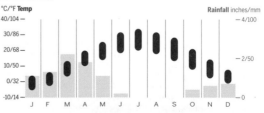

are widely available, though not necessarily in familiar brands. The hardest thing will be trying to keep children entertained in a country where journeys are long and attractions often rather 'adult'. Parents should explain fairly clearly to their daughters aged nine or older that they'll have to wear hejab.

Eating with the family is the norm in Iran, and taking your kids into a restaurant will not only be welcome but can bring you more-attentive service. While few menus include special meals for children, staff often tailor the size of the meal to the size of the child. Most food is not spicy.

If you have small children and plan on using taxis, you'll probably have to bring your own baby seat. Few vehicles have seatbelts in the back, so it's worth asking for them when you book. High chairs are rare and childcare agencies and nappy-changing facilities almost non-existent. Breastfeeding in public is not a great idea.

Customs Regulations

Contrary to popular belief, Iranian officialdom is fairly relaxed about what foreigners take into and out of the country; at airports, your bags probably won't be searched at all. However, don't take this to mean you can load your luggage with vodka, bacon and porn. You are allowed to import, duty-free, 200 cigarettes and 50 cigars, and a 'reasonable quantity' of perfume. And of course zero alcohol, which remains strictly illegal.

You'll probably get away with any book, no matter how critical of the government, as long as it doesn't have too much female skin or hair visible on the cover.

You should have no trouble bringing in your laptop, smartphone, shortwave radio, iPad and video equipment if it doesn't look professional. Visitors are supposed to

declare cash worth more than US$1000. In practice few do and the authorities aren't really interested.

Export Restrictions

Officially, you can take out anything you legally imported into Iran, and anything you bought, including handicrafts other than rugs up to the value of US$160 (hang on to your receipts), as long as they are not for 'the purpose of trade'. Many traders will undervalue goods on receipts issued to foreigners. A 'reasonable number' of rugs can be exported with no limit on value.

You can also take out 150g of gold and 3kg of silver, without gemstones. If you want to exceed these limits, you will need an export permit from a customs office. Officially you need permission to export anything 'antique' (ie more than 50 years old), including handicrafts, gemstones and coins. No more than IR200,000 in Iranian cash is allowed to be taken out of Iran.

Sanctions mean that in theory you can't take more than US$100 worth of goods purchased in Iran into the USA.

Electricity

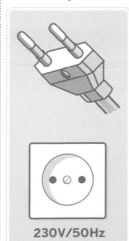

230V/50Hz

Embassies & Consulates

It's important to realise what your own embassy – the embassy of the country of which you are a citizen – can and can't do if you get into trouble. Generally speaking, it won't help if the trouble is remotely your own fault. Remember that you are bound by the laws of the country you are in and your embassy won't be sympathetic if you end up in jail after committing a crime locally, even if such actions would be legal in your own country. Don't expect support for feminist or political statements you make in Iran, for example. In genuine emergencies you might get some assistance after other channels have been exhausted. If you have your money and documents stolen it will assist with a new passport, but forget a loan for onward travel.

For a list of Iranian embassies around the world, see the **Iranian Ministry of Foreign Affairs** (www.mfa.ir).

Embassies & Consulates in Iran

Many embassies ask travellers to register their presence by phoning in and asking for the consul. If you do, let them know when you leave, too. In a genuine emergency call the number here, wait until the message gives you the emergency number, and call that. The following have representation in Tehran:

Afghan Embassy (Map p44; ☑021-8873 7050; www. afghanembassy.ir; cnr 4th & Pakistan Sts, off Beheshti Ave; ⊙8am-2pm Sat-Wed; ⓂShahid Beheshti); Mashhad branch (Map p261; ☑051-3859 7551; www.cg-afg.com; Akhund Khorasani 23; ⊙8am-2pm Mon-Thu)

Armenian Embassy (Map p44; ☑021-6670 4833; www.iran. mfa.am; cnr Ostad Shahriar & Razi Sts; ⊙9am-6pm Sun-Thu; ⓂTheatr Shahr) Tourist visas also available on the border or at Yerevan airport.

Australian Embassy (Map p44; ☎021-8386 3666; www.iran.embassy.gov.au; 2 23rd St, off Khaled Eslamboli St; ☺7.30am-noon & 12.30-3.30pm Sun-Wed, to 2.45pm Thu; MMosalla)

Azerbaijani (Map p52;☎021-2256 3146; www.tehran.mfa.gov.az; 16 Rastovan St; ☺9am-12.30pm Sat-Wed; MShariati); Tabriz branch (https://evisa.gov.az; Aref St, Valiasr) A 30-day tourist visa is issued in Tehran, usually requiring an invitation certified in Baku; call for details. Visas not available at land borders.

Dutch Embassy (Map p52; ☎021-2366 0000; http://iran.nlembassy.org; 60 West Arghavan St; ☺7.30am-4pm Sun-Wed, to 1.30pm Thu; MNobonyad)

French Embassy (Map p44; ☎021-6409 4000; www.ambafrance-ir.org; 64 Nofl Loshato St; ☺8.30am-noon Mon-Thu; MTeatr-e Shahr)

German Embassy (Map p38; ☎021-3999 0000; www.teheran.diplo.de; 324 Ferdowsi St; ☺7am-3.30pm Sun-Thu; MSa'di)

Indian Embassy (Map p44; ☎021-8875 5103; www.indianembassy-tehran.ir; 46 Miremad St, cnr 9th St; ☺9am-12.30pm Sun-Thu; MShahid Beheshti)

Iraqi Embassy (Map p44;☎021-8893 8865; www.mofamission.gov.iq; Valiasr Ave; MMeydan-e Valiasr) Visas depend on the prevailing situation in Iraq.

Italian Embassy (Map p44; ☎021-6672 6955; www.ambteheran.esteri.it; 68 Nofl Loshato St; ☺9am-1pm Sun-Thu; MTeatr-e Shahr)

Japanese Embassy (Map p44; ☎021-8871 7922; www.ir.emb-japan.go.jp; cnr Bucharest & Fifth Sts, Arzhantin; ☺8.30-10.30am & 3-4pm Sat-Thu)

New Zealand Embassy (Map p52;☎021-2612 2175; www.mfat.govt.nz/en/countries-and-regions/middle-east/iran/new-zealand-embassy; cnr 2nd Park Alley, Sosan St, North Golestan Complex, Aghdasiyeh St; ☺8.30am-12.30pm & 1-3pm Sun-Thu)

Pakistani Embassy (Map p44; ☎021-6694 1388; www.mofa.gov.pk/iran; 1 Etemadzadeh Ave; ☺8.30am-1.30pm Sat-Wed; MMeydan-e Enghelab Eslami) Embassy not issuing visas to nonresidents; consulates have not issued visas for several years.

Swiss Embassy (Map p52; ☎021-2200 6002; www.eda.admin.ch/tehran; 2 Yasaman St, off Sharifi Manesh Ave; ☺8am-noon Sun-Thu; MSadr) Handles US affairs.

Tajikistani Embassy (Map p52; ☎021-2283 4650; www.tajembiran.tj; 10, 3rd Alley, Shahid Zein-aly St, Niyavaran; ☺9am-noon Mon, Wed, Thu & Sun) North of Niyavaran Palace; issues tourist visas for one/two/four weeks for US$30/40/50. Takes a week; bring a letter of introduction from your embassy.

Turkish Embassy (Map p38; ☎021-3595 1100; http://tehran.emb.mfa.gov.tr; 337 Ferdowsi St; ☺9am-5pm Sun-Thu; MSa'di)

Turkmen Embassy (Map p52; ☎021-2220 6306; http://iran.tmembassy.gov.tm; 5 Barati St, off Vatanpour St; ☺9.30-11am Sun-Thu; MTajrish, then taxi); Mashhad branch (Map p261; ☎051-3854 7066; Do Shahid St, off Dah-e Dey Sq; ☺8.30-noon Mon-Thu & Sat) A five-day transit visa or a tourist visa are issued either the same day or after a week (yes, inconsistent) with a letter of introduction (eg from www.stantours.com), photos and copies. Once approval has been given, speed of stamping depends on the price paid.

UK Embassy (Map p44;☎021-6405 2000; www.gov.uk; 198 Ferdowsi St; ☺7.30am-2pm Sun-Thu; MSa'di)

Uzbek Embassy (Map p52; ☎021-2229 9780; www.uzbekembassy.ir; 15 4th Dead End, off Aqdasieh St; MNobonyad) See website for details of what is needed to secure a visa and associated fees. It's near the Sadaf Shopping Centre.

Food

For more about eating and drinking in Iran, see Iranian Cuisine (p302).

LGBTI Travellers

There is no reason why LGBTI travellers shouldn't visit Iran. There are no questions of sexuality on visa application forms.

Iran certainly has an LGBTI community, but it's one that, by necessity, is barely visible in general society. While Islamic law doesn't ban being gay, it in no way condones intercourse between two people of the same gender. Homosexual acts are illegal for both men and women – if caught, locals and foreigners alike could face corporal punishment and the death penalty.

However, Iran does recognise transgender individuals and permits sexual reassignment surgery. In fact, more sex change operations are carried out in Iran than any other country in the world except Thailand, with the government chipping in for

EMERGENCY & IMPORTANT NUMBERS

Drop the 0 when dialling an area code from abroad.

SERVICE	NUMBER
Ambulance	☎115
Fire	☎125
Police	☎110
Iran country code	☎98
International access code	☎00
Local directory	☎118

half the cost and recognising the changed sex on birth certificates.

Naturally, LGBTI residents are extremely cautious of how 'out' they are, and it's advisable for gay and lesbian visitors to err on the side of caution and adopt a similar low profile. Arranging meetings with Iranian gays and lesbians is possible; dating apps such as Grindr and Scruff are not censored.

It makes sense not to advertise that you're part of a same-sex couple. Most hoteliers won't ask, though you might find in some places discretion is the better part of valour when seeking a double bed.

Insurance

In 2011 it became compulsory to have travel insurance to get a visa to Iran. When looking for a policy, make sure Iran is actually covered (ie specifically mentioned). If it's not, or if you're unsure, buy the official insurance for US$16 at the airport; the insurance desk is opposite the visa desk (you should visit the insurance desk first). Some insurers, particularly in the USA, consider the region a 'danger zone' and either exclude it altogether or insist on exorbitant premiums. Travel in areas such as Kordistan and Sistan va Baluchestan might not be covered if your country's foreign office warns against travelling there.

Internet Access

In Iran, internet cafes are known as *cafenets* (previously *coffeenets*), although there are fewer such places with each passing year as everyone has mobile internet and wi-fi is increasingly common. In Tehran, for example, there are virtually no *cafenets* left as pretty much all cafes, teahouses and hotels have wi-fi. Speeds are variable, but most cities have ADSL connections.

> ### EATING PRICE RANGES
>
> The following price ranges refer to a main course in most of Iran.
>
> **$** less than US$5 (IR200,000)
> **$$** US$5–US$10 (IR200,000–IR375,000)
> **$$$** more than US$10 (IR375,000)
>
> In Tehran and central Iran, prices are higher:
>
> **$** less than US$10 (IR375,000)
> **$$** US$10–US$20 (IR375,000–IR700,000)
> **$$$** more than US$20 (IR700,000)

Viruses, worms, Trojans and key-loggers (if not Stuxnet) are widespread, so be wary of sticking your USB stick into any local machines.

Wi-fi is increasingly available in hotels and cafes, and it's usually (but not always) free. Upmarket coffee shops invariably have wi-fi, and whether you pay for it or not seems to depend a little on how much you pay for your coffee – the more expensive your espresso, the less likely you are to have to pay to get connected.

Banned Websites

Access to thousands of websites is blocked by the government. At the time of writing, these included the following:

➡ Facebook
➡ Twitter
➡ BBC and most Western news services

At the time of writing, Skype, Yahoo! Messenger and Instagram were accessible, but most Iranians use telegram, me or whatsapp to communicate with each other. Many, perhaps even most, Iranian businesses in the tourist sector have an Instagram page.

To get around blocked websites, most Iranians use a VPN client – set one up on your device before you leave home, although it can slow things down considerably, which can be particularly frustrating where the wi-fi is already slow. If you don't, you'll find access to many websites to be

difficult; *cafenets* can sometimes get around the wall. For news, try Al Jazeera's English service www.aljazeera.com.

And it's not just Iran's government that does the blocking. Try not to use internet banking or even PayPal while you're in Iran, as international banking sites routinely block any IPs coming from Iran. The same also happens sometimes with Gmail.

Legal Matters

Like most things in Iran, the legal system is based on Islamic principles. The system, however, is not the strictest interpretation of Sharia law. Most of the same activities that are illegal in your country are illegal in Iran, but the penalties can be much harsher. For most minor crimes foreigners will probably be deported, though this is not an absolute. A few years ago a German businessman was sentenced to death for having sex with an unmarried Muslim woman, though he was eventually released after serving about two years in jail. The penalties for drug or alcohol use and smuggling are harsh. Carrying the smallest amount of hashish can result in a minimum six-month jail sentence; don't expect assistance from your embassy or a comfortable cell. Trafficking heroin or opium carries the death penalty.

There are two 'crimes' that foreigners may not be aware of. Homosexual activity is illegal and has resulted in the death penalty for some Iranians. Deliberate refusal to wear correct hejab (the Islamic dress code for women) can also result in a public flogging (although a foreigner will probably be deported).

Maps

Gita Shenasi (Map p44; ☎021-6670 3221; www.gitashenasi.com; 20 Ostad Shahriar St; ⊙8am-6.30pm Sat-Wed, to 1pm Thu; ⋈Teatr-e Shahr) in Tehran publishes maps of all major towns and cities, country maps and some mountain ranges. Some are in English, while others list streets and suburbs in English and everything else in Farsi. Maps are harder to find outside Tehran.

Gita Shenasi's *Iran Road Map* (1:2,250,000) is updated annually and is highly detailed. Outside Iran, look for the excellent, if dated, *Reise Know-How Iran* (1:1,500,000).

If you're carrying a smartphone, the **maps.me app** (www.maps.me) is excellent for most places in Iran, although it's not always perfect.

Money

The official unit of currency is the Iranian rial, but Iranians almost always talk in terms of tomans, a unit equal to 10 rials. With inflation soaring, we sometimes convert all prices into US dollars, although fewer Iranian businesses are doing this with each passing year.

For all intents and purposes, Iran for the visitor is a purely cash economy. No credit cards. No travellers cheques. Just bring cold, hard cash – preferably in high-denomination euros or US dollars printed since 1996. Apart from some hotels, carpet shops and tour agencies where you can pay in dollars or euros, all transactions are in rials. Where prices are quoted in euros we will do the same. Other major currencies, such as British pounds, Australian or Canadian dollars, Swiss francs and UAE dirhams, can be changed in Tehran and other big cities, if not smaller towns. However, Turkish lira are treated with scorn everywhere except close to the Turkish border; ditto for the Afghan, Azerbaijani, Turkmen and Pakistani currencies.

Whichever currency you choose, the most important thing to remember is to bring as much cash as you're likely to need, then a bit more. Getting your hands on money once you're inside Iran is a nightmare.

ATMs

Although Iran has a functioning network of ATMs (cashpoint machines), they can only be used with locally issued bank cards, so are useless to travellers unless you open a local account.

Banks

At the time of writing banks had been limited to changing money at a fixed rate, called the First Market, which was far lower than the floating market rate to be had at exchange shops. How long these mandated rates last is anybody's guess.

Although it sometimes seems as if every fourth building is a bank, only a few banks will actually change your money and then usually only US dollars, euros or, less often, British pounds in cash (and only after the day's rates arrive from Tehran between 9am and 10am). The best bet will always be your town's central branch (*markazi*) of Bank Melli (BMI), or the central branches of the other major banks: Bank Mellat, Bank Tejarat, Bank Sepah and Bank Saderat. You need your passport; bank staff will help with the Farsi paperwork.

Cash

There are coins for IR1, IR2, IR5, IR10, IR20, IR50, IR100, IR250, IR500, IR1000 and ITR5000. So rare are IR1

IF YOU ARE ARRESTED

In most cases, the primary motives for arresting a foreigner are usually curiosity, suspicion and the desire to appear powerful. In the unlikely event you are arrested:

➡ Keep cool, you are a tourist (*jahangardi*) and this is just a misunderstanding.

➡ It's best not to reply to, or appear to understand, any questions in Farsi.

➡ When you can understand the questions, they will likely be very detailed and you will be expected to answer. Do so politely, patiently, openly and diplomatically. Be complimentary about Iran and Iranians.

➡ Answer your interrogators so that their curiosity is satisfied, their suspicion allayed and their sense of their own self-importance flattered.

➡ Take special care not to incriminate yourself or anyone else, especially anyone Iranian, with a careless statement. Do not volunteer to show your photos if they include images of Iranians, who could be unwittingly dragged into something. Equally, don't actively try to hide them as this will raise suspicions.

➡ If things get heavy, ask to contact your embassy in Tehran.

coins (no longer minted) that they are considered lucky, despite being utterly worthless. Coins are marked only in Farsi numerals, while notes come in Persian and European numerals. There are notes for IR100 (rare), IR200 (rare), IR500, IR1000 (two varieties), IR2000 (two varieties), IR5000 (two varieties), IR10,000, IR20,000, IR50,000, IR100,000 and IR500,000.

Usually no-one cares what state rial notes are in, then out of the blue someone will reject one because it has a tiny tear or is too grubby. On the other hand, foreign currencies will be rejected if they are not clean and without any tears whatsoever.

Credit & Debit Cards

Um, no. Sanctions mean your (Western-issued) credit card will be useless in Iran. The only exceptions are a handful of carpet shops with foreign accounts, but if they can help at all (it's far from guaranteed) you'll pay a hefty 10% plus service charge for the privilege. Bring enough cash.

This can, at times, be rather annoying because locals now pay for just about everything, even very small purchases, using their local debit cards. The practice is so widespread that some places are even surprised when you try to pay in cash (and seem flummoxed by the whole concept of giving change). Some ticket machines (eg to use the Metro in Mashhad) don't even accept cash and will only accept locally issued cards for payment.

International Transfers

Sanctions have made it practically impossible to transfer money into or out of Iran without the assistance of a worldwide network of shady money dealers.

Money Changers

The easiest way to change money is at an official money-exchange office, in your hotel, with a taxi driver or in the jewellery section of the bazaar where the whole deal is done in seconds. In most banks it can take considerably longer. There's an exchange office offering correct (ie non-bank) rates on the departure level of Tehran's Imam Khomeini International Airport.

OFFICIAL MONEYCHANGERS

Exchange shops are reliable and can be found in most cities, usually signed in English and with rate boards in the window. When we went to press their rates were decided on the floating market, officially called the Second Market, which at that time bought you considerably more rials than changing at the bank (First Market) rate. The process is completely paperwork free.

BLACK MARKET

Changing money on the street is illegal and as long as exchange shops are allowed to trade money at market rates it makes little sense to do this. That said, the volatile state of the rial means there will be plenty of people prepared to buy your foreign exchange on the black market.

If you do change money on the street, expect to be treated like a total moron with no idea of current rates. You should demand at least the same rate as you'd get in the exchange shop and expect the changer to take a 'service fee'. Count the rials carefully (there are often notes missing or folded over), and don't hand over your bills until you're sure the count is correct.

Taxes & Refunds

In Iran, quoted prices and tariffs usually include all local taxes, but always ask if you're unsure.

There is no system of sales-tax refunds for tourists who purchase items in Iran.

Travellers Cheques

American Express. Leave home without it! Like credit cards, travellers cheques are useless in Iran.

Opening Hours

Opening and closing times can be erratic, but you can rely on most businesses closing Thursday afternoons and Friday (the Iranian weekend). Sights, especially government-operated museums and landmarks, open for longer during the warmer months.

The opening hours of many sights and business change between No Ruz (21 March) and 21 September, when many closing times are pushed back by an hour. In hotter areas many businesses close their doors from about noon until 4pm – along the blistering Persian Gulf coast doors stay shut until about 5pm – but businesses then operate in the relative cool of evening until about 8pm or 9pm.

Hours will generally accord (more or less) with the following:

Banks & Government Offices 8am to 2pm Saturday to Wednesday, 8am to noon Thursday

Museums 9am to 6pm summer, until 4pm or 5pm winter, closed on Monday

Post Offices 7.30am to 3pm Saturday to Thursday; some main offices open later

Private Businesses 8am or 9am to 5pm or 6pm Saturday to Wednesday, until noon Thursday; often closed over lunch

Restaurants Lunch noon to 3pm, dinner 6pm or 7pm to 10pm, or whenever the last diner leaves

Shops 9am to 8pm Saturday to Thursday, but likely to have a siesta between 1pm and 3.30pm and possibly close Thursday afternoon

Telephone Offices 8am to 8pm or 9pm; close earlier in small towns

Travel Agencies 9am to 5pm or 6pm Saturday to Wednesday, 7.30am to noon Thursday

Photography

Memory cards are widely available, especially in larger towns.

Photographing People

Most Iranians are happy to have their picture taken provided you ask first. However, where lone women are concerned it doesn't matter how nicely you ask, the answer will usually be no. Exceptions might be made for women photographers.

Offering to take pictures of your Iranian friends and post or email to them later is greatly appreciated – as long as you remember to post or email them. If you're not going to do it, don't promise to do so.

Restrictions

Avoid photographing airports, naval dockyards, nuclear reactors, roadblocks, military installations, embassies or consulates, prisons, telephone offices or police stations – basically, any government building at all. A group of Polish travellers were detained for hours in Bandar Abbas for taking a picture of the port, other travellers were arrested in Howraman-at-Takht for unknowingly taking a photo of a hill that happened to be the Iraqi border. If you get caught, don't try to be anything except a dumb tourist.

Post

Postage is less reliable and much more expensive than it once was and can take quite a while. Postcards can reach Europe in four or five days, but as some readers have reported they might also take two months. Post boxes are rare except outside post offices. Poste restante is unreliable. If you're sending mail to an Iranian address that's complicated or remote, try to get the address in Farsi.

Parcels

Sending a parcel from Iran can involve much form shuffling, but your package will usually arrive. Take your passport and unwrapped goods to the parcel post counter (daftar-e amanat-e posti) at the main post office (postkhuneh-ye markazi) in a provincial capital before 2pm. They will be checked, packaged and signed for in triplicate. There are three parcel services – pishtaz (express), havayi (airmail) and surface. Rates can vary, but a 5kg parcel to anywhere by surface mail will cost less than US$100; air mail is more expensive. The customs officer on duty generally has discretion over what can be posted abroad, so be nice.

Public Holidays

Public holidays commemorate either religious or secular events. It's worth staying aware of the dates, especially if you are planning to extend your visa. Government offices and just about everything else will close for the morning, at least, on a holiday, but many small businesses open after lunch. Transport functions fairly normally and hotels remain open, but many restaurants will close. Holidays are sometimes extended for a day if they fall near the Iranian weekend. In Tehran, public holidays are sometimes announced at short notice when air pollution reaches dangerous levels. In recent years that has been in mid-July and late November/early December. These holidays affect government offices, schools, universities, sporting arenas and can (but not always) include museums.

Islamic events are based on the lunar calendar and dates move forward 10 or 11 days each year.

Religious Holidays

Religious holidays follow the Muslim lunar calendar, which means the corresponding dates in the Western calendar move forward by 10 or 11 days every year.

Tasua (9 Moharram, 19 September 2018)

Ashura (10 Moharram, 20 September 2018) The anniversary of the martyrdom of Hossein, the third Shiite imam, in battle at Karbala in October AD 680. This is

RIALS OR TOMANS?

No sooner have you arrived in Iran than you will come up against the local practice of talking about prices in tomans, even though the currency is denominated in rials. One toman is worth 10 rials, so it's a bit like shopkeepers in Europe asking for '10' whenever they wanted €1.

To make matters worse, taxi drivers and shopkeepers will often say 'one' as shorthand for IR10,000. However, before you consider cancelling your trip on the grounds of commercial confusion, rest assured that after a few days you'll understand that the five fingers the taxi driver just showed you means IR50,000. And as you start to get a feel for what things cost, you'll understand that if something sounds too good to be true – or too bad – it probably is.

In the interim, you can always have the price written down, and then to double-check ask whether it's in rials or tomans – using a calculator is handy, too, as the numbers show in Western rather than Arabic numerals.

And just when you've mastered the rial, remember that there are plans to replace it with the toman as Iran's official currency over the coming years.

celebrated with religious theatre and sombre parades.

Arbaeen (20 Safar, 10 November 2018) The 40th day after Ashura.

Martyrdom of the Prophet Mohammed (28 Safar, 19 November 2018)

Martyrdom of Imam Reza (30 Safar, 9 November 2018)

Birth of the Prophet Mohammed (17 Rabi'-ol-Avval, 20 November 2018)

Martyrdom of Fatima (3 Jamadi-l-Okhra, 19 February 2018) Fatima was the daughter of Prophet Mohammed.

Birth of Imam Ali (13 Rajab, 30 March 2018)

Ascension of Holy Prophet (27 Rajab, 13 April 2018) Maabath.

Birthday of Imam Mahdi (15 Shaban, 1 May 2018)

Martyrdom of Imam Ali (21 Ramazan, 5 June 2018)

Eid al-Fitr (1 Shavval, 15 June 2018) The Festival of the Breaking of the Fast that marks the end of Ramazan. After sunset on the last day of Ramazan large meals are consumed across the country.

Martyrdom of Imam Jafar Sadegh (25 Shavval, 9 July 2018)

Eid-e Ghorban (10 Zu-I-Hejjeh, 22 August 2018) Marks the day when Abraham offered to sacrifice his son. Expect to see plenty of sheep being butchered.

Qadir-e Khom (Eid-al-Ghadir; 18 Zu-I-Hejjeh, 30 August 2018) The day Prophet Mohammed appointed Imam Ali as his successor while returning to Mecca.

RAMAZAN (RAMADAN)

During the month known in Iran as Ramazan, Muslims are expected to perform a dawn-to-dusk fast that includes abstaining from all drinks (including water) and from smoking. This is seen less as an unpleasant ordeal than a chance to perform a ritual cleansing of body and mind. Some people, especially in cities, don't fully observe the fast, but most do for at least part of the month. Some Muslims are exempted from the fast (eg pregnant and

menstruating women, travellers, the elderly and the sick), as are non-Muslims, but they mustn't eat or drink in front of others who are fasting.

Ramazan can be a trying period, particularly if it falls in summer when the days are that much longer and the heat and hunger tend to shorten tempers. Businesses and shops keep odd hours. However, public transport continues to function and travellers are exempt from the fast so you don't need to worry about finding food on flights, trains or bus trips, and many hotels keep their restaurants open. Other restaurants either close altogether or open only after dark. Many shops selling food remain open throughout Ramazan, so you can buy food to eat in your room.

Although you shouldn't have many problems in larger cities, in rural areas finding any food might be difficult during daylight hours.

Secular Holidays

Secular holidays follow the Persian solar calendar, and usually fall on the same day each year according to the Western calendar.

Magnificent Victory of the Islamic Revolution of Iran (11 February, 22 Bahman) The anniversary of Khomeini's coming to power in 1979.

Oil Nationalisation Day (20 March, 29 Esfand) Commemorates the 1951 nationalisation of the Anglo-Iranian Oil Company.

No Ruz (21–24 March, 1–4 Farvardin) Iranian New Year.

Islamic Republic Day (1 April, 12 Farvardin) The anniversary of the establishment of the Islamic Republic of Iran in 1979.

Sizdah be Dar (2 April, 13 Farvardin) 'Nature Day' is the 13th day of the Iranian New Year, when Iranians traditionally leave their houses for the day.

Heart-Rending Departure of the Great Leader of the Islamic Republic of Iran (4 June, 14 Khordad) Commemorates the death of Ayatollah Khomeini in 1989. About 500,000 Iranians flock to Tehran,

Qom (where he trained and lived) and the village of Khomein (where he was born).

Anniversary of the Arrest of Ayatollah Khomeini (5 June, 15 Khordad) In 1963 Khomeini was arrested after urging Muslims of the world to rise up against the superpowers.

NO RUZ

No Ruz, the Iranian New Year, is a huge family celebration on a par with Christmas in the West. From a practical point of view, Iran virtually shuts down between 21 March (the beginning of new year) and Sizdah be Dar (2 April). Finding hotel accommodation (especially midrange and top end) is very tough from about 17 March until 2 April and all forms of long-distance public transport are heavily booked, though savaris run more frequently making some shorter trips relatively easy. Government offices and most businesses, including many restaurants, close from 21 to 25 March inclusive, and many stay shut the full two weeks. It's not impossible to travel during No Ruz, but think twice before heading to popular tourist destinations such as Esfahan, Mashhad, Yazd, Shiraz and anywhere on the Persian Gulf or Caspian coasts. Mountain areas such as rural Kordistan and primarily business cities such as Tehran and Kermanshah remain relatively uncrowded. On the positive side, museums and tourist sites stay open longer hours while some normally closed attractions will open.

IRANIAN CALENDARS

Three calendars are in common use in Iran: the Persian solar calendar is the one in official and everyday use; the Muslim lunar calendar is used for Islamic religious matters; and the Western (Gregorian) calendar is used in dealing with foreigners and in some history books. Newspapers carry all three dates. When entering Iran the stamp in your passport will be in Farsi and refer to the Persian calendar. Be sure to confirm the Western date so you don't overstay your visa; check www.payvand.com/calendar.

Persian Calendar

The modern Persian solar calendar, a direct descendant of the ancient Zoroastrian calendar, is calculated from the first day of spring in the year of the Hejira, the flight of the Prophet Mohammed from Mecca to Medina in AD 622. It has 365 days (366 every leap year), with its New Year (No Ruz) falling on 21 March according to the Western calendar. The names of the Persian months are as follows:

SEASON	PERSIAN MONTH	APPROXIMATE EQUIVALENT	SEASON	PERSIAN MONTH	APPROXIMATE EQUIVALENT
spring	Farvardin	21 Mar–20 Apr	autumn	Mehr	23 Sep–22 Oct
(bahar)	Ordibehesht	21 Apr–21 May	(pa'iz)	Aban	23 Oct–21 Nov
	Khordad	22 May–21 Jun		Azar	22 Nov–21 Dec
summer	Tir	22 Jun–22 Jul	winter	Dei	22 Dec–20 Jan
(tabestan)	Mordad	23 Jul–22 Aug	(zamestan)	Bahman	21 Jan–19 Feb
	Shahrivar	23 Aug–22 Sep		Esfand	20 Feb–20 Mar

Muslim Calendar

The Muslim calendar starts from the month before the Hejira and is based on the lunar year of 354 or 355 days, so it is out of step with the Persian solar calendar by some 40 years.

Zoroastrian Calendar

The Zoroastrian calendar works to a solar year of 12 months of 30 days, with five additional days. The week has no place in this system, and each of the 30 days of the month is named after and presided over by its own angel or archangel. The 1st, 8th, 15th and 23rd of each month are holy days. As in the Persian calendar, the Zoroastrian year begins in March at the vernal equinox and except for Andarmaz, which replaces Esfand, the months are the same.

Smoking

Smoking is banned in all public places and has been since 2007. It's also banned in cars, although enforcement on this is somewhat lax. The ban also extends to smoking *qalyans* (water pipes), which has hit teahouses and coffee shops hard, with many now empty and devoid of atmosphere. Enforcement is more lax in rural teahouses.

Telephone

Iran's country code is ☑98. To dial out of Iran call ☑00; if calling from outside Iran, drop the initial 0 from all area codes. Phone numbers and area codes change with disconcerting regularity, but in general numbers include a three-digit area code and a seven-digit number. The exception is Tehran, where ☑021 is followed by an eight-digit number.

More than 90% of Iranians have mobile-phone access and most travellers buy a SIM card on arrival. If you need a payphone, cards are available in newsstands, though most are for domestic calls only. In our experience, every second card phone is broken. Local calls are so cheap that most midrange and better hotels, bus and airport terminals have a public telephone permitting free local calls.

International calls are also relatively cheap (US$0.20) per minute to most countries. These rates can be had at small, private telephone offices (usually open from about 7.30am until 9pm), where you give the number to the front desk and wait for a booth to become available. You'll normally be charged a minimum of three minutes. In many cities international calling cards are available from newsstands, grocery stores and *cafenets* (internet cafes).

Mobile Phones

Iran has several mobile-phone networks but only two – government-owned MCI and MTN Irancell (www.irancell.ir), which is owned by the Iranian government, and South African group MTN – enjoy wide coverage.

Irancell has a one-month tourist SIM card sold at a booth upstairs in Tehran's Imam Khomeini International Airport for IR500,000. The SIM gives IR200,000 worth of calls and texts (which should cover most eventualities over the course of a month) plus 5GB of data. Top up your credit at vendors displaying yellow and blue MTN signs; vendors will usually charge about 10% more than the card's face value. Full pricing is available in English on Irancell's website.

Irancell SIMs allow GPRS data transfer after a free registration process, and WiMAX has been rolled out in several cities. In our experience the GPRS service was unreliable and download speeds slow. As a general rule, 4G is available in big cities and 3G in mid-sized ones, while there's very basic pedal power in rural places, if at all.

Time

Time throughout Iran is 3½ hours ahead of Greenwich Mean Time (GMT), so noon in Tehran is 3.30am in New York; 8.30am in London; 10.30am in Turkey; 11.30am in Azerbaijan; noon in Afghanistan; 1.30pm in Pakistan and Turkmenistan (note this when preparing to cross borders); and 6.30pm in Sydney.

Daylight saving is observed between No Ruz (usually 21 March) and 22 September.

Toilets

Most Iranians have squat toilets at home, but the majority of better hotels have thrones or a choice of loos. Almost all public toilets are squats and while some are regularly cleaned, others are definitely not. Still, there are usually enough options that you won't have to enter anywhere too stinky. Mosques, petrol stations, bus and train stations and airport terminals always have toilets, sans toilet paper.

Fortunately, most small grocery stores stock toilet paper or tissues. All but the cheapest guesthouses supply toilet paper too, though sometimes you'll need to ask. That said, it's worth remembering that the wise traveller carries an emergency stash of TP. Whatever you use, most plumbing is not designed for paper so put your used sheets in the bin not the bowl.

Tourist Information

The ominous-sounding Ministry of Culture and Islamic Guidance is responsible for 'cultural affairs, propaganda, literature and arts, audiovisual production, archaeology, preservation of the cultural heritage, tourism, press and libraries'. As the list suggests, tourism is not its top priority.

Cultural Heritage offices, universally known as Miras Faranghi in Farsi and often housed in restored historic buildings in provincial capitals, dispense information. They

don't see too many walk-in tourists but will usually try to find someone who speaks English and search around in filing cabinet drawers until you have a showbag full of brochures, maps, postcards and other promotional paraphernalia. Some cities also have more proactive private or semi-private tourist offices, where basic information is available in English and guides and tours can be arranged.

There are small information booths in train stations and bus terminals, where staff are usually good on timetable information, and international airports, where they might speak English and have a map, but little else.

Travellers with Disabilities

Facilities aimed at travellers with disabilities are rare, and while Iranians are always willing to help, visiting here can be something of an obstacle course. Wheelchair ramps are starting to appear, although they remain exceptional. Only the more upmarket hotels are guaranteed to have elevators big enough for wheelchairs; disabled accessible toilets are very rare indeed. Bring your own medications and prescriptions.

For more information on travelling with disabilities, check out the **Society for Accessible Travel & Hospitality** (www.sath.org). Based in the US, it offers assistance and advice.

Visas

See p27 for details on getting and extending a visa.

Transport

GETTING THERE & AWAY

International sanctions have made Iran increasingly isolated, but it is fairly simple to get into the country on a plane, by train from Turkey or across numerous border crossings from neighbouring countries to the north.

Flights and tours can be booked online at lonelyplanet. com/bookings.

Entering the Country

Assuming you have a visa, most immigration and border officials are efficient and tourists rarely get too much hassle. Land borders can take longer if you're on a bus or train. Women need to be adequately covered from the moment they get off the plane or arrive at the border.

Arriving without a visa is risky, as the visa-on-arrival process sees a lot of people turned away.

Passports

Iran will not issue visas to Israeli passport holders, and people with an Israeli passport will be turned away at the border (you won't get on a flight to Iran with an Israeli passport). Similarly, having an Israeli stamp in any other passport will see you turned away or put on the next flight out. And it's not just Israeli stamps – they check carefully for exit stamps out of Jordan or Egypt at border points that imply that you must have entered Israel.

Air

The vast majority of international flights come to Tehran. However, some travellers are choosing to start or end their trip in Shiraz, saving some backtracking.

Airports & Airlines
INTERNATIONAL AIRPORTS

Tehran's Imam Khomeini International Airport (IKIA) sees most of Iran's international air traffic. It's small, so delays are possible. Elsewhere, Shiraz, Esfahan, Mashhad, Tabriz, Bandar Abbas and Kish (in that order) are potentially useful arrival or departure points, while Abadan, Ahvaz and Zahedan are less useful.

Iran Air is the national airline and has the Homa, a mythical bird, as its symbol. As the government-owned carrier, it offers service with an Islamic flavour (ie no pork, no alcohol and no exposed hair on the hostesses).

Note that Caspian Airlines, Kish Air and Taban Air have all had fatal crashes in the past 10 years.

TICKETS & ROUTES

Buying tickets in Iran for flights from Iran is best done through an agent – you can only buy tickets online if you're using an Iranian credit

---

CLIMATE CHANGE & TRAVEL

Every form of transport that relies on carbon-based fuel generates CO_2, the main cause of human-induced climate change. Modern travel is dependent on aeroplanes, which might use less fuel per kilometre per person than most cars but travel much greater distances. The altitude at which aircraft emit gases (including CO_2) and particles also contributes to their climate change impact. Many websites offer 'carbon calculators' that allow people to estimate the carbon emissions generated by their journey and, for those who wish to do so, to offset the impact of the greenhouse gases emitted with contributions to portfolios of climate-friendly initiatives throughout the world. Lonely Planet offsets the carbon footprint of all staff and author travel.

or debit card. The Middle East is a popular staging point, with several airlines connecting Tehran, Esfahan and Shiraz to the world via various Gulf airports. East and Southeast Asia also have quite a few services, but there are no direct flights from North or South America. Instead, most people come through Europe, where a host of airlines have regular flights to Tehran, or the Middle East.

INTERNATIONAL AIRLINES FLYING TO & FROM IRAN

Aegean (www.aegeanair.com) Athens

Aeroflot (www.aeroflot.com) Moscow

Air Arabia (www.airarabia.com) Sharjah

Air Asia (www.airasia.com) Malaysia

Air India (www.airindia.com) Delhi

Alitalia (www.alitalia.com) Rome

Ariana Afghan Airlines (www.fly ariana.com) Kabul, Mazar-e Sharif

AtlasGlobal (www.atlasglb.com) İstanbul

Austrian Airlines (www.aua. com) Vienna

Azerbaijan Airlines (www.azal. az) Baku

Emirates (www.emirates.com) Dubai

Etihad Airways (www.etihadair ways.com) Abu Dhabi

KLM (www.klm.com) Amsterdam

Kuwait Airways (www.kuwait-airways.com) Kuwait City

Lufthansa (www.lufthansa.com) Frankfurt, Munich, Zürich

Pegasus (www.flypgs.com) İstanbul

Qatar Airways (www.qatarair ways.com) Doha

Saudi Arabian Airlines (www. saudiaairlines.com) Jeddah, Riyadh

Syria Air (www.syriaair.com) Damascus

Tajik Air (www.tajikairlines.com) Dushanbe

Turkish Airlines (www.turkishair lines.com) İstanbul

Ukraine International Airlines (www.flyuia.com) Kyiv

IRANIAN AIRLINES

All airlines are based in Tehran except for Taban Air, which is in Mashhad.

Caspian Airlines (www.caspian. aero) Damascus, Dubai, İstanbul, Kyiv, Yerevan

Iran Air (☎021-4662 1888; www. iranair.com) Amsterdam, Ankara, Baku, Beijing, Beirut, Cologne, Copenhagen, Damascus, Doha, Dubai, Frankfurt, Gothenburg, Hamburg, İstanbul, Karachi, Kuala Lumpur, Kuwait, London, Milan, Mumbai, Paris, Stockholm, Tashkent, Vienna

Kish Air (www.kishairline.com) Damascus, Dubai, İstanbul

Mahan Air (www.mahan.aero) Almaty, Baghdad, Bangkok, Bir-mingham, Damascus, Delhi, Dubai, Dusseldorf, İstanbul, Kabul, Kuala Lumpur, Phuket, Shanghai

Taban Air (www.taban.aero) International flights to cities in Central Asia and the Middle East

Land

It's possible to arrive by land from seven countries. Crossing from Turkey is easy and from Armenia, Azerbaijan and Turkmenistan is do-able with varying degrees of hassle. The borders to Afghanistan and Pakistan are straightforward, but check security before you head to these – both were off-limits at the time of writing. Foreigners cannot cross into Iraq proper, though the

border to Iraqi Kurdistan is open intermittently.

Border Crossings
AFGHANISTAN

The border at Dogharon, 20km east of Taybad, is open but we strongly warn against crossing this border.

ARMENIA

The border between Iran and Armenia is only 35km long, with one crossing point in Iran at Norduz (p96). Armenian visas are issued at the border, though sometimes the bus leaves before you have your visa! Apart from that, it's pretty smooth.

AZERBAIJAN

The Azeri border has at least three recognised crossings. You can cross between Astara (Azerbaijan) and Astara (Iran), and Culfa (Azerbaijan) and Jolfa (p95) (Iran), the latter leading to the exclave of Nakhchivan, from where you cannot enter Armenia and must fly to get to Baku. The third option, good if you want to go to Jolfa from Baku, is at Bilesuva, the border used by Baku–Nakhchivan buses and plenty of Azeris on their way to Tabriz. Visas are *not* issued at any of these land borders.

Direct buses between Tehran and Baku, via Astara, are available but are not such a good idea because you'll probably get stuck for hours while your conveyance gets a full cavity search, which is considerably less interesting than it sounds. Taking one bus to the border, crossing as a pedestrian and finding another bus is *much* easier.

The train line is meant to open from Baku to Rasht in 2018 but don't hold your breath.

IRAQ

Border crossings to Iraqi Kurdistan are open to foreign tourists at Haj Omran, Bashmaq and Sayran Ban. Parvis Khan, Mehran and Khosravi are the border crossings into Iraq. Western government advisories contain strong warnings against travel in the areas in which all of these border crossings are located.

PAKISTAN

Along the 830km border with Pakistan, the only recognised crossing for foreigners is between Mirjaveh (Iran) and Taftan (Pakistan). Crossing this border is considered highly dangerous for Western travellers.

TURKEY

The main road crossing to/from Turkey is at Gürbulak (Turkey) and Bazargan (Iran; p81), where there are hotels, moneychanging facilities and regular transport on either side of the border, though staying in nearby Maku is more pleasant.

Foreigners can also cross at Esendere (40km from Yüksekova, Turkey) and Sero, near Orumiyeh (p91) in Iran. There is nowhere to stay on either side and transport can be infrequent. Motorists usually cross at Bazargan. See the boxed text for more information.

TURKMENISTAN

There are three border posts open to foreigners along this 1206km-long frontier. From west to east, there is inconvenient and little-used Incheh Borun/Gyzyl-Etrek, Bajgiran crossing linking Mashhad and the Turkmen capital Ashgabat, and Sarakhs and Saraghs for those heading east; the area around the latter should be visited with caution. You must change transport at all three crossings. See the boxed text (p255) for more information.

The new train line from near Gorgan crossing at Gyzyl-Etrek has officially opened but there are no passenger services yet.

The paperwork and organisation involved in travelling to Turkmenistan is a hassle; **Stantours** (www.stantours. com) seems to be the best at making it all go (relatively) smoothly.

Bus

Travelling by bus you have two options: long haul or short hops.

Buses between Tehran and İstanbul and/or Ankara (about 36 to 42 hours) cost about US$60. They leave from Terminal-e Jonub and go via Terminal-e Gharb; several bus companies offer the service, but usually it's just one bus that runs. Those in the know swear it's better to take the Ankara bus, which is full of students and embassy workers, rather than the İstanbul bus, which is full of traders and therefore more likely to be taken apart at customs.

Alternatively, take it more slowly and enjoy eastern Turkey and western Iran

along the way. By taking a bus to – but not across – either border you'll avoid having to wait for dozens of fellow passengers to clear customs. It's usually possible to cross from Erzurum (Turkey) to Tabriz (Iran) in one day if you start early. It takes longer in winter when high mountain passes near the border can be snowbound.

Car & Motorcycle

To bring your own vehicle into Iran, you must be more than 18 years old and have an international driving permit. For the vehicle, you'll need a *carnet de passage* (temporary importation document).

Assuming your papers are in order, crossing into and out of Turkey is usually pretty straightforward. Third-party insurance is compulsory, and if you don't already have it, it can be bought in Maku, near the border. If you already have insurance check that it's valid for Iran (this is increasingly unlikely due to sanctions) and accredited with Iran Bimeh, the Iranian Green Card Bureau.

No one but the police is allowed to have a motorbike with an engine larger than 150cc. However, foreigners in transit can ride bikes of any size. With big bikes so rare, expect to attract plenty of attention.

Shipping vehicles across the Persian Gulf is possible but tedious, but a reasonable number of people do it nonetheless. Rules and ferry times change regularly.

Lonely Planet Thorn Tree (www. lonelyplanet.com/thorntree) Plenty of trip reports.

Africa Overland Network (www. africa-overland.net) Asia branch has links to blogs by overlanders.

Horizons Unlimited (www. horizonsunlimited.com) Search the HUBB forum, which has details on borders, fuel, shipping and repair shops.

Train

The train from İstanbul to Tehran via Ankara and Tabriz

CHECKPOINTS

If you're travelling from Bandar Abbas, you're likely to have to stop at checkpoints designed to catch smugglers. In some cases a customs official or policeman will get onto the bus and walk up and down, presumably looking for obvious smugglers or 'illegal aliens', before waving the bus on. However, searches can be much more thorough and time consuming.

is called the Trans-Asia Express. It runs weekly in either direction and, at the time of writing, trains on the 2968km journey departed İstanbul on Tuesday, and left Tehran on Wednesday; it takes 70 hours and costs about €50 each way. Seating is in comfortable 1st-class couchettes with four berths. Check www.raja.ir or the Turkish railways website at www.tcdd.gov.tr for the latest info.

The Trans-Asia Express is two trains: an Iranian train between Tehran and Van, on the shores of Lake Van in eastern Turkey, and a Turkish train from Tatvan to Ankara and İstanbul. It's evoked some strong feelings among readers, usually relating to the concept of 'express', although complaints have been fewer in recent years. Delays are likely in winter when snow can block the tracks and low temperatures can freeze the plumbing. However, there's a distinctly romantic touch to such a long train trip, and in either direction it's a great way to meet Iranians.

Sea

Iran has 2410km of coastal boundaries along the Persian Gulf, Gulf of Oman and Caspian Sea, but there are relatively few ways to enter or leave Iran by sea.

The main shipping agency for trips across the Persian Gulf is **Valfajr-8** (www. valfajr.ir), which operates car ferries and catamarans between Bandar Abbas and Sharjah once or twice a week (other routes listed on the website no longer run), as well as car ferries between Bandar-e Lengeh and Dubai. As services are infrequent, oft-delayed and more expensive than flying, few people bother.

NFC (☎076-3522 3322; www. nfc.om) operates a car ferry from Bandar Abbas to Khasab and Muscat (both Oman), but services are fairly unreliable.

GETTING AROUND

Air

Domestic air fares in Iran are low and flights on most routes are frequent. For possibilities, check out www.parvazyab. com, though you'll need your best Farsi.

Airlines in Iran

Iran Air is the largest among a growing roster of domestic airlines and boasts an extensive network of flights, covering most provincial capitals. Domestic prices are set by the government, so it doesn't matter which airline you fly, the price will be the same. For tickets it's best to use one of the many travel agencies, where you'll get all the options, rather than an airline office.

Iran's domestic airlines:

ATA (www.ataair.ir)

Atrak (www.atrakair.com)

Caspian Airlines (www.caspian. aero)

Iran Air (☎021-4662 1888; www. iranair.com)

Iran Airtours (www.iat.aero)

Iran Aseman (www.iaa.ir)

Kish Air (www.kishairline.com)

Meraj Airlines (www.merajair lines.ir)

Mahan Air (www.mahan.aero)

Qeshm Air (www.qeshm-air.com)

Taban Air (www.taban.aero)

When making a booking, check the aircraft type and avoid any clunking old Tupolevs that have yet to fall out of Iran's skies. Mahan Air, Iran Air and Iran Aseman are the most reliable and have the most routes. Whichever airline you choose you'll find delays are common. Despite this, get to the airport at least an hour ahead of domestic departures.

Getting a domestic ticket from outside Iran is difficult. Sanctions mean paying for a seat online (if online booking is available) doesn't work. It is theoretically possible to call an Iran Air office outside Iran and get a booking reference, which you then pay for at an Iran Air office in Iran or at Mehrabad Airport in Tehran. More reliably, use any Iranian-based tour agency.

Bicycle

Excellent roads, friendly people and a relatively small risk of theft mean Iran sounds like an ideal cycling destination. And that's what most cyclists report. It's not, however, all easy. Vast distances, dodgy traffic and hot, tedious stretches of desert road – not to mention seasonal winds – can get tiring. And in recent years some cyclists have reported a more hostile road environment, particularly from young men on motorbikes. For women, you'll need to stay covered up or expect unwanted attention. Male cyclists report that wearing cycling gear when actually on the road is OK, as long as you have clothes at hand to cover up as soon as you stop.

As you head east you'll need to carry plenty of water and food to last the long desert stretches, a decent map and a phrasebook. Camping is possible but there's no guarantee your presence will be welcome – it's better to ask to pitch your tent at a mosque. Spare parts can be hard to find and there is nowhere to rent bicycles for long distances, so bring your own.

Boat

The only ferry services are between Iran's Persian Gulf coast (usually Bandar Abbas) and Kish, Qeshm and Hormoz Islands. Routes include the following:

➡ Bandar Abbas to Qeshm and Hormuz Islands

➡ Hormuz to Qeshm Islands

➡ Bandar-e Pol to Laft-e Kohneh (Qeshm)

→ Bandar-e Charak to Kish Island

During No Ruz, there are also car ferry services from Bandar-e Lengeh to Kish Island.

Bus

In Iran, if you can't get somewhere by bus (or minibus), the chances are no one wants to go there. More than 20 bus companies offer thousands of services on buses that are cheap, comfortable and frequent. The quality of bus drivers does vary, but the government does its best to minimise 'insh'Allah' (God willing) attitudes by aggressively enforcing speed limits. Speeds are recorded and drivers must stop and show this log to highway police every 100km or so. Fares are set by the government so variations are small. Except on very short trips, standing is not allowed.

Don't be confused by the names of the destinations on a bus. It's common for a bus travelling between, for example, Khorramabad and Ahvaz, to have 'Tehran-İstanbul' written on the front or side in English. Similarly, phrases such as 'Lovely bus' are not always a fair reflection of reality. There are no bus passes.

A useful resource for bus information is the Farsi-only www.payaneha.com.

Bus Companies & Types

Most bus companies are co-operatives and were formerly known as Cooperative Bus Company No X (Sherkat-e Ta'avoni Shomare X), or whatever number it is. Most now have more varied names, but in the terminal they might still direct you to, for example, 'ta'avoni hasht' (cooperative number 8). The best ta'avo-nis, with the most extensive networks, are **TBT** (Taavoni 15) and **Iran Peyma** (www.iranpeymaesfahan.com), often

with the word 'Ta'avoni' or 'Bus No One' written on it.

For a bit more comfort, **Seiro Safar** (www.en.seiro safar.ir) offers newer, better buses for a little extra cost, though most travellers don't bother seeking out a specific company and just take whichever is the next bus going their way.

There are two main types of bus:

Mahmooly Meaning 'normal', these are Volvo, Scania or similar intercity coaches. The driver is accompanied by one or two attendants, who hand out packaged food and handle luggage. Most have toilets. Older, 1960s-era Mercedes *mahmooly* buses have mostly been retired on account of their pollution.

VIP More luxurious because they have seats that recline almost fully and more service. They operate on major routes, such as Tehran to Esfahan or Mashhad, and cost about 50% more than a *mahmooly*.

Minibus

Minibuses are often used for shorter distances linking larger cities and towns to surrounding villages. Sometimes they're an alternative to the bus, but usually there's no choice; just take whatever is going your way. Minibuses are particularly popular along the Caspian Sea coast, and between Caspian towns and Tehran.

Minibuses are marginally more expensive than buses, and can be faster because they have fewer passengers and spend less time dropping off and picking up. On the downside, they're uncomfortable and usually leave only when they're full, which can mean a wait.

Bus Terminals

Most bus terminals are located at the edge of town and are easily reached by shuttle or private taxi. Some cities have more than one bus terminal; if in doubt, ask at your hotel or charter a taxi to the relevant terminal. Tell the

driver '*terminal-e* (your destination)' and he'll know where to drop you – pronounce 'terminal' with a prolonged 'aal' at the end.

Bus terminals are filled with the offices of individual bus companies, though timetables are rarely in English. Just ask 'Shiraz?', 'Esfahan?' or wherever and you'll be directed to the right desk, or listen for your destination being screamed out when a bus is about to leave. Terminals always have somewhere selling food, and larger terminals might have a police station, left-luggage facility and even a hotel.

If you're leaving a secondary town, such as Zanjan or Kashan, you may need to go to a major roundabout to board a passing bus, rather than at the terminal. Locals will point you to the right place.

Reservations

You can buy tickets up to a week in advance from bus company ticket offices in town or at the terminal. Between major cities, such as Esfahan and Tehran, buses leave at least every hour between about 6am and midnight. In medium-sized towns, such as Hamadan and Kerman, buses to nearer locations leave every hour or so, but longer trips (and any cross-desert trip) will often be overnight. In smaller places, where there may be only one or two buses a day to your destination, it is essential to book ahead.

There are often no-shows for bus trips, so seats can magically appear on otherwise full buses just before departure. Alternatively, you might be offered the back seat.

Tickets are almost always in Farsi, so learn the Arabic numbers to check the day of departure, time of departure, bus number, seat number, platform number and fare...or ask a local.

The Journey

Expect to average about 60km/h on most journeys.

On most trips of more than three hours, you'll stop at roadside restaurants serving cheap food. Ice-cold water is normally available on the bus and is safe to drink. Every two hours or so the driver will stop to have his tachograph checked by the police as a precaution against speeding. If it's summer, try to get a seat on the side facing away from the sun.

Car & Motorcycle

Self-drive 'holidays' don't really exist in Iran unless you bring your own car, which is exactly what a steady stream of travellers used to do en route between Europe and Asia. The trail is largely empty these days, thanks to the dangers of travelling in southeastern Iran and (more particularly) southwestern Pakistan. When it was still a well-worn trail, most reported the country driving was great and the city driving was not. If you're considering an overland journey these sites have the stories of those who've gone before:

➡ www.africa-overland.net/Asia

➡ www.horizonsunlimited.com

Bring Your Own Vehicle

If you are driving your own vehicle, you should always slow down and get ready to stop at roadblocks. Usually if you wind down your window, smile nicely, and give the officials your best 'I-don't-know-what-to-do-and-I-don't-speak-Farsi' look, you will be waved straight through. At worst you'll have to show your passport, licence and vehicle documents. Be sure to find a hotel with safe parking when in the southeast.

Hossein Ravanyar of **Iran Overland** (www.iranoverland.com) is a guide/fixer who specialises in helping people with carnet trouble and getting their cars across the border at the Astara crossing.

Driving Licences

To drive in Iran you need an international driving licence. Get one from the national automobile association in your home country.

Fuel & Spare Parts

While fuel in Iran is not as dirt cheap as it once was, it will still be a bargain compared with what you pay at home. Except in the desert, you'll find large towns with *benzin* (petrol) stations at least every 100km. Not all stations sell diesel and there is usually nothing written on the pump to differentiate it from *benzin* – be sure to ask. Fuel quality is poor – drivers told us most *benzin* was just 71 octane – so don't expect the same mileage as at home. More problematic, though, are the long queues in towns within 100km or so of a border, where well-organised smuggling operations leave little for locals. Iranian motor oil can also be of dubious quality. International brands are safer.

Expect to pay around IR10,000 to IR12,000 per litre.

Even the tiniest settlements have repair shops. The price for repair work is open to negotiation but you won't have much choice when it comes to spare parts. In the height of summer, scalding heat makes tyre blowouts fairly common.

Hire

It's theoretically possible to rent a car but unusual. Instead, 'car rental' usually means chartering a taxi and/or private driver, either privately or through a travel agency.

Insurance

Your vehicle will need a *carnet de passage* and a green card, both of which you should organise before you arrive.

Road Conditions

Road surfaces are generally excellent. On the other hand, driving at night is more dangerous because of occasional unmarked potholes and the risk of running into tractors and other vehicles crawling along the road with no lights. On intercity roads most signs are in English and Farsi. All cities have street signs, many in English and Farsi.

Road Hazards

Iranian drivers in the cities... Camels in the deserts... Unmarked speed bumps everywhere. The last, often at the edges of towns, are both highly annoying and dangerous, and you'll often be completely unaware they exist until your car suddenly gets airborne as you launch over the bump.

If you're in an accident the Iranian involved will probably call the local traffic police. If you're alone, call the emergency number – ☑110 for police, ☑115 for ambulance. You should never move the vehicle from the road until the police have come to make their report. As a foreigner, you'll probably be held responsible.

Road Rules

Lanes? What are they? Driving across Iran is not a task to be taken lightly. In theory, everyone drives on the right but this can't be depended upon; faced with a one-way street going the wrong way, the average Iranian driver sees nothing wrong with reversing down it. Take 10 Iranian drivers and an otherwise deserted road and they will form a convoy so tightly packed that each can read the speedometer of the car in front. 'Optimum braking distance' is not widely understood.

Take comfort, however, in the knowledge that most foreign drivers make it across Iran without too much trouble.

Hitching & Ride-Sharing

Hitching is never entirely safe in any country, and we don't recommend it. Travellers who decide to hitch should understand that they are taking a small but potentially serious risk and in Iran, women should not even consider it.

For men, however, it's doable. Hitching, as understood in the West, is a novel concept in Iran. Although you will often see people standing by the roadside, they are actually waiting for space in a bus, minibus or shared taxi, for which they expect to pay. Occasionally drivers will offer foreigners a free ride in return for practising their English or out of simple hospitality. Like anywhere, you're most likely to find rides in more remote areas. Host drivers will be typically generous, possibly sharing food and cigarettes, all while refusing attempts to pay for them. You should be prepared to pay something, however, and make the offer, although it will usually be turned down. In such a case it's nice to have something small to thank them with.

When flagging down a ride, rather than using the thumb out sign (which could be construed as offensive), wave your hand down with palm down, as if patting the air down.

Local Transport

Bus & Minibus

Most Iranian towns and cities have local bus services. Because local buses are often crowded and can be difficult to use unless you know exactly where you're going, most travellers use the Metro, where possible, or shared and private taxis instead.

Bus numbers and destinations are usually only marked in Farsi, so you need to do a lot of asking around – most people will be happy to help (even if you don't entirely understand their reply). Except in Shiraz and (sometimes) in Tehran, tickets must be bought at little booths along main streets, or at local bus terminals, before you get on the bus. Tickets cost a few cents.

Small children of both genders and all women have to sit at the back of the bus. This segregation can be complicated if you are travelling as a mixed couple and need to discuss when to get off. You must give your ticket to the driver either when you get on or off, depending on the local system. Women must pass

their tickets to the driver while leaning through the front door of the bus and then board the bus using the back door.

Minibuses service local suburban routes and are quite often so crammed with passengers that you can't see out to tell where you're going. You normally pay in cash when you get on. Men and women get a seat anywhere they can; there is no room for segregation. Minibuses stop at normal bus stops or wherever you ask them.

Metro

Metros are the great hope for Iranian cities slowly being strangled by traffic. The Tehran Metro is growing and Mashhad's smaller metro is operating. The first phases of underground railways in Shiraz and Esfahan are scheduled, insh'Allah (God willing), to be operational shortly but, be warned – they've been saying that for years and were originally slated to begin services in 2013... Other cities with metros in the pipeline include Tabriz, Kermanshah and Ahvaz.

Taxi

City taxis come in three main incarnations in Iran.

SHUTTLE (SHARED) TAXI

In most towns and cities, shared or shuttle taxis duplicate or even replace local bus services. They usually take

---

IS THIS SEAT FREE?

Choosing where to sit on Iranian transport can be fraught with difficulty. On city buses, even married couples must sit separately: men at the front of the bus, women at the back.

In contrast, on intercity buses and minibuses, seating is arranged so that women sit next to women and men next to men, unless they're couples or family. A woman is not expected to sit next to an unrelated man even if there's only one spare seat left on the bus; people will move around until the gender mix is right.

But sometimes the opposite sex is impossible to avoid. In shared taxis, people pop in and out of the front and back like pinballs in an attempt to keep unrelated men and women apart. But when this proves impossible, you'll end up next to someone of the opposite sex and no one will get too upset. On the metro, women can choose the women's only carriages or squeeze in with the men. And on sleeper trains you might find yourself in a mixed compartment if you don't specify that you want a single-sex compartment.

up to five passengers: two in the front passenger seat and three in the back. Kia Prides and Samand make up the bulk of shuttle taxis. Note that shuttle taxis operate in cities, while savaris offer a similar service between towns.

Shuttle taxis travel between major *meydans* (squares) and along main roads, so the key to using them is to learn the names of the *meydans* along your intended route. There is a certain art to finding a shuttle taxi going your way. Start by stepping onto the road far enough for the driver to hear you shout your destination, but close enough to the kerb to dash back in the face of hurtling traffic. If the driver has a spare seat, he'll slow down for a nanosecond while you shout your one-word destination – usually the name of a *meydan*. If he's going your way he'll stop.

When you want to get out simply say *'kheili mamnun'* (thank you very much) or make any other obvious noise. Pay during the trip or when you get out; drivers appreciate exact change.

The government-regulated fares range from a few cents for short trips to a couple of dollars, depending on the distance, the city (Tehran is the most expensive) and the traffic. Try and see what other passengers are paying before handing over your money.

If you get into an empty shuttle taxi, particularly in Esfahan and Tehran, it might be assumed you want to charter it privately. Similarly, if everyone else gets out the driver might decide you are now a private fare. Clarify what you want by saying *'dar baste'* (closed door) or *'nah dar baste'*.

When trying to hail a shuttle taxi, don't bother with anything along the lines of 'Iran Hotel, on the corner of...': the driver will have lost interest after the word 'hotel', picked up someone else and be halfway there before you know it. Use a major landmark or a town square as a destination,

DAR BAST NA!

If you hail an empty taxi the driver will probably think you want to hire it privately. He might ask you: *'Dar baste?'*, which literally means 'Closed door?', or perhaps *'agence?'* If you want to share, make your intentions clear by leaning in and telling him simply *'Nah dar baste'*, or 'No closed door'. He'll soon let you know if he's interested or not.

even if you are getting off before then. Shout it quickly and loudly: 'FeDOSe!' will do for Ferdosi St or Sq; similarly, 'eHESHTe!' for Beheshti St or Sq; and so on. The driver will either ignore you, or give you a quick beep on the horn and pull over for half a second while you leap in.

PRIVATE TAXI

Any taxi without passengers, whether obviously a shared taxi or a more expensive private taxi (usually yellow), can be chartered to go anywhere in town; an act usually called *'service'* or *'agence'*. Unless it's a complicated deal, including waiting time, simply hail the vehicle, tell the driver where you want to go, and ask *'chand toman?'*. Immediately offer about 60% of what he suggests but expect to end up paying about 75% or 80% of the originally quoted price.

If your destination has no known street address, tell the driver the name of the place and the nearest square, main road or other landmark.

Many locals in Iran's major cities now use the app Snapp (www.snapp.ir) to arrange rides with any driver who's part of the service – it works similarly to Uber, but you will be given a fare estimate when you confirm the ride and can pay in cash.

AGENCY TAXIS

Agency taxis, or 'telephone' taxis, are ordered by phone. Any hotel can arrange an agency taxi (often with the manager's brother behind the wheel). These are the most expensive taxis but you get a better car, the comfort of knowing there will be some-

one to complain to if anything goes wrong and, possibly, a driver who speaks English. One reader wrote to say that lone women are advised to get someone to call them a taxi if they're travelling after dark, thus avoiding being hooted at or ignored by dozens of drivers as they try to hail one. Demand is such that Tehran and other cities (Yazd among them) have women-only taxis – female drivers, female passengers, no groping.

Private Intercity Taxi

Almost every car in the country is available for private hire. Needless to say, prices are open to negotiation. One way to avoid getting ripped off is to ask the driver of a savari for the price per person of a certain trip then multiply it by four or five.

To hire a taxi for the whole day costs between about US$50 and US$150, depending on factors including your ability as a negotiator, the quality of the car, the distance you plan to drive and where you are. The smaller the town, the cheaper the price.

Savari (Shared Intercity Taxi)

You can almost always find a savari for a trip between towns less than three hours apart. Savari means 'shared taxi' and is usually applied to intercity versions of the species. Speed is the main advantage because savaris are generally less comfortable than buses. Sometimes two people will be expected to squeeze into the front passenger seat, though for longer journeys a total of four passengers is normal.

Savaris rarely leave with an empty seat unless a passenger (or all passengers) agrees to pay for it. These days most savaris are Kia Prides (or the rebadged Saipa Saba) and bigger Peugeot 405s. Peugeots usually cost a bit more.

As a general rule, savaris cost two to three times more than *mahmooly* buses. This is still cheap and worth using for quick trips, especially through dull stretches of countryside. As usual, lone women will normally be given the front seat.

Savaris usually leave from inside, or just outside, the relevant bus terminal, or at major squares at the beginning of whichever road they're about to head down. If in doubt, charter a private taxi and tell the driver *'savari'* and your destination.

Train

Travelling by train is an inexpensive way to get around Iran and meet Iranians.

Iran's first line was the trans-Iranian railway, built in the 1930s to connect the Caspian Sea at Bandar-e Torkaman with the Persian Gulf at Bandar-e Imam Khomeini. A useful way of getting to Sari or Gorgan from Tehran, the route goes through mountains and passes, and is one of the great engineering achievements of the 20th century. It has recently been joined by another engineering marvel: the line between Esfahan and Shiraz that bores its way through the Zagros mountainscape. The line is part of an ambitious program to expand Iran's rail network that in recent years has seen lines open from Qazvin to Astara via Rasht, Mashhad to Bafq and Bam to Zahedan (though the connecting service into Pakistan has not run for years due to security issues).

Routes

Tehran is the main hub and most services begin or end in the capital. There is at least one daily service to Mashhad, Esfahan, Tabriz, Bandar Abbas and Kerman. Trains usually depart on time, but arrival times for stops en route are often in the middle of the night and, as a result, most travellers take the bus.

Classes & Costs

The majority of trains have two classes, though a significant minority have only one. If you decide a 2nd-class compartment is too crowded for you, you can often upgrade to 1st class along the way, provided there's space. A seat in 2nd class costs a bit less than a *mahmooly* bus, and a 1st-class seat is a bit less than a VIP bus.

On overnight trains (usually to/from Tehran), the 1st-class carriages have sleeper couchettes (*ghazal*) with four or six bunks. Solo women should strongly consider requesting a single-sex sleeper. On most 1st-class services, meals are served in your compartment and aren't too bad. Long-distance trains also travel with a restaurant car.

The most comfortable trains are on the busy Tehran to Mashhad route. The Simorgh, for example, is more expensive than other 1st-class options but includes dinner, breakfast, a particularly comfortable bed and the mixed blessing of a TV. You can ask to be seated in a nonsmoking compartment.

Reservations

Train ticketing is on an integrated system and tickets can be booked at railway stations up to a month in advance. Especially for trains leaving on Thursday, Friday and public holidays, it's recommended you book ahead through one of the train stations around the country. At the time of writing, online bookings were not possible.

USEFUL RAIL JOURNEYS

FROM	TO	FARE	DURATION	DEPARTURES
Esfahan	Shiraz	IR500,000	9hr	daily (morning or evening)
Mashhad	Yazd	IR950,000	18½hr	every 2nd evening
Tehran	Esfahan	IR350,000	7½hr	every second day (overnight)
Tehran	Gorgan	IR500,000/300,000 1st/2nd class	10hr	daily (overnight)
Tehran	Kerman	IR700,000/500,000 1st/2nd class	8–13hr	14 daily
Tehran	Tabriz	IR500,000	13hr	daily (overnight)
Yazd	Kerman	IR215,000	6hr	6am daily

Health

Due in part to its dryness and relative isolation, your chances of getting seriously ill with a virus or other infectious disease in Iran are fairly small.

The most common reason for travellers needing medical help is as a result of accidents. If you are unfortunate enough to need a hospital, Iran is home to some of the best in the Middle East. Many doctors have been trained in Europe or North America and, especially in the larger cities, you shouldn't have too much trouble finding one who speaks English. In remoter areas, medical facilities are more basic.

Before You Go

Insurance

Find out in advance if your insurance plan will make payments directly to providers or reimburse you later for overseas health costs, because banking sanctions mean it will be very difficult for insurers to pay doctors direct in Iran. It's also worth ensuring your travel insurance will cover repatriation home or to better medical facilities elsewhere, if necessary. Your insurance company might be able to locate the nearest source of medical help, but it's faster to ask your hotel or, in an emergency, call your embassy or consulate. Travel insurance usually covers emergency dental treatment.

Not all insurance covers emergency aeromedical evacuation home or to a hospital in a major city, which may be the only way to get medical attention for a serious emergency.

Recommended Vaccinations

The World Health Organization recommends that all travellers regardless of the region they are travelling in should be covered for diphtheria, tetanus, measles, mumps, rubella and polio, as well as hepatitis B. While making preparations to travel, take the opportunity to ensure that all of your routine vaccination cover is complete. However, in Iran outbreaks are rare.

Medical Checklist

Following is a list of other items you should consider packing in your medical kit.

➡ Acetaminophen/paracetamol (Tylenol) or aspirin

➡ Adhesive or paper tape

➡ Antibacterial ointment (eg Bactroban) for cuts and abrasions

➡ Antibiotics (if travelling off the beaten track)

➡ Antidiarrhoeal drugs (eg loperamide)

➡ Antihistamines (for hay fever and allergic reactions)

➡ Anti-inflammatory drugs (eg ibuprofen)

➡ Bandages, gauze, gauze rolls

➡ DEET-containing insect repellent for the skin

➡ Iodine tablets (for water purification)

➡ Oral rehydration salts

➡ Permethrin-containing insect spray for clothing, tents, and bed nets

➡ Pocket knife

➡ Scissors, safety pins, tweezers

➡ Steroid cream or cortisone (for allergic rashes)

➡ Sun block

➡ Syringes and sterile needles (if travelling to remote areas)

➡ Thermometer

Websites

World Health Organization (www.who.int/ith) The superb, free *International Travel and Health* is revised annually.

MD Travel Health (www.redplanet.travel/mdtravelhealth) Travel health recommendations updated daily.

The Centers for Disease Control and Prevention (www.cdc.gov) Another useful website.

In Iran

Availability & Cost of Health Care

There are few, reciprocal medical arrangements between Iran and other countries so be prepared to pay for all your medical and dental treatment. The good news is that costs are negligible. The quality of hospitals varies from place to place, but in Tehran, Esfahan and Shiraz, in particular, you'll find international-standard hospitals and well-trained doctors. Wherever you are, locals will direct you to the nearest and/or most appropriate treatment centre.

Medical care is not always readily available outside major cities. Medicine, and even sterile dressings or intravenous fluids, may need to be bought from a local pharmacy, which are usually very well stocked. Nursing care may be limited as this is something families and friends are expected to provide.

Standards of dental care are variable and there is an increased risk of hepatitis B transmission via poorly sterilised equipment. Travel insurance usually only covers emergency dental treatment.

Infectious Diseases

The following infectious diseases are present in Iran, but reports of travellers being infected are extremely rare.

DIPTHERIA

Diphtheria is spread through close respiratory contact. It causes a high temperature and severe sore throat and, sometimes, a closure of the throat requiring a tracheotomy to prevent suffocation. Vaccination is recommended for those likely to be in close contact with the local population in infected areas. The vaccine is given as an injection alone, or with tetanus, and lasts 10 years. Diptheria is present in Iran.

HEPATITIS A

Hepatitis A is present in Iran and is spread through contaminated food (particularly shellfish) and water. It causes jaundice and, although it is rarely fatal, can cause prolonged lethargy and delayed recovery. Symptoms include dark urine, a yellow colour to the whites of the eyes, fever and abdominal pain. Hepatitis A vaccine (Avaxim,

VAQTA, Havrix) is given as an injection: a single dose will give protection for up to a year while a booster 12 months later will provide a subsequent 10 years of protection.

HEPATITIS B

Infected blood, contaminated needles and sexual intercourse can all transmit hepatitis B. It can cause jaundice, and affects the liver, occasionally causing liver failure. All travellers should make this a routine vaccination. (Many countries now give hepatitis B vaccination as part of routine childhood vaccination.) The vaccine is given singly, or at the same time as the hepatitis A vaccine (Hepatyrix). A course will give protection for at least five years. It can be given over four weeks, or six months.

HIV & AIDS

HIV remains mercifully rare in Iran but the growing use of prostitutes and, more problematically, the large number of intravenous drug users, means the HIV rate is rising. For some longer-term visa types, Iran requires a negative HIV test.

MALARIA

There is little malaria in Iran, but there is a reasonably high risk of catching the disease in the country's southeast, including Bandar Abbas. Still, it's worth knowing that malaria almost always starts with shivering, fever and sweating. Muscle pains, headache and vomiting are common. Symptoms may occur anywhere from a few days to three weeks after the infected mosquito bite. The illness can start while you are taking preventative tablets if they are not fully effective, and may also occur after you have finished taking your tablets.

RABIES

Rabies is present in Iran and any dog bites or licks on broken skin should be treated with suspicion as rabies can be fatal. Animal handlers

should be vaccinated, as should those travelling to remote areas where a reliable source of post-bite vaccine is not available within 24 hours. Three injections are needed over a month. If you have not been vaccinated you will need a course of five injections starting within 24 hours of the injury. Vaccination does not provide immunity; it merely buys more time to seek appropriate medical help.

TUBERCULOSIS

Tuberculosis (TB) is found in Iran, especially in the southeast. TB is spread through close respiratory contact and occasionally through infected milk or milk products. BCG vaccine is recommended for those likely to be mixing closely with the local population, though it is not a guarantee against infection.

Traveller's Diarrhoea

While water is safe to drink almost everywhere in Iran, avoiding tap water unless it has been boiled, filtered or chemically disinfected can help you avoid diarrhoea. Freshly prepared meals are best, while pre-prepared dishes like *khoresht* should be avoided by those with fragile stomachs.

If you develop diarrhoea, be sure to drink plenty of fluids, preferably an oral rehydration solution containing lots of salt and sugar. A few loose stools don't require treatment, but if you start having more than four or five stools a day, you should start taking an antibiotic (usually a quinolone drug) and an antidiarrhoeal agent (such as loperamide). If diarrhoea is bloody, persists for more than 72 hours, is accompanied by fever, shaking, chills or severe abdominal pain you should seek medical attention.

Environmental Hazards

HEAT ILLNESS

Heat exhaustion occurs following heavy sweating and excessive fluid loss with inadequate replacement of fluids and salt. Travellers will be especially susceptible during Iran's oven-hot summers, particularly if they are engaging in a greater level of exercise than usual. Be especially careful on desert treks out of places like Yazd.

Symptoms include headache, dizziness and tiredness. Dehydration is already happening by the time you feel thirsty – aim to drink sufficient water such that you produce pale, diluted urine. Electrolyte replacement sachets are the easiest and fastest way to treat dehydration; they are available in Iran, though it makes sense to carry them from home. Alternatively, fluid replacement with water or fruit juice or both, and cooling by cold water and fans is recommended. The treatment of the salt-loss component consists of salty fluids as in soup or broth, and adding a little more table salt to foods than usual.

Heatstroke is much more serious. This occurs when the body's heat-regulating mechanism breaks down. An excessive rise in body temperature leads to sweating ceasing, irrational and hyperactive behaviour and eventually loss of consciousness and death. Rapid cooling by spraying the body with water and fanning is an ideal treatment. Emergency fluid and electrolyte replacement by intravenous drip is usually also required.

INSECT BITES & STINGS

Mosquitoes may not carry malaria but can cause irritation and infected bites. Using DEET-based insect repellents will prevent bites. Mosquitoes also spread dengue fever. Bees and wasps only cause real problems to those with a severe allergy (anaphylaxis). If you have a severe allergy to bee or wasp stings you should carry an adrenaline injection or similar.

There are plenty of scorpions in Iran's deserts and they can cause a painful bite, though contrary to popular misconception, they are rarely life threatening.

Mercifully, Iran doesn't seem to suffer too badly from bed bugs, though occasionally they do pop up (as opposed to appearing – who's ever seen one of the critters?) in hostels and cheap hotels. They lead to very itchy, lumpy bites. Spraying dubious-looking mattresses with insecticide will help get rid of them, or use a sleep sheet.

Scabies might also be found in cheap accommodation. These tiny mites live in the skin, particularly between the fingers. They cause an intensely itchy rash. Scabies is easily treated with lotion available from pharmacies; people who you come into contact with also need treating to avoid spreading scabies between asymptomatic carriers.

AIR POLLUTION

If you have severe respiratory problems, speak with your doctor before travelling to any heavily polluted urban centres such as Tehran. If troubled by pollution, leave the city for a few days to get some fresh air.

Travelling with Children

All travellers with children should know how to treat minor ailments and when to seek medical treatment. Make sure the children are up to date with routine vaccinations, and discuss possible travel vaccines well before departure as some vaccines are not suitable for children aged under one year old.

If your child is vomiting or experiencing diarrhoea, lost fluid and salts must be replaced. It may help to take rehydration powders for reconstituting with boiled water.

You won't see many dogs in Iran, but if you do, children should avoid them, and other mammals, because of the risk of rabies. Any bite, scratch or lick from a warm-blooded, furry animal should immediately be thoroughly cleaned. If there is any possibility that the animal is infected with rabies, immediate medical assistance should be sought.

Lonely Planet's *Travel With Children* (2015) is packed with useful information including pre-trip planning, emergency first aid, immunisation and disease information and what to do if you get sick on the road.

Women's Health

Emotional stress, exhaustion and travelling through different time zones can all contribute to an upset in the menstrual pattern. If using oral contraceptives, remember some antibiotics, and diarrhoea and vomiting can stop the pill from working and lead to the risk of pregnancy. Apart from condoms you should bring any contraception you will need. Tampons are almost impossible to find in Iran, but sanitary towels are available in cities.

Travelling during pregnancy is usually possible but be sure to have a check-up before embarking on your trip. The most risky times for travel are during the first 12 weeks of pregnancy, when miscarriage is most likely, and after 30 weeks – most airlines will not carry a traveller more than about 32 weeks pregnant. Antenatal facilities vary between cities in Iran and there are major cultural and language differences. Taking written records of the pregnancy, including details of your blood group, are likely to be helpful if you need medical attention. Ensure your insurance covers pregnancy, delivery and postnatal care.

Language

The official language of Iran is called Farsi by its native speakers, although in the West it's commonly referred to as Persian. As the language of Iran, and also Afghanistan and Tajikistan, Farsi has around 70 million speakers, but only about 50 million claim it as their first language. The dialect of Farsi spoken in Afghanistan (known as Dari) is very similar to the standard Farsi of Iran, while Tajik (the variety spoken in Tajikistan) is usually considered a separate language.

Farsi is written and read from right to left in the Perso-Arabic script. If you read our coloured pronunciation guides as if they were English, you'll be understood. Note that a is pronounced as in 'act', aa as the 'a' in 'father', e as in 'bet', ee as in 'see', o as in 'tone' and oo as in 'zoo'. Both gh (like the French 'r') and kh (like the 'ch' in the Scottish *loch*) are guttural sounds, pronounced in the back of the throat, r is rolled and zh is pronounced as the 's' in 'pleasure'. The apostrophe (') indicates the glottal stop (like the pause in the middle of 'uh-oh'). The stressed syllables are indicated with italics.

BASICS

Hello.	سلام	sa·*laam*
Goodbye.	خدا حافظ	kho·daa·haa·*fez*
Yes.	بله	ba·*le*
No.	نه	na
Please.	لطفا	lot·*fan*
Thank you.	متشکرم	mo·te·shak·*ke*·ram

WANT MORE?

For in-depth language information and handy phrases, check out Lonely Planet's *Farsi (Persian) Phrasebook*. You'll find it at **shop.lonelyplanet.com**, or you can buy Lonely Planet's iPhone phrasebooks at the Apple App Store.

Excuse me.	ببخشید	be·bakh·*sheed*
Sorry.	متاسفم	mo·ta·as·*se*·fam
How are you?	حالتون چطور هست؟	haa·le·toon che·to·re
Fine, thanks. And you?	خوبم خیلی ممنون	khoo·bam khey·*lee* mam·*noon*
	شما چطور هستید؟	sho·*maa* che·to·reen
What's your name?	اسمتون چی هست؟	es·me·toon chee·ye
My name is ...	اسم من ... هست	es·*me* man ... hast
Do you speak English?	شما انگلیسی حرف	sho·*maa* een·gee·lee·see
	می زنید؟	harf *mee*·za·need
I don't understand.	من نمی فهم	man ne·*mee*·fah·mam
Can I take a photo?	می توانم عکس	*mee*·too·nam aks
	بگیرم؟	be·*gee*·ram

ACCOMMODATION

Where's a ...?	... کجاست؟	... *ko*·jaast
campsite	محل	ma·hal·*le*
	چادر زدن	chaa·*dor* za·dan
guesthouse	مهمان	meh·maan·
	پذیر	pa·*zeer*
hotel	هتل	ho·*tel*
Do you have a ... room?	شما اتاق	sho·*maa* o·taa·*ghe*
	دارید؟ ...	... *daa*·reen
single	یک خوابه	yek khaa·*be*
double	دو خوابه	do khaa·*be*
twin	دو نفره	do na·fa·*re*
How much is it per ...?	... برای هر	ba·raa·ye har ...
	چقدر هست؟	che·ghadr hast
night	شب	shab
person	نفر	na·*far*

Can I get another (blanket)?
می توانم (پتو) mee·too·nam (pa·too)
ی دیگر بگیرم؟ ye dee·ge be·gee·ram

The (air conditioning) doesn't work.
(تهویه مطبوع) (tah·vee·ye·ye mat·boo')
کار نمی کند kaar ne·mee·ko·ne

DIRECTIONS

Where's the ...? ... کجاست؟ ... ko·jaast
bank بانک baank
market بازار baa·zaar
post office ... اداره ی پست ... e·daa·re·ye post

Can you show me (on the map)?
می توانید mee·too·neen
(در نقشه به) (dar nagh·she) be
من نشان بدهید؟ man ne·shun be·deen

What's the address?
آدرس اش چی هست؟ aad·re·sesh chee hast

Could you please write it down?
لطفا می توانید lot·fan mee·ta·vaa·need
آن را بنویسید؟ aan raa be·ne·vee·seed

How far is it?
تا اونجا چقدر taa oon·jaa che·ghadr
راه هست؟ raah hast

How do I get there?
چطور به اونجا بروم؟ che·tor be oon·jaa be·ram

Turn left/right.
بپیچ چپ/راست be·peech chap/raast

It's ... اون ... هست oon ... hast
behind ... پشت ... posh·te ...
in front of ... جلوی ... je·lo·ye ...
next to ... کنار ... ke·naa·re ...
on the corner گوشه goo·she·ye
opposite ... مقابل ... mo·ghaa·be·le ...
straight ahead مستقیم mos·ta·gheem

EATING & DRINKING

Can you recommend a ...?
می توانید یک mee·too·neen yek
پیشنهاد ... ... peesh·na·haad
کنین؟ ko·neen

cafe کافه kaaf·fe
restaurant رستوران res·too·raan
I'd like a/the ..., please.
لطفا من ... lot·fan man ...
می خواهم mee·khaam
nonsmoking section
قسمت غیر ghes·ma·te ghey·re
سیگاری see·gaa·ree
table for (four)
یک میز برای yek meez ba·raa·ye
(چهار نفر) (chaa·haar)

SIGNS

Entrance	ورود
Exit	خروج
Open	باز
Closed	بسته
Information	اطلاعات
Toilets	توالت
Men	مردانه
Women	زنانه

What would you recommend?
شما چی پیشنهاد sho·maa chee peesh·na·haad
می کنید؟ mee·ko·neen

What's the local speciality?
غذای مخصوص gha·zaa·ye makh·soo·se
محلی چی یه؟ ma·hal·lee chee·ye

Do you have vegetarian food?
شما غذای sho·maa gha·zaa·ye
گیاه خواری دارید؟ gee·yaah·khaa·ree daa·reen

I'd like (the) ..., please.
لطفا من ... lot·fan man ...
را می خواهم ro mee·khaam
bill صورت حساب soo·rat he·saab
drink list لیست lees·te
نوشیدنی noo·shee·da·nee
menu منو me·noo
that dish آن غذا oon gha·zaa

Could you prepare a meal without ...?
می توانید یک mee·too·neen yek
غذای بدون gha·zaa·ye be·doo·ne
درست کنید؟ ... ... do·rost ko·neen
butter کره ka·re
eggs تخم مرغ tokh·me·morgh
meat stock آبگوشت aab·goosht

I'm allergic to ...
من به ... man be ...
حساسیت has·saa·see·yat
دارم daa·ram
dairy produce لبنیات la·ba·nee·yaat
nuts آجیل aa·jeel
seafood غذای gha·zaa·ye
دریایی dar·yaa·yee
coffee ... قهوه ... ghah·ve ...
tea ... چای ... chaa·yee ...
with milk با شیر baa sheer
without sugar بدون شکر be·doo·ne she·kar

... water آب ... aa·be ...
boiled جوش joosh
mineral معدنی ma'·da·nee

(orange) juice	(آب) پرتقال	aa·be (por·te·ghaal)
soft drink	نوشابه	noo·shaa·be

EMERGENCIES

Help!	!کمک	ko·mak
Go away!	!برو کنار	bo·ro ke·naar

Call ...!	... صدا کنید!	... se·daa ko·neen
a doctor	یک دکتر	yek dok·tor
the police	پلیس	po·lees

I'm lost.
من گم شده ام   man gom sho·dam

Where are the toilets?
توالت کجاست؟   too·vaa·let ko·jaast

I'm sick.
من مریض هستم   man ma·reez has·tam

I'm allergic to (antibiotics).
من به   man be
(آنتی بیوتیک)   (aan·tee·bee·yoo·teek)
حساسیت دارم   has·saa·see·yat daa·ram

SHOPPING & SERVICES

Where's a ...?	... کجاست؟	... ko·jaast
department store	فروشگاه زنجیره ای	foo·roosh·gaa·he zan·jee·re·yee
grocery store	بقالی	bagh·ghaa·lee
newsagency	روزنامه فروشی	rooz·naa·me foo·roo·shee
souvenir shop	کادو فروشی	kaa·do foo·roo·shee
supermarket	فروشگاه	foo·roosh·ghaah

I'm looking for ...
... من دنبال   man don·baa·le ...
می گردم   mee·gar·dam

Can I look at it?
می توانم به آن   mee·too·nam be oon
نگاه کنم؟   ne·ghaah ko·nam

Do you have any others?
چیز دیگر هم   chee·ze dee·ge ham
دارید؟   daa·reen

It's faulty.
آن خراب هست   oon kha·raa·be

How much is it?
آن چقدر هست؟   oon che·ghadr hast

Can you write down the price?
می توانید قیمت   mee·too·neen ghey·mat
را بنویسید؟   ro be·ne·vee·seen

That's too expensive.
آن خیلی گران هست   oon khey·lee ge·roon hast

What's your lowest price?
پایین ترین   paa·yeen·ta·reen
قیمت تون چند هست؟   ghey·ma·te·toon chan·de

There's a mistake in the bill.
در صورت حساب   dar soo·rat·he·saab
اشتباه شده   esh·te·baah sho·de

Where's an ATM?
خود پرداز کجاست؟   khod·par·daaz ko·jaast

What's the exchange rate?
نرخ ارز چی هست؟   ner·khe arz chee hast

Where's the local internet cafe?
کافی نت محلی   kaa·fee ne·te ma·hal·lee
کجاست؟   ko·jaast

How much is it per hour?
برای هر ساعت   ba·raa·ye har saa·'at
چقدر می شود؟   che·ghadr mee·she

Where's the nearest public phone?
نزدیکترین تلفن   naz·deek·ta·reen te·le·fo·ne
عمومی کجاست؟   oo·moo·mee ko·jaast

I'd like to buy a phonecard.
می خواهم یک کارت   mee·khaam yek kar·te
تلفن بخرم   te·le·fon be·kha·ram

TIME & DATES

What time is it?
ساعت چنده؟   saa·'at chan·de

It's (two) o'clock.
ساعت (دو) هست   saa·'at (do) hast

Half past (two).
(دو) و نیم   (do) vo neem

At what time ...?
چه ساعتی...؟   che saa·'a·tee ...

At ...
در ...   dar ...

yesterday ...	... دیروز	dee·rooz ...
tomorrow ...	... فردا	far·daa ...
morning	صبح	sobh
afternoon	عصر	asr
evening	شب	shab

Monday	دو شنبه	do shan·be
Tuesday	سه شنبه	se shan·be
Wednesday	چهار شنبه	chaa·haar shan·be
Thursday	پنج شنبه	panj shan·be
Friday	جمعه	jom·'e

QUESTION WORDS

When?	کی؟	key
Where?	کجا؟	ko·jaa
Who?	کی؟	kee
Why?	چرا؟	che·raa

NUMBERS

1	١	یک	yek
2	٢	دو	do
3	٣	سه	se
4	٤	چهار	chaa·haar
5	٥	پنج	panj
6	٦	شش	shesh
7	٧	هفت	haft
8	٨	هشت	hasht
9	٩	نه	noh
10	١٠	ده	dah
20	٢٠	بیست	beest
30	٣٠	سی	see
40	٤٠	چهل	che·hel
50	٥٠	پنجاه	pan·jaah
60	٦٠	شصت	shast
70	٧٠	هفتاد	haf·taad
80	٨٠	هشتاد	hash·taad
90	٩٠	نود	na·vad
100	١٠٠	صد	sad
1000	١٠٠٠	هزار	he·zaar

Arabic numerals, used in Farsi, are written from left to right (unlike script).

Saturday	شنبه	shan·be
Sunday	یک شنبه	yek shan·be

TRANSPORT

Is this the ... to (Rasht)?	این ... برای (رشت) هست؟	een ... ba·raa·ye (rasht) hast
boat	کشتی	kesh·tee
bus	اتوبوس	oo·too·boos
plane	هواپیما	ha·vaa·pey·maa
train	قطار	gha·taar
What time's the ... bus?	... اتوبوس کی هست؟	oo·too·boo·se ... key hast
first	اول	av·val
last	آخر	aa·khar

One ... ticket, please.	... یک بلیط لطفا	yek be·leet ... lot·fan
one-way	یک سره	yek sa·re
return	دو سره	do sa·re

How long does the trip take?
مسافرت چقدر طول می کشد؟ · mo·saa·fe·rat che·ghadr tool mee·ke·shad

What station/stop is this?
این کدام ایستگاه هست؟ · een koo·doom eest·gaah hast

Please tell me when we get to (Sari).
لطفا وقتی به (ساری) می رسیم به من بگویید · lot·fan vagh·tee be (saa·ree) mee·re·seem be man be·goo·yeen

How much is it to ...?
... برای چقدر می شود؟ · ba·raa·ye ... che·ghadr mee·she

Please take me to (this address).
لطفا من را (به این آدرس) ببر · lot·fan man ro (be een aad·res) be·bar

Please ... here.	... لطفا اینجا	lot·fan een·jaa ...
stop	توقف کن	ta·vagh·ghof kon
wait	منتظر باش	mon·ta·zer baash

I'd like to hire a ...	... من می خواهم یک کرایه کنم	man mee·khaam ... yek·ke·raa ye ko nam
4WD	چهار دبلیو دی	chaa·haar daa·bel·yoo dee
car	ماشین	maa·sheen

How much for ... hire?	... کرایه چقدر می شود؟	ke raa ye·ye ... che·ghadr mee·she
daily	روزانه	roo·zaa·ne
weekly	هفتگی	haf·te·gee

Is this the road to (Enghelab)?
(این راه به (انقلاب می رود؟ · een raah be (en·ghe·laab) mee·re

I need a mechanic.
من یک مکانیک لازم دارم · man yek me·kaa·neek laa·zem daa·ram

I've run out of petrol.
من بنزین تمام کر ده ام · man ben·zeen ta·moom kar·dam

FARSI ALPHABET

Farsi is written from right to left. The form of each letter changes depending on whether it's at the start, in the middle or at the end of a word or whether it stands alone.

Word-Final	Word-Medial	Word-Initial	Alone	Letter
ـا	ـا	ا	ا	alef
ـب	ـبـ	بـ	ب	be
ـپ	ـپـ	پـ	پ	pe
ـت	ـتـ	تـ	ت	te
ـث	ـثـ	ثـ	ث	se
ـج	ـجـ	جـ	ج	je
ـچ	ـچـ	چـ	چ	che
ـح	ـحـ	حـ	ح	he
ـخ	ـخـ	خـ	خ	khe
ـد	ـد	دـ	د	daal
ـذ	ـذ	ذـ	ذ	zaal
ـر	ـر	رـ	ر	re
ـز	ـز	زـ	ز	ze
ـژ	ـژ	ژـ	ژ	zhe
ـس	ـسـ	سـ	س	se
ـش	ـشـ	شـ	ش	she
ـص	ـصـ	صـ	ص	saad
ـض	ـضـ	ضـ	ض	zaad
ـط	ـطـ	طـ	ط	taa
ـظ	ـظـ	ظـ	ظ	zaa
ـع	ـعـ	عـ	ع	eyn
ـغ	ـغـ	غـ	غ	gheyn
ـف	ـفـ	فـ	ف	fe
ـق	ـقـ	قـ	ق	ghaaf
ـك	ـكـ	كـ	ك	kaaf
ـگ	ـگـ	گـ	گ	gaaf
ـل	ـلـ	لـ	ل	laam
ـم	ـمـ	مـ	م	meem
ـن	ـنـ	نـ	ن	noon
ـو	ـو	و ـ	و	ve
ـه	ـهـ	هـ	ه	he
ـی	ـیـ	یـ	ى	ye

GLOSSARY

Here, with definitions, are some unfamiliar words and abbreviations. Generally the Farsi words in this book are transliterations of colloquial usage. See Language (p362) for other useful words and phrases.

agha – sir; gentleman
Allah – Muslim name for God
aramgah – resting place; burial place; tomb
arg, ark – citadel
astan-e – sanctuary; threshold
ateshkadeh – a Zoroastrian fire temple where a flame was always kept burning
ayatollah – Shiite cleric of the highest rank, used as a title before the name; literally means a 'sign or miracle of God'
azad – free; liberated
azadi – freedom

badgir – windtower or ventilation shaft used to catch breezes and funnel them down into a building to cool it
bagh – garden
bandar – port; harbour
Bandari – indigenous inhabitant of the Persian Gulf coast and islands
bastan – ancient; ancient history; antiquity
bazar – bazaar; market place
bazari – shopkeeper in the bazaar
behesht – paradise
boq'eh – mausoleum
borj – tower
bozorg – big, large, great
burqa – a mask with tiny slits for the eyes worn by some Bandari women

caliphate – the dynasty of the successors of the Prophet Mohammed as rulers of the Islamic world
caravanserai – an inn or way-station for camel trains; usually consisting of rooms arranged around a courtyard

chador – literally 'tent'; a cloak, usually black, covering all parts of a woman's body except the hands, feet and face
coffeenet – internet cafe
cuneiform – ancient wedge-shaped script used in Persia

dar baste – literally closed door, used in taxis to indicate you want a private hire
darvazeh – gate or gateway, especially a city gate
darya – sea
dasht – plain; plateau; desert, specifically one of sand or gravel

enqelab – revolution

Farsi – Persian language or people
Ferdosi – one of the great Persian poets, born about AD 940 in Tus, near Mashhad; wrote the first epic poem, the Shahnamah
fire temple – see ateshkadeh

gabbeh – traditional rug
golestan – rose garden; name of poem by Sa'di
gonbad – dome, domed monument or tower tomb; also written 'gombad'

Hafez – one of the great Persian poets, born in Shiraz in about AD 1324
hajj – pilgrimage to Mecca
halal – permitted by Islamic law; lawful to eat or drink
hammam – bath, public bathhouse; bathroom
Hazrat-e – title used before the name of Mohammed, any other apostle of Islam or a Christian saint
hejab – veil; the 'modest dress' required of Muslim women and girls
Hossein – the third of the 12 imams recognised by Shiites as successors of the Prophet Mohammed
Hosseinieh – see takieh

imam – 'emam' in Farsi; religious leader, also title of one of the 12 descendants of Mohammed who, according to Shiite belief, succeeded him as religious and temporal leader of the Muslims
Imam Reza – the eighth Shiite imam
imamzadeh – descendant of an imam; shrine or mausoleum of an imamzadeh
insh'Allah – if God wills it
istgah – station (especially train station)
iwan – 'eivan' in Farsi; barrel-vaulted hall opening onto a courtyard

Jameh Mosque – Masjed-e Jameh in Farsi; meaning Congregational Mosque, sometimes mis-translated as Friday Mosque

kabir – great
kalisa – church (sometimes cathedral)
kavir – salt desert
khalij – gulf; bay
khan – feudal lord, title of respect
khan-e sonnati – traditional house
kuche – lane; alley
Kufic – ancient script found on many buildings dating from the about the 7th to 13th centuries

madraseh – school; also Muslim theological college
majlis – Iranian Parliament
manar – minaret; tower of a mosque
markazi – centre; headquarters
masjed – mosque; Muslim place of worship
Masjed-e Jameh – see Jameh Mosque
mehmankhaneh – hotel
mehmanpazir – a simple hotel
mehmansara – government-owned resthouse or hotel
mihrab – niche inside a mosque indicating the direction

of Mecca; in Iran, specifically the hole cut in the ground before the niche

minbar – pulpit of a mosque

Moharram – first month of the Muslim lunar calendar, the Shiite month of mourning

mosaferkhaneh – lodging-house or hotel of the cheapest, simplest kind; 'mosafer' means traveller or passenger

muezzin – person at mosque who calls Muslims to prayer

mullah – Islamic cleric; title of respect

No Ruz – Iranian New Year's Day, celebrated on the vernal equinox (usually 21 March)

Omar Khayyam – Famous as a poet, mathematician, historian and astronomer; his best-known poem is the *Rubaïyat*

pasazh – passage; shopping arcade

Persia – old name for Iran

Persian – adjective and noun frequently used to describe the Iranian language, people and culture

pik-up – utility with a canvas cover

pol – bridge

qal'eh – fortress; fortified walled village

qalyan – water pipe, usually smoked in traditional teahouses

qanat – underground water channel

qar – cave

Quran – Muslim holy book

Ramazan – ninth month in the Muslim lunar calendar; the month of fasting

rial – currency of Iran; equal to one-tenth of a *toman*

rud, rudkhuneh – river; stream

Rumi – famous poet (born in 1207) credited with founding the Maulavi Sufi order – the whirling dervishes

ruz – day

Sa'di – one of the great Persian poets (AD 1207–91); his most famous works are the *Golestan* (Rose Garden) and *Bustan* (Garden of Trees)

sardar – military governor

savari – private car; local word for a shared taxi, usually refers to longer trips between cities

shah – king; the usual title of the Persian monarch

shahid – martyr; used as a title before the forename of a fighter killed during the Islamic Revolution or the Iran-Iraq War

shahr – town or city

shuttle taxi – common form of public transport within cities; they usually run on set routes

ta'arof – ritualised politeness

takht – throne, also the day-bed-style tables in teahouses

takieh – building used during the rituals to commemorate the death of Imam Hossein during Moharram; sometimes called a *Hosseinieh*

tappeh – hill; mound

terminal – terminal; bus station

toman – unit of currency equal to 10 *rials*

vakil – regent

yakh dan – mud-brick ice house

zarih – the gilded and latticed 'cage' that sits over a tomb

ziggurat – pyramidal temple with a series of tiers on a square or rectangular plan

Zoroastrianism – ancient religion, the state creed before the Islamic conquest; today Zoroastrians are found mainly in Yazd, Shiraz, Kerman, Tehran and Esfahan

zurkhaneh – literally 'house of strength'; a group of men perform a series of ritualised feats of strength, all to the accompaniment of a drumbeat

Behind the Scenes

SEND US YOUR FEEDBACK

We love to hear from travellers – your comments keep us on our toes and help make our books better. Our well-travelled team reads every word on what you loved or loathed about this book. Although we cannot reply individually to your submissions, we always guarantee that your feedback goes straight to the appropriate authors, in time for the next edition. Each person who sends us information is thanked in the next edition – the most useful submissions are rewarded with a selection of digital PDF chapters.

Visit **lonelyplanet.com/contact** to submit your updates and suggestions or to ask for help. Our award-winning website also features inspirational travel stories, news and discussions.

Note: We may edit, reproduce and incorporate your comments in Lonely Planet products such as guidebooks, websites and digital products, so let us know if you don't want your comments reproduced or your name acknowledged. For a copy of our privacy policy visit lonelyplanet.com/privacy.

OUR READERS

Many thanks to the travellers who used the last edition and wrote to us with helpful hints, useful advice and interesting anecdotes: Adriaan van Dijk, Adrian Incichen, Adrien Bitton, Adrien Ledeul, Agapi Galenianou, Alan & Lynn Taylor, Alan Keltner, Alberto Ibanez, Alexis Haneke, Alfred Schupp, Amanda Löwenberg, Amir Qaredaghi, Ana Hocevar, Ana Louro, Andrew Coker, Andrew Rerttman, Angus Lee, Ankur Agarwal, Anna Zavyalova, Anne Ataii, Anton Kerst, Arlo Werhoven, Arne Gerberding, Aurélien Grollemund, Bas Geelen, Basia Jóźwiak, Bastiaan Bijl, Basudeb Banerjee, Behnaz Shaabani, Bojan Bokal, Cale Lawlor, Catherine Waters, Chevallier Elodie, Chiara Pentini, Christian Kayed, Christina Gade, Cinzia Mina, Damjan Sinigoj, David Cassan, David Droob, David Treller, Desislava Slavcheva, Dominik Hetzer, Edda Senior, Edo Willemse, Elise Vonk, Elizabeth van Tilborg, Eloise de la Croix, Ester Vila, Eugenio Ariztia, Eva Anita Steiger, Farnoush Sheykhani, Florian Siebeck, Franca Gilissen, Franco Pagnoni, Frank Westerhof, Frans Ewals, Geert van Waveren, Gert Fisahn, Gilda Gazor, Greg Minshall, Hadrien Cazeaux, Helen Carmichael, Helena Foito dos Santos, Helena Henneken, Henry Bacon, Hojat Kermani Nejad, Hon Chiu Vincent Ko, Ian Thomson, Ioannis Mamoukaris, Jaap Hooijkaas, Jacek Janczarek, Jan Setnan, Jan-Pieter Visschers, Jascha de Ridder, Jason Pemberton, Jeanne Watt, Jenny Hess, Jessie Toose, Jim Lowther, John Pasturel, Jonas Keil, Joris Tieleman, Julia Dorenwendt, Julian Madsen, Kaldia Douag, Kamran Hasani, Katharina Lüke, Kay Martin, Klaas Flechsig, Larissa Chu, Leigh Dehaney, Leonie Gavalas, Lianne Bosch, Lisandra Ilisei, Luis Maia, Luzius Thuerlimann, Maarten Jan Oskam, Maksymilian Dzwonek, Manfred Henze, Marc Verkerk, Marcel Althaus, Marei Bauer, Marianne Schoone, Mario Sergio Dd Oliveira Pinto, Marjolijn Polman, Martin Hausmann, Mary Gavan, Mehmet Gavremoglu, Michael Chow, Mike van kruchten, Mina Rahimi, Mirka Badinska, Mohammad Afshinfar, Mohammad Ebrahimi, Mohsen Rezaie-Atagholipour, Momo Nedderwedder, Monica Coppi, Monica Santosuosso, Monika Marek, Nga Bellis, Nicholas James, Nick Lubout, Olav Wissink , Oleg Zhernovoy, Olivia-Petra Coman, Olivier Drouin, Parniyan Fakharzadeh, Parto Shahvandi, Paul Downing, Paul Faust, Paul Tjiam, Paul-Noël Dumont, Petros Mouchas, Phuong Tran, Pier Giorgi, Regi & Andi Keller, Regine Fisahn, Remko Donga, Rens Geerse , Reto Vogt, Ricardo Puerto, Richard & Joan Williams, Roderick van de Weg, Roëlla de Ruiter, Ronald De Hertogh, Rouhollah Fallahi, Roya Moradifar, Ryan Mckechnie, Ryan Teo, Ryo Kakiuchi, Sadra Beygi , Sebastian Lopienski, Shahireh Nozari, Simon Coombe, Simon Walo, Simone Zoppellaro, Siska D'hoore, Stefan Gruber, Stefanie Mikkers, Stela Prodanovic, Stephane Baudemont, Susanne Janssen, Svein Skalevag, Sveta Selivanova, Terry Hooper, Thessi Summer, Thibaud Marcesse, Thomas Nash, Thomas Sarosy, Thomas Schneider, Tim Rom, Tobias Leupold, Tobias Wolski, Tom De Mits, Tomasz Kozaczek, Ursula Streit, Vida Pirlou, Xavier law, Xin Tian Yong, Yao Zhang, Yasi Ayat, Yorian Bordes

WRITER THANKS

Simon Richmond

Many thanks to the following for their assistance in preparation for and during my research in Iran: Andrew Burke, Gabe Kaminski, Laili Sadr, Mathew Scott, Yi-Juan Koh, William Lodder, Navid, Sogand, Matin, Shirin, Ali, Farah, Ramin, Armin, Masoud, Jalal and Berzhad.

Jean-Bernard Carillet

A huge thanks to everyone who helped out and made this trip an enlightenment, especially Mojtaba, Eric, Amir, Ibrahim, the young couple met on Qeshm and all the people I met on the road. At Lonely Planet I'm grateful to Helen for her trust, and to the hard-working editors. At home, a *gros bisou* to Eva and lots of love to Morgane, whose support was essential.

Mark Elliott

Many, many thanks to gallant guides Shahram and Mojtaba, to Helen, Dylan and Megan for making things possible and to Sally Kingsbury and my unbeatable parents for so much love and support. Thank you also to countless kind Iranians and travellers who were so generous with their time, hospitality and information, notably Vali, Reza and family, Rino, Ahmad, Amir, Jalal, Mohammad and Akbar.

Anthony Ham

A big thank you to my editor, Helen Elfer, for trusting me to write about such a wonderful part of the world. And to my co-authors – Mark Elliott, Jean-Bernard Carillet, Simon Richmond, Jenny Walker and Steve Waters – who together represent some of the finest writers writing guidebooks anywhere.

Jenny Walker

Iran is acknowledged as a country of wonders – and this includes the legendary hospitality extended to visitors. A general thanks, then, to all who helped contribute to the information in the Central Iran chapter. Specific thanks to Bijan Nabavi for setting the scene, to Mostafa Ramezanpoor for attention to detail and most especially to Mojtaba Heidari for his extreme efforts in extreme circumstances – not forgetting his signature coffee stops! Biggest thanks to beloved Sam (Owen), husband, co-researcher and fellow traveller.

Steve Waters

Thanks to all the beautiful Iranian people who smoothed my way, picked me up when I was miles from nowhere, bought me tea and chocolates, or *chelo kabab,* who taught me lessons in humility, patience and honesty, who told me subversive jokes, made me laugh, shared their food and persevered with my mangled Farsi. And thanks to Rahel, Kaz, Hamish, Megan and Roz for being yourselves.

ACKNOWLEDGEMENTS

Climate map data adapted from Peel MC, Finlayson BL & McMahon TA (2007) 'Updated World Map of the Köppen-Geiger Climate Classification', Hydrology and Earth System Sciences, 11, 163344.

Cover photograph: Masjed-e Sheikh Lotfollah (Sheikh Lotfollah Mosque), Esfahan, JPRichard/Shutterstock ©

THIS BOOK

This 7th edition of Lonely Planet's *Iran* guidebook was researched and written by Simon Richmond, Jean-Bernard Carillet, Mark Elliott, Anthony Ham, Jenny Walker and Steve Waters. The previous edition was written by Andrew Burke, Virginia Maxwell and Iain Shearer. This guidebook was produced by the following:

Destination Editors Helen Elfer, Lauren Keith
Product Editors Joel Cotterell, Anne Mason
Senior Cartographer David Kemp
Book Designer Nicholas Colicchia
Assisting Editors Sarah Bailey, Imogen Bannister, Carly Hall, Ali Lemer, Kristin Odijk, Gabrielle Stefanos, Ross Taylor, Saralinda Turner

Assisting Cartographer Julie Dodkins
Cover Researcher Naomi Parker

Thanks to Jordan Hallewell, Indra Kilfoyle, Kate Mathews, Claire Naylor, Karyn Noble, Martine Power, Kirsten Rawlings, Alison Ridgway, Shadi Salehian

Index

NOTES

NOTES

Map Legend

Sights

- Beach
- Bird Sanctuary
- Buddhist
- Castle/Palace
- Christian
- Confucian
- Hindu
- Islamic
- Jain
- Jewish
- Monument
- Museum/Gallery/Historic Building
- Ruin
- Shinto
- Sikh
- Taoist
- Winery/Vineyard
- Zoo/Wildlife Sanctuary
- Other Sight

Activities, Courses & Tours

- Bodysurfing
- Diving
- Canoeing/Kayaking
- Course/Tour
- Sento Hot Baths/Onsen
- Skiing
- Snorkelling
- Surfing
- Swimming/Pool
- Walking
- Windsurfing
- Other Activity

Sleeping

- Sleeping
- Camping

Eating

- Eating

Drinking & Nightlife

- Drinking & Nightlife
- Cafe

Entertainment

- Entertainment

Shopping

- Shopping

Information

- Bank
- Embassy/Consulate
- Hospital/Medical
- Internet
- Police
- Post Office
- Telephone
- Toilet
- Tourist Information
- Other Information

Geographic

- Beach
- Gate
- Hut/Shelter
- Lighthouse
- Lookout
- Mountain/Volcano
- Oasis
- Park
- Pass
- Picnic Area
- Waterfall

Population

- Capital (National)
- Capital (State/Province)
- City/Large Town
- Town/Village

Transport

- Airport
- Border crossing
- Bus
- Cable car/Funicular
- Cycling
- Ferry
- Metro station
- Monorail
- Parking
- Petrol station
- Subway station
- Taxi
- Train station/Railway
- Tram
- Underground station
- Other Transport

Note: Not all symbols displayed above appear on the maps in this book

Routes

- Tollway
- Freeway
- Primary
- Secondary
- Tertiary
- Lane
- Unsealed road
- Road under construction
- Plaza/Mall
- Steps
- Tunnel
- Pedestrian overpass
- Walking Tour
- Walking Tour detour
- Path/Walking Trail

Boundaries

- International
- State/Province
- Disputed
- Regional/Suburb
- Marine Park
- Cliff
- Wall

Hydrography

- River, Creek
- Intermittent River
- Canal
- Water
- Dry/Salt/Intermittent Lake
- Reef

Areas

- Airport/Runway
- Beach/Desert
- Cemetery (Christian)
- Cemetery (Other)
- Glacier
- Mudflat
- Park/Forest
- Sight (Building)
- Sportsground
- Swamp/Mangrove

Jenny Walker
Central Iran A member of the British Guild of Travel Writers and the Outdoor Writers and Photographers Guild, Jenny has written extensively on the Middle East for Lonely Planet for more than a decade. With her husband, Wing Commander (retired) Sam Owen, she also authored *Off-Road in the Sultanate of Oman* – a country they have made their home for nearly 20 years.

Steve Waters
Western Iran Travel and adventure have always been Steve's life, and he couldn't imagine a world without them. Steve has been using Lonely Planet guidebooks for more than 30 years in places as diverse as Iran, Central Asia, Kamchatka, Tuva, the Himalaya, Canada, Patagonia, the Australian Outback, NE Asia, Myanmar and the Sahara. Little wonder then that he finally got a gig with the company! Steve has contributed to *Iran, Indonesia* and the past four editions of *Western Australia,* and come any September you're likely to find him in a remote gorge somewhere in the Kimberley.

OUR STORY

A beat-up old car, a few dollars in the pocket and a sense of adventure. In 1972 that's all Tony and Maureen Wheeler needed for the trip of a lifetime – across Europe and Asia overland to Australia. It took several months, and at the end – broke but inspired – they sat at their kitchen table writing and stapling together their first travel guide, *Across Asia on the Cheap*. Within a week they'd sold 1500 copies. Lonely Planet was born.

Today, Lonely Planet has offices in Franklin, London, Melbourne, Oakland, Dublin, Beijing and Delhi, with more than 600 staff and writers. We share Tony's belief that 'a great guidebook should do three things: inform, educate and amuse'.

OUR WRITERS

Simon Richmond

Tehran Journalist and photographer Simon Richmond has specialised as a travel writer since the early 1990s and first worked for Lonely Planet in 1999 on their *Central Asia* guide. He's long since stopped counting the number of guidebooks he's researched and written for the company, but countries covered including Australia, China, India, Iran, Japan, Korea, Malaysia, Mongolia, Myanmar (Burma), Russia, Singapore, South Africa and Turkey. For Lonely Planet's website, he's penned features on topics from the world's best swimming pools to the joys of urban sketching.

Jean-Bernard Carillet

Persian Gulf Jean-Bernard is a Paris-based freelance writer and photographer who specialises in Africa, France, Turkey, the Indian Ocean, the Caribbean and the Pacific. He loves adventure, remote places, islands, the outdoors, archaeological sites and food. His insatiable wanderlust has taken him to 114 countries across six continents, and it shows no sign of waning. It has inspired lots of articles and photos for travel magazines and some 70 Lonely Planet guidebooks, both in English and in French.

Mark Elliott

Southeastern Iran, Northeastern Iran Mark Elliott had already lived and worked on five continents when, in the pre-Internet dark ages, he started writing travel guides. He has since authored (or co-authored) around 60 books including dozens for Lonely Planet. He also acts as a travel consultant, occasional tour leader, video presenter, speaker, interviewer and blues harmonicist.

Anthony Ham

Plan Your Trip, Understand and Survival Guide chapters Anthony is a freelance writer and photographer who specialises in Spain, East and Southern Africa, the Arctic and the Middle East. When he's not writing for Lonely Planet, Anthony writes about and photographs Spain, Africa and the Middle East for newspapers and magazines in Australia, the UK and US.

OVER PAGE MORE WRITERS

Published by Lonely Planet Global Limited
CRN 554153
7th edition – September 2017
ISBN 978 1 78657 541 8
© Lonely Planet 2017   Photographs © as indicated 2017
10 9 8 7 6 5 4 3 2 1
Printed in China